HARVEY C. FREEDMAN CPA, CGA

CAROL SMITH MBA, CPA, CMA

LEARNING ── ○ # 2015

SAGE 50 ACCOUNTING
○ ──────── A MODULAR APPROACH

Covers Sage 50 Premium Accounting 2015 🍁 Canadian Edition

NELSON
EDUCATION

Learning Sage 50 Accounting: A Modular Approach

by Harvey C. Freedman and Carol Smith

**Vice President, Editorial
Higher Education:**
Anne Williams

Publisher:
Anne-Marie Taylor

Marketing Manager:
Dave Stratton

Developmental Editor:
Linda Sparks

Project Manager:
Becky Pembry-Spratley

Proofreader:
Susan James

Design Director:
Ken Phipps

Managing Designer:
Franca Amore

Cover Design:
Sharon Lucas

Cover Image:
aleksandarvelasevic/Getty
Royalty Free

Compositor:
Diane van Ingen

**Library and Archives Canada
Cataloguing in Publication Data**

Freedman, Harvey C., author
Learning Sage 50 accounting : a modular approach / Harvey C. Freedman (CPA, CGA), Carol Smith (MBA, CPA, CMA). -- Canadian edition.

Includes index."Covers Sage 50 Premium Accounting 2015."ISBN 978-0-17-670346-2 (paperback)

1. Sage 50 accounting (Computer file)–Textbooks. 2. Accounting--Computer programs–Textbooks. 3. Small business–Accounting--Computer programs–Textbooks. I. Smith, Carol (Carol C.), author II. Title. III. Title: Sage 50 accounting.

HF5679.F728 2015
657'.9042028553
C2015-904420-0

ISBN-13: 978-0-17-670346-2
ISBN-10: 0-17-670346-2

DEDICATION

This book is dedicated to all the volunteers in your community who give their time and effort to help those in need. If you are a volunteer, I offer my own thank you. We all appreciate the work you do to make your community a wonderful place to live.

ACKNOWLEDGMENTS

I would like to thank the individuals below who contributed to making this textbook a success. On behalf of the team, I hope that you find using this book a rewarding experience.

My wife **Marlene**, who reviewed the manuscript, my sons **Jeremy** and **Jason**, granddaughters **Jordan, Jessica,** and **Harper,** for their support and encouragement while the book was in progress. I realize that I did not spend as much time with you as I would have liked.

Carol Smith, Professor at Humber Institute of Technology and Advanced Learning, my colleague, who was the technical reviewer for this textbook. She reviewed the manuscript and offered numerous suggestions, ideas, and helpful criticisms to make the textbook easy to understand.

Rosemary Imola, Professor at Mohawk College, who was the keystroke reviewer, checked the manuscript and the slideshows, and offered numerous suggestions and helpful criticisms to make the textbook easy to understand.

Sage 50 Accounting staff— **Melissa Lutman, Jim Collins, Joel Reisler** and other members of Sage 50 Accounting Education and Technical Support for their ongoing technical assistance.

Students, who always come up with new ways of looking at the same information and whose suggestions help make the textbook material more effective.

Diane van Ingen, desktop technician, who contributed many suggestions and ideas to help make this textbook visually appealing.

Rebecca Pembry-Spratley, for creating the slideshows.

Anne-Marie Taylor, Susan Calvert, Linda Sparks, Vicki Gould, Joanne Woods, and **Susan James** of Nelson Education for their assistance on this project.

Harvey Freedman

> *Tell me and I forget.*
> *Show me and I remember.*
> *Let me do it and I understand.*
> *- Zen Proverb*

CREDITS

Becky Pembry-Spratley, Project Manager
Rosemary Imola, Keystroke Tester and Reviewer (Slideshows)
Diane van Ingen, Desktop Technician

Preface

This textbook is a comprehensive introduction to *Sage 50 Premium Accounting 2015 Release 1* using the **modular approach**. Step-by-step instructions are provided for using all the features in each of the following Sage 50 modules:

1. COMPANY
2. RECEIVABLES
3. PAYABLES
4. EMPLOYEES & PAYROLL
5. INVENTORY & SERVICES
6. PROJECTS
7. BANKING

The textbook also includes Month-End and Year-End processing, Project Costing, Account Reconciliation, and Foreign Currency. Conversion from a manual accounting system or from another accounting software is covered as well.

www **Students**: To access the online resources at www.nelson.com/student, you must use the access code provided with your text or purchase one online at www.nelsonbrain.com.

Instructors, as with previous editions, please ask your educational representative from Nelson for access to the site. Log into http://replocator.nelson.com to find your educational rep.

Modular Approach

The modular approach has been chosen to provide the following benefits:

1. ALL types of transactions in each Sage 50 module are studied in independent chapters. This allows a flexible training program design, as the chapters can be presented in any order.

2. By having each chapter parallel a module in Sage 50, this textbook minimizes confusion and maximizes student success by providing a direct path to software mastery.

3. Because every function in one module is in one chapter, it is easy to find specific functions when required at a later time. The textbook therefore serves as an effective learning device as well as an easy reference.

The authors have purposely kept away from the case study approach to avoid scattering topics among various chapters.

Perpetual Inventory Is In! (Move Over, Periodic Inventory!)

Perpetual inventory systems are used throughout the book to reflect the approach used in current accounting textbooks, as dictated by present-day business practices and trends. The examples, therefore, are up-to-date, realistic, and practical.

Acknowledging that there is still a need for understanding Periodic Inventory system entries, we have included comprehensive material in on-line appendices using real-life business cases.

Lesson Format

The lessons are designed so that step-by-step instructions immediately follow the transaction description or source document. This format results in easy-to-follow lessons and no confusion because it does not require flipping of pages forward and backward.

After each chapter, challenge exercises are provided, which many instructors use in assessing students' mastery of the software functions.

8	Stain	Stain Company	Yes	Yes	Yes		Yes		
	Hair	Charlie's Hair Styling	Yes	Yes	Yes		Yes		
	Vet	Vet Services	Yes	Yes	Yes		Yes		
	Bears	Bears Company	Yes	Yes	Yes		Yes		
10	Magazines	Rama Magazines	Yes		Yes		Yes		
	Gravel	City Gravel	Yes	Yes			Yes		
12	China	China Company	Yes	Yes	Yes				Yes
14	Saddles	Saddles Company	Yes		Yes		Yes		

* Data files to be created by student.

Other Features

- At the end of the textbook is a **Glossary** containing Accounting and Sage 50 Accounting Terminology used in the chapters.

- A **Table of Contents** at the beginning of each chapter provides a detailed list of the topics in the chapter. A detailed index is also provided at the end of the textbook for your easy reference.

- **Review questions** are given at the end of each chapter to help you assess your own learning and prepare yourself for tests.

- Chapter 6 (Shirts & Ties) is a **Comprehensive Challenge Exercise** that requires you to set up a company from scratch and record transactions from source documents. You may also use the 06 Shirts data file, with Perpetual Inventory.

- The **List of Relevant Appendices** at the end of most chapters guides you to the online appendices relevant to the functions in the particular chapter.

Appendices

Various appendices provide you with additional information that would be useful to you, both in your current course and when using Sage 50 Accounting on the job.

Appendix 1 (end of Chapter 1 in textbook), *Taxes (HST, GST, and PST)*
Appendix 2 (in textbook), *Sage 50 Premium Accounting 2015.0 Student Version Installation Instructions.*

WWW **Appendix 2015** The following appendices are provided in your course materials at www.nelson.com/student.

Appendix 2015 A   Basics of Accounting—Perpetual Inventory System
Appendix 2015 B   Basics of Accounting—Periodic Inventory System
Appendix 2015 C   What's New in Sage 50 Premium Accounting 2015.0
Appendix 2015 D   Printing a Tax (HST) Report
Appendix 2015 E   Budgets—General Ledger
Appendix 2015 F   Periodic Inventory Entries
Appendix 2015 G   Updating Inventory and COGS Balances for Companies Using Periodic Inventory System
Appendix 2015 H   INVENTORY & SERVICES Module Setup Perpetual Inventory for Sarah's Kitchen Stores (4B)
Appendix 2015 I   Checklists for Task Completion
Appendix 2015 J   Work Logbook for Sage 50 Premium Accounting 2015
Appendix 2015 K   Graphs Feature
Appendix 2015 L   Setting Up a New Company File using a Sage 50 Premium Accounting Template
Appendix 2015 M   Post-Dated Cheques
Appendix 2015 N   Adding a Salesperson's Name to an Invoice
Appendix 2015 O   Security—Passwords
Appendix 2015 P   Payroll Garnishment
Appendix 2015 Q   Names Fields

HST, GST, and PST are explained in Appendix 1, *Taxes (HST, GST, and PST)* located at the end of Chapter 1. The chapters will help to ensure that you understand the procedures for recording the HST, GST, and PST collected from Sales, and the HST, GST, and PST paid on buying merchandise for resale and other goods and services.

Software

The Sage 50 Premium Accounting Software 2015.0 Student Version for use at home is available as a download from the Sage 50 Accounting website. Do NOT load the software until you have read Appendix 2, *Sage 50 Premium Accounting 2015.0—Student Version Installation Instructions,* at the back of this textbook, for system requirements and instruction on loading the software, as well as restrictions on its use.

Caution: Do not load the Sage 50 Accounting software until you have read Appendix 2, *Sage 50 Premium Accounting 2015.0—Student Version Installation Instructions,* at the back of this textbook.

Tips for Making the Most of Your Sage 50 Premium Accounting Training

- When you see a number and a symbol similar to **7➢**, it means there is something on the line or paragraph in bold for you to type or a key or keys you must press.

- It is important that you follow the instructions in the order that they are given (don't jump around). Read each section before you do the work on the computer to get an idea of what will be done. This will help you avoid errors that could be prevented by knowing information presented a little further in the book. Ask your instructor if you are not sure. Asking your fellow students may help, but the final results are your responsibility, not your classmates'.

- Your instructor will have a Solutions Manual available for you to check your work. If you realize you have made an error after posting a transaction, don't panic; you can correct the error. Review Chapter 13, *Correcting Transaction Errors After Posting*, on ways to correct posted entries.

- Your transaction listing may not match the Solutions Manual exactly (e.g., you made a mistake), but the financial statements, Income Statement, and Balance Sheet must be the same as the solution.

- Always back up your data after every work session, either in the classroom or at home. This can save you hours of extra work. Look for the Backup icon to remind you to back up.

- Answer the **Before Moving On** questions at the end of each chapter before moving to the next chapter. This will help you understand the reasons behind the keystrokes and aid you in preparing for tests.

For the Instructors

We have provided for you a comprehensive Instructor's Support Package. The items below are products of years of teaching experience and a strong desire to make your teaching experience not only easier but also more enjoyable.

These are the items that you will find in the Instructor Resource section at www.nelson.com/instructor. For your convenience, the student resources are also included in this section of the Nelson website.

- Instructor's Manual
  - Tips before your class starts
  - Tips for every chapter in the textbook
  - Tips—Challenge Cases, Tests, and/or Assignments
  - Tips—Additional Cases
  - Review of transactions for Sage 50 Premium Accounting 2015

- Chapter Exercise Solutions
  - Chapter Solutions
  - Challenge Solutions
  - Appendices Solutions
  - Chairs Solutions

- Additional Case Studies & Solutions
  - Case 1—Security Guards Inc. (G/L, A/R, A/P, Payroll)
  - Case 2—Blankets Company   (G/L, A/R, A/P, Inventory & Services)
  - Case 3—Becky's Bags   (G/L, A/R, A/P, Inventory & Services, Projects)
  - Case 4—Engine Repairs Ltd. (G/L, A/R, A/P, Inventory & Services, Reconciliation & Deposits)
  - Case 5—Steel Roof Deck Inc. (G/L, A/R, A/P, Payroll, Inventory & Services, Projects)
  - Case 6—Alvin's Paints Ltd.   (Set up new Company: G/L, A/R, A/P, Payroll, Inventory & Services)

- Test Banks & Solutions
  - Before Moving On Solutions to questions in the textbook
  - Multiple-Choice Questions and Solutions
  - True-False Questions and Solutions
  - Quizzes on the Slideshows and Solutions
  - Mid-Term and Final Exam (Test 1/Test 2)—test document, data files, and solutions

- Data Files
  - Textbook Chapters
  - Challenge Exercises

- Online Appendices

- PowerPoint Slideshows (with quizzes)

Your Feedback

Please send comments, suggestions, or corrections to the author at: freedmanh@rogers.com

Updates

www You may access the Publisher's website to download files related to this text. Please also consult this site for information or links that were not available to us at publication time. The Publisher's website is: www.nelson.com/student

Table of Contents

Chapter 1
Getting Started and COMPANY Module

Appendix 1
Taxes (HST, GST and PST)

Chapter 2A
RECEIVABLES Module—Basics

Chapter 2B
RECEIVABLES Module—Beyond Basics
Santos Luggage **143**

Chapter 3A
PAYABLES Module—Basics
Tyson's Toys **185**

Chapter 3B
PAYABLES Module—Beyond Basics

Chapter 4A
Setting Up a New Company
Sarah's Kitchen Stores **273**

Chapter 4B
INVENTORY & SERVICES Module
Setup Perpetual Inventory for Sarah's Kitchen Stores (4B) 347

Chapter 5
Review of COMPANY, PAYABLES & RECEIVABLES Modules
Sarah's Kitchen Stores **349**

Chapter 9
Month-End/Year-End Processing

Chapter 10
Year-End Closing
Kafa2 Sweaters... **515**

Chapter 11
PROJECTS* Module Setup and Transactions
HotTubs Company Ltd. **529**

Chapter 12
BANKING Module – Reconciliation & Deposits
Wedding Flowers Company **557**

Chapter 13
Correcting Transaction Errors After Posting 579

Chapter 14
Foreign Currency
Saddles Company 601

Appendix 2
Sage 50 Premium Accounting 2015.0–
Student Version Installation Instructions 617

Glossary..625

Index...633

Appendix A-AH..www.nelson.com/student

Chapter 1

Getting Started and COMPANY Module

Photos Company

Learning Objectives

After completing this chapter you will be able to:

☐ Use the General Journal to enter and post transactions using the Double-Entry method.
☐ Display General Journal entries.
☐ Advance the Session Date.
☐ Adjust a wrong Journal entry after posting.
☐ Set up, use and remove a recurring entry.
☐ Use the Additional Transaction Details feature.
☐ Display and print relevant reports.
☐ Save and back up the data file.
☐ Record backup information in a logbook.

Learning Sage 50 Premium Accounting 2015.0: A Modular Approach (formerly *Sage Simply Accounting*), which we will refer to as Sage 50 Premium Accounting 2015.0, is sold in five different business versions: **First Step, Pro, Premium, Quantum** and **Accountants' Edition**.

FREE to you, as a download program from the Sage 50 server, is the **Sage 50 Premium Accounting Release 2015.0**, which we will refer to as the Student Version (Sage 50 Premium Accounting Release 2015.0).

> *See Appendix 2 at the back of the textbook for computer system requirements, restrictions and installation instructions.*

The Premium Educational Version (installed in your school lab) and the Student Version, which is available as a download, are the same program. *Note*: The 2015.0 version will work with Windows Vista, Windows 7 and Windows 8, but will not work with earlier Windows versions.

When you start Sage 50 Premium Accounting 2015.0 at school, you will see the following in the bottom left of the window:

> **Registered to**: _____
> **2015.0**
> **Serial Number** _____
> **Payroll Taxes Effective: Jul 1, 2014**

Note: This window will display only for a few seconds.

If you are using the Student Version you will see:

> **Student version**
> **xxx days remaining**
> **2015.0**
> **Payroll Taxes Effective Jul 1, 2014**

You will learn the features of the **Premium** version in this textbook. The Premium software is available as a 2-user networking software. Features such as multi-user mode and departmental accounting will be discussed, but you will not be given exercises using these features.

The first chapter, **Photos Company**, explains basic concepts to give you an idea of how Sage 50 Premium Accounting 2015.0 works using double-entry accounting. The exercises allow you to try out some of the basic techniques in recording transactions, using folders and windows, in the Sage 50 Premium Accounting 2015.0 General Ledger.

The contents of this chapter are as follows:

As you go through the text, you will come across the following icons that are accompanied by special notations. Study each one carefully.

 This icon alerts you to general information, usually relevant accounting or GAAP (Generally Accepted Accounting Principles) notation. You will find the information box as a sidebar at the left of the main text.

 This icon signals caution, VERY IMPORTANT information or a reminder for you to do something that may affect processing results.

 Whenever you see this icon, run the slideshow relevant to the topic under study. It will help you to better understand concepts and procedures in the chapter.

www This icon indicates the availability of specific course material for download by opening your course materials at www.nelson.com/student. View the Appendix relevant to the topic under study. It will help you to better understand concepts and procedures.

 This icon will indicate that you will purposely make an error that you will learn how to correct later.

This icon will indicate that you will correct an error that you purposely made earlier.

 This icon will remind you to back up your data.

 This icon will remind you to update your logbook. A logbook form is in your course materials at www.nelson.com/student. Appendix 2015 J, *Work Logbook for Sage 50 Premium Accounting 2015;* there you will log the page number and topic that you last completed.

 You will see these icons together to remind you to back up your data and update your logbook form.

Sage 50 Premium Accounting 2015.0 Overview

Accrual Basis accounting
Generally Accepted Accounting Principles (GAAP) stipulate that revenue should be recognized and recorded when a service has been provided or a product has been delivered (for cash or on credit). Expenses should be recognized and recorded when a service has been provided or products have been delivered (for cash or on credit). This is the main premise of the **accrual** method.

Cash Basis accounting
Revenue is recognized and recorded when cash is received, and expenses are recognized and recorded when paid. This method is contrary to the accrual method and is not consistent with GAAP. The cash basis method can be used by farmers and fishermen, but is not accepted for income tax purposes.

The accrual method has been used in this book because it records revenues and expenses (when incurred, and provides appropriate reports that show profits or losses) at a specified accounting period, based on the time when actual business transactions occur and not when cash is received or paid. The accrual method is accepted for income tax purposes.

Sage 50 Premium Accounting 2015.0 is a simple, secure and integrated accounting software package designed to simplify bookkeeping functions using double entry accounting, i.e., Debit entries must equal Credit entries. You can view and/or print various financial statements and other reports whenever needed.

Subledgers, when in use, are linked to the GENERAL LEDGER (e.g., ACCOUNTS RECEIVABLE in Chapters 2A, 2B, and ACCOUNTS PAYABLE in Chapters 3A, 3B). This means that when a transaction is processed in any of the subledgers, the General Ledger is automatically updated. The Accounts Payable and Accounts Receivable subledgers may be linked to the INVENTORY & SERVICES subledger (Chapters 2A, 2B, 3A, 3B, and 8).

Sage 50 Premium Accounting 2015.0 provides a choice of either the **Cash** method or the **Accrual** method of accounting. This text uses the **Accrual** method (see side note box).

There are some powerful features of Sage 50 Premium Accounting 2015.0 that offer many advantages over using manual bookkeeping. For example:

1. Data entry errors may be easily corrected.
2. Controls are provided to prevent data entry errors, such as addition errors or duplicate invoice numbers, transposition of numbers..
3. Posting transactions is automatically performed by clicking the **Post** [Post] icon or the [Post ▼] icon, depending on which module you are working in, and all ledgers are updated immediately.
4. Records are updated immediately.
5. Standard financial statements and reports may be printed at any time.

Company data files for you to work with are supplied in your course materials at www.nelson.com/student. See Exercise 1-1a. Your instructor will explain which data files should be downloaded to your storage device and then extracted. If you have a damaged data file or if you want to repeat a chapter from the beginning you can extract the file again.

WWW This text assumes that you are familiar with basic accounting. If you require help in this area, information on the Basics of Accounting can be found in Appendix 2015 A, *Basics of Accounting—Perpetual Inventory System* in your course materials at www.nelson.com/student.

As you work through each section of this textbook, you will learn how to use Sage 50 Premium Accounting 2015.0 in a business setting. The purpose of the procedures and various features is explained in simple terms. A thorough knowledge of this software will make you a valuable employee.

In Chapter 4A students should be aware that they will create a new sole proprietorship retail company data file using "Let me build the list of accounts myself after the company is created."

Sage 50 Premium Accounting 2015.0 also has multiple company templates available to help save you time when creating a company in, "Have Sage 50 Premium Accounting 2015.0 create a list of accounts based on your business type." These templates will create a Chart of Accounts that matches the company's type of ownership—sole proprietorship, partnership or incorporated company—and industry type. Refer to Appendix 2015 L, *Setting Up a New Company File using a Sage 50* **WWW** *Premium Accounting Template* in your course materials at www.nelson.com/student.

Run **Slideshow 1—Getting Started and the COMPANY Module** by opening your course materials at: www.nelson.com/student. It will give you a general overview of Sage 50 Premium Accounting and how the COMPANY Module is used to journalize transactions in the General Journal.

From this point on, Sage 50 Premium Accounting 2015.0 will be referred to as "Sage 50 Accounting."

Getting Started

A basic understanding of Windows is required if you wish to use Sage 50 Accounting effectively. You can find a glossary of accounting and Sage 50 Accounting terminology at the back of the book.

If the Sage 50 Accounting software has been installed using the Typical method (most common option) on the school computer/or network, the program is located in the path:

C:/Program Files/Sage 50 Premium Accounting Version 2015

It is assumed that:

1. You have access to the Sage 50 Accounting software.

2. You will be storing your data files on a storage device. This text designates the storage device as drive **C:**. If your drive is any other than C: replace **C:** with the appropriate drive letter when doing your exercises.

Throughout the text, you will see capitalized wording such as RECEIVABLES, PAYABLES, INVENTORY & SERVICES, EMPLOYEES & PAYROLL, PROJECTS (DIVISIONS), BANKING, and COMPANY. These refer to the module being discussed.

When you see a number followed by an arrowhead, such as 1➤, 2➤, it means there is something on the line or the paragraph for you to do on the keyboard or with your mouse button. Icons will alert you to special notations.

Click	Means to click the left mouse button **once**.
Double-click	You must click the left mouse button **twice** quickly (without pausing).

Words you have to type or keys you have to press are shown in **BOLD**.

Throughout the text you will see shaded references similar to: See Exercise 7-8. These references are shaded to help you find them quickly in the textbook.

Read the instructions and explanation in the exercises before executing the keystrokes on your computer to avoid making errors.

VERY IMPORTANT:

Always back up your data at the end of EVERY work session, either in the classroom or at home. This can save you hours of redoing work (see side note box). Answer the questions at the end of each chapter before moving on to the next chapter. This will help you understand the reasons for the various procedures. It will also aid you in preparing for tests.

A detailed index is provided at the end of the book for your easy reference.

A practical storage device to back up data is a USB storage device (see picture below). These are available in varying storage capacities. The plugs into a USB port and can be easily plugged in and taken out. Ask your instructor where the USB port is located on your computer.

Most schools have an anti-virus program that protects the files in the school network. If your school does not, you should be aware that your files could be corrupted if there is a virus in the system. It is imperative, therefore, that you back up your data regularly.

If you do some of your work at home, you should invest in an anti-virus program with regular updates to ensure that your files will not be damaged, and that you do not take corrupted data to school, which can infect the network system.

Exercise 1-1a—Downloading the Master Data Files Using the Internet

Please refer to the access code instructions to be able to log into www.nelson.com/student.

WWW

The Master company data files you need to work through the exercises in this book are contained on the Nelson Education website. Each of the company data files is compressed using WinZip and is in self-extracting executable (exe) format. You need to download and unzip these files onto your storage device using the procedure below, which assumes that you are loading the data files to the C: drive. If you are loading the data files to a different storage device, use the procedure below, substituting the drive letter of the device for C. (See side note box.)

> Backup files, created in Exercise 1-24, can be used to restore a data file (see Appendix 2015 Z, *Restoring a Data File from a Backup Data File* in your course materials at **www.nelson.com/student**) if it becomes damaged or if you want to start an exercise again.

WWW

1 ➤ Using Windows Explorer, create two folders, **Sage 50 Exe**, where the Exe files will be located, and **Sage 50 Data 2015**, where the data files will be located on the C: drive, or other drive as requested by your instructor.

2 ➤ Start your web browser (Internet Explorer, Firefox, etc.).

WWW

3 ➤ In the locator bar, type **www.nelson.com/student**, press `Enter`. You will be taken to the NelsonBrain website.

4 ➤ In the box labelled "**Register**" enter the **access code** printed on your Premium Website Access Card, included with your text.

5 ➤ **Register** as a new user or log in if you already have a NelsonBrain account.

6 ➤ To access course materials, click on the **Open** button. This opens the online course materials for the text.

7a ➤ To download all the data files used in the text, you could select **Download the Chapter Data and Challenge files in one ZIP file**, or go to step 7b.

7b ➤ To download files individually, **scroll** down to Chapter 1. You should also see the Challenge Exercises that are available. Click on **01 Photos**, click **Save**, locate your **Sage 50 Exe** folder, and click **Save** and **Close**. Follow the prompts for "Download" or "Save" as presented to you by your computer.

Repeat the procedure to download appropriate files required by your instructor.

8 ➤ When you have finished downloading/saving files from the website, locate your **Sage 50 Exe** folder.

Exercise 1-1b—Extracting the Master Data Files

1 ➤ Go to the folder where your downloads are located. Double-click on the **01 Photos.exe** file.

You may see the following Security Warning window.

If you use **Windows Explorer** or **My Computer**, you will notice that the **01 Photos folder** contains a Photos folder with an extension of **SAJ** and a file with an extension of **SAI**. Inside the SAJ folder are 3 folders and additional files. The **mysql** folder contains the database and the **Sage 50 Accounting 2015** folder contains the Sage 50 data files. Together these files contain information about the company, accounts, transactions, etc. When you open the data file, Exercise 1-2, step 10, you use only the **SAI** file in the window.

If you move your mouse to hover over the SAI file, you will see information that this is a Sage 50 Data File.

If you see this window, click **Run**.

 The WinZip Self-extractor, Unzip command will create the Photos data file in the Sage 50 Data 2015 folder on your storage device. If you want to load the data files in a different drive/folder, change the field **C:\Sage 50 Data 2015** to your specific location, or click **Browse** to locate the specific storage space.

2 ➤ Click **Unzip**.

The following window indicates that the data files have been successfully unzipped and are ready for you to use.

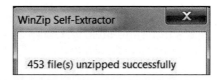

The data folder in your C:\ storage location should have the following name:

Folder	Company Name	Module used (Main)
01 Photos	Photos Company	COMPANY

3 ➤ Click **OK**, then **Close**.

To copy other company files (e.g., 02 2A Luggage-PI-2A) to your storage space (e.g., C:\Sage 50 Data 2015), repeat the above steps.

Refer to Appendix 2, at the back of the text, for instructions on installing the Student version of the Sage 50 Premium Accounting 2015 program.

Using Windows Explorer, locate the Sage 50 Data 2015 folder and the 01 Photos data file.

Starting the Sage 50 Premium Accounting 2015 Program

 www In a business setting, you may be required to enter a password before you can access a Sage 50 Accounting data file. Passwords prevent unauthorized people from having access to your program and the company data. The exercises in this textbook do not require a password. Information on using a password can be found in Appendix 2015 O, *Security—Passwords* in your course materials at www.nelson.com/student. See your instructor for more information.

⚠ Read the instructions and explanation in each exercise before attempting to record data using the Sage 50 Accounting program. If you ignore the instructions and explanation, you may make errors that could easily have been avoided.

Remember...

Click   means to click the left button once.

Double-click means to click the left button twice rapidly.

Exercise 1-2—Starting the Sage 50 Premium Accounting 2015 Program

---

⚠ Do NOT open the Sage 50 Accounting 2015 file from the Windows Explorer or My Computer windows. Use the procedure shown in this exercise.

You need to tell the Sage 50 Premium Accounting 2015 program where to locate the company data files that you will be using. You will start by using the Photos Company data folder.

Your instructor will advise you how to access Sage 50 Premium Accounting 2015 in the classroom. If you are using your home computer, there are 2 ways to open a data file (Method 1 and Method 2).

ⓘ The location of the Sage 50 Premium Accounting 2015 icon and/or name depends upon how your Windows program groups are set up for application software.

Method 1

1 ➤ Click the **Start** icon (see side note box).

2 ➤ In the left hand column, move the mouse to the [📊 Sage 50 2015 Premium Accounting Version ▶] icon and hold it until the Recent files list displays to the right of the icon.

3 ➤ As this is the first time to open a file (Photos.SAI), it will not display in the list. Click the **Sage 50** icon in step 2. You are taken to Fig. 1-1a, Sage 50 Accounting start window.

The Sage 50 Accounting Start Window

ⓘ If you have used the Photos.SAI file before, it will appear on the list. It is the specific company file you worked on last. Click **Photos.SAI.** You move to step 9 or 10 (i.e., New Session date window) depending on which method (1 or 2) you use to open the file.

Fig. 1-1a: Sage 50 Accounting start window. (See side note box.)

Fig. 1-1b: Sage 50 Accounting start window, with Open last company.

a) **Open the sample company** to help you learn Sage 50 Accounting. Used if you want to open the sample company (Universal Construction) that was installed in the computer. (You may not have access to the sample companies.)

b) **Create a new company**. Used when you need to create a new company. You will use this option in Chapter 4A.

c) **Restore from backup**. Used when you want to open a backup file (e.g., to replace a damaged data file). Instructions on using this feature are in Appendix 2015 Z, *Restoring a Data File from a Backup Data File* in your course materials at www.nelson.com/student.

WWW

d) **Select an existing company**. Used when you want to open a company that is on your storage space. (See this exercise at step 5.)

e) **Open the last company you worked on**. This option may not be applicable in a classroom setting. If the student before you was working on a different company, this choice may not be appropriate.

f) **Do not show this Select Company window at startup**. Do NOT click this selection. This option is explained in Chapter 4A.

4 ➤ Click **Select an existing company**.

5 ➤ Click **OK**. You may then see the Open Company window, Fig. 1-2.

Fig. 1-2: Open Company window.

Remember, if your data folders are located on another drive such as **D:**, **E:** or another letter, substitute your drive letter for **C:**.

6 ➤   In the left pane, locate and click the **Sage 50 Data 2015** folder (Fig. 1-2).

7 ➤   In the right panel double-click the folder .

8 ➤   In the right panel double-click the file name. (*Note*: In Fig. 1-2, you may not see the **SAI** extension in the file name box.) You should see Fig. 1-3, New Session Date window.

Wait for the program to load. A Session Date box appears.

If you are using the Sage 50 Premium Accounting Student Version, see the note at the left. The Fig. 1-3, New Session Date window appears. (See side note box.)

Fig. 1-3: New Session Date window.

> If you are using the Student Version, the program can be used for a period of 14 months (425 days) from the date that you install the program.
>
> The number of days remaining will display on the left side when you start the program.

Sage 50 Accounting uses the date format as defined by Windows. The author has used the long date format: **mm/dd/yyyy** (month, day, year) format. (Sage 50 Accounting allows the date to be displayed using an abbreviated name, i.e., Apr 10, 2019 instead of 04/10/2019).

To change the date you have three choices.

⚠ Do NOT click this field. If you click this field and OK by mistake, you enter the Photos data file. The next time you open this company, the Session Date window will NOT display and you will have to change the session date inside the data file.

To correct the mistake, and have the session date displayed as above, each time you open the data file, from the top menu bar click **Setup, User Preferences, View**, click on the 3ʳᵈ item at the bottom, ☑ Show Change Session Date at Startup and click **OK** to return to the Home window.

1.   You may type the date in the **Date for this Session** box.
2.   You may click the ▼ arrow and select the appropriate date from a range of dates. See Method 2, step 10.
3.   You may click the Calendar button.

⚠ The most efficient way to enter a date is by using choice 3, the Sage 50 Accounting Calendar. It is fast and it helps you avoid making date format errors.

You will click the ▼ arrow in the next step only to understand the concept of range of dates relevant to the Session Date.

9 ➤   Click the ▼ arrow. A drop-down list of dates appears.

Fig. 1-4: Multiple Session Dates to be explained.

The location of the Sage 50 Premium Accounting 2015 icon and/or name depends upon how your Windows program groups are set up for application software.

Method 2

1 ➤ Click the **Start** icon ![start icon], in the left hand column, move the mouse to the to the ▶ All Programs icon.

2 ➤ Scroll to and click ![Sage]. (See side note box.)

3 ➤ Move the mouse and click on ![Sage 50 Premium Accounting Version 2015].

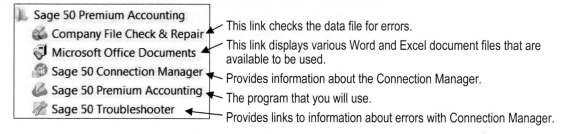

Sage 50 Premium Accounting
- Company File Check & Repair — This link checks the data file for errors.
- Microsoft Office Documents — This link displays various Word and Excel document files that are available to be used.
- Sage 50 Connection Manager — Provides information about the Connection Manager.
- Sage 50 Premium Accounting — The program that you will use.
- Sage 50 Troubleshooter — Provides links to information about errors with Connection Manager.

4 ➤ Click on the next ![Sage 50 Premium Accounting Version 2015]

5 ➤ You are taken to Fig. 1-1b, Sage 50 Accounting start windows, with Open last company.

6 ➤ Click on **Select an existing company**, and **OK**.

7 ➤ In the right panel double-click the folder ![01 Photos].

8 ➤ In the right panel double-click the ![Photos.SAI] file name. (*Note*: In Fig. 1-2, you may not see the **SAI** extension in the file name box.) You should see Fig. 1-3, New Session Date window.

9 ➤ Click **OK**. Wait for the program to load. A Session Date box appears.

10 ➤ Click the ![down arrow] arrow. A drop-down list of dates appears.

Range of Dates

The Photos Company is using a calendar fiscal year.

Start of the fiscal year is: Jan 01, 2019
End of the fiscal year is: Dec 31, 2019

Apr 01, 2019   This is the first day of the current month.

Apr 10, 2019   This is the last date that the Photos Company data file was used. This is known as the **Session Date**. In a business environment, the Session Date is the current date when you are entering transactions. This date will change as you change the Session Date.

Dec 31, 2019   The end of Photos Company's fiscal year.

Jan 01, 2020   The start of Photos Company's next fiscal year. You must be careful NOT to select this. If you type or accept Jan 01, 2020, the start of Photos Company's next fiscal year, Sage 50 Accounting will automatically perform year-end procedures, closing the Revenue and Expense accounts for the previous fiscal year to zero. In addition, the net profit or loss will be updated in the appropriate Equity account, e.g., Capital, Retained Earnings, etc.

You will now use the Calendar button ▦ to enter the Session Date. Although you can type the Session Date 04102019, Apr10, or select the appropriate date from the drop-down options, using the Calendar is by far the most efficient way.

11 ➤   Click the **Calendar** button ▦ to close the drop-down list of dates. Click it a second time and the calendar for the current month appears. To move to future months, click the ▶. To move back, click the ◀. Try going forward and backward now.

12 ▶   Move the Calendar to April. For this exercise, you need to enter **Apr 18, 2019** as your Session Date. Click **18**. Your window should resemble the next screen:

13 ➤   Click **OK**.

  The Warning window advises you if the date you entered is more than one week (7 days) past the previous session date. However, it will not advise you if you have entered a new month or if you have entered the wrong date. If you have made an error in the date, the program will give you the opportunity to change it at this point by clicking **Cancel**.

14 ➤   If the date is correct, click **OK** to accept the new Session Date.

You will see the Getting Started window in front of the Sage 50 Accounting Home window.

In addition to the Getting Started window, Fig. 1-5a, you may receive additional windows. If you do, steps 17 and 18 apply. If not, step 18.

Fig. 1-5a: Getting Started; Welcome to Sage 50 Accounting window.

15 ➤ A Product Enhancement Program window may also appear. Click **Close** to continue.

You may also see a window regarding Pop-up messages. *Note*: Some of the Pop-up messages can be turned off (Not display). See Exercise 1-3, Turn Off Message Centre Pop-up Alerts. *Note*: Support Pop-up Alerts cannot be turned off.

Your current data file is for Photos Company. The Getting Started: Welcome to Sage 50 window should look like Fig. 1-5a. The Sage 50 Accounting **Home** window will be Fig. 1-5b. A brief explanation of the menus and icons is shown after step 24. You are welcome to experiment clicking on menu items or icons as you proceed with this overview.

Do not make any changes to any of the windows, as they may affect the data used in the practice exercises later in the chapter. To exit from this window or any window, click the ⬚X⬚ in the top-right corner. If you click ⬚X⬚ from the Home window, Fig. 1-5b, Sage 50 Accounting saves the work you completed and closes the file.

The Welcome to Sage 50 window is divided into 4 parts.

If you click on various choices, the Welcome to Sage 50 window may disappear.

You should see the ⬚ icon on the bottom taskbar. Click on the icon to return to the Home Window.

Explore Sage 50 This section contains videos to learn about various parts of Sage 50 Accounting. If you have used an older version of Sage Simply Accounting (2014 or prior), you will want to review the "What's New in Sage 50 Premium Accounting 2015" link, and the Learning Centre. Also see Appendix 2015 C, *What's New in Sage 50 Premium Accounting 2015 (Release 2015.0)* in your course materials at www.nelson.com/student. The other selections will be discussed in various chapters.

Add Business Records This section contains links to add items identified. This text will show you how to add records in each chapter: Accounts in Chapter 1, Customers in Chapter 2A, etc. The link to Open the Setup Guide will be discussed in Chapter 4A.

Customize Sage 50 This section contains links that you will see in various chapters. Set Company Preferences, Schedule data backups, Customize your invoices and other business forms will be discussed in Chapter 4A.

Learn How to This section contains links to Help documents. You will be shown how to set up INVENTORY & SERVICES in Chapter 8 and Appendix 2015 H, *INVENTORY & SERVICES Module Setup Perpetual Inventory for Sarah's Kitchen Stores (4B)*, PROJECTS (can also be called DIVISIONS) in Chapter 11, PAYROLL in Chapter 7, and Security (Users and permissions) in Appendix 2015 O, *Security—Passwords* in your course materials at www.nelson.com/student.

16 ➤ To not see the Getting Started; Welcome to Sage 50 Accounting window at startup and go directly to the Home window (Fig. 1-5b), click the ☑ **Show this window on startup** (this will remove the checkmark), then click **Close**.

Note: For other companies the ☐ **Show this window on startup**, has been unchecked to not display on Startup. You will go directly to the Home page. If you have clicked the button as indicated ☑ and you want to see the Welcome to Sage 50 Accounting window, from the menu bar on the home window, click **Setup**, **Getting Started Guide**.

A feature in Sage 50 Accounting is the Message icon 🖂 at the bottom right of the Home window. By clicking on this icon you can view messages from Sage 50 Accounting that may be appropriate for individual companies. The number identifies the number of messages that have not been viewed. This feature is not available for students.

Home Window—Enhanced View

Fig. 1-5b: Sage 50 Premium Accounting HOME Enhanced View window.

Company Name: The internal data file company name [Photos Company, Student's Name] displays, above the module bars, near the top left side, as part of the Home window. You will be changing the "Student's Name" to your own name in Exercise 1-5. Your name will then display in the Home window and other journals.

Look at the top right side to see the location of the Session Date. [Session Date: Apr 18, 2019] You will change the date using this feature in Exercise 1-9.

If you have seen previous versions of Sage Simply Accounting (2007 and prior), you will notice a big change in the Home window.

17 ➤ On the right side, on the Support & Services line, click on the [−] at the end of the line. The section reduces to a single line and hides the information until you need it. This works with the 2 sections on the right.

18 ➤ To expand the section that is hidden, click on the [+].

You can still see and use the previous version Home page, now known as the Classic View.

19 ➤ To see the **Classic View** window, at the top right side click [Switch to Classic View].

Home Window—Classic View

Fig. 1-5c: Sage 50 Premium Accounting HOME Classic View window.

20 ➤ To return to the **Enhanced View** window, click [Switch to Enhanced View].

When you click the ⊠ button (Exit) in the top right corner of the Home window, Sage 50 Accounting **saves** all entries in memory to the data file in the storage location and closes the program.

Menu Bar

Each menu item contains a drop-down list of options related to the menu heading. You can display the menu list by clicking the menu item. Try clicking each menu item now.

Toolbar on Enhanced window Fig. 1-5b

Note that there is a row with 5 icons below the Menu Bar (this text calls them **Toolbar icons**). The icons are designed to allow easy access to changing to another company data file, backing up the current data file, opening the Daily Business Manager DBM (shown in Chapter 2A), closing any open Sage 50 Accounting journals or reports and for the business user Chat with Support, which requires a business prepaid service plan. When you move your mouse over a toolbar icon, an information box appears below it with a brief explanation. Position your mouse over each of the icons and read the explanation that appears.

Modules

In Sage 50 Accounting and this text, a module is referred to as a bar in the Home window. Each module will have different views for Tasks, Accountant's Tasks, and Related Tasks depending on the module selected. Click on each of the modules to see the differences. These will be explained in this and other chapters. The COMPANY module will be discussed in this chapter. Each module can be hidden or revealed as needed. You will see how this works in later chapters.

21 ➤ Click on the **RECEIVABLES** module and look at the Tasks area and the Customers icon.

History: This symbol beside an icon indicates that you can enter historical transactions in the record. Until you finish entering history, you can continue to change the account balances or other information you entered. In this chapter, the COMPANY module is ready to record journal entries. The other modules (RECEIVABLES, PAYABLES, INVENTORY & SERVICES, EMPLOYEES & PAYROLL) have the icon, which means that these records are available to record historical transactions.

Note: You cannot start a new fiscal year if the subsidiary ledgers do not agree with the General Ledger. This text does not record transactions until the module has been set up.

22 ➤ Click the **DASHBOARD** module. This module by means of graphs and columns displays company information for Revenues Year to Date: (line graphs), Revenue vs. Payroll Expenses (column graphs), and in later chapters will display Pie Charts for Aged Receivables and Payables.

23 ➤ Click the **COMPANY** module.

Tasks

Projects This feature can also be called Divisions, Territories or another appropriate name. This feature will allow revenues and expenses to be allocated and accumulated for projects, divisions, salesperson's territories, etc. (see Chapter 11).

Daily Business Manager This feature allows the user to add notes for future reference and shows other Memo information, Recurring Invoices, Payments Due and Sales Due. You can also view various Business Performance ratios. You will be shown how to use this feature in Chapter 2A, Exercise 2A-9 through 2A-12, or hide the option in Chapter 2A, Exercise 2A-13.

Data Management You can right-click on any icon that shows the ▼ to see details of the features. This feature allows the user to Back up a data file, Restore a data file, Advanced Database Check, Consolidate Company (used when combining different businesses owned by one owner—this feature is not shown in this text) and Import and Export Records.

Accountant's Tasks

Chart of Accounts The General Ledger (G/L) for a company. This ledger allows you to keep a complete G/L system from which you can produce financial statements. The G/L uses the following account grouping: Assets, Liabilities, Equities, Revenues, and Expenses. This feature allows you to View, Add, Modify, and Remove accounts. You can also add accounts from inside journals.

General Journal This is the journal that you will use in this chapter.

You would normally use the Sage 50 Accounting General Journal only to make entries that cannot be made in subledgers and their associated journals. You use the double-entry method to record these entries, which are usually banking transactions and those that relate to accrued adjustments.

Transactions pertaining to sales and purchases are entered in the RECEIVABLES module (Chapters 2A, 2B) and PAYABLES module (Chapters 3A, 3B) respectively. You will learn how to record sales-related transactions in the RECEIVABLES module and purchases-related transactions in the PAYABLES module.

Some small companies, although not very many, use only the General Ledger and none of the subledger modules. Photos Company is one of them.

Accountant's Copy This feature allows the user to create a data file to be sent to the accountant for month-end or year-end entries. When the accountant sends you the updated data file, you can use the Import Entries from Accountant item. You can also Cancel the Accountant's copy. This feature is not shown in this text.

Related Tasks

Settings This feature will allow you to change default settings in the software. This will be explained in more detail in Chapter 4A.

Form Designer This feature will allow you to change default settings in various Sage 50 Accounting forms. This feature is discussed in Appendix 2015 N, *Adding a Salesperson's Name to an Invoice* in your course materials at www.nelson.com/student.   **WWW**

Support & Services

Support & Services Refer to the Installation Instructions in Appendix 2 at the back of the textbook. Please note that support or services through SAGE Software Inc. are not available for student version software.

Reports

Report Centre This feature allows the user to select a report from the Report Centre window, without having to click **Reports** from the menu bar and select from various types of reports. This feature also lets you see what the report will look like before you display it. You can also click the drop-down arrow at Reports to see the reports that are available in this module. Each module will have different reports available.

Recently viewed reports This section will display the last 4 reports the user viewed. You can click any report in this section and it will display and can be printed.

The various tasks and journals are explained in the appropriate chapters, such as Sales and Receipts, where transaction information is recorded and posted. Each of the modules must be properly set up.

24 ➤ Click on the **Learning Centre**. Depending on the configuration of your computer, you may see the next window. The window is divided into 7 active parts (from left to right).

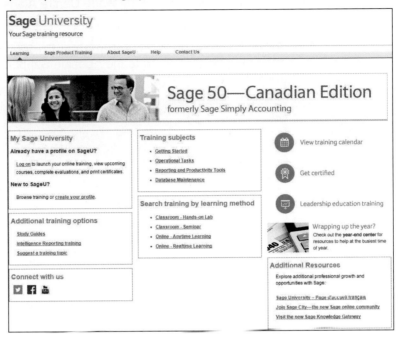

Fig. 1-5d: Learning Centre window.

 Note: This window may have a different configuration than the one displayed. (i.e., the My Sage University and other sections may be in different columns or rows; classroom courses may be in the 2nd row on the left. Other configurations are also possible.

This feature allows the user to use various tutorials.

My Sage University you need a profile (online account) to access information.

Additional training options this section contains information regarding study guides available for purchase; webcasts, and various training courses are available.

Training subjects this section contains training courses available for a fee.

Search training by learning method this section contains various learning methods are available, i.e., hands on in a computer lab, seminars or online courses.

View training calendar This section displays courses that are available by date on-line or in a classroom, for a fee.

Get certified this section is for users who want to be certified.

Leadership education training this section contains information about Sage 50 Accounting courses in various locations, for a fee.

Additional Resources – Sage University a forum is available for student questions; does not require a service plan.

25 ➤ Click ⊠ to close.

26 ➤ On the left side, click on the **Company** module.

Exercise 1-3—Turn Off Message Centre Pop-up Alerts

---

1 ➤   You will now turn off the Message Centre Alerts pop-ups. They would be used in the retail market.

2 ➤   From the menu bar, click **Setup, User Preferences, Pop-ups** and you will see the Message Centre. Note the * beside Support Alerts. Support Alerts cannot be turned off.

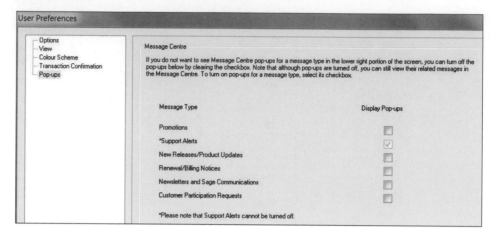

3 ➤   Click **each box** to remove the checkmark ☐ from the **Display Pop-ups** column.

4 ➤   Click **OK** to return to the home window.

Using Sage 50 Accounting HELP

Sage 50 Accounting provides 5 ways to find Help within the program. It is assumed that the COMPANY module is selected on the left.

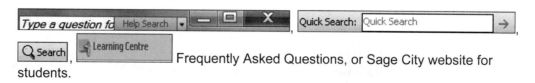

Frequently Asked Questions, or Sage City website for students.

Exercise 1-4a—Using Help—Type a Question for Help

---

1 ➤   [Type a question for Help Search] This help field, at the top right of the window, enables the user to enter questions for assistance as if he or she were talking to the software. Click the Help Search ▼. Select either Sage 50 Help (default) or On Line Community. Click in the field and type your question such as: **How many expense accounts are in the ledger?** Press Enter. If you select Sage 50 Help, you will see 1,186 responses.

2 ➤   Click on ⊠ in the top right corner to **Exit**, and return to Fig. 1-5b, Home window.

Exercise 1-4b—Using Help—Search

1 ➤   In **Quick Search:** [Quick Search] type **expense**, and click the **→** (Quick Search) button, or press **Enter**. The Search button searches all reports and customer, vendor, and other modules for instances of the information requested (expense).

A report with a list of 11 accounts with the word "Expense" in the name will appear and the Advanced Search Results Summary report will display the information next.

> **Number of Matches: 11**
> Search <All Fields> Contains expense

2 ➤   As you move your mouse over the information, a magnifying glass appears. **Double-click** on any item in the window and Sage 50 Accounting will drill down (this will be explained in more detail in Exercise 1-17) to the information and display it. In this situation, the General Ledger, where you can change account information, will appear.

3 ➤   Click **X** **twice** to return to the Home window. If you can see the **⊠ Close other windows** icon on the tool bar, you can also click the icon and you will be returned to the Home window.

Exercise 1-4c—Using Help—Database Search Tool

1 ➤   Click on **🔍 Search**. The Basic and Advanced tabs will display. Click the **▼** to see a list of records or transactions you can search for. This feature is not used in this text.

2 ➤   Click **Cancel**, to return to Fig. 1-5b, Home window.

Exercise 1-4d—Using Help—Learning Centre

1 ➤   Click the **Learning Centre** module icon. Scroll over **Help** in the toolbar and click on **FAQs** to access a list of items. You may have to scroll up or down to see more items.

2 ➤   Click on the **Company** module to return to Fig. 1-5b, Home window.

The **F1** key for Help does not work in the Enhanced Home window.

Exercise 1-4e—Using Help—Sage City for Students

Sage 50 Accounting has a website for students to access for help.

http://sagecity.na.sage.com/sage_students/default.aspx

Type the link (sage[underscore]students/default.aspx). Press **Enter**. Hold the **Ctrl** key down and click on the link. You can join a group and get access to Student Forums, Videos, Knowledge base, etc.

Revising Company Information

Sage 50 Accounting allows you to make changes in the company information; e.g., the address needs to be changed if the company has moved, phone numbers may have changed, or the company may have installed additional phones. In the next exercise, you will change the company name information to include your name.

WWW   For a quick reference guide on various exercises throughout the textbook, refer to Appendix 2015 R, *Quick Reference Guide* in your course materials at www.nelson.com/student.

Photos Company, Student's Name
Trial Balance As at Apr 18, 2019

Account	Debits	Credits
1100 Bank Account	4,135.00	-
1110 Bank Credit Card	750.00	-
1200 Accounts Receivable	3,050.00	-
1260 Inventory	22,100.00	
1300 Prepaid Expenses	432.00	-
1520 Photo Equipment	31,500.00	-
1525 Accum Deprec- Photo Equipment	-	8,750.00
1580 Office Equipment	8,250.00	-
1585 Accum Deprec- Office Equipment	-	1,300.00
2200 Accounts Payable	-	2,565.00
2710 Bank Loan Payable (Long Term)	-	12,000.00
3100 Capital Terrie Chikowski	-	35,822.00
3120 Additional Investment T. Chikowski	-	0.00
3560 Drawings Terrie Chikowski	1,000.00	-
4100 Sales	-	31.267.00
4220 Sales Returns	100.00	
4240 Sales Discounts	120.00	-
5010 Cost of Goods Sold	16,628.00	-
5070 Purchase Discounts	-	489.00
5180 Bank Charges Expense	75.00	
5220 Office Supplies Expense	85.00	
5240 Telephone Expense	136.00	
5260 Rent Expense	1,500.00	
5399 Wages/Salaries Expense	1,200.00	-
5400 Repairs & Maintenance Expense	97.00	
5440 Advertising Expense	735.00	
5490 Depreciation Expense	300.00	-
	----------------	------------------
	92,193.00	92,193.00
	=========	=========

Exercise 1-5—Changing Company Information

As you and your fellow students in class start printing reports, there could be confusion as to which printout belongs to whom, because you will all have the same heading, **Photos Company**, **Student's Name**. You will now change the company name to include your name, so you can easily identify your own printout.

You may use the same technique shown here to change any company information.

1 ➤ In the lower Related Tasks area, click on the **Settings** icon; in the left pane click on **Information**. The Company Information window will appear.

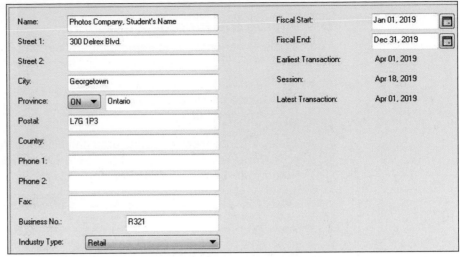

Name:	Photos Company, Student's Name		Fiscal Start:	Jan 01, 2019
Street 1:	300 Delrex Blvd.		Fiscal End:	Dec 31, 2019
Street 2:			Earliest Transaction:	Apr 01, 2019
City:	Georgetown		Session:	Apr 18, 2019
Province:	ON ▼ Ontario		Latest Transaction:	Apr 01, 2019
Postal:	L7G 1P3			
Country:				
Phone 1:				
Phone 2:				
Fax:				
Business No.:	R321			
Industry Type:	Retail ▼			

Fig. 1-6: A portion of the Company Information window.

2 ➤ In the Name box, highlight **Student's Name** and type your **last name** (surname) and **first name** (given), then click **OK**. The company name will be changed accordingly and now will appear at the top of the modules on the left side of the Home window.

Example: | Photos Company, Guida Marisa |

⚠ You should follow the name change procedure for each new company you work on. You only need to do this once for each company.

To Display Reports

Shortcuts: You will be shown how to create a list of reports (Customize) that you may use often in Exercise 1-22a, Creating Custom Report Shortcuts. You can add or remove items in the list.

Most new companies will start by setting up the various modules, e.g., COMPANY, RECEIVABLES, PAYABLES, EMPLOYEES & PAYROLL. Some new companies, however, may start with only the COMPANY module and eventually add the other modules when they determine that they have enough transactions for these modules to warrant the effort to set them up.

As mentioned earlier, the COMPANY module allows you to enter transactions into a complete General Ledger system (double entry), and allows financial statements to be displayed and/or printed at any time. (See side note box.) Note that the other modules are not active for the Photos Company (you can tell because the History symbol 🖋 is showing with the Tasks icons inside each of the other modules).

Financial Statements for a company are generated from previously entered data, and may be displayed or printed for a range of dates or a specific day.

To start this exercise you need to be at the Photos Company Home window.

Exercise 1-6a—Displaying Reports Using Recently Viewed Reports Area

---

Displaying the Income Statement

You can display an Income Statement for any period of time:

- one day or a few days
- a week or a few weeks
- one month or a few months
- year-to-date

1 ➤ The Recently viewed reports area can display with the last 4 reports listed. In the **Reports** field, click ▾, select **Income Statement**, click **Display**. The report will display. Only the top portion is shown.

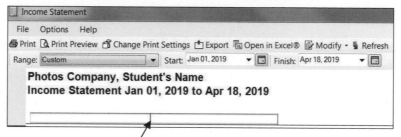

By clicking on the dividing line, you can move the columns to the left or right to change the way the columns display and/or print in statements.

2 ➤ To modify the Income Statement, click on the **Modify** icon.

Fig. 1-7: Modify Options menu.

3 ➤ Click on **Report Options**. You will see the following window.

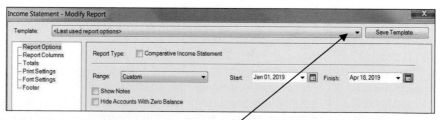

The settings on the left side are the same as those in the Modify icon drop-down area.

Comparative Income statements will be discussed and shown in Chapter 3B.

You can customize the Income Statement Print settings and/or Font settings. The same customization information applies for the Balance Sheet. There is no exercise for changing Print and Font settings.

Template drop-down ▾: Click ▾ and two choices appear:

<Default report options>
<Last used report options>

<Default report options> Options used by Sage 50 Accounting without changes.

<Last used report options> The options used the last time you requested the report will be used to display the report this time.

Save Template button — You are able to save a report with any changed settings (date, terms, etc.) as a template and it can be retrieved later with the same settings.

☐ **Show Notes** — Do NOT Change. You are able to add specific notes to viewed and printed statements. See Appendix 2015 U, *Adding Notes/Footers to Statements* for more information in your course materials at www.nelson.com/student.

WWW

☐ Hide Accounts With Zero Balance — By clicking this field, General Ledger accounts with zero balances will not display when printing reports. Leave blank.

As noted previously at Exercise 1-2, you can change the date in reports using either the ▼ or the calendar feature.

4 ➤ **Range** — Click ▼ and a list of various reports dates appears. Click the ▼ again to use the **Custom** selection.

5 ➤ **Start** — Leave the date as **Jan 01, 2019**, the start of the fiscal year.

6 ➤ **Finish** — Using the calendar, change the date to **April 10, 2019** (because you have not yet entered data in April).

7 ➤ Click **OK** to display an Income Statement for the period Jan 01, 2019 to Apr 10, 2019 (see side note box). **DO NOT PRINT AT THIS TIME. You will print an Income Statement in Exercise 1-20**.

To view the lower part of the statement, you can use the vertical scroll bar, and/or the maximize button ☐. (See side note box.) Scroll back to the top of the Income Statement.

8 ➤ A management feature for the Financial Statements is now available. You will notice the symbol ▣ to the left of the wording ▣ **Revenue**, ▣ **Cost of Goods Sold**, and ▣ **Store & Admin Expenses** .

> *Note*: This feature will hide the individual accounts and display the section total. The Revenue and Store & Admin Expense sections can be hidden for the Purchasing Manager. The Cost of Goods Sold & the Store & Admin Expense sections can be hidden for the Sales Manager, and so on.
>
> This feature will also work with the Balance Sheet.

9 ➤ To hide individual amounts, click on the ▣ for the **Cost of Goods Sold** & the **Store & Admin Expense** sections. The Revenue section Sales accounts are still displayed. This report can be printed and distributed to managers in the Sales departments. Other reports can be distributed as needed.

10 ➤ To display the previously hidden section, click on the ⊞ **(expand)** button.

11 ➤ To close the Income Statement, click the ☒ **EXIT** button and return to the Home window. The Recently viewed reports area displays the Income Statement that you just viewed.

ⓘ You can view other parts of the report by scrolling down.

In the lower left corner of the displayed statement is the wording: **Generated On**: with the current date. When the statement is printed, the wording changes to **Printed On:** with the current session date.

Displaying the Balance Sheet

Exercise 1-6b—Displaying the Balance Sheet Using the Report Menu

You can display a Balance Sheet only at a certain date, not for a range of dates. To use another method of displaying reports, follow this procedure.

1 ➤ From the Menu bar, click **Reports**, move to **Financials**, move to **Balance Sheet**, then **click**.

You can customize the Balance Sheet Print settings and/or Font settings.

> The wording **Generated on**: with the current date will appear at the bottom of all displayed reports.

2 ➤ **Template**   Click the ▼ and select **Default Report Options** to match the window above.

3 ➤ **As at**   Click the ▼ to see the range of dates that are available. Change to **Custom**.

4 ➤ **Date**   Using the calendar, change the date to **Apr 10, 2019** (because you have not yet entered data in April). (See side note box.)

> As discussed previously, the individual amounts can be hidden. If you click on the ⊟ at Photo Equipment, two accounts are hidden and only the subtotal (Net Book Value) appears.

5 ➤   Click **OK** to display a Balance Sheet. (See side note box.) Notice that account 3120 Additional Investment T Chikowski, displays with a zero balance.

If you had clicked the 1-6a exercise, ☐ Hide Accounts With Zero Balance account #3120 would not have displayed. You may want to try this feature now.

DO NOT PRINT AT THIS TIME; you will print a Balance Sheet in Exercise 1-20.

6 ➤ To close the Balance Sheet, click the ☒ **EXIT** button and return to the Home window.

Exercise 1-6c—Displaying the Income Statement Using the Report Centre

1 ➤ Click the **Report Centre** icon.

2 ➤ In the COMPANY module, the default is Financials with 5 Income Statements indicated. Notice the 5 types of Income Statements that can be displayed.

3 ➤ Using **Standard**. A sample of a similar Income Statement is displayed on the right.

4 ➤ Click on **Display**; the Photos Income Statement is displayed. The dates will need to change depending on your situation.

5 ➤ **Start date**   Leave the date as **Jan 01, 2019**.

6 ➤ **Finish date**   Change to **Apr 10, 2019** (because you have not yet entered data in April). The statement dates should change. If they did not, click the **Refresh** ⟳ Refresh icon (top right) to update the information. The statement date is revised.

<table>
<tr><td>

</td><td>

7 ➤   Range

Change to **This Calendar Year**. The Start date stays at Jan 01, 2019, and the Finish date changes to the Session Date Apr 18, 2019.

DO NOT PRINT AT THIS TIME. You will print in Chapters 2A and 2B. (See side note box.)

8 ➤

Click **X** to exit the Income Statement and return to the Report Centre. Other reports can be printed from the Report Centre. Click **Close** to return to the Home window.

</td></tr>
</table>

Processing Transactions in the COMPANY Module

In Sage 50 Accounting, it is only in the **GENERAL Journal** that you use double entry recording (enter both debit and credit items).

To record transactions, see Exercise 1-7, which follows these steps:

1. Enter the data into a **Journal**. Each entry must have equal debits and credits; otherwise, Sage 50 Accounting will not allow you to post the entry.

2. View the entry to make sure it is correct. Sage 50 Accounting will allow you to make corrections if necessary.

3. When the entry is correct, click the **Posting** icon [Post], and the entry is automatically posted to the appropriate accounts in the General Ledger.

Correcting Errors

Correcting Errors

A: BEFORE Posting:
Click the field(s) that require changing and change the amounts or wording.

B: Reverse Entry. To Correct Errors AFTER Posting—Cancelling the entry:
If you make an error in the journal entry and realize after you have posted it that it is completely in error and should be cancelled, use the **Reverse entry** feature. (See Exercise 2A-19.)

The Reverse entry reverses the original entry (debits and credits), which cancels the original entry.

C: Adjust a previously posted entry. To Correct Errors AFTER Posting—

Correcting the entry **Exercise 1-13:**
If you make a minor error(s) in a journal entry and realize it after you have posted it, you can use an **Adjustment** entry to open the original entry and correct the error(s) and post the correction. This adjustment entry reverses the original entry (debits and credits) and records the correct entry. See Exercise 1-13, *Correcting an Entry*.

Correction Method A. In this exercise you will record, from a bank debit memo, the bank charges for printing new company cheques. Study the transaction:

Apr 18, 2019	**Received from the bank, new company cheques with a $31.00 bank debit memo, dated April 17, 2019, for the printing charge.**

The correct journal entry is:

Dr	Bank Charges Expense	31.00	
Cr	Cash in Bank		31.00

In order to show you how to correct errors before posting entries, you will deliberately make two errors (an account number at step 6 and an amount at step 12) and correct them before posting.

For this chapter only, HST is ignored. This will allow you to focus on understanding the basics of Sage 50 Accounting at this early stage of your learning.

Exercise 1-7—Entering Transactions in the General Journal

To start this exercise, you need to be at the Photos Company home window.

General Journal

1 ➤ Click the **General Journal** icon.

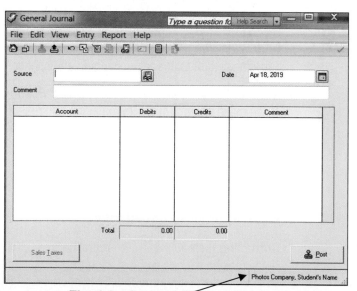

Fig. 1-8: General Journal window.

The name of the company is displayed on the bottom taskbar of the journals. This feature can be turned off and will be discussed in Chapter 4A.

When you hold your mouse over each of the toolbar icons, a display below each icon indicates what it is used for. Try it now.

The [Tab] key is used to move to the next field in all journal screens.
If you want to move to a specific field, click the appropriate field or box.

Source: This field indicates where the information was taken from. It could be a bank debit or credit memo, an invoice number, a cheque number, return or adjustment numbers, a memo, etc.

2 ➤ **Source**   Type **Bank Debit Memo** as the source, press the [Tab] key. You move to the icon. This icon will allow you to search for previously posted transactions. You are then able to reverse and correct previously posted General Journal entries. This will be shown to you in Exercise 1-13; press [Tab] to move to the Date field.

3 ➤ **Date**   This is the date the transaction occurred. You may not always enter transactions on the day they occurred, depending on business volume. Although the printed cheques were received on the 18th, the bank charged (debited) our account on the 17th. The debit memo was issued on April 17; therefore, the transaction date is Apr 17, 2019. Using the calendar, change the date to **Apr 17, 2019**. [Tab] to move to the Comment field.

Comment The comment line should include details of **who**, **what**, and/or **why** you are making the entry. In this entry you need to record information about the printed cheques and any other important information. You may have to abbreviate the comments because the comments field only allows 65 characters.

4 ➤ **Comment**   Type **Printing charges new cheques SN** (where SN is your initials), press [Tab] to move to the Account field.

Account: If you knew the account number, you would type it in this field.

 To see a list of General Ledger accounts, press the [Enter] key or double-click the **Account** field.

You can also search for an account number or account name description. You will search by number.

To use this feature, type the account number (as you will do at step 6) and the lower portion of window will display the accounts near the number. You could also scroll down to find the account you need. It is easier to search by Number (see step 6).

To bypass the search field and use only the lower portion of the window, you would click the **Bypass Search Field** box in the top right and the setting will take effect the next time you use the **Select Account** feature.

5 ➤ Double-click the **Account** field or press [Enter].

A portion of the General Ledger chart of accounts list is shown next.

Select Account		
Select account:		☐ Bypass Search Field
Search		
[ ] ⦿ Number ◯ Name		
Account Name	**Account Class**	
<Add new account>		
1100 Bank Account	Bank	
1110 Bank Credit Card	Asset	
1200 Accounts Receivable	Accounts Receivable	
1260 Inventory	Asset	

You may need to scroll down using the ☑ scroll bar to the right of the Accounts box. You will notice that the first line indicates **<Add new account>**. The <Add new account> field can be used when you cannot find an appropriate account and decide that a new account in the ledger is needed. This option is explained in Exercise 1-10b and Chapter 4A.

Study the following table, which shows the account numbering system in Sage 50 Accounting:

Account Number Starts with	Type of Account	Normal Balance	To Increase Account	To Decrease Account
1	Asset	Debit	+ Debit	- Credit
2	Liability	Credit	+ Credit	- Debit
3	Equity	Credit	+ Credit	- Debit
4	Revenue	Credit	+ Credit	- Debit
5	Expense	Debit	+ Debit	- Credit

You are going to choose the wrong account and then correct the account before posting.

ℹ️ From a Select Account window, in the lower portion, you could also scroll down to 5220 Office Supplies Expense and double-click, or click **Select**.

6 ➤ In the **Search** field type **5** (you will notice that the lower window moves to the 5 account numbers.) Type **2** and you move further into the 5 section account numbers. You should be at the line for Office Supplies Expense. If there were other numbers (e.g., 5220) you would continue entering numbers or scroll to the account needed. Press ⌨Enter or click **Select**. (See side note box.)

5220 Office Supplies Expense is entered in the Account field and the cursor has moved to the Debits column (0.00) for the amount.

Oops, wrong account number. This is an error that needs to be corrected.

You will now correct the account number.

7 ➤ To delete the wrong account, click **5220 Office Supplies Expense** and press the ⌨Delete key.

8 ➤ Repeat steps 5 and 6 to locate and select (double-click) **5180 Bank Charges Expense** account. The account number has been corrected.

9 ➤   In the Debits column enter the amount **31** and press . Sage 50 Accounting puts in the missing 00 after the decimal point. (If the amount was 50.25, you would need to enter 50, decimal point, 25 then Tab.) The cursor moves to the Comment column.

10 ➤   **Comment**   Use this column when you want to record additional comments for each account. Type **Printing charge new cheques**. (See side note box.) Press Tab to move to the Account field.

> This field may be left blank if the information for the transaction is already included in the Comment line. We have shown it here for illustrative purposes only.

11 ➤   Double-click the **Accounts** field and select **1100 Bank Account**. The amount **31.00** automatically appears in the credit column. The software calculates the net amount of the Debit and Credit entries entered, and displays the amount needed to make debits and credits equal. **Bank Account** is credited because when money is deducted from the account (by debit memo or cheque) Bank Account decreases.

You will enter the wrong amount in the current field to allow you to observe what happens when you try to post an entry with unequal debits and credits.

---

12 ➤   Change the **Bank Account** amount from 31.00 to **55.00**, Tab. This is an error that you will fix in step 15.

Notice that the totals at the bottom of the General Journal are not equal.

Total	31.00	55.00

13 ➤   Click the Post button. Study the Error message box that appears:

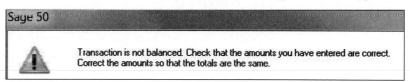

Sage 50

⚠ Transaction is not balanced. Check that the amounts you have entered are correct. Correct the amounts so that the totals are the same.

14 ➤   Click **OK** to return to the General Journal.

You will now enter the correct amount.

---

15 ➤   Click on **55.00**, and type **31**, then press Tab. The Totals at the bottom of the Journal are now equal.

Do not post at this time.

Congratulations! You have entered a complete journal entry. Compare your window with Fig. 1-9.

The Sales Taxes button Sales Taxes is greyed out because HST is not used in this entry. This button will be discussed in Chapter 3B.

Fig. 1-9: General Journal Entry.

DO NOT POST YET. You need to verify your entry first.

Displaying a Journal Entry

Before posting, it is best to check the accuracy of your journal entry. If there is an error, it may be easily corrected before posting.

There are two ways to correct an entry before posting:

1. Highlight the wrong entry item in the General Journal window and type the correct information.

2. If the entry has quite a few errors, it is best to start over. Click the **Undo** icon. A message box will appear, verifying that you want to discard the entry. Click **Yes** to discard the entry, then retype the complete entry.

Exercise 1-8—Displaying a Journal Entry

---

1 ➤ Click **Report** on the Menu Bar.

2 ➤ Click **Display General Journal Entry Ctrl + J** (Ctrl + J is a keyboard shortcut to display the entry). You can press **Ctrl + J** from Fig. 1-9 without having to complete steps 1 and 2. You will notice many other shortcuts in drop-down menus.

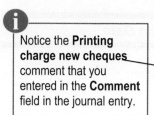

Notice the **Printing charge new cheques** comment that you entered in the **Comment** field in the journal entry.

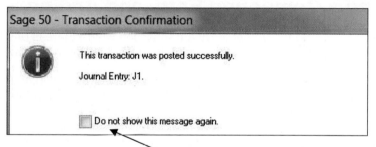

General Journal Entry Apr 17, 2019 (J1)

Account Number	Account Description	Debits	Credits
5180	Bank Charges Expense	31.00	-
	Printing charge new cheques		
1100	Bank Account	-	31.00
Additional Date:	Additional Field:		
		31.00	31.00

Sage 50 Accounting assigns a journal entry number, beginning with J1, to posted entries. This entry is displayed as J1. There are no previous Journal entries recorded in this data file.

The **Additional Date** and **Additional Field** information is displayed in all journal windows even if you don't enter information in these fields. The use of these fields will be explained in Exercise 1-12.

Review the entry to make sure it is correct. If it is not correct, you need to close this window and therefore correct the entry on the General Journal window before posting.

3 ➤ To exit, click the X box to return to the Journal window.

4 ➤ Click the **POST** button; the screen flickers and the following window appears.

> **Sage 50 - Transaction Confirmation**
>
> ⓘ   This transaction was posted successfully.
>
> Journal Entry: J1.
>
> ☐ Do not show this message again.

This confirmation window is used to Indicate that the entry was posted as Journal 1 (J1) to the General Ledger. Many students are not sure if they have posted the entry and record another entry. After you are comfortable knowing your entries are posted, you could check the **Do not show this message again** box.

⚠️ If you click the "Do not show this message again" box by mistake, you can return the Transaction Confirmation window by clicking **Setup**, **User Preferences**. In the left-hand window, click **Transaction Confirmation**, and click the right-hand box, then **OK**.

5 ➤ Click **OK** to accept the posting confirmation. The screen flickers, and returns to a blank journal window.

6 ➤ To exit to the Home window, click the X.

HST is ignored in this chapter and will be covered later in the text.

To Advance the Session Date

The current Session Date is April 18 and you need to record transactions dated for the week ending April 25. You do not need to exit the program to move or advance the date. You can advance the date from the Home window.

Exercise 1-9—Advancing the Session Date

---

1 ➤ Click the calendar at 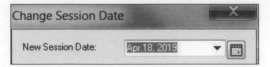 icon.

> **Change Session Date**   X
>
> New Session Date: Apr 18, 2019   ▼   ▦

2 ➤ Using the calendar, change the date to **Apr 25, 2019**, and click **OK**. You may see a backup information window. If you do, click **No**. You do not need to back up at this time.

You may see the Sage 50 Accounting Survey window, now or later in the course. *Note*: If you select **Remind me again in... days**, you have a selection of 1, 3, 7 or 10 days. You will need an active Internet connection to participate.

With any selection, click **OK**.

Recording a Compound Entry and Adding a New Account

So far, you entered a transaction where there is one Debit account and one Credit account. A compound entry uses three or more accounts.

The next transaction is a payment for a bank loan. Payments are normally recorded in the PAYABLES module. The PAYABLES module records all purchases and payments by credit, cash, cheque, credit card, or debit card. This transaction is entered in the General Journal because the bank debited the company bank account and a cheque is not being issued. You will be shown how to record payments by cheque in the PAYABLES module in Chapter 3A.

Exercise 1-10a—Recording a Compound Entry

Study the following transaction:

> **Apr 22, 2019** **Received debit memo, dated today, from the bank, indicating a $215.00 payment was made on the bank loan that includes interest of $76.44. The loan was received on March 22.**

The correct compound entry is:

Dr	Bank Loan Payable (Long Term)	138.56	
Dr	Bank Loan Interest Expense	76.44	
Cr	Cash in Bank		215.00

A new General Ledger account for Bank Loan Interest Expense will be created as part of Exercise 1-10b.

1 ➤ Click on the **General Journal** icon.

2 ➤ **Source**   Type **Bank Debit Memo** as the source, and press `Tab`, `Tab` to move to the Date field.

3 ➤ **Date**   Using the calendar, change the date to **Apr 22, 2019**. `Tab` to move to the Comment field.

4 ➤ **Comment**   Type **Bank Loan Payment (Long Term)**, press `Tab` to move to the Account field.

5 ➤ **Account**   Type **2710 (**Bank Loan Payable (Long Term), `Tab`**.**

6 ➤ **Debits**   Type **138.56,** `Tab`.

7 ➤ **Comment**   **Principal repayment,** `Tab`.

Exercise 1-10b—Adding a New General Ledger Account

---

1 ➤ **Account**   Double-click the **column** or press `Enter` and click on <**Add new account**>, click **Select**.

Enter information shown in Fig 1-10a.

Add an Account

Your company uses the following account numbering system:

Asset accounts   1000-1999
Liability accounts   2000-2999
Equity accounts   3000-3999
Revenue accounts   4000-4999
Expense accounts   5000-5999

Enter the account number and name for the account you want to add.

Number   5190

Name   Bank Loan Interest Expense

Fig 1-10a: Add an Account window.

Number   The owner has decided to add a new account, number 5190, for the Bank Loan Interest Expense. You must make sure that it fits one of the numbering sequences as noted in the window. This account follows after account 5180 for Bank Charges Expense. There is room to add other accounts between 5180 and 5190 later.

Name   This is the name of the new account.

2 ➤ When the Add an Account window resembles Fig. 1-10a, click **Next>**.

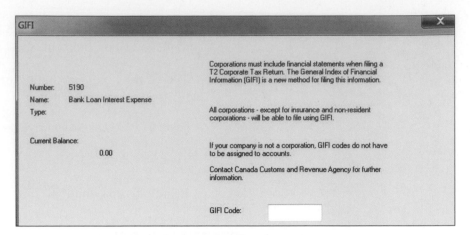

Fig. 1-10b: GIFI Code window.

Type   The default type of account code will be Group Account. It can be
                  changed in step 5 or 6. Account Groups will be explained in more
                  detail in Chapter 4A.

Current   0.00. This is a new account for Photos Company. You cannot add a
Balance   balance to a new account in this company data file. The file is in Ready
                  mode for the Company folder. You can create a balance for a company
                  that is being created (History). This is discussed in Chapter 4A.

If your business was a corporation, you would need to number the account based on
the GIFI codes as identified by Canada Revenue Agency (CRA). This section
assumes that the business is not a corporation. If your business is a corporation,
contact your accountant or Canada Revenue Agency for further information about
the GIFI numbering sequences.

  3 ➤ Photos Company is not a corporation; therefore, leave the GIFI field empty.
          Click **Next >**.

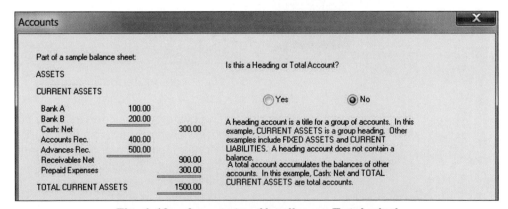

Fig. 1-10c: Accounts—Heading or Total window.

If the account to be added is a Heading or a Final Total of a section, you would click
Yes. Account 5190 is an account used to accumulate Bank Loan Interest Expense
and is not a Heading or a Total account. Headings and Total accounts will be
discussed in more detail in Chapter 4A.

  4 ➤ With a setting of **No**, click **Next>**.

          If the account being added is to be added with another account to create a
          subtotal, similar to Bank A and Bank B shown next, then you would click **Yes**.
          This is similar to Prepaid Expenses Account 5190 and will not require a subtotal.

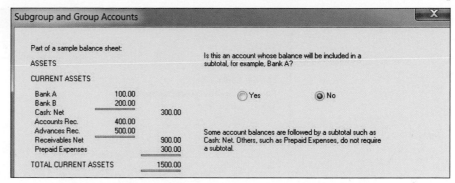

Fig. 1-10d: Subgroup and Group Accounts window.

5 ➤ With a setting of **No**, click **Next>**.

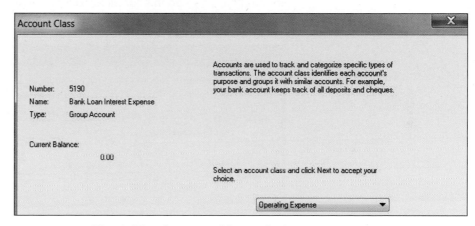

Fig. 1-10e: Account Class window.

Sage 50 Accounting has selected Operating Expense as the Account Class. You will learn more about account classes in Chapter 4A.

6 ➤ Click the ▼ and you will see various Account classes. Select the account class **Expense**, click **Next>**.

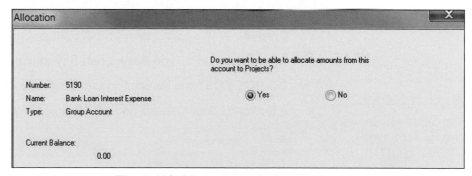

Fig. 1-10f: Allocation window.

7 ➤ If you needed to allocate project revenue and expenses to this account, you would accept the Yes default selection. This business does not use the PROJECT module; therefore, change the setting to **No**. Click **Next>**.

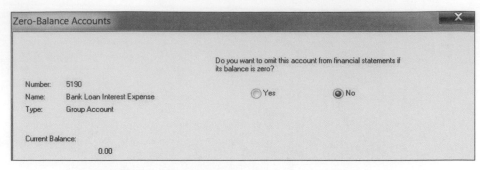

Fig. 1-10g: Zero-Balance Accounts window.

8 ➤ If you wanted accounts with zero balances to appear on financial statements, you would click No. If you do not want accounts with zero balances to appear on financial statements you would click Yes. With a setting of **No**, click **Next>**. Note that you can do this for all accounts with zero balances, as shown in Exercise 1-6a at step 3.

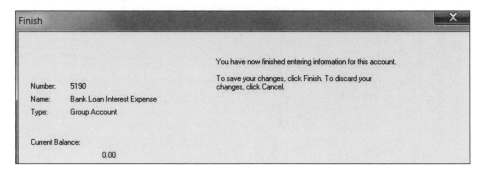

Fig. 1-10h: Finish window.

9 ➤ Click **Finish** to add the account to the General Ledger and the account column. Continue recording the entry as shown next.

10 ➤ **Account**   Tab .

11 ➤ **Debits**   Type **76.44**, Tab to Account.

12 ➤ **Account**   Type **1100** (Bank Account), Tab .

13 ➤ **Credits**   Tab to accept **215.00** and move to Comment.

14 ➤ **Comment**   Type **Bank Loan Payment**.

DO NOT POST the transaction until you complete the next exercise.

A portion of your General Journal window should resemble the following:

You could have used the Sage 50 Accounting calculator to confirm the amounts. 215.00 – 76.44 = 138.56

Source	Bank Debit Memo			Date	Apr 22, 2019	
Comment	Bank Loan Payment (Long Term)					

Account	Debits	Credits	Comment
2710 Bank Loan Payable (Long Term)	138.56	--	Principal repayment
5190 Bank Loan Interest Expense	76.44	--	
1100 Bank Account	--	215.00	Bank Loan Payment

15 ➤ Don't forget to display the entry. Notice that this entry is J2 and is a compound entry.

General Journal Entry Apr 22, 2019 (J2)

Account Number	Account Description	Debits	Credits
2710	Bank Loan Payable (Long Term)	138.56	-
	Principal repayment		
5190	Bank Loan Interest Expense	76.44	-
1100	Bank Account	-	215.00
	Bank Loan Payment		
Additional Date:	Additional Field:		
		215.00	215.00

Note: In Sage 50 Accounting, the Additional Date and Additional Field will be shown in the journal entry display (as above) even when no information has been entered in the fields. See Exercise 1-12, step 7.

16 ➤ Click X to return to the General Journal screen.

DO NOT POST YET! Continue with the next exercise.

Recurring Entries

A recurring entry refers to a transaction that may repeat many times during the year. The bank loan payment transaction is a good example. You know that you will be paying the bank loan payment on a regular basis. If you enter the above entry as a recurring entry, the next time your bank debits your account for the loan payment you can recall the entry, change the date and amounts, and it will be ready to post. It saves time and helps you avoid errors.

Exercise 1-11—Creating a Recurring Entry

1 ➤ To store this entry for future use, click the 3rd icon on the left side of the toolbar, **Store as recurring transaction** 💾. The next window is where you will identify the name you wish to associate with this entry and the frequency with which you want Sage 50 Accounting to remind you when it will reoccur.

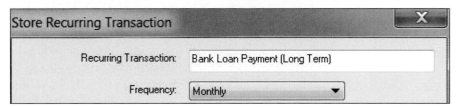

2 ➤ Notice that in the Recurring Transaction box, the comment you entered in the General Journal is automatically entered. Change the recurring transaction name to **Bank Loan Payment Monthly** Tab .

3 ➤ **Frequency** Click the ▼ to see the various choices available for how often you want this entry to appear. Leave Frequency as **Monthly**.

4 ➤ Click **OK**. The entry is now saved for future use. You will be using a different recurring entry in Exercise 1-16.

5 ➤ **Post** when correct.

6 ➤ You will see the J2 Transaction confirmation window. Click **OK**.

Owner Investment in Business

The owner's investment may be recorded in the General Journal as the funds were transferred, by the bank, from her personal account to the business to show the personal investment.

Exercise 1-12—Journalizing Owner Investment in Business

Apr 24, 2019	Mrs. Chikowski decided to invest an additional $2,000.00 in the business, as she is going to purchase a new photo machine from another business. She is transferring $2,000.00 from her personal bank account to the company's bank account and asked you to record the investment.

If you closed the General Journal prior to this exercise, click on the General Journal icon.

If you did not close the General Journal, you should be at a blank General Journal window.

   1 ➤ **Record** the investment based on the following window.

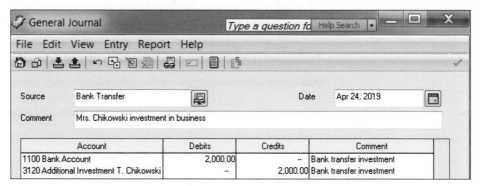

   2 ➤ On the icon bar, click the **Enter Additional Information** ☑ icon and the Additional Information window appears.

This feature allows you to record additional information about the transaction, such as other dates and other information (e.g., voucher dates and voucher approvals, or entry recorded by person's name) that may be useful for the audit trail, or for future reference. This text does not use this feature in all entries.

   3 ➤ **Additional Date** Select **Apr 24, 2019**, the day the transaction was recorded. `Tab`.

   4 ➤ **Additional Field** Type **Mrs. Chikowski phone call message SN** (replace SN with your initials).

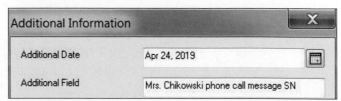

5 ➤ Click **OK**. Notice that the Additional Information window is gone and the General Journal window shown does not have any indication of the information just entered. This will be explained in the next 2 steps.

6 ➤ When your entry resembles the previous investment window, click **Report, Display General Journal Entry**.

General Journal Entry Apr 24, 2019 (J3)

Account Number	Account Description	Debits	Credits
1100	Bank Account	2,000.00	-
	Bank transfer investment		
3120	Additional Investment T. Chiko...	-	2,000.00
	Bank transfer investment		
Additional Date: Ap...	Additional Field: Mrs. Chikowski ph...		
		2,000.00	2,000.00

7 ➤ Notice the additional information at the bottom. The additional information entered displays in the General Journal Entry window, and is retained by the system. Click X to close the entry. You will notice that the additional information is not shown in the General Journal.

8 ➤ When your entry is correct, click **Post**, and click **OK** to accept **J3**.

Correcting an Entry—Cancel or Adjusting

When you realize that an error has been made after you have posted a transaction, you can use the Reverse entry or Adjust the entry features in Sage 50 Accounting. Sage 50 Accounting makes this task very easy.

Exercise 1-13—Correcting an Entry

Apr 25, 2019 **Mrs. Chikowski advised you that she decided to increase the investment in the business to $3,000.00, when she was at the bank (April 24). She gave you the $3,000 bank transfer document.**

In Exercise 1-12 you posted the following:

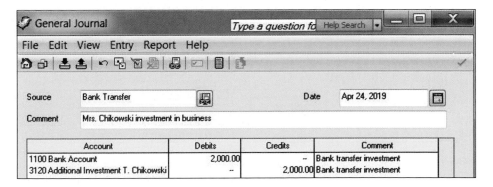

The investment was recorded for the wrong amount. Do not panic. You can reverse or correct an entry after it has been posted.

You have three ways to correct this:

1. You can manually reverse entry J3 by reversing the debits and credits. Then enter a new entry to record the entry correctly. You could make an error in the reversal and need to correct this error as well.

2. You can use the Reverse entry feature to allow Sage 50 Accounting to reverse the debits and credits to cancel J3. Then you enter the correct entry if needed. Refer to Exercise 2A-19, *Correcting a Receipt Error,* or Exercise 2A-21, *Cancelling a Posted Invoice.*

Refer to Chapter 13, Exercise 13-2, *Correcting General Journal Entries.*

3. You can use the Adjust a previously posted entry feature to adjust and correct J3. This will allow you to correctly record the entry. You do not need to reverse J3.

This exercise will use method 3 to adjust the J3 entry.

1 ➤ Click the **Adjust a previously posted entry** icon. It is on the toolbar and the following window appears.

In business, you choose the dates of the entries you want to see displayed or sort by Source field description, Journal entry number or Amount.

You could leave the other fields blank and click OK to see what entries have been previously recorded.

2 ➤ Leave the other fields blank to see the entries recorded, click **OK**. Entries 1, 2, and 3 have been recorded previously and are displayed.

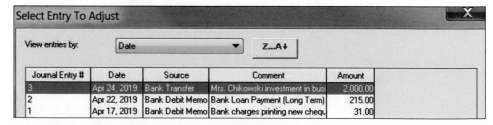

3 ➤ You would click the entry that you need to reverse. **J3** should be highlighted in blue; click **Select**. Note that the previous entry with details appears and the header of the entry identifies the Source field.

4 ➤ Change Debits and Credits to **3000.00**. You can change any fields (source, date, comments, account names and/or amounts). Do NOT change the date.

5 ➤ Display the Journal entry. Note that the entry number is **J5**. J4 is the reversal entry and J5 is the correct entry.

General Journal Entry Apr 24, 2019 (J5)

Account Number	Account Description	Debits	Credits
1100	Bank Account	3,000.00	-
	Bank transfer investment		
3120	Additional Investment T. Chiko...	-	3,000.00
	Bank transfer investment		
Additional Date: Ap...	Additional Field: Mrs. Chikowski ph...		
		3,000.00	3,000.00

6 ➤ **Exit** the display window.

7 ➤ Click **Post**, click **OK** to accept confirmation number J5, click X and return to the Home window.

Displaying Corrected Entries with Reversals

When necessary, you can display entries that have been posted and subsequently corrected. The following exercise will show you how to display both the original incorrect entries and reversing entries. Later in the exercise, you will learn how to display the corrected entries only, without the incorrect entries.

This text uses displaying corrections as the default. However, your instructor may advise you to display only the correct entries without showing any of the entries you have reversed.

Exercise 1-14—Displaying Corrected Entries

---

1 ➤ At the Reports area, click ▼ and select **All Journal Entries**, click **Display**. The display shows J1, J2, and J5. We want to see what happened to the reversal and correction. Click the ☑ Modify ▼ button, select **Report Options**. Click the **Corrections** field.

Corrections: Make sure the field
```
Show
☑ Corrections
☐ Additional Information
```
is checked.

Additional Information: Leave the field blank. We will concentrate on the correction and not the Additional Information area.

---

2 ➤ Change the Start date and Finish date to **Apr 24, 2019**. This exercise will focus on the Investment correction entry. The All Journal Entries Modify Report window should appear as shown next:

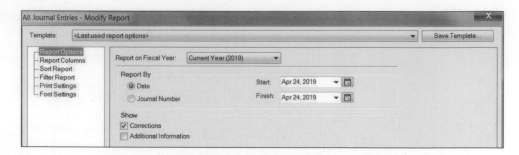

In a job situation, you would display and print all entries (with corrections) because this provides an audit trail (history) of entries that were recorded and changed. Notice that the Additional Information field is not checked.

3 ➤ Click **OK** and the following window will appear (see side note box):

The original (incorrect) journal entry was **J3**.

The reversing journal entry is **J4.**

The new correct journal entry (correction) is **J5.**

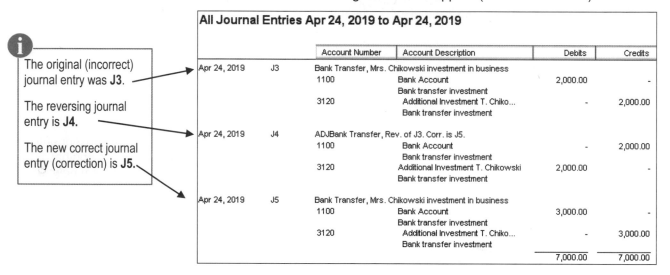

J4 shows as the reversing entry and **J5** is the corrected Journal entry. The amount **7,000.00** at the bottom of the entry is the total of the debits and credits displayed. This will be explained in more detail later.

4 ➤ In order to prepare for the next steps, click the Modify ▾ icon and select **Report Options**. The All Journal Entries—Modify Report window (seen at step 2) reappears.

To Show Corrected Entries Only

Notice that the Show ☑ Corrections box is checked, which is now the default.

5 ➤ You do not want to show the original incorrect entry and the reversing entry in the report; therefore, click the Show ☑ Corrections box to remove the check mark.

6 ➤ Click **OK**. Entry 3, with the error, and entry 4, the reversing entry, will not be displayed. Only the corrected entry J5 is displayed, as shown next.

All Journal Entries Apr 24, 2019 to Apr 24, 2019

		Account Number	Account Description	Debits	Credits
Apr 24, 2019	J5		Bank Transfer, Mrs. Chikowski investment in business		
		1100	Bank Account	3,000.00	-
			Bank transfer investment		
		3120	Additional Investment T. Chiko...	-	3,000.00
			Bank transfer investment		
				3,000.00	3,000.00

Now, if you wish to display all entries, from a specific date only, without corrections (e.g., Apr 17, 2019), follow the next step.

7 ➤ Click the **Modify** icon, select **Report Options**, and the All Journal Entries Modify Report window reappears. Change the Start Date to **Apr 17, 2019** and make sure the ✓ has been removed from Corrections. Click **OK**.

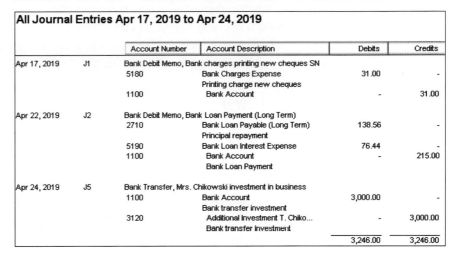

All Journal Entries Apr 17, 2019 to Apr 24, 2019					
		Account Number	Account Description	Debits	Credits
Apr 17, 2019	J1		Bank Debit Memo, Bank charges printing new cheques SN		
		5180	Bank Charges Expense	31.00	-
			Printing charge new cheques		
		1100	Bank Account	-	31.00
Apr 22, 2019	J2		Bank Debit Memo, Bank Loan Payment (Long Term)		
		2710	Bank Loan Payable (Long Term)	138.56	-
			Principal repayment		
		5190	Bank Loan Interest Expense	76.44	-
		1100	Bank Account	-	215.00
			Bank Loan Payment		
Apr 24, 2019	J5		Bank Transfer, Mrs. Chikowski investment in business		
		1100	Bank Account	3,000.00	-
			Bank transfer investment		
		3120	Additional Investment T. Chiko...	-	3,000.00
			Bank transfer investment		
				3,246.00	3,246.00

Entry 3, with the error, and entry 4, the reversing entry, will not be displayed. Only the correct entries are displayed.

8 ➤ Exit the display window.

To Remove a Recurring Transaction Entry

Exercise 1-15—Removing a Recurring Transaction Entry

You previously created a recurring transaction entry for Bank Loan Payment Monthly. This exercise will show you how to delete a recurring transaction entry, but you will not actually remove it.

1 ➤ Click the **General Journal** icon.

2 ➤ Click the 4th icon on the left ⬆ (Recall recurring transaction) and the following window appears.

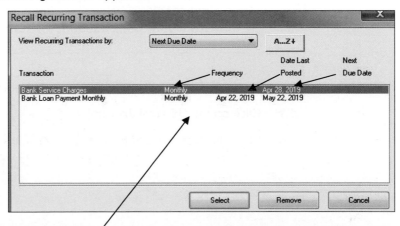

Note: See the above arrows. Due to a computer graphic card problem, some displays will have the column headings in the wrong location. Sage is aware of the problem.

3 ➤ View Recurring Transactions by: Click the ▼ and a drop-down list of report options is displayed. Leave the choice as **Next Due Date**. Click the A...Z↓ and the report will be sorted automatically in descending or ascending order.

4 ➤ Return the display to ascending as shown in step 3.

5 ➤ Click the **Bank Loan Payment Monthly** listing, then click the Remove button and a warning message box appears.

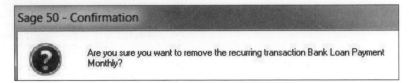

6 ➤ Click No, as you do not want to remove this item. This exercise is only to show you how you could remove a recurring entry. Click **Cancel** and you are returned to the General Journal window.

7 ➤ If the Home window is showing, you can click the ⊠ Close other windows icon to close the General Journal window and any other Sage 50 Accounting windows and return to the Home window. If you cannot see the ⊠ Close other windows icon, click X to return to the Home window.

8 ➤ Advance the date to **Apr 30**. If the Sage 50 Accounting—Backup window, appears, click **No**, as you do not need to back up now.

Using a Recurring Transaction

ℹ
The amount for bank charges can be received from a Bank Debit memo, (sent by mail and/or email). If the business has bank internet access the amount can be located when the bank account is displayed.

Bank charges are levied each month and, as shown in Exercise 1-16, in the Recall Recurring Transaction window, an April 28 bank charges recurring transaction was set up for future use on April 28. You will also use a recurring entry in Chapter 3B. (See side note box.)

Exercise 1-16—Using a Recurring Transaction

Apr 30, 2019   **You received a Bank Statement with a Debit memo dated April 29, 2019 from the bank advising that they have deducted $22.46 from your bank account for service charges.**

To use the Bank Charges recurring entry, complete the following steps:

1 ➤ Click on the **General Journal** icon.

2 ➤ From the **General Journal** window, click the **Recall recurring transaction** icon, 4th icon on the left, and the following window appears.

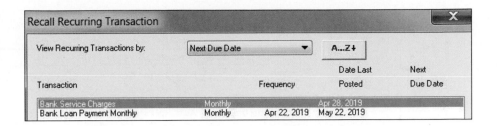

3 ➤ **Bank Service Charges** should be highlighted in blue; click **Select** and the General Journal window appears with the recurring transaction information.

4 ➤ **Date** Change the date to **Apr 29, 2019**. This is the date the money was removed from the bank account.

5 ➤ Change the **date** and the **amount** as shown in the journal below.

6 ➤ Click the **Enter Additional Information** [icon] icon.

This feature allows you to record additional information about the transaction, such as other dates and other information (e.g., voucher dates and voucher approvals, or entry recorded by person's name) that may be useful for the audit trail, or for future reference. This text does not use this feature in all entries.

7 ➤ **Additional Date** Change the date to **Apr 29, 2019**, the day the service charges were taken from the account.

8 ➤ **Additional Field** Type **Recorded by SN** (replace SN with your initials).

9 ➤ Click **OK**.

10 ➤ When your entry resembles the above window, click **Report, Display General Journal Entry**.

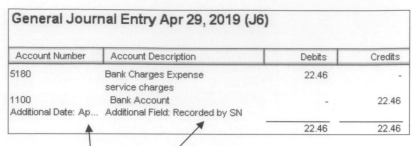

General Journal Entry Apr 29, 2019 (J6)

Account Number	Account Description	Debits	Credits
5180	Bank Charges Expense	22.46	-
	service charges		
1100	Bank Account	-	22.46
Additional Date: Ap...	Additional Field: Recorded by SN		
		22.46	22.46

11 ➤ Notice the additional information. Click ⊠ to close the entry.

12 ➤ When your entry is correct, click **Post**.

You will see the Confirmation message shown next:

Sage 50 - Confirmation

The recurring transaction Bank Service Charges has been changed. Posting this transaction will update its next due date. Do you wish to continue?

> **ⓘ**
>
> You have recorded the bank charges for the period ending April 29. The recurring Due date (May 28th) is from the initial creation date. If the date or other information needs to change, the recurring entry could be resaved with the new information. Many businesses set up several recurring entries to help save time; you change only fields that need changing, and post.

13 ➤ Click **Yes**; J6 posting confirmation window appears. Click **OK**. The entry will be available for next month. (See the Next Due Date window in step 14.)

14 ➤ Click the 📤 **Recall recurring transaction**. (See side note box and Next Due Date field.) As mentioned in Exercise 1-15, the column headings are in the wrong location, e.g., Frequency should be over the wording Monthly.

Recall Recurring Transaction				X
View Recurring Transactions by:	Next Due Date ▼	A...Z↓		
			Date Last	Next
Transaction		Frequency	Posted	Due Date
Bank Loan Payment Monthly		Monthly	Apr 22, 2019	May 22, 2019
Bank Service Charges		Monthly	Apr 29, 2019	May 28, 2019

15 ➤ Click **Cancel** and ⊠ to return to the Home window.

Drill Down (Trace Back)

From an Income Statement, Balance Sheet or other reports, you can drill down (trace back) one level at a time to review a transaction in order to see the relevant information (including amounts) in the report.

This drill down feature works in all modules.

Exercise 1-17—Drill Down (Trace Back)

Your manager has asked you to review the transactions you entered earlier, using the Income Statement. The following instructions will show you various techniques in tracing back transactions.

1 ➤ Display the **Balance Sheet** for Photos Company for **Apr 29, 2019** (see Exercise 1-6b).

2 ➤ As you move your cursor over the accounts, the cursor changes to a magnifying glass.

3 ➤ Move down to the **Equity section**, **Additional Investment—T. Chikowski** account and double-click.

The General Ledger Report for account 3120 displays for the same time period.

General Ledger Report Apr 01, 2019 to Apr 29, 2019 Sorted by: Transaction Number						
Date	Comment	Source #	JE#	Debits	Credits	Balance
3120	**Additional Investment T. Chikowski**					- Cr
Apr 24, 2019	Mrs. Chikowski investment in business	Bank Transfer	J5	-	3,000.00	3,000.00 Cr

If you hide the error and reversing entry (J3 and J4) from the Journal Entries display as shown in Exercise 1-14, they will still display in the General Ledger report if the Show Corrections box is checked ✓.

This report is sorted by Transaction Number (default). As shown in Exercise 1-18, *Displaying and Printing the General Journal*, the report can be sorted by date. Using the Drill down feature, this report does not display the Adjusting entries (J3 and J4).

4 ➤ Position the cursor on Source # field, **Bank Transfer** and double-click. The ⟨General Journal - Journal Entry Lookup⟩ that created the entry is displayed. (See side note box.) Click X to return to the step 3 window.

If you want to see the original and reversing entries, on the Modify icon, click on **Report Options** and click on ☑ Corrections. Click **OK** to see the original, reversing and correcting entry.

In the RECEIVABLES and PAYABLES modules, Chapters 2A, 2B, 3A, and 3B, when the journal entry is displayed, you will be able to see the aged report for that firm if you click the Customer or Vendor name.

5 ➤ If you want to see the General Journal entry (debit and credit) display ⟨General Journal Display⟩, double-click on **J5**, or the Amount or Comment field. You are taken to the journal window. Click X X to return to the Balance Sheet.

6 ➤ Click X to return to the Home window.

Display and Print the General Journal

It is a good idea at this point to print a report of entries you have recorded from Session Date Apr 17 to Apr 29. The printed copy provides proof of what has been recorded in the company file.

Exercise 1-18—Displaying and Printing the General Journal

The Reports area will display only All Journal entries. Use the following procedure to display and print only General Journal entries from the COMPANY module.

Although you might know that there are no transactions between April 1 to 17, you should use the beginning of the month for the Start Date to ensure that your system does not have entries posted before the entries you processed.

You should be at the Home window to start this exercise.

1 ➤ Click the **Report Centre** icon, in the left pane, click on **Accounts**, click on **General Journal Entries**. If you were sure of the setting to change, you could click on **Modify this report** to change a setting. You will do this in step 2. Click **Display**.

2 ➤ To change a setting, click on **Modify** icon, **Report Options**. The Start Date should be **Apr 01, 2019** (the first day of the month) and the End Date should be **Apr 30, 2019** (current Session Date).

When you choose the ✓ show **Additional Information,** the **Additional Date** and **Additional Field** will display in all entries regardless if you used the field or not.

In the future, if you do not want the **Additional Date** and **Additional Field** to appear in Journal windows or printouts, make sure the field is unchecked.

3 ➤ Make sure the boxes are ✓ to have this information shown in the report. (See side note box.)

There are a number of reports that can be customized to the user's requirements.

```
Report Options
Report Columns
Sort Report
Filter Report
Print Settings
Font Settings
```

Start of Information Section

There are no exercises in this text to use features other than Report Options. If you customize any of the reports, you must return to the original default choice, otherwise, future displays and/or reports will be different from what is shown in the text.

Report Options   Shown previously.

Report Columns   Customize column settings for this report. This feature will allow you to change the width of the columns, and the columns to be displayed/printed in reports. In the left pane, click on **Report Columns**, click on **Custom report column settings** button.

Sort Report—Custom sort order

Click **Sort Report**, and **Custom sort order**. This feature allows you to sort columns (fields) in reports.

Click **Filter Report**, and click **Use your filter specification**.

This feature allows you to prepare reports in modules with various columns equal to the data requested; e.g., customers with balances over $1,000.00.

Print Settings — Custom page orientation and **Custom margins**

Click **Print Settings,** click **Custom page orientation**.

This feature allows you to set Portrait or Landscape and to Customize the margins as the default print setting.

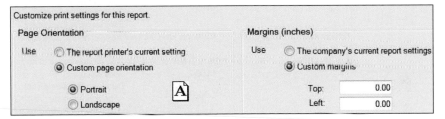

End of Information Section

Font Settings—Custom font settings

4 ➤ Click **Font Settings**, click **Custom font settings**.

This feature allows you to change report fonts and colours, sizes, Bold, Italicize and Align information left, centre or right.

5 ➤ Click **OK** to display the Journal Entries.

You may experiment with any of the customizations, but you must return to the default settings choice; otherwise, future displays and/or reports will be different from what is shown in the text.

General Journal Apr 01, 2019 to Apr 30, 2019

		Account Number	Account Description	Debits	Credits
Apr 17, 2019	J1		Bank Debit Memo, Bank charges printing new cheques SN		
		5180	Bank Charges Expense	31.00	-
			Printing charge new cheques		
		1100	Bank Account	-	31.00
Additional Date:		Additional Field:			
Apr 22, 2019	J2		Bank Debit Memo, Bank Loan Payment (Long Term)		
		2710	Bank Loan Payable (Long Term)	138.56	-
			Principal repayment		
		5190	Bank Loan Interest Expense	76.44	-
		1100	Bank Account	-	215.00
			Bank Loan Payment		
Additional Date:		Additional Field:			
Apr 24, 2019	J3		Bank Transfer, Mrs. Chikowski investment in business		
		1100	Bank Account	2,000.00	-
			Bank transfer investment		
		3120	Additional Investment T. Chiko...	-	2,000.00
			Bank transfer investment		
Additional Date: Apr 24, 2019		Additional Field: Mrs. Chikowski phone call message SN			
Apr 24, 2019	J4		ADJBank Transfer, Rev. of J3. Corr. is J5.		
		1100	Bank Account	-	2,000.00
			Bank transfer investment		
		3120	Additional Investment T. Chikowski	2,000.00	-
			Bank transfer investment		
Additional Date: Apr 24, 2019		Additional Field: Mrs. Chikowski phone call message SN			
Apr 24, 2019	J5		Bank Transfer, Mrs. Chikowski investment in business		
		1100	Bank Account	3,000.00	-
			Bank transfer investment		
		3120	Additional Investment T. Chiko...	-	3,000.00
			Bank transfer investment		
Additional Date: Apr 24, 2019		Additional Field: Mrs. Chikowski phone call message SN			
Apr 29, 2019	J6		Bank Debit Memo, Bank Service Charges		
		5180	Bank Charges Expense	22.46	-
			service charges		
		1100	Bank Account	-	22.46
Additional Date: Apr 29, 2019		Additional Field: Recorded by SN			
				7,268.46	7,268.46

Fig. 1-11: General Journal Transactions (no hidden entries).

> The total amount: i.e., 7,268.46, is the sum of journal entries 1 to 6, and verifies the equality of debits and credits only. The total does not indicate the accuracy of the values recorded.

The total amount at the bottom (7,268.46), which is the sum of journal entries 1 through 6, does not have to equal your numbers if you have made more entries. (See side note box.)

To make sure you have processed your entries correctly, you must compare your entries to each entry in the solution set. (You cannot rely on the debit and credit column totals.)

You can use the 🔍 Print Preview icon on the toolbar to view the report before printing to make sure it is what you want. If you see … on some lines, click X to return to the General Journal Display. You can click the top report header and move the columns to display the missing information. If you expand the columns, watch for the right column (dotted line) that indicates a page break.

6 ➤ To print this report, you can click **Print** in the Print Preview window, or return to the General Journal Display and click the 🖶 Print icon. Wait for the Print dialogue box to disappear before moving on.

7 ➤ **Exit** to the Home window.

Display and Print the General Ledger Report

The General Ledger report displays the transactions posted to each General Ledger account.

The report could be printed by Transaction Number (the default) or by Date. The date feature would be useful if entries were recorded on a random date basis. The date report would place all entries with the same date together, regardless of the date when they were recorded. There is no exercise for the date feature. The report can also be printed with each account on a separate page (see step 3).

Exercise 1-19—Displaying/Printing the General Ledger Report

To print all entries in the General Ledger:

ℹ️ You can also view and print from the menu bar, click **Reports**, **Financials**, **General Ledger**.

1 ➤ In the Reports Area, click ▼, select **General Ledger**, click **Display**. (See side note box.)

2 ➤ The report displays with the default of Apr 01, 2019 to Apr 30, 2019 and the default of printing with Transaction Number and Show transaction comment.

3 ➤ A feature in Sage 50 Accounting is the ability to print each account on a separate page. This feature is demonstrated, but not completed, in order to save paper in a classroom setting.

From the General Ledger Report window, click the **File** menu, and click on the
Separate Each Account on a New Page when Printed item. You are returned to the General Ledger Report window and you can see the ...... page separators.

4 ➤ Click the **File** menu and you will see a ✓ beside
Separate Each Account on a New Page when Printed .

Click ✓ Separate Each Account on a New Page when Printed again to remove the ✓ check mark and you are returned to the General Ledger Report window with only 1 page separator lower in the report.

5 ➤ Click the 🖶 Print icon to print the report without printing on separate pages.

To display the report with journal line comments, instead of transaction comments, or if you wanted to print only 1 General Ledger account, follow these steps.

6 ➤ Click on the **Modify** button, click on **Report Options**. To print only 1 account (e.g., 1100 Bank Account) in the middle pane, scroll up to **1100 Bank Account** and **click**. The other accounts turn white. If you also wanted to print account 3120 Additional Investment T. Chikowski, **scroll down** to 3120 and press **CTRL** and click on **3120**. It turns blue like 1100. You could also change the lower setting to **Show line comment**.

7 ➤ Click **OK**. Only 2 accounts are displayed. Compare the Comments column in this report with the Comments printed in the report in step 5. It is not possible to print the G/L report with both Comments in a report.

8 ➤ **Exit** from the display window.

If you wanted to see the report with the Corrections displayed, you would click the **Modify** button, select **Show corrections**, and **OK**. Many businesses will prefer to see the GL report without the corrections showing. Management may want to concentrate on the correct entries.

Exercise 1-20—Printing Financial Statements

> **Print Reports in Excel©**
> If your instructor requires reports in Excel©, view Appendix 2015 AH, *How to Convert Company Reports into Microsoft Excel©* at www.nelson.com/student.

1 ➤ Refer to Exercise 1-6a and 1-6b, and **print**:

- Income Statement for period Jan 01, 2019 to Apr 30, 2019. Net Income = $10,650.10.

- Balance Sheet as at Apr 30, 2019. Total Assets: $62,898.54.

(See side note box.)

Exercise 1-21—Display the Recurring Transactions Report

---

1 ➤ Click the **Report Centre** icon; in the left pane, click on **Recurring Transactions**. Select **General**, at the bottom under the right pane, click **Display**.

The report as shown next indicates the Module type.

Recurring Transactions

Type	Description	Frequency	Last Processed	Due Date
General	Bank Loan Payment Monthly	Monthly	Apr 22, 2019	May 22, 2019
General	Bank Service Charges	Monthly	Apr 29, 2019	May 28, 2019

2 ➤ Click **X** and **Close** to exit to the Home window.

Exercise 1-22a—Creating Custom Report Shortcuts

Look at the Recently viewed reports: area on the right side under Reports. This area displays the last 4 reports that are viewed in all modules. In future chapters, the section may no longer display the Income Statement and Balance Sheet links.

This exercise will create shortcuts (a maximum of 10 reports or reports and blank separators) under the Shortcuts area on the left side of the Home window for the Income Statement and Balance Sheet, which are used often. Other reports can be added as you will see in this exercise.

1 ➤ From the Home window, in the Shortcuts area, click on **Customize**. The Customize Shortcuts window appears.

2 ➤ Click the ⊞ beside **Reports**, click the ⊞ at **Financials**, click the ⊞ at **Income Statement,** click on **Standard**.

3 ➤ Click **Add>**. The Standard item moves to the right side of the Shortcuts display window.

4 ➤ Click **OK**. In the Shortcuts pane you will see:

> **Shortcuts**   Customize
> Income Statement Rep...

5 ➤ Repeat the procedure to add a Standard Balance Sheet Report, and a Gross Margin—Standard report (under Income Statement) to display the following:

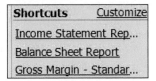

Exercise 1-22b—Removing a Report Shortcut

---

1 ➤ In the Shortcuts area, click on **Customize**. The Customize Shortcuts window appears.

2 ➤ In the right side pane, click on **Gross Margin – Standard**.

3 ➤ Click the **Remove** button, and the item is removed.

Exercise 1-22c—Adding a Blank Space between Reports

This exercise will add a blank space between reports. Note you can have only 10 reports, or a combination of reports and blank separator spaces equalling 10.

  1 ➤ In the Shortcuts right pane window, click on the first **Standard** Item.

  2 ➤ Click on the **Add Separator** button, and the window changes to:

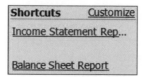

  3 ➤ Click **OK** and the Shortcuts area changes to:

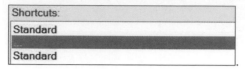

  4 ➤ To remove the expander …, click **Customize**, click on the blank line with … Click on the **Remove** button. Click **OK**.

The left side now displays.

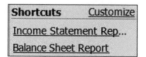

You can add reports from any of the modules shown in the left-hand pane.

Saving Your Work

If there is a power outage during your work session, you can lose what you have done before the power went out. To avoid this, you can save your work periodically during the work session.

The saving techniques in the next exercise may also be used for copying and backing-up purposes. The main difference between the copy and backup functions is file size: when you copy the company file to another storage device, the copy has the same file size as the original; when you use the backup function in Sage 50 Accounting, the file is compressed in a CAB file and your data file gets smaller (similar to a zip file).

Exercise 1-23—Saving Your Work

New feature in 2015. Note you cannot save a data file to an SAJ folder.

To start this exercise, you need to be at the Photos Company Home window.

1 ➤ Click the **File** selection on the Main Menu. Study the different methods of saving:

Save As Saves a copy of the current company data under a different file name on your hard drive, USB or other storage device. You have an option of changing the location and company name from the default file name of NEW.SAI.

DO NOT USE THIS FEATURE in your exercises in this book, because all future saves will be made to the new location and company name. If you leave the default settings, all future saves will be made to that same folder, but with a name **New.SAI**. When you open the file, the name on the top menu bar will be *New*.

If you use this feature outside class, change the file name from *New* to a more descriptive name such as:

E:\Sage 50 2015 Backup\Backup_01_Photos_Sep_09_2015a_SN

E:\Sage 50 2015 Backup is the drive and folder where you will keep the backup copies of your work. Refer to Exercise 1-24, step 3.

Backup_01_Photos_Sept_09_2015a refers to the name of the file, with the actual date that the student is working on the material and not the data file date and will help in identifying the saved file. If you were making a second backup on the same day, you would change 2015a to 2015b. Record in your logbook (see Exercise 1-25) the page you get to in the text.

Save a Copy This feature is similar to the Save As choice. You can save the current company data under a different file name and location, and at the same time you will continue to work in the original storage location with the original company data file.

For the copy file, you should change the company name to a descriptive name such as:

Backup_01_Photos_Sep_09_2015a_SN
(The actual date you are making the backup.)

Be sure your storage device has enough space available. Use a USB storage device as discussed in the "Getting Started" section on page 1-5.

Backup There are a number of options to back up. You can click this **Backup** option, or click on the 🗐 Backup icon on the tool bar, or you can click ▼ on Data Management in the Tasks area and select Backup. In the next exercise you will back up using the Data Management option. Backing up will compress (make your data file smaller) for saving on your USB storage device.

Restore Restore a data file from a previous saved file. You can also restore a data file by clicking ▼ on Data Management in the Tasks area and select Restore. See Appendix 2015 Z, *Restoring a Data File from a Backup Data File* in your course materials at www.nelson.com/student.

WWW

Exit	Save work and exit Sage 50 Accounting. You can also Exit and Save by clicking on the ⊠ in the Home window on the top.
	The computer stores the entries in the RAM memory of the computer. When you request a display of a Financial Statement, Ledger account or click ⊠ to exit, the program will add the entries in memory to the current balance of the accounts, and will update the files on your storage location.

2 ➤ Click anywhere on the Home page to exit the menu list for File.

🖫 Backup This tool bar option is the same as **File, Backup** on the menu bar, or the Backup option in the Data Management icon. See the next exercise.

Why Back Up?

You have just spent a considerable amount of time recording entries and learning about the Sage 50 Accounting software. What would you do if your hard drive crashed or you lost your storage device? It is always safest to have your backup stored in a different location from your original data.

WWW If you need to restore your data files, see Appendix 2015 Z, *Restoring a Data File from a Backup Data File* in your course materials at www.nelson.com/student.

Here are other recommendations:

- Use a USB storage device for storage of backups. Keep the protective tab for the computer end. This may reduce the possibility of damage from accidental spilling of pop, coffee, etc.

- Keep your storage device(s) at room temperature. Do not leave them in an automobile where they can be subjected to extreme hot or cold temperatures.

- Do not take your storage device out of the drive before you have completed the Exit or backup procedure. If you remove the device during the procedure you may lose some of the work you have just completed!

Backup Procedures

You will need to become familiar with the mechanics of backing up. There are a number of ways to back up your data.

As noted previously, Sage 50 Accounting has provided a number of ways to back up your company's working data from your hard drive.

In the next exercise, you will use the Data Management option to back up. As noted, it will condense (compress) your data and back up the information to a USB storage device that your computer supports. (See side note box.)

ⓘ
You can back up many company folders to the USB device.

Exercise 1-24—Backing up Your Data

This exercise assumes that you are using a USB storage device for storage of the backup files.

1 ➤ Click the ▼ at **Data Management**, select **Backup** and a window similar to the following will appear.

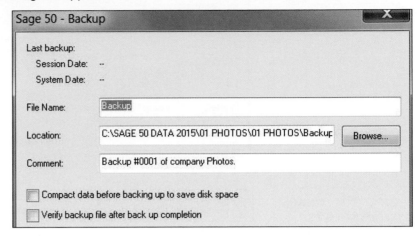

The location name may be truncated (reduced) (e.g., Sage~1\Photos\Backup) depending on your computer configuration.

Last backup:

Session Date:	The date is blank, as you have not backed up previously. The window would indicate the Session Date that was used on a previous backup.
System Date:	The date is blank as you have not backed up previously. The window would indicate the computer system date that was used on a previous backup.
2 ➤ **File Name**:	Change the File Name to: **Backup_01_Photos_Sep_09_2015a_SN**. This will identify the backup with a company name and date the backup was created. We are assuming an actual working date of Sep 09, 2015. The **01** refers to the chapter number of the data file and the 2015a refers to the first backup of the data file. If you were creating a second backup for the same day and chapter, you would use the next letter 2015b, then 2015c for the third backup if needed. This will allow you to have a backup for different saving points in the chapter in case you want to redo an Exercise that you have completed or your data file became corrupt. The **SN** (Student's Name) would be your initials as identification in case your instructor requires you to submit a backup file.
3 ➤ **Location**:	Change the location to: **E:\SAGE 50 2015\Backup**. All backup files will be located in this folder.

Newer computers have DVD and CD-ROM drives and the drive letter available for the USB device may not be E. If your storage device's drive letter is different, substitute the appropriate drive letter for E. Use a backup file name that includes the company name and use the actual date the backup was created (in this example, September 09, 2015).

4 ➤ **Comment**	Do NOT change the Comment field. This identifies this backup as the first backup of the Company file named Photos. In future backups, Sage 50 Accounting will update the backup by increasing the number accordingly; i.e., 0002, 0003, etc.

Do NOT change. You would ✓ this box if your drive and/or data file was fragmented and you wanted Sage 50 Accounting to defrag the file before backing up. This procedure is not necessary in the classroom. (See side note box.)

Fragmented means that portions of this file or many data files are not together on the drive. Fragmentation can slow down the performance of the computer.

There is no exercise for this feature.

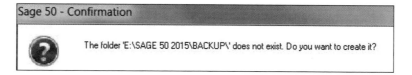 Check this box ✓. Verification of the backup file is important. If it was not verified, data corruption could occur during the backup and you would not know until you needed to use the backup. With the ✓, if data corruption occurred during the backup, the verification would display a warning message.

5 ➤ Click **OK** and the following Confirmation window appears:

> Sage 50 - Confirmation
>
> ❓ The folder 'E:\SAGE 50 2015\BACKUP\' does not exist. Do you want to create it?

6 ➤ Click **Yes**. The backup may take a few minutes to complete.

7 ➤ When successful, a Backup complete window appears as shown next.

> Sage 50 - Information
>
> ⚠️ Backup complete.

8 ➤ Click **OK** and you are returned to the Home window.

9 ➤ **Exit** by clicking the X box in the top-right corner of the Home window.

10 ➤ Change the selection to **No**, as you have already backed up. This is also a reminder to back up if you forget.

 Do NOT select this. If you select this choice the Backup window will not display when you close Sage 50 Accounting for this company. You can reset this choice, and this will be discussed in Chapter 4A.

11 ➤ Click **OK** to close the company.

When you click the EXIT $\boxed{X}$ box in the top-right corner of the Home window, Sage 50 Accounting saves all entries in memory to the data file in the storage device and closes the company and the program.

Go to the E: drive, or the drive letter of where you put your file, then double-click the **Sage 50 2015\BACKUP** folder. You should see the file:

> Backup_01_Photos_Sep_09_2015a_SN1.CAB

This means a Photos backup CAB file was created with the creation date September 9, 2015. Sage 50 Accounting added the **1** in 2015a_SN1 to indicate this is the first backup file in a series. There is no second backup (series) file for Photos. Depending on the configuration of your computer, you may not see the CAB file extension.

You should back up your work on a USB drive or other storage device on a regular basis to reduce the chance of losing data.

 From this point onward, back up whenever you see the icon at the left, before you leave the classroom, or when you are moving to another exercise and you want to save the file at that point.

If there are any error messages during the Backup process, complete the Backup procedure again. If the same error messages or others appear, there may be some damage to the storage device. Write the error message(s) on paper and have your instructor look at the storage device and messages.

Using a Logbook or Diary

A logbook may be used to maintain a list of the work you have finished, and what backup drive you used on a specific date. This will be useful in determining where to start on your next work session. If you have a drive failure or you lose your backup drive, you can refer to your logbook to find out which drive and file name you used last.

Exercise 1-25—Maintaining a Logbook

WWW A logbook form is provided in Appendix 2015 J, *Work Logbook for Sage 50 Premium Accounting 2015* in your course materials at www.nelson.com/student.

1 ➤ Enter the information from the backup that you completed in the previous exercise in the logbook. See the next example.

Date	Backup	Data Information Where you get to each class	Name of File in Storage Location
Sept 9	*1*	*Finished Ex. 1-13, page 1-43*	01_Photos_Sep_09-2015a
Sept 9	*2*	*Finished Ex. 1-23, page 1-58*	01_Photos_Sep_09-2015b
Sept 15	*1*	*Finished Ex. 2A-14, page 2A-105*	02_Luggage_Sep_15_2015a
Sept 26	*2*	*Chapter 2A finished, page 2A-142*	02_Luggage_Sep_26_2015b

It is recommended that you copy the backup file from the USB drive to your own computer as another form of backup away from the main computer. This will reduce the amount of work you have to redo if your storage location data is damaged or lost.

Back up your data and update your logbook now.
Remember, if it is important, back it up.

Backing up in an Office Environment

Most companies store their working data files on the hard drive of the computer and back up daily to a hard drive of another computer, USB device, CD-ROM, DVD, or other storage device. The important thing is to ensure that the backup is not on the same storage device as the working data file and that the backup is kept at a different location. This way, if anything happens to one storage device, there is still a means to retrieve the company data.

It is very important to record in a daily log the backup number and important information about the day or session. Information such as last cheque, last sales invoice, last purchase invoice recorded, should also be recorded in the log. This way, if the working data file becomes damaged, you will have a record of what was entered on each of the backup disks.

Here is one backup procedure:

1. Use a set of 7 folders on an external storage device. Label one folder for every working day of the week: **Sunday, Monday**, **Tuesday**, **Wednesday**, **Thursday**, **Friday, Saturday**. It is assumed that many businesses record accounting information 7 days a week.

2. Prepare another set of 5 folders labelled **Week 1** to **Week 5**.

3. Prepare another set of 12 folders labelled for each month of the year: **January**, **February**, **March**, etc.

4. At the end of each day, back up your data into the appropriate backup folder; e.g., on Monday copy your data into the Monday backup folder, etc.

5. At the end of the week, copy the Saturday data file to a folder labelled Week 1, etc. to Week 5 (some months have 5 Saturdays).

6. At the end of each month, another backup should be made on the appropriate folder and dated.

The backup storage device should be stored off site.

In a classroom situation, while you are learning to use the software, making a backup of your data at the end of every work session will be sufficient.

Do not take your storage device out of the drive before the light on your backup storage device goes off, because the backup procedure will not have been completed. If you remove the storage device, you may lose some of the work you have just completed.

Update your logbook regularly, identifying the page you last worked on, and which backup destination drive is being used on a specific date.

Summary

Some of the benefits of computerized bookkeeping, compared to manual bookkeeping, are:

1. Data entry errors may be easily corrected.

2. Controls are provided to prevent data entry errors, such as addition errors, duplicate invoice numbers, or transposition of numbers.

3. Posting transactions is automatically performed by clicking the Post icon, and all ledgers and journals are updated immediately.

4. Standard financial statements and reports may be printed at any time.

When starting Sage 50 Accounting, you are required to enter a date, which is the work session date. For each transaction you enter, you must enter the actual Transaction date, which could be either the same date as the Session Date or earlier.

Sage 50 Accounting is an integrated accounting system. The system contains **modules** that are similar to ledgers and subledgers in a manual system. The modules in Sage 50 Accounting are:

- RECEIVABLES subledger with Sales and Receipts journals.

- PAYABLES subledger with Purchases and Payments journals.

- INVENTORY & SERVICES subledger with Build, Adjust, and Transfer journals.

- EMPLOYEES & PAYROLL subledger with Payroll Cheque and Pay Remittance journals. To automatically calculate payroll taxes, businesses must purchase a Payroll ID code to activate Automatic payroll calculations.

- PROJECTS module with Sales, Purchases, Paycheques, and General Journal.

- BANKING ledger with Receipt, Deposits, Transfer Funds, and Bank Reconciliation journals.

- COMPANY ledger with General Journal.

- In previous versions, there was a module TIME SLIPS (formerly called TIME & BILLING); it is now located in the RECEIVABLES and EMPLOYEES & PAYROLL modules.

To save your work and exit from Sage 50 Accounting, click the X in the top-right corner.

Budgets: Sage 50 Accounting has a feature to record and display budget amounts. Information on Budget input and display can be found in Appendix 2015 E, *Budgets—General Ledger* in your course materials at www.nelson.com/student. See your instructor for more information.

WWW

This chapter (Photos Company) uses only the GENERAL module and does not have a subledger section for each customer or vendor.

In Chapters 2A & 2B, using the RECEIVABLES module, Santos Luggage Company sales and payments are recorded in the RECEIVABLES subledger. Individual customer detail is available and will include details of inventory items sold.

In Chapters 3A & 3B, using the PAYABLES module, Tyson's Toys records all purchases of merchandise for resale, services (e.g., rent paid, telephone bill, owner's withdrawals and goods for business use) in the PAYABLES subledger module. Individual Vendor transaction detail is available and will include details of inventory items and services purchased.

If a company is using the RECEIVABLES and PAYABLES modules, the General Journal would be used only for bank service charges, owner investments and adjustments that do not relate to specific customers or suppliers (vendors).

To View Corrections

To view corrections that need to be made to the text, please go to:

WWW   www.nelson.com/student

Click on **Corrections**. Corrections to the text, if any, will be listed.

Before Moving On . . .

Read the following questions and make sure you know the answers to them; otherwise, read the corresponding part in the chapter before moving on:

1.   What is the best way to open the Sage 50 Accounting program and data files?

2.   Describe Toolbar icons.

3.   The firm's year-end (fiscal year) is on December 31, 2019. You received on January 22, a bank debit memo dated January 20, 2019, for service charges on the bank account:

     What would be your **Session Date**? _____ Your **Transaction Date**? _____

4.   What important information does the **Source** field indicate?

5.   What is the **Comment field** (box) used to record?

6.   What is the **Comment column** used to record?

7.   Describe two ways to display a list of accounts when entering a General Journal entry.

8.   An Income Statement may be displayed/printed for only 1 day, a month at a time, or a time period that can be several months or parts of a month (e.g., January 1 to February 17). Explain why.

9.   Why would you use the **Drill Down** feature in Sage 50 Accounting?

10. Describe an effective backup routine in an office environment.

11. A logbook/diary, as discussed in this chapter, is used for what purpose?

12. How or where can you get help in Sage 50 Accounting?

Relevant Appendices

WWW The following appendices are available in your course materials at
www.nelson.com/student.

Appendix 2015 A	**Basics of Accounting—Perpetual Inventory System**
Appendix 2015 C	**What's New in Sage 50 Premium Accounting 2015 (Release 2015.0)**
Appendix 2015 E	**Budgets—General Ledger**
Appendix 2015 H	**INVENTORY & SERVICES Module Setup Perpetual Inventory for Sarah's Kitchen Stores (4B)**
Appendix 2015 J	**Work Logbook for Sage 50 Premium Accounting 2015**
Appendix 2015 L	**Setting Up a New Company File using a Sage 50 Premium Accounting Template**
Appendix 2015 N	**Adding a Salesperson's Name to an Invoice**
Appendix 2015 O	**Security—Passwords**
Appendix 2015 R	**Quick Reference Guide**
Appendix 2015 U	**Adding Notes/Footers to Statements**
Appendix 2015 Z	**Restoring a Data File from a Backup Data File**
Appendix 2015 AE	**Recording Chapter 1 Transactions with Perpetual Service Items**
Appendix 2015 AH	**How to Convert Company Reports into Microsoft Excel©**

Challenge Exercise 01 C1-1, Driving School
(General Ledger Review)

1 ➤ Refer to Exercise 1-1b to unzip the **01 C1-1 Driving.exe** file.

2 ➤ Open the **01 C1-1 Driving** file.

The Driving School is a sole-proprietorship business, owned by Tanya Gauci. You should record the following transactions in the General Journal (double-entry accounting). You will learn how to record some of these entries more efficiently in the RECEIVABLES and PAYABLES modules in Chapters 2A, 2B, 3A and 3B. The fiscal year is Jan 1 to Dec 31. Use appropriate additional Info and comment fields in 3 transactions.

Note: This assignment does not involve HST, similar to Photos Company.

This business uses the **Track Additional Transaction Details** feature where necessary.

3 ➤ **Record** and **Post** the following transactions in the General Journal for the month of January using the Double-Entry method.

Jan 2   Purchased $80.00 worth of office supplies from Kanwal Supplies and issued cheque #652. Note that these supplies are assumed to be used up by the end of the month.

Jan 2   Issued $80.00 invoice #324 to YOUR name (your name in the comment line) for 2 hours of driving lessons before your driving test. Cheque #113 received.

Jan 3   Issued $600.00 cheque #653 to Uptown Mall for rent of a store in the mall.

Jan 5   Issued $50.00 invoice #325 and received cheque #748 from Vito Campize for one-hour driving lesson ($40.00) and rule book test ($10.00) for his daughter.

Jan 6   Issued $320.00 cheque #654 to Capilano Advertising for advertisements being delivered to homes in the area today.

Jan 8   A new client, Naomi Regalea, took a 3-hour driving lesson. Received her $120.00 cheque #522 for invoice #326.

Jan 9   Issued $120.00 cheque #655 to Morton Medina (driving teacher) for wages.

Jan 11   Purchased 2 driving lesson DVDs at $75.00 each for use in the Beginners Driving Lesson course approved by the government. They will be used in the course starting tomorrow. Cheque #656 issued to Major Film Labs.

Jan 12   Record the $308.00 Bank Debit memo for a payment on the bank loan. This amount includes interest of $32.40.

Jan 12   Beginners Driving Lessons course started today. Received $250.00 cash from customers and deposited $250.00 in the bank today.

4 ➤ **Print** the following:
   a) Journal Entries All for the period, Jan 02 to Jan 12, **with additional information**
   b) Income Statement for the period Jan 02 to Jan 12
   c) Balance Sheet as at Jan 12
   d) General Ledger for all accounts to Jan 12

WWW   Note: After completing Chapters 1, 2A and 3A students can download Appendix 2015 AE, *Recording Chapter 1 Transactions with Perpetual Service Items* in your course materials at www.nelson.com/student, and record the same transactions using the Perpetual Service feature.

Challenge Exercise 01 C1-2, Astrology Readings
(General Ledger Review)

1 ➤ Refer to Exercise 1-1b to unzip the **01 C1-2 Readings.exe** file.

2 ➤ Open the **01 C1-2 Readings** file.

The Astrology Readings is a sole-proprietorship business, owned by Harriet Patel. You should record the following transactions in the General Journal (double-entry accounting). You will learn how to record some of these entries more efficiently in the RECEIVABLES and PAYABLES modules in Chapters 2A, 2B, 3A and 3B. The fiscal year is Jan 1 to Dec 31.

Note: This assignment does not involve HST, which is similar to Photos Company.

3 ➤ **Record** and **Post** the following transactions in the General Journal for the month of January using the Double-Entry method:

Jan 4   Paid $500.00 rent for the month to Eastwood Mall Inc. Issued cheque #131.

Jan 4   Manager advised the rent has increased to $520.00 on new lease. Reverse and correct the previous entry to the correct amount. Cheque #132 issued.

Jan 4   Paid $50.00 to YourTown Newspaper for an advertisement in today's paper. Invoice #7622. Cheque #133 issued.

Jan 5   Issued invoice #231 for astrology reading to YOUR name (your name in the comment line). Received your cheque #788 in the amount of $130.00.

Jan 6   Issued invoice #232 for astrology reading for Sylvia Ciuciura. Received cash in the amount of $130.00.

Jan 7   Paid $20.00 for special computer paper from Grand Supplies on invoice #8964. Cheque #134 issued. Charge to Astrology Printouts Expense because it will be used by the end of the month.

Jan 9   Received $43.00 telephone bill for regular service from Metro Phones. Cheque #135 issued.

Jan 9   Issued invoice #233 for astrology reading for Ying Xiang. Received her cheque #465 in the amount of $120.00.

Jan 26   Issued $100.00 cheque #136 to Jeremy Design Studio, for graphic design work on new advertising brochure. Received invoice #356.

Jan 31   Issued invoice #234 for astrology reading for John Harwood. Received his cheque #611 in the amount of $125.00.

4 ➤ **Print** the following:
   a) Journal Entries All for Jan 01 to 31, **with corrections**
   b) Income Statement for Jan 01 to 31
   c) Balance Sheet as at Jan 31
   d) General Ledger at Jan 31

Note: After completing Chapters 1, 2A and 3A students can download Appendix 2015 AE, *Recording Chapter 1 Transactions with Perpetual Service Items*, in your course materials at www.nelson.com/student and record the same transactions using the Perpetual Service feature.

WWW

Information on HST or GST Goods and Services Tax

The Goods and Services tax (GST), currently at 5%, or blended (Harmonized—HST) with some provincial taxes at different rates (e.g., Ontario at 13%) is levied by the federal government of Canada through the CRA, Customs and Revenue Agency, on most goods and services in Canada.

The HST rate of 13% is used in this text and reflected in the solutions. When on the job be sure to use the appropriate HST or GST and PST rates.

Refer to Figure 1-10 or 3B-29 for a chart of the tax rates levied by various governments and the dates when changes if any are to be implemented.

Some goods and services are not taxed as follows:

1. **Tax exempt** (i.e., GST/HST is not calculated on these goods. GST/HST is, therefore, not collected or paid). Examples: child care; most health, medical and dental services provided by licensed physicians or dentists for medical reasons; music lessons; legal aid services; educational services leading to a certificate or a diploma.[1]

2. **GST/HST taxable at a zero rate** (zero-rated; i.e., the current GST/HST rate on these goods or services is zero percent; therefore, GST/HST is not collected or paid). Examples: basic groceries—milk, bread and vegetables; agriculture products—grain and raw wool; prescription drugs; medical devices including hearing aids, artificial teeth. Companies claim the GST/HST that they pay or is payable on purchases. [2]

Tax codes used in this text are:

HS   Harmonized at 13%
HI   Harmonized at 8%
No Tax Used on some items (paying HST or GST to the Receiver General, drawings or withdrawals to the owner, etc.).

(PST) Provincial Sales Tax

Provinces (except Alberta) levy a provincial sales tax (PST), which is included in the HST, and may include or exclude the GST in the price on which the PST is calculated. The companies in this text exclude the GST in calculating the PST. PST also may be called Retail Sales Tax (RST).

HST or GST Charged on Sales

HST or GST is charged on goods or services regardless of whether they are sold to a retail customer (consumer) or to another company (merchandiser, wholesaler or service company). The **HST Charged on Sales** or **GST Charged on Sales** is entered as a liability.

---

[1] Canada Revenue Agency. (2013, April 12). Retrieved June 30, 2015, from Exempt goods and services:
www.cra-arc.gc.ca/tx/bsnss/tpcs/gst-tps/gnrl/txbl/chrts/xmpt/menu-eng.html

[2] Canada Revenue Agency. (2013, April 12). Retrieved June 30, 2015, from Zero-rated (0%) goods and services: www.cra-arc.gc.ca/tx/bsnss/tpcs/gst-tps/gnrl/txbl/menu-eng.html

HST or GST Paid on Purchases

When a company buys goods for resale or for its own use, HST or GST is paid on the purchase price, regardless of whether or not the purchased item is intended for resale. The **HST Paid on Purchases or GST Paid on Purchases** is entered as a contra-liability.

Method of Recording HST or GST

A business may use the **Regular** method of recording HST or GST, in which the HST or GST is recorded on each sale and purchase. At the end of the reporting period the business will either send the difference (more HST or GST collected than paid) or claim a refund (more paid than collected) to the Receiver General of Canada. Depending on the size of the business, it will report on a monthly, quarterly or annual basis.

A business may use the **Quick** method, which calculates the HST or GST to be paid based on a rate of 1 to 5 percent of net sales. Grocery and convenience stores are typical examples of businesses that use the Quick method.

The companies in this text use the Regular method of recording the GST.

To avoid double taxation, a business is allowed to deduct the **HST or GST Paid on Purchases** from the **HST or GST Charged on Sales**. The usual business practice is to locate the **HST or GST Paid on Purchases** account in the liability section of the Balance Sheet, with the **HST or GST Charged on Sales**. Some companies use one account only, HST or GST Payable, to record both the HST or GST collected and paid.

Registration

A business with annual sales of more than $30,000 in a single calendar quarter or in four consecutive calendar quarters, which exceed the small supplier limit, **must** register to collect the HST or GST. Registering will allow a business to recover any HST or GST paid on its purchases. Registration is optional for a business in which sales are less than $30,000.[3]

Accounting Examples Using the Regular Method of Recording HST

In this chapter the cents are not shown, and it is assumed the province is Ontario, with an HST rate of 13%.

If Brittany Company buys merchandise **for resale** from Dustin Company, the entry on each company's books is shown in Appendix Fig. 1-1.

Brittany Company			**Dustin Company**		
buys goods			**sells** goods		
Dr Inventory	200		Dr Cash or Accounts Receivable	226	
Dr HST Paid on Purchases	26		Cr Sales		200
Cr Cash or Accounts Payable		226	Cr HST Charged on Sales		26
			Dr Cost of Goods Sold	100	
			Cr Inventory		100

Appendix Fig. 1-1

---

[3]   Canada Revenue Agency. (2014, January 20). Retrieved June 30, 2015, from Mandatory registration: www.cra-arc.gc.ca/tx/bsnss/tpcs/gst-tps/rgstrng/menu-eng.html

If Brittany Company **sells** merchandise, including HST, to Chad Company, another merchandising company, the entries on each company's books are shown in Appendix Fig. 1-2.

Brittany Company			Chad Company		
sells goods			**buys** goods		
Dr Cash or Accounts Receivable	565		Dr Inventory	500	
Cr Sales		500	Dr HST Paid on Purchase	65	
Cr HST Charged on Sales		65	Cr Cash or Accounts Payable		565
Dr Cost of Goods Sold	250				
Cr Inventory		250			

Appendix Fig. 1-2

- Most firms add the HST to the selling price of the goods or services on the invoice.

- The $500 price, plus 13% HST, equals invoice amount of $565.

HST or GST Paid to the Federal Government

The clerk will determine the amounts in the two HST or GST accounts, at the report date, and calculate the difference as being a payment to be made (see Appendix Fig. 1-3 and Exercise 3B-32). If a refund is requested, the business would submit the HST return and claim a refund. See information box in Exercise 3B-31.

For Brittany Company, at reporting time (month or quarter), the value of **HST Paid on Purchases** ($26) is subtracted from **HST Charged on Sales** ($65), and the difference ($39) is paid to the government, the Receiver General, by the appropriate date. See Exercise 3B-32.

Assuming different dollar values:

If the **HST Paid on Purchases** ($420) is subtracted from HST Charged on Sales ($390), the difference ($30) is reported to the government, and a refund is claimed.

HST Examples for Showing Remittances

The Receiver General is set up as a vendor in the PAYABLES module. To record the payment of HST, Brittany Company must reduce the amount in both HST accounts, and the difference will be paid by cheque using the Make Other Payment option to the Receiver General for Canada. See Appendix Fig. 1-3 and Exercise 3B-32.

DR HST Charged on Sales	65	
CR HST Paid on Purchases		26
CR Cash		39

Appendix Fig. 1-3

HST—What Account Do You Charge?

A common question that comes up when you buy goods or services is, which account is the HST (Harmonized Sales Tax) posted to?

You pay the HST; therefore, it should go into the HST Payable account—or should it?

To answer that question, look at the following Ontario example:

Business Supplies
85 Shaw Avenue   **INVOICE**
Toronto, ON M2W 3A6   **4557**
Phone 416-333-2255 ❖ Fax 416-333-2211

SOLD TO:
Taras Rai   P.O. _____
21 Nina Drive   Date: _April 5, 2016_
Rexdale, ON M9N 1Z2   Shipped By: _Our Truck_

#	ITEM	QTY.	DESCRIPTION		AMOUNT
	various	1	Various Office Supplies	$	100.00
				HST (13%)	13.00
Terms: On Receipt			TOTAL	$	113.00

	Personal	**Business**
Office supplies bought above	$100.00	$100.00
HST Paid (included in invoice)	13.00	13.00
Total paid	$113.00	$113.00
Rebate from Provincial Government	nil	nil
Rebate from Federal Government	nil	13.00 (Federal)
The true cost	$113.00	$100.00

You cannot get any other rebates from governments, therefore:

- the personal true cost of the office supplies becomes $113.00
- the business true cost of the office supplies becomes $100.00

If the true cost of supplies for business is $100.00, then the cost of the supplies and HST should be charged as follows.

The business entry would be:

Office Supplies On Hand (Asset)	$100.00	
HST Paid on Purchases	13.00	
Cash or Bank or Accounts Payable		$113.00

PST—Provincial Sales Tax; RST—Retail Sales Tax

Provinces (except Alberta) levy a Provincial Sales Tax (PST). It may also be called Retail Sales Tax (RST), and may include or exclude the GST in the price on which the PST is calculated. As noted previously, some provinces blend (harmonize) their PST with the GST (the tax is called HST). The following discussion is for provinces that collect the PST from retailers.

The Provincial Sales Tax, normally referred to as PST or RST, is collected by the selling company on goods or services sold within the province. The company that sells the product or service is required by the provincial government to collect the tax at the time of sale, and forward the amount collected to the provincial taxation office in the following month.

If Brittany Company **purchases** merchandise for resale from other vendors, the merchandise purchased is exempt from provincial tax (PST). This means that Brittany Company does not pay PST on items purchased that are going to be resold to customers. A purchasing firm (e.g., Brittany) would apply for a PST exemption certificate, and the certificate number would have to be given to a seller to advise them that the goods were purchased PST-Exempt.

If Brittany Company **sells** merchandise to a final consumer (Retail sale) the entry to record the sale is shown as in Appendix Fig. 1-4. It is assumed that the PST is calculated only on the selling price and not on the selling price plus GST.

Retail Sale with PST @ 8% and GST at 5%

Brittany Company			Mrs. Marion Chaiken
sells goods			**buys** goods for her personal use.
Dr Cash or Accounts Receivable 452			Does not keep accounting records
Cr Sales		400	and, therefore, does not record entries.
Cr GST Charged on Sales		20	
Cr PST Charged on Sales		32	
Dr Cost of Goods Sold	200		
Cr Inventory		200	

Appendix Fig. 1-4

If Brittany Company **sells** *different* merchandise to another merchandising company, the PST-exemption entry to record the sale is shown as in Appendix Fig. 1-5.

Merchandiser/Wholesaler

Brittany Company			Delta Company		
sells goods			**buys** goods		
Dr Cash or Accounts Receivable 525			Dr Inventory	500	
Cr Sales		500	Dr GST Paid on Purchases	25	
Cr GST Charged on Sales		25	Cr Cash or Accounts Payable		525
Dr Cost of Goods Sold	250				
Cr Inventory		250			

Appendix Fig. 1-5

PST Paid to the Provincial Government

Brittany Company will determine the amounts in the PST account at the report date. As shown in Appendix Fig. 1-4, Brittany Company owes the provincial government $32.

To record the payment, Brittany Company would set up a Vendor, the Minister of Finance of the province, and would issue a cheque in Payments using Make Other Payment option and record the following entry. See Appendix Fig. 1-6.

```
Dr PST Charged on Sales     32
Cr    Cash                       32
```

Appendix Fig. 1-6

GST Sales Tax

Assume that Brittany Company is in Manitoba with a GST tax of 8%. The wholesale entries are as shown in Appendix Fig. 1-7.

```
Brittany Company                      Ditlove Company
sells goods                           buys goods
Dr Cash or Accounts Receivable 432    Dr Inventory              400
Cr   Sales                   400      Dr GST Paid on Purchases  32
Cr   GST Charged on Sales     32      Cr    Accounts Payable          432
Dr Cost of Goods Sold     200
Cr   Inventory            200
```

Appendix Fig. 1-7

When goods for resale are **purchased**, entries similar to the following are recorded:

```
Brittany Company                      Darwin Company
buys goods                            sells goods
Dr Inventory           300            Dr Cash or Accounts Receivable  324
Dr GST Paid on Purchases   24         Cr   Sales                  300
Cr   Cash or Accounts Payable   324   Cr   GST Charged on Sales    24
                                      Dr Cost of Goods Sold     150
                                      Cr    Inventory           150
```

Appendix Fig. 1-8

At the end of the recording period for Brittany Company, the net GST is remitted to the Receiver General with a procedure similar to HST as shown in Appendix Fig. 1-9.

Note: The provincial portion of the GST is not paid separately.

```
Dr GST Charged on Sales     32
Cr   GST Paid on Purchases       24
Cr   Cash                         8
```

Appendix Fig. 1-9

PST—What Account Do You Charge?

A common question that comes up when you buy goods or services is: which account is the PST (Provincial Sales Tax) posted to?

You pay the PST; therefore, it should go into the PST Payable account—or should it?

To answer that question, look at the following Manitoba example:

Business Supplies
856 Tranner Avenue   **INVOICE**
Brandon, MB, M2W 3A6   **3658**
Phone 204-783-4689 ❖ Fax 204-783-8528

SOLD TO:
  Geraldine Anrason   P.O. _____
  2561 Louise Avenue   Date: _April 5, 2016_
  Brandon, MB   R7A 6C3   Shipped By: _Our Truck_

#	ITEM	QTY.	DESCRIPTION	AMOUNT
	various	1	Various Office Supplies	$ 100.00
			GST 5%	5.00
			PST 8%	8.00
Terms: On Receipt			TOTAL	$ 113.00

	Personal	**Business**
Office supplies bought above	$100.00	$100.00
PST Paid (included in invoice)	8.00	8.00
GST Paid (included in invoice)	5.00	5.00
Total paid	$113.00	$113.00
Rebate from Provincial Government	nil	nil
Rebate from Federal Government	nil	5.00(Federal)
The true cost	$113.00	$108.00

You cannot get any other PST rebates from governments, therefore:

- the personal true cost of the office supplies becomes $113.00
- the business true cost of the office supplies becomes $108.00

If the true cost of supplies for business is $108.00, then the cost of the supplies and GST should be charged as follows.

The business entry would be:

Office Supplies On Hand (Asset) $108.00
GST Paid on Purchases   5.00
    Cash or Bank $113.00

HST, GST, and PST Rates by Province and Territory

HST, GST and PST rates by Province and Territory (at July 1, 2015)				
	HST	GST	PST/QST	Total
NS Nova Scotia	15.0	-	-	15.0
QC Quebec	-	5.0	9.975	14.975
PE Prince Edward Island	14.0	-	-	14.0
MB Manitoba	-	5.0	8.0	13.0
NB New Brunswick	13.0	-	-	13.0
NL Newfoundland & Labrador	13.0	-	-	13.0
ON Ontario	13.0	-	-	13.0
BC British Columbia	-	5.0	7.0	12.0
SK Saskatchewan	-	5.0	5.0	10.0
AB Alberta	-	5.0	-	5.0
NT North West Territories	-	5.0	-	5.0
NU Nunavut	-	5.0	-	5.0
YT Yukon	-	5.0	-	5.0

Appendix Fig. 1-10: Provincial and Territory tax rates.

Chapter 2A

RECEIVABLES Module—*Basics*

Santos Luggage

Learning Objectives

After completing this chapter you will be able to:

☐ Process sales quotes, orders, invoices and sales returns using the Perpetual Inventory System.

☐ Add new customers and make changes to existing customers' data files.

☐ Process customers' receipts in full or partial payment of invoices with or without cash discounts, and record cash and/or ATM (bank card) or credit card sales.

☐ Process deposits from customers for sales orders.

☐ Reverse and correct errors in invoices and cheques.

☐ Use Daily Business Manager and other Sage 50 Accounting special features.

☐ Display and print various Receivable reports and journals.

Note: The Harmonized Sales Tax (HST) is being charged based on percentages available at time of preparation of this textbook. See Exercise 2A-6, step 18.

Note: You will be recording inventory transactions using the Perpetual Inventory System. Setup of Inventory will be shown in Chapter 8, Printers, and Appendix 2015 H, *INVENTORY & SERVICES Module Setup Perpetual Inventory for Sarah's Kitchen Stores (4B).*

The contents of this chapter are as follows:

Comparison of Periodic and Perpetual Inventory Systems

In the following examples HST, GST and/or PST is NOT included in the transactions. This will highlight the differences between the two systems.

Transactions

Periodic Inventory

Buy Merchandise for resale

	Ref		
Dr. Purchases	A	400	
Cr. Accounts Payable	B		400

Return part of goods

	Ref		
Dr. Accounts Payable	C	100	
Cr. Purchase Returns	D		100

At this point, we have $300 of goods (at cost) available for sale in both systems. Periodic (Net Purchases) Perpetual (Inventory [Asset])

We sell goods for $320 costing $200

	Ref		
Dr. Accounts Receivable	E	320	
Cr. Sales	F		320

Perpetual Inventory

Buy Merchandise for resale

	Ref		
Dr. Inventory (Asset)	L	400	
Cr. Accounts Payable	M		400

Return part of goods

	Ref		
Dr. Accounts Payable	N	100	
Cr. Inventory (Asset)	O		100

We sell goods for $320 costing $200

	Ref		
Dr. Accounts Receivable	P	320	
Cr. Sales	Q		320
Dr. Cost of Goods Sold	R	200	
Cr. Inventory (Asset)	S		200

General Ledger Accounts (Periodic)

Accounts Receivable

Ref	Debit	Credit	Balance
E	320		320 Dr

Accounts Payable

Ref	Debit	Credit	Balance
B		400	400 Cr
C	100		300 Cr

Sales

Ref	Debit	Credit	Balance
F		320	320 Cr

Purchases

Ref	Debit	Credit	Balance
A	400		400 Dr

Purchase Returns

Ref	Debit	Credit	Balance
D		100	100 Cr

General Ledger Accounts (Perpetual)

Accounts Receivable

Ref	Debit	Credit	Balance
P	320		320 Dr

Inventory (Asset)

	Ref	Debit	Credit	Balance
Purchase of goods	L	400		400 Dr
Return of goods	O		100	300 Dr
Goods sold	S		200	100 Dr

Accounts Payable

Ref	Debit	Credit	Balance
M		400	400 Cr
N	100		300 Cr

Sales

Ref	Debit	Credit	Balance
Q		320	320 Cr

Cost of Goods Sold

Ref	Debit	Credit	Balance
R	200		200 Dr

Fig. 2A-1a: Comparison of Periodic and Perpetual Inventory Systems.

Trial Balance

Accounts Receivable	320	
Inventory (Asset)	100	
Accounts Payable		300
Sales		320
Cost of Goods Sold	200	
	620	620

Income Statement

Sales	320
Cost of Goods Sold	200
Gross Margin	120

Balance Sheet

Accounts Receivable	320	
Inventory (not sold)	100	
Assets		420
Accounts Payable	300	
Net Income	120	
Liabilities & Owner Equity		420

Trial Balance

Accounts Receivable	320	
Accounts Payable		300
Sales		320
Purchases	400	
Purchase Returns		100
	720	720

Income Statement

Sales		320
Beginning Inventory		0
Purchases	400	
Purchases Returns	100	
Net Purchases		300
Goods Available for Sale		300
Less: Ending Inventory (count)		-100
Cost of Goods Sold		200
Gross Margin		120

Balance Sheet

Accounts Receivable	320	
Inventory (not sold)	100	
Assets		420
Accounts Payable	300	
Net Income	120	
Liabilities & Owner Equity		420

Fig. 2A-1b: Comparison of Periodic and Perpetual Inventory Systems.

RECEIVABLES Module Overview and Company Profile

This chapter, Parts A (Basics) and B (Beyond Basics), uses **Santos Luggage** and will guide you through recording transactions that affect the amount of money owed to the company, involving Accounts Receivable subledgers and the General Ledger, as well as updating inventory items on hand.

Below are two main types of transactions recorded in the RECEIVABLES module with the corresponding journals:

1. Sales of merchandise or services   - Sales Quotes
    (Sales Journal)   - Sales Orders
                                           - Sales Invoices on credit (on account)
                                           - Sales Invoices paid by Cash/Cheque
                                           - Sales Invoices paid by Credit Card (Part B)
                                           - Sales Invoices paid by Bank Debit Card

2. Receipts from customers   - Partial payment
    (Receipts Journal)   - Full payment with or without cash discounts
                                           - Deposits against a future invoice (Part B)

WWW

Slideshow 2A—RECEIVABLES Module Basics will help you understand how the RECEIVABLES module works. It will also give you a review of the GAAP applicable to accounts receivable transactions. Run it now; you will find it in your course materials at www.nelson.com/student.

Santos Luggage

Santos Luggage has been selling luggage and accessories, for over 10 years, to various stores (wholesale) and has an outlet store at the back of the warehouse to sell slightly damaged items and samples to retail customers. A $15.00 handling fee is charged to the customer if their cheque is returned by the bank. The business has an acceptable level of receivables outstanding based on selling to large stores with cash discounts for prompt payment.

WWW

Santos Luggage uses the Perpetual Inventory Average Cost method for calculating inventory remaining in the warehouse and Outlet Store. Periodic Inventory Entries will be demonstrated in Appendix 2015 F, *Periodic Inventory Entries* in your course materials at www.nelson.com/student.

Assume that you are a part-time bookkeeper and work at Santos Luggage on a variable time schedule. Some days you work for an hour; some days you work for three hours, and other days you work the whole day.

The owner, Mrs. Santos, has decided, at this time, to *not* use the Track Additional Transaction Details feature of the software.

WWW

For companies that use periodic inventory systems, inventory and COGS balances are not updated on a continuous basis as goods are bought and sold. Therefore, in order to present correct financial statements (Income Statement, Balance Sheet), inventory balances must be updated via manual entries. The values for these manual entries are derived from the physical count of goods. This adjustment is covered in Appendix 2015 G, *Updating Inventory and COGS Balances for Companies Using Periodic Inventory System* in your course materials at www.nelson.com/student.

Opening the RECEIVABLES Module Part A

In a job situation, it is most likely that you would work on an accounting system that has already been set up. Santos Luggage's RECEIVABLES module is ready to use. In this chapter, you will access the RECEIVABLES module of Santos Luggage and enter transactions related to inventory sales and receipts of payment from customers.

Exercise 2A-1—Opening the RECEIVABLES Module

---

1 ➤ Refer to Exercise 1-1b to unzip the **02 2A Luggage-PI-2A.exe** file.
Note: PI identifies the Perpetual Inventory file.

2 ➤ Start **Sage 50 Accounting**.

3 ➤ At the **Select Company** window, click **Select an existing company** button, **OK**.

> **ℹ**
> Review Exercise 1-2 if you need help to open a data file.

4 ➤ At the Sage 50 Accounting **Open Company** window, in the **Look in** box, locate your student location drive and folder, **Sage 50 Data 2015**. Double-click on the **Sage 50 Data 2015** folder. (See side note box.)

5 ➤ Double-click the 📁 02 2A Luggage-PI-2A folder. You will see a
📁 02 2A Luggage-PI-2A.SAJ folder and a 📄 02 2A Luggage-PI-2A.SAI file in the window. The image at the left of Luggage may be different, depending on the configuration of your computer, and the SAI may be in lowercase.

6 ➤ Click on 📄 02 2A Luggage-PI-2A.SAI. The lower **File name** box will change to: 📄 02 2A Luggage-PI-2A.SAI. (.SAI may not display or may be in lowercase.)

7 ➤ Click **Open** to open the **02 2A Luggage-PI-2A.SAI** file.

8 ➤ The Session date will be **Feb 29, 2016**. This is the date when the file was last used. Click **OK**.

Study the Santos Luggage Home window:

Fig. 2A-2: Santos Luggage-PI-A, Enhanced Home window.

Notice that on the right side, in the Customers window, the name of the customer, telephone number, and current balance are displayed. You can click on each of the column headings to sort the column in ascending or descending order. If you right click the **column**, you will see 2 check boxes for Telephone or Balance. Clicking the **check mark** will hide the column. You can bring back the hidden column by right clicking a **column** that is not hidden and clicking the **column** that is hidden and it will display.

Notice at the bottom of the Customers section, ☑ Include inactive customers.

In a business it would be better to have only the active accounts display. You will see in Exercise 2A-23, in the customer's record, a setting to identify inactive customers. Santos Luggage does not have any inactive customers at this time.

The History symbol appears for some icons in the **PAYABLES** and **EMPLOYEES & PAYROLL** modules. This means that the historical information has not been completed, but you are still able to record transactions.

9 ➤ On the left, click on the following modules: **PAYABLES, INVENTORY & SERVICES, EMPLOYEES AND PAYROLL, PROJECTS, BANKING,** and **COMPANY**.

10 ➤ Click the **RECEIVABLES** module on the left.

Notice that the History symbol (see side note box) does not appear for **RECEIVABLES, INVENTORY & SERVICES, BANKING,** and **COMPANY** modules. This signifies that history has been completed, and you can record transactions.

11 ➤ Remember to change the company name to include your name; e.g., **Santos Luggage, Guida Marisa**.

Exercise 2A-2—Displaying Inventory Summary

---

12 ➤ To view the items in stock that Santos Luggage sells, from the menu bar, click **Reports, Inventory & Services, Summary, 1300 Inventory** should be selected in blue, As at **Today**, click **OK**. The report should display as follows:

Inventory Summary As at Feb 29, 2016

Item No. △	Description	Unit	Quantity	Cost	Value
Brief-R	Briefcase-regular	Each	43	50.00	2,150.00
Brief-W	Briefcase-wide	Each	40	60.00	2,400.00
Carry-sm	Carry-on bag-small	Each	124	10.50	1,302.00
Lap-BP	Laptop Back Paks	Each	92	35.00	3,220.00
Locks-1	Locks-combination	Each	107	2.00	214.00
Power-1	Power Adapters	Each	52	5.25	273.00
Suit w/w R	Suitcase w/w Regular	Each	222	28.00	6,216.00
Suit-w/w L	Suitcase w/w Large	Each	255	31.00	7,905.00
					23,680.00

13 ➤ Click ☒ to return to Home page.

Printing Reports

An Income Statement shows the current financial position re SALES, COST OF GOODS SOLD, and EXPENSES.

As you have seen in Chapter 1, an Income Statement may be viewed or printed at any time. However, for the Income Statement to be accurate, the ending inventory needs to be updated to the correct value of goods on hand that have not been sold.

For companies that use perpetual inventory systems, such as Santos Luggage (Chapters 2A and 2B) and Tyson's Toys (Chapters 3A and 3B), inventory and Cost of Goods Sold (COGS) balances are updated as goods are bought and sold. Inventory adjustments are necessary if, and only if, there exist differences between the continuous inventory records and actual physical count. These differences arise from occurrences such as faulty inventory bar codes, manually inputted inventory bar codes, goods that become unsellable, etc. If a perpetual inventory system is in place, a physical count must be done at least once per year to ensure continuous records accurately reflect inventory levels. This inventory adjustment is covered in Chapter 8.

Exercise 2A-3—Printing Reports

1 ➤ Print the following:

a. Income Statement for period **Jan 01, 2016** to **Feb 29, 2016**. (See side note box.)

b. Balance Sheet at **Feb 29, 2016**.

2 ➤ Display a Trial Balance and compare it to Fig. 2A-3 to make sure it agrees with the values shown in Fig. 2A-3. From the Menu bar, click **Reports**, **Financials**, **Trial Balance**; leave the date at Feb 29, 2016, then **OK**.

You should notice that in the Income Statements, there are no ENDING INVENTORY accounts; only the Cost of the Goods Sold is shown. You should also note the Balance Sheet has a value of Inventory on hand (account #1300; $23,680.00).

See Figs. 2A-1a and 2A-1b at the beginning of the chapter for the Comparison of Periodic and Perpetual Inventory Systems. The chapters in this text will use the Perpetual Inventory System.

Study the Santos Luggage Trial Balance. (First, see side note box.)

The published solution for this chapter includes inventory values and COGS inventory values based on the inclusion of updated inventory values using the Perpetual Inventory System. It is assumed the inventory values for Santos Luggage are correct and do not need adjusting for this chapter.

Note: If a Periodic Inventory system was in use, adjusting entries would be required. Refer to Appendix 2015 G, *Updating Inventory and COGS Balances for Companies Using Periodic Inventory System* for additional information located in your course materials at www.nelson.com/student .

www

The majority of the transactions in this chapter will affect the accounts shaded in Fig. 2A-3:

1020 Bank Chequing Account,
1030 Visa Credit Card Bank Account,
1200 Accounts Receivable,
1210 Allowance for Doubtful Accounts,
1300 Inventory,
2630 HST Charged on Sales, and Income Statement accounts,
4100 to 4510 Sales accounts, and
5010 Cost of Goods Sold.

When you have confirmed that the Trial Balance is correct, exit to the Home window.

Santos Luggage-PI-2A, Student's Name			
Trial Balance As At Feb 29, 2016		**Debits**	**Credits**
1020	Bank Chequing Account	19,436.86	-
1030	Visa Credit Card Bank Account	600.00	-
1200	Accounts Receivable	12,656.00	
1210	Allowance for Doubtful Accounts		2,440.00
1300	Inventory	23,680.00	-
1320	Prepaid Supplies	712.00	-
1420	Office/Warehouse Furniture/Equip...	25,163.00	
1425	Accum. Deprec Office/Ware Furn/E...	-	4,100.00
2200	Accounts Payable	-	11,255.00
2630	HST Charged on Sales	-	1,120.00
2640	HST Paid On Purchases	525.00	-
3100	Capital, Maria Santos	-	62,724.68
3160	Additional Investment	-	0.00
3180	Drawings, Maria Santos	2,200.00	-
4100	Sales	-	40,125.00
4150	Sales-Discounts	320.00	-
4200	Sales-Returns & Allowances	355.00	-
4510	Handling Fee		15.00
5010	Cost of Goods Sold	24,320.00	-
5080	Purchase Discounts	-	335.00
5090	Inventory Adjustment	-	
5310	Wages Expense	8,000.00	-
5320	Advertising Expense	432.00	-
5330	Bank Charges & Interest	95.00	-
5340	Credit Card Charges	34.30	-
5350	Rent Expense	800.00	-
5370	Bad Debt Expense	0.00	-
5410	Office/Warehouse Supplies Expense	216.00	-
5450	Rent Expense Warehouse	2,000.00	-
5460	Utility Expense	263.89	-
5550	Telephone Expense	305.63	-
		122,114.68	122,114.68

Fig. 2A-3: Santos Luggage-A Trial Balance.

3 ➤ Click ⊠ to return to the Home window.

Displaying and Printing the Customer Aged Report

To find out the status of your company receivables, you can display and/or print the Customer Aged Report. Sage 50 Accounting groups receivables calculated from the date of the invoice to the current Session Date, and provides a list of accounts that are **Current**, **31 to 60** days overdue, **61 to 90** days overdue, and **91+** days overdue.

Sage 50 Accounting provides two options: **Summary** and **Detail**. Your choice depends on the purpose for which you need the reports. At this point, if you wished to acquaint yourself with the company customers, their purchasing pattern, their balances, and what accounts are overdue, you would then select **Detail**. You will display/print both report options in this exercise.

> When displaying this report, it is important the Session Date is correct; otherwise, the aging will not be accurate.

Depending on the type of printer that is connected to the computer or network, you may see two dotted lines, one dotted line on the right side of 61 to 90 and another on the right of 91+. This means the report will print on 2 pages. This will be adjusted in step 3.

61 to 90	91+
-	-
-	-

Exercise 2A-4—Displaying/Printing Customer Aged Report

The default Detail report does not display Terms. In this exercise, you will display a **Detail** Customer Aged Report and modify it to display terms. Later you will display a **Summary** report. Observe the type of information each report provides, so you can determine which type you will need in the future.

1 ➤ On the left, click on **RECEIVABLES**, at the right in **Reports,** Customer List, click ▼, select **Customer Aged Detail**, click **Display**. You will see the Customer Aged Detail window. The display may show a dotted line on the left side of 91+. This means the report may print on 2 pages. (See side note box.)

2 ➤ Click the **Modify** icon, click on **Report Options**. Click **Include Terms**. All customers should be in blue, meaning they have been selected. Click **OK**. The report will display with the right side showing 2 columns (dotted lines) and a portion will print on the second page.

Columns shown on the report	
Column Name	Width
Source	19
Date	14
Terms	15
Transaction Type	17
Total Balance Owing	14
Current	14
31 to 60	14
61 to 90	11
91+	11

3 ➤ To reduce the size of the columns, double-click on the divider line at **Source, Date**, **Transaction Type**, **Total**, **Current**, **31-60**, **61 to 90** and **91+**. To save printed paper you may have to move some of the divider line columns manually to the left, until the page divider line disappears. See Fig. 2A-4. This will happen with a number of reports.

(See side note box with revised column widths used in the 2A-4 report.)

Do **NOT** Print now. To print this report with an earlier date, you would change the **Date** accordingly. This is useful when the session date was advanced and you want to produce a report for a previous period. Do not change the Feb 29, 2016 date.

4 ➤ At the top left, at **As at:**, click ▼ and you will see a number of choices. Select **Today**. The Date should be **Feb 29, 2016**. (See side note box.)

If you are able to change the printer to display/print in landscape mode, click **File**, **Printer Setup**, (on some computers you click Properties), and click the appropriate boxes on your system. You will have to ask your faculty member which of the appropriate items to click to print in landscape mode. This text assumes you are printing in portrait mode (default). Click **OK**.

You should now see the Customer Aged Detail report. Note the information it provides. (See side note box beside Fig. 2A-4.)

Customer Aged Detail As at Feb 29, 2016								
Source	Date	Terms	Transaction Type	Total	Current	31 to 60	61 to 90	91+
Havarah Leather Goods								
2253	Feb 26, 2016	2%/10, Net 30	Invoice	2,373.00	2,373.00	-	-	-
Total outstanding:				2,373.00	2,373.00	-	-	-
Royes Luggage Inc.								
2212	Jan 31, 2016	2%/10, Net 30	Invoice	1,017.00	1,017.00	-	-	-
2256	Feb 27, 2016	2%/10, Net 30	Invoice	1,243.00	1,243.00	-	-	-
Total outstanding:				2,260.00	2,260.00	-	-	-
Sandler Travel Stores								
2197	Jan 26, 2016	2%/10, Net 30	Invoice	4,407.00	-	4,407.00	-	-
Total outstanding:				4,407.00	-	4,407.00	-	-
Spiller Luggage Stores								
2230	Feb 20, 2016	2%/10, Net 30	Invoice	3,616.00	3,616.00	-	-	-
Total outstanding:				3,616.00	3,616.00	-	-	-
Total unpaid invoices:				12,656.00	8,249.00	4,407.00	-	-
Total deposits/prepaid order:				-	-	-	-	-
Total outstanding:				12,656.00	8,249.00	4,407.00	-	-

Fig. 2A-4: Customer Aged Detail Report (reduced column sizes).

> **ℹ**
> The arrow is pointing at **Total deposits/prepaid order:** this refers to all customers.
>
> If there are no deposits paid by customers, deposits/prepaid order will display blanks (-).

DO NOT PRINT NOW. You will print this report at the end of the chapter.

5 ➤ To save these column settings and have the same report style available for another time, click the **Modify** icon, click **Report Options**, at the top, click **Save Template** button. In the Save Template as: type `Receivable Aged Detail on 1 page`, click **Save** and **OK**. This template displays.

You will see Fig. 2A-4, with a header change identifying your saved report.

`Customer Aged Detail As at Feb 29, 2016 - Receivable Aged Detail on 1 page`

You can repeat these steps for other module reports as well.

6 ➤ To exit your template, click X, and you will see the Fig. 2A-4 report.

7 ➤ To display the Summary report click the **Modify** icon, click **Report Options**, at Report Type, click **Summary button** (the customers should be blue), the date should be **Feb 29, 2016,** click **OK**. (See side note box.)

> **ℹ**
> Do **NOT** print now.
> To display/print this report with an earlier date, you would change the **As at: Date** accordingly. This would be useful if the Session Date was advanced and you want to produce a report for a previous period. For now, do not change the Feb 29, 2016 date.

The Customer Aged Summary report displays. This report does not need to have the column sizes reduced.

Customer Aged Summary As at Feb 29, 2016					
Name	Total	Current	31 to 60	61 to 90	91+
Havarah Leather Goods	2,373.00	2,373.00	-	-	-
Royes Luggage Inc.	2,260.00	2,260.00	-	-	-
Sandler Travel Stores	4,407.00	-	4,407.00	-	-
Spiller Luggage Stores	3,616.00	3,616.00	-	-	-
Total outstanding:	12,656.00	8,249.00	4,407.00	-	-

Fig. 2A-5: Customer Aged Summary window.

You will notice that the **Detail** report shows the individual invoices owed by each customer, and that the **Summary** report shows only the total owed by each customer. You will print the Detail report at the end of the chapter.

8 ➤ **Exit** the Summary window, **exit** the Customer Aged Detail default window, and return to the Home window.

9 ➤ To see your saved template report, at **Reports**, click ▼, select **Customer Aged Detail**, click **Display**. The Customer Aged Detail window will display without the terms displayed. Click the **Modify** icon, click **Report Options**. To the left of the **Save Template** button, click ▼, and select Receivable Aged Detail on 1 page . Click **OK**.

10 ➤ Click X to **exit** your Detail window and click X to **exit** to the Home window.

The RECEIVABLES Journals

The following types of transactions are entered in the three Sales journals:

Sales Quotes	a form sent to a customer indicating the price of products or services as requested by the customer.

Sales Orders	a confirmation of a commitment to purchase by a customer. A sales order can be issued without a previously issued sales quote. The product will be delivered at a later date, at which time a sales invoice will be issued.

Sales Invoices Pay Later	a sale on account (credit), which may or may not be issued without a sales Quote and/or a Sales Order.
Sales Invoices Paid by	a sale fully paid by cash, bank debit card, cheque, credit card or Pre-Authorized Debit
Sales Invoices Adjustment	an entry to record a return of goods or an adjustment to the sales price, also called a Credit Memo.

The following types of transactions are recorded in the **Receipts Journal**:

Receipts	Payments (receipts) from customers on invoices, which may or may not be previously recorded.

Receipts can be:

1. Full payment of sales invoice on credit (Invoice-Pay Later) with or without cash discounts.
2. Partial payment of sales invoice on credit (Invoice-Pay Later) with or without partial cash discounts.
3. Deposits against a future sales invoice (Part B).

The Sales Journals

A customer may request a quote from a vendor (the selling company) to confirm/guarantee sales prices. The vendor prepares a **sales quote**, which is recorded in the Sales Quote Journal. The sales quote is printed and sent to the customer. When you record the sales quote, neither the customer subledger nor any ledger account is updated with an accounting entry, as no sale has been made at this point. Although a sale is not made at this time, a record of the sales quote is useful for sales staff for follow-up purposes. Copies of printed quotes need to be kept because Sage 50 Accounting does not provide a printed report of outstanding quotes.

When the customer confirms that the quote has been accepted, the quote can be converted into a **sales order**. At this point, the customer subledger and ledger accounts are still not updated with an accounting entry. The sales order is recorded in the company's Sales Order Listing and can be printed as a **Pending Sales Order** report. It is best to record the sales order to avoid the shipment getting missed in case there may be a delay in the delivery, or if the customer does not send a Purchase Order form. The Sales Order can also be displayed in the Daily Business Manager detail (see Exercise 2A-9).

> When a sales quote is converted into a sales order, the information on the **sales quote** is automatically entered into the **sales order** window. Likewise, sales order information is entered into the **sales invoice** window upon conversion.

When the goods/services are delivered, the sales order is converted into a **sales invoice**. At this time, an accounting entry is made and the sales transaction is posted to the corresponding ledger accounts and customer subledgers. (See side note box.)

Sales Quote ⟶ **Sales Order** ⟶ **Sales Invoice**

In the Sales Journal, the following options are available for **Payment Method**:

Option	*Payment Method*	*Linked with Account*
Pay Later	on credit	Accounts Receivable
Cash	when paid in cash	Bank account
Cheque	when paid by cheque	Bank account
Pre-Authorized (PAD)	when paid by **Pre-A**uthorized **D**ebit (PAD)	Bank Debit Card account
Bank Debit Cd	when paid by ATM (debit card)	Bank Debit Card account
Visa Credit	when paid by credit card	Bank Credit Card account

When you record entries in the Sales Journals, you enter only one part of the entry. The program knows you are in the RECEIVABLES module and will debit or credit the appropriate account (Receivable or other account shown above) and appropriate taxes, as required.

For example: If you had recorded a credit sale (invoice #239) transaction for a $70.00 Laptop Back Pak to J. Tang, the entry in the General Journal (double entry) would have looked similar to the following.

Account	Debits	Credits	Comment
1200 Accounts Receivable	70.00	–	
4100 Sales	–	70.00	

Source: Invoice 239   Date: Feb 29, 2016
Comment: Sale of Laptop Back Pak to J. Tang

To properly enter this type of transaction in the RECEIVABLES module, you need to enter the Item Number and Quantity. The Base Price (**credit** amount), Price, Amount, and Accounts. In this example: 4100 Sales account, will be filled in automatically.

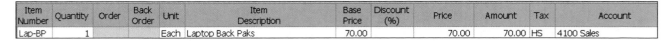

Item Number	Quantity	Order	Back Order	Unit	Item Description	Base Price	Discount (%)	Price	Amount	Tax	Account
Lap-BP	1			Each	Laptop Back Paks	70.00		70.00	70.00	HS	4100 Sales

In the RECEIVABLES module, Sage 50 Accounting will automatically debit the 1200 Accounts Receivable Account. *Note*: You cannot enter a credit sale transaction in the General Journal (or any transaction affecting 1200 Accounts Receivable (control account)), once you have activated (added customer history) and are using the RECEIVABLES module.

Exercise 2A-5—Deleting Columns (Customizing) and Resizing the Sales Journal

---

1 ➤ Right click on the **Sales Invoice** icon. Notice the selections. Select **Create Invoice**. The Sales Invoice Journal will appear.

Study the basic format of the Sales Journal - Sales Invoice as shown next.

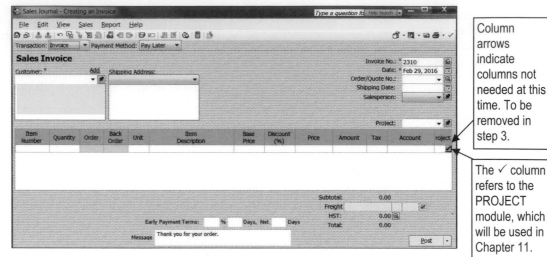

Fig. 2A-6: Sample Sales Invoice window.

Customizing the Sales Journal Window

WWW The **Item Number** column is used when the company records quotes, orders, sales or purchases of merchandise using the **perpetual** inventory system. The other system, periodic inventory, is discussed in Appendix 2015 F, P*eriodic Inventory Entries* in your course materials at www.nelson.com/student. Sage 50 Accounting requires detailed records of goods (merchandise) being sold or purchased and will use the **Item Number** column with the Perpetual Inventory system.

You need to customize the Sales Journal window to include only columns for information you will enter in the Sales Journal.

Exercise 2A-5 will show you how to hide the **PROJECTS** columns (see arrows in Fig. 2A-6) to customize the Sales Journal window for Santos Luggage. You may use the same procedure to hide any other column that you do not wish to appear on your sales journal. For example, a **service** company would not use **Ship Date**, **Order**, **Back Order**, and **Unit**. A service company would hide these columns to streamline invoices.

Follow the steps below to hide the **PROJECTS** columns.

2 ➤ Click the **Customize Journal** icon 🔲 and the Customize Journals window will appear; click on **Columns**. Form settings styles will be shown after step 8.

Show form settings for:

| Professional Style |
| Retail Style |
| **Standard Style** |

For Standard Style, do not show these columns

☐ Item Number   ☐ Unit   ☐ Description
☐ Quantity Shipped   ☐ Quantity on Order   ☐ Quantity on Back Order
☐ Base Price   ☐ Disc. %   ☐ Price
☐ Tax Code   ☐ Account   ☐ Projects

You can change the width and order of columns in the transaction window. Click and drag the column headings or border lines with your mouse.

The above settings are for display only.
If you would like to change the printed invoice form, click Form Options.

[Form Options...]

In the Perpetual Inventory System, leave the Item Number box blank. In the Periodic Inventory System the box would be checked.

> **(i)** Notice that the **Projects** column no longer displays on the customized window.

3 ➤ You will not need the Projects field. Click the **Projects** box and a ✓ will appear. (See side note box.)

4 ➤ On the left side of the window, click on the ⊞ at **Sales Orders**, then **Columns**. (The author has completed step 3 for you, as well as, for the Retail and Professional styles.) You could also, in the left pane, select **Quotes**, then click **Columns**. Note that there is no Projects box under Sales Quotes.

5 ➤ Click **OK** when you are finished. The column area will now display similar to the following: (See step 7 to change the column widths.)

Item Number	Quantity	Order	Back Order	Unit	Item Description	Base Price	Discount (%)	Price	Amount	Tax	Account

Fig. 2A-7a: Customized Sales Journal window (before sizing).

6 ➤ In order to show more information in the Description and Acct fields, type the information as shown in Fig. 2A-7b. Place your mouse over a column heading dividing line between 2 columns (e.g., Description), then use the windows ⊞ icon to drag the column left or right to resize the columns to the approximate size as shown. This information will be deleted in step 8, but the column widths will remain the same size.

Item Number	Quantity	Order	Back Order	Unit	Item Description	Base Price	Discount (%)	Price	Amount	Tax	Account
Suit w/w R				Each	Suitcase w/w Regular	56.00		56.00		HS	4200 Sales- Returns & Allowance:

Fig. 2A-7b: Customized Sales Journal window (after sizing).

7 ➤ When you have the columns to this approximate size, click the ↶ (undo icon) and you will see the following.

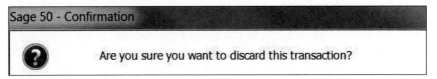

Sage 50 - Confirmation

(?)   Are you sure you want to discard this transaction?

8 ➤ Select **Yes** to return to a blank invoice. The column sizes remain as you have set them up.

Sales Invoice Styles

1 ➤ From the menu bar, click **View, Invoice Style** and you will see that there are 3 invoice template styles available.

The headings that will appear on a Standard Invoice window are:

Item Number	Quantity	Order	Back Order	Unit	Item Description	Base Price	Discount (%)	Price	Amount	Tax	Account

2 ➤ Click on **Retail**. You will see that the Order and Back Order columns are not displayed.

Quantity	Unit	Item Description	Base Price	Discount (%)	Price	Amount	Tax	Account

The **Retail** template could be used in a business that does not use Sales Quotes or Orders.

3 ➤ Click on **View, Invoice Style**, and click on **Professional**. You will see that the Order and Back Order columns from the Standard template and Item, Quantity, Unit, Base Price, Disc % and Price columns are not displayed from the Retail template.

Item Description	Amount	Tax	Account

The **Professional** template could be used in a business that sells services (Accounting, real estate, legal, etc.), and does not sell and list items or units.

In this text we will use the **Standard** style, and have modified the columns to not display Project Allocation.

4 ➤ Click on **View, Invoice Style** and click on **Standard**.

5 ➤ **Exit** to the Home window.

Entering Transactions in the RECEIVABLES Module

A common question asked is, "When should transactions be entered?" The answer depends on the volume of transactions. Smaller volumes (10 to 20 transactions a week) may be entered weekly, anything more than 10 a day should probably be done on a daily basis.

Another factor is the type of transaction. In general, you would like your accounting records to be up to date, especially when it concerns customers; therefore, sales quotes, orders, invoices, and adjustments (including sales returns and discounts) must be entered with the date the transaction (entry) took place, to record cash discounts and full payment dates properly. The sales receipt dates may not be correct for cheques received, e.g., date stamp of receipt or deposit date on the cheque is not the same as the date on the cheque. If the invoice date is not recorded properly, the aging of invoices will not be accurate.

Recording a Sales Quote

One thing to remember about a Sales Quote is that a sales transaction has not taken place; therefore, a quote does not affect the company accounts. The quote is a record of an inquiry—with no commitment on the part of the customer to buy.

When a company sells items to a business that will resell the items to others, the buying company pays the HST on these goods.

Exercise 2A-6—Recording a Sales Quote

---

1 ➤ Change the Session date to **Mar 01, 2016**.

There are 4 different ways to create a Quote. The same choices apply to Sales Orders, Sales Invoices, or Receipts.

a) Right click on the Sales Quote icon, select Create Quote.

b) At the Sales Quote icon, click the ⏷, notice the 3 choices, select Create Quote.

c) Click the Sales Quote icon to go directly to the Sales Quote window.

d) At the Sales Invoice icon, click the ⏷, notice the 3 choices, select Create Invoice, at Transaction click the ⏷, select Quote.

This text will use method c) to Create Sales Quotes, Sales Orders, and Sales Invoices.

2 ➤ Click the **Sales Quotes** icon. The Sales Quote Journal will appear.

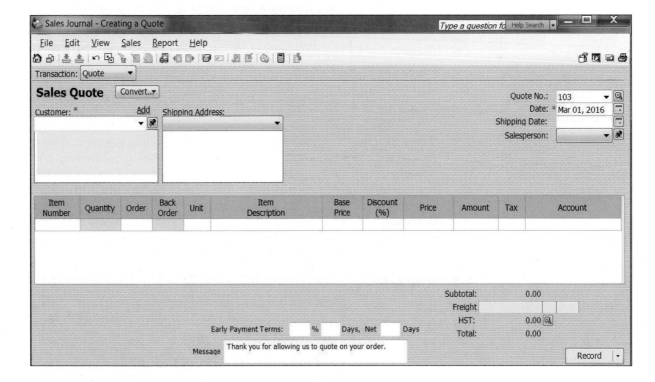

Study this transaction:

> **Mar 01, 2016** Luggage 4U has requested a quote for the following items that are to be picked up by their van on March 3. Their purchasing manager was very specific that the goods must be received by March 3 or the order will not be accepted. Their delivery van driver will pick up the quote before 2:30 p.m. today. Your manager has asked you to complete the Sales Quote, as the items requested are in stock and have been put aside for this customer: Total Quote $1,525.50.
>
> 5 Laptop Back Paks at $70.00 each
> 8 Suitcase w/w (with wheels) Large at $62.00 each
> 9 Suitcase w/w Regular in red colour at $56.00 each
>
> **Add HST at 13% on all items. Terms are 2/10, net 30.**

To record the quote, complete the following steps:

Note: The Red * on screen refers to required information in the window.

ℹ

You can also press the first letter of the company name. Sage 50 Accounting will display the customer list with the names beginning with this letter.

If you select <One-time customer> while you are creating a sales quote or sales order, the window will change to a Sales Invoice.

You would click the red stick pin 📌 to enter sales information for the same customer on the next invoice. You do not have to choose the customer again until you need to enter information for a new customer.

---

3 ➤ Customer Click the ▼ arrow to display the list of customers to choose from. Notice that the customers are displayed in alphabetical order and require no customer numbers. You may have to move ▲ or ▼ to see more customers. (Also see side note box.) Click to select **Luggage 4U**.

The address details for Luggage 4U are automatically shown in the Customer and Shipping Address fields. You will be shown how to record this information in Exercise 2A-23.

4 ➤ Press the [Tab] key once to move to the red stick pin (see side note box), and [Tab] again to move to the **Shipping Address** field. When you choose a customer in step 3, the Shipping Address field changes to:

| <Mailing Address> | ▼ |

If you click the ▼ the field can be changed to Ship-to Address. The shipping address could be inserted here if the goods are being ordered by a Head Office and the goods are to be shipped to one of the stores. This feature will be demonstrated in Exercise 2A-23. Leave the choice as **Mailing Address**.

5 ➤ Shipping Address Pressing the [Tab] key moves the cursor to each line of the address. If there were no changes in this field you could use the mouse to click the next field, **Quote No**.

6 ➤ Quote No. The number **103** is displayed, which is the number of the next quote in Santos Luggage company's records. [Tab] once to move to the Select Order or Quote button 🔍. (This will be explained in Exercise 2A-8.) You will learn how to insert the automatic numbering in Chapter 4. [Tab] again to move to the **Date** field.

7 ➤ **Date**
This is the date the quote is given to the customer. The date should be **Mar 01, 2016.** This date is important because quotes, with sale items, may expire within a set number of days from the quote date. [Tab] [Tab] to move to the **Shipping Date** field.

8 ➤ **Shipping Date**
This is the date agreed upon that the goods will be shipped to the customer. Use the calendar icon and change the date to **Mar 03, 2016**. [Tab] [Tab] to move to the **Salesperson** field.

9 ➤ **Salesperson**

WWW
You will not use this field in these exercises. See Appendix 2015 N, *Adding a Salesperson's Name to an Invoice* in your course materials at www.nelson.com/student, for information on the steps you would need to complete to have this field available. Not all companies would make use of this field. [Tab] [Tab] to move to the **Item Number** field.

10 ➤ **Item Number**
Double-click or press [Enter] to display the Inventory/Service items listing. You will be able to see the quantity of items available for sale. Select **Laptop Back Paks**, code **Lap-BP**. You move to the Order field.

Quantity
This column will be used when goods are shipped to the customer.

11 ➤ **Order**
Type **5**, [Tab].

Back Order
The Back Order column is skipped on a Sales Quote or a Sales Order. It is used when a sales invoice is being produced and some of the goods ordered by the customer (part of the order) are not available. The goods will be shipped when stock arrives.

12 ➤ **Unit**
Each is displayed. [Tab].

13 ➤ **Description**
Laptop Back Paks is displayed. [Tab].

14 ➤ **Base Price**
This field represents the price before any sale discounts are given to a customer. [Tab] to accept **70.00**.

15 ➤ **Discount %**
This field would be a sale discount percentage and does NOT represent a discount for paying an invoice within the discount terms. This field will be explained in Exercise 2B-34. [Tab].

16 ➤ **Price**
[Tab] to accept price of 70.00.

17 ➤ **Amount**
This field represents the calculated amount from fields **Order** times **Price**. [Tab] to accept 350.00.

18 ➤ **Tax**
The HS tax code is displayed (see side note box). Press [Enter]. A list of Tax Codes and information is displayed (see below).

> **Select Tax Code**
>
> Select Tax Code:
>
> - No Tax
> HS - HST at 13% added to invoice
> HI - HST at 8% added to invoice

ℹ️ **HST** refers to the **Harmonized Goods and Services Tax** applied by the federal government to goods and services sold.

HST rate of 13% is used in this text and reflected in the solutions. This rate, however, may have changed since the publication date. When on the job, be sure to use the appropriate HST rates.

For additional information on HST, GST, and PST, refer to Appendix 1, *Taxes (HST, GST, and PST)*.

The codes **HS** and **HI** are created by the company and may be different for each company. A company may make up any two-letter combination and wording for a tax code.

The Harmonized Sales Tax (abbreviated HST) is being charged based on percentages available at time of preparation of this textbook.

No tax	This includes items that are HST-exempt (no HST charged), HST Non- Taxable (no HST charged) and HST taxable (HST with a rate of 0%).
HS	Price of goods **plus** HST. The HST is not included in the selling price and must be added to the selling price of the items; e.g., Selling price of $200.00 plus 13% HST of the price ($26.00). Taxes total $26.00.
HI	This code applies on a sale where HST at a reduced rate of 8% is charged. (An example of this is when you buy or sell insurance. HST at 8% Sales Tax is charged.) The HI code will be used in Chapter 3B.

19 ➤   Select **HS**. This means the selling price does not include HST.

20 ➤ Account   Account 4100 Sales is displayed. Each item of inventory has a default Sales account. You may want to use a different account than the one displayed (e.g., for Sales Returns). Press [Enter]. The G/L chart of accounts should be displayed. You may have to scroll using [▼] or [▲] to see more accounts. Sage 50 Accounting is looking for an account to credit. Select account **4100 Sales** by double-clicking on it. You can also type **4** and the selection window changes to accounts beginning with 4. If needed, you could then type **1** and the account window would change to accounts beginning with 41. [Tab].

21 ➤   Enter the next two items on the quote. The tax code and the sales account will be the same for all items (w/w means *with wheels*).

     8   **Suitcase w/w Large at $62.00 each**
     9   **Suitcase w/w Regular at $56.00 each 'Add wording' in red colour**

Note the **Description** field when you add the wording **in red colour**. Sage 50 Accounting will word wrap the required information to the next line(s) if the information does not fit on one line. You can use the [✛] icon and drag left or right to resize the column as required. (See side note box.)

> By moving the [✛] to the right, you can expand the column if you want the column wider. Do not change the column width for this exercise.

22 ➤   Remove the words: **in red colour**.

Message box. This field displays a variety of messages you want customers to see on quotes, orders, and invoices. Note the default for quotes. You will be shown how to enter other default comments in Chapter 4.

The **Early Payment Terms** box should display **2.00%, 10 days, Net 30 days**, the terms previously agreed upon with the customer. If the terms are different from the default, click the appropriate box, and change as required. *Note*: This field will be referred to as "Terms" in subsequent locations in the text.

       Freight   Santos Luggage does not charge for delivery; therefore, this field is not used.

23 ➤ Shipped by   On the icon bar, click [✉] the **Track Shipments** icon.

24 ➤	**Shipper**	Click the ▾ arrow to display a list of shippers. Select **Your Vehicle** (the customer's vehicle).
	Tracking Number	This will be blank because there is no need to track the shipment, since it is being picked up by the customer's vehicle. The software can track shipments; however, this text does not provide an exercise for tracking shipments on the Internet. Click **OK**.
		You will notice that the Shipping information does not display in the window. It prints on the printed Quote.

When you have completed entering the above information, the window display should look as follows:

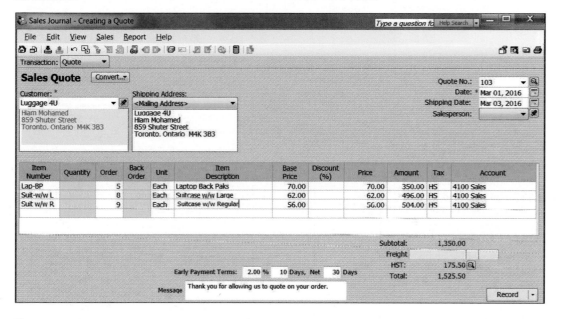

If your business uses pre-printed forms bearing the company name and/or logo and other relevant information, you would click the 🖨 from the Quote window. The information being printed on the Pre-printed form will look similar to Fig. 2A-8.   *Note*: You do not need to print the quote.

25 ➤ To display the Quote using the Custom Sage 50 Accounting Form document, click on 🔲 **Print Preview**. You may see the following error message.

> **Sage 50**
>
> ⚠ To use Print Preview, you must select a Sage 50 Form. To do this, click the Reports _Forms button on the toolbar. Then, on the page for the form you want to preview, select Custom Forms and change the Form Type to Sage 50 Form.

The settings for the Sage 50 Accounting Custom Forms have not been selected.

26 ➤ Click **OK**, click 🗄 (4th icon from right side)

> Change the default printer settings for your reports (Ctrl+Shift+F) .

27 ➤ Change from Pre-printed to **Custom Forms** 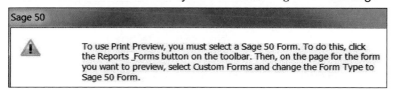 . At Description field, click the ▾ and select **Sales Quote with discount**. Repeat in the email form Description, to **Sales Quote with discount**. Click **OK**.

28 ➤ Click **OK**, click on Print Preview . The Quote information ◆ Sage 50 Forms Designer is
      similar to Fig. 2A-8. You may have to scroll down to see the information at the
      bottom.

29 ➤ Click **X** to exit the Quote and return to the Quote window.

Do not record; continue with Exercise 2A-7.

Santos Luggage-PI-2A, Student's name   **QUOTE**
635 Semple Avenue
Toronto, Ontario M9L 1V5

                                                Quote No.:   103
                                                Date: Mar 01, 2016
                                                Page: 1
                                                Ship Date: Mar 03, 2016

Sold To: **Ship To:**

    Luggage 4U   Luggage 4U
    Hiam Mohamed   Hiam Mohamed
    859 Shuter Street   859 Shuter Street
    Toronto, Ontario M4K 3B3   Toronto, Ontario M4K 3B3

Business No.:   V8956325

Item No.	Quantity	Unit	Description	Tax	Unit Price	Amount
Lap-BP	5	Each	Laptop Back Paks	HS	70.00	350.00
Suit w/w R	9	Each	Suitcase w/w Regular	HS	56.00	504.00
Suit-w/w L	8	Each	Suitcase w/w Large	HS	62.00	496.00
			Subtotal:			1,350.00
			HS - HST at 13% added to invoice			
			HST			175.50

Santos Luggage-PI-2A, Student's name HST: #V8956325

Shipped by Your Vehicle		
Terms: 2%/10, Net 30. Due Mar 31, 2016.		
Comments Thank you for allowing us to quote on your order.	**Total Amount**	1,525.50
Sold By:		

*Fig. 2A-8: Sales Quote information viewed/printed using a Sage 50 form.
(See side note box.)*

Pre-printed forms will
normally have the
company name and
address printed on the
form. The information
shown in Fig. 2A-8
indicates the company
name printed by Sage
50 Accounting. If you
are required to print the
forms in the
lab/classroom, the
name printed by Sage
50 Accounting will
allow you to identify
your printouts in class.

Edit Notes...
**To Cut, Copy, and
Paste**:
Select (highlight) the text
with the left mouse
button. Choose **Edit**
from the top menu of the
window and then select
either **Cut** (to remove) or
Copy. The text is
temporarily copied to the
Windows clipboard, and
can be retrieved using
the Paste feature.
Reposition the cursor,
click **Edit**, then **Paste** to
place the text at the new
cursor location.

Revising the Sales Quote Form

You can use Windows features such as Cut (selects text inside one column at a time),
Copy, and Paste from the Edit menu of the Sales Journal window (see side note box).
You can cut, copy, and paste text from one Sage 50 Accounting window to another, or
from a Sage 50 Accounting window to another program (e.g., word processing). It will
save time in typing information.

Using the Edit menu, you can Insert or Remove a line in the Sales Quote, Sales Order, or
Sales Invoice.

In the following exercise you will use the Insert and Remove feature for the information in
a row within a Quote.

Exercise 2A-7—Revising the Sales Quote Form

The manager has asked you to move the Regular suitcase to the middle line of the invoice before you record the quote.

1 ➤ Click on **Suit-w/w L** in the Item Number column, then click **Edit, Insert Line**.

A blank line appears as the second line of the invoice. The new line can be entered at the top, or between any items on the invoice. If you are not replacing any item, you could enter the item(s) you want as the second sales item.

2 ➤ In the Item Number column, select item code **Suit-w/w R**. Type **9**, Tab .

3 ➤ In the Item Number column, select item code **Suite-w/w R** at the bottom. Click **Edit**, **Remove Line** to remove the bottom sales item. You could press the *Delete* key to remove the sales information from each of the columns for the Regular suitcase. (See side note box.)

The Quote information area should now resemble Fig. 2A-9.

Item Number	Quantity	Order	Back Order	Unit	Item Description	Base Price	Discount (%)	Amount	Tax	Account
Lap-BP		5		Each	Laptop Back Paks	70.00		350.00	HS	4100 Sales
Suit w/w R		9		Each	Suitcase w/w- Regular	56.00		504.00	HS	4100 Sales
Suit-w/w L		0		Each	Suitcase w/w Large	62.00		496.00	HS	4100 Sales

Fig. 2A-9: Revised Quote information area.

4 ➤ Make corrections to any fields, if necessary.

5 ➤ To display the Sales Journal entry created by this quote, click **Report**, then **Display Sales Journal Entry**. The window should display:

Sales Journal Entry Mar 01, 2016

Account Number	Account Description	Debits	Credits

There is no data to report.

See the Mini-guide at the end of Chapter 2B, after Challenge Exercises. This form will help you identify when entries are recorded in the RECEIVABLES module and which journal they are recorded in. You can find the document at Appendix 2015 V1, *Perpetual Mini-Guide Receivables—Payables* in your course materials at www.nelson.com/student.

6 ➤ **Exit** from the Sales Journal Entry window.

7 ➤ At the Record button click ▾, you will see the following:

Record ▾
✓ Record
Print & Record

. You are able to Record or Print and Record the Purchase Order. To save paper, select and click **Record**.

You will see the see the same Print & Record buttons at: Sales Orders and Purchase Orders. You will see a similar window to Print & Post at Sales Invoices.

More Edit Notes...

To Move a Whole Column to a New Position:
Click and hold down the left mouse button positioned on a column heading. Drag the column to a new position, then release the mouse button.

Restoring the Original Column Width and Positions:
There is no Sage 50 Accounting window feature to restore a window back after a column is changed. The View menu, Restore feature will return the window to the original default column size.

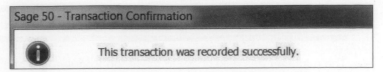

Notice that the confirmation window says Transaction was recorded successfully, but it does not indicate a Journal entry #.

There is no entry made in the company records, because a sale has not taken place. At this point, the customer has requested a formal price quote and will decide whether to buy the goods at the quoted price. Santos Luggage must now wait for the customer to make a decision.

8 ➤   Click **OK** and **Exit** from the Sales Journal-Quote window to the Home window.

Converting a Sales Quote into a Sales Order

> If you are processing multiple sales orders, the order number now increments by 1 automatically to save you time and keep track of your work.

When you record a Sales Quote, it is recorded in the Sales Quote database and it will remain there until it is converted into a Sales Order or Sales Invoice, or it is deleted. When converting a Sales Quote into a Sales Order, the details are automatically forwarded to the Sales Order, but may be revised.

Remember that a **Sales Order** does NOT affect the company books because no goods were shipped. The order, when recorded, goes to a Sales Order listing. (See side note box.)

Exercise 2A-8—Converting a Sales Quote into a Sales Order

The Purchasing Manager of Luggage 4U confirmed, by fax, to your Sales Manager the approval of Quote #103. To change the sales quote into a sales order, complete the following steps:

Sales Orders ▼

> The sales quote is recorded in the Sales Quote database of the program and cannot be printed as a report. You will be able to see a list of Quotes as shown in Exercise 2A-8. The Sales Quote does NOT get posted to the General Ledger.

1 ➤   Advance the Session date to **Mar 02, 2016**.

2 ➤   At **Sales Orders**, click the ▼ to display the 3 choices. Click the **Create Order** item, or click the **Sales Order** icon. The Sales Journal—Creating an Order will appear.

3 ➤   **Order No.**   Click the **Order No. finder** 🔲 icon.

(See side note box.)

You could also open Sales Quote 103 and click the ▼ [Convert...▼] to convert the Sales Quote to a Sales Order.

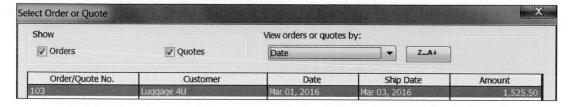

This window will display details about previously recorded customer quotes and orders for all customers. Quote **103** is the only outstanding quote at this time.

4 ➤ **View orders or quotes by:** Click the ⬇ and you will see the different columns the report can be sorted by. Note that the report can also be sorted in ascending or descending order.

5 ➤ Click **Select** or **double-click 103** to accept the Quote.

The Sales Journal—Creating an Order window fills with the details from the Sales Quote.

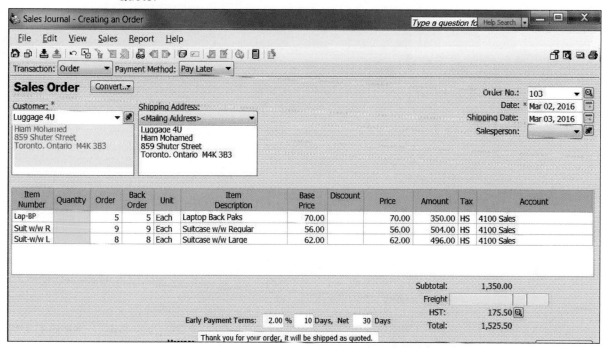

Fig. 2A-10: Sales Order window—filled in.

Back Order The Back Order column shows **5**, **9** and **8** respectively, the quantity ordered. This means that 5, 9 and 8 of the specified items are back ordered (not yet shipped since this is only a Sales Order form). The goods are due to be shipped to the customer on March 3, 2016. Do NOT change values in this column. Sage 50 Accounting will keep track of the amounts.

All other details of the order are the same as entered in the quote. At this point, the quote could be revised. For example, the buyer might decide to increase or decrease the quantity. The price could also be changed if the final selling price was lower. Remember that a quote is a commitment by the seller to provide a product or service at the agreed-upon price for the period of the quote (usually shown in **Ship Date**). If there is a price hike after the sales quote is issued and before the Ship Date, the buyer is protected from price increases. However, a price lower than the price quoted is to the advantage of the buyer, so it can be changed without consulting the buyer. For now, do not change any fields.

6 ➤ To display the Sales Journal entry created by this Sales Order, click **Report**, **Display Sales Journal Entry**. The window should display:

Sales Journal Entry Mar 02, 2016			
Account Number	Account Description	Debits	Credits

There is no data to report.

Similar to the Sales Journal Entry window for the sales quote, an entry to the company books has not been created, because a sale has not yet taken place.

> ℹ️ To correct a Sales Order, refer to Chapter 13, Exercise 13-3.

7 ➤ **Exit** from this window by clicking the ☒ button.

8 ➤ Make corrections to the sales order, if necessary. (See side note box.)

9 ➤ Click the [Record ▾] button. This records the sales order in the Pending Sales Order listing and does NOT post to the General ledger. Do not print the order.

Study the message that appears when you click the Record button:

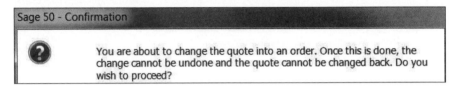

Sage 50 - Confirmation

❓ You are about to change the quote into an order. Once this is done, the change cannot be undone and the quote cannot be changed back. Do you wish to proceed?

10 ➤ Click **Yes** to proceed. The Confirmation window says the Transaction was recorded successfully, but it does not indicate a Journal Entry #, as a sale has not taken place. Click **OK**.

11 ➤ **Exit** from the Sales Order window.

Daily Business Manager

The Daily Business Manager (DBM) ⊞ DBM is located on the **icon tool bar**. The Daily Business Manager is a business tool that can be displayed when you start Sage 50 Accounting (the default setting), and/or when you advance the session date, or when you need to display the window. This window is very helpful for managing customer receivables in a business setting. You will see that outstanding Sales Orders are displayed in this window.

Exercise 2A-9—Using the Daily Business Manager (DBM)

1 ➤ Change the Session date to **Mar 03, 2016**.

2 ➤ Click ⊞ DBM the **Daily Business Manager** icon and the DBM will appear as shown next.

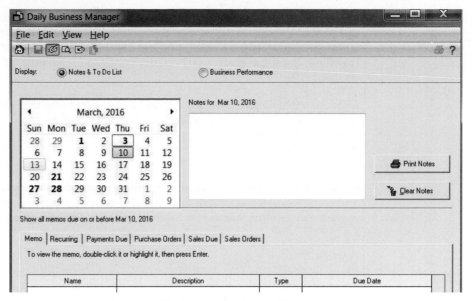

Fig. 2A-11: Daily Business Manager window.

The lower window will list reminders about tasks you need to do, for the next 7 days, relating to the various tabs shown (Memo, Recurring, Payments Due, etc.).

The **Reminder** date Mar 10, 2016 for all tabs is calculated from the **Session** date, Mar 03, 2016. *Note:* Sales Quotes will not display.

3 ➤ Click each of the tabs in the lower half of the window.

Memo	Lists general information that has been placed in the customer file. This will be explained later in this chapter.
Recurring	Lists all recurring entries that are due within the next 7 days. Santos Luggage has not used recurring entries.
Payments Due	Shows all invoices that must be paid on or before Mar 10, 2016. This would include invoices for which discounts are available, if paid within the terms agreed upon (e.g., 2/10, net 30) when purchased. There are no items listed: Santos Luggage does not use the PAYABLES module.
Purchase Orders	Shows all purchase orders that are due to be shipped to your company on or before Mar 10, 2016. Santos Luggage does not use the PAYABLES module.
Sales Due	This tab lists overdue sales invoices and sales invoices that are due to be paid within the next 7 days.
	If you double-click on an invoice, you will be taken to the Receipts Journal. Exit from the Receipts Journal window to discard the receipt. (See side note box.)
Sales Orders	The display shows the Outstanding Order #103 for Luggage 4U. If you double-click any column, you will be taken to a filled-in Sales Invoice. It is assumed that you want to record a sale. Exit from the Sales Invoice window to discard the invoice.

> ℹ️ Sandler Travel Stores' invoice was due to be paid on Feb 25, 2016 and is now 7 days overdue. Someone from your company will have to contact this customer to follow up about the outstanding invoice.

By studying the information in the various tabs, you may find items that need to be followed up.

You can also use the Daily Business Manager to manage your daily tasks. The window to the right of the calendar will display messages that can be used to remind you to call customers, back up data files, prepare special reports for management, and more. However, those messages will not appear automatically. You will need to make notes for yourself.

Exercises 2A-10 and 2A-11 illustrate how you can use the Daily Business Manager to view outstanding invoices, orders, and memo notes to assist employees, and provide graphical analysis for management.

To use the **Notes** feature, follow the steps in the next exercise.

Exercise 2A-10—Using the Notes Feature of the DBM

1 ➤ In the calendar on the left side of your screen, click **8** (Mar 08, 2016).

2 ➤ Click in the **Notes for Mar 08, 2016** box near the top. Type **Prepare draft newspaper advertisement for local paper**.

3 ➤ In the calendar on the left, click **March 10**. Type **Finalize newspaper advertisement for local paper**.

4 ➤ Click **March 8**. The previous message you typed is displayed.

Exercise 2A-11—Using the Business Performance Feature of the DBM

1 ➤ **Display**   Click the 🔘 **Business Performance** button.

There are three Business Performance Measurements (ratios) shown in the top portion. A graphical representation of the measurements is shown in the lower portion. There are no entries made to this point; therefore, the graphs are a straight line.

2 ➤ Click the **Daily Business Manager Options** 🔍 icon. The **Business Performance** tab should be selected.

3 ➤ Management may like to see different measurements graphically. To set up a new measurement from the left window, click **Sales (Past 7 Days)**, click **Select >**, then **OK**. It is now moved to the right side pane. In Exercise 2B-28, you will return to this Business Performance window to see the graphical display.

4 ➤ To exit, click **X** to return to the Home window.

Exercise 2A-12—Displaying the DBM

1 ➤ In the menu bar, click **Setup, User preferences, View** in the left-side pane, and at Daily Business Manager, click **At Start Up**, to display the ✓. Notice the other choice is after Changing the Session Date, which would be appropriate in a business setting. Click **OK**. The module is displayed the next time you start up (open) the company file.

From this point on, it is assumed that the DBM will **not** display each time you open the company. See Exercise 2A-13. Your faculty member may ask you to display the DBM each time you open the file.

Exercise 2A-13—Hiding the DBM

As noted in this Exercise, we do not want the DBM to appear each time we open the company file.

1 ➤ From the Home window, click **Setup**, **User Preferences**, **View**, at Daily Business Manager, click **At Start Up** to remove the ✓. Click **OK**. The DBM will be hidden next time you open the file.

Viewing the Pending Sales Orders Report

This report can also be viewed in **Summary** style, which does not list the description and Item code. The item column in the Detail report may have to be expanded to display more information. The report may print on two pages.

You need to view and/or print the Pending Sales Orders Report regularly to make sure that no sales order is missed.

Exercise 2A-14—Viewing the Pending Sales Orders Report

---

1 ➤ From the **Home** window, click **Report Centre**, the left pane should be **Receivables,** click **Pending Sales Orders Detail by Customer**, click the blue **Modify this report**. Change the **Date** to **Mar 10, 2016, OK**. This report will assist management in displaying all outstanding (pending) sales orders due within 1 week from the current Mar 03, 2016 session date. (See side note box.)

Orders with shipping dates due later than the date specified (Mar 10, 2016) will not display.

Pending Sales Orders Detail by Customer As at Mar 10, 2016

Sales Order Number	Sales Order Date	Ship Date	Amount Original O...	Item	Description	Unit	Back Orde...
Luggage 4U							
103	Mar 02, 2016	Mar 03, 2016	1,525.50				
				Lap-BP	Laptop Back Paks	Each	5.00
				Suit w/...	Suitcase w/w Regular	Each	9.00
				Suit-w/...	Suitcase w/w Large	Each	8.00
			1,525.50				
			1,525.50				

2 ➤ **Exit** to the Home window.

IMPORTANT: BACK UP your data after every work session and update your logbook.

Producing a Sales Invoice from a Sales Order

It is common practice to print multi-copy sales invoices and/or sales orders for distribution to the customer and various departments in the company as illustrated in Fig. 2A-12.

Santos Luggage
635 Semple Avenue
Toronto, Ontario M9L 1V5
Phone: (416)698-3333 ✦ Fax (416)698-3345

INVOICE
Invoice No. : 2310
Date: Mar 01, 2016
Ship Date: Mar 03, 2016
Page: 1
Re: Order No. 103

SOLD TO
Luggage 4U
Hiam Mohamed
859 Shuter Street
Toronto, Ontario M4K 3B3

Business No.: V8956325

SHIP TO
Luggage 4U
Hiam Mohamed
859 Shuter Street
Toronto, Ontario M4K 3B3

ITEM	SHIP	ORDER	B/O	UNIT	DESCRIPTION	TAX	PRICE	AMOUNT
Lap-BP	5	5			Laptop Back Paks	HS	70.00	$ 350.00
Suit w/w R	9	9			Suitcase w/w Regular	HS	56.00	504.00
Suit-w/w L	8	8			Suitcase w/w Large	HS	62.00	496.00
					Subtotal			1,350.00
					HS- HST at 13% added to invoice			
					HST			175.50
					Terms: 2%/10, Net 30.			

Shipped by Your Vehicle.
    Thank you for your order

TOTAL $ 1,525.50

| Copy 1 Customer |
| Copy 2 Accounting |
| Copy 3 Sales |
| Copy 4 Packing Slip |

Fig. 2A-12: Sales Invoice Form and Distribution Schedule.

Exercise 2A-15—Converting a Sales Order to a Sales Invoice

All goods ordered by Luggage 4U on Sales Order #103 are ready to be shipped. To record the sale, complete the following steps:

1 ➤ Right click the **Sales Invoices** icon, click **Create Invoice**. The Sales Journal-Creating an Invoice window appears.

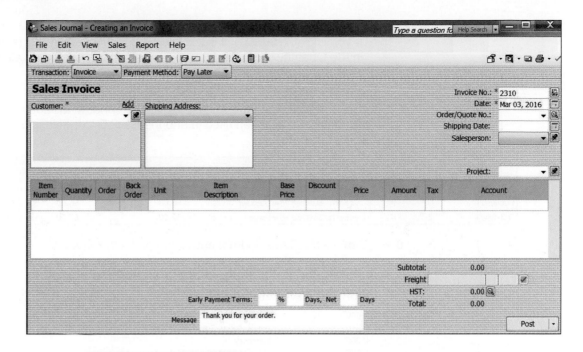

Note: The [Project: ▼] *field will be used in Chapter 11.*

> **Transaction**: Do NOT change the default from Invoice.

2 ➤ Order/Quote No. Click the **Finder** 🔍 icon.

As in Exercise 2A-8, this window will display details about previously recorded customer quotes and orders for all customers. Order 103 is the only outstanding order. Note: you may need to click the [☐ Orders] field to see the Sales Order.

3 ➤ Click **Select** or double-click to accept Order #103. The Sales Invoice window fills with the details from Sales Order #103 recorded previously.

4 ➤ Payment Method Click the ▼ arrow and 6 choices appear:

- *Pay Later* for a sale on credit.
- *Cash* used when cash is received as payment.
- *Cheque* used when a cheque is received as payment.
- *Pre-Authorized* used when a client signs an agreement to authorize an **Debit** **(PAD)** automatic transfer of funds to a business.
- *Bank Debit Cd* used if a Bank Debit card is received as payment.
- *Visa Credit* used if the Visa Credit Card is used as payment. This is the credit card that Santos Luggage accepts.

Because it is on account (on credit), select **Pay Later**, [Tab].

The full order is ready to ship. You can complete the invoice in one of two ways:

a. If you clicked in the **Quantity** column you would enter the quantity of each item shipped, [Tab] and continue entering the quantity shipped. Note that the Back Order column changes to blank because there are no goods back ordered.

Note: At this time, before shipping, the Quantity column for quantity of goods to be sold (shipped) can be increased or decreased.

b.   If you click the ⬜ (Fill Backordered quantities) icon, Sage 50 Accounting will fill in the Quantity columns for you. This would be used when all the items ordered are filled and there are no back orders.

5 ➤   Click the ⬜ icon and the middle portion window will change to the following. The quantity field has been filled in and the Back Order field is blank, as the goods are being shipped.

Item Number	Quantity	Order	Back Order	Unit	Item Description	Base Price	Discount (%)	Price	Amount	Tax	Account
Lap-BP	5	5		Each	Laptop Back Paks	70.00		70.00	350.00	HS	4100 Sales
Suit w/w R	9	9		Each	Suitcase w/w- Regular	56.00		56.00	504.00	HS	4100 Sales
Suit-w/w L	8	8		Each	Suitcase w/w Large	62.00		62.00	496.00	HS	4100 Sales

6 ➤   Display the Sales Journal entry created by this invoice.

Sales Journal Entry Mar 03, 2016 (J1)

Account Number	Account Description	Debits	Credits
1200	Accounts Receivable	1,525.50	-
5010	Cost of Goods Sold	675.00	-
1300	Inventory	-	675.00
2630	HST Charged on Sales	-	175.50
4100	Sales	-	1,350.00
Additional Date:	Additional Field:		
		2,200.50	2,200.50

ⓘ **J1** (Journal Entry #1) indicates that this is the first Sage 50 Accounting journal entry in the Santos Luggage Company records.

Notice the automatic debit to 1200 Accounts Receivable account made by Sage 50 Accounting. Also notice the automatic credit to the HST CHARGED ON SALES calculated by Sage 50 Accounting, based on the HST code or rate previously entered. The automatic linking to the debit and credit General Ledger accounts will be explained in Chapter 4A.

Notice that the Cost of Goods account #5010 is increased by $675.00, and the Inventory account #1300 is decreased by the amount of the goods sold.

Sage 50 Accounting combines two journal entries into one entry when an inventory sale is recorded.

1. The Sales entry:		
Accounts Receivable	1,525.50	
HST Charged on Sales		175.50
Sales		1,350.00
2. The Cost of Goods Sold entry:		
Cost of Goods Sold	675.00	
Inventory		675.00

> 5 Back Paks @ 35 = 175
> 9 Suitcase/R @ 28 = 252
> 8 Suitcase/L @ 31 = 248
>   675

7 ➤   **Exit** from the entry window.

In this text, you will not need to print Invoices or Packing Slips.

8 ➤   Click the 🔽 on the right beside the Printer icon. You will see:

✓	Print Invoice	Ctrl+P
	Print Packing Slips	Ctrl+Shift+P
	Print Invoice and Packing Slip	Ctrl+Shift+K

The current default is to print an Invoice. This can be changed. You will see this in Chapter 4. To save paper, do NOT print the Invoice. Click the 🔍 Print Preview icon and notice that the Order No. displays and prints on the right side of the display.

9 ➤ Click **OK** on the far right to exit this window.

In this text, we will not need to print Invoices or Packing Slips.

Sage 50 Accounting now prints the Ship Date and Order No. on the invoice.

WWW If the business processes invoices in a batch (printing and posting a number of sales invoices at one time), refer to Appendix 2015 AB (Printing in Batches) and AC (Batch Processing) in your course materials at www.nelson.com/student.

10 ➤ Click the **Post** button to post the invoice.

The next information box informs you that the complete sales order has been filled (no back order), and that the sales order will be removed from the Sales Order Listing.

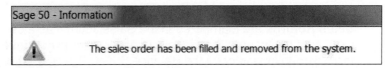

Sage 50 - Information

⚠ The sales order has been filled and removed from the system.

11 ➤ Click **OK**.

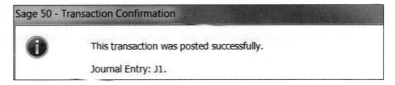

Sage 50 - Transaction Confirmation

ⓘ This transaction was posted successfully.

Journal Entry: J1.

The Transaction Confirmation window displays that Journal entry J1 was posted successfully. Click **OK**.

12 ➤ The next window informs the user that there is a need to reorder some items of inventory. The manager should be contacted.

	Advisor:	Entries just processed caused one or more inventory items to drop below the reorder point. Print the Inventory Item Quantity report to see which items to reorder.

13 ➤ Click inside the box to continue. **Exit** to the Home window. From the menu bar click **Reports**, **Inventory & Services**, **Quantity**, **Inventory by Asset** should be selected, click **OK**. There is a minor problem, in that the To Order report column indicates that no item of inventory needs to be ordered.

Inventory Quantity

Item No.	Description	Unit	Quantity	Minimum	On Purc...	On Sale...	To Order
Brief-R	Briefcase-regular	Each	43	10	0	0	-
Brief-W	Briefcase-wide	Each	40	10	0	0	-
Carry-sm	Carry-on bag-small	Each	124	10	0	0	-
Lap-BP	Laptop Back Paks	Each	87	10	0	0	-
Locks-1	Locks-combination	Each	107	10	0	0	-
Power-1	Power Adapters	Each	52	10	0	0	-
Suit w/w R	Suitcase w/w Regular	Each	213	50	0	0	-
Suit-w/w L	Suitcase w/w Large	Each	247	10	0	0	-

14 ➤ **Exit** from the Inventory Quantity report to the Home window.

Journalizing Sales Returns

Sometimes customers return goods that are damaged, goods that were delivered but not ordered, or goods delivered in excess of what was ordered. This type of transaction is referred to as a **Sales Return** and is recorded as a negative Sales Invoice.

	They are a CUSTOMER to you
Sale to your customer	Dr Accounts Receivable Dr Cost of Goods Sold Cr Inventory Cr HST Charged on Sales Cr Sales
Sales Returns from your customer (Issue a Credit Note to the customer.)	Dr Inventory Dr HST Charged on Sales Dr Sales Returns & Allowances Cr Accounts Receivables Cr Cost of Goods Sold

Sales Returns are journalized in the Sales Journal as a decrease to Sales (in the Sales section of the Income Statement). In addition, **returned inventory** items will need to be increased to inventory on the Balance Sheet. The **HST Charged on Sales** must also be reduced accordingly (in the Balance Sheet). Follow the steps in the next exercise.

Exercise 2A-16—Journalizing a Sales Return

> **Mar 03, 2016**   Havarah Leather Goods returned 2 Laptop Back Paks. Santos Luggage does not charge a Restocking Fee. The Back Paks were originally purchased on invoice #2253 at 70.00, plus HST. We sent Havarah Leather Goods our credit memo #124 dated today in the amount of $158.20, and referenced it to invoice #2253Rt.

1 ➤   Right-click the **Sales Invoice** icon, select **Create Invoice**.

2 ➤   **Sold To**   Select **Havarah Leather Goods**, `Tab`. Click in the **Invoice No.** field.

3 ➤   **Invoice No.**   Many firms enter the Invoice number with a return code (Rt) or other codes as shown below. This cross-references the return with the original sales invoice.

      Change to **2253Rt CM124**. When displaying the customer detail the invoice number will show first in the column. `Tab` `Tab` to Date.

Other invoice codes used to identify action taken are:

Ad Adjustment		**Al** Allowance Granted		**Co** Correction	
Dp Deposit		**NS** NSF		**Rt** Returned goods	
Rv Reversal		**TS** Transfer		**Wo** Write-off	

4 ➤   **Date**   **Mar 03, 2016** is the date the goods were received by our firm.

      `Tab`. You should not backdate the return to the original date of the sale (Feb 26, 2016). You want your records to reflect dates when transactions actually happened. Double-click in the **Item Number** field. Select **Laptop Back Paks**.

5 ➤ Quantity   Type **-2** (negative) (2 items returned), [Tab].

6 ➤ Unit   Each [Tab].

7 ➤ Description   Type **Laptop Back Paks not needed**, [Tab].

8 ➤ Base Price   70.00 is the original selling price. [Tab] [Tab] [Tab] to Amount as there is no % discount.

9 ➤ Amount   [Tab] to accept **-140.00**. The minus sign before the invoice amount will make this entry a **Debit** to the account selected and a **Credit** to Accounts Receivable.

10 ➤ Tax   [Tab]. The **HS** code is still valid for a sales return.

11 ➤ Account   The default **4100 Sales** revenue account cannot be used because this is not a sale. It is a return of some or part of a sale. Many companies use a separate account to keep a record of returns.

Press [Enter]. The G/L accounts should be displayed.

Select account **4200 Sales – Returns & Allowances**. [Tab] to accept.

> The Early Payment terms fields would need to change when goods are returned within the 10 days of the discount period.

12 ➤ Early Payment Terms   Leave the 2.00%. Change the terms to **4** days and **Net 24 days**. The goods were sold on Feb 26, and the returns were accepted on Mar 3. Six days have passed since the goods were sold, therefore, there are 4 days remaining in the discount period. (See side note box).

13 ➤ Message   Click in the **Message** field. The default comment code is not appropriate for a return. Change the comment by highlighting the current comment and typing **Return accepted, not needed**.

[Tab]. You could leave the comment space blank, but it is best to enter a note for future reference.

> The Information about Mrs. Santos approving the return will not print on the customer return invoice.

14 ➤ Click the **Enter Additional information** [✓] icon and type the information shown. (See side note box.)

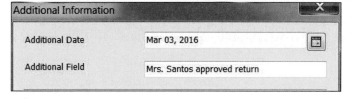

Additional Information		X
Additional Date	Mar 03, 2016	🗓
Additional Field	Mrs. Santos approved return	

15 ➤ Click **OK**.

16 ➤ View the Sales Journal Entry as shown next.

Sales Journal Entry Mar 03, 2016 (J2)

Account Number	Account Description	Debits	Credits
1300	Inventory	70.00	-
2630	HST Charged on Sales	18.20	-
4200	Sales- Returns & Allowances	140.00	-
1200	Accounts Receivable	-	158.20
5010	Cost of Goods Sold	-	70.00
Additional Date: Ma...	Additional Field: Mrs. Santos appro...		
		228.20	228.20

17 ➤ **Exit** from viewing the Sales Journal entry.

The invoice window display should appear as follows:

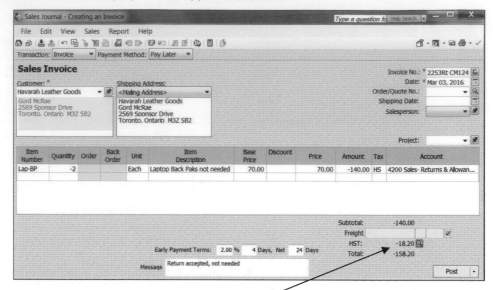

Notice that HST originally charged on this invoice has been reduced by the amount corresponding to the return. Negative **-18.20** is 13% of the $140.00 returned goods.

18 ➤ **Post** when correct, click **OK** for the J2 confirmation window and **Exit** to the Home window.

19 ➤ **Recently Viewed Reports Area**

Display the Havarah Leather Goods Customer Aged Detail report at March 3, 2016, with terms. Click on **Customer Aged**, the report displays. Click the **Modify** icon, **Report Options**, select **Havarah Leather Goods**, **Detail** button should be selected. **Include Terms** ✓ should be selected, click on **OK**. Notice the **2253Rt** reference, and the amount is shown with a minus.

Customer Aged Detail As at Mar 03, 2016

Source	Date	Terms	Transaction Type	Total	Current
Havarah Leather Goods					
2253	Feb 26, 2016	2%/10, Net 30	Invoice	2,373.00	2,373.00
2253Rt CM124	Mar 03, 2016	2%/4, Net 24	Invoice	-158.20	-158.20
Total outstanding:				2,214.80	2,214.80
Total unpaid invoices:				2,214.80	2,214.80
Total deposits/prepaid order:				-	-
Total outstanding:				2,214.80	2,214.80

20 ➤ **Exit** the Aged Detail window and return to the Home window.

Remember to back up your data and update your logbook at the end of every work session.

The Receipts Journal

The Receipts Journal is used to record all types of payments from customers:

- Payment without discount
- Payment with discount(s)
- Deposits (see Exercise 2B-29)

Most companies that have a large volume of sales invoices have a procedure to record receipts of payments. Upon receipt of the customer's cheque, it is usually stamped on the back with a notation "For Deposit Only" or "For Deposit to the Account of (company)." This prevents unauthorized persons from using the cheque for any other purpose.

For accurate bookkeeping and consistency with the bank reconciliation process, the receipt should be recorded when it is actually received (date stamp) and deposited. If the receipt date is no more than 2-3 days past the end of the discount period, then it is usually appropriate to permit the discount on an invoice. This business practice reflects the normal 2-3 day grace period allowed for mail delivery. In some businesses, manager approval may be required before processing this discount override. In Sage 50 Accounting, you would need to type the amount of the discount into the ***Discount Taken*** field to process it.

The date of receipt may be backdated one or two days to accommodate a sales discount. This would apply when a customer's cheque was mailed on the tenth day from the invoice date. There may also be a delay in mail delivery or a cheque received on a Monday when the due date was on a Saturday or Sunday.

The receipts are usually deposited daily to update customer balances owing. A record of each receipt is detailed in the bank deposit book.

Journalizing a Receipt with Cash Discount

Cheques for payment of an invoice are usually accompanied by an advice, a detachable form that provides the details of the payment.

Fig. 2A-13 illustrates a cheque received for this transaction, accompanied by an advice. The date and security stamps on the back of the cheque are also shown. You will use the details shown on the cheque and the advice to journalize the payment.

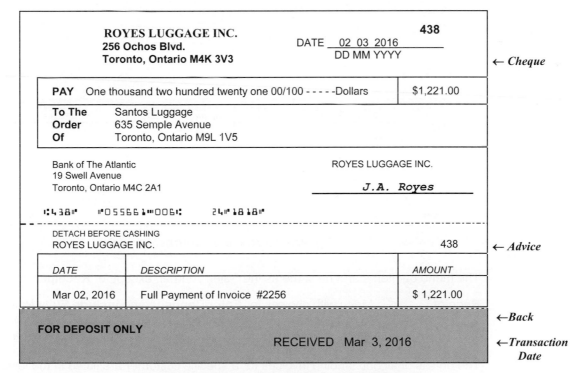

Fig. 2A-13: A Payment Cheque with Advice.

Exercise 2A-17—Recording a Receipt with Discount

Study the following transaction:

> **Mar 03, 2016   Received from Royes Luggage Inc. cheque #438 for $1,221.00 in full payment of invoice #2256.**

There are 3 different ways to create Receipts:

Receipts ▼

1 ➤ A) At the **Receipts** icon, click the ▼, notice the 3 choices. Select **Create Receipt**. In the **From** field, click ▼ and select the customer. The screen fills with the outstanding invoices. Click **X** to return to the Home window.

B) Click the **Receipts** icon, to go directly to the Receipts Journal window. In the **From** field click ▼ and select the customer. The screen fills with the outstanding invoices. Click **X** to return to the Home window.

C) In the **Customers** area, click the ▼ or right click on the **customer from whom we received the cheque**, select **Receive Payments**. The screen fills with the outstanding invoices. Click **X** to return to the Home window.

2 ➤ Using step 1, method **C**, click the ▼ at **Royes Luggage Inc.**, select **Receive Payments**. (See side note box.) The Receipts Journal will display the name and address of the customer as shown:

If you are going to process a number of cheques from the same customer, you can click on the red pushpin 📌 to keep the same customer on the next receipt.

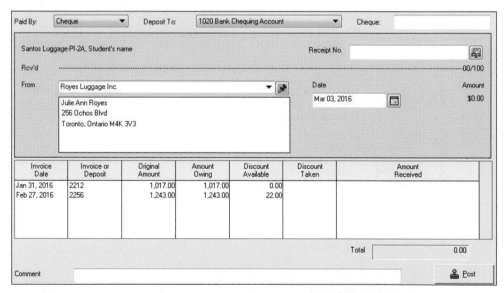

Fig. 2A-14: Receipts Journal window.

The menu bar items are the same as the Sales Journal, except for **Receipt**.

Receipt   Menu with choices for **Enter Deposits** and **Include Fully Paid Invoices/Deposits** in the top detail section of the Receipts window. You can adjust a previously posted receipt or look up (view) a receipt.

The details of all outstanding invoices for a specific customer are listed in the lower section, including the original Invoice Date. Royes Luggage Inc. has two invoices that have not been paid in full. The company is paying only invoice # 2256 at this time.

When a customer/vendor takes a 2% discount for paying an invoice within terms of 2/10, net 30, HST regulations consider the discount a finance charge and not a reduction to the HST portion.

The terms for this client are 2/10, net 30, (i.e., a discount of 2% if the invoice is paid within 10 days, or the full amount due in 30 days). The discount is calculated on the invoice amount **before** taxes (HST not included). HST is not affected by discounts taken. See side note box.

Invoice #2256 amounts to $1,100.00 for various luggage goods, plus HST of 143.00 totalling $1,243.00. The 2% discount is calculated on the luggage sold at $1,100.00, which equals $22.00. (See side note box.) To summarize:

Invoice #2256	
Luggage Sold	$1,100.00
HST	143.00
Total	$1,243.00
Discount	
.02 x $1,100.00 =	$22.00
Cheque received	
1,243.00 less 22.00 =	$1,221.00

3 ➤   Paid By: Click the ▼ and 5 choices are available. Select **Cheque**, and [Tab] to the next field.

4 ➤   Deposit To: Click the ▼. Sage 50 Accounting allows the receipt to be deposited to one of many bank accounts. This would be useful if the business has Canadian, U.S. and other currency bank accounts; e.g., euro, Mexican peso, etc. and accounts for depositing credit card receipts.

Santos Luggage uses two bank accounts:

  1020 Bank Chequing Account is used for normal receipts from customers.

  1030 Visa Credit Card Bank Account is used to deposit credit card receipts at a different bank.

5 ➤   Select **1020 Bank Chequing Account** and [Tab] to Cheque.

6 ➤   Cheque   This field will show the cheque number received from the customer.

The cheque number will appear in the All Journal Entries or Journal Entries Receipts entries.

Change the window to the following:

X

You will see an error message about the **Receipt No.** field in step 15. It will be corrected in step 17.

7 ➤   Receipt No.   Leave blank. This field can also be used for a receipt number if the firm records cheques received with a sequence number.

8 ➤   Date   The date should be Mar 03, 2016, the date the cheque was received. (This company is not using the additional information fields.) Change the date to **Mar 09, 2016**.

The **Discount Available** column should be **0.00** for both, indicating that the discount period has passed for both invoices. Sage 50 Accounting will calculate the discount available within the days allowed by the terms of the invoice.

9 ➤   Change the date back to **Mar 03, 2016** and the correct discount of 22.00 shows in the **Discount Available** column. [Tab].

If the customer's cheque amount is less than the amount showing in the **Amount Owing** column and the discount amount shown is **0.00**, you should change the date back a few days (e.g., March 01) to see if the cheque reflects a discount taken by the customer.

Ask your manager what to do if a cheque is received a day or two late and misses the discount period. In most cases the manager will allow the discount.

---

10 ➤	**Invoice Date**	The cursor jumps to this field. *Note*: The payment is being made for invoice #2256 dated Feb 27, 2016. Use the ↓ key on the keyboard to move down to invoice 2256 dated Feb 27, 2016 that is being paid. You can also use your mouse to position the cursor on 2256. [Tab].
	Invoice or Deposit	This field indicates the invoice number or deposit number issued.
	Original Amount	This field indicates the original amount of each invoice.
	Amount Owing	This field indicates the balance remaining on each invoice if partial payments have been received.
	Discount Available	This field indicates the amount of any cash discounts available based on the terms agreed upon. This client's terms are 2/10, net 30. Most firms calculate the cash discount amount on the invoice price ($1,100.00) before taxes. The correct discount is $22.00.
11 ➤	**Discount Taken**	The cursor jumps to this field. If the **Discount Available** field is blank, it indicates that no discount is available for this invoice. You can override the **Discount Taken** field by typing in an amount. [Tab] to accept the discount of 22.00. (See side note boxes.)
12 ➤	**Amount Received**	The field now shows 1,221.00, the amount of the outstanding invoice after the discount has been taken off, and is also the amount of the cheque received. [Tab] to accept the receipt of 1,221.00 against this outstanding invoice.
	Total	This field (greyed out) shows the total of the Amount Received column. It should agree with the cheque received.

[Side note 1]

The **Early Payment Discount**, for payment within the discount period, is automatically calculated and entered in the **Discount Available** field. When the discount is accepted in the **Discount Taken** field, the amount is linked to the **Sales Discount** account. You will see the linking in Chapter 4A.

[Side note 2]

All other discounts—staff, seniors, quantity, trade, etc.—need to be entered in the Sales Journal Discount % column. You will see this in Exercise 2B-34.

If the cursor was on the invoice 2212 line and you pressed the [Tab] key twice by mistake to move to the Amount Received column, the amount of 1,017.00 appears in the Amount Received field. Press the *Delete* key to remove the amount.

---

13 ➤ Display the Receipts Journal Entry. Click **Report**, then **Display Receipts Journal Entry**. The entry should appear as follows:

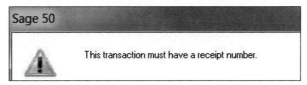

Receipts Journal Entry Mar 03, 2016 (J3)			
Account Number	Account Description	Debits	Credits
1020	Bank Chequing Account	1,221.00	-
4150	Sales -Discounts	22.00	-
1200	Accounts Receivable	-	1,243.00
Additional Date:	Additional Field:		
		1,243.00	1,243.00

The G/L account numbers did not need to be entered. All payments received will automatically be debited to the **Deposit To:** bank account identified in step 5, and credited to ACCOUNTS RECEIVABLE.

All merchandise cash discounts will be debited to Sales-Discounts.

14 ➤ When finished viewing, **exit** from the entry window. (See side note box.) To change any of the amounts, click the incorrect field and enter the correct information. Remember to view the entry to make sure you have made the changes properly.

15 ➤ Click the 📧 (e-mail icon at the top-right corner of the window) and a message box appears. This is related to step 7 earlier.

Sage 50
⚠ This transaction must have a receipt number.

Sage 50 Accounting requires a Receipt Number in the Receipt No. field to post the transaction.

Most companies like Santos Luggage do not use receipt numbers, but record the **cheque number** in the **Receipt No.** field for easy verification (Audit trail). Using this method, they can see the cheque number in the journal entry as shown at step 22 and still be able to use the Reconciliation & Deposit Journal at a later time.

16 ➤ Click **OK** to return to the Receipts Journal.

17 ➤ **Complete your window** as shown next: Press the [Tab] key.

nt ▼	Cheque:	438
Receipt No.	438	🖥

All companies in this text use this method of recording cheque numbers in both fields.

✓ This will now correct the error message seen at step 15.

18 ➤ Click the 📧 (e-mail icon) again and the following message appears.

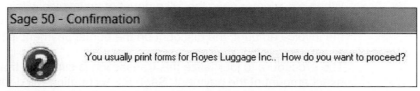

Sage 50 - Confirmation
❓ You usually print forms for Royes Luggage Inc.. How do you want to proceed?

19 ➤ This is to advise you that you normally print forms for Royes Luggage Inc.

There is no exercise to e-mail the receipt. Click **Cancel** to return to the Receipt Journal window.

20 ➤ **Post** when correct, click **OK** to accept the confirmation for J3. In future exercises, when the instruction is to Post, it also means to accept the confirmation.

21 ➤ **Exit** from the Receipts Journal.

22 ➤ **View** the Receipts Journal Entry. At **Reports**, click ▼, select **Receipts Journal Entries**, click **Display**. (See side note box.)

> If there were other receipt entries and you wanted to display certain ones, click the **Modify** icon, **Report Options**, change the dates as required, or click Journal Number and change the information as required.

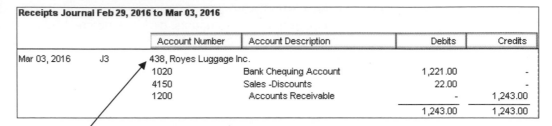

Receipts Journal Feb 29, 2016 to Mar 03, 2016		Account Number	Account Description	Debits	Credits
Mar 03, 2016	J3	438, Royes Luggage Inc.			
		1020	Bank Chequing Account	1,221.00	-
		4150	Sales -Discounts	22.00	-
		1200	Accounts Receivable	-	1,243.00
				1,243.00	1,243.00

The 438 cheque number is shown in the posted entry.

23 ➤ **Exit** from the Receipts Journal window.

24 ➤ View the Customer Aged Detail report only for Royes Luggage Inc. In the Customers area at **Royes Luggage Inc.**, click ▼, select **Display Customer Aged Detail Report**. The Detail report displays only Royes Luggage Inc.

Notice how the Payment and Discount appear, with a minus sign, and the Discount wording in the Transaction Type column in Fig. 2A-15.

Customer Aged Detail As at Mar 03, 2016						
Source	Date	Transaction Type	Total	Current	31 to 60	61 to 90
Royes Luggage Inc.						
2212	Jan 31, 2016	Invoice	1,017.00	-	1,017.00	-
2256	Feb 27, 2016	Invoice	1,243.00	1,243.00	-	-
438	Mar 03, 2016	Discount	-22.00	-22.00	-	-
438	Mar 03, 2016	Payment	-1,221.00	-1,221.00	-	-
Total outstanding:			1,017.00	-	1,017.00	-

Fig. 2A-15: Customer Aged Detail.

Cheque number **438** is shown on both the **Discount** and **Payment** lines.

25 ➤ **Exit** from the Customer Aged Detail report. Notice that in the Customer Area on the Home page, the Balance for Royes Luggage Inc. now displays as 1,017.00.

Journalizing a Partial Receipt with No Discount

When a customer pays the full amount of an invoice within the discount period, the discount as per the terms of sale is allowed. However, if the customer pays only part of the invoice amount, the discount on the partial payment is normally not allowed.

The procedure to journalize this transaction is similar to that in Exercise 2A-17. Enter the exact amount of the payment. Sage 50 Accounting will deduct the partial payment from the invoice without discount and will show the remaining amount outstanding.

Exercise 2A-18—Journalizing a Partial Receipt without a Discount

You are going to enter the wrong amount for the cheque and then correct the error after posting. You will later also make an error in an invoice and correct it after posting.

Study this transaction and complete the following steps:

> **Mar 03, 2016**   Received cheque #159, in the amount of $2,000.00, from Sandler Travel Stores as a partial payment on its outstanding invoice #2197 from January 26, 2016.

1 ➤   Using the ▼ in the Customers area, click on **Receive Payments** for Sandler Travel Stores.

2 ➤   Cheque   Type **159** for the customer's cheque number, [Tab] to accept. The cursor moves to the From area.

3 ➤   Receipt No.   Type **159,** [Tab] [Tab].

4 ➤   Date   [Tab] [Tab] to accept Mar 03, 2016.

5 ➤   Invoice Date   At Jan 26, 2016, for Invoice **2197,** [Tab].

Discount Available   There is no discount available, because it is more than 10 days since the invoice date of Jan 26, 2016.

6 ➤   Discount Taken [Tab] to leave the field blank.

(See side note box.)

> A firm may allow a discount under special circumstances, even when the discount period has passed. If a customer asks for a discount or if you receive a payment showing an unauthorized discount, consult your manager.

To practise correcting an error after posting a transaction, you will deliberately make an error and then correct it later.

---

7 ➤   Amount Received   Type **2200.00** (This amount is not correct. You will correct it in the next exercise.) [Tab] to show a receipt of $2,200.00 against invoice #2197.

8 ➤   View the entry.

Receipts Journal Entry Mar 03, 2016 (J4)

Account Number	Account Description	Debits	Credits
1020	Bank Chequing Account	2,200.00	-
1200	Accounts Receivable	-	2,200.00
Additional Date:	Additional Field:		
		2,200.00	2,200.00

9 ➤   Exit to the Receipts Journal and **Post** J4 with the error.

You will be at a blank Receipt window.

10 ➤   From   Select **Sandler Travel Stores**. You will see that the **Amount Owing** column is reduced by the partial payment.

Invoice Date	Invoice or Deposit	Original Amount	Amount Owing
Jan 26, 2016	2197	4,407.00	2,207.00

You have just realized that you have made an error in the amount, as the Amount Owing should have been $2,407.00. Complete the next exercise to reverse and correct the error in posting.

Exercise 2A-19—Correcting a Receipt Error

You will now correct the error that you deliberately made in the last exercise. You have two choices.

1. You can use the **Adjust Receipt** icon as shown in this exercise. This would be useful if the amount of the invoice is to be changed.

2. You could use the **Reverse Receipt entry** icon to reverse and cancel the entry. This method would be useful if you posted the error to the wrong customer or you wanted to cancel the entry with the error and start the entry again. Refer to Chapter 13 to reverse a cash receipt.

> **i** To correct a Sales Receipt, refer to Chapter 13, Exercise 13-5.

---

1 ➤ **Receipt No.** Click the **Lookup a Receipt** icon. The Search, Receipt Lookup window appears.

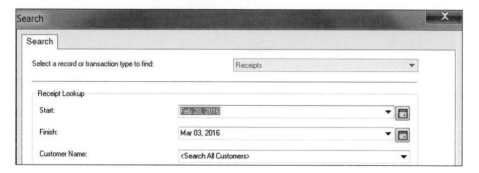

2 ➤ Click **OK**. The **Select a Receipt** window appears.

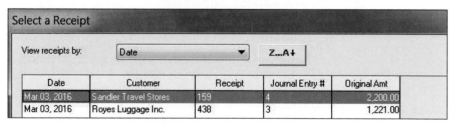

Date	Customer	Receipt	Journal Entry #	Original Amt
Mar 03, 2016	Sandler Travel Stores	159	4	2,200.00
Mar 03, 2016	Royes Luggage Inc.	438	3	1,221.00

3 ➤ Select **Sandler Travel Stores**.

4 ➤ The **Receipts Journal - Receipt Lookup** window appears and the **Paid By:**, **Deposit To:**, **Cheque:**, **Receipt No.**, **From** and **Date** fields are greyed out.

5 ➤ Click the **Adjust Receipt** icon. The top header changes to **Receipts Journal - Adjusting Receipt 159** and only the lower portion of the **From** field is greyed out. The customer cannot be changed, because we are reversing an entry to their account.

6 ➤ Click the **Amount Received** column and change the amount to **2000.00**, Tab.

If you display the entry, it will display as J6. **Exit** the entry.

7 ➤ **Post** when correct.

8 ➤ **Exit** from the Receipts Journal.

9 ➤ **Display** the Customer Aged Detail report for **Sandler Travel Stores.**

Source	Date	Transaction Type	Total	Current	31 to 60
Customer Aged Detail As at Mar 03, 2016					
Sandler Travel Stores					
2197	Jan 26, 2016	Invoice	4,407.00	-	4,407.00
159	Mar 03, 2016	Payment	-2,000.00	-	-2,000.00
Total outstanding:			2,407.00	-	2,407.00

Note that only the correct posting of -2,000.00 displays.

10 ➤ **Exit** from the Customer Aged Detail.

11 ➤ Display the **Receipts Journal Entries** as shown in Exercise 2A-17.

The default display is to NOT show corrections (e.g., J4 and J5). To see the Corrections, click **Modify, Report Options,** click **Corrections** to have a ✓, click **OK**. You will notice that J5 is the reversing entry for J4 (the error) and J6 is the correct entry.

12 ➤ **Exit** from the Receipts Journal window and return to the Home window.

Remember to back up your data and update your logbook at the end of your work session.

Exercise 2A-20—Recording a Minor Repair (Service) Invoice

Study the following transaction:

> **Mar 03, 2016** Received from Mr. Larry Johns, cheque #614 ($16.95) for $15.00 plus HST for a minor lock repair, with a 30-day warranty. This entry will use the inventory service item feature. We do not expect to do other business with Mr. Johns.

1 ➤ Click the **Sales Invoices** icon.

2 ➤ **Transaction** [Tab] to accept Invoice and move to Payment Method.

3 ➤ **Payment Method** Click the ▼ and select **Cheque,** [Tab] to Cheque No.

4 ➤ **Cheque No.** Type **614,** [Tab] to Customer.

5 ➤ **Customer** Type **Mr. Larry Johns,** [Tab].

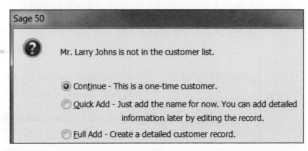

6 ➤ We do not expect to do other business with Mr. Johns; therefore, use the **Continue** selection. Click **OK**.

7 ➤ **Item Number** Double-click this field or press Enter. Notice that the Qty On Hand field for Service Type HF-1 (Handling Fee) and MR-1 (Minor Repair) is --. This is a service field and not inventory on-hand. You will learn how to set up the Service feature in Chapter 8.

8 ➤ Select **MR-1, Minor Repair**. Notice that the fields are filled in; however, the Quantity, Amount and Total fields are not filled in.

9 ➤ **Quantity** Type **1** Tab. The Total field is now 16.95.

10 ➤ **Change** the Item Description field as shown next.

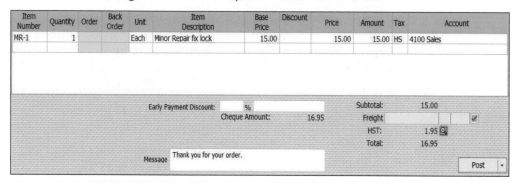

Item Number	Quantity	Order	Back Order	Unit	Item Description	Base Price	Discount	Price	Amount	Tax	Account
MR-1	1			Each	Minor Repair fix lock	15.00		15.00	15.00	HS	4100 Sales

Early Payment Discount: ___ %
Cheque Amount: 16.95
Message: Thank you for your order.

Subtotal:	15.00
Freight	☑
HST:	1.95
Total:	16.95

Post ▾

11 ➤ View the Sales Journal entry. It should appear as follows:

Sales Journal Entry Mar 03, 2016 (J7)

Account Number	Account Description	Debits	Credits
1020	Bank Chequing Account	16.95	-
2630	HST Charged on Sales	-	1.95
4100	Sales	-	15.00
Additional Date:	Additional Field:		
		16.95	16.95

12 ➤ **Exit** from the display window.

13 ➤ **Post** when correct and **Exit**.

Cancelling an Invoice After Posting

There may be situations where you need to cancel an invoice. You posted a sale to the wrong customer, or a customer decides they don't want/need the product just purchased. This would be different from a sales return. The customer did not take the merchandise out of the store, so it is technically not a sales return.

1 ➤ Advance the date to **Mar 04, 2016**.

2 ➤ **Record** and **Post** the following transaction.

Mar 04, 2016 **A clerk from Havarah Leather Goods is being sent to pick up 2 Laptop Back Paks.**

Record and Post the sale (invoice #2312) in the regular way at $70.00 each, plus HST. Terms 2/10, n30. Invoice total $158.20.

Exercise 2A-21—Cancelling a Posted Invoice

1 ➤ In this exercise, you will cancel the invoice, based on the following information.

To correct a Sales Invoice, refer to Chapter 13, Exercise 13-4.

Mar 04, 2016 **The Havarah Leather Goods clerk changes the order to 3 extra large Laptop Back Paks. Your store does not carry this particular item and your supplier does not stock this item. The clerk confirms with his boss that the order for 2 Laptop Back Paks is to be cancelled.**

2 ➤ Click the **Lookup an Invoice** icon and the Invoice Lookup Search window appears. A portion is shown next.

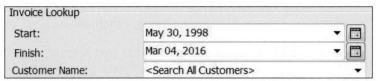

A range of dates and/or customers, invoice numbers or Journal entry numbers may be selected at this point. In this exercise you will view all posted invoices.

3 ➤ Click **OK**. The Select an Invoice window is displayed listing the invoices you have entered in this chapter. *Note*: Only a partial window is shown.

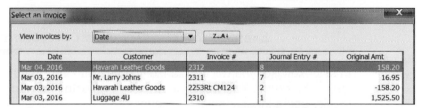

4 ➤ **Select** invoice **2312**. The invoice details are inserted into the Sales Journal-Invoice Lookup window for *review only*.

The icon remains the same, but the wording in each Journal window will change.

If you reverse a receipt the same icon is named "Reverse Receipt."

5 ➤ You want to cancel invoice 2312; therefore, click the **Reverse Invoice** entry icon. (See side note box.)

6 ➤ Click **Yes**.

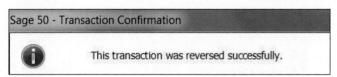

7 ➤ Click **OK**. The window returns to a blank invoice. The reversing entry has been posted; therefore, the original entry has been reversed.

8 ➤ **Exit** the invoice and return to the Home window.

9 ➤ Display the **Sales Journal Entries** for Mar 04, 2016 (change the Start date) with Corrections ✓. Click **Modify**, **Report Options**, click **Corrections**, change the **Start Date** to **Mar 04, 2016**, **OK**.

Sales Journal Mar 04, 2016 to Mar 04, 2016				
	Account Number	Account Description	Debits	Credits
Mar 04, 2016 J8	2312, Havarah Leather Goods			
	1200	Accounts Receivable	158.20	-
	5010	Cost of Goods Sold	70.00	-
	1300	Inventory	-	70.00
	2630	HST Charged on Sales	-	18.20
	4100	Sales	-	140.00
Mar 04, 2016 J9	ADJ2312, Rev. of J8. Corr. is J9.			
	1300	Inventory	70.00	-
	2630	HST Charged on Sales	18.20	-
	4100	Sales	140.00	-
	1200	Accounts Receivable	-	158.20
	5010	Cost of Goods Sold	-	70.00
			456.40	456.40

Journal entry 9 has cancelled Sales journal entry 8. The above information will not display in the Customer Aged Detail report as there was no sale.

This procedure can also be used to cancel Sales Quotes, Sales Orders, Receipts, Purchase Quotes, Purchase Orders, Purchase Invoices, and Payments.

10 ➤ **Exit** the Sales Journal window and ☒ to return to the Home window.

The Customer's Ledger

When you set up a customer account in the RECEIVABLES module, you are creating a ledger for that customer. When you enter sales or payment transactions referring to the particular customer in the RECEIVABLES module, the corresponding customer's ledger will be updated.

Exercise 2A-22—Viewing a Customer's Ledger

In this exercise, you will familiarize yourself with the Customers window and view a customer ledger. You would need to view a customer's ledger when you receive an inquiry about the customer's account.

1 ➤ Advance Session date to **Mar 05, 2016**.

2 ➤ In the **Tasks** area, at **Customers** icon, click ▼ to see the 4 choices. Select **View Customers**. As discussed in previous Exercises, you can also click the Customers icon to go directly to the Customers window. Study Fig. 2A-16.

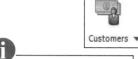

The find customer feature: Click the **magnifying glass on the left**, and the **Find Customer Search** window appears. You would use this if you want to find a specific customer in a long list of similar names (e.g., Smith, Singh, etc.).

The FIND icon is a quick way to locate an item from a long list. Sage 50 Accounting provides this facility in various fields in most windows. Use it. It can save you time!

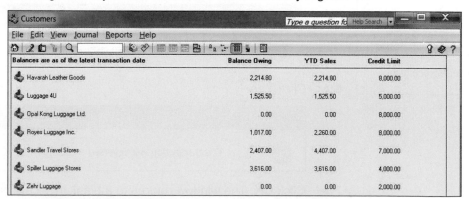

Fig. 2A-16: Customers Summary Information.

This window shows summary information about the customer, including the credit limit the customer is allowed.

You will see that the Customers window has the following menu bar choices: (Also see side note box.)

File	Menu with choices for opening a customer, creating a new customer or removing a current customer (only if balance is nil and prior invoices have been cleared).
Edit	Menu item allows you to search for a customer record.
View	Menu choice for displaying customer information (changing the size of the icons for the display). **Icon** displays 2 customers on a line, **Small icon** displays 3 customers on a line, or **Name** displays customer detail information as shown in Fig. 2A-16. If you maximize the window, depending on the monitor, resolution and icon you are using, you may see 2, 3 or 4 customer names on a line, and Restore Window to default setting.
Journal	Menu choice of either the **Sales** or **Receipts** Journal for data entry. (Icons are also provided on the toolbar for this.)
Reports	A drop-down menu listing reports available for display.
Help	The Sage 50 Accounting Help menu.

3 ➤ Return to the **Home** window.

Adding a New Customer Record

Sage 50 Accounting allows you to create two basic types of customers and add new customers in two different ways:

1. **Regular Customer** You create individual ledgers for customers who buy from the company more than once during the accounting period. The ledger would include the customer's name, address and other details of the company. You can enter a new customer:

    A) using the Customers icon
    B) using the Sales Invoice Journal

    In Exercise 2A-23, you will create a ledger for a new regular customer using method B.

2. **One-time Customer** There are two options available when you need to record a sale to a customer who is not likely to buy again. These options are available when you use the Sales Invoice icon, and select Create Invoice. When you enter a name of a customer that is not in the Customers List you have two choices.

    a) **<One-time customer>** (see Exercise 2B-30) with customer information *not retained* in the customer list.

    Sage 50 Accounting allows you to record the details of the individual sale including the customer's name and address (in the lower box), but Sage 50 Accounting will not create a ledger for the customer. You can view the record of the sale (Journal entry) at a later time, as it will be in the list of transactions.

When you record a sale using this option, Sage 50 Accounting will allow you to enter a cash sale only (cash, cheque, bank debit card or credit card). Payment from the customer for the sales amount is journalized at the same time as the sale.

b) Type the customer's name and use the **Continue** button (see Exercise 2B-31) with customer information *retained* for the new customer in the Journal Entry report but not in the customer list. Sage 50 Accounting will not create a ledger for the customer.

Exercise 2A-23—Creating a Regular Customer Ledger and a Sales Invoice

---

Study this transaction:

Mar 05, 2016 **You have made a sale to a new customer. The details are: A-Your Name Luggage Rack; Contact: Your Name; 256 Trillium Way, Oakville, Ontario, L6J 2H8; telephone 905-699-8000, extension 2563; fax number 905-699-8010; credit limit $3,000.00 Invoice 2312 $400.02; terms 2/10, net 30.**

The goods ordered and shipped on this first order are:

6 Carry-on bag–small	**@ $21.00 each, plus HST**
3 Suitcase w/w Large	**@ $62.00 each, plus HST**
4 Power Adapters	**@ $10.50 each, plus HST**

The goods **are to be picked up by their own delivery truck and delivered** to the Hamilton store, operated by **Jackie Welland**, as follows: **939 Fennel Avenue West, Hamilton, Ontario, L9N 3T1.**

Note: You will be recording the Hamilton Store information in the Customer Ledger Address tab.

Your Name Luggage Rack is a good example of a regular customer, as they are likely to buy from you again. Since there is no existing ledger for this new customer, you need to create a Customer Ledger, and then record the sale.

Sales Invoices

1 ➤ Click the **Sales Invoices** icon, at **Customer**: type, **A-Your Name Luggage Rack**, (The **A-** is used to place your name at the beginning of the customer list regardless of the first letter of your name.) `Tab`. The following window will display.

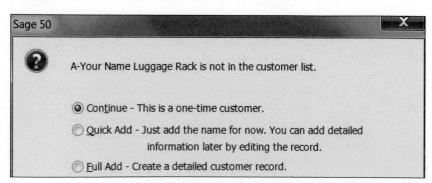

This is where you would identify the customer type by clicking the appropriate button:

Continue

You would select this when you type the name of the one-time customer in the **Customer** field. It allows you to continue recording the sale without adding the customer to the customers list. Remember, however, that if you select this option, you can enter only a cash, cheque, debit card, or credit card sale.

Quick Add

This feature will add the customer to the Customers Ledger but will omit details about the customer (address, phone number, terms, credit limit, etc.), **Tab** . The cursor will move to the **Shipping Address** field. Type the customer address and complete the invoice. You can use this feature with a quote or order. You will need to go back to the customer account and add the details later.

Full Add

This feature will add the customer to the Customers Ledger and will open the Receivables Ledger window to record details about the customer. When the details have been entered, you are returned to the previous window. You can then produce the invoice. *Note:* The address information will be automatically entered from the Customer Ledger information. You can use this feature with a quote or order.

Cancel

To cancel the current operation. Sage 50 Accounting will then allow you to enter a different customer name.

2 ➤ Select **Full Add, OK**. The Receivables Ledger window will open with the name of the customer displayed.

Address tab

3 ➤ Enter the information for A-Your Name Luggage Rack, as shown next:

Customer:	A-Your Name Luggage Rack		

Address | Ship-to Address | Options | Taxes | Pre-Authorized Debit | Statistics | Memo | Import/Export | Additional Info

Contact:	Your Name	Phone 1:	(905) 699-8000 2563
Street 1:	256 Trillium Way	Phone 2:	
Street 2:		Fax:	(905) 699-8010
City:	Oakville	E-mail:	
Province:	Ontario	Web Site:	
Postal Code:	L6J 2H8	Salesperson:	
Country:		Customer Since:	Mar 05, 2016

> In this window, you can add a new customer's details on various tabs. You can also click the ✏ Edit icon to amend details on the tabs for a customer.

Customer	Entered previously, **Tab** .
Contact	Your name as the contact person for this company.
Postal Code	When you type **L6J2H8** or l6j2h8 and press **Tab** , the postal code will format automatically.

Enter the phone/fax numbers without dashes. Sage 50 Accounting will automatically format them with a dash and brackets as you press **Tab** .

Phone	Type **9056998000** (without dashes) and [Tab].
	To add the extension number **2563** to the phone number, click at the end of the phone number, press the space bar and type the extension number (up to 10 numbers), [Tab] [Tab]. If you type the number and extension as 90569980002563 and then press [Tab], the number and extension will not format.
Fax	Type **9056998010** (without dashes) and press [Tab].
E-mail	Leave blank. This text does not show sending e-mail.
Web Site	Leave blank. This text does not show accessing a customer's website.
Salesperson **WWW**	As discussed earlier, this field is not used in this chapter. See Appendix 2015 N, *Adding a Salesperson's Name to an Invoice* in your course materials at www.nelson.cm/student.
Customer Since	This feature lets clerks see, at a glance, when the customer started buying goods from Santos Luggage. *Note*: Santos Luggage has not updated previous customers. It is assumed that they have been customers for many years.
☐ Inactive Customer	When a customer no longer buys merchandise from you, you can click this field to not have them display in the Home Page Customers section, if the ☑ Include inactive customers is not already checked.

Ship-to Address

4 ➤ Click the **Ship-to Address** tab. This window information would be used when you are sending the invoice to the mailing address of a company (usually the Head Office) and always send the goods to a different store location.

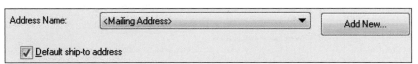

The address information is greyed out as it is assumed that this is the default mailing address and shipping address for all invoices.

5 ➤ Click the **Add New** button, Type the Address Name information as shown next. Each customer can have up to 100 different shipping addresses. You can also add shipping addresses from the invoice. This is shown later in this Exercise (after step 21), Journalizing the Sale, step 1.

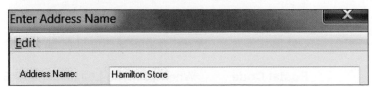

6 ➤ Click **OK**. You are returned to the Receivables ledger.

7 ➤ Enter the information shown next. Ignore Phone and other information.

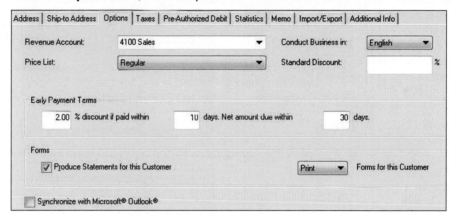

Add New   This button would be used when you want to add an address name.

Rename   This button would be used when you want to change an address.

Remove   This button would be used when you want to remove an address.

Options

8 ➤   Click the **Options** tab, and complete the information as shown.

Revenue Account	When you use the Perpetual Inventory System, the default Revenue account will be received from the Inventory item. The Revenue account 4100 Sales shown here will display in the Sales Quotes, Orders, or Invoice window for non-inventory items.
Price List	Sage 50 Accounting Premium supports 100 different price lists. This is discussed in Chapter 8. Santos Luggage does not use this feature.
Conduct Business in	This field indicates the ability to have screen displays and printouts in French for the customer. Santos Luggage has not had requests to conduct business in French.
Standard Discount	This field would indicate the discount that would apply to each item the customer buys. This is not to be confused with a cash discount for paying early (within term time limits). This discount is for good customers who buy a lot of goods and deserve a reduction to the selling price. If an amount is entered here, it will appear in the Discount % column for the customer. Santos Luggage will not be using this field in Chapter 2A. See Exercise 2B-34 after step 7 for a discussion of the Quantity or Trade Discount.

<table>
<tr><td>**Early Payment Terms**</td><td>When customers are given time to pay for the goods or services they purchase, it is called purchasing goods on credit. The time is normally 30 days.</td></tr>
</table>

Some customers are allowed special terms of 2/10, net 30. This means that if customers pay the balance owing within 10 days they can deduct 2% of the cost of the goods bought as a cash discount; otherwise, the balance is to be paid within 30 days. These terms with discount are referred to as **Early Payment Terms. 2/10 net 30** is the default.

A-Your Name Luggage Rack is a new customer, and as a general practice, your company allows payment terms of 2/10 net 30 days to new customers to provide an incentive to pay early.

Do NOT change from the default.

ⓘ

If you email invoices and orders to your customers, the invoice or order number is now included in the filename, allowing you and your customer to keep better track of files.

Produce Statements for this Customer	Do NOT change. A ✓ in the box will allow you to print a summary statement to be sent to a customer. You will learn how to produce a customer statement in Exercise 2B-40.
9 ➤ **Forms for this Customer**	Click ▼ . There are two choices: **E-mail** and **Print**. Leave the choice as **Print**. (See side note box.)
Synchronize with Microsoft® Outlook®	When this box is ✓, the customer's e-mail address will be placed in the Microsoft® Outlook® Mailing address list. Do NOT change. There is no exercise for this feature.

Taxes

10 ➤ Click the **Taxes** tab and complete the information as shown.

Indicate which taxes this customer is exempt from by entering Yes for Tax Exempt.

Tax	Tax Exempt	Tax ID	
HST	No		

Choose the tax code that includes the taxes that you normally charge this customer:

HS - HST at 13% added to invoice   ▼

Tax	HST, do NOT change. This is the tax code used with this client.
Tax Exempt	HST, do NOT change. This customer is not exempt from HST.
Tax ID	This field would be used if the customer was exempt from the HST. An identification number would be given to the customer by the provincial and/or federal government.

11 ➤ In the lower box, click the ▼ and a list of Tax codes appears. Select **HS - HST at 13% added to Invoice**. The HS code will appear on the first line of the sales invoice.

Pre-Authorized Debit

12 ➤ Click the **Pre-Authorized Debit** tab. Santos Luggage does not have any Debit agreements with clients. This could be used when customers buy the same inventory items on a regular basis.

Tell me more about Pre-Authorized Debits

☐ This customer has a signed active pre-authorized debit agreement with my company

Statistics

13 ➤   Click the **Statistics** tab and enter the information as shown.

 This is the customer's credit limit.

Many companies give each customer a maximum credit balance. When the customer's balance is larger than its preset limit, a warning message box will appear when you try to post a new sale to the customer's account. Although a customer may have exceeded its limit, sales to that customer can still be processed, but you would first consult your manager on how to properly handle this situation. Management may require a payment from the customer to reduce the Accounts Receivable before any additional sales can be made, or your manager may approve the extended credit limit based on financial records of the customer.

You should check the sale and payment history of customers on a regular basis to ensure that each customer is making payments within the agreed terms.

Memo

The open space allows you to make notes about the customer. Click in the open box and the status bar informs you that you can use up to 255 characters to make your note.

14 ➤   Click the **Memo** tab and enter the information as shown.

You will see this memo note in Exercise 2B-28, step 2.

15 ➤   To-Do Date: This is the date (10 days from the date of the sale, plus two days for late mail delivery) that you want to be reminded to deal with the information in the box. Select **Mar 17**.

16 ➤   Display this memo in the Daily Business Manager   Click the box to enter a ✓ in this field. This ✓ will allow the above messages to appear in the Daily Business Manager display.

Import/Export

17 ➤   Click the **Import/Export** tab.

Address	Ship-to Address	Options	Taxes	Pre-Authorized Debit	Statistics	Memo	Import/Export	Additional Info

☐ This customer has Sage 50 and can import invoices and quotes

☐ This customer uses my item numbers on orders

Match the customer's item number to my item number or an account number for importing orders:

Customer's Item No.	My Item No.	My Account	

This customer has...	Leave this box blank. You would ✓ this box if you know the customer uses Sage 50 Premium Accounting 2015, and can import your quotes and invoice information. The text does not have an exercise for importing or exporting information to another company. This feature is not used often.
This customer uses my item numbers...	You would click in the box to insert a ✓ only if your company uses the Perpetual Inventory System in recording sales and you know the customer uses the item numbers of your goods when ordering from your company. This feature is not used often.

Additional Info

18 ➤ Click the **Additional Info** tab. The fields in this window allow you to add additional information that will display when the customer is selected in a transaction. Complete the information as shown.

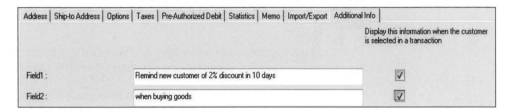

WWW See Appendix 2015 Q, *Names Fields* in your course materials at www.nelson.com/student for more information.

19 ➤ Click 💾 Save and Close . The customer account is created and you are returned to a Sales Invoice window.

20 ➤ The Sales Invoice window, with the name and address you entered and with the **HS** tax code and the **4100** default **Sales** account indicated, is displayed. `Tab`.

21 ➤ The Additional Info Note window for fields 1 and 2 will appear in front of the Sales Invoice window. If the Info window is partially hidden, click on the box, and then click **Close**. You can also click **Close** later.

Journalizing the Sale

Now that you have completed the new customer file, follow these steps to journalize the sale to this customer:

Transaction	Do not change the default **Invoice**.
Payment Method	Do not change the default **Pay Later**.
1 ➤ Shipping Address	The goods are being shipped to the Hamilton store. Click the ▼ and select **Hamilton Store**. The address field changes. `Tab`.
Invoice	The next invoice number is **2313**.
Date	**Mar 05, 2016** This is the date the goods are shipped to the Customer.
Order/Quote No.	This field will be blank, as no previous sales quotes or orders were received from this customer.

Shipping Date   This date field can be left blank as the goods were not ordered on a Sales Quote or Sales Order, and the goods are being shipped the same day as the invoice date.

A-Your Name Luggage Rack ordered the following items:

     6 Carry-on bag–small   @ $21.00 each, plus HST
     3 Suitcase w/w Large   @ $62.00 each, plus HST
     4 Power Adapters   @ $10.50 each, plus HST

The goods are to be picked up by their own delivery truck and delivered to the Hamilton store.

---

2 ➤ Item Number   Double-click or press [Enter]. Select **Carry-sm**.

3 ➤ Quantity   Type **6,** [Tab]. (These are the units being sold and shipped.) The invoice line is filled in.

     Order   This column is skipped. The goods are ordered and shipped.

     Back Order   This column is skipped. There are no goods back ordered on this invoice.

4 ➤ Unit   The field can be changed or left as the default, [Tab].

5 ➤ Description   The field can be changed or left as the default, [Tab].

6 ➤ Base Price   The price can be changed or left as the default, [Tab].

7 ➤ Discount   This customer is not being given a discount on goods purchased. Leave blank. [Tab].

8 ➤ Price   This field would be the individual price after a discount (step 7) is given, [Tab].

9 ➤ Amount   This field represents the calculated amount from fields **Quantity** times **Price**. [Tab] to accept **126.00**.

10 ➤ Tax   The default code **HS** is entered as you set this up earlier. This is correct. [Tab] to accept.

     HST is not included in the selling price of each item. (See the side note box in Exercise 2A-6, for a discussion of the tax codes.)

11 ➤ Account   4100 Sales is shown as the default General Ledger account number. This was set up in the inventory records. If you want to change the account number, double click or press [Enter]. The G/L chart of accounts available should be displayed. You may have to move ▲ or ▼ to see more accounts. Select or type account **4100** Sales and [Tab] to accept 4100.

12 ➤   Enter the remaining sales information from step 1.

     When you enter the invoice lines, Sage 50 Accounting will input the default tax code and account number from the inventory file. You are able to change the tax code and/or account number as needed.

Subtotal	This field is the subtotal of the Amount column (goods being sold without taxes).	
Freight	Your company does not charge for delivery and, therefore, does not use this field.	
Early Payment Terms	Should show **2.00%**, **10 days**, **Net 30 days**, the terms you set up earlier. If the terms are different, you can click on these fields and enter the correct terms.	
Message	This field would display a variety of messages you want the customers to see on quotes, orders and invoices. The default for all invoices is shown. You will learn how to enter this type of information in Chapter 4.	

13 ➤ **Track Shipments** Click the 🖾 **Track Shipments** icon. Click ▼ and a drop-down list of shipping companies is displayed. Select **Your Vehicle**, ⎡Tab⎤. The shipped information will not display in the Invoice window, but will print on the invoice.

14 ➤ **Tracking Number** This will be blank because there is no need to track the shipment if it is being picked up by the customer's vehicle. Click **OK**.

15 ➤ When you have completed recording the above information, the window display should look like Fig 2A-17.

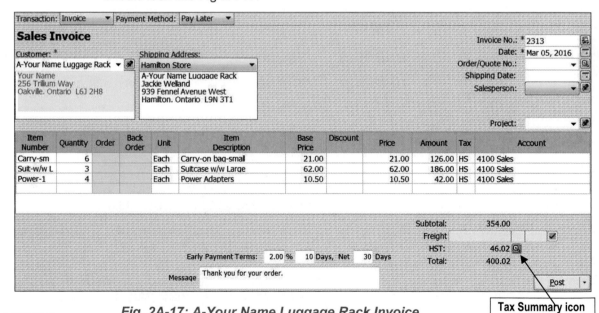

Fig. 2A-17: A-Your Name Luggage Rack Invoice.

Tax Summary icon

When an invoice is created to record cash register summary tapes, there may be a few cents difference in the HST amounts. As stated in the **Tax Summary** window, the amount field can be changed. If in doubt, use the Sage 50 Accounting calculator and make the changes, if necessary.

16 ➤ To see information about the taxes, click the **Tax Summary** icon 🔍 and the summary displays as shown next. This would be a summary of the HST fields to the left. (See side note box.)

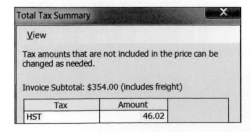

17 ➤ Click **OK**.

18 ➤ Display the Sales Journal entry created by this invoice. The window should display as follows:

Sales Journal Entry Mar 05, 2016 (J10)			
Account Number	Account Description	Debits	Credits
1200	Accounts Receivable	400.02	-
5010	Cost of Goods Sold	177.00	-
1300	Inventory	-	177.00
2630	HST Charged on Sales	-	46.02
4100	Sales	-	354.00
Additional Date:	Additional Field:		
		577.02	577.02

Recording this invoice allows the preparation of a journal entry, given that a sale has taken place. Notice the automatic debit to the Accounts Receivable account made by Sage 50 Accounting. Notice that the automatic credit to the HST Charged on Sales, calculated by Sage 50 Accounting, is based on the HST code or rate entered. Notice also the Cost of Goods Sold and Inventory accounts needed in this sale.

19 ➤ **Exit** from this window by clicking the ☒ button.

20 ➤ Make corrections to any fields that have errors in them. Click the **Post** icon. The entry will be posted to the customer's account in the RECEIVABLES module and will also be posted to the General Ledger, and inventory items are updated.

21 ➤ **Exit** to the Home window.

22 ➤ If the Additional Info window is displayed, **close** it now.

Additional Transactions

1 ➤ Advance the Session date to **Mar 06, 2016**.

Process the following transactions:

Mar 06, 2016	**Sold to Zehr Luggage Terms 2/10, net 30, 10 Suitcases w/w Large at $62.00 each, 4 Suitcases w/w Regular at $56.00, plus HST on all items. Invoice 2314, $953.72.**

Mar 06, 2016	**You made a sale to a new customer, Hanlan's Luggage Store, contact: Liam Hanlan, 2318 Avondale Drive, Oakville, Ontario, L6H 5A1; telephone 905-399-5000, Revenue Account 4100, Terms No %, 0 days, Net amount 0 days, HS code. Credit limit $3,000.00, and they paid by business cheque #739. Record this as a sale and then record the receipt separately. You will see how to combine this into one transaction in Chapter 2B, Exercise 2B-30.**
	The goods ordered and shipped on this first order are: **6 Carry-on bag–small at $21.00 each, $126.00 plus HST ($142.38)**

When a business has a lot of customers and they cannot see all of them in the Customers area, you can scroll down the listing and/or expand the area. In the Reports area, click the ▣ minimize icon. The Reports area is minimized. *Note*: This will work only for the current session. To expand the Reports area, click the ⊞ expand icon.

2 ➤ Advance the Session date to **Mar 07, 2016**.

Mar 07, 2016	**Zehr Luggage returned 3 Suitcases w/w Large. Record the Sales Return. You do not need to record a return to the manufacturer. Purchases Returns will be shown in Chapter 3A, Tyson's Toys.**
	Issued Credit Memo #125, with reference to original sales invoice. Terms amended to 9 days, net 29 days.
	–3 Suitcases w/w Large at $62.00, plus HST (net return –$210.18).

Exercise 2A-24—Correcting a Posted Sales Invoice

Study this transaction:

Mar 07, 2016	**Mr. Hanlan called and stated that the order (invoice #2315) received has a wrong selling price of $21.00 for each bag. Mrs. Santos had forgotten to advise you that the price, for this one time only, should have been $20.50 each. When you correct the invoice, Hanlan's Luggage will have a credit balance in their account, as they paid for the goods when they were picked up yesterday.**

Original Sales Journal Entry

Sales Journal Entry Mar 06, 2016 (J12)

Account Number	Account Description	Debits	Credits
1200	Accounts Receivable	142.38	-
5010	Cost of Goods Sold	63.00	-
1300	Inventory	-	63.00
2630	HST Charged on Sales	-	16.38
4100	Sales	-	126.00
Additional Date:	Additional Field:		
		205.38	205.38

There are different ways to correct a posted invoice containing an incorrect price or quantity.

A. Use the Lookup an invoice icon, Adjust Invoice icon feature. Sage 50 Accounting will reverse the previous sale(s) item and record a new one for the corrected price or quantity. All items on the original invoice would be shown. Refer to Chapter 13, Correcting Transaction Errors After Posting. The customer receives two invoices (original and revised).

B. Correct the item(s) assuming one or two items in a new invoice. This method makes it easier for the customer to see that the price/quantity changed. The customer would receive two invoices (original and revised).

C. Reverse (Cancel) the original invoice (refer to Exercise 2A-21), then issue a correct invoice. If the invoice contains many items, this takes too long and is a waste of an employee's time. The customer receives two invoices (original and revised).

Method **A** will be shown as follows:

1 ➤ Click the **Sales Invoices** icon.

2 ➤ Click the **Look up an invoice** icon .

3 ➤ Search   Click **OK**.

4 ➤ Invoice   Select Invoice #**2315**.

5 ➤   Click the **Adjust Invoice** icon.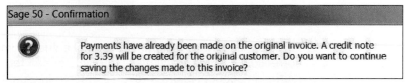

6 ➤   **Base Price**   Change the Base Price to **20.50**, `Tab`.

7 ➤   **Invoice**   Change the invoice number to a code as discussed in Exercise 2A-16. Invoice No.: * 2315Co

8 ➤   **Message**   Type **Price Correction per Mrs. Santos**.

Item Number	Quantity	Order	Back Order	Unit	Item Description	Base Price	Discount	Price	Amount	Tax	Account
Carry-sm	6			Each	Carry-on bag-small	20.50		20.50	123.00	HS	4100 Sales

Subtotal:	123.00
Freight	☑
HST:	15.99 🔍
Total:	138.99
Amount Owing:	-3.39

Early Payment Terms: ___ % ___ Days, Net ___ Days

Message: Price correction per Mrs. Santos

[Post ▾]

9 ➤   Display the Sales Journal entry created by this correction. The window should display as follows:

Sales Journal Entry Mar 06, 2016 (J16)

Account Number	Account Description	Debits	Credits
1200	Accounts Receivable	138.99	-
5010	Cost of Goods Sold	63.00	-
1300	Inventory	-	63.00
2630	HST Charged on Sales	-	15.99
4100	Sales	-	123.00
Additional Date:	Additional Field:		
		201.99	201.99

10 ➤   **Exit** from this window by clicking the ☒ button.

11 ➤   Click the **Post** button.

Sage 50 - Confirmation

❓   Payments have already been made on the original invoice. A credit note for 3.39 will be created for the original customer. Do you want to continue saving the changes made to this invoice?

12 ➤   The Credit Note Number can be changed if required. To continue click **Yes**.

Enter the Credit Note Source Number

Customer payments have been received for the original invoice. To reverse this invoice, a credit note for 3.39 will be created for the original customer.

Please enter a source number for the credit note.

Credit Note Number: CN-2315Co

13 ➤   2 journal entries (J15 and J16) were created, click **OK**.

14 ➤   **Exit** to the Home window.

15 ➤   In the Customers section, at **Hanlan's Luggage Store** click the ▼ and select **Display Customer Aged Detail** to display the report.

Customer Aged Detail As at Mar 07, 2016

Source	Date	Transaction Type	Total	Current	31 to 60
Hanlan's Luggage Store					
2315Co	Mar 06, 2016	Invoice	138.99	138.99	-
739	Mar 06, 2016	Payment	-142.38	-142.38	-
Overpayment	Mar 06, 2016	Payment	3.39	3.39	-
CN-2315Co	Mar 06, 2016	Invoice	-3.39	-3.39	-
Total outstanding:			-3.39	-3.39	-

Original Accounts Receivable Amount	$142.38
Correction of Invoice due to price	138.99
Reduction to cost of merchandise including tax	- 3.39 (overpaid)

Original cost of Carry-on bag-small	$ 21.00 each
Price reduced to	20.50 each
Net reduction	-.50 each

Reduced price for 6 items x -.50	= $-3.00
HST on -3.00	-.39
Total reduction	-3.39

16 ➤ **Exit** from this window by clicking the ☒ button, and return to the Home window.

Remember to back up your data and update your logbook at the end of your work session.

Printing Reports When Needed

The following reports may be printed for management's information and for filing for the audit trail.

- Journal Entries may be printed in one of two ways (see Exercise 1-18).

    a) **All Journal Entries** will print all journal entries from all modules (with or without corrections). All transactions, in the time period requested, are numbered in this journal in sequential order (even if entered in a subledger; i.e., RECEIVABLES or PAYABLES module).

    b) **General Journal Entries** will print journal entries entered in the COMPANY module only.

1 ➤ To save time and paper, **print** only the following:

    a) All Journal Entries (with corrections)   Mar 01 to Mar 07
    b) Income Statement for   Jan 01 to Mar 07
    c) Balance Sheet at   Mar 07
    d) Customer Aged Detail, all customers with terms at Mar 07
    e) General Ledger   Mar 01 to Mar 07

Your instructor may request printouts of the Sales and/or Receipts Journals. See Exercise 2B-41.

Refer to the Glossary for a complete list of Accounting and Sage 50 Premium Accounting 2015 Terminology for the Receivables chapter.

Relevant Appendices, Part A

WWW

The following appendices are available in your course materials at www.nelson.com/student.

Appendix 2015 F	**Periodic Inventory Entries**
Appendix 2015 G	**Updating Inventory and COGS Balances for Companies Using Periodic Inventory System**
Appendix 2015 N	**Adding a Salesperson's Name to an Invoice**
Appendix 2015 Q	**Names Fields**
Appendix 2015 V1	**Perpetual Mini-Guide Receivables—Payables** (in Excel)
Appendix 2015 AB	**Printing in Batches**
Appendix 2015 AC	**Batch Processing**

Summary, Part A

Here is a summary of the transactions entered in this chapter:

Transaction:	Journal/Ledger:	Remarks:
Sales Quotes	*Sales Quotes*	Creates a quote (with inventory) that may be printed and sent to a customer. Sage 50 Accounting records it in the Sales Quote database, but does not post to the General Ledger.
Sales Order	*Sales Orders*	Creates a sales order record (with inventory) when an order is received from a customer. May be created by converting an existing sales quote. Sage 50 Accounting records in the Sales Order Listing, but does not post to the General Ledger.
Sale on Account	*Sales Invoices*	Records SALES (with inventory). Sage 50 Accounting automatically debits Accounts Receivable and credits the appropriate tax accounts, and increases the Cost of Goods Sold and decreases the Inventory.
Sales Adjustment	*Sales Invoices*	Use Adjustment icon.
Return on Account/ Credit Memo	*Sales*	Enter the memo as a minus amount with HST.
Receipt	*Receipts*	Select the invoice(s) paid.
Receipt with Discount	*Receipts*	Apply the receipt against the original invoice less the discount amount calculated on the sales amount before taxes.
New Customer	*Customers*	Remember to select an appropriate Revenue account and appropriate tax code for each customer.
Cancel an Invoice	*Sales*	Use the **Reverse Invoice** icon to reverse the original invoice. Can also be seen in Chapter 13.
Revise a Cash Receipt	*Receipts*	Use **Lookup** to find the original receipt and adjust the amounts as required. Can also be seen in Chapter 13.

Before Moving On ... Part A

Read the following questions and make sure you know the answers to them; otherwise, review the corresponding section in the chapter before moving on.

1. What types of transactions are journalized in the RECEIVABLES module?

2. What is the main difference in journalizing transactions between the RECEIVABLES module and the COMPANY module?

3. What occurs when you post journal transactions in the RECEIVABLES module?

4. Why would a business need to use more than one bank account?

5. Explain the concept of aging in customer accounts.

6. Name at least two uses of the Customer Aged Detail report.

7. What is the difference between a sales quote and a sales order?

8. The default Revenue account is used for what purpose?

9. What is a cheque payment advice?

10. When recording a return of inventory (e.g., product), which journal do you record the transaction in: Sales Quote, Sales Order, Sales Invoice, or Receipts Journal?

11. What is the entry for a Sales Return?

Challenge Exercise 02 C2A-1, Clocks
(RECEIVABLES and COMPANY Modules)

Clocks is a business that sells various type of clocks (e.g., table, desk, grandfather) and is open 7 days a week.

You do *NOT* need to print Sales invoices or receipts. Terms are varied for different customers. HST is 13%.

   1 ➤ Refer to Exercise 1-1b to unzip the **02 C2A-1 Clocks.exe** file.

   2 ➤ Open the **02 C2A-1 Clocks** file, and enter the following Accounts Receivable transactions for May:

May 1   Sold 10 desk clocks, model #256, code DC-01 at $30.00 each, plus HST, to Carney's Clocks. Invoice #212 issued with terms 2/10, net 30.

May 1   Issued Sales Quote #136 to **Your Name** (Your actual name must appear). Terms net 5 days. Other information: 623 Autumn Breeze Way, Mississauga, Ontario, L5B 9P2. Phone and fax numbers may be left blank. Credit limit $2,500.00 for a grandfather model AC clock, code GF-AC, at $2,000.00, plus HST. Free delivery and setup of the clock. Your Name will return from a business trip on Friday, May 4 and will advise about the quote on the clock. Ship date Tuesday, May 8.

May 4   **Your Name** accepted quote #136 and ordered the grandfather clock. The order was increased to include 2 travel alarm clocks, code TC-01, at $35.00 each, plus HST.

May 5   Issued invoice #213 for sale of one antique-style desk clock, code DC-AS for $140.00, plus HST, to Carlton Shippers. Cheque #258 received.

May 8   The grandfather and travel alarm clocks on Order #136 were delivered to **Your Name** and the grandfather clock was installed. Invoice #214 was left at the home.

May 9   Issued sales order #137 to wholesale customer Sandy's Clock Town, for 10 desk clocks model #899, code DC-03, at $62.50 each, plus HST. The clocks are scheduled to be shipped May 14. Terms are net 2/10, net 30 days.

May 10 Your Name returned one of the travel alarm clocks, as it does not work. Your Name does not want a replacement. Credit his/her account.

May 11 Received cheque #847 from Carney's Clocks to pay for outstanding invoice #212.

May 13 Received cheque #148, as payment from Your Name re: invoice #214.

May 14 Issued invoice #215 to Sandy's Clock Town for 7 desk clocks for their order. Three clocks are back ordered and will be shipped on May 23. (Close the confirmation window advising that you are below the re-order point for this item.)

   3 ➤ When you have recorded the above entries, **print** the following reports:

       a)   Customer Aged Detail, all customers, with terms at May 14
       b)   All Journal Entries for May 1 to 14
       c)   Sales Journal Entries for May 1 to 14
       d)   Receipts Journal Entries for May 1 to 14
       e)   Income Statement for Jan 1 to May 14
       f)   Pending Sales Order Detail, by customer, May 14

Challenge Exercise 02 C2A-2, Dog Walkers
(RECEIVABLES and COMPANY Modules)

Dog Walkers is a business that looks after pets during the day or evening, or when the owners are away for a period of time. The business takes the dogs for walks and to play in parks.

You do *NOT* need to print Sales invoices or receipts.

Note: All invoices are left at the residence or business at the end of each week (5-day walking) or at the end of the walking period if the period is less than a week. Terms are varied for different customers. HST is 13%.

1 ➤ Refer to Exercise 1-1b to unzip the **02 C2A-2 Walkers.exe** file.

2 ➤ Open the **02 C2A-2 Walkers** file, and enter the following Accounts Receivable transactions for May.

May 1   Issued Sales Quote #362 to Ms. Sadia Kalirai for 3 walking services at $20.00, plus HST per day, starting on Friday, May 4. Terms net 3 days.

May 2   Left invoice #782 for 4-day walking services for Ms. Rachel Tran's dog, at $20.00 plus HST per day with terms of net 3 days.

May 2   Ms. Sadia Kalirai accepted quote #362.

May 5   Received cheque #829 from Ms. Rachel Tran for invoice #782.

May 6   Issued and left invoice #783, on order #362, for $67.80 (3 days service at $20.00 per day plus HST) at Ms. Sadia Kalirai's home.

May 7   Issued sales order #363 to a new business client, Your Name Transport (Your Name must appear), to take their 2 security dogs for walks. The first Sales order is for a minimum of 10 days for the month. Use May 31 as the Ship Date. The dogs are to go on longer walks and the charge will be $40.00 plus HST per visit. Other information: 889 Ancaster Avenue, Stoney Creek, Ontario, L8E 6Z9. Phone and fax numbers may be left blank. Terms are 2% 10 days net 20 days. (Special terms arranged for business clients.) Credit limit $500.00.

May 8   Received $41.00 Bank Debit memo re: service charges on the Bank account.

May 8   Received cheque #529 from Ms. Kalirai for invoice #783.

May 11   Issued invoice #784 against sales order #363 to Your Name Transport for 3 days walking.

May 21   Received cheque #8961 from Your Name Transport for invoice #784.

May 21   Issued invoice #785 to Mr. Manpreet Foss for 2 days walking services at $20.00 per day, plus HST. Mr. Foss paid by cheque #603.

3 ➤ When you have recorded the above entries, **print** the following:

    a) Customer Aged Detail, all customers, with terms, at May 21
    b) All Journal Entries for May 1 to 21
    c) General Journal Entries for May 1 to 21
    d) Sales Journal Entries for May 1 to 21
    e) Pending Sales Order Detail, by Customer, May 31
    f) Income Statement for Jan 1 to May 21

Chapter 2B

RECEIVABLES Module—*Beyond Basics*

Santos Luggage

Learning Objectives
After completing this chapter you will be able to:

☐ Revise (increase or decrease) invoices for quantity or prices.
☐ Track Additional Information in transactions.
☐ Use the Daily Business Manager and other Sage 50 Accounting special features.
☐ Journalize Deposits with a Sales Order.
☐ Journalize Cash/Cheque/Bank Debit Card sales.
☐ Journalize Credit Card Sales.
☐ Journalize a Customer Account Write-Off and/or NSF Cheques.
☐ Apply Deposits to Invoices.
☐ Journalize a Cash Sale with a Discount and/or Credit Card Receipts.
☐ Journalize Owner Investment.
☐ Journalize non-merchandise receipt.
☐ Process deposits from customers for sales orders.
☐ Use Display and print various Receivable reports and journals.
☐ Set up an inventory service item.

This chapter is a continuation of Chapter 2A. You should download the 02 2B Luggage-PI-2B data file for use with this chapter.

The contents of this chapter are as follows:

Opening the RECEIVABLES Module, Part B

In this chapter (2B), you will access the RECEIVABLES module of Santos Luggage and enter transactions related to sales, receipts of payment from customers, and other Receivable transactions, starting from March 8.

The 02 2B Luggage-PI-2B.exe file contains the ending balances of the General Ledger accounts, Customers files, and Inventory items from Chapter 2A of this text (see Trial Balance shown on next page). These balances will be the starting point of the PI-2B file, and journal entries will start at J1.

Exercise 2B-25—Opening the 02 2B Luggage-PI-B data file

> Review Exercise 1-2 if you need help to open a data file.

1 ➤ Refer to Exercise 1-1b to unzip the **02 2B Luggage-PI-2B.exe** file.

2 ➤ Start **Sage 50 Accounting**.

3 ➤ At the Select Company window, click **Select an existing company** button, and **OK**.

4 ➤ At the Sage 50 Accounting **Open Company window**, in the left panel, locate your student location drive and the 📁02 2B Luggage-PI-2B folder.

5 ➤ **Double-click** the 📁02 2B Luggage-PI-2B folder. The 📁 02 2B Luggage-PI-2B.SAJ folder and the 📄02 2B Luggage-PI-2B.SAI file should appear in the right pane. The image at the left of Luggage may be different, depending on the configuration of your computer, and the SAI may be in lowercase.

6 ➤ Double-click the 📄02 2B Luggage-PI-2B.SAI file icon.

7 ➤ The Session date will be Mar 07, 2016. Click **OK**.

8 ➤ Remember to change the company name to include your name; e.g., **Santos Luggage, Guida Marisa**.

Santos Luggage-P1-2B, Student's Name
Trial Balance As At Mar 07, 2016

		Debits	Credits
1020	Bank Chequing Account	22,817.19	-
1030	Visa Credit Card Bank Account	600.00	-
1200	Accounts Receivable	11,920.47	-
1210	Allowance for Doubtful Accounts		2,440.00
1300	Inventory	22,506.00	-
1320	Prepaid Supplies	712.00	-
1420	Office/Warehouse Furniture/Equip...	25,163.00	
1425	Accum. Deprec. Office/Ware Furn/E...	-	4,100.00
2200	Accounts Payable	-	11,255.00
2630	HST Charged on Sales	-	1,426.80
2640	HST Paid On Purchases	525.00	-
3100	Capital, Maria Santos	-	62,724.68
3160	Additional Investment	-	0.00
3180	Drawings, Maria Santos	2,200.00	-
4100	Sales	-	42,811.00
4150	Sales-Discounts	342.00	-
4200	Sales-Returns & Allowances	681.00	-
4510	Handling Fee	-	15.00
5010	Cost of Goods Sold	25,494.00	-
5080	Purchase Discounts	-	335.00
5090	Inventory Adjustments	0.00	-
5310	Wages Expense	8,000.00	-
5320	Advertising Expense	432.00	-
5330	Bank Charges & Interest	95.00	-
5340	Credit Card Charges	34.30	-
5350	Rent Expense	800.00	-
5370	Bad Debt Expense	0.00	-
5410	Office/Warehouse Supplies Expense	216.00	-
5450	Rent Expense Warehouse	2,000.00	-
5460	Utility Expense	263.89	-
5550	Telephone Expense	305.63	-
		125,107.48	125,107.48

Slideshow 2B—RECEIVABLES Module Beyond Basics demonstrates the use of Sage 50 Accounting special features and more transaction processing techniques. Run it now.

Using Sage 50 Accounting Special Features

Sage 50 Accounting has some special features that maximize efficiency in your everyday tasks and optimize the use of computerized accounting software. You learned earlier how to use the Daily Business Manager. Below are special features relevant to tasks involving sales and customers.

The Lookup Feature

The **Invoice Lookup** feature shown in the next exercise can be used when management wants to view previously posted invoices in order to verify details. This is especially useful if the paper copy of the invoice(s) cannot be located, or to locate a previously posted invoice that you wish to correct.

Exercise 2B-26a—Processing a Transaction with an Increase in Quantity

---

In this exercise you will record a transaction while the customer, Mr. Tran, is still in the store and the order is being prepared. After the invoice is **Posted**, the customer decided to increase the quantity for the carry-on bags. You could prepare a new invoice for the additional items, but the customer wants all the items on one invoice.

You will be shown how to correct the posted invoice in the exercise that follows.

1 ➤ Advance the Session date to **Mar 08, 2016**.

2 ➤ **Record** and **Post** the following transaction.

On future invoices, if **Shipped by** details are not provided, do NOT enter any information. Also assume **Mailing address** and **Ship to** address are the same if not specified.

Mar 08, 2016	**Sold 15 Carry-on bag–small at $21.00 each and 3 Power Adapters at $10.50 each, plus HST, to a new customer, Tran's Luggage Warehouse, contact person is Huong Tran, 875 Burke Avenue, Markham, Ontario L2S 2Y9. Phone number 905-768-3620, the default Revenue account is 4100, price list is Regular, terms are 2/10, net 30, tax code is HS, credit limit is $1,500.00. Invoice #2316 for $391.55 including $45.05 HST.**

To Correct a Posted Invoice

✓ You will now correct the invoice that you just posted.

Exercise 2B-26b—Correcting a Posted Invoice (Lookup Feature)

It is assumed that you are still in the Sales Journal-Creating an Invoice window.

1 ➤ **Invoice**   Click the 🖼 **Invoice Lookup** icon and the Search window appears.

2 ➤ Click **OK**, and the Select an Invoice Window appears.

3 ➤ With **Invoice 2316** highlighted, click **Select**. The Sales Journal-Invoice Lookup window appears with the original 2316 invoice. (See side note box.)

If other invoices were posted, you could use the 🔲🔲 **Look up previous** or **Look up next** icons to move forward or backward in the list of invoices.

4 ➤ Click the 🖼 **Adjust Invoice** icon. (The icon is identical to the Adjust Receipt icon used previously.) The 🖼 Sales Journal - Adjusting Invoice 2316 banner appears at the top.

5 ➤ Change the 15 Carry-on bag–small to **18**, [Tab]. The Invoice total changes to $462.74, which includes $53.24 HST.

6 ➤ **Post** this transaction. You may see the following window.

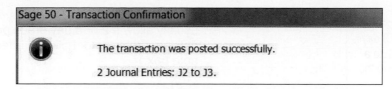

Sage 50 - Transaction Confirmation

(i) The transaction was posted successfully.

2 Journal Entries: J2 to J3.

The J2 and J3 are referencing the reversal and correction entries. **Exit** to the Home window.

To Track Additional Transaction Details

This feature is the same as the feature you used in Chapter 1, Exercise 1-12. You will be able to add additional information about transactions when required.

Exercise 2B-27—Using the Additional Transaction Details

Mrs. Santos has decided to have the **Additional Date and Information** fields available and used when appropriate. You have been asked to use this feature.

> **Mar 08 2016** **Received cheque #1256 dated Mar 07, 2016 in the amount of $2,175.60 (after a net $39.20 discount after the return) from Havarah Leather Goods on Invoice #2253. Use additional transaction detail information as noted in this exercise.**

1 ➤ Click the **Receipts** icon.

2 ➤ **From** Click the ▼ and select **Havarah Leather Goods**. **Record** this transaction using the **Mar 08, 2016** date as the transaction date (the actual date the cheque was deposited — this will match up to the bank statement). **Don't forget to input cheque #1256 into the cheque number and receipt fields**.

The cheque was mailed by the customer on the 10th day of the discount period and should be given the discount. In steps 3 and 8, at the Discount Taken field, you will type the Discount taken amount to override the blank amount shown.

Invoice Date	Invoice or Deposit	Original Amount	Amount Owing	Discount Available	Discount Taken	Amount Received
Feb 26, 2016	2253	2,373.00	2,373.00	0.00		
	2253Rt CM124	-158.20	-158.20	0.00		

(i)

Note the Invoice Date column. Sage 50 Accounting does not display the date of the return or other credits.

3 ➤ Change the date to **Mar 07, 2016** and the Discount Available field changes to 42.00 with the return discount -2.80 as a negative. (See side note box.)

Invoice Date	Invoice or Deposit	Original Amount	Amount Owing	Discount Available	Discount Taken	Amount Received
Feb 26, 2016	2253	2,373.00	2,373.00	42.00		
	2253Rt CM124	-158.20	-158.20	-2.80		

4 ➤ Change the date back to **Mar 08, 2016**. You will note that the **Discount Available** field is back to 0.00, [Tab].

5 ➤ **Invoice or Deposit** At invoice 2253, [Tab].

6 ➤ Discount Taken Type **42.00** to allow the discount, ⎡Tab⎤. Management will usually allow a 2 or 3 day grace period as there could be mail delivery problems or holidays affecting the delivery. (See side note box.)

> If it is longer than 3 days, you need to speak to a manager to approve the discount.

7 ➤ Amount Received ⎡Tab⎤ to accept 2,331.00. The cursor moves to the 2253Rt CM124 Discount Taken line.

Original Purchase $ 2,100.00	Discount available $ 42.00
Less Return (140.00)	Return Discount lost (2.80)
Net Sale $ 1,960.00 x 2% = $39.20	Net Discount $ 39.20

8 ➤ Discount Taken Type **-2.80**, ⎡Tab⎤ to allow the negative discount on the return.

9 ➤ Amount Received ⎡Tab⎤ to accept -155.40. The lower portion should resemble the following:

Invoice Date	Invoice or Deposit	Original Amount	Amount Owing	Discount Available	Discount Taken	Amount Received
Feb 26, 2016	2253	2,373.00	2,373.00	0.00	42.00	2,331.00
	2253Rt CM124	-158.20	-158.20	0.00	-2.80	-155.40
					Total	2,175.60

10 ➤ Click the **Additional Information** icon 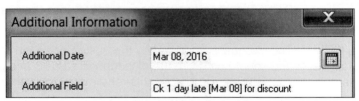 and record the information to show that a cheque dated on the 7th was received and deposited on the 8th.

Additional Information	✕
Additional Date	Mar 08, 2016 🗓
Additional Field	Ck 1 day late [Mar 08] for discount

11 ➤ Click **OK**. Display the Receipts Journal Entry.

The journal entry window should look like the following:

Receipts Journal Entry Mar 08, 2016 (J4)

Account Number	Account Description	Debits	Credits
1020	Bank Chequing Account	2,175.60	-
4150	Sales -Discounts	39.20	-
1200	Accounts Receivable	-	2,214.80
Additional Date: Ma...	Additional Field: Ck 1 day late (Mar...		
		2,214.80	2,214.80

12 ➤ Exit the journal window. You can leave the Comment field blank. **Post** this transaction.

1 ➤   **Record** and **post** the following transaction:

Mar 08, 2016   **Sold to Havarah Leather Goods, 10 Briefcase-regular at $100.00 each, 3 Briefcase-wide at $120.00 each, 3 Carry-on bag–small at $21.00 each, 15 Suitcase w/w Large at $62.00 each, plus HST. Terms are 2/10, net 30. HST in the amount of $305.89 is added to the goods sold to give a final invoice total of $2,658.89.**

---

2 ➤   Advance the date to **Mar 10, 2016**.

3 ➤   **Record** and **post** the following transaction:

Mar 10, 2016   **Sold to Royes Luggage Inc., 10 Laptop Back Paks at $70.00 each, 10 Locks-combination at $3.50 each (reduce the Base Price), and 14 Suitcase w/w Regular at $56.00, each plus HST. Terms are 2/10, net 30. HST in the amount of $197.47 is added to the goods sold to give a final invoice total of $1,716.47.**

---

4 ➤   When finished processing the transaction, **Exit** from the Sales Journal and return to the Home window.

Exercise 2B-28—Using the Daily Business Manager (DBM)

---

1 ➤   Advance the Session date to **Mar 17, 2016**.

2 ➤   In Exercise 2A-23 at step 15 you identified Mar 17 as the date to display the memo note in the Daily Business Manager. To see the note, click the **Daily Business Manager** (DBM) icon on the tool bar at the top. Click the **Notes & To Do List** bullet (it may be selected when you open the DBM), then select **Mar 17**. If the Memo tab information is not displayed in the lower window, click the **Memo** tab. The clerk would advise management about the memo note for further action.

3 ➤   **Display**   In Exercise 2A-11, you were shown how to display the Business Performance window. Select **Business Performance**. You can now see that the straight line (in Exercise 2A-11) has changed with the entries you have recorded.

4 ➤   **Display**   Click **Sales (Past 7 Days)** to see another change. This information can be very helpful for management when planning staff work schedules.

5 ➤   Return to the Home window.

Journalizing a Deposit

Assume you have received an order of 40 Suitcases with wheels Large for March 29 (a future date) of $2,480.00, plus HST of $322.40 for a total of $2,802.40. The customer pays a deposit of $1,000.00 to ensure that the goods are delivered on time. The deposit is usually applied toward the final price.

When you record a deposit of $1,000.00 before a sale is completed, it is entered as a **credit** in the customer RECEIVABLES Ledger. Since there is no sale, it is, in essence, a negative receivable and the money is owed to the customer until the corresponding service is rendered or goods are delivered.

Exercise 2B-29 will show you how to record a deposit as you record a Sales Order.

Remember: A deposit cannot be recorded on a Sales Quote.

A deposit transaction is not a sale but rather a deposit on a future sale.
Sage 50 Accounting would record the following entry as an example:

Dr BANK ACCOUNT $1,000.00
        Cr ACCOUNTS RECEIVABLE $1,000.00

This, in effect, gives the customer a **credit** balance of $1,000.00.

When the goods or services are delivered, the sale is recorded with a **debit** invoice ($2,802.40) in the customer RECEIVABLES Ledger.

When the remaining outstanding balance ($1,802.40) on the invoice is received, the $1,802.40 receipt and the $1,000.00 prepayment are applied to the total invoice of $2,802.40, to clear the invoice from the outstanding list. (The invoice would then be fully paid.)

Exercise 2B-29—Journalizing a Deposit with a Sales Order

You will now journalize the $1,000.00 deposit as you record the Sales Order.

Study the transaction:

Mar 15, 2016 **Opal Kong Luggage Ltd. has placed an order for 40 Suitcase w/w Large. The cost will be $62.00 each, plus HST. Total order including HST is $2,802.40. Requested shipping date is Mar 29, 2016. We have received Opal Kong Luggage Ltd.'s cheque #433 for a $1,000.00 deposit (or prepayment) on this Order.**

To Record the Sales Order

1 ➤   Create an Order using the **Sales Order** icon.

2 ➤   **Transaction**   Do NOT change, from Order.

3 ➤   **Customer**   Select **Opal Kong Luggage Ltd.**, [Tab].

       Before you continue, look at the Date and Shipping Date fields. There is no field between them.

4 ➤   **Payment**   Select **Cheque.** You will now see the
      Method   fields `Deposit Ref. No.: *` [   ] between the Date and Shipping Date fields. You will also see
       `Deposit Applied:` [   ] field in the lower section. You will use these fields in steps 8 and 12 of this exercise. [Tab].

      Deposit To   Do NOT change.

5 ➤ Cheque No.   Type **433**, `Tab` .

6 ➤ Order No.   Order number 104 displays/ `Tab` `Tab` . New in 2015: Sage 50 Accounting creates the Order numbers..

7 ➤ Date   Select **Mar 15, 2016**, the day the cheque is received. `Tab` `Tab` .

8 ➤ Deposit Ref No.   **Dp SO#104** refers to Deposit Special Order #104. Some companies will use the number of the cheque received and others may use a deposit reference number, which is different than the cheque number received. `Tab` .

9 ➤ Complete the rest of the information as follows:

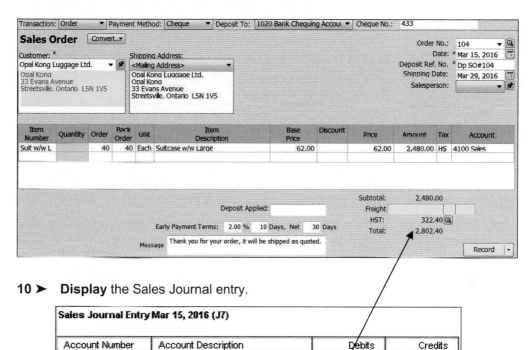

10 ➤ **Display** the Sales Journal entry.

Sales Journal Entry Mar 15, 2016 (J7)			
Account Number	Account Description	Debits	Credits
There is no data to report.			

11 ➤ J7 reports no data because no goods have been sold. **Exit** to the Sales Order window.

12 ➤ Enter the $1000.00 information in the lower part of the window as shown.

Deposit Applied: 1,000.00 The amount will be applied to the client record.

Notice that the Sales Order Total (2,802.40) has not changed. The order is still for the full amount.

Amount Owing   The field **Amount Owing** may not be seen until after the Sales Order has been recorded.

13 ➤ **Display** the Sales Journal entry; it should look like the following. The entry records the money received on the Sales Order.

Sales Journal Entry Mar 15, 2016 (J7)

Account Number	Account Description	Debits	Credits
1020	Bank Chequing Account	1,000.00	-
1200	Accounts Receivable	-	1,000.00
Additional Date:	Additional Field:		
		1,000.00	1,000.00

14 ➤ **Exit** from the entry and **Record** the transaction.

15 ➤ **Exit** to the Home window.

16 ➤ Display the **Customer Aged Detail Report** for Opal Kong for **Mar 17, 2016** (see Exercise 2A-4: Displaying/Printing Customer Aged Report).

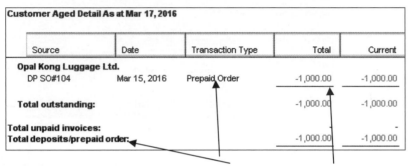

Customer Aged Detail As at Mar 17, 2016

Source	Date	Transaction Type	Total	Current
Opal Kong Luggage Ltd.				
DP SO#104	Mar 15, 2016	Prepaid Order	-1,000.00	-1,000.00
Total outstanding:			-1,000.00	-1,000.00
Total unpaid invoices:			-	-
Total deposits/prepaid order:			-1,000.00	-1,000.00

The Opal Kong report shows a deposit (Prepaid Order) of **-1,000.00** in two places.

17 ➤ **Exit** from the Aged Detail Report and return to the Home window.

Journalizing Cash/Cheque/Bank Debit Card Sales

This type of sale can be recorded in the Sales Journal as a One-time customer, because you do not expect to have repeat sales with the customer. This option is appropriate because there is no need to keep detailed computer records for a One-time customer. However, the sales record is useful for the audit trail or for inquiries of goods sold, etc.

When you use this option, Sage 50 Accounting automatically allows you to enter only a sale paid by cash, cheque, credit or bank debit card. This means that nothing (name or amounts) will be posted to the ACCOUNTS RECEIVABLE account in the G/L. The One-time customer transaction will appear in the journal and ledger printouts similar to:

Mar 15, 2016	J8	456, 2319, <One-time customer>

The sales invoice will, however, record the name/address of the customer in the lower box and can be viewed at a later time.

The next cash transaction exercise shows you how to enter the name of a One-time customer in the lower **Sold to** field. This allows you to have the One-time customer wording (instead of name) as shown above to appear in journal entries.

Exercise 2B-30—Journalizing a Retail Sale (by cheque)

> **Mar 15, 2016** Mrs. Arlene Hirsch has purchased from the outlet store
> 2 Suitcase w/w Large at $80.00, 2 Carry-on bag–small at
> $28.00, and 2 Locks-combination at $4.50 each, plus HST.
> Cheque #456 for $254.25 was accepted.

1 ➤ Create an invoice using the **Sales Invoices** icon.

    Transaction Do NOT change the default Invoice.

2 ➤ Payment Method Select **Cheque**, ⌨Tab.

3 ➤ Deposit to Do NOT change, ⌨Tab to accept 1020 Bank Account.

4 ➤ Cheque Type **456**. ⌨Tab.

5 ➤ Customer Click the ▾ and select **<One-time customer>**. ⌨Tab ⌨Tab.

For audit trail information and verification purposes you should type in the name of the customer (as shown) and address information. The manager, however, decided you do not need the cash customer's address. Enter the information as shown next.

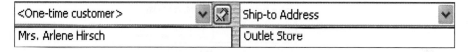

<One-time customer> ▾ 🔲	Ship-to Address ▾
Mrs. Arlene Hirsch	Outlet Store

6 ➤ Ship-to-Address Type **Outlet Store**. This indicates that the customer has picked up the goods from the Outlet Store. ⌨Tab, and click the Invoice field.

7 ➤ Invoice ⌨Tab to accept 2319. ⌨Tab to Date.

8 ➤ Date Select **March 15, 2016**. ⌨Tab and click the **Item Number** field.

9 ➤ Enter the information shown in Fig. 2B-18.

The Sales Invoice window should appear as follows: (See side note box.)

Transaction: Invoice	Payment Method: Cheque	Deposit To: 1020 Bank Chequing Accoul	Cheque No.: * 456

Sales Invoice

Invoice No.: * 2319
Date: * Mar 15, 2016
Shipping Date:
Salesperson:

Customer: *
<One-time customer>
Mrs. Arlene Hirsch

Shipping Address:
Ship-to Address
Outlet Store

Division:

Item Number	Quantity	Order	Back Order	Unit	Item Description	Base Price	Discount	Price	Amount	Tax	Account
Suit w/w	2			Each	Suitcase w/w Large	80.00		80.00	160.00	HS	4100 Sales
Carry-sm	2			Each	Carry-on bag-small	28.00		28.00	56.00	HS	4100 Sales
Locks-1	2			Each	Locks-combination	4.50		4.50	9.00	HS	4100 Sales

Early Payment Discount: ____ %

Cheque Amount: 254.25

Subtotal:	225.00
Freight	
HST:	29.25
Total:	254.25

Message: Thank you for your order.

Post

Cheque Amount: 254.25

in the bottom middle indicates the amount of cash, cheque, or bank debit card received.

Fig. 2B-18: Retail Sale (by cheque) Invoice window.

The Early Payment Discount field would be used for a customer who received terms of 2/10, net 30 days, and who buys today and pays today. Mrs. Hirsch does not receive this discount.

10 ➤ **Display** the Sales Journal Entry. The window should appear as follows:

Sales Journal Entry Mar 15, 2016 (J8)

Account Number	Account Description	Debits	Credits
1020	Bank Chequing Account	254.25	-
5010	Cost of Goods Sold	87.00	-
1300	Inventory	-	87.00
2630	HST Charged on Sales	-	29.25
4100	Sales	-	225.00
Additional Date:	Additional Field:		
		341.25	341.25

11 ➤ **Exit** from the display window.

12 ➤ **Post** when correct and **Exit** to the Home window.

Journalizing a Credit Card Sale

Credit Card sales are, in essence, **cash** sales. However, journalizing them is a bit different from a sale where the customer pays cash or uses a bank (debit) card. When a customer pays with a credit card, the vendor's credit card company charges the vendor a fee for the privilege of accepting the credit card. This is called a **discount charge**. The credit card discount rate varies depending on the dollar volume of sales processed by the vendor.

When journalizing this type of sale, the sale amount is reduced by the amount of the credit card company's discount fee, and the discount fee is entered as a separate item.

Depending on the arrangement with the credit card company, your bank may credit your account for this type of sale, or you may be required to deposit credit card receipts at your bank.

Exercise 2B-31—Journalizing a Credit Card Sale

Santos Luggage has arranged to have credit card receipts credited automatically to their bank account.

The credit card discount fee for Santos Luggage is 3.5% of the sales amount (including taxes) and is entered in a separate account; e.g., 5340 Credit Card Charges. In Chapter 4, you will see how to set up a credit card and discount fee rate.

> **Mar 17, 2016**   **Another sale from the Outlet Store. Mr. Jerry Tyson, of Tyson's Toys, used his business credit card to purchase 1 Briefcase-wide for $135.00, plus HST. The invoice total was $152.55, including taxes.**

1 ➤   Create an invoice using the **Sales Invoice** icon.

     Transaction   Do NOT change Invoice.

2 ➤   **Payment Method**   Select **Visa Credit**. Santos Luggage accepts the Visa Credit Card. [Tab].

3 ➤   **Customer**   Type **Mr. Jerry Tyson**, [Tab], **Continue**, click **OK**. This is similar to selecting <One-time Customer>, but as noted previously, the customer's name will appear in the printouts, similar to Visa Credit, 2320, Mr. Jerry Tyson. This is the author's recommended way to record this type of transaction, as the customer's name will display and print in the journals and G/L. To ensure privacy, do NOT type credit card numbers on-screen. They should be recorded on paper only. Type **Outlet Store** as shown. [Tab].

     Invoice   **2320** is correct.

     Date   **Mar 17, 2016** is correct.

4 ➤   Enter the information shown next:

Item Number	Quantity	Order	Back Order	Unit	Item Description	Base Price	Discount (%)	Price	Amount	Tax	Account
Brief-W	1			Each	Briefcase-wide	135.00		135.00	135.00	HS	4100 Sales

     Discount   There is no discount on this sale.

     Tax   Mr. Tyson is purchasing this for personal use. He pays 13% HST.

The window should display the following:

Fig. 2B-19: Sales Journal—Sales Invoice for credit card sale (see side note box).

ℹ Because you selected **Visa Credit** in the **Paid By** box on the sales invoice when you journalized the transaction, Sage 50 Accounting automatically deducted the $5.34 discount fee (invoice total of $152.55 x 3.5%) and posted it to **5340 Credit Card Charges**. The remainder $147.21 is debited to **1030 Visa Credit Card Bank Account**.

The **Total** and **Visa Credit Amount** of $152.55 on the sales invoice remain the same.

5 ➤ Display the Sales Journal entry.

Sales Journal Entry Mar 17, 2016 (J9)

Account Number	Account Description	Debits	Credits
1030	Visa Credit Card Bank Account	147.21	-
5010	Cost of Goods Sold	60.00	-
5340	Credit Card Charges	5.34	-
1300	Inventory	-	60.00
2630	HST Charged on Sales	-	17.55
4100	Sales	-	135.00
Additional Date:	Additional Field:		
		212.55	212.55

6 ➤ **Exit** from the display window.

7 ➤ **Post** when correct and **Exit** to the Home window. You may see the Sage 50 Accounting *Credit Cards Processing with Sage Payment Solutions* window information. This feature requires the user to pay a user fee for this service. This feature will not be discussed in this text. Click **Do Not Show Me again**, to exit to the Home window.

8 ➤ Advance the Session date to **Mar 18, 2016**.

Journalizing a Customer Account Write-Off

A write-off may be either a reduction by the full amount or by a partial amount from a specific invoice or the balance in the customer ledger. When all attempts to collect the amount from the customer have failed due to bankruptcy, business closing, etc., the account balance of the customer would be written off.

If there is a dispute over the goods or services supplied, a partial or full write-off on the specific invoice may be made. In the next exercise, a portion of an invoice will be written off after you received notification from the customer's lawyer that the company declared bankruptcy and the cheque received, a partial payment of an invoice, will be the final amount paid.

> **Mar 18, 2016 Received cheque #3431 for $904.00 and a letter from Spiller Luggage Stores' lawyer advising our company that Spiller Luggage had a severe (uninsured) fire at their store, and they have declared bankruptcy. The cheque received is the final amount to be received.**
>
> **Maria Santos, the owner, reviewed the letter and advised you to write off the $2,712.00 difference to the following accounts:**
>
> | | |
> |---|---|
> | **Allowance for Doubtful Accounts** | **$2,400.00** |
> | **HST ON SALES** | **$ 312.00** |
> | **Total to be written off** | **$2,712.00** |
>
> **Mrs. Santos advised you to record a notation in the client memo file that $2,712.00 has been written off.**

ℹ️ The user could confirm the invoice/balance outstanding and related details (e.g., invoice #, date) by viewing the Customer Aged record for Spiller Luggage Stores before writing off the account.

To record the write-off properly, you should do it in three steps:

1. Update the customer memo notes if required.
2. Record the write-off.
3. Record the receipt.

Mrs. Santos has asked you to first enter a note in the customer's file, then record the write-off and record the receipt.

Exercise 2B-32—Recording a Note in a Customer's File

Record a Note in a Customer's File

Refer to Exercise 2A-23, step 14, which specifically describes the memo tab in the customer's Receivables Ledger file.

1 ➤ In the Customers area, click the ▼ at **Spiller Luggage Stores** click **View Customer Record**.

2 ➤ Click the **Memo** tab, and enter the following information.

> Mar 18, 2016 Received $904.00 cheque ($800.00 plus $104 HST) from customer's lawyer regarding business bankruptcy. Wrote off the account balance of $2,712.00 per memo from Mrs. Santos.

> **To-Do Date**   Leave blank. No need to have this information reported later.
>
> Management may want to remove the Spiller account information from the Customer's section of the Home window. You would click the ☐ Inactive Customer icon.
>
> *Note*: The Home window ☑ Include inactive customers must also be unchecked. Do NOT click the box for now.

3 ➤ Click **Save and Close**, return to the Home window.

Exercise 2B-33a—Journalizing a Partial Write-Off

Follow this procedure to write off the $2,712.00 difference for invoice #2230 using a negative invoice.

1 ➤ In the **Customers** area, click the ▼ at Spiller Luggage Stores, click **Create Invoice**.

Transaction	Do NOT change from **Invoice**.
Payment Method	Do NOT change from **Pay Later**. (You must use **Pay Later** to match the write-off to the previous sale.)

> When writing off an account, the individual sale items are not adjusted. The customer has the inventory and the balance owing will not be paid.

2 ➤ **Invoice** Type **2230Wo**, [Tab] [Tab]. Sage 50 Accounting does not allow the entry of an invoice number twice, so adding **Wo** (code for **w**rite-**o**ff) to the original invoice number allows you to reference the write-off to the original sales invoice. (See side note box.)

3 ➤ **Date** [Tab] to accept Mar 18, 2016 (18th is the date the decision was made to write off the amount). Click on **Item Description**.

4 ➤ **Item Description** Type **Write-off partial invoice balance**. [Tab]. Click on **Amount**.

5 ➤ **Amount** Type **-2400.00**. The minus sign before the amount will make this entry a Debit to the account selected. [Tab] to accept.

6 ➤ **Tax** [Tab] to select code **HS**.

7 ➤ **Acct** Press [Enter]. Select account **1210 Allowance for Doubtful Accounts**, [Tab]. (See side note box.)

8 ➤ **Terms** Remove **2, 10, 30**. There is no discount on a write-off.

9 ➤ **Message** Type **Write-off approved by Mrs. Santos**. [Tab].

> Alternatively, some companies employ the Direct Write-Off method and write off accounts as they become uncollectible. Bad Debt Expense is charged when the customer's account is closed. The **Allowance** method, used in this text, is the GAAP preferred method.
>
> The Allowance for Doubtful Accounts now has a balance of 40.00 (original balance 2,440 -2,400). The Allowance would need adjusting to increase the amount for future uncollectable customers.
>
> The allowance is adjusted to **Bad Debts Expense** when required or at year-end, depending on circumstances.
>
> Refer to your Accounting text for this discussion.
>
> Actual Accounts Receivable write-offs reduce **Allowance for Doubtful Accounts**.

10 ➤ Display the Sales Journal Entry.

Sales Journal Entry Mar 18, 2016 (J10)

Account Number	Account Description	Debits	Credits
1210	Allowance for Doubtful Accounts	2,400.00	-
2630	HST Charged on Sales	312.00	-
1200	Accounts Receivable	-	2,712.00
Additional Date:	Additional Field:		
		2,712.00	2,712.00

11 ➤ **Exit** from the display window.

12 ➤ **Post** after verifying accuracy and **Exit** to the Home window.

Exercise 2B-33b—Journalizing the Receipt

1 ➤ In the Customers area, click the ▼ at **Spiller Luggage Stores**, click **Receive Payments**.

2 ➤ **Cheque**   Type **3431**, [Tab].

    From   Spiller Luggage Stores is filled in.

3 ➤ **Receipt No.**   Click in the field, type **3431**, [Tab] [Tab].

4 ➤ **Date**   [Tab] [Tab] to accept **Mar 18, 2016**.

5 ➤ **Invoice Date**   [Tab] to accept Feb 20, 2016.

6 ➤ **Discount Taken** [Tab], there is no discount.

7 ➤ **Amount Received**   [Tab] to accept the original 2230 invoice $3,616.00.

8 ➤ **Discount Taken** [Tab], there is no discount.

If your invoice 2230Wo line has a **-48.00 Disc. Available** amount showing, it means that you did not remove the 2% terms in the previous exercise. Use the [*Delete*] or [*Backspace*] key to remove **-48.00**.

9 ➤ **Amount Received**   [Tab] to accept the write-off of **-2,712.00**. The lower portion of the Receipts window will look similar to the following:

Invoice Date	Invoice or Deposit	Original Amount	Amount Owing	Discount Available	Discount Taken	Amount Received
Feb 20, 2016	2230	3,616.00	3,616.00	0.00		3,616.00
	2230Wo	-2,712.00	-2,712.00	0.00		-2,712.00
					Total	904.00

The **Total** box 904.00 at bottom will indicate the amount of the cheque received, which is the net amount of invoice 2230 ($3,616.00), less the write-off allowed (-2,712.00).

10 ➤ Display the Receipts Journal entry.

Receipts Journal Entry Mar 18, 2016 (J11)			
Account Number	Account Description	Debits	Credits
1020	Bank Chequing Account	904.00	-
1200	Accounts Receivable	-	904.00
Additional Date:	Additional Field:		
		904.00	904.00

11 ➤ **Exit** from the display window.

12 ➤ **Post** when correct and **Exit** to the Home window.

13 ➤ **Display** the Customer Aged Detail Report, using the ▼ in the Customers area for Spiller Luggage Stores at March 18.

The screen should look as follows:

Customer Aged Detail As at Mar 18, 2016				
Source	Date	Transaction Type	Total	Current
Spiller Luggage Stores				
2230	Feb 20, 2016	Invoice	3,616.00	3,616.00
3431	Mar 18, 2016	Payment	-3,616.00	-3,616.00
2230Wo	Mar 18, 2016	Invoice	-2,712.00	-2,712.00
3431	Mar 18, 2016	Payment	2,712.00	2,712.00
Total outstanding:			-	-

The lower portion of the report has hyphens (-) to indicate no dollar values.

Notice that cheque **3431** has been applied to both the **invoice 2230** and **invoice 2230Wo**. For future reference, the negative invoice 2230Wo is shown to be applied to original invoice 2230.

14 ➤ The following procedure works with the RECEIVABLES AND PAYABLES modules and assumes that you want to display details of the original invoice(s). **Double-click** on any item on the invoice **2230Wo** line. The original invoice that created the $ values is displayed with a **PAID** image. This will assist you in verifying if payment was received on an invoice.

15 ➤ **Exit** the Invoice Lookup, and **Exit** the Aged Detail report.

Journalizing a Cash Sale with a Discount

You learned earlier how to journalize a payment for a sale on credit with a discount. In this exercise, you will learn how to journalize a cash sale with a discount; e.g., a senior's discount. This procedure would also apply if the business was giving a discount to a firm for buying a lot of merchandise or services (trade discount).

Exercise 2B-34—Journalizing a Cash Sale with a Discount (Senior)

Santos Luggage has had a number of inquiries from senior citizens who want to buy various luggage articles, and would appreciate a senior's discount, similar to what other businesses allow. Mrs. Santos has decided that it would be appropriate to offer a 10% discount to senior citizens (this is not the same as a cash discount for paying early on credit sales).

These sales will be recorded in the Sales Journal by typing the customer's name and using the **Continue** button because the business wants a record of the customer's name in the entry, similar to other entries made from the Outlet Store. See Exercise 2B-31 **Customer** area.

Mar 18, 2016   Mr. Ronald Peddle, a senior citizen, used his senior's card to purchase 2 Suitcase w/w Large at $80.00 each, before a 10% senior's discount. HST would be added to the price after the discount as follows:

Suitcase w/w Large, 2 @ $80.00	$ 160.00	
Senior's discount less 10%	$ (16.00)	
Net Sales amount before taxes		$144.00
HST 13% on $144.00		$ 18.72
	Amount to be paid	$162.72

Mr. Peddle paid the bill in full with his cheque #749.

You will record the sale with the regular selling price and also show the discount. *Note*: The cash discount on goods is not a discount for paying within the invoice terms. However, only the $72.00 net amount for each suitcase (total $144.00) is posted to the Sales account. Follow these steps:

1 ➤   Create an invoice using the **Sales Invoices** icon.

     Transaction   Do NOT change from Invoice.

2 ➤   **Paid By**   Select **Cheque**, [Tab] to Deposit To.

3 ➤   **Deposit To**   Do NOT change the default 1020 Bank Chequing Account, [Tab] to Cheque.

4 ➤   **Cheque No.**   Type **749**, [Tab].

5 ➤   **Customer area**   Type **Mr. Ronald Peddle**, [Tab], **Continue**, then click **OK**, then [Tab], [Tab], to move to the address area and type **2569 Plaster Lane**, [Tab], type **Mississauga, ON**, [Tab], type **L5N 3K7**, [Tab]. Click the **Ship-to Address** field.

6 ➤   **Ship-to Address**   If you click the ▼ there will not be an address listed. A cash sale customer would not require a Ship-to Address. [Tab] to move to the lower box. Type **Outlet Store**, [Tab]. Click on **Item Number**.

7 ➤   **Item Number**   Complete the information as shown next.

Item Number	Quantity	Order	Back Order	Unit	Item Description	Base Price	Discount (%)	Price	Amount	Tax	Account
Suit-w/w L	2			Each	Suitcase w/w Large	80.00	10.00	72.00	144.00	HS	4100 Sales

Other Information:

An early payment discount (2% 10 days, net 30, for paying within the discount terms) is recorded in the Receipts Journal as it is linked to the Sales Discount account in the General Ledger.

Discount (%)	This column is used to record reductions in the price of the goods being sold to businesses that buy a lot of goods or services (quantity or trade discounts). This column is also used for the senior's discount, and the amount is calculated by Sage 50 Accounting (discount % column) and reduces the amount in the Price column. Base price less the discount % column equals the revised price. (See side note box.) The Price column would show the reduced price for each item on the invoice.
Tax	**HS** Retail Sale 13% HST is calculated on the reduced price of goods in the Price column.

Do NOT type an amount in the Early Payment Discount field. This field is linked to the Sales Discount account for paying within the 2% 10 days discount terms and is not applicable to quantity, trade or senior's discounts.

The Sales Invoice window for the senior's discount should look like the following:

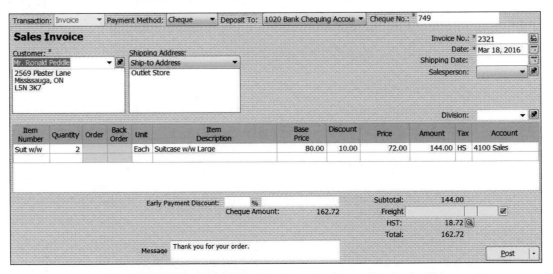

Fig. 2B-20: Sales Invoice window—Senior's Discount.

8 ➤ **Display** the Sales Journal Entry. It should resemble the following:

Sales Journal Entry Mar 18, 2016 (J12)

Account Number	Account Description	Debits	Credits
1020	Bank Chequing Account	162.72	-
5010	Cost of Goods Sold	62.00	-
1300	Inventory	-	62.00
2630	HST Charged on Sales	-	18.72
4100	Sales	-	144.00
Additional Date:	Additional Field:		
		224.72	224.72

Some firms may want to keep track of the dollar value of discounts given to seniors and would create a new General Ledger account, **Senior's Discount**. Mrs. Santos has decided that she does not need this type of account.

9 ➤ **Exit** from the display window and **post** the entry when correct.

10 ➤ **Exit** to the Home window. (See side note box.)

Additional Transactions

1 ➤ Record and **Post** the following transaction information.

The Additional Info note box for **A-Your Name Luggage Rack** (normally appears when you tab the customer field, or click on any source field) appears to remind you to discuss the 2% discount in 10 days with the customer. **Close** the Additional Info box.

Mar 18, 2016	**Sold to the Oakville branch of A-Your Name Luggage Rack the following: 4 Suitcase w/w Large @ $62.00 each, plus HST Total Invoice including HST of $32.24, is $280.24. Credit terms 2%/10 n30.**

Mar 18, 2016	**Havarah Leather Goods returned 2 Briefcase—regular ($100.00 plus HST each on invoice #2317). Total return is $226.00 including HST of $26.00. Credit terms net 20.**

Mar 18, 2016	**Judy Morrison, a staff member, purchased 1 Suitcase w/w Large at $80.00 less a 23% staff discount, plus HST. Cheque # 225 received.**

Additional Transactions

1 ➤ Advance the Session date to **Mar 21, 2016**.

2 ➤ Record and **Post** the following transaction information.

Mar 21, 2016	**Receipt from Havarah Leather Goods from sale on March 08, less the return. Note cheque #786 dated March 18. Allow the discount of $43.06 on invoice #2317 net of returns ($47.06—$4).**

Mar 21, 2016	**Sale, at the Outlet Store, to Henry Taylor of 2 Suitcase w/w Large at $70.00 plus HST. Cheque # 683 received.**

Journalizing a Customer's NSF Cheque

When a customer's cheque is returned by the bank as **NSF** (**N**ot **S**ufficient **F**unds), it means the customer did not have enough money in their bank account to cover the cheque that they had sent to you for payment. They still owe you money for the invoice that you now show as paid in your records.

To correct this situation, enter in the Sales Journal an increase (Debit) to **Accounts Receivable** in the amount of the NSF cheque plus bank charges and/or any handling charges, if any, and a decrease (Credit) to **Bank Account** (or Cash) for the total amount owing. To keep track of the fact that the entry is due to an NSF cheque, you can use the same invoice number as the original invoice with the code NS or NSF; e.g., Invoice # 12345NSF.

Do NOT use the Reverse Entry icon. You do NOT want to reverse the original sale. The sale has taken place; only the payment is not valid.

Exercise 2B-35—Journalizing an NSF Customer Cheque

---

1 ➤   Advance the Session date to **Mar 25, 2016**.

Study this transaction:

> **Mar 23, 2016**   **You were notified by the bank debit memo (shown next) that Mrs. Arlene Hirsch's cheque #456 in the amount of $254.25 was returned NSF (Not Sufficient Funds). The bank did not charge a service fee on this transaction. Santos Luggage charges an additional handling fee of $15.00 to the customer for the NSF transaction.**
>
> **She will send you a replacement cheque to cover the above. Her new home is at: *993 Ashdown Crescent, Toronto M3H 2K8*, new phone number *905-585-6366*.**

> To locate the details of the entry made in the accounting records, when the cheque was originally received, use the Reports, Journal Entries All to display the entries. Locate the entry with the amount of the original cheque $254.25. You can then drill down to locate the original entry and invoice number. Verify the information before recording the NSF cheque.

TD Bank
2589 Forestor Lane
Toronto, ON M2P 3X3   D A T E __Mar 23, 2016__

To: Santos Luggage-B Student's Name
         635 Semple Avenue
         Toronto, ON
         M9L 1V5

Item returned NSF Not Sufficient Funds
Cheque #456 Mrs. Arlene Hirsch   Amount: _$- 254.25_

                                                   Signed: _____M. Lee_____

⑈125⑈ ⑈5869 003 525⑈758 6⑈   ⑈000000 · 254.25 ⑈

Some banks deduct an NSF service fee for processing the returned cheques from the person or company that issued the NSF cheque. They may also charge a service fee to the company that deposits a cheque that becomes NSF. In this case, the amount deducted from the company bank account will be added to the receivable the customer owes your firm (original account receivable $254.25 plus the service fee, e.g., $10.00) with an offsetting credit of $264.25 to the bank account. This means you require your customer to reimburse your company for both the NSF cheque *and* the bank-deducted service fee.

If the bank did NOT charge a fee to process an NSF cheque, the entry would be
similar to: 1200 Accounts Receivable   254.25
                1020   Bank Chequing Account   254.25

If the bank did charge a fee to process an NSF cheque, the entry would be similar to:
                1200 Accounts Receivable   264.25
                1020   Bank Chequing Account   264.25

When you recorded the cheque on Mar 15, 2016 from Mrs. Hirsch, you journalized the entry as an **Invoice Paid by Cheque** for a **One-time customer** in the Sales Journal, and made the following entry:

Account Number	Account Description	Debits	Credits
Sales Journal Entry Mar 15, 2016 (J8)			
1020	Bank Chequing Account	254.25	-
5010	Cost of Goods Sold	87.00	-
1300	Inventory	-	87.00
2630	HST Charged on Sales	-	29.25
4100	Sales	-	225.00
Additional Date:	Additional Field:		
		341.25	341.25

The bank, by the debit memo, has reduced our bank account balance by $254.25 (the amount of the $254.25 NSF cheque, without a service fee). Santos Luggage charges a Handling Fee of $15.00 (for the NSF cheque); therefore, Mrs. Hirsch now owes the company the $254.25 plus $15.00. As this handling fee (to cover extra staff costs) is not earned in the ordinary course of business, it will be separated from the regular revenue on the Income Statement. We need to set up Mrs. Hirsch as a customer and show this amount as being outstanding until her replacement cheque is recorded.

When you record the NSF cheque, you will record the following entry:

1200	Accounts Receivable	269.25*	
1020	Bank Chequing Account		254.25
4510	Handling Fee		15.00
	(* 254.25 +15.00)		

2 ➤ Using the **Sales Invoices** journal icon, create an Invoice as follows:

3 ➤ **Customer** Type **Mrs. Arlene Hirsch**, ⌨Tab.

4 ➤ Select **Full Add** and set up **Mrs. Hirsch** as a customer with the **address information** provided; customer since **Mar 15, 2016**. Leave Revenue Account field blank, terms will be **0%** discount, and **Net amount due within 4 days**. Use **No** Tax code. Credit Limit **0.00**.

There is no sale when you record an NSF cheque. The sale took place on March 15, and you are now recording the fact that the customer owes you the money originally received.

She will have a **0.00** credit limit, and the memo note could be:

> Replacement cheque for NSF cheque required from customer, plus Handling Fee. NSF cheque #456 received in Outlet Store. Friend of employee (put in your name).

To-Do date Select **Mar 29, 2016**, as a reminder to verify that the cheque was received.

Display this Memo Click this field to place a ✓ in the box.

Click the **Save and Close** button when done.

5 ➤ Invoice   Type **2319NS Cheque 456** and [Tab] [Tab]. Remember that
                       Sage 50 Accounting prevents the entry of an invoice number
                       twice, so adding NS or NSF (for **N**ot **S**ufficient **F**unds) to the
                       invoice number will allow you to enter the original invoice
                       number twice. This will also indicate to you, later, that this
                       entry is a re-entry of a previous sale due to an NSF cheque.
                       The 456 represents the cheque number that was received
                       NSF. 456 is recorded for tracing purposes, if required.

6 ➤ Date   Select **Mar 23, 2016,** [Tab]. Click on **Item Description**.

7 ➤ Item   Type **NSF cheque #456,** [Tab]. Click on **Amount**.
   Description

8 ➤ Amount   Type **254.25,** [Tab] [Tab] to Account. This will leave a blank Tax
                       field. This is the same as double-clicking and selecting - No Tax.

9 ➤ Account   Press [Enter]. Select **1020 Bank Chequing Account**. This
                       results in a credit to the Bank Account [Tab].

10 ➤ Item   **Double-click** and select **HF-1 Handling Fee (Service item),**
   Number   [Tab]. This results in a credit to the Account.

11 ➤ Quantity   Type **1,** [Tab].

12 ➤ Message   **Remove** the information, [Tab]. The lower section should
                       look like the following:

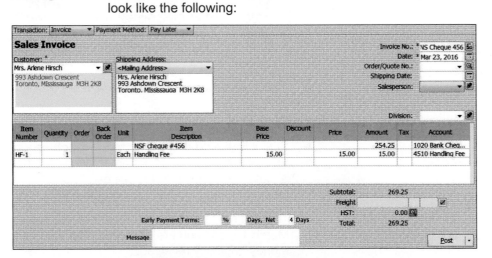

Fig. 2B-21: NSF Sales Invoice.

13 ➤ Display the Sales Journal Entry. The window should appear as follows:

Sales Journal Entry Mar 23, 2016 (J18)

Account Number	Account Description	Debits	Credits
1200	Accounts Receivable	269.25	-
1020	Bank Chequing Account	-	254.25
4510	Handling Fee	-	15.00
Additional Date:	Additional Field:		
		269.25	269.25

Notice that there is no amount posted to the Sales account. The sale was
recorded on March 15, 2016. The credit to the Bank Account shows that the
payment from Mrs. Hirsch was NSF. This entry reverses the bank deposit

entry of March 15, and debits (increases) the customer's Accounts Receivable account for the amount of the cheque plus the Handling Fee.

WWW

Refer to Appendix 2015 AG, *Writing Off Handling Fee Revenue* in your course materials at www.nelson.com/student.

> An alternate method to record a returned cheque is to reverse the payment transaction (see Chapter 13, *Correcting Transaction Errors after Posting*).
>
> The invoice method shown in this exercise is preferred by many businesses because it allows you to send an invoice to the customer advising them that they owe you the money.

14 ➤ **Exit** the Sales Journal Entry window and **Post** the entry.

You should receive the following warning message. (The credit limit was set to 0.00.) (See side note box.)

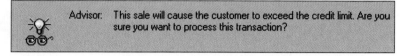

Advisor: This sale will cause the customer to exceed the credit limit. Are you sure you want to process this transaction?

15 ➤ Click **Yes**. You entered a 0.00 credit limit for this customer.

16 ➤ **Exit** from the Sales Journal. Return to the Home window.

More Transactions

1 ➤ **Journalize** and **Post** the following transactions:

Mar 24, 2016 **Cheque #186 from Sandler Travel Stores in the amount of $2,407.00 for Jan 26, 2016 invoice #2197 received and deposited to the bank**.

Mar 24, 2016 **Debit memo received from the bank identifying Henry Taylor's cheque #683 was returned NSF. Santos Luggage charged a $15.00 Handling Fee. Mrs. Santos sent a letter to Mr. Taylor requesting a replacement cheque for the NSF cheque, plus the Handling Fee. Use Full Add with terms of net 4 days, and credit limit of 0.00 to add the customer.**

1 ➤ Advance the Session date to **Mar 29, 2016**.

Applying an Invoice to a Deposit

On March 15, 2016 Opal Kong Luggage Ltd. placed a $2,802.40 sales order with a deposit of $1,000.00. The customer ledger shows a **-1,000.00** balance.

When the goods are shipped, you convert the sales order into a sales invoice for $2,802.40.

The $2,802.40 sales invoice less the deposit of $1,000.00 you recorded earlier will leave a receivable balance owing of $1,802.40.

Exercise 2B-36—Applying an Invoice to a Deposit

Here is the full transaction description:

Mar 25, 2016 **The order of 40 Suitcase w/w Large for Opal Kong Luggage Ltd. was picked up by their vehicle this morning. Issue invoice for $2,802.40 as per sales order #104.**

1 ➤ Convert Sales Order #104 to an invoice #2325 (see Caution information below). **Record** and **Post** the invoice, as the order has been filled. The Sales Invoice window lower portion should display as shown next. (*Note*: Don't forget to change the date to March 25.)

Sage 50 Accounting may have changed the **Paid By** field to **Cheque** (last used selection when the Sales Order was created). Change it to **Pay Later**.

Item Number	Quantity	Order	Back Order	Unit	Item Description	Base Price	Discount	Price	Amount	Tax	Account
Suit w/w L	40	40		Each	Suitcase w/w Large	62.00		62.00	2,480.00	HS	4100 Sales

	Subtotal: 2,480.00
Deposit Applied: 1,000.00	Freight ☑
	HST: 322.40
Early Payment Terms: 2.00 % 10 Days, Net 30 Days	Total: 2,802.40
Message: Thank you for your order.	Amount Owing: 1,802.40 Post ▾

The **Total** field shows the invoice amount as the correct $2,802.40. See Step 2 Journal entry.

The **Amount Owing** field now shows the balance owing (after deduction of the deposit). You will also see it reduced in Step 4, when you display the Aged Detail report. However, the printed invoice does not show the reduced balance.

2 ➤ Display the Sales Journal entry; it will look similar to the following:

Sales Journal Entry Mar 25, 2016 (J21)

Account Number	Account Description	Debits	Credits
1200	Accounts Receivable	2,802.40	-
5010	Cost of Goods Sold	1,240.00	-
1300	Inventory	-	1,240.00
2630	HST Charged on Sales	-	322.40
4100	Sales	-	2,480.00
Additional Date:	Additional Field:		
		4,042.40	4,042.40

3 ➤ **Exit** the entry, **Post** the sale. The information box "The sales order has been filled and removed from the system" displays. Click **OK**. You may see a report that the inventory is low. Ignore the message.

4 ➤ **Exit** to the Home window. **Display** a **Customer Aged Detail** report at March 25, for Opal Kong Luggage Ltd., and note how Sage 50 Accounting displays the deposit and sale. The report should display as follows:

Customer Aged Detail As at Mar 29, 2016				
Source	Date	Transaction Type	Total	Current
Opal Kong Luggage Ltd.				
Dp SO#104	Mar 15, 2016	Prepaid Order	-1,000.00	-1,000.00
2325	Mar 25, 2016	Applied	1,000.00	1,000.00
2325	Mar 25, 2016	Invoice	2,802.40	2,802.40
2325	Mar 25, 2016	Payment	-1,000.00	-1,000.00
Total unpaid invoices:			1,802.40	1,802.40
Total deposits/prepaid order:			-	-
Total outstanding:			1,802.40	1,802.40
Total unpaid invoices:			1,802.40	1,802.40
Total deposits/prepaid order:			-	-
Total outstanding:			1,802.40	1,802.40

Dp SO#104 and **Prepaid Order**	This is the deposit received when Opal Kong Luggage placed their order on the 15th.
Applied	The **Prepaid** amount is transferred from the Sales Order record to the invoice, when you converted the sales order into a sales invoice, shown at line 4 (in the Aging report) as a payment.
Invoice	This is the regular **$2,802.40** Invoice recorded previously.
Payment	This is from the **Applied** amount discussed above.

You will note that the amount **Unpaid by Ms. Kong** in this transaction is **1,802.40** ($2,802.40 sale less the $1,000.00 deposit).

5 ➤ **Exit** from the display and return to the Home window.

Journalizing Credit Card Receipts

A credit card received as a payment on any ACCOUNTS RECEIVABLE amount owing may be recorded directly to a specific credit card account, which may be linked to one of the bank accounts. In your company's Chart of Accounts, 1030 Visa Credit Card Bank Account is linked to the Visa Credit Card. If you record a payment using a credit card from Visa, it updates the 1030 Visa Credit Card Bank Account.

Exercise 2B-37—Journalizing a Credit Card Receipt

Study the following transaction:

> **Mar 29, 2016 Mrs. Hirsch came in to pay her account. She decided to pay her account (NSF cheque) using her Visa card. Process her payment using the credit card.**

1 ➤ Using Mrs. Arlene Hirsch from the Customers Area, use **Receive Payments**.

2 ➤ **Paid By** Select **Visa Credit**, [Tab].

  From Mrs. Arlene Hirsch is selected.

3 ➤ **Receipt No.**   This is a credit card receipt, which does not have a cheque or invoice number. You do NOT want to record the Authorization code from the credit card company on this document because of privacy concerns. Click the field, type **Visa**. [Tab] [Tab] to Date.

4 ➤ **Date**   [Tab] to accept. [Tab] to Invoice Date.

5 ➤ **Invoice Date**   [Tab] [Tab] to Amount Received.

Discount Taken There is no discount on this invoice (NSF cheque).

6 ➤ **Amount Received**   [Tab] to accept 269.25.

7 ➤ **Comment**   Type **Paid by Visa Credit Card**.

The Receipt window should look like the following:

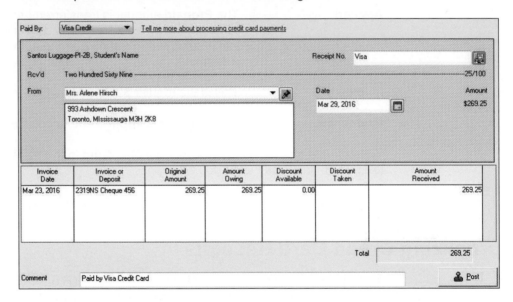

8 ➤ **Display** the Receipts Journal entry. It should resemble the following:

Receipts Journal Entry Mar 29, 2016 (J22)

Account Number	Account Description	Debits	Credits
1030	Visa Credit Card Bank Account	259.83	-
5340	Credit Card Charges	9.42	-
1200	Accounts Receivable	-	269.25
Additional Date:	Additional Field:		
		269.25	269.25

9 ➤ **Exit** from the display window and **Post** the entry when correct.

10 ➤ **Exit** to the Home window.

11 ➤ Advance Session date to **Mar 31, 2016**.

Owner Investment in Business

The owner's investment may be recorded by either of the following methods:

1. Recording a General Journal entry to show the personal investment where funds have been transferred by the bank. (See Exercise 1-12.)

2. Setting up a customer ledger with the owner's name and recording a sales invoice (using the Capital account or Additional Investment by Owner account) paid by cheque whenever the owner invests more money into the business.

Method #1 is the preferred method.

Exercise 2B-38—Journalizing Owner Investment in Business

> **Mar 31, 2016** Mrs. Santos has decided to invest an additional $6,000.00 into the business, as she is going to purchase a large number of suitcases from a company that is going out of business. She therefore transferred $6,000.00 from her personal bank account to the company's bank account. She brought the bank transfer form as a source document for the business.

The General Journal method will be used to record the investment.

1 ➤ Click on the **COMPANY** module and click on the **General Journal** icon. **Record** and **Post** the investment based on the following window.

| Source | Bank Transfer | | | Date | Mar 31, 2016 | |

| Comment | Mrs. Santos investment in business | | | | | |

Account	Debits	Credits	Comment
1020 Bank Chequing Ac	6,000.00	--	Bank transfer investment
3160 Additional Investme	--	6,000.00	Bank transfer investment

2 ➤ **View** the General Journal entry. The window should appear as follows:

General Journal Entry Mar 31, 2016 (J23)

Account Number	Account Description	Debits	Credits
1020	Bank Chequing Account	6,000.00	-
	Bank transfer investment		
3160	Additional Investment	-	6,000.00
	Bank transfer investment		
Additional Date:	Additional Field:		
		6,000.00	6,000.00

3 ➤ **Exit** from viewing the General Journal entry.

4 ➤ **Post** when correct and **Exit** to the Home page.

Additional Transactions

Process the following three transactions:

Mar 31, 2016 Mrs. Santos visited the Royes Luggage Inc. store yesterday, and discussed the problems (conditions of goods received) with their manager. Mrs. Santos and the manager agreed that there is a problem with the goods. Mrs. Santos will give a Sales price allowance for the goods on invoice #2212, in the amount of $100.00 plus HST. Mrs. Santos received Royes Luggage Inc.'s cheque #496 in the amount of $904.00 as payment for this invoice, less the allowance. There are no discount terms on this allowance as it is more than 10 days from the purchase date.

1. Record the allowance.
2. Record the cheque received.

Mar 31, 2016 Sold to Luggage 4U, to be picked up today, 5 Suitcase w/w Large at $62.00 plus HST, and 4 Power Adapters at $10.50 each plus HST. Issued invoice #2326 for $397.76 including 45.76 HST, terms 2/10 net 30 days.

Mar 31, 2016 Sold to Hanlan's Luggage Stores, 3 Suitcase w/w Regular at $56.00 plus HST, and 2 Suitcase w/w Large at $62.00 each plus HST. Issued invoice #2327 for $329.96 including 37.96 HST, terms 2/10 net 30 days. Change the terms in the customer record before recording this sale.

Recording a Receipt for a Non-Merchandise Item

This procedure is not to be used for Owner Investment, as this is not a sales-related event. Owner Investment should be recorded in the General Journal. See Exercise 1-12, Journalizing Owner Investment in Business.

There will be situations when the business receives a cheque(s) for goods that are not being resold (e.g., sale of your old equipment, rebate cheque, etc.). (See side note box.)

This next exercise shows you how to enter the rebate information as a cash transaction (refer to Exercise 2B-30), as an invoice is normally created for the cheque received. The name of the firm issuing the cheque will appear in journal entries.

Exercise 2B-39—Journalizing a Non-Merchandise Cheque (Rebate Cheque)

Mar 31, 2016 Mrs. Santos handed you a $10.20 mail-in-rebate cheque #2897561. The rebate cheque (without an HST rebate) is for a case of computer paper the business purchased last month from the Office Supply Store.

You would not create a customer ledger for the Office Supply Store, as they are a vendor in the PAYABLE module.

1 ➤ Create an invoice using the **Sales Invoice**s icon.

    Transaction   Do NOT change the default Invoice.

2 ➤ **Payment Method** Select **Cheque**, `Tab`.

3 ➤ **Deposit to**   Do NOT change, `Tab` to accept 1020 Bank Chequing Account.

4 ➤ **Cheque**   Type **2897561**, `Tab`.

5 ➤ **Customer**   Enter the information shown next.

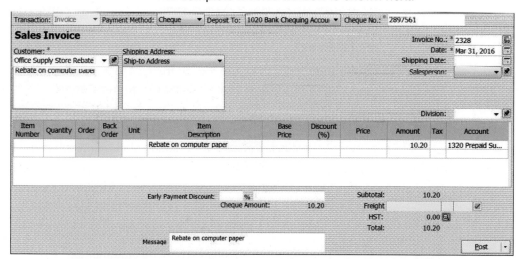

6 ➤ Enter the information shown next.

Item Number	Quantity	Order	Back Order	Unit	Item Description	Base Price	Discount (%)	Price	Amount	Tax	Account
					Rebate on computer paper				10.20		1320 Prepaid Supplies

    Tax   You will not be able to recover tax (HST) on a rebate. This field should be blank.

7 ➤ **Account**   Select **1320 Prepaid Supplies**, as this is the account that was charged when the computer paper was purchased.

8 ➤ **Message**   Type **Rebate on computer paper**.

    The complete Invoice window is shown next.

9 ➤ **View** the Sales Journal Entry. The window should appear as follows:

Sales Journal Entry Mar 31, 2016 (J28)

Account Number	Account Description	Debits	Credits
1020	Bank Chequing Account	10.20	-
1320	Prepaid Supplies	-	10.20
Additional Date:	Additional Field:		
		10.20	10.20

10 ➤   **Exit** from the display window.

11 ➤   **Post** when correct and **Exit** to the Home window.

The following would appear in the Reports, Journal Entries - All display.

2897561, 2328, Office Supply Store Rebate

Printing Customer Statements

Many businesses send their customers a statement, which is a record of the transactions recorded in their account. This will give customers a chance to check their own records and investigate any invoices that do not agree. It is also a very effective reminder to customers of any overdue amounts. Statements may be printed or e-mailed for all customers or for individual customers at any time during the month.

If a firm prints statements for mailing, it can use the built-in Sage 50 Accounting custom forms or it can purchase pre-printed forms from a printing company, which can include the company logo and will have shaded column headings where Sage 50 Accounting can print the information that is shown in Fig. 2B-22. A brochure of various forms available is included in the software manufacturer's package. You can order the forms through Sage 50 Accounting, or you could take the brochure to a commercial printer to have forms customized for your company. You can also e-mail a version of the statement to the customer if you have their e-mail address.

Remember that statements may be printed at any time (whenever there is a customer account inquiry, to collect an overdue account, etc.), not only at the end of the month. To reduce paper use, your instructor may request you to print only one statement (on plain paper) for an individual customer to allow you to see what will print on pre-printed forms.

Exercise 2B-40—Printing Customer Statements

For practice, you will print one customer statement on blank paper. Be sure your printer is ready.

1 ➤   From the Home window, in the **Customers** area, at **Royes Luggage Inc.**, click on ▾ and click on **View Customer Record**.

2 ➤   Click the **Options** tab, click the ▾ at Print ▾ Forms for this Customer . There are 2 choices E-mail / Print for creating statements indicated on the Receivable Ledger Options tab.

3 ➤   Make sure the **Produce Statements for this Customer** box is (✓). Statements for customers can be e-mailed/printed only if this box is (✓).

4 ➤   **Exit** from the Receivables Ledger window. Return to the home window.

There are two options for printing statements:

a)   In the Tasks area, click on the ▾ at Customer's icon, click on View Customers. From the menu bar, click Reports, Customer Statements and you will see the Customer Statements window displayed.

b)   From the Home window menu bar, click Reports, Receivables, Customer Statements and you are at the Customer Statements window.

The top portion is shown here:

Print   Print statements for customers identified as Print in Options.
E-mail   E-mail statements for customers identified as E-mail in Options.
By Preference   Will prepare and send statements based on preference in Options.

You also have the option to ☐ Include due dates. The lower portion is shown here:

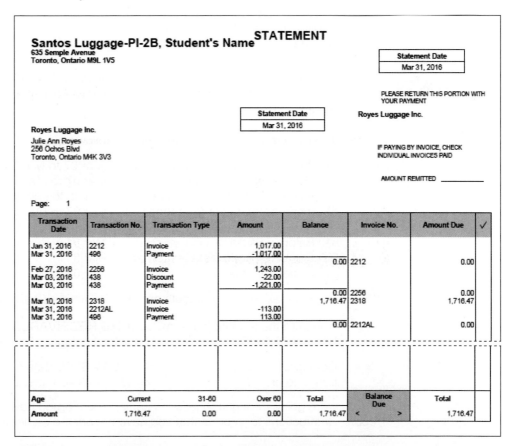

Provide statements for
◉ Selected customers
○ Selected customers with outstanding balances
○ Selected customers with overdue balances

Selected Customers   You have a choice of printing statements for customers you select.

Outstanding balances   Will print statements with a balance of 1 cent or more.

Overdue balances   Will print/e-mail statements with overdue balances (e.g., 31-60 days or more.

5 ➤ Using either a or b method, make sure the ◉ Print button, in the top-left corner, is selected. Select **Royes Luggage Inc.**, then **OK**. The statement should print.

Your printout on plain paper should resemble Fig. 2B-22. This form can be printed or emailed to your customers.

Santos Luggage-PI-2B, Student's Name **STATEMENT**
635 Semple Avenue
Toronto, Ontario M9L 1V5

Statement Date
Mar 31, 2016

PLEASE RETURN THIS PORTION WITH YOUR PAYMENT

Statement Date
Mar 31, 2016

Royes Luggage Inc.

Royes Luggage Inc.
Julie Ann Royes
256 Ochos Blvd
Toronto, Ontario M4K 3V3

IF PAYING BY INVOICE, CHECK INDIVIDUAL INVOICES PAID

AMOUNT REMITTED _____

Page: 1

Transaction Date	Transaction No.	Transaction Type	Amount	Balance	Invoice No.	Amount Due	✓
Jan 31, 2016	2212	Invoice	1,017.00				
Mar 31, 2016	496	Payment	-1,017.00				
				0.00	2212	0.00	
Feb 27, 2016	2256	Invoice	1,243.00				
Mar 03, 2016	438	Discount	-22.00				
Mar 03, 2016	438	Payment	-1,221.00				
				0.00	2256	0.00	
Mar 10, 2016	2318	Invoice		1,716.47	2318	1,716.47	
Mar 31, 2016	2212AL	Invoice	-113.00				
Mar 31, 2016	496	Payment	113.00				
				0.00	2212AL	0.00	

Age	Current	31-60	Over 60	Total	Balance Due	Total
Amount	1,716.47	0.00	0.00	1,716.47	< >	1,716.47

Fig. 2B-22: Customer Statement information.

To charge customers interest on overdue balances: view Appendix 2015 AF, *Calculating Interest on Overdue Receivable Balances* for the steps in changing the settings for this method in your course materials at www.nelson.com/student.

Notice how Sage 50 Accounting displays information for sales (Invoices) and receipts (Payment and Discount). Information for invoice #2212 is shown in two places (2212AI), as the report lists invoices by date order.

Be sure to back up your data and update your logbook at the end of every work session.

Printing Period-End Reports

The following reports may be printed for management's information and for filing for the audit trail.

- Journal Entries may be printed in one of two ways (see Exercise 1-18).
  - a) **All Journal Entries** will print all journal entries from all modules (with or without corrections). All transactions, in the time period requested, are numbered in this journal in sequential order (even if entered in a subledger; i.e., RECEIVABLES or PAYABLES module).
  - b) **General Journal Entries** will print journal entries entered in the COMPANY module only.
- The General Ledger—complete general ledger listing of transactions for the month.
- The Receivable Sales Journal for the month.
- The Receivable Receipts Journal for the month.
- The Balance Sheet as at March 31.
- The Income Statement for the year to March 31.
- The Customer Aged Detail report.
- The Aged Overdue Receivables Detail.

www The HST Report—all transactions in the month with HST are shown in this report: for more information see Appendix 2015 D, *Printing/Filing a Tax (HST) Report* in your course materials at www.nelson.com/student.

1 ➤ To save time and paper, **print** only the following:

   a) All Journal Entries, with corrections Mar 07 to Mar 31
   b) General Journal entries   Mar 07 to Mar 31
   c) Income Statement for period   Jan 01 to Mar 31
   d) Income Statement for period   Mar 07 to Mar 31 for Sales Manager.
      Hide details of Cost of Goods Sold and Office/Warehouse Expenses.
   e) Balance Sheet at   Mar 31
   f) Customer Aged Detail report at   Mar 31
   g) General Ledger   Mar 07 to Mar 31

Your instructor may request printouts of the Sales and/or Cash Receipts Journals.

2 ➤ Compare the amount in the ACCOUNTS RECEIVABLE account on the Balance Sheet with the Customer Aged Detail total balance. They should be the same.

3 ➤ Compare your printouts with the RECEIVABLES data files for Santos Luggage provided on the Solutions Disk with your instructor.

As you were going through the lessons earlier, you learned how to print some of the reports. Instructions for reports that you have not printed earlier follow.

Exercise 2B-41—Printing Period-End Reports

Printing a Gross Margin Income Statement

The **Gross Margin Income Statement** can also be called the **Gross Profit Income Statement** and is an income statement that breaks down Expenses into two categories: **Cost of Goods Sold** (takes into account items that refer to goods purchased for resale) and **Expenses** (referred to as purchases of goods/services not for resale).

1 ➤ Click **Report Centre**, click **Financials,** click the **+** at Income Statement, select **Gross Margin—Standard**, click **Modify this Report**.

2 ➤ The Start and Finish dates should be **Jan. 01, 2016** and **March 31, 2016**. You can change the dates to display the report for different dates. Click **OK** to display the Income Statement.

3 ➤ Click the **Print** icon to print the report. Note the change in wording for various lines; Net Sales and Total Revenue to: TOTAL REVENUE and TOTAL OPERATING REVENUE. A GROSS MARGIN line has been added, along with the information below the Total Expenses line. Refer to your accounting textbook for discussion of these changes, as this text does not explain the various changes.

4 ➤ **Exit** from the display window.

Printing the Sales Journal

1 ➤ Move to **Receivables, Sales Journal Entries. Click Modify this Report.** The **Start date** should be **Mar 07, 2016** (the day the file was started). If required, click **Modify**, **Report Options**, to add or remove the ✓ at Corrections. Click **OK** to display the Sales Journal entries.

2 ➤ Click the **Print** icon to print the report.

3 ➤ **Exit** from the display window.

Printing the Receipts Journal

1 ➤ Move to **Receipt Journal Entries**. Click **Modify this Report**. The **Start date** should be **Mar 07, 2016** (the day the file was started). If required, click **Modify, Report Options**, to add or remove the ✓ at Corrections. Click **OK** to display the Receipt Journal entries.

2 ➤ Click the **Print** icon to print the report.

3 ➤ **Exit** from the display window and return to the Home window.

Viewing/Printing Graphs

Sage 50 Accounting also has a Graph feature that allows you to view and/or print your data in graph format.

WWW Additional information on using the graph feature (pie and bar charts) can be found in Appendix 2015 K, *Graphs Feature* in your course materials at www.nelson.com/student.

Exercise 2B-42—Viewing/Printing Graphs

Viewing Graphs

1 ➤ From the Home page, menu bar, click **Graphs**.

2 ➤   Click **Receivables by Customer**, **Select All**, **OK**. A pie chart will display.

The Generated on date will correspond to the date you display the graph.

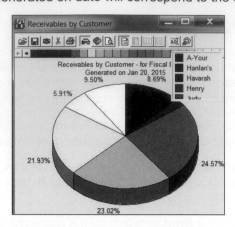

3 ➤   At this point, you may print the graph by clicking the **Print** button.
The Legend will not print with the graph.

4 ➤   **Exit** from the graph display.

Summary, Part B

Here is a summary of the transactions entered in Chapter 2B.

Transaction:	*Journal/Ledger*	*Remarks:*
Deposit	*Receipts*	Enter a deposit when you receive a partial payment with the Sales Order.
Cash Sale	*Sales*	Select **Transaction Invoice** and **Paid by: Cash/Cheque** with Payments; **One-time Customer,** or type the **customer's name** in the Sold to field and click **Continue** for an automatic cash/cheque sale.
Credit Card Sale	*Sales*	Select **Transaction Invoice**, and choose the Credit Card Company in the **Paid by** drop-down box.
Write-off	*Sales*	Enter write-off as a minus amount with HST.
NSF cheque	*Sales*	Enter a revised invoice or new invoice for the original cheque (plus bank charges) with *no* taxes. Select the **Cash in Bank** account *(not* Sales).
Post-dated cheques	*Receipts*	The post-dated entry (debit Bank, credit Accounts Receivable) will not appear in reports until the date the cheque is deposited.
www		More information is found in Appendix 2015 M, *Post-Dated Cheques* in your course materials at www.nelson.com/student.
Revise an Invoice		Use **Lookup** to find the original invoice and adjust with the corrected amounts. Can also be seen in Chapter 13.
Service Invoice		Enter a Service inventory invoice, with HST.

Review **Slideshows 2A** and **2B**.

Before Moving On, Part B

Read the following questions and make sure you know the answers to them; otherwise, review the corresponding section in the chapter before moving on.

1. What is a deposit? In what circumstances would a business require a deposit? Where do you record the deposit?

2. Which of the following business events does not need a negative amount to record the transaction?

   a) A retail sale invoice for a pair of sunglasses was issued for $172.89 ($153.00 plus taxes) and should have been issued for the correct amount of $152.55 ($135.00 plus taxes).
   b) Write off a customer balance due to the bankruptcy of the customer.
   c) Record a sale with HST to a customer.
   d) Return of an unopened DVD movie by a customer.

3. How would you record a senior's discount?

4. Give the journal entry (or entries) for a $210.00 NSF cheque for which the bank has added bank charges of $15.00 (no HST) to your company bank statement. Indicate the Sage 50 Accounting module in which the entry is made.

5. What is a customer account write-off? In what circumstances would a business write off a customer account?

6. A customer wants to pay an outstanding invoice in the amount of $339.00 (which includes $39.00 of HST) with a credit card. Which journal would you use to record it and what entry is made in the accounting records, assuming the bank charges 3% for processing credit cards?

7. Your manager would like you to prepare a Gross Margin Income Statement. What is it?

8. How do you record a quantity discount for a good customer?

Relevant Appendices, Part B

WWW The following appendices are available in your course materials at www.nelson.com/student.

Appendix 2015 D	**Printing/Filing a Tax (HST) Report**
Appendix 2015 K	**Graphs Feature**
Appendix 2015 M	**Post-Dated Cheques**
Appendix 2015 V1	**Perpetual Mini-Guide Receivables—Payables** (in Excel)
Appendix 2015 AF	**Calculating Interest on Overdue Receivable Balances**
Appendix 2015 AG	**Writing Off Handling Fee Revenue**

Challenge Exercise 02 C2B-1, Brides
RECEIVABLES and COMPANY Modules

1 ➤ Refer to Exercise 1-1b to unzip the **02 C2B-1 Brides.exe** file.

2 ➤ Open the **02 C2B-1 Brides** file and enter Receivable transactions for May for a company that sells bridal gowns, other dresses, accessories, and repairs (alterations) to dresses as needed. HST is 13%. Brides Company does not print Sales invoices or receipts.

Note: All sales are picked up in person; therefore, leave **Shipped by** field blank.

May 3   Issued Sales Order #30 to Marlene's Bridal Fashions for 4 bridesmaid dresses, style BM-126. Each dress will sell for $410.00, plus HST. Accept default terms 2/10, net 30. Total order $1,853.20. Delivery date will be May 27.

May 3   Received cheque #689 for $3,330.00 (net of $60.00 discount) as payment in full from Bev's Bridal Shop re outstanding invoice #381.

May 5   Retail sale to credit card customer Navneet Banwait of 1 bridal gown, style BG-253, for $1,200.00 and 4 accessories, code AC-30, at $30.00 each (all items plus HST). Credit card authorization #D1962 for $1,491.60.

May 6   Sold 3 bridal gowns, style BG-224, to Brenda's Dresses at $800.00 each, plus HST. Terms 2/10, net 30 days. Invoice total $2,712.00.

May 9   Sold 3 bridal gowns, style BG-362, at $800.00 each and 10 accessories, code AC-25, at $25.00 each, plus HST, to new customer, *Your Actual Name Dresses*, contact *Your Actual Name*, 967 Spadina Street, Markville, Ontario, L3X 2Z9. Phone and fax number are 905-826-3820. Credit limit will be $5,000.00 with terms of 2/10, net 30 days, Invoice total $2,994.50.

May 14 *Your Actual Name Dresses* returned 10 accessories. Return accepted, and credit note referring to invoice #784 sent to customer.

May 19 Sold a party dress, style PD-04, at $250.00, plus HST, to Mrs. Petra Kurek for an engagement party. Mrs. Kurek qualifies for the 10% senior's discount. Cheque #556 received.

May 19 *Your Actual Name Dresses* cheque #613, as payment in full, was received.

May 24 The bank advised that Mrs. Kurek's cheque #556 for $254.25 was returned "Account Closed." Charged a $15.00 Handling Fee. Mrs. Kurek will be sending a certified cheque to cover the error. Use any address information for Mrs. Kurek.

May 24 A new customer, Saira Heggie (any address information is acceptable), ordered a dress at $900.00, plus HST. Bridal gown, code BG-143, to be delivered by June 12. Sales Order #31 was issued and a $300.00 cheque, #134, was received as a deposit. Leave discount terms blank.

May 25 The bridesmaid dresses ordered on sales order #30 arrived and were picked up by Marlene's Bridal Fashions. Invoice amount per the May 3 order.

May 31 The owner, Mrs. Mehta, gave you a bank transfer for $4,000.00, which is for her additional investment in the business.

May 31 Marlene's Bridal Fashions sent in a bridesmaid dress for alterations. Issued next invoice for 2 units of 20 minutes (alterations), at $30 each, plus HST.

3 ➤ When you have recorded the above entries, print the following:
    a) Customer Aged Detail Report as at May 31
    b) All Journal Entries, for the monthly activity
    c) General Journal Entries, for the monthly activity
    d) Sales Journal Entries for May
    e) Receipts Journal Entries for May
    f) Income Statement for May 1 to May 31
    g) Pending Sales Order Detail by Customer at June 12

Challenge Exercise 02 C2B-2, Skis
RECEIVABLES and COMPANY Modules

---

1 ➤ Refer to Exercise 1-1b to unzip the **02 C2B-2 Skis.exe** file.

2 ➤ Open the **02 C2B-2 Skis** file and enter Receivable and General Ledger transactions for March for a company that sells skis and related sporting equipment. HST is 13%.

Note: All sales are picked up in person; therefore, leave **Shipped by** field blank.

Mar 2   Retail sale of 1 pair of Blanchard skis and bindings, code SB-103, $550.00 plus HST, to Miss Devon Cutronia. Received her Universal credit card for payment.

Mar 3   Issued Sales Order #212 to Jordan's Sports Equipment for 10 Jock Snowboards, code JSB-050, at $500.00 each plus HST. Snowboards shipping date will be March 31, terms 2/10, net 30 days. (Note special price for long-time customer.)

Mar 5   Owner Hong Duong invested an additional $5,000 in the business. Received a bank transfer receipt showing the money was put in the bank account today.

Mar 5   Sold to Mr. Lopez a package containing 1 pair of used skis, bindings, and poles, code US-104, for $300.00 plus HST. The manager allowed a 10% senior's discount. Cheque #326 received.

Mar 6   As a new customer, **Your actual Last (Family) name Skiing Lodge** (add any address) ordered and received 3 Norseman Snowboards, code NSB-045, at $510.00, and 3 ski goggles (glasses), code SG-02, at $60.00 each. All items plus HST. Credit limit $7,000 and terms 2/10, net 30.

Mar 9   **Your actual Last (Family) name Skiing Lodge** returned 1 Norseman Snowboard, code NSB-045, ($510.00 plus HST) because it has a tiny crack in the middle. The board has not been used and the manager approved a credit to the account.

Mar 16 Sold one set of ski poles, code SP-03, to Mr. Obi for $56.00 plus HST. Received his cheque #985 in full payment.

Mar 16 Received cheque #638 from **Your actual Last (Family) name Skiing Lodge** as payment on the goods ordered on the 6th and the return on the 9th.

Mar 23 Bank advised that Mr. Obi's cheque #985 was returned NSF. Sent registered letter to Mr. Obi advising him of the returned cheque with a Handling Fee of $15.00. The mailing address was 689 Copton Court, Mountsberg, Ontario L9Z 2B8.

Mar 26 Received a $13.10 bank debit memo for bank service charges to Mar. 23.

Mar 31 Only 8 snowboards ordered by Jordan's Sports Equipment on the 3rd arrived. The other 2 Jock Snowboards are to be delivered within 5 days. Called Jordan's and they agreed to accept the 8 boards received. Issued next sales invoice for this order, and the company picked up the boards.

3 ➤ When you have recorded the above entries, print the following:

    a) Customer Aged Detail report as at Mar 31
    b) All Journal Entries, for the monthly activity
    c) General Journal Entries, for the monthly activity
    d) Income Statement for the year-to-date activity, for the Sales Manager. Hide appropriate information.
    e) Sales Journal Entries
    f) Pending Sales Order Detail by Customer at March 31

Challenge Exercise 02 C2B-3, House Sitters

RECEIVABLES and COMPANY Modules

House Sitters is a service business that looks after your house or apartment while you are away. The business waters plants; looks after pets; makes sure the furnace, water heater and air conditioning are working; brings in the mail and newspapers, and so on.

House Sitters Company does *NOT* print Sales invoices or receipts.

Note: All invoices are left at the residence or business on the day the client returns. Terms are varied for different customers. HST is 13%.

1 ➤ Refer to Exercise 1-1b to unzip the **02 C2B-3 Sitters.exe** file.

2 ➤ For this review assignment open the **02 C2B-3 Sitters** file, and enter the following Accounts Receivable transactions for May.

May 1   Completed 4-day sitting for Hagos Aulakh at $30.00 plus HST per day. Invoice #177, in the amount of $135.60 with terms of net 5 days.

May 3   Received $101.70, cheque #752, as payment from Winston Chun re outstanding invoice #170.

May 6   Left invoice #178 in the amount of $101.70, at Mr. & Mrs. Thomas Royes' home for service for three days at $30.00 plus HST per day. Terms net 5 days.

May 6   Received $135.60, cheque #829 from Mr. Hagos Aulakh for invoice #177.

May 9   Received $101.70, cheque #256 from Mr. & Mrs. Thomas Royes as payment for invoice #178.

May 10 Completed 2-day sitting for Mrs. Manpreet Foss at $30.00 plus HST per day. Invoice #179, in the amount of $67.80 with terms of net 3 days, was left in the house.

May 12   Mrs. Foss paid invoice #179 in full with $67.80 cash.

May 18   A new business client, **Your Actual Name Ceramics**, requested us to check her store 3 times a day at $30.00 plus HST per visit. She will be out of town May 19 and 20. Other information: 889 Ancaster Avenue, Stoney Creek, Ontario A0A 3C3, phone and fax numbers may be left blank. Terms are 2%, 10 days, net 30. (Special terms arranged for business clients.) Credit limit $300.00.

May 20 Issued invoice #180, for $203.40, for **Your Actual Name Ceramics**.

May 28 Received **Your Actual Name Ceramics** cheque #158, in the amount of $199.80, as payment in full for invoice #180 with a discount taken of $3.60.

May 31 Completed 2-day sitting for Hagos Aulakh at $30.00 plus HST per day. Invoice #181 issued for $67.80 with terms net 5 days.

3 ➤ When you have recorded the above entries, **print** the following:
   a)   Customer Aged Detail, all customers, with terms, at May 31
   b)   All Journal Entries, for May 1 to 31
   c)   Sales Journal Entries for May 1 to 31
   d)   Receipts Journal Entries for May 1 to 31
   e)   Income Statement for Jan 1 to May 31

Mini-Guide for Transactions in Chapters 2A and 2B

Mini-guide (in Excel) for Perpetual transactions in Sage 50 Premium Accounting 2015***

***Not all types of transactions listed here.

***Study Suggestion – Add additional transactions from your chapters.

Receivable Events	Entry	Module	Journal	Comments	You fill in the Text Ref
Customer asks for price quote	No entry	RECEIVABLE	Sales, Orders & Quotes	No sale, customer asking for prices	
Customer confirms quote & places order for later delivery	No entry	RECEIVABLE	Sales, Orders & Quotes	No sale, price confirmed for future delivery	

Sale of Merchandise entry	A/Rec
	  Sales
	  HST collected on Sales
		RECEIVABLE	Sales, Orders & Quotes	May be preceded by sales quote
				May be preceded by sales order
				May be a sale without prior quote or order	

and Cost of Goods Sold entry	Cost of Goods Sold Inventory			Automatic entry by Sage 50 Accounting Automatic entry by Sage 50 Accounting	
Sales Rtn of Merchandise	Sales Rtns & Allowances HST collected on Sales A/Rec	RECEIVABLE	Sales, Orders & Quotes	Add "Rt" to invoice number If credit memo issued, then add "CMxxx"	
and Cost of Goods Rtn entry	Inventory Cost of Goods Sold			Automatic entry by Sage 50 Accounting Automatic entry by Sage 50 Accounting	
Receipt (no discount)	Cash A/Rec	RECEIVABLE	Receipts	-can be partial or full receipt -can be after a return	
Receipt, with discount	Cash Sales Discount A/Rec	RECEIVABLE	Receipts	-full receipt -can be after a return	

Chapter 3A

PAYABLES Module—*Basics*

Tyson's Toys

Learning Objectives

After completing this chapter you will be able to:

☐ Record purchase orders, invoices, and returns, using the Perpetual Inventory system.
☐ Add new vendors and make changes to existing vendors.
☐ Record payments to vendors in full or partial payment of invoices, with or without cash discounts.
☐ Record payments to other suppliers.
☐ Display and print various payable reports (vendor balances outstanding, etc.) and journals.

The contents of this chapter are as follows:

The PAYABLES Module Overview

The PAYABLES module consists of the Vendors Ledger, the Purchase Quotes (Tyson's Toys does not use the Purchase Quotes Journal), Purchase Orders, Purchase Invoices, Payments Journals, and the INVENTORY module. The Vendors Ledger is the same as the Accounts Payable (A/P) subledger in a manual accounting system.

Purchase Quotes and Purchase Orders are recorded (not posted) in the database. Purchase Invoices and Payments Journal transactions are posted to the individual vendor ledger accounts and to the linked accounts in the General Ledger.

The following transactions are normally recorded in the **Purchase** journals:

- Purchase quotes, purchase orders, and/or purchase invoices on credit from vendors (suppliers), using the Perpetual Inventory system.

- Prepayments with a purchase order.

- Purchases on company credit card.

The following are recorded in the **Payments** journal:

- Payments to vendors (suppliers):
    - partial payment of an invoice.
    - full payment of an invoice with discount.
    - full payment, no discount.
    - cash purchase paid with a cheque, credit card, or debit card.

- Payments for expenses: all other payments, such as rent, electricity, water bills, owner drawings, tax payments (HST) to the government.

At any time, reports (e.g., Aged Vendor reports, etc.) can be produced that show the balances that are payable to vendors. Remember, the total of all payable balances to vendors must match the balance of the ACCOUNTS PAYABLE account in the General Ledger.

In working with the PAYABLES module, you must be very careful in determining the difference between purchases of **goods for resale** (also referred to as merchandise) and purchases of **services or goods not for resale**.

> **Slideshow 3A—PAYABLES Module Basics** is designed to help you understand how the PAYABLES module works and the GAAP related to it. Notice the similarities (and differences) between the RECEIVABLES and PAYABLES modules. Run the slideshow now.

Company Profile—Tyson's Toys

Jerry Tyson and his wife, Helen, owners of Tyson's Toys, sell wooden toys for children from a store in the local mall. Helen works in the store and also travels to toy conventions in search of new toys to sell in their store and to promote their business.

Only the COMPANY, PAYABLES, and INVENTORY & SERVICES modules, for the month of April, are used in the following exercises in Chapters 3A and 3B.

Jerry normally waits until the last day of the invoice terms to pay for goods purchased on credit. Helen has been trying to get him to pay the outstanding invoices so that he can take advantage of the 2% discount. However, he has been focusing on selling the toys rather than good money management. With your help he can manage the business more effectively.

In Part A, Tyson's Toys uses the data folder **03 3A Toys-PI-3A**. Cost of inventory on hand can be viewed using inventory reports.

The business does not use the Track Additional Details feature to record information.

Study Tyson's Toys Trial Balance.

Tyson's Toys-PI-3A, Student's Name
Trial Balance As At Mar 31, 2016

		Debits	Credits
1010	Bank Chequing Account	11,425.00	-
1020	Bank Savings Account	580.60	-
1200	Accounts Receivable	12,899.00	-
1310	Toys and Parts Inventory	6,907.29	-
1330	Prepaid Office Supplies, etc.	625.00	-
1340	Prepaid Insurance	0.00	-
1510	Store Equipment	25,138.45	-
1515	Accum. Deprec. Store Equipment	-	11,393.00
1520	Office Furniture/Equipment	2,812.60	-
1525	Accum. Deprec. Office/Furniture/Equi	-	1,605.00
2200	Accounts Payable	-	10,666.96
2210	Visa Credit Card Payable	-	0.00
2550	HST Charged On Sales	-	1,738.25
2560	HST Paid On Purchases	650.14	-
2610	Bank Loan Payable	-	14,310.86
3100	Capital Jerry Tyson	-	11,924.65
3120	Drawings Jerry Tyson	3,500.00	-
3200	Capital Helen Tyson	-	11,924.65
3210	Drawings Helen Tyson	3,500.00	
4100	Sales	-	34,191.08
4150	Sales - Discount	212.30	-
4200	Sales - Returns & Allowances	604.00	-
5010	Cost of Goods Sold	16,623.00	-
5080	Purchase Discounts	-	289.93
5090	Inventory Adjustments	0.00	-
5310	Rent Expense	6,000.00	-
5340	Advertising Expense	516.00	-
5345	Bank Loan Interest	301.00	-
5350	Bank Charges	135.00	-
5355	Credit Card Expense	0.00	-
5360	Insurance Expense	303.00	-
5370	Auto Lease Expense	1,200.00	-
5440	Office/Store Supplies Expense	750.00	-
5450	Telephone Expense	912.00	-
5460	Utility Expense	1,250.00	-
5470	Bad Debts Expense	0.00	-
5480	Delivery Expense	1,200.00	-
		98,044.38	98,044.38

Fig. 3A-1: Trial Balance, Tyson's Toys-PI-3A.

Session Date

In Chapters 2A and 2B you entered transactions for Santos Luggage at various times and advanced the Session Date as needed. Tyson's Toys has adopted a policy of entering its Accounts Payable transactions on a daily basis, unless you are not available.

Advance the Session Date as noted in the instructions for each exercise.

Starting Sage 50 Accounting for Payables

Exercise 3A-1—Opening the PAYABLES Module

> **Review Exercise 1-2** if you need help to open a data file.

1 ➤ Refer to Exercise 1-1b to unzip the **03 3A Toys-PI-3A.exe** file.

2 ➤ Start **Sage 50 Accounting**.

3 ➤ At the Select Company window, click **Select an existing company** button and click **OK**.

4 ➤ At the **Sage 50 Accounting - Open Company** window, in the left pane, locate your student location drive and the Toys folder ⌂03 3A Toys-PI-3A.

5 ➤ Double-click the ⌂03 3A Toys-PI-3A folder. The 📁 03 3A Toys-PI-3A.SAJ folder and the 📄03 3A Toys-PI-3A.SAI file should appear in the right pane. (The image at the left of Toys may be different depending on the configuration of your computer and the SAI may be in lower case.)

6 ➤ Double-click the 📄03 3A Toys-PI-3A.SAI file icon.

7 ➤ The **Session Date** window will be **Mar 31, 2016**. Click **OK**.

Study the Tyson's Toys Home window. The other modules are hidden.

> The Accounts Payable ledger does not have the **History** symbol. This means that the historical information has been entered and agrees with the GL. You are able to record transactions.

Fig. 3A-2: Tyson's Toys-A Home window.

8 ➤ Remember to revise your company information to add *your name* to the company information in order to have your name printed on your printouts. Refer to Exercise 1-5 if you need help. **This is the last reminder. It is assumed that you will add your name to each of the company records from here on.**

To Display the Vendor Aged Report

As in the RECEIVABLES module, you can find out the status of the company payables by displaying and/or printing the Vendor Aged Report. Similarly, Sage 50 Accounting groups payables calculated from the date of the invoice to the current Session Date. It provides a list of accounts that are **Current**, **31 to 60** days overdue, **61 to 90** days overdue, and **91+** days overdue.

Also, as in the RECEIVABLES module, Sage 50 Accounting provides two options: **Summary** and **Detail**. Your choice depends on the purpose for which you need the reports. At this point, if you wished to acquaint yourself with the balances owing to vendors, and which vendor invoices are overdue, you would select **Detail**. In the next exercise you will display the Detail Vendor Aged report.

When printing this report, it is important that the **Session Date** is correct; otherwise, the aging will not be accurate.

Exercise 3A-2—Displaying the Detail Vendor Aged Report

1 ➤ From the menu bar click **Reports**, **Payables**, **Vendor Aged**, **Detail** should be selected. Click on **Terms**. If necessary, **Select All** to highlight all Vendors in blue, click **OK**.

Compare the window display to Fig. 3A-3. Notice that the screen shows columns that are based on the age of the invoices. As in the RECEIVABLES module, the aging schedule can be changed. This is covered in Chapter 4A. Notice that the Detail Report has the session date (As at date); this is what the aging of invoices is based on.

As at date

Vendor Aged Detail As at Mar 31, 2016

Source	Date	Terms	Transaction Type	Total	Current	31 to 60	61 to 90	91+
City Office Supplies								
1235	Mar 02, 2016	2%/10, Net 30	Invoice	154.57	154.57	-	-	-
Total outstanding:				154.57	154.57	-	-	-
Jason's Transport Service								
6691	Mar 01, 2016	Net 30	Invoice	1,356.00	1,356.00	-	-	-
Total outstanding:				1,356.00	1,356.00	-	-	-
Lanting Speciality Toys								
6198	Feb 22, 2016	2%/10, Net 30	Invoice	1,057.68	-	1,057.68	-	-
6211	Feb 25, 2016	2%/10, Net 30	Invoice	3,403.56	-	3,403.56	-	-
Total outstanding:				4,461.24	-	4,461.24	-	-
Markham Toy Manufacturing								
1622	Mar 22, 2016	2%/10, Net 30	Invoice	1,154.86	1,154.86	-	-	-
1638	Mar 30, 2016	2%/10, Net 30	Invoice	1,127.74	1,127.74	-	-	-
Total outstanding:				2,282.60	2,282.60	-	-	-
Thompson Toy Makers								
886	Mar 15, 2016	2%/10, Net 30	Invoice	2,412.55	2,412.55	-	-	-
Total outstanding:				2,412.55	2,412.55	-	-	-
Total unpaid invoices:				10,666.96	6,205.72	4,461.24	-	-
Total prepayments/prepaid order:				-	-	-	-	-
Total outstanding:				10,666.96	6,205.72	4,461.24	-	-

Fig. 3A-3: Tyson's Toys Vendor Aged Detail window.

As in the RECEIVABLES module, the aged report will show the total for each vendor when there are two or more invoices listed.

2 ➤ **Exit** from the display window.

Displaying and Printing the Income Statement

As part of your task in getting acquainted with the company, you would display and/or print the Income Statement.

Exercise 3A-3—Displaying/Printing Income Statement and Balance Sheet

---

1 ➤ Display and **print** the **Year-to-date Income Statement** with start and end dates of **Jan 01, 2016** and **Mar 31, 2016**. **Keep this printout,** because you will be using it to compare with the Income Statement printed in Exercise 3B-36. Do NOT hide any amounts.

2 ➤ Display and **print** the **Balance Sheet at Mar 31, 2016**. **Keep this printout,** because you will be using it to calculate the HST amounts in Exercise 3B-31. Do NOT hide any amounts.

Exercise 3A-4—Displaying/Printing Inventory Items in Stock

---

1 ➤ To view the items in stock that Tyson's Toys sells, from the menu bar, click **Reports, Inventory & Services, Summary. 1310 Toys and Parts Inventory** should be selected in blue, at **Report On**, click **Latest Transaction**, click **OK**. The report should display as follows:

Inventory Summary Mar 31, 2016

Item No. △	Description	Unit	Price	Quantity	Cost	Value	Margin %
Cars-Lg	Cars-Large	Each	64.00	44	32.00	1,408.00	50.00
Cars-Med	Cars-Medium	Each	44.95	50	22.71	1,135.50	49.48
Cars-SM	Cars-Small	Each	29.90	65	15.08	980.20	49.57
Doors-Sm	Doors-Small	Each	2.40	147	1.20	176.40	50.00
Trailer-Tr	Trailer-Truck	Each	19.50	70	10.00	700.00	48.72
Trucks-LG	Trucks- Large	Each	59.00	50	30.00	1,500.00	49.15
Trucks-SM	Trucks Small	Each	28.00	57	14.32	816.24	48.86
Truck-WL	Truck - wheels	Each	1.99	30	0.99	29.70	50.25
Var-Odd	Various-Odd parts	Each	2.49	125	1.29	161.25	48.19
						6,907.29	

2 ➤ **Exit** to the Home window.

Vendor Invoices Guidelines and Procedures

Tyson's Toys follows common accounting procedures in processing transactions in the PAYABLES module, using the Perpetual Inventory system.

When journalizing vendor invoices in the Purchases Journal, you must know which G/L account the purchase should be charged to. The following guidelines are used by Tyson's Toys:

- Toys and Parts purchased, to be sold to customers (stores and retail), are charged to account #**1310 Toys and Parts Inventory**.

- Other payables (rent, advertising, utilities [water, gas, electricity], etc.) are charged to the appropriate expense account.

- Any goods or services paid for in advance (e.g., office supplies, insurance) are charged to a **PREPAID ASSET** account.

When a purchase invoice is received, the invoice is usually stamped on the back with the date of receipt and an approval stamp (see Fig. 3A-11).

The purchase invoice is then sent to a department manager or other supervisor who is authorized to approve payment and will assign a G/L account number to the amount(s) purchased. It is then signed or initialled, dated, and sent to the Accounting Department for recording and issuing of the cheque. The co-owner, Jerry Tyson, then reviews the relevant documents and signs the cheque(s) for payment.

The PAYABLES Journals

The PAYABLES Module has four journals: **Purchase Quotes, Purchase Orders, Purchase Invoices,** and **Payments Journals**. The following options are available in the Purchase Journals when entering transactions:

Purchase Quotes   used to record a form received from a vendor indicating the price of products or services at which they will sell the product or service to you. Tyson's Toys does not use this Journal.

Purchase Orders (PO)   used to record a confirmation of a commitment to purchase. You would normally send a copy of the purchase order to a vendor. You may record a purchase order even though there is no purchase quote recorded earlier.

The following options are available in the Home window in the Purchase Journal— Purchase Invoices when entering transactions:

Create Invoice   used to enter a purchase on account (credit). A purchase quote and/or a purchase order may or may not have been issued earlier. When a purchase invoice is posted, an accounting entry is recorded that affects both General Ledger and Payables subsidiary ledger accounts.

Find Invoice   look up a posted invoice.

Adjust Invoice   using a negative invoice, this is used to record a return of goods or an adjustment to the purchase price, also called a **Debit Memo**. Similar to the Create Invoice option above, when an Adjustment invoice is posted, an accounting entry is recorded that affects both General Ledger and Payables subsidiary ledger accounts.

When entering the Purchase Journal—Purchase Invoice window, the following option is available.

Payment Method (Chapter 3B)   You can record a purchase with Pay Later, Cash, Cheque, Direct Deposit, or Visa Credit.

The following options are available in the Payments Journal icon, when entering transactions:

Pay Purchase Invoices   used to record payments to vendors for invoices previously recorded using the Purchase Invoice—Pay Later option.

Pay Credit Card Bills   used to record payments where a credit card is used for invoices previously recorded. Tyson's Toys does not use this feature.

Pay Expenses (Also known as) **Make Other Payment**	used to record payments for invoices or debit/credit memos that have not been recorded previously; e.g., rent, drawings, purchases paid by cash, cheque, credit card, direct deposit, or bank debit card.
Pay Remittances (Chapter 7)	used to record payments for payroll deductions (e.g., CPP, EI, Income Tax and Union Dues).

When entering the Payments Journal window, you can record a payment with the following options:

Type	Pay Purchase Invoices, Pay Credit Card Bill, Make Other Payment (Pay Expenses from home window), and Pay Remittance.
By	You can record a payment by Cash, Cheque, Direct Deposit, or Visa Credit.

The Purchase Invoice Journal

This journal is intended to look like a future invoice, and is used to record purchases. Purchase orders and purchase invoices windows are similar. Similar windows were seen in sales quotes, sales orders, and sales invoices in the RECEIVABLES module.

Similar to the Sales Journal, when you record entries in the Purchases Journal, you enter only one part of the entry. The program knows you are in the PAYABLES module and will automatically debit or credit the Accounts Payable account and appropriate taxes.

Customizing the Purchase Orders Journal

As with the Sales Journals, you may also customize the Purchase Journals. Tyson's Toys uses the **Perpetual Inventory** system, and uses the **Item** column. The ☑ division column is not used in this chapter. It will be used in Chapter 11.

Exercise 3A-5—Customizing the Purchase Invoice Journal

---

1 ➤ Advance the Session date to **Apr 01, 2016**.

2 ➤ As in the RECEIVABLES module, you can click the ▼ to see the choices available. Click the **Purchase Invoices** icon and the Purchases Invoice window displays.

3 ➤ Click the **Customize** 🔲 icon, click on **Columns**. Make sure a ☑ appears in the **Division** box to not display this column.

4 ➤ Click **OK** when you are finished.

5 ➤ Type the following into the columns shown. Resize the columns as shown in Fig. 3A-4.

Item Number	Quantity	Order	Back Order	Unit	Item Description	Price	Tax	HST	Amount	Account
					Cheques Special order					1330 Prepaid Office Supplies etc.

Fig. 3A-4: Customized Purchases Journal window (after sizing).

6 ➤ When you have the columns to this approximate size, click the 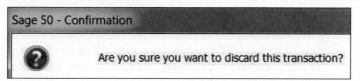 and you will see the following.

Sage 50 - Confirmation

? Are you sure you want to discard this transaction?

7 ➤ Select **Yes** to return to the Purchase Invoice window.

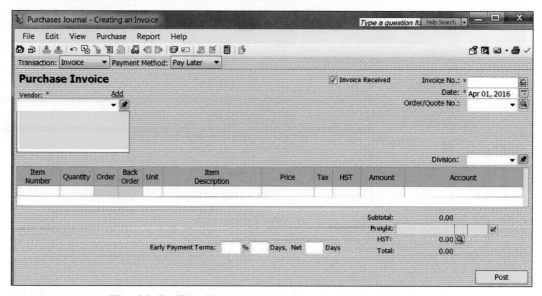

Fig. 3A-5: The Purchase Invoice Journal window.

Toolbar Icons

The toolbar icons are similar to the icons seen in the RECEIVABLES module Fig. 2A-6, Sample Sales Invoice window.

1 ➤ Click X to return to the Home window.

2 ➤ Click the **Purchase Orders** icon.

Entering Purchase Orders

> When a purchase quote is converted into a purchase order, the information on the purchase quote is automatically entered into the Purchase Order window. Likewise, purchase order information is entered into the Purchase Invoice window upon conversion.

A purchase order is a commitment by a purchaser to buy goods, merchandise or services, at the agreed-upon price, terms, and date. The goods are to be delivered, or services provided, within the stated time period.

In the PAYABLES module you can:

1. enter a Purchase Quote;

2. convert it into a Purchase Order (PO); then

3. convert the PO into a purchase invoice.

(See side note box.)

Purchase Quote ⟶ Purchase Order ⟶ Purchase Invoice
Purchase Order ⟶ Purchase Invoice
Purchase Invoice

Similar to the RECEIVABLES module, the purchase quote and the purchase order do not affect the subledgers; they are simply recorded in a Purchase Quote or Purchase Order Listing.

Tyson's Toys records purchase orders; it does not record purchase quotes. Although there are no serious consequences if you do not record purchase quotes, it is important to record purchase orders in order to make sure that all ordered goods or services are provided by the vendor(s). Remember, PURCHASES are goods for resale. If you do not receive your shipments from your vendors, you might not have anything to sell!

Exercise 3A-6—Entering a Purchase Order

> **Apr 01, 2016**   Jerry Tyson issued purchase order #82 to Markham Toy Manufacturing for 35 Trucks Small for $14.32 each, plus HST. The trucks will be delivered on Apr 5. Credit terms are 2/10, net 30.

Some firms may use a numbering sequence for purchase orders that reflects the date; e.g., 100401 (for PO#100 for Apr 1). Mr. Tyson has decided to use the numerical sequence included in Sage 50 Accounting. The next PO is **#82**.

When entering a purchase transaction, from a Purchase invoice, in the Purchases Journal, Sage 50 Accounting will automatically **credit** the Vendor account and ACCOUNTS PAYABLE in the G/L with the total invoice amount (including taxes).

1 ➤ **Transaction**   Click the ▼ arrow and note that the choices are similar to the Receivables Journal, select **Order**. [Tab].

2 ➤ **Payment Method**   Click the ▼ arrow and note the five choices available. If you use the Cash, Cheque, Direct Deposit, or Visa Credit option, the software assumes you are making a prepayment (a payment in advance to a vendor) on the Purchase Order. (See side note box.) Leave the choice as **Pay Later**. [Tab] to Vendor.

3 ➤ **Vendor**   Select **Markham Toy Manufacturing**. [Tab].

> ℹ️ Sage 50 Accounting records money **paid** on a future order in the PAYABLES module (Chapter 3B) as a **Prepayment**. In the RECEIVABLES module (Chapter 2B), Sage 50 Accounting records money **received** on a future order as a **Deposit**.

Note that the address for Tyson's Toys is recorded in the **Shipping Address** box. If the goods are to be shipped to a different address, you will need to type the information in the box, as there is no field available to list different addresses, as there is in the RECEIVABLES module.

Notice that the **Tax** has already been filled in, based on the Vendor Options Tab. You can change the tax and account fields when necessary.

	Order No.	82 will be the next Purchase Order number. Do NOT change.
	Date	The date is correct.
4 ➤	**Shipping Date**	Click the **calendar** and choose **Apr 05**, [Tab] [Tab].
5 ➤	**Item Number**	Double-click or press **Enter**. Select **Trucks-SM**.
	Quantity	This field is skipped because we have not received the goods that were ordered.
6 ➤	**Order**	Type **35**, [Tab]. The row is filled in.
7 ➤	**Back Order**	These are items that have not been received from a purchase order. [Tab] to accept 35.
8 ➤	**Unit**	The cost price is per each truck. [Tab].
9 ➤	**Description**	The description can be changed if needed. Leave the name as indicated. [Tab] to accept the name.
10 ➤	**Price**	[Tab] to accept 14.32.
11 ➤	**Tax**	Press [Enter] or double-click. You will see tax codes like those used in Santos Luggage, Chapters 2A and 2B. Select **HS**. [Tab].
12 ➤	**HST**	The HST amount should be 65.16, which is 13% of 501.20 (35 pieces x 14.32 = 501.20) in the Amount column, [Tab] to accept.
13 ➤	**Amount**	This column should be 501.20 (35 pieces times the cost of 14.32) with a total amount of 566.36 including HST, [Tab] to accept.
14 ➤	**Account**	The default account, **#1310 Toys and Parts Inventory**, is displayed (see side note box). You will be shown how to set a default account in Exercise 3A-9. [Tab] to accept **1310**.
15 ➤	**Terms**	Verify that the terms **2% 10** Days Net **30** Days are recorded correctly. Correct if necessary.

The purchase order is now complete and is displayed in Fig. 3A-6.

> ℹ
>
> A default account is the account that is used most often with each vendor.
>
> This is a purchase of **goods for resale** and should be charged to the #1310 Toys and Parts Inventory account.

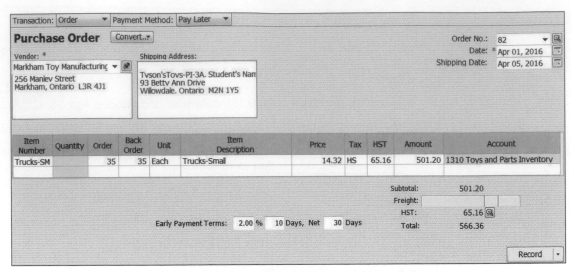

Fig. 3A-6: Purchase Order window with order.

16 ➤ Display the **Purchases Journal Entry**. It should be as shown in Fig. 3A-7.

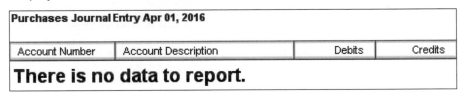

Purchases Journal Entry Apr 01, 2016			
Account Number	Account Description	Debits	Credits
There is no data to report.			

Fig. 3A-7: Purchases Journal Entry window.

There is no journal entry created with a PO, because the goods have not been purchased. When the goods arrive, the PO is converted into a purchase invoice and a journal entry is then created and posted.

17 ➤ **Exit** from the Purchases Journal Entry window.

The Reports and Forms Options have been set at Pre-printed. You do NOT need to print the Purchase Order.

18 ➤ After verifying that the PO is correct, click the **Record** button.

19 ➤ Click **OK** to exit the Transaction Confirmation window. **Exit** the Purchase Order window to return to the Home window.

Exercise 3A-7—Revising a Purchase Order

Apr 01, 2016   Jerry Tyson reviewed purchase order #82 to Markham Toy Manufacturing and decided to increase the order to 40 Trucks small for $14.32 each, plus HST. The other information did not change.

1 ➤ Click the **Purchase Orders** icon.

2 ➤ **Order No**   Click 🔍 **Find Order** icon. The Select Order or Quote window appears with **Quote 82** highlighted. Click **Select** and the window changes to the PO with 35 items back ordered.

> ℹ️ To correct or cancel a Purchase Quote, Purchase Order, or Purchase Invoice after recording, you would repeat this procedure, which is also appropriate for a Quote or Invoice. You may refer to Chapter 13, *Correcting Transaction Errors After Posting*.

3 ➤ Click the 🗑 **Adjust purchase order** icon.

The header changes to: Adjusting Order 82 .

4 ➤ **Order**   Change the quantity to **40**, Tab , and the Subtotal amount changes to 572.80 and the total changes to 647.26. Mr. Tyson is pleased with the change.

5 ➤ After verifying that the PO is correct, click the **Record** button.

6 ➤ Click **OK** to exit the Transaction Confirmation window, and **exit** to the Home window. (See side note box.)

Pending Purchase Order Report

It is good practice to view/print the Pending Purchase Order report to ensure that all goods you have ordered are either received or have been scheduled for shipping by the vendor(s).

Exercise 3A-8—Viewing/Printing Outstanding Purchase Orders

1 ➤ To display the Pending PO report, click **Report Centre,** from the Payables tab, select **Pending Purchase Orders Summary by Vendor**, click **Display**. The report will display that there is no data to report. Sage 50 Accounting defaults to the last time the report was used: Apr 01, 2016. Click the **Modify** button, **Report Options** and change the Date to: **Apr 08, 2016** (a week in the future; all items should be in blue (if not, click Select All), click **OK**.

Pending Purchase Orders Summary by Vendor As at Apr 08, 2016			
Purchase Order Number	Purchase Order Date	Ship Date	Amount Original Order
Markham Toy Manufacturing			
82	Apr 01, 2016	Apr 05, 2016	647.26
			647.26
			647.26

Fig. 3A-8: Purchase Order Summary window.

This report displays the outstanding Purchase Orders and the dates the goods are expected to be shipped.

2 ➤ **Exit** from the Pending Purchase Order window and return to the Home window.

The Vendors Subledger

Before you can enter transactions for a vendor, you need to create a Vendors Subledger account for that vendor. The procedure is very similar to creating a customer subledger in the RECEIVABLES module.

Exercise 3A-9—Entering a New Vendor

1 ➤ Advance the Session date to **Apr 05, 2016**.

Study this transaction:

Apr 05, 2016   **Mr. Tyson issued PO #83 to a new vendor A-Your Name Toy Parts, contact A-Your Name, 956 West Credit Avenue, Mississauga, Ontario, L6X 3K9. Phone number 905-820-3865 extension 2056, Fax 905-820-3866. Ordered 100 Truck wheels (to be sold as parts) at 99 cents plus HST per wheel, terms 2/10, net 30. Total Purchase Order is $111.87 and the wheels are to be shipped on Apr 15.**

Before you can enter a transaction for Your Name Toy Parts, you need to enter a new Vendor account in the Vendors (Accounts Payable) subledger.

> Notice that in the PAYABLES module, there is no **Continue** button.
>
> You can enter a one-time vendor while entering a Purchase Invoice transaction. As in the RECEIVABLES module, the purchase from a one-time vendor must be paid at the same time as the date of purchase in cash, cheque, credit card, or debit card.
>
> If you select **<One-time vendor>** when you create a Purchase Quote or Purchase Order, the window changes to a Purchase Invoice screen.

2 ➤ From the Home window click on **Purchase Orders** ▼ and select **Create Order**.

3 ➤ Transaction   Do NOT change from **Order,** `Tab` `Tab` `Tab`.

4 ➤ Purchased From   Type **A-Your Name Toy Parts,** `Tab`. Type **A-** in front of your name. This puts your name at the top of the vendors. (See side note box—there is no Continue button.)

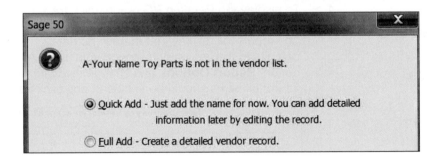

5 ➤ Similar to the RECEIVABLES module, you can create a new vendor in the Payables ledger as you enter transactions. Click **Full Add**, **OK**.

Address

6 ➤ Enter the appropriate information as shown in Fig. 3A-9.

> ⚠ Enter the phone/fax numbers without dashes. Sage 50 Accounting will automatically format them with a dash and brackets as you press `Tab`. Refer to Exercise 2A-23 to record the extension number.

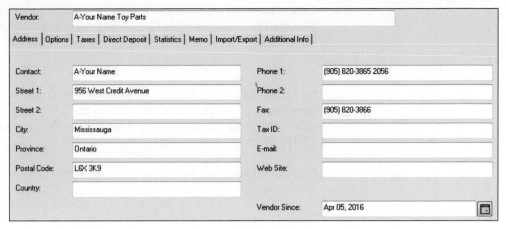

Fig. 3A-9: Payables Ledger window—Address tab.

Tax ID	This field would be used for subcontractor tax numbers required by Canada Revenue Agency for T5018 forms. Tyson's Toys does not use subcontractors for selling toys.
E-mail	Not used.
Web Site	Not used.
Vendor Since	As noted in Receivables, this field lets the user know how long they have been using that particular vendor. It is assumed that previous vendors have been used for a long time.

Options

7 ➤ Click the **Options** tab, and enter information as shown:

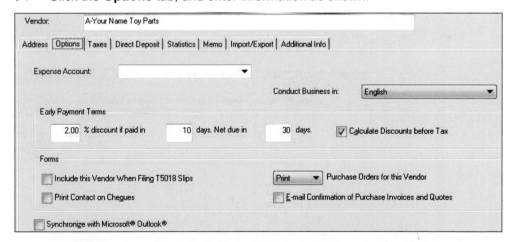

Expense Account	Leave blank. The default account will be #1310 Toys and Parts Inventory, which is from the Inventory item default. The account can be changed if an item of Expense is purchased.
Conduct Business in	There is the ability to have screen displays and printouts in French for the customer. Tyson's Toys has not had any requests to conduct business in French. Do NOT change.
Early Payment Terms	Type as shown. This is the discount for paying within the terms time period.

8 ➤	**Calculate Discounts before Tax**	Checking this box instructs Sage 50 Accounting to calculate discounts on the price before tax, when the company pays within the early payment terms. **Click** the box. A ✓ will appear, `Tab`.
	Include this Vendor when Printing T5018 Slips	Do NOT change. This box would be ✓ to include this vendor when printing the T5018 slips. Leave blank, as Tyson's Toys does not use subcontractors and does not need T5018 forms.
	Print Contact on Cheques	Do NOT change. You would click this box to print the contents of the "Contact" field on the cheques printed for this vendor. Mr. Tyson does not want to print the contact name on cheques produced by the program; therefore, you may leave the box blank.
	Purchase Orders for this Vendor	Do NOT change. You have a choice of sending a purchase order by e-mail or printing and mailing the purchase order. Leave choice as Print.
	E-mail Confirmation of Purchase Invoices and Quotes	Do NOT change. This box would be ✓ if the vendor was able to e-mail you their quotes and/or invoices. Leave blank, as this text does not have an exercise to receive e-mail.
	Synchronize with Microsoft® Outlook®	Do NOT change. As discussed in Chapter 2A, when this box is ✓, the vendor's e-mail address will be placed in the Microsoft® Outlook® Mailing address list. There is no exercise for this feature.

Taxes

9 ➤ Click the **Taxes** tab. This tab will indicate the appropriate taxes that are applied to purchases from this vendor.

10 ➤ Enter the information as shown. Select Tax code **HS**.

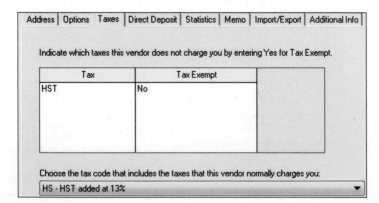

Direct Deposit

11 ➤ Click the Direct Deposit tab. Do NOT change. This feature would allow you to make payments to individual vendors. There is no exercise for this feature.

12 ➤ Click the **Statistics** tab. Do NOT change. This tab will show the value of purchases and payments with each vendor.

Memo

13 ➤ Click the **Memo** tab. Do NOT change. This tab will allow you to keep information about the vendor and have the information shown in the Daily Business Manager.

Import/Export

14 ➤ Click the **Import/Export** tab. Do NOT change. This tab is similar to the Import/Export tab in RECEIVABLES. It refers to importing quotes and invoices from your vendors with your firm's item numbers.

Additional Info

15 ➤ Click the **Additional Info** tab. Do NOT change. This tab could show additional information about the vendor. Refer to Appendix 2015 Q, *Names Fields* in your course materials at www.nelson.com/student for more information.

16 ➤ Click 🖫 Save and Close button to save this vendor in the Payables Ledger and return to a Purchase Order window.

17 ➤ You can now enter purchase order **#83** information for A-Your Name Toy Parts.

100 Truck wheels at 99 cents plus HST per wheel, terms 2/10, net 30. Total Purchase Order is $111.87 and the wheels are to be shipped on Apr 15.

18 ➤ View the Journal entry. There is no journal entry created, as no goods have been purchased. This is only an order to purchase goods. The vendor may not be able to supply the parts.

19 ➤ At the **Record** button, click the ▼. You have a choice to Record or Print & Record the Purchase order when correct. Click **Record** and **Exit** to the Home window.

You can also create a new vendor as follows:

a) From the Home window, click the **Vendors** ▼ arrow, select **View Vendors**. The Vendors window (Fig. 3A-10) displays icons and information for all vendor accounts.

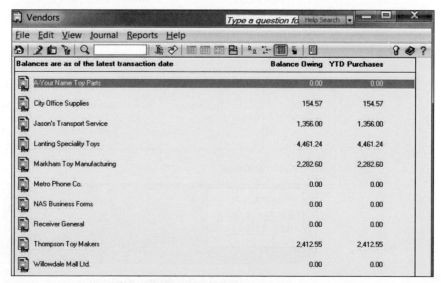

Fig. 3A-10: Vendors window.

The new toolbar icons at the top of the Vendors window mean the following:

Purchases: Displays a blank Purchases Journal for entry of purchase invoices. If a vendor icon is highlighted and this icon is clicked, the vendor address details are automatically inserted in the blank Purchases Journal.

Payments: Displays a blank Payments Journal for entry of a payment to a vendor. If a vendor icon is highlighted and this icon is clicked, the vendor address details are automatically inserted in the blank Payments Journal.

b) From the **Vendors** window, click the **Create** icon [icon] , and the Payables Ledger window appears similar to Fig. 3A-9, with a red asterisk beside Vendor* and a red * asterisk Required Field to the right.

c) **Enter** the appropriate vendor information.

d) **Exit** the Vendors window and return to the Home window.

End of Information section.

Purchase with No Purchase Order (PO)

Sage 50 Accounting will also allow you to enter a purchase in the Purchases Journal without a Purchase Quote or a Purchase Order.

Study the sample Vendor invoice:

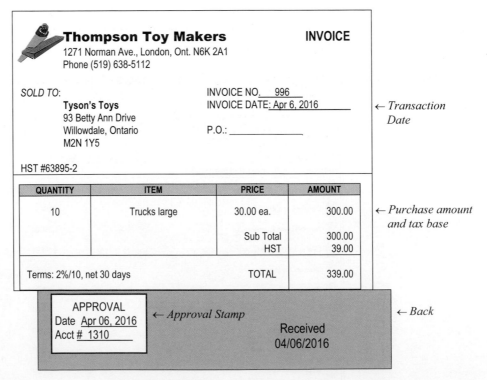

Fig. 3A-11: Vendor invoice.

Exercise 3A-10—Recording a Purchase with NO Purchase Order (PO)

Remember that a **purchase** refers to buying goods for resale. Buying services and goods that are not for resale are recorded as **expenses or prepayments**.

1 ➤ Advance the Session date to **Apr 06, 2016**.

The vendor invoice in Fig. 3A-11 is a credit purchase of toy trucks for resale and should be charged to the Inventory account (1310 Toys and Parts) in the G/L.

There are three ways to create a Purchase invoice.

a) Click the ▾ at Purchase Invoices icon, view the choices, select Create Invoice, at Vendor: select your vendor. The window fills with the vendor name and address.

b) Click on Purchase Invoices icon to open the Purchase Invoice Journal, at Vendor: select your vendor. The window fills with the vendor name and address.

c) In the Vendor section, at top right, scroll to the vendor, click the ▾, select Create Invoice. The window fills with the vendor name and address.

When Tyson's Toys buys goods, the HST the business pays is recorded separately from the HST collected on Sales. Other companies may put the HST collected and HST paid in the same account.

At the end of a period (e.g., month, quarter) the business subtracts the HST PAID ON PURCHASES from the HST COLLECTED FROM SALES. (Calculation of HST amount is shown in Exercise 3B-31.) If the HST collected (e.g., $800.00) is more than the HST paid (e.g., $300.00) the difference ($500.00) is sent to the government (shown in Exercise 3B-32 for remittance entry preparation and posting). If the HST collected (such as $700.00) is less than the HST paid (e.g., $900.00) the difference ($200.00) is requested from the government.

HST PAID ON PURCHASES is a Contra Liability account on the Balance Sheet, and has a debit balance.

We will use method **c)** for this transaction.

2 ➤ In the Vendors section, move to **Thompson Toy Makers**, click the ▾ select **Create Invoice**. The window fills with the vendor name, address and Tax code.

3 ➤ Transaction `Tab` to accept Invoice.

4 ➤ Payment Method Click ▾ . Note that the choices are similar to the Receivables Journal. Accept **Pay Later**, `Tab`.

5 ➤ Vendor `Tab` to accept **Thompson Toy Makers**, `Tab`.

6 ➤ Invoice Received It is assumed that all invoices have been received, `Tab`.

7 ➤ Invoice Type **996**, the invoice number, `Tab` `Tab`.

8 ➤ Date `Tab` `Tab` to accept Apr 06, 2016 (the date of the purchase).

9 ➤ Order/ Quote No. `Tab` `Tab` (a previous purchase order was not issued).

10 ➤ Division Division: [▾] 📎 `Tab` `Tab` . This field is used in Chapter 11.

11 ➤ Item Number Select **Trucks-Large**.

12 ➤ Quantity Type **10**, `Tab`.

Item Number	Quantity	Order	Back Order	Unit	Item Description	Price	Tax	HST	Amount	Account
Trucks-LG	10			Each	Trucks-Large	30.00	HS	39.00	300.00	1310 Toys and Parts Inventory

Order		Not used if PO is not issued.
Back Order		Not used if PO is not issued.
13 ➤ Unit		[Tab], to accept Each.
14 ➤ Description		[Tab], to accept Trucks-Large
15 ➤ Price		[Tab], to accept 30.00
16 ➤ Tax		[Tab] to accept HS.

17 ➤ HST   The HST amount. We have purchased $300.00 of toy trucks to resell to customers, 13% HST on the $300.00 is calculated.

[Tab] to accept **39.00**.

18 ➤ Amount   [Tab] to accept 300.00. The 300.00 is the calculated amount of Quantity multiplied by Price.

Account   You cannot change the default account inventory account **1310 Toys and Parts Inventory**.

19 ➤ Terms   Verify that the terms 2%/10, net 30 days are recorded correctly. Correct the terms if the record is incorrect.

20 ➤ Click **Report**, **Display Purchases Journal Entry**. The display window should appear as follows:

Purchases Journal Entry Apr 06, 2016 (J1)

Account Number	Account Description	Debits	Credits
1310	Toys and Parts Inventory	300.00	-
2560	HST Paid On Purchases	39.00	-
2200	Accounts Payable	-	339.00
Additional Date:	Additional Field:		
		339.00	339.00

Notice the automatic credit to Accounts Payable. Check to make sure that the details on your screen are the same.

21 ➤ **Exit** from the Journal Entry window. Changes can be made to the invoice, if required, by clicking on the field to be changed, and entering the revised details. Make sure you display the entry again, after changes, to make sure that it is correct.

(See side note box.)

22 ➤ **Post** when correct and **Exit** to the Home window.

> ℹ️ To correct or cancel a recorded purchase quote, purchase order, or posted purchase invoice, refer to Chapter 13. A procedure similar to Exercises 2A-19 and/or 3A-7 (revising) and 2A-21 (cancelling) could also be followed.

Viewing a Vendor Account

Sometimes you may need to view a vendor account; e.g., you want to take advantage of a discount so you need to check the date of the invoice, or you want to know how much you owe a particular vendor. At any time, you can display or print the details in a vendor account.

As in the RECEIVABLES module, you can display a **Vendor Aged** report.

Exercise 3A-11—Displaying a Vendor Account

To display the Vendor Report for Thompson Toy Makers, you have two choices:

a) If the Vendor Aged is listed in the *Recently Viewed Reports* area, click on it. This will display all vendors.

b) If the Vendor Aged is not listed in the *Recently Viewed Reports* area, use step 1 to display only Thompson Toy Makers.

  1 ➤ Click **Report Centre**, from the Payables tab select, **Vendor Aged Detail**, click **Modify this report**, click on **Thompson Toy Makers** (it remains blue). The date should be Apr 06, 2016, click **OK**. The report could be displayed with Include Terms.

       Notice that the 2 invoices are in the Current (0 to 30 days) column.

  2 ➤ **Exit** from the display window and return to the Home window.

Purchase of Services/Goods Not for Resale

Inevitably you need to purchase goods not for resale, such as shipping supplies. Although these items may be related to your sales, the items themselves are not for resale; therefore, they should be recorded differently.

Other examples of items not for resale are office supplies, printed cheques for paying bills, customer bags, utilities (Electricity, Water).

Journalizing Purchases for Goods Not for Resale

When a firm purchases goods or services that will be used by the business and not sold to customers, the HST that is part of the invoice price becomes part of the HST recoverable; e.g., supplies used in the office and store, telephone, electricity.

HST is calculated on the invoice amount of goods or services. Remember, HST paid on purchases is recoverable from the Federal Government. For example:

Value of supplies purchased	300.00
HST paid and recoverable	39.00
Total cost of goods and taxes	**339.00**
HST to be recovered	39.00
True cost of amount paid for supplies	300.00

Sage 50 Accounting allows you to record the cost price and HST to match the information from the purchase invoice, and the software does the rest.

Exercise 3A-12—Recording Purchase of Goods Not for Resale

Apr 06, 2016   Mr. Tyson ordered and received 1 box of 1,000 cheques, form
style number #10188, from NAS Business Forms. The special
printing of cheques, on Invoice #4556 dated today, is in the
amount of $300.00, plus HST $39.00. Terms are 2/10, net 30.
A purchase order number was not issued for this purchase.

Note: Charge 1330 Prepaid Office Supplies because the
cheques have not been used. The cost will be charged to an
expense (adjustment) as they get used.

NAS Business Forms

8599 Hammel Avenue   INVOICE **4556**
Toronto, Ont. M8W 3X9
Phone 416-983-2265 ❖ Fax 416-983-2266

SOLD TO:

Tyson's Toys   P.O. _____
93 Betty Ann Drive   Date: __Apr 06, 2016__
Willowdale, Ont. M2N 1Y5

#	UNIT CODE	QTY.	DESCRIPTION	AMOUNT
1	10188	1000	Cheques Special Order	$ 300.00
			HST	39.00
Terms: 2/10, net 30			TOTAL	$ 339.00

Fig. 3A-12: Purchase of non-merchandise.

1 ➤ Use the Purchase Invoices icon, and **Record** the entry as shown in Fig. 3A-13.
You cannot use the Item Number column as the cheques are not part of inventory
for sale.

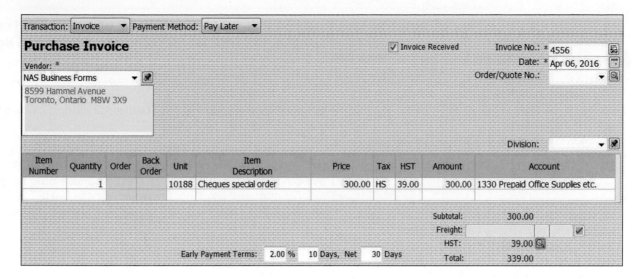

Fig. 3A-13: Purchases Journal window.

2 ➤ View the Purchases Journal Entry. Sage 50 Accounting calculates the cost of the cheques correctly.

Purchases Journal Entry Apr 06, 2016 (J2)			
Account Number	Account Description	Debits	Credits
1330	Prepaid Office Supplies etc.	300.00	-
2560	HST Paid On Purchases	39.00	-
2200	Accounts Payable	-	339.00
Additional Date:	Additional Field:		
		339.00	339.00

> If you make an error in a recorded purchase quote or order, or in a posted invoice, you can use the icon to revise (Exercise 3A-7) or cancel the quote, order, or invoice. You can also Reverse the entry. Refer to Exercise 2A-21, which would be similar, but use the appropriate Purchases, Quotes, Orders, or Invoices Journal instead. See also Chapter 13 for how to make corrections.

3 ➤ When your entry is complete, **Post** the transaction and return to the Home window. (See side note box.)

Purchase of Services

A non-merchandise transaction such as rent, utility (electricity or water) expenses, accountant's fees, drawings, or HST payments, should be entered in the Purchases Journal, if it will be paid later just as any other purchase, or in the Payments Journal, if it is paid when you get the bill/invoice. A vendor subledger should be created for each non-merchandise supplier.

Exercise 3A-13—Recording Purchase of Services—Cheque Issued

This exercise illustrates the steps to record a cheque issued for a service.

1 ➤ Advance the Session date to **Apr 07, 2016**.

> **Apr 07, 2016**   **Mr. Tyson will pick up a cheque payable to Willowdale Mall Ltd. for $2,000.00 plus 13% HST, for the monthly mall rent at 93 Betty Ann Drive.**

The term *Pay Expenses* is not exactly correct. You use this choice to pay expenses that are being paid without being recorded as a payable: rent cheques; office supplies that are purchased and not being used during this accounting period; Owner's Drawings, which is not a business expense; and/or other miscellaneous expenses that are being paid by cheque.

2 ➤ From the Home window at the **Payments** icon, click the ▼ arrow and there are 6 choices.

Pay Purchase Invoices	Pays Invoices previously posted
Pay Credit Card Bills	Pays Credit Card bills previously posted
Pay Expenses	Pays other bills not previously posted (see side note box)
Pay Remittances	Pays Government amounts previously posted—HST (see Exercise 3B-32) and Income Tax, CPP, EI (see Chapter 7)
Find Payment	Finds payments previously posted
Adjust Payment	Adjusts a payment previously posted (see Exercise 3A-16)

3 ➤ Select **Pay Expenses**. (See side note box.)

4 ➤ The choice at top left is Make Other Payment. Click the ▼ to see the choices available. Select **Make Other Payment**. `Tab`.

5 ➤ By   Click the ▼ to see the choices available. Select **Cheque**, `Tab`.

6 ➤ From   If the company used more than 1 bank account you would click the ▼ arrow and select a bank account. Tyson's Toys uses only 1 bank account. `Tab`.

7 ➤ To the Order of   Select **Willowdale Mall Ltd.**, `Tab`.

Cheque No.   The next cheque number is 2511. Cheque #2511 was set up as part of the company defaults. You will learn how to do this in Chapter 4A.

Note: Effective Jan 1, 2007, the Canadian Payments Association (CPA) has issued guidelines for cheque dates. Sage 50 Accounting has adopted the same DDMMYYYY standard that Canadian cheque printers have adopted.

8 ➤ Date   Click this field. You could select a different date. `Tab` `Tab` to accept the date and move to Acct. The Payments Journal window shows the cheque date as Apr 07, 2016, but the printed cheque will display the date as follows:

    0 7 0 4 2 0 1 6   based on the CPA cheque guidelines. D D M M Y Y Y Y   (See side note box.)

9 ➤ Acct   `Tab` to accept this field because this is the default expense account. If you needed to change this column, you would double-click on **5310** and change it to the appropriate account number. Do NOT change.

10 ➤ Description   Type **Mall rent for April**, `Tab`.

11 ➤ Amount   Type **2000.00**, `Tab`.

12 ➤ Tax   `Tab` to accept code HS.

13 ➤ HST   `Tab` to accept HST calculated amount (260.00).

14 ➤ Invoice Ref   Type **Lease 04-2016**, Tab. This field can contain appropriate invoice numbers, memo codes, or other descriptive notations that help describe why the payment is being made. This information will display in the Vendor Aged Report. You cannot use the same Invoice Reference twice; therefore, **04-2016** would indicate the month and year of the lease payment.

15 ➤ Comment   Type **Mall rent for Apr at 93 Betty Ann Drive**. Tab. This field can be used to record an additional comment on the cheque at the bottom of the detail section. See the Make Other Payment window next. See next information note (under cheque) re printed journal.

 In the printed Journal, the comment field will display to the right of the vendor name; e.g., 2511, Willowdale Mall Ltd.: Mall rent for Apr at 93 Betty Ann Drive .

16 ➤ Display the **Payments Journal Entry**. The window should appear as follows:

Payments Journal Entry Apr 07, 2016 (J3)

Account Number	Account Description	Debits	Credits
2560	HST Paid On Purchases	260.00	-
5310	Rent Expense	2,000.00	-
1010	Bank Chequing Account	-	2,260.00
Additional Date:	Additional Field:		
		2,260.00	2,260.00

Notice that Sage 50 Accounting has automatically credited the Bank Chequing account.

17 ➤ Exit the display and **Post** when correct.

18 ➤ Exit to the Home window.

A bill with amounts this large should be accrued as an adjustment at the end of each month. You have advised the accountant and they will begin recording monthly accruals starting at the end of this month. (Adjustments like this will be discussed in Chapter 9.)

Exercise 3A-14—Recording Purchase of Services—Pay Later

This exercise illustrates the steps necessary to record an invoice to be paid later. To record this transaction, the procedure is similar to Exercise 3A-10. You will use the Purchase Invoices icon. (See side note box.)

> **Apr 07, 2016** The March telephone bill was received today. The bill, with no invoice number but dated Mar 31, was from Metro Phone Company. This bill was not accrued in the month of March. The amounts of the bill were: Phone service rental and long distance charges $352.00, HST $45.76. Phone bill is due for payment on Apr 24, 2016. Total amount $397.76.

1 ➤ From the Home window click the **Purchase Invoices** icon.

2 ➤ **Vendor**   Click the ▾ arrow and select **Metro Phone Co.**, `Tab`.

Use an appropriate code for other bills or memos that do not have an invoice number (e.g., for electricity bill use **Hydro0410**, for water bill use **Water0410**).

3 ➤ **Invoice No.**   Type **PHMar31**, `Tab` `Tab`. This coding indicates that the invoice is from the phone company (PH), and that the date the information was sent by the phone company was March 31. (See side note box.)

Date: If you use a Mar 31, 2016 date and try to post the entry, you will get the following message:

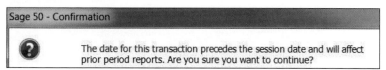

This means that the entry will go back to March 2016 data and change the account postings. The reports dated Mar 31, 2016 have already been printed and sent to the various managers and owners, and would now be incorrect. It is better to date this type of entry as being received on Apr 01, 2016.

The advanced date (Apr 1) would not have a significant effect on the financial results of April.

This approach is reasonable as long as the amount is not significant. A significant transaction amount (large dollar value) would have to be recorded in March; otherwise, the reports may be misleading. Some companies may want to backdate this type of entry. If so, revised reports would be required for all managers and necessary staff. Be sure to provide an explanation to the managers and staff as to why the previous report was revised.

End of Information section.

4 ➤ **Date**   Select **Apr 01, 2016,** `Tab` to accept.

5 ➤ **Quantity**   Type **1,** `Tab` `Tab` to Description.

6 ➤ **Description**   Type **Phone bill to Mar 31,** `Tab`.

7 ➤	**Price**	Type **352.00**, the invoice amount before taxes, Tab.
8 ➤	**Tax**	Tab to accept HS code.
9 ➤	**HST**	Tab to accept 45.76.
10 ➤	**Amount**	Tab to accept 352.00.
11 ➤	**Acct**	The default account **5450 Telephone Expense** is displayed.

If you need to select a different account number, press Enter or double-click. Remember, Sage 50 Accounting will debit the account chosen, Tab. The cursor moves to the next line of the purchase invoice. No more entries are required.

The total at the bottom should equal the total phone bill of **$397.76**.

12 ➤	**Terms**	Leave % blank, leave **Days** blank, type **23** in **Net _Days** box (payment due by Apr 24). There are no discount rates for phone service.

The Purchase Invoice window should appear as follows:

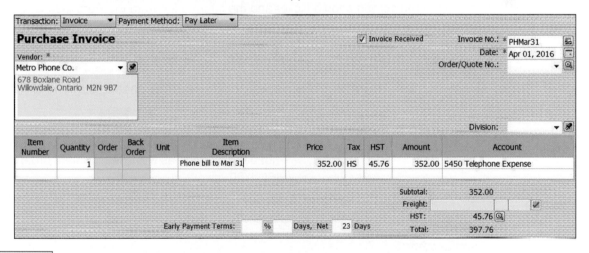

This transaction has been posted to Apr 2016. This does not follow the Matching Principle. However, if a March date is used, all of the reports for March will be changed. In cases like this, most companies would prefer to date this transaction as Apr 1, 2016 so that reports for Mar 2016 are not changed.

Monthly accruals should be recorded by the accountant.

13 ➤ Display the Purchases Journal Entry as follows:

Purchases Journal Entry Apr 01, 2016 (J4)

Account Number	Account Description	Debits	Credits
2560	HST Paid On Purchases	45.76	-
5450	Telephone Expense	352.00	-
2200	Accounts Payable	-	397.76
Additional Date:	Additional Field:		
		397.76	397.76

Sage 50 Accounting has automatically credited Accounts Payable. Check the accuracy of the details.

14 ➤ Exit the Journal window, **Post** when correct and **Exit** from the Purchases Journal window. (See side note box at step 13.)

Recording Arrival of Goods Ordered on a Purchase Order

When goods on a purchase order arrive, an invoice usually accompanies them. This is now a purchase transaction; therefore, it should be recorded (and posted).

Exercise 3A-15—Recording a Purchase Invoice from a PO

> **Apr 07, 2016 The items ordered from Markham Toy Manufacturing on purchase order #82 arrived today with Invoice #1693 dated Apr 06, 2016. Record the transaction with a purchase date of Apr 06, 2016, because the 2% discount period starts on the 6th.**
> **Mr. Tyson was aware the trucks would arrive late.**

Enter the appropriate information into the fields as required.

1 ➤ From the Home window click the **Purchase Invoices** icon.

2 ➤ **Order/Quote No**. Click 🔍 **Look up an Order/Quote**. Select **82**.

The screen should flicker and the information from the Purchase Order is displayed in the window.

3 ➤ Invoice   Type **1693**, [Tab] [Tab].

4 ➤ Date   Type or select **Apr 06, 2016**, [Tab].

5 ➤ Quantity   Type **40**, [Tab] or use the [icon]. The Back Order column is now blank because it shows the correct amount of items that have not been shipped as Nil. The complete order has been received.

The Purchases Journal window should appear as follows:

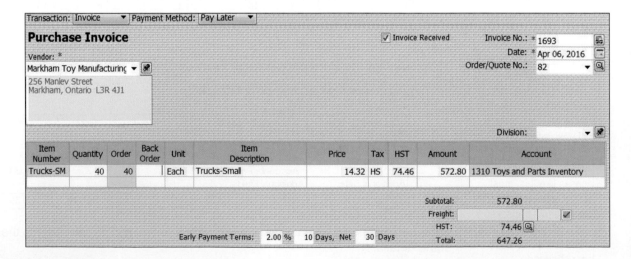

6 ➤ View the Purchases Journal entry. The display window should appear as follows:

Purchases Journal Entry Apr 06, 2016 (J5)			
Account Number	Account Description	Debits	Credits
1310	Toys and Parts Inventory	572.80	-
2560	HST Paid On Purchases	74.46	-
2200	Accounts Payable	-	647.26
Additional Date:	Additional Field:		
		647.26	647.26

7 ➤ **Exit** from the Journal entry window and **Post** when correct.

A message box appears.

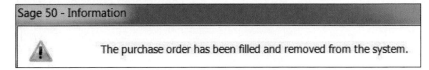

Sage 50 - Information

⚠ The purchase order has been filled and removed from the system.

8 ➤ Click **OK**. Click **OK** again, to accept the confirmation window. The window flickers and returns to a blank Purchases Journal.

9 ➤ **Exit** to the Home window.

Back up your data and update your logbook (located at the back of this textbook) now. **Remember, if it is important, back it up**.

Adjusting a Cheque

There may be situations where a cheque was printed with the wrong amount, or to the wrong vendor. This exercise will show you how to adjust the Payment to the correct amounts. You could have cancelled the cheque (using the Reverse Cheque icon) and then issued a new cheque. In this exercise we will adjust the cheque and change the cheque number. You cannot reprint a cheque using the same cheque number.

Exercise 3A-16—Adjusting a Posted Cheque

This exercise illustrates the steps to adjust a cheque.

> **Apr 07, 2016**   **Mr. Tyson realized that he did not tell you the rent increased to $2,100.00 plus 13% HST as of April 1. Cancel cheque #2511 and issue a corrected cheque #2512 payable to Willowdale Mall Ltd. for the monthly mall rent at 93 Betty Ann Drive.**

1 ➤ From the Home window click the ▼ at the **Payments** icon.

2 ➤ Select **Adjust Payment**, and the Search window opens. Click **OK**.

3 ➤ Select **cheque 2511**, and a payment window with this header appears.

> 💷 Payments Journal - Adjusting Other Payment 2511

4 ➤ Cheque No.   Change the cheque number to **2512** (the next cheque), `Tab`.

If there was an error in the vendor name, you could click the `▼` arrow and select the correct vendor.

5 ➤ Amount   Type **2100.00**, `Tab`.

HST   The amount changes to 273.00 (2,100.00 x 13%).

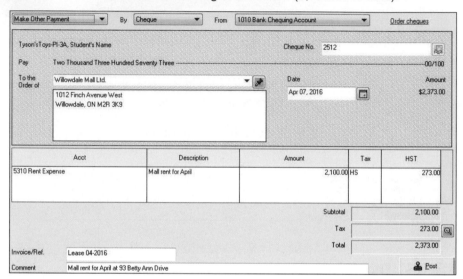

6 ➤ View the Payments Journal entry. The display window should appear as follows:

Payments Journal Entry Apr 07, 2016 (J7)

Account Number	Account Description	Debits	Credits
2560	HST Paid On Purchases	273.00	-
5310	Rent Expense	2,100.00	-
1010	Bank Chequing Account	-	2,373.00
Additional Date:	Additional Field:		
		2,373.00	2,373.00

7 ➤ Exit from the Journal entry window and **Post** when correct.

8 ➤ Exit to the Home window.

9 ➤ Click **Report Centre**, **Banking**, **Cheque Log**, **Modify this report**, the Start Date should be **March 31** and a Finish Date of **April 7**, click **OK**.

Cheque Log for 1010 Bank Chequing Account from Mar 31, 2016 to Apr 07, 2016

Cheque No.	Che... Type	Payee	Amount	Cheque Date	Times Prin...	Entered... system	JE#	JE Date
2511	Payment	Willowdale Mall Ltd.	2,260.00	Apr 07, 2016	0	Reversed	J3	Apr 07, 2016
2512	Payment	Willowdale Mall Ltd.	2,373.00	Apr 07, 2016	0	Yes	J7	Apr 07, 2016

Notice that each cheque is shown as not being printed.

Good Audit Trail information, cheque 2511 is shown as Reversed, for the managers, accountants, and owners.

10 ➤ Exit to the Home window.

Journalizing Purchase Returns

There are times when you may return merchandise for the same reasons that your customers would return goods you have shipped (they were damaged, defective, or not as ordered). This type of transaction should be recorded in the Purchase Returns account. You may send a return invoice (DEBIT MEMO) (to the vendor along with the returned goods because you are **debiting** your ACCOUNTS PAYABLE account. The vendor would then credit the ACCOUNTS RECEIVABLE account in their books that corresponds to your company. They may send you a credit invoice (CREDIT MEMO) to verify the transaction.

Study this summary (without taxes).

Transactions	Recorded in YOUR books	Transactions	Recorded in THEIR books*
	They are a VENDOR to you		**You are a CUSTOMER to them**
Purchases from your vendor	Dr Inventory Cr Accounts Payable	Sale to you	Dr Accounts Receivable Dr Cost of Goods Sold Cr Inventory Cr Sales
Purchase Returns to your vendor (Received their Credit Note)	Dr Accounts Payable Cr Inventory	Sales Return from you (Issue Credit Note to the customer)	Dr Sales Returns & Allowances Dr Inventory Cr Accounts Receivable Cr Cost of Goods Sold
	They are a CUSTOMER to you		**You are a VENDOR to them**
Sale to your customer	Dr Accounts Receivable Dr Cost of Goods Sold Cr Inventory Cr Sales	Purchase from you	Dr Inventory Cr Accounts Payable
Sales Returns from your customer (Issue a Credit Note to the customer)	Dr Sales Returns & Allowances Dr Inventory Cr Accounts Receivable Cr Cost of Goods Sold	Purchase Return from you (Received your Credit Note)	Dr Accounts Payable Cr Inventory

*Assuming they use Perpetual Inventory.

Exercise 3A-17—Recording Purchase Returns

> **Apr 07, 2016**   Returned 13 Trucks small, received this morning from Markham Toy Manufacturing due to paint peeling. The cost of each returned item is $14.32, plus HST from invoice #1693. Markham Toy Manufacturing faxed us their credit memo #CM265 today in the amount of $ -210.36.

Record the entry as follows:

1 ➤ From the Home window, click the **Purchase Invoices** icon.

2 ➤	Purchased From	Select **Markham Toy Manufacturing** vendors, [Tab].	
3 ➤	Invoice	Many firms would enter the old invoice number 1693 with an Rt code; i.e., **1693Rt**. Some firms, in addition, may also enter the credit memo number. Type **1693Rt CM265**. This coding method shows both the original invoice and the credit note. [Tab].	
	Date	**Apr 07, 2016** is the date goods are returned.	

Item Number	Quantity	Order	Back Order	Unit	Item Description	Price	Tax	HST	Amount	Account
Trucks-SM	-13			Each	Trucks-Small-returned paint peeling	14.32	HS	-24.20	-186.16	1310 Toys and Parts Inventory

		Subtotal:	-186.16
		Freight:	☑
Early Payment Terms:	2.00 % 9 Days, Net 29 Days	HST:	-24.20 🔍
		Total:	-210.36

4 ➤	Item Number	**Double-click** and select **Trucks-SM** (Trucks-Small).
5 ➤	Quantity	Type **-13** (minus), [Tab]. The minus sign represents the return of the trucks.
6 ➤	Unit	[Tab] to accept Each.
7 ➤	Description	Type new information: **returned paint peeling**, [Tab].
8 ➤	Price	[Tab] to accept **14.32**.
9 ➤	Tax	[Tab] to accept HS.
10 ➤	HST	[Tab] to accept -24.20. The HST PAID ON PURCHASES account will be credited (reduced).
11 ➤	Amount	[Tab] to accept -186.16 (negative).
12 ➤	Account	You use account 1310 Toys and Parts Inventory because we are reducing (decreasing) the inventory. [Tab]. This account will be credited because of the minus amount. The cursor moves to the next line of the purchase invoice. No more entries are required. (See side note box.)

> ℹ️ A credit memo received is entered as a **negative** purchase invoice, which **reduces** Cost of Goods Sold in the Income Statement.

13 ➤	Terms	Change to **2%, 9 days, net 29 days** to match the original terms on invoice #1693. *Note*: Some firms would not change terms.

The lower portion of the window should appear as shown at step 3.

> ℹ️ Entering a *negative* amount in the **Quantity** column results in a **debit** to **Accounts Payable**, and **credits** to **HST Paid on Purchases** and **Toys and Parts Inventory**.

14 ➤ Display the Purchases Journal Entry as follows: (See side note box.)

Purchases Journal Entry Apr 07, 2016 (J8)

Account Number	Account Description	Debits	Credits
2200	Accounts Payable	210.36	-
1310	Toys and Parts Inventory	-	186.16
2560	HST Paid On Purchases	-	24.20
Additional Date:	Additional Field:		
		210.36	210.36

15 ➤ **Post** when correct. **Exit** from the Purchases Journal window and return to the Home window.

Save your work on a regular basis and update your logbook.

Reviewing the Vendor Record

To view the return memo (negative purchase invoice) just recorded and posted, display the Vendor Aged detail as follows:

1 ➤ In the Vendors area, click ▼ at **Markham Toy Manufacturing, Display Vendor Aged Detail Report**, click **Modify, Report Options, Include Terms** and **OK** to display the detail for Markham Toy Manufacturing.

Notice that the return memo is displayed in the "Current" column because of the date used to enter the transaction.

Vendor Aged Detail As at Apr 07, 2016

Source	Date	Terms	Transaction Type	Total	Current	31 to 60
Markham Toy Manufacturing						
1622	Mar 22, 2016	2%/10, Net 30	Invoice	1,154.86	1,154.86	-
1838	Mar 30, 2016	2%/10, Net 30	Invoice	1,127.74	1,127.74	-
1693	Apr 06, 2016	2%/10, Net 30	Invoice	647.26	647.26	-
1693Rt CM265	Apr 07, 2016	2%/9, Net 29	Invoice	-210.36	-210.36	-
Total outstanding:				2,719.50	2,719.50	-
Total unpaid invoices:				2,719.50	2,719.50	-
Total prepayments/prepaid order:				-	-	-
Total outstanding:				2,719.50	2,719.50	-

2 ➤ **Exit** from the display window.

Viewing/Printing Special Reports

> *Exercise 3A-18—Viewing/Printing a Pending Purchase Orders Report*

Outstanding Purchase Orders

This report displays the outstanding Purchase Orders and the dates the goods are expected to be shipped. It is good to print this report periodically to ensure that no purchase orders are missed. The information in this report is also used for budgeting, particularly forecasting future receipts to ensure that cash is available for payment of bills.

1 ➤ To display this report, click **Report Centre, Payables, Pending Purchase Orders Detail by Vendor, Modify this report**, change the date to: **Apr 15, 2016** (just over 1 week in the future), **OK**. The Pending PO (A-Your Name Toys Parts) is displayed and includes a description of the items being purchased and Back ordered (100 wheels have been ordered). Note that this report is different than the Summary report in Exercise 3A-8.

2 ➤ **Exit** from the Pending Purchase Orders window and return to Home window.

Another Transaction

1 ➤   **Record** and **Post** the following transaction: Return to the Home window.

> **Apr 07, 2016** Per special arrangements, Mr. Tyson sent back 30 Trailer-Truck at $10.00 each plus HST, to Lanting Speciality Toys, that were originally purchased on invoice #6198 dated Feb 22, 2016. Total return including HST is -339.00 (negative). There are no terms on this return.
>
> *Note:* **You may have to change the Price from 1.00 to 10.00.**

The Payments Journal

Payments to vendors for invoices that were previously recorded are entered in the **Payments** Journal. The Payments Journal is also used to record payments for prepayments and cash purchases where invoices are paid at time of purchase (invoices that have not been previously recorded and require a cheque). For cash purchases, you would record the invoice and the cheque at the same time.

Journalizing a Vendor Payment

When entering a vendor payment, Sage 50 Accounting will automatically record a debit to ACCOUNTS PAYABLE and a credit to CASH IN BANK for the amount of the payment.

Sage 50 Accounting can print cheques with an advice; however, Sage 50 Accounting prints only the details of the cheque and advice. The cheques have to be formatted and printed with the bank codes according to bank specifications, ideally on preprinted cheques.

You can also select an option to display a reminder window to print cheques before posting. This has not been done for Tyson's Toys but will be covered in Chapter 4A.

Exercise 3A-19—Recording a Vendor Payment

---

1 ➤   Click the **Payments** icon from the Home window to open the Payments Journal.

Toolbar Icons

The new icon in the Payments Journal is:

 Enter vendor prepayments   Allows you to record payments in advance of receiving goods and/or services. Used with or without a purchase order (see Exercise 3B-29).

ℹ️   📄 The **Include Fully paid invoices prepayment** icon means that any invoice recorded as a Purchase Invoice (not paid using the Pay Expense selection) that was previously fully paid and not cleared (from the data file) will be displayed in the **Original Amt.** column. This feature allows a review of the invoice and payment activity for this vendor. (If you check the box while entering payments, the journal will be reset and amounts will have to be re-entered.)

> ℹ️ To issue a prepayment, click the **Enter vendor prepayments** icon and two vendor Prepayment fields display. Vendor Prepayment Reference No., is the cheque number and/or other information required and the other field is the amount of the prepayment.

Process the following transaction:

> **Apr 07, 2016 Mr. Tyson made arrangements to pay Lanting Speciality Toys for Invoice #6198 and the return of goods from that invoice. Cheque #2513 issued (see below).**

As the information in Fig. 3A-14 indicates, cheque 2513 is paying only Invoice #6198 less the #6198 return. Invoice #6211 is not being paid at this time.

Enter the payment as follows:

If you are going to process a number of cheques to the same vendor, you can click on the red pushpin 📌 to keep the same vendor on the next cheque.

2 ➤ To the Order of

Select **Lanting Speciality Toys**. Notice the program shows all unpaid invoices for this vendor (supplier). [Tab] . (See side note box.)

Cheque No.

2513 is the next available cheque number for Tyson's Toys. If the cheque number is different, you would type the correct number.

Date

The date is correct.

3 ➤ Due Date

Click on **Mar 23, 2016** for invoice **6198**. [Tab] .

The Due Date column displays the net 30 days due date, not the discount period date.

Due Date * 30 days from Invoice date	Invoice or Prepayment	*Invoice Date*	*Discount Date*
Mar 23, 2016	6198	*Feb 22, 2016*	*Mar 03, 2016*
Mar 26, 2016	6211	*Feb 25, 2016*	*Mar 06 2016*
***	6198Rt	*Apr 07, 2016*	*- none- **

*   February 2016 is a leap year

**   The 6198Rt (return) does not have a discount date, as the discount period for the original purchase has passed.

*** Sage 50 Accounting does not display the Due Date for negative invoices (returns and Allowances), therefore, the Mar 23, 2016 date is not shown.

Discount Available

The cursor does not stop in this field, as it is an information column that shows if a discount is available (this invoice is more than 10 days from the purchase date and, therefore, over the discount period).

4 ➤ Discount Taken

As discussed above, there is no discount on this invoice, [Tab] to leave blank.

5 ➤ Payment Amount

The amount **1,057.68**, which is the amount of invoice 6198, appears in this field and is highlighted.

6 ➤ Discount Taken

i *If the Disc. Available column has a -6.00 discount showing, it was because you forgot to remove the terms from the return you recorded in the previous entry. Press Delete to remove the -6.00.*

The cursor drops to the next invoice and the Discount Taken column. The current payment is for invoice 6198 and the return 6198Rt associated with the same invoice. Use the down arrow key ↓ to move to the **Discount Taken** field on the line for **6198Rt. [Tab]** . (See side note box.)

If you pressed [Tab] by mistake before moving down, and 3,403.56 appears in the Payment Amount column, press the *Delete* key to remove 3,403.56 from the column.

7 ➤ Payment Amount

The amount of **-339.00** is highlighted, [Tab] . The total of the cheque to be issued is $718.68. If other invoices were listed and required payment, you would use the ↑ or ↓ key to move to the invoices that were being paid, and repeat the above procedure.

8 ➤ Comment

This field (maximum 39 characters) could be used to record an additional comment, which will appear at the bottom of the detail section on the cheque. (See Fig. 3A-14.)

Type **Payment as discussed with Mr. Lanting**, [Tab] .

The lower portion window should display as follows:

i *The Due Date field does not display the date of the debit note (return or allowance). See Exercise 2B-27, step 3.*

Due Date	Invoice or Prepayment	Original Amount	Amount Owing	Discount Available	Discount Taken	Payment Amount
Mar 23, 2016	6198	1,057.68	1,057.68	0.00		1,057.68
Mar 26, 2016	6211	3,403.56	3,403.56	0.00		
	6198Rt	-339.00	-339.00	0.00		-339.00

Total 718.68

Comment: Payment as discussed with Mr. Lanting

🖳 Post

Fig. 3A-14 Lower portion of Payments Journal.

9 ➤ Display the Payments Journal Entry.

Payments Journal Entry Apr 07, 2016 (J10)

Account Number	Account Description	Debits	Credits
2200	Accounts Payable	718.68	-
1010	Bank Chequing Account	-	718.68
Additional Date:	Additional Field:		
		718.68	718.68

Notice that Sage 50 Accounting has automatically debited Accounts Payable and credited the Bank Account.

10 ➤ Exit from the display window.

Do NOT print a cheque at this time. Pre-printed cheques can be printed on 8-1/2 x 11 paper with one or two advice stubs. If the cheque has two stubs, one advice stub may be sent to the vendor and the second advice stub would be attached to the invoice with other documentation required to approve the payment. If only one advice stub is used, it will be sent to the vendor with the cheque.

11 ➤ **Post** when correct.

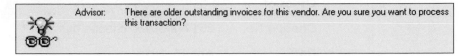

> Advisor: There are older outstanding invoices for this vendor. Are you sure you want to process this transaction?

To correct or cancel a posted cheque refer to Exercise 3A-16, or see Chapter 13, for PAYABLES corrections.

The message box informs you that there are older invoices that should have been paid first. Mr. and Mrs. Tyson have made arrangements to pay invoice #6211 by Apr 16. In a business setting, the clerk would advise a supervisor that an older invoice has not been paid, and the supervisor would take appropriate action.

12 ➤ We want to pay this invoice less the return; therefore, click **Yes**.

13 ➤ **Exit** to the Home window. (See side note box.)

To Review the Vendor Record

14 ➤ Display the **Vendor Aged Detail** report, without terms, for Lanting Speciality Toys.

Vendor Aged Detail As at Apr 07, 2016

Source	Date	Transaction Type	Total	Current	31 to 60	61 to 90
Lanting Speciality Toys						
6198	Feb 22, 2016	Invoice	1,057.68	-	1,057.68	-
2513	Apr 07, 2016	Payment	1,057.68	-	-1,057.68	-
6211	Feb 25, 2016	Invoice	3,403.56	-	3,403.56	-
6198Rt	Apr 07, 2016	Invoice	-339.00	-339.00	-	-
2513	Apr 07, 2016	Payment	339.00	339.00	-	-
Total outstanding:			3,403.56	-	3,403.56	-

15 ➤ **Exit** from the display window to the Home page.

16 ➤ Advance the Session date to **Apr 15, 2016**.

Payment with Merchandise Discount

Note: If a cheque is being issued for a partial payment, in most situations the vendor would not allow a discount on the partially paid invoice.

Many firms take a cash discount on the price of the goods before HST. Most firms will not allow a discount on the HST. You would set a default for the Sage 50 Accounting program to specify how to calculate discounts (to include or not include HST). Tyson's Toys has set Sage 50 Accounting to allow cash discounts before taxes. You saw this step when you set up a new vendor in Exercise 3A-9.

Exercise 3A-20—Recording a Payment with Merchandise Discount

> **Apr 15, 2016 Issued cheque #2514 to Thompson Toy Makers for $2,745.55 in payment of Invoices #886 and #996. Tyson's Toys took a cash discount on Invoice #996. Mr. Tyson wants the cheque to arrive before the end of the discount period.**

Tyson's Toys calculates the cash discount on the $300.00 merchandise purchased on invoice #996, before taxes; therefore, the discount available on this invoice is $6.00, which is 2% of $300.00.

1 ➤ Click the **Payments** icon from the Home window to display the Payments Journal.

2 ➤ **To the Order of**   Select **Thompson Toy Makers**, [Tab].

Cheque No.   **2514** (the next cheque number).

Date   **Apr 15, 2016**.

The lower portion of the journal is displayed in Fig. 3A-15 and the Discount Available column shows 6.00.

Due Date	Invoice or Prepayment	Original Amount	Amount Owing	Discount Available	Discount Taken	Payment Amount
Apr 14, 2016	886	2,412.55	2,412.55	0.00		
May 06, 2016	996	339.00	339.00	6.00		

Fig. 3A-15: Payments Journal window showing discount.

> If you advance the date more than 10 days from the date of the invoice, the automatic discount calculation will report zero discount available.

3 ➤ **Date**   Change the date to **Apr 16, 2016**. The discount remains at 6.00.

4 ➤ Change the date to **Apr 17, 2016**. The Discount Available field now shows 0.00. (See side note box.)

5 ➤ Change the date back to **Apr 15, 2016**, [Tab]. The Discount Available field now shows 6.00.

6 ➤ **Due Date**   The cursor should be at Apr 14, 2016 in this field, [Tab].

7 ➤ **Discount Taken** There is no discount because it is more than 10 days from the invoice date for invoice #886. [Tab].

8 ➤ **Payment Amount**   [Tab] to accept 2,412.55.

The cursor should be in the **Disc. Taken** field.

9 ➤ Double-click **6.00** in the **Disc. Available** field. The screen drills down to the original invoice. You can see the original purchase amount of $300.00 and can verify the discount of 2%. Sage 50 Accounting does the calculation automatically.

10 ➤ **Exit** from the Purchases Journal – Invoice Lookup window, [Tab].

11 ➤ **Discount Taken** [Tab] to accept 6.00.

12 ➤ **Payment Amt**. [Tab] to accept $333.00.

The amount of the cheque should be $2,745.55. The lower portion of the Payments Journal window should resemble Fig 3A-16:

Due Date	Invoice or Prepayment	Original Amount	Amount Owing	Discount Available	Discount Taken	Payment Amount
Apr 14, 2016	886	2,412.55	2,412.55	0.00		2,412.55
May 06, 2016	996	339.00	339.00	6.00	6.00	333.00
					Total	2,745.55

Fig. 3A-16: Payments Journal window.

13 ➤ Click **Report**, click **Display Payments Journal Entry**. The display window should appear as follows:

Payments Journal Entry Apr 15, 2016 (J11)			
Account Number	Account Description	Debits	Credits
2200	Accounts Payable	2,751.55	-
1010	Bank Chequing Account	-	2,745.55
5080	Purchase Discounts	-	6.00
Additional Date:	Additional Field:		
		2,751.55	2,751.55

Notice the Debit to Accounts Payable and the Credit to Purchase Discounts.

14 ➤ **Exit** from the display window. If the cheque was printed on pre-printed forms, with Easy-Align, it would resemble Fig. 3A-17. You Do NOT need to print the cheque.

Tyson's Toys-PI-3A, Student's Name
93 Betty Ann Drive
Willowdale, Ontario M2N 1Y5

CHEQUE NO.   2514

DATE 1 5 0 4 2 0 1 6
       D D M M Y Y Y Y

Two Thousand, Seven Hundred Forty Five and 55/100 $**2,745.55

Thompson Toy Makers
1271 Norman Avenue
London, Ontario N6K 2A1

Tyson's Toys-PI-3A, Student's Name

Thompson Toy Makers   Apr 15, 2016   2514

	Discount	Amount Paid
886		2,412.55
996.	6.00	333.00
		Total 2,745.55

Fig. 3A-17: Information printed on Easy-Align pre-printed cheque form (note Discount).

15 ➤ **Post** when correct, and **Exit** the Payments Journal.

16 ➤ Display the **Vendors Aged Detail** Report (no terms) for this vendor at Apr 15, 2016.

The report should look like the following (note the Discount):

Vendor Aged Detail As at Apr 15, 2016						
Source	Date	Transaction Type	Total	Current	31 to 60	61 to 90
Thompson Toy Makers						
886	Mar 15, 2016	Invoice	2,412.55	-	2,412.55	-
2514	Apr 15, 2016	Payment	-2,412.55	-	-2,412.55	-
996	Apr 06, 2016	Invoice	339.00	339.00	-	-
2514	Apr 15, 2016	Discount	-6.00	-6.00	-	-
2514	Apr 15, 2016	Payment	-333.00	-333.00	-	-
Total outstanding:			-	-	-	-

To display details of a recorded invoice, you could double-click on any item on the invoice **996** line. The invoice that created the $ values is displayed with a PAID image. This will assist you in not paying an invoice twice. To see the cheque that paid the invoice, you would double-click on the Payment line. The Cheque Lookup window will appear.

17 ➤ **Exit** from the Vendor Aged Detail display window.

Printing Reports When Needed

It is normal to print some of the following reports during the month and file them for your audit trail:

- All Journal Entries Apr 1 to Apr 15.
- Vendor Aged Detail report, all vendors, with terms, at Apr 15.
- Purchases Journal Apr 1 to Apr 15.
- Payments Journal Apr 1 to Apr 15.
- Cheque Log Apr 1 to Apr 15.

Exercise 3A-21—Printing Period-End Reports

Make sure the printer is ready. You should be at the Tyson's Toys Home window to start this exercise.

1 ➤ **Print the All Journal Entries** report as shown in previous chapters.

2 ➤ **Print the Vendor Aged Detail** at Apr 15. To ensure that everything is correct, you should compare the Balance Sheet Accounts Payable amount with the total of the Vendor Aged Detail report. They should be the same.

3 ➤ If required by your instructor, at Apr 15, refer to Exercise 3B-37 to View and/or Print the Purchases Journal, Payments Journal, and/or Cheque Log.

Summary, Part A

Here is a summary of tasks and transactions in Chapter 3A:

Transaction	Journal	Remarks
Purchase Quote	Purchase Quotes	Enter amounts as positive, including HST where applicable. Does not update the General Ledger. Can be changed to a Purchase Order.
Purchase Order	Purchase Orders	Similar to Purchase Quote. Enter amounts as positive. A purchase order can be entered without a purchase quote being recorded. Does not update the General Ledger.
Purchase	Purchase Invoices	A purchase can be entered by changing a Purchase Order to an invoice, or can be recorded without recording a purchase order. Enter amounts as positive. HST amounts are entered in appropriate fields. Updates the General Ledger.
Purchase Return	Purchase Invoices	Enter amount as a minus amount. HST is recorded as a negative amount. Updates the General Ledger.
Payment to Recorded invoice	Payments	Select the invoice(s) to be paid. Updates the General Ledger.
Payment with Discount	Payments	Applies a payment against the original invoice and the calculated discount.
New Vendor (Supplier)	Vendors Ledger	At the Taxes tab, change the Tax Exempt status for HST where necessary and select the appropriate tax code. Select an appropriate default expense account.

Before Moving On ... Part A

Read the following questions and make sure you know the answers to them; otherwise, read the corresponding part in the chapter before moving on:

1. Name the types of transactions that are recorded in the PAYABLES module.

2. Describe the procedure for approving vendor invoices from the time they are received until they are paid. What is the significance of this procedure?

3. What types of entries are **not** recorded in the PAYABLES module? (Ignore Sales entries.)

4. When journalizing non-merchandise purchases with HST, how is the **HST** recorded?

5. Give the journal entry for a merchandise purchase return of $300.00 plus HST of $39.00.

6. Describe briefly the steps in recording an invoice payment in full, net of a cash discount. Assume that: a) merchandise for resale was purchased, and b) discounts are calculated on pre-tax amounts.

7. What happens when you post journal transactions in the PAYABLES module?

8. When journalizing non-merchandise purchases with HST, on what amount is **HST** based?

Relevant Appendices, Part A

www The following appendices are available by opening your course materials at www.nelson.com/student.

Appendix 2015 Q **Names Fields**

Appendix 2015 V1 **Perpetual Mini-Guide Receivables—Payables** (in Excel)*

Refer to Mini-guide at the end of Chapter 3B for transactions.

Challenge Exercise 03 C3A-1, Wheelchairs
(PAYABLES and COMPANY Modules)

Wheelchairs is a business that sells various kinds of wheelchairs to wholesale and retail customers.

Note: The business is open 7 days a week. HST is 13%.

1 ➤ Refer to Exercise 1-1b to unzip the **03 C3A-1 Wheelchairs.exe** file.

2 ➤ Open the **C3A-1 Wheelchairs** file, and enter the following Accounts Payable transactions.

Mar 1   Issued Purchase order #81 to Your Name Chairs (Your name must appear) for 8 new model wheelchairs, code WC-CP-3, at $1,500 each, plus HST. Ship date is Mar 4. Other information: 156 Octavia Street, Belleville, Ontario, K8P 1H3, phone and fax numbers may be left blank. Terms are 2% 10 days, net 30 days, calculate discounts before tax.

Mar 1   Issued $2,250.00 plus HST cheque to Gordon Mall Management for lease rent for March.

Mar 4   Received 7 wheelchairs, code WC-CP-3, from Your Name Chairs from PO#81. Invoice #4568 received. The other chair is back ordered and should be delivered by Mar 25.

Mar 5   Returned 1 wheelchair from PO#81, as there is a crack in the frame. Credit note CN-56 received by fax.

Mar 6   Purchased and received from The Paper Place, 2 boxes of invoices, that will be used during the year. Invoice #2256 received for $300 plus HST, Terms 2/10, net 30.

Mar 7   We discovered that ¼ of the invoices (value $75.00) received on invoice #2256 were printed without logos. The Paper Place manager agreed to an allowance (2256Al) of $75.00 plus HST, which can be used to reduce the cost of the current order.

Mar 13 Received Belleville Hydro bill #1565-3 for $112.00 plus HST. Service bill dated Mar 12, and payment date is Mar 27.

Mar 14 Issued next cheque to Your Name Chairs for amount owing, less the return.

Mar 18 Purchased from Avery Parts, 6 items, code RP-01. Invoice #8897 received in the total amount of $120.00 plus HST. Terms 2/10, net 30.

Mar 20 Received a bank debit memo, dated today, regarding the loan payment of $400.00, which includes $67.00 of interest.

3 ➤ When you have recorded the above entries, **print** the following:
  a) Vendor Aged Detail, all vendors, with terms at Mar 20
  b) All Journal Entries for Mar 1 to 20
  c) General Journal Entries, for Mar 1 to 20
  d) Purchase Journal Entries for Mar 1 to 20
  e) Income Statement for Jan 1 to Mar 20
  f) Pending Purchase Order Detail, by Vendor report, with terms Mar 20

Challenge Exercise 03 C3A-2, Radios
(*PAYABLES and COMPANY Modules*)

Radios is a business that sells various kinds of radios to wholesale and retail customers.

Note: The business is open 7 days a week. HST is 13%.

1 ➤   Refer to Exercise 1-1b to unzip the **03 C3A-2 Radios.exe** file.

2 ➤   Open the **03 C3A-2 Radios** file, and enter the following Accounts Payable transactions.

Jun 1   Issued $2,000 plus HST cheque to Royal Mall Management for lease rent for June.

Jun 1   Purchased from Town Printing Co. 4,000 advertising flyers at $ .35 (35 cents each) plus HST, on Invoice #9974, terms 2/10, net 30. The flyers are being distributed today.

Jun 4   Received 20 radios model #26583, code R-265, from Radio Manufacturing Ltd., at $40.00 each plus HST on Invoice #5380, with terms 2/10, net 30.

Jun 4   Ordered on Purchase Order #135, 15 radios, code R-83, at $83.00 plus HST, from new vendor Your Name Radio Wholesale. (Your name must appear). Ship date is Jun 06. Other information: 688 Coleman Street, Belleville, Ontario, K8P 7P3, phone and fax numbers may be left blank. Terms are 2% 10 days, net 30 days, calculate discounts before tax.

Jun 6   Complete order received from Your Name Radio Wholesale on Invoice #3865 dated today.

Jun 7   Returned 1 radio from the Your Name Radio Wholesale order of June 6, as one of the speakers is broken. Credit note CN-86 received.

Jun 14   Issued next cheque to Radio Manufacturing Ltd. for Invoice #2583.

Jun 15   Purchased from Oksana Radio Sales, 2 Outside radios, code R-65, at $150.00 each plus HST on Invoice #3489. Terms 2/10, net 30.

Jun 15   Issued next cheque to Your Name Radio Wholesale for amount owing, less the return.

Jun 20   Issued next cheque to Gananoque Telephone for telephone service $160.00 and Yellow Pages advertising $40.00, plus HST. Service bill dated June 19.

Jun 20   The owner does not want the cheque mailed to Gananoque Telephone, as there is an error in the advertising amount. Reverse the cheque. We have requested a revised invoice.

3 ➤   When you have recorded the above entries, **print** the following:
   a)   Vendor Aged Detail, all Vendors, with terms at Jun 20
   b)   All Journal Entries for Jun 1 to 20, **with Corrections**
   c)   Purchase Journal Entries for Jun 1 to 20
   d)   Income Statement for Jan 1 to Jun 20

Chapter 3B

PAYABLES Module—*Beyond Basics*

Tyson's Toys

Learning Objectives

After completing Chapter 3B you will be able to:

☐ Continue to record purchase orders, invoices and returns.
☐ Continue to add new vendors and make changes to existing vendors.
☐ Record payments to vendors in full or partial payment of invoices with or without cash discounts.
☐ Record payments to other suppliers (one-time vendor, owner for drawings, etc.).
☐ Record tax payments for HST to the Federal Government.
☐ Record prepayments to vendors.
☐ Display and print various payable reports (vendor balances outstanding, etc.) and journals.

This chapter is a continuation of Chapter 3A. You should download the 03 3B Toys-PI-3B data file for use with this chapter.

The contents of this chapter are as follows:

Opening the PAYABLES Module, Part B

In this Chapter (3B), you will access the PAYABLES module of Tyson's Toys and enter transactions related to purchases, payments to vendors, one-time payments and other payable transactions, using the Perpetual Inventory System where appropriate starting from April 15.

The 03 3B Toys-PI-B.exe file contains the ending balances of the General Ledger accounts and Vendor files from Chapter 3A of this text (see Trial Balance on the following page). These balances will be the starting point of the B file and journal entries will start at J1.

View **Slideshow 3B—PAYABLES Module Beyond Basics** to prepare for more transaction processing in the PAYABLES module. Pay particular attention to the Accounting principles related to the various tasks.

Starting Sage 50 Accounting for Payables

Exercise 3B-22—Opening the 03 3B Toys-PI-3B data file

Review Exercise 1-2 if you need help to open a data file.

1 ➤ Refer to Exercise 1-1b to unzip the **03 3B Toys-PI-3B.exe** file. (See side note box.)

2 ➤ Start **Sage 50 Accounting**.

3 ➤ At the Select Company window, click **Select an existing company** button and **OK**.

4 ➤ At the Sage 50 Accounting **Open Company** window, in the left pane, locate your student location drive, and the Toys folder 03 3B Toys-PI-3B .

5 ➤ Double-click the 03 3B Toys-PI-3B folder. The 03 3B Toys-PI-3B.SAJ folder and the 03 3B Toys-PI-3B.SAI file should appear in the right pane. The image at the left of Toys may be different, depending on the configuration of your computer.

6 ➤ Double-click the 03 3B Toys-PI-3B.SAI file icon.

7 ➤ The **Session Date** window will be **Apr 15, 2016.** Click **OK**.

8 ➤ Display the **Trial Balance**. The following is the Tyson's Toys Trial Balance at the end of Chapter 3A.

Study Tyson's Toys Trial Balance.

Tyson's Toys-PI-3B, Student's Name
Trial Balance As At Apr 15, 2016

		Debits	Credits
1010	Bank Chequing Account	5,587.77	-
1020	Bank Savings Account	580.60	-
1200	Accounts Receivable	12,899.00	-
1310	Toys and Parts Inventory	7,293.93	
1330	Prepaid Office Supplies, etc.	925.00	-
1340	Prepaid Insurance	0.00	-
1510	Store Equipment	25,138.45	-
1515	Accum. Deprec. Store Equipment	-	11,393.00
1520	Office Furniture/Equipment	2,812.60	-
1525	Accum. Deprec. Office/Furniture/Eq	-	1,605.00
2200	Accounts Payable	-	8,370.39
2210	Visa Credit Card Payable	-	0.00
2550	HST Charged On Sales	-	1,738.25
2560	HST Paid On Purchases	1,058.16	-
2610	Bank Loan Payable	-	14,310.86
3100	Capital Jerry Tyson	-	11,924.65
3120	Drawings Jerry Tyson	3,500.00	-
3200	Capital Helen Tyson	-	11,924.65
3210	Drawings Helen Tyson	3,500.00	
4100	Sales	-	34,191.08
4150	Sales - Discount	212.30	-
4200	Sales - Returns & Allowances	604.00	-
5010	Cost of Goods Sold	16,623.00	-
5080	Purchase Discounts	-	295.93
5090	Inventory Adjustments	0.00	-
5310	Rent Expense	8,100.00	-
5340	Advertising Expense	516.00	-
5345	Bank Loan Interest	301.00	-
5350	Bank Charges	135.00	-
5355	Credit Card Expense	0.00	-
5360	Insurance Expense	303.00	-
5370	Auto Lease Expense	1,200.00	-
5440	Office/Store Supplies Expense	750.00	-
5450	Telephone Expense	1,264.00	-
5460	Utility Expense	1,250.00	-
5470	Bad Debts Expense	0.00	-
5480	Delivery Expense	1,200.00	-
		95,753.81	95,753.81

Fig. 3B-18: Trial Balance, Tyson's Toys-PI-3B.

Cash Flow Projection Report

The Cash Flow Projection report shows how the bank account is expected to change by anticipated payments to outstanding vendor accounts, and expected customer payments (receipts) to be received within the number of days specified, as well as recurring entries and other payments that will affect the bank balance. (See Bank Account projection in step 1 and side note box beside step 1.)

Exercise 3B-23—Viewing/Printing a Cash Flow Report

> **Apr 15, 2016** Mr. Tyson is concerned about the amount of money he will have in the bank and the amount he owes his suppliers. He has asked you to print a Cash Flow report.

i

The Cash Flow **Summary** report shows a summary of amounts that will affect the bank account balance. This chapter shows only Accounts Payable transactions and does not show any receipts from Accounts Receivable.

1 ➤ To display the Cash Flow report, click **Report Centre, Financials**, **Cash Flow Projection Summary**, **Display**. This report does not indicate when the account will be in a negative position. (See side note box.)

1010 Bank Chequing Account. Cash flow projection from Apr 15, 2016 to May 15, 2016

Description	Balance
Balance as of Apr 15, 2016	5,587.77
Total receipts	0.00
Total payments	-8,356.65
Total recurring general journal transactions	-884.20
Total recurring other payment transactions	0.00
Ending balance	-3,653.08
Net change in cash balance:	-9,240.86
Lowest balance in the account:	-3,653.09
Highest balance in the account:	5,587.77

i

An overdraft occurs when you have issued cheques for more money than you have in your bank account.

2 ➤ Click **Modify**, **Report Options**, select **Detail**, **1010 Bank Account** is selected, click **OK**. The report shows the balance per day (Total for the day) and that the bank account will go into a negative position, (overdraft), on Apr 16 if current ACCOUNTS PAYABLE vendors are paid on time. Mr. and Mrs. Tyson are drafting a payment plan with the bank and all vendors. (See side note box.)

3 ➤ **Print** the Report.

4 ➤ **Exit** from the Cash Flow Projection window, return to the Home window.

Credit Card Purchase

Similar to credit card sales in the RECEIVABLES module, credit card purchases are considered cash purchases.

In Chapter 2B, the credit card company charges the vendor (Mrs. Santos) a fee for each transaction for allowing a customer to use a credit card. In the case of the customer who uses a credit card to pay for a purchase, the customer does not pay a fee for every transaction. The credit card company usually collects an annual fee from the credit card holder. Study how the credit card purchase transaction is recorded in the next exercise.

Exercise 3B-24—Recording a Credit Card Purchase

Apr 15, 2016	Mrs. Tyson purchased a second new briefcase (wide) for $135.00, plus 13% HST, for a total price of $152.55 from Santos Luggage. Mrs. Tyson used her business credit card to pay for the purchase. Received Invoice #2319.

Follow these steps to record the transaction:

1 ➤ From the Home window, click the **Purchase Invoices** icon.

Transaction Do NOT change.

2 ➤ Payment method Select **Visa Credit**, `Tab`.

3 ➤ Vendor Type **Santos Luggage** `Tab`, **Continue** should be selected. Click **OK,** then `Tab` `Tab`.

4 ➤ Type **635 Semple Avenue** `Tab`, **Toronto, ON** `Tab`, **M9L 1V5**. `Tab`.

5 ➤ Invoice No. For a credit card transaction, some vendors will issue a regular invoice and other vendors will issue a cash register receipt. Type **2319**, because Santos Luggage issued Invoice #2319, `Tab` `Tab`.

6 ➤ Date `Tab` to accept **Apr 15, 2016**, `Tab` to Division.

7 ➤ Division This field is used in Chapter 11. `Tab` `Tab` to Item Number.

8 ➤ Item Number This column would be used when purchasing goods for resale. The briefcase is not for sale. `Tab`.

9 ➤ Quantity Type **1**, `Tab`.

10 ➤ Unit Type **each**, `Tab`.

11 ➤ Item Description Type **Briefcase wide**, `Tab`.

12 ➤ Price Type **135.00**, `Tab`.

13 ➤ Tax	Select **HS**, [Tab].
14 ➤ HST	[Tab] to accept 17.55.
15 ➤ Amount	[Tab] to accept 135.00.
16 ➤ Account	Select **5440 Office/Store Supplies Expense**.

> Some firms may have specific expense accounts to charge this type of item. This item would not be charged to an asset account due to the low dollar value (the amount is not material). Your instructor will explain in more detail.

(See side note box.)

The lower portion of the window appears as follows:

Item Number	Quantity	Order	Back Order	Unit	Item Description	Price	Tax	HST	Amount	Account
	1			each	Briefcase wide	135.00	HS	17.55	135.00	5440 Office/Store Su...

The following is shown at the bottom of the Invoice window:

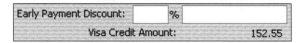

Early Payment Discount:	%
Visa Credit Amount:	152.55

There is no Early Payment Discount on this purchase. The Early Payment Discount referred to here is for a regular customer who has 2%/10 day terms. The discount does not apply to a Visa purchase.

17 ➤ Display the entry as follows.

> Because you selected **Visa Credit** in the **Paid By** field, Sage 50 Accounting automatically entered a credit to 2210 Visa Credit Card Payable, instead of a credit to ACCOUNTS PAYABLE.

Purchases Journal Entry Apr 15, 2016 (J1)

Account Number	Account Description	Debits	Credits
2560	HST Paid On Purchases	17.55	-
5440	Office/Store Supplies Expense	135.00	-
2210	Visa Credit Card Payable	-	152.55
Additional Date:	Additional Field:		
		152.55	152.55

(See side note box.)

18 ➤ Post when correct, and **Exit** to the Home window.

Payment with Non-Merchandise Discount

At this point, it is important to differentiate between **Purchase Discount** and **Cash Discount**.

A **Purchase Discount** account is used **ONLY** to show **reductions** (for paying within the discount period) to the cost of merchandise to be resold. When you are able to take a cash discount on goods or services that are **not for resale** (non-merchandise items, e.g., office supplies) and, therefore, not charged to the Toys and Parts Inventory account, you should not record the discount to the Purchase Discount account.

Sage 50 Accounting will allow an automatic discount entry to only 1 account. The Purchase Discount account has been set up as the default discount account.

Before you can record a payment with a discount on goods that are not for resale, e.g., Office Supplies, Advertising Expense, etc., you need to record a negative invoice. This invoice is charged to the same account, e.g., office supplies, which is a reduction to the original account where the cost was charged.

There are two steps to record a payment that involves a non-merchandise discount:

1. Record a negative purchase invoice for the discount. There are two ways to calculate the discount:

    i) You can use the lookup feature to view the details of the original invoice, and manually calculate the discount.

    ii) You can use the Payment cheque icon to view the items that are owing for each vendor, and let *Sage 50 Accounting* calculate the discount for you. ***Do NOT post the transaction. This method is used to calculate the discount only.***

2. Record the payment including the discount using method (i) above.

Exercise 3B-25—Recording a Payment with Non-Merchandise Discount

> **Apr 15, 2016** **Paid $333.00 with your cheque #2515 to NAS Business Forms in payment of their invoice #4556, taking a cash discount because you are paying within the credit terms. The amount of the discount is $6.00 (2% of the $300.00 printing costs).**

The discount of $6.00 is a reduction of the cost of the printed cheques and is not charged to the Purchase Discounts account.

Note that this purchase of non-merchandise items was originally entered, in Exercise 3A-12 Journal entry 2, as shown:

Purchases Journal Entry Apr 06, 2016 (J2)			
Account Number	Account Description	Debits	Credits
1330	Prepaid Office Supplies etc.	300.00	-
2560	HST Paid On Purchases	39.00	-
2200	Accounts Payable	-	339.00
Additional Date:	Additional Field:		
		339.00	339.00

To record the payment with a cash discount:

Step One: *Record the Discount*

<table>
<tr><td>1 ➤</td><td></td><td>Click Purchase Invoices icon.</td></tr>
<tr><td>2 ➤</td><td>Payment method</td><td>Select Pay Later to match original invoice.</td></tr>
<tr><td>3 ➤</td><td>Vendor From</td><td>Select NAS Business Forms, <kbd>Tab</kbd>.</td></tr>
<tr><td>4 ➤</td><td>Invoice No.</td><td>Type 4556Di, <kbd>Tab</kbd> <kbd>Tab</kbd>. (See side note box.)</td></tr>
<tr><td>5 ➤</td><td>Date</td><td><kbd>Tab</kbd> to accept Apr 15, 2016,</td></tr>
<tr><td>6 ➤</td><td>Quantity</td><td>Type 1, <kbd>Tab</kbd>.</td></tr>
<tr><td>7 ➤</td><td>Unit</td><td>Type Each, <kbd>Tab</kbd>.</td></tr>
<tr><td>8 ➤</td><td>Item Description</td><td>Type Discount on Invoice #4556, <kbd>Tab</kbd>.</td></tr>
<tr><td>9 ➤</td><td>Price</td><td>Type -6.00 (negative amount to reduce the cost of supplies), <kbd>Tab</kbd>.</td></tr>
<tr><td>10 ➤</td><td>Tax</td><td>There are no taxes on a discount. Delete HS. <kbd>Tab</kbd> to Amount.</td></tr>
<tr><td>11 ➤</td><td>Amount</td><td><kbd>Tab</kbd> to accept -6.00. <kbd>Tab</kbd> to Account.</td></tr>
<tr><td>12 ➤</td><td>Account</td><td>The default account 1330 Prepaid Office Supplies, etc., appears in this field. The cheques were originally charged (posted) to this account; therefore, <kbd>Tab</kbd> to accept. This will reduce the cost of the supplies.</td></tr>
<tr><td>13 ➤</td><td>Terms</td><td>Remove 2% 10 Days, Net 30 Days. There are no terms when claiming a discount, <kbd>Tab</kbd>.</td></tr>
</table>

> **Di** is added to the end of the invoice number to distinguish the discount as relating to a cash discount for non-merchandise items, and not a purchase discount for goods purchased for resale.

Your Purchases Journal display should be as follows:

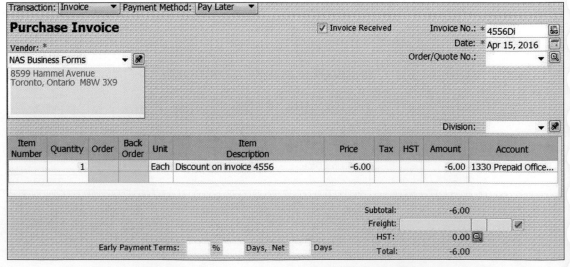

Fig. 3B-19: Purchases Journal showing discount.

14 ➤   **Display** the Journal entry; it should appear as follows:

Purchases Journal Entry Apr 15, 2016 (J2)			
Account Number	Account Description	Debits	Credits
2200	Accounts Payable	6.00	-
1330	Prepaid Office Supplies etc.	-	6.00
Additional Date:	Additional Field:		
		6.00	6.00

Notice the **credit** to PREPAID OFFICE SUPPLIES, etc., and the **debit** to ACCOUNTS PAYABLE.

15 ➤   **Exit** from the Journal Entry window.

16 ➤   **Post** when correct, and **Exit** to the Home window.

Step Two: Journalize the Payment

17 ➤   Click the **Payments** icon.

18 ➤   **Pay to the order of**   Select **NAS Business Forms,** [Tab].

Cheque No.   2515 is the next cheque number.

Date   Apr 15, 2016 is the correct date.

19 ➤   **Due Date**   **Click** May 06, 2016. We want to pay invoices #4556 and #4556Di; therefore, press [Tab].

20 ➤   **Discount Taken**   Automatic calculation shows 6.00. Accepting the discount amount in this column means you want the discount to be charged to the Purchase Discount account. We have recorded a 6.00 non-merchandise discount on the next line.

Press the [*Delete*] key to remove the 6.00, [Tab].

21 ➤   **Payment Amount**   [Tab] to accept $339.00, the amount of the original invoice.

22 ➤   **Discount Taken**   The cursor moves to the Discount Taken field for invoice **4556Di,** [Tab].

23 ➤   **Payment Amount**   [Tab] to accept -6.00. This will reduce the amount paid (i.e., payable less non-merchandise discount). The cheque amount total at the bottom (333.00) correctly pays the invoice balance owing in full.

The lower portion of the Payments Journal should resemble Fig. 3B-20.

Due Date	Invoice or Prepayment	Original Amount	Amount Owing	Discount Available	Discount Taken	Payment Amount
May 06, 2016	4556	339.00	339.00	6.00		339.00
	4556Di	-6.00	-6.00	0.00		-6.00
					Total	333.00

Fig. 3B-20: Payment with Prepaid Office Supplies discount.

24 ➤ **Display** the Journal entry; it should appear as follows:

The discount on this payment was charged to PREPAID OFFICE SUPPLIES in step 11.

Payments Journal Entry Apr 15, 2016 (J3)

Account Number	Account Description	Debits	Credits
2200	Accounts Payable	333.00	-
1010	Bank Chequing Account	-	333.00
Additional Date:	Additional Field:		
		333.00	333.00

25 ➤ **Exit** from the Payments Journal Entry window.

26 ➤ **Post** when correct and **Exit** to the Home window.

27 ➤ **Display** the Vendor Aged Detail report for NAS Business Forms at Apr 15, 2016 and it should appear as follows. Do NOT click Include Terms. The report should appear similar to Fig. 3B-21.

Vendor Aged Detail As at Apr 15, 2016

Source	Date	Transaction Type	Total	Current	31 to 60
NAS Business Forms					
4556	Apr 06, 2016	Invoice	339.00	339.00	-
2515	Apr 15, 2016	Payment	-339.00	-339.00	-
4556Di	Apr 15, 2016	Invoice	-6.00	-6.00	-
2515	Apr 15, 2016	Payment	6.00	6.00	-
Total outstanding:			-	-	-

Fig. 3B-21: Vendor Aged Detail.

28 ➤ **Exit** from the Vendor Aged Detail window.

29 ➤ Advance the date to **Apr 16, 2016**.

More Transactions

If you make an error in a cheque amount and realize it after you have posted the payment, refer to Exercise 2A-19 (correct) and 2A-21 (cancel).

1 ➤   **Record** and **Post** the following transactions:

(See side note box.)

Apr 16, 2016	**Received invoice #646 dated today, in the amount of $384.93 for 15 Cars medium at $22.71 each plus HST, from Thompson Toy Makers. A PO was not issued. Terms 2/10, net 30.**

Apr 16, 2016	**The complete Purchase Order #83 of truck wheels from A-Your Name Toy Parts arrived in good condition with invoice #65839 for $111.87 dated today.**

2 ➤   Advance the date to **Apr 18, 2016**.

Apr 18, 2016	**Cheque issued to pay Lanting Specialty Toys $3,403.56 on invoice #6211.**

Apr 18, 2016	**After receiving numerous telephone calls from Jason's Transport Service, Mr. Tyson paid their invoice #6691 with the next cheque.**

Apr 18, 2016	**Cheque issued to pay City Office Supplies for invoice #1235 in full.**

Purchase and Payment to a One-time Vendor

Similar to the RECEIVABLES options, Sage 50 Accounting allows you to enter a purchase and payment to a vendor you may not deal with again (One-time vendor). For example, you may hire a company to deliver advertising flyers, or you may purchase curtains for the office from a store.

You can enter this type of purchase/payment by using either the:

1. **Cheque** option in the **Purchase Invoices** Journal, or
2. **Make Other Payment** option in the **Payments** Journal.
3. Click the ⏷ in **Payments**, select **Pay Expenses,** the Make Other Payment option is shown.

The Payments Journal, option 2, will be used in this exercise.

Sage 50 Accounting will record the transaction to the appropriate General Ledger account, but this type of entry will not be displayed in the Vendor Aged Detail report because no vendor was set up. The journal entry may be viewed in the Payments Journal or the Journal Entries–All report.

Exercise 3B-26—Recording a Purchase from a One-time Vendor

---

1 ➤ Advance date to **Apr 19, 2016**.

> Apr 19, 2016   **Issued cheque to Alan Cohen & Associates, 2340 Eglinton Avenue East, Toronto ON M6E 2L6 for work done on setting up our website. The invoice #589 dated today, was for $412.00 plus HST $53.56, for a total invoice of $465.56. Mr. Tyson is not sure if he will deal with this firm again.**

2 ➤ Click the **Payments** icon.

3 ➤ At | Pay Purchase Invoices   ▼ |, select **Make Other Payment,** [Tab].

4 ➤ **Cheque**   Select **Cheque,** [Tab] [Tab].

5 ➤ **To the**   Type **Alan Cohen & Associates,** [Tab], click **Continue,**
   Order of   then [Tab].

6 ➤ In the box, type the address as indicated above. This information would appear on the cheque if it were printed. Also, the payee name is recorded in the Payments Journal for audit trail purposes. [Tab]

   Cheque No.   The next cheque is 2519.

   Date   Apr 19, 2016.

7 ➤ **Account**   Select **5340 Advertising Expense**.

8 ➤ **Description**   Type **Setup Website**, <kbd>Tab</kbd>.

9 ➤ **Amount**   Type **412.00**, <kbd>Tab</kbd>.

10 ➤ **Tax**   Type **HS**, <kbd>Tab</kbd>.

11 ➤ **HST**   <kbd>Tab</kbd> to accept **53.56**.

12 ➤ **Invoice/Ref.**   Type **589**, <kbd>Tab</kbd>.

> The **Comment** field replaces the **Vendor name** in the Journal entry display and printout. If you use the comment field, always use the vendor name as part of the comment.

13 ➤ **Comment**   Type: **Alan Cohen & Associates created our website**, <kbd>Tab</kbd>. (See side note box.)

14 ➤ The Payments Journal window should resemble the following:

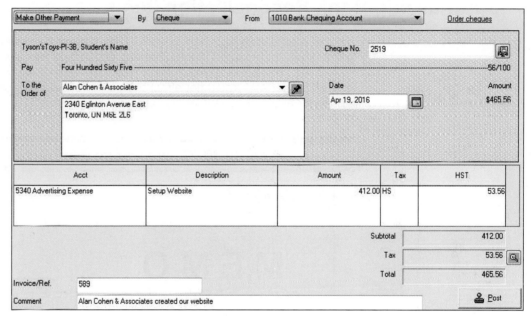

15 ➤ **Display** the Payments Journal Entry. The display window should appear as follows:

Payments Journal Entry Apr 19, 2016 (J9)

Account Number	Account Description	Debits	Credits
2560	HST Paid On Purchases	53.56	-
5340	Advertising Expense	412.00	-
1010	Bank Chequing Account	-	465.56
Additional Date:	Additional Field:		
		465.56	465.56

> To correct or cancel a vendor **Make Other Payment**, see Chapter 13.

16 ➤ **Exit** the Payments Journal Entry window.

17 ➤ **Post** after verifying accuracy.

A warning message box appears.

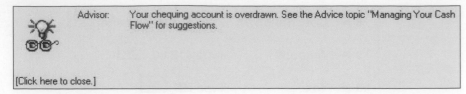

Advisor: Your chequing account is overdrawn. See the Advice topic "Managing Your Cash
            Flow" for suggestions.

[Click here to close.]

18 ➤ Mr. & Mrs. Tyson have previously made arrangements to issue cheques when
      they do not have enough money in their bank account. (This can be called a line of
      credit or overdraft protection.) You will see this message window when you post
      cheques later in this chapter. Accept the message by **clicking inside the box** to
      continue.

19 ➤ **Exit** the Payments Journal.

Journalizing Bank Reconciliation Items

Bank charges and various items recorded on the bank statement (e.g., any special
charges) but not recorded in the company accounting records would need to be
entered into your Sage 50 Accounting files. This type of entry would be entered in the
General Ledger and would not affect the Vendors Ledger because it does not concern
any vendor and a cheque is not issued.

Exercise 3B-27—Recording Bank Reconciliation Entries

Study the next memo:

MEMO

Date: Apr 19, 2016

To: Jerry Tyson

From: Student's name, Accounting Clerk

The Bank Reconciliation is complete. I will make an
adjustment for the monthly service charge of $31.15,
processed by the bank on April 18.

SN

Fig. 3B-22: Memo about unrecorded item.

Entering Service Charges

> ℹ️ Tyson's Toys has set up a General Journal recurring entry for regular monthly service charges.

1 ➤ Click on the **COMPANY** module, click the **General Journal** icon.

(See side note box.)

2 ➤ Click the **Recall Recurring Transaction** icon 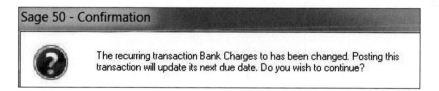 and the Recall Recurring Transaction window will appear as follows:

3 ➤ Select **Bank Charges to**, and the General Journal window will fill in with the recurring information.

> ℹ️ The entry date (Apr 18) is the date the bank took the bank charges from your account.

Change the fields to resemble the following window. (See side note box.)

4 ➤ **Post** after verifying accuracy. A Confirmation box will appear.

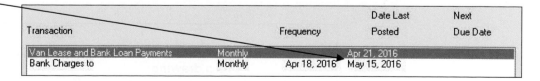

5 ➤ Click **Yes**. Click the **Recall Recurring Transaction** icon 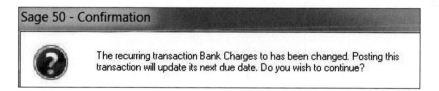. The recurring entry has been posted and will be updated to the next scheduled due date of May 15, 2016. (See side note box.) *Note*: As indicated previously, the headings Frequency, etc., are not above the correct information.

> ℹ️ Recurring due dates update from the original date and do not correspond to the date last used/posted.

6 ➤ Click **Cancel** and **Exit** to the Home window.

Journalizing Partner's/Proprietor's Drawings

Although proprietorship withdrawals are not considered a normal vendor transaction, they are entered in **the PAYABLES module because this module is used to keep track of all payments made by the business.** Sole proprietorships or partnerships use an account called DRAWINGS or WITHDRAWALS when an owner withdraws money for personal use.

Jerry and Helen Tyson will be withdrawing money on a regular basis; therefore, vendor accounts should be set up. At any time Jerry or Helen can check their vendor account to see what amounts they have withdrawn during the year.

Exercise 3B-28—Recording Owner's Drawings

---

1 ➤ Advance the Session date to **Apr 20, 2016**.

Study the following memo:

MEMO

Date: Apr 20, 2016

To: Accounting

From: Jerry Tyson

Please issue a cheque to me as a personal draw in the amount of $900.00.

Jerry

Fig. 3B-23: Memo requesting personal draw.

Apr 20, 2016   Issued next cheque to the owner, Jerry Tyson, for $900.00 as a drawing.

Recording the Withdrawal

Other payments that
would use the **Make
Other Payment** option
are Rent, HST payments
to Receiver General,
Insurance, purchases
paid by cash, cheque,
and credit card.

2 ➤ Click on the **PAYABLES** module, click the **Payments** icon to display the Payments Journal.

(See side note box.)

3 ➤ At `Pay Purchase Invoices ▼`, select **Make Other Payment**, `Tab`.

4 ➤ **To the Order of**   Type **Jerry Tyson**, `Tab`.

5 ➤ Select **Full Add**. The **Address** tab (Home address), is **556 Betty Ann Drive, Willowdale, Ontario, M2N 1Y7**. Click **Options** tab, **Expense Account**, select **3120 Drawings Jerry Tyson**, click **Taxes** tab, change **Tax Exempt** to **Yes** for **HST**, **No tax** should be selected (there are no taxes on owner's withdrawals).

Click `Save` and `Close` when complete and you are returned to the Payments Journal, `Tab`.

Date   Apr 20, 2016.

6 ➤ **Description**   Type **Draw Apr 20, 2016**, `Tab`.

7 ➤ **Amount**   Type **900.00**, `Tab`.

Tax   Leave blank; there is no tax when an owner withdraws money from the business.

8 ➤ **Invoice/Ref**   Jerry or Helen would normally give you a memo to request a cheque indicating the reason for issuing the cheque. This is important for the audit trail. They will be giving you a number of memos during the year, and you will need to identify which memo was your authority to issue for each cheque. Type **Memo Apr 20** or Draw # 1, April (draw Apr, 1st draw of month), `Tab`.

 Leave the **Comment** field blank for this and the other cheques that follow.

The Payments Journal should look like Fig. 3B-24.

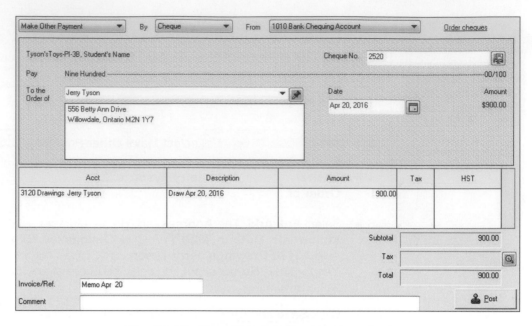

Fig. 3B-24: Jerry Tyson's Draw entry window.

9 ➤ Display the journal entry and it should appear as follows:

Payments Journal Entry Apr 20, 2016 (J11)

Account Number	Account Description	Debits	Credits
3120	Drawings Jerry Tyson	900.00	-
1010	Bank Chequing Account	-	900.00
Additional Date:	Additional Field:		
		900.00	900.00

10 ➤ **Exit** from the Payments Journal Entry window.

11 ➤ **Post** when correct.

12 ➤ **Exit** from the Payments Journal, and **Exit** to the Home window.

This entry could be displayed in the **Vendor Aged Detail**. You do not need to view the Aged report at this time.

Recording a Purchase Order with a Prepayment to a Vendor

It is common business practice to give a prepayment to a vendor against future invoices to show the commitment to purchase items (special orders) or use their services.

In the Sage 50 Accounting PAYABLES module, this type of transaction is called a **Prepayment**. In RECEIVABLES it is called a **Deposit**.

Although we will use the Purchase Order paid by Cheque option in this Exercise, the cheque will not be issued in Sage 50 Accounting. A manual cheque will need to be issued. An alternative method is noted in a side note box beside Exercise 3A-19 starting with: To issue a prepayment...

Exercise 3B-29—Recording a Purchase Order and Prepayment Cheque

Apr 20, 2016   A local service club has ordered 16 Trucks- Large. The trucks need to be received on Apr 28, 2016. Issue a Purchase Order (#84) to Thompson Toy Makers for these trucks at $30.00 each plus HST, Total $542.40. Terms 2/10, Net 30. Thompson requires a $200.00 prepayment.

To issue the Purchase Order and a prepayment cheque to Thompson:

1 ➤ Click the **Purchase Orders** icon from the home window.

     Transaction   **Order**, do NOT change.

2 ➤ **Payment Method**   Select **Cheque,** a new field displays above Shipping Date

     Prepay Ref. No. 2521   2521 is the next cheque # or reference # for the prepayment.

3 ➤ **Vendor**   **Select Thompson Toy Makers.**

4 ➤ **Shipping Date**   Select **Apr 28, 2016**.

5 ➤ **Item Number**   Select **Trucks– Large**.

6 ➤ **Order**   Type **16**, [Tab].

Item Number	Quantity	Order	Back Order	Unit	Item Description	Price	Tax	HST	Amount	Account
Trucks-LG		16	16	Each	Trucks- Large	30.00	HS	62.40	480.00	1310 Toys and parts Inve...

The Purchase Order will fill in the information above.

7 ➤ Prepayment Applied: Type **200.00**, [Tab].

The Prepayment will be applied to the final invoice.

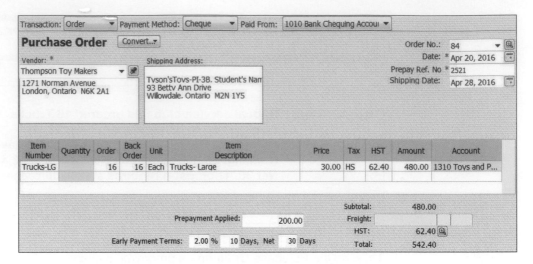

8 ➤ The Purchases Journal–Purchase Order Entry should appear as follows:

Purchases Journal Entry Apr 20, 2016 (J12)

Account Number	Account Description	Debits	Credits
2200	Accounts Payable	200.00	-
1010	Bank Chequing Account	-	200.00
Additional Date:	Additional Field:		
		200.00	200.00

9 ➤ **Exit** the Purchases Journal–Purchase Order Entry window.

10 ➤ **Record** when correct and **Exit** to the Home window.

11 ➤ Display the Vendor Aged Detail Report for **Thompson Toy Makers** at
      Apr 20. The lower portion is shown next. The Prepayment (Prepaid Order) is
      identified separately.

2521	Apr 20, 2016	Prepaid Order	-200.00	-200.00
Total unpaid invoices:			384.93	384.93
Total prepayments/prepaid order:			-200.00	-200.00
Total outstanding:			184.93	184.93

12 ➤ Advance the Session date to **Apr 21, 2016**.

Recording Lease Payments

Because Tyson's Toys pays the lease of their van on a monthly basis, they have set
up a recurring transaction entry for this transaction.

Exercise 3B-30—Recording a Lease Payment

Apr 21, 2016   Received Bank Debit memo dated Apr 21, 2016 in the amount
of $852.00 for the van lease payment ($400.00 plus $52.00
HST) and $400.00 payment on the bank loan ($304.59 to
reduce the loan and $95.41 interest).

You will use the **Recall Recurring Transaction** option, which has been set up for this transaction earlier.

1 ➤ Click on the **COMPANY** module. Click on the **General Journal** icon.

2 ➤ Click the **Recall recurring transaction** icon 📤 and the Recall Recurring Transaction window will appear as follows:

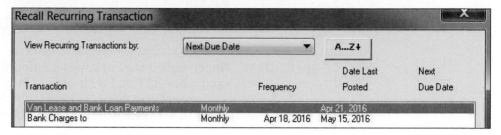

3 ➤ Select **Van Lease** and **Bank Loan Payments**, and the General Journal window is filled in.

4 ➤ Make necessary changes as shown in Fig. 3B-25.

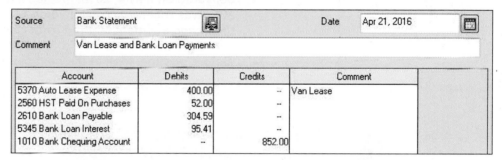

Fig. 3B-25: Van Lease and Bank Loan Payment entry.

5 ➤ In order to update the HST taxes properly, for the HST report, when using the General Journal, click the **Sales Taxes** button.

6 ➤ **Enter** the information as shown next. This will update the HST report, which can be seen in Appendix 2015 D, *Printing/Filing a Tax (HST) Report* by opening your course materials at www.nelson.com/student.

WWW

7 ➤ Click **OK**. You will notice a blue ☑ in the [✓ Sales Taxes] button. This means that the Sales Taxes will be updated for the HST report.

8 ➤ **Post** when correct, click **Yes** to update the recurring entry.

9 ➤ **Exit** the General Journal to the Home page.

More Transactions

1 ➤ Advance the date to **Apr 29, 2016**.

2 ➤ **Record** and **Post** the three transactions below.

Apr 26, 2016   **Paid $109.89 to A-Your Name Toy Parts for invoice #65839**.

Apr 27, 2016   **Received 3 boxes of various coloured paper at $56.00 each, plus HST and 3 binders ½ inch at $4.00 each plus HST, from City Office Supplies. Invoice #2640 dated Apr 27, 2016 with terms of 2/10 n30. Total invoice $203.40.**

Apr 28, 2016   **Received 14 of the trucks ordered on PO #84, from Thompson Toy Makers. The other 2 trucks will be delivered on May 4, 2016. Invoice #1007 dated Apr 27, 2016 was received. Total invoice $474.60. You will need to change Payment Method from Cheque to Pay later.**

Before posting, look at the next caution window.

Sage 50 Accounting remembers the last setting you used for the **Paid By** field. You may have to click the **Paid By** ▼ and change it to **Pay Later**.

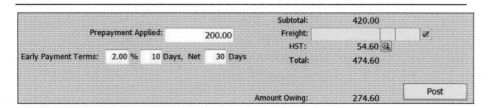

Notice that the Prepayment made on Apr 20 has been applied to the invoice total of 474.60, which leaves an amount owing of 274.60.

Journalizing HST Remittance

The Federal Government (Canada Revenue Agency) requires that **GST/HST CHARGED ON SALES** be paid to the government (**Receiver General**) on a regular basis. *Note*: Depending on the size of businesses, they may need to file the GST/HST electronically, effective for all reporting periods ending on or after July 1, 2010. This text will demonstrate the issuance of a cheque to pay the GST/HST. The text will not demonstrate the steps if you use NETFILE, TELEFILE, Electronic Data Interchange or Internet File Transfer to file your returns.

Companies are allowed to subtract from the payment any **GST/HST PAID ON PURCHASES** (this includes all goods and services). This is why many companies keep track of HST Paid on Purchases separately from HST Charged on Sales Invoices.

The balance of the HST PAID ON PURCHASES account is a **debit** (meaning **receivable**) and HST CHARGED ON SALES is a **credit** (meaning **payable**). However, both accounts are typically located in the Liabilities section of the Balance Sheet.

In a job situation, the task of reconciling HST PAID ON PURCHASES and HST CHARGED ON SALES and journalizing HST remittance may be part of your routine responsibilities. You may or may not receive a memo from your supervisor when it is time to reconcile. It depends on the procedure that has been set up at your company.

Exercise 3B-31—Calculating the HST Remittance

Study the following memo:

MEMO

Date: Apr 29, 2016
To: Accounting Clerk
From: Helen Tyson

Please pay the Receiver General the net March 31 HST balance.

Helen

Fig. 3B-26: HST Remittance memo.

Apr 29, 2016	Paid the Receiver General the net HST payable outstanding at the end of March 2016.

First, you must find out the General Ledger account balances for HST CHARGED ON SALES and HST PAID ON PURCHASES at the end of March. In a normal business environment you would display the Balance Sheet or the Trial Balance at the end of March.

Chapter 3 was split into parts 3A and 3B. As part 3B starts at Apr 15, 2016 you cannot display a Mar 31, 2016 Balance Sheet in Part 3B. In Exercise 3A-3 you were asked to print a Balance Sheet at Mar 31 and retain it for use in this Exercise. If you cannot locate the Mar 31, 2016 Balance Sheet, refer to the Mar 31, 2016 Trial Balance in Fig 3A-1 for the HST amounts.

In a business environment, you could also print a HST report as shown in Appendix 2015 D, *Printing/Filing a Tax (HST) Report* in your course materials at www.nelson.com/student. The Tyson's Toys 3A data file was started at Mar 31; therefore, there are no transactions recorded for March. There will be a message that there is no data to report.

Calculating HST Remittance

1 ➤ Refer to the Balance Sheet printed in Exercise 3A-3.

2 ➤ Circle the amounts for **HST CHARGED ON SALES** and **HST PAID ON PURCHASES**. The net HST amount owing should be $1,088.11.

HST Charged on Sales	1,738.25
HST Paid on Purchases	- 650.14
Net HST amount owing	1,088.11

OR:

Refer to the Trial Balance (Fig. 3A-1) at the end of Mar 31, 2016, and write on a piece of paper the balances for HST CHARGED ON SALES and HST PAID ON PURCHASES, and calculate the difference. It should amount to **$1,088.11**.

There may be situations when the HST paid on purchases/services is higher than the HST collected on sales.

HST on Sales	$1,730.00
HST on Purchases/Services	$1,750.14
HST overpaid (refund requested)	$ 20.14

In this situation, the business would submit the HST return and claim a refund.

In a business environment you could also print the Balance Sheet or Trial Balance noted above as proof of the amounts used. Print the Income Statement for the dates specified on the HST Tax Form. The Sales and Purchase information will be used to fill in the tax form. This would be attached to the documentation for the cheque request and would be part of the audit trail information.

The Receiver General has been set up as a vendor for regular HST payments. Using a vendor will retain information in the PAYABLES module about payments made. This record can be used by Canada Revenue Agency auditors to verify that a payment has been made.

Note: When remitting the HST/GST to the Receiver General you would issue a cheque as shown in this exercise. When requesting a refund, more HST/GST paid than received, a Sales Invoice is recorded, with the HST on Sales entered as a negative value and HST Paid on Purchases entered as a positive value. The invoice balance is the refund requested from the Receiver General.

In this situation, the business would submit the HST return and claim a refund.

Exercise 3B-32—Recording the HST Remittance

To record the amount payable to the Receiver General, you would use the same procedure as in the payment to Mr. Tyson in Exercise 3B-28.

1 ➤　Click the **Payments** icon.

2 ➤　Select **Make Other Payment**, ⌨Tab.

By Cheque	Do NOT change.
From	1010 Bank Chequing Account. Do NOT change.

3 ➤　**To the Order of**　　Select **Receiver General** and ⌨Tab.

　　　　Acct　　The default account **2550 HST Charged on Sales** appears. HST Charged on Sales is a 2 series Liability account number. The program treats all 2 series numbers as **Liability** accounts, which have normal **credit** balances. We need to **debit** the HST CHARGED ON SALES account and transfer the amount to the ACCOUNTS PAYABLE account. Do NOT change.

4 ➤　**Description**　　Type **Payment for Mar HST on Sales**, ⌨Tab.

5 ➤　**Amount**　　Type **1738.25**, ⌨Tab. (A positive number will debit the account used.)

6 ➤　**Tax**　　HS code is not used when paying the Receiver General. ⌨Tab.

7 ➤　**Acct**　　Select **2560 HST Paid on Purchases**.

8 ➤　**Description**　　Type **Payment for Mar HST on Purchases**, ⌨Tab.

9 ➤　**Amount**　　Type negative **-650.14** (a negative amount will credit the account used), ⌨Tab.

10 ➤　**Invoice/Ref**　　We need to create a visual record of what is taking place. Some companies would use codes similar to: HST@Mar 31, 2016 (Net HST at the end of March), Mar HST 2016 (March HST being paid) or HST1QTR2016 (HST 1st Quarter of year).

　　　　Type **Mar HST 2016**, ⌨Tab. The window should resemble Fig. 3B-27:

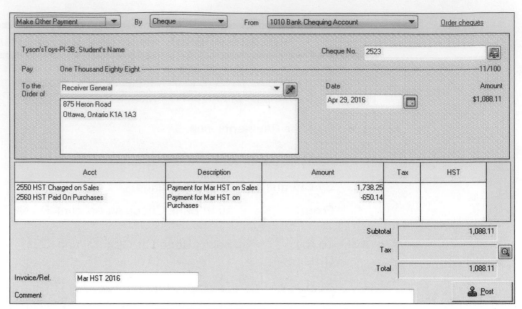

Fig. 3B-27: HST Payment window.

11 ➤ **Display** the Journal Entry and the window should appear as follows:

Payments Journal Entry Apr 29, 2016 (J17)

Account Number	Account Description	Debits	Credits
2550	HST Charged on Sales	1,738.25	-
1010	Bank Chequing Account	-	1,088.11
2560	HST Paid On Purchases	-	650.14
Additional Date:	Additional Field:		
		1,738.25	1,738.25

12 ➤ **Exit** from the Payments Journal Entry window. You could store this transaction as a recurring entry for future periods.

13 ➤ **Post** when correct and **Exit** from the Payments Journal and **Exit** to the Home window.

Viewing the Vendor Aged Report

1 ➤ The above entry can be displayed using the Vendor Aged Detail report. Your screen display for the Receiver General, should be similar to:

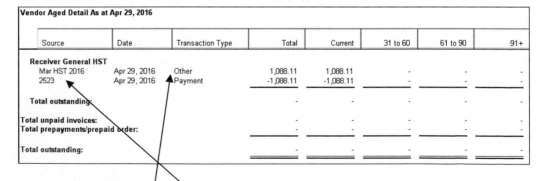

Notice the Source **Mar HST** information.

Also notice **Other** in the Transaction Type column. Future payments should have similar audit trail information.

2 ➤ **Exit** the Vendor Aged Detail Report.

Journalizing an Invoice with Reduced HST

Current federal HST legislation exempts insurance from HST at a rate of 5%; therefore, at present there is HST on insurance for this company of operating in Ontario 13% − 5% = 8% (using the HI tax code). However, this legislation may change, so watch for HST changes in the future.

Insurance is normally paid in advance, and the cost is charged to PREPAID EXPENSES and then charged to INSURANCE EXPENSE every accounting period over the life of the insurance policy.

Exercise 3B-33—Recording an Invoice with Reduced HST

Study this transaction and the invoice below:

> **Apr 29, 2016**   Received the following invoice #4799 from Meadows Insurance Brokers Inc. HST is applicable on insurance invoices at 8%.

Meadows Insurance Brokers Inc.

197 Larange Avenue, Suite 125   **INVOICE**
Toronto, Ontario M8Z 4R9   **4799**
Phone/Fax (416) 233-5886

SOLD TO: Tyson's Toys
           93 Betty Ann Drive   Date:___Apr 28, 2016___
           Willowdale, ON M2N 1Y5

COVERAGE	
Renewal Policy #3224321 To insure building at 93 Betty Ann Drive, Willowdale, Ontario	
Coverage for the period Apr 01, 2016 through Mar 31, 2017	$1,200.00

	HST	96.00
Terms: upon receipt	TOTAL	$1,296.00

Fig. 3B-28: Insurance Invoice.

As the company will be buying additional insurance during the year, you will set up **Meadows Insurance Brokers Inc.** as a vendor, using the Full Add option.

The invoice will be allocated to prepaid expense based on the following:

- $1,296.00 divided by 12 months equals $108.00 per month.

- April expense (#5360 Insurance Expense) account will be $108.00 and as the remaining $1,188.00 prepaid amount expires (gets used up), it will be charged to INSURANCE EXPENSE.

You could set up a recurring adjusting General Journal entry for the insurance expense portion for future use.

Recording Payment for Insurance

1 ➤   Click the **Payments** icon.

2 ➤   Select **Make Other Payment**.

3 ➤ **To the Order of**   Type **Meadows Insurance Brokers Inc.**, `Tab`.

4 ➤ Click `Full Add`. Use Invoice information to complete the data fields.

5 ➤ Click the **Options** tab. Expense Account field, select **1340 Prepaid Insurance**.

6 ➤ Click the **Taxes** tab. **Tax Exempt** field for HST. Do NOT change from No.

7 ➤ **Tax code.**   Select **HI** (HST at 8%). Click `Save and Close` when complete, `Tab`.

     Cheque No.   2524, the next cheque number.

     Date   Apr 29, 2016, the date the cheque is being issued.

     Acct   Account 1340 Prepaid Insurance is shown since you created this in step 5.

8 ➤ **Description**   Type **Insurance - Building Prepaid**, `Tab`.

9 ➤ **Amount**   Type **1,100.00**, `Tab`.

> ℹ️ The $1,100 charged to **Prepaid Expenses** is for the 11 months from May 1, 2016 to Mar 31, 2017. As the insurance expires in future months, this amount will be reduced and allocated to **Insurance Expense**.

10 ➤ **Tax**   `Tab` to accept HI.

11 ➤ **HST**   `Tab` to accept 88.00.

12 ➤ **Acct**   Select **5360 Insurance Expense**.

13 ➤ **Description**   Type **Insurance - Building Expense**, `Tab`.

14 ➤ **Amount**   Type **100.00**, `Tab`.

15 ➤ **Tax**   `Tab` to accept HI.

16 ➤ **HST**   `Tab` to accept 8.00.

17 ➤ **Invoice/Ref**   Type **4799**, `Tab`.

The lower portion of the Payments window should appear as follows:

Acct	Description	Amount	Tax	HST
1340 Prepaid Insurance	Insurance - Building Prepaid	1,100.00	HI	88.00
5360 Insurance Expense	Insurance - Building Expense	100.00	HI	8.00
		Subtotal		1,200.00
		Tax		96.00
		Total		1,296.00

Invoice/Ref.   4799

Comment

Post

18 ➤ Display the Payments Journal Entry. It should look like the following:

Payments Journal Entry Apr 29, 2016 (J18)			
Account Number	Account Description	Debits	Credits
1340	Prepaid Insurance	1,188.00	-
5360	Insurance Expense	108.00	-
1010	Bank Chequing Account	-	1,296.00
Additional Date:	Additional Field:		
		1,296.00	1,296.00

19 ➤ **Exit** from the Payments Journal Entry window.

20 ➤ **Post** after verifying accuracy, and **Exit** to the Home window.

Additional Transaction

Record and **Post** the following transaction:

> **Apr 29, 2016** **Returned 3 binders ½ inch at $4.00 each plus taxes, to City Office Supplies. Original Invoice #2640. Binders too small.**
> *Note:* Use a purchase invoice with a negative amount to Prepaid Office Supplies.

Exercise 3B-34—Creating an Inventory Item When Recording a Purchase Invoice

> **Apr 29, 2016** **Purchased 125 large doors (new inventory item) at $1.27 each, plus HST, from A-Your Name Toy Parts. A PO was not issued. Received their invoice #9765 dated today, for $179.39 (including $20.64 HST), terms net 30 for this invoice.**

To add a new item of inventory when recording a Purchase Invoice, follow these steps:

1 ➤ Click the **Purchase Invoices** icon.

2 ➤ **Vendor**   Select **A-Your Name Toy Parts**.

3 ➤ **Invoice No**   Type **9765**, [Tab].

4 ➤ **Item Number**   Double-click and select **<Add new inventory/Service>**.

5 ➤ **Number**   Type **Doors-Lg**, [Tab].

6 ➤ **Description**   Type **Doors Large**, [Tab].

Quantities tab

7 ➤ **Minimum Level** Type **10**, [Tab].

Pricing tab

8 ➤ Click the **Pricing Tab**, at Regular type **2.50**, [Tab]. The other amounts should be 0.0000

Linked tab

9 ➤ Click the **Linked**, [Tab].

10 ➤ **Asset**   Select **1310 Toys and Parts Inventory**.

11 ➤ **Revenue**   Select **4100 Sales**.

12 ➤ **COGS**   Select **5010 Cost of Goods Sold**.

13 ➤ Click [Save and Close]. You are returned to the Purchase Invoice window.

14 ➤ **Quantity**   Type **125**, [Tab] to **Price**.

15 ➤ **Price**   Type **1.27**, [Tab].

The window should look like the following.

Item Number	Quantity	Order	Back Order	Unit	Item Description	Price	Tax	HST	Amount	Account
Doors-Lg	125			Each	Doors Large	1.27	HS	20.64	158.75	1310 Toys and Parts I...

16 ➤ Change the default terms from 2/10 n30 to **net 30**.

17 ➤ Display the Purchases Journal Entry; it should appear as follows.

Purchases Journal Entry Apr 29, 2016 (J20)

Account Number	Account Description	Debits	Credits
1310	Toys and Parts Inventory	158.75	-
2560	HST Paid On Purchases	20.64	-
2200	Accounts Payable	-	179.39
Additional Date:	Additional Field:		
		179.39	179.39

18 ➤ **Exit** from the Journal Entry window.

19 ➤ **Post** when correct, and **Exit** to the Home window.

Exercise 3B-35—Making a Credit Card Payment

---

1 ➤ Advance the date to **Apr 30, 2016**.

> Apr 30, 2016   **The Visa Credit Card payment is due today. Issue next cheque using the Pay Credit Card Bills feature. The outstanding payable item is the briefcase purchased on Apr 15 on Invoice #2319.**
> *Note:* Use a purchase invoice with a negative amount to Prepaid Office Supplies.

2 ➤ At the **Payments** icon, select **Pay Credit Card Bills**.

Pay Credit Card Bill ▼	By	Cheque ▼	From	1010 Bank Chequing Account ▼	Order cheques

3 ➤ **To the Order of**   Select **Visa Credit**.

Credit Card Payable Account Balance	As noted, the balance of the 2210 Credit Card Payable account is $152.55.
Additional Fees and Interest	This field would be used for additional amounts that are owed. (Annual fees, Interest on outstanding balances, etc.)

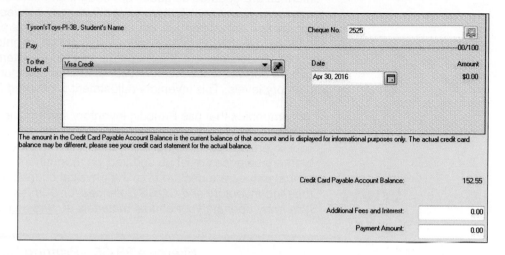

4 ➤ Payment Amount You would enter the amount of the outstanding balance that Mr. Tyson is going to pay. Type **152.55**. Tab .

5 ➤ Display the Payments Journal- Entry, it should appear as follows.

Payments Journal Entry Apr 30, 2016 (J21)

Account Number	Account Description	Debits	Credits
2210	Visa Credit Card Payable	152.55	-
1010	Bank Chequing Account	-	152.55
Additional Date:	Additional Field:		
		152.55	152.55

6 ➤ Exit from the Journal Entry window.

7 ➤ Post when correct, and **Exit** to the Home window.

Transaction

Record and **Post** the following transaction:

> Apr 30, 2016 Paterson's Wood Working, 698 Beech Avenue, Suite 6, Toronto, Ontario, M4E 9A3, delivered and installed 2 new Store Equipment (display) cabinets. They were ordered by Mrs. Tyson to display new and current toys. A PO was not issued. The cabinets cost $900.00 each, plus HST. Received $2,034.00, invoice #2696 dated today, with terms net 10 days.

Printing Reports

An Income Statement shows the current financial position re: SALES, COST OF GOODS SOLD and EXPENSES.

As you have seen in previous chapters, an Income Statement may be viewed or printed at any time. However, for the Income Statement to be accurate, the ending inventory needs to be updated to the correct value of goods on hand that have not been sold.

- For companies that use Perpetual Inventory systems, inventory and COGS balances are updated as goods are bought and sold. Inventory adjustments are necessary, if and only if, there exist differences between the continuous inventory records and actual physical count. These differences arise from occurrences such as faulty inventory bar codes, manually inputted inventory bar codes, goods that become unsellable, etc. If a Perpetual Inventory system is in place, a physical count must be done at least once per year to ensure continuous records accurately reflect inventory levels. This inventory adjustment is covered in Chapter 8.

- For companies that use Periodic Inventory systems, inventory and COGS balances are not updated on a continuous basis as goods are bought and sold. Therefore, in order to present correct financial statements (Income Statement, Balance Sheet), inventory balances must be updated via manual entries. The values for these manual entries are derived from the physical count of goods. See Appendix 2015 G, *Updating Inventory and COGS Balances for Companies Using Periodic Inventory System* by opening your course materials at www.nelson.com/student.

www

Exercise 3B-36—Printing Reports

---

1 ➤ Print the following:

    a. Income Statement for period **Jan 01, 2016** to **Apr 30, 2016**.

    b. Balance Sheet at **Apr 30, 2016**.

2 ➤ Print a Trial Balance. Click **Reports, Financials, Trial Balance**, Date: **Apr 30, 2016**. Click **OK**, then **Print** Report.

You should notice that in both Income Statements, Cost of Goods Sold accounts (5010) have different values, as they are updates on each sale and purchase. You should also notice that both Balance Sheets have a Current Asset Toys and Parts Inventory (#1310). The dollar values have different values due to updates on each sale and purchase.

Comparative Income Statement

To print a Comparative Income Statement, follow these steps:

1 ➤ Click **Report Centre**, **Financials**, click the **+** at **Income Statement**, select **Comparative 2 Period**, click **Modify this report**. A new Options window appears.

2 ➤ To see what changes occurred in the period Apr 16 to April 30, as well as the year-to-date information, change the **First Period Start** date to **Apr 16, 2016**, [Tab], change the Report On item as shown, then click **OK**.

The Comparative Income Statement is displayed. The first column of amounts is the activity that occurred from the entries you recorded from April 16 to the 30th. The other column is the year-to-date values in the accounts.

3 ➤ **Exit** to the Home window.

Other Period-End/Month-End Reports

At the end of the month it is normal to print the following additional reports for the month and file them for your audit trail:

- The All Journal Entries for the transactions entered Apr 15 to April 30.
- The General Journal entries for Apr 15 to Apr 30.
- The Balance Sheet as at Apr 30, 2016.
- The General Ledger for Apr 15 to Apr 30.
- The Vendor Aged Detail report, *with terms*, as at Apr 30, 2016.
- The Purchases Journal for Apr 15 to 30 — includes cash purchases.
- The Payments Journal for Apr 15 to 30.
- The Cheque Log for Apr 15 to Apr 30.

Exercise 3B-37—Printing Period-End Reports

Make sure the printer is ready. You should be at the Tyson's Toys Home window to start this exercise.

1 ➤ **Print** the **All Journal Entries** as shown in previous chapters.

2 ➤ **Print** the **General Ledger for Apr 16-30** as shown in previous chapters.

3 ➤ **Print** the **Vendor Aged Detail** at **Apr 30, 2016**. To make sure that everything is correct, you should compare the Balance Sheet Accounts Payable amount with the total of the Vendor Aged Detail report. They should be the same.

Viewing and Printing the Purchases Journal

To print the **Purchases Journal** for Apr 2016:

1 ➤ Click **Report Centre, Payables, Purchase Journal Entries, Modify this report**.

    By Date   Do NOT change.

2 ➤ **Start**   Select **Apr 15, 2016**, `Tab`.

3 ➤ **Finish**   `Tab` to accept Apr 30, 2016.

4 ➤ Click **Corrections** or **Additional Information** if required. Click **OK** to display the Purchases Journal.

5 ➤ **Print** the report.

6 ➤ **Exit** from the display window. (See side note box.)

Viewing and Printing the Payments Journal

To print the **Payments Journal** for Apr 2016:

1 ➤ Click **Report Centre, Payables, Payment Journal Entries, Modify this report**.

    By Date   Do NOT change.

> When you see the magnifying glass with the + sign in any of the reports, it means you can drill down (if you click the **Journal entry number**) to see the original invoice that made up the entry.
>
> If you drill down from the account number or name, you will see the ledger account and all entries that make up the account. Try drilling down for one or two entries.

2 ➤ **Start**   Select **Apr 15, 2016,** Tab .

3 ➤ **Finish**   Tab to accept Apr 30, 2016.

Click the boxes shown. Payments options will be discussed in Chapter 7, Payroll.

4 ➤ Click **OK** to display the Payments Journal.

5 ➤ **Print** the report.

6 ➤ **Exit** from the display window.

Viewing and Printing a Cheque Log

1 ➤ Click **Report Centre**, **Banking**, **Cheque Log**, **Modify this report**, select the options as shown next:

2 ➤ **Range**   Click the ▼. You may have to scroll up or down to see the choices available. Notice the Last Calendar Year. Sage 50 Accounting can display and print cheque log reports from the current year, as well as previous-year activity. There is no exercise for viewing or printing previous-year activity. Select the options as shown above.

3 ➤ Click **OK** and the cheque log will display.

4 ➤ You may **Print** this report, and return to the Home Window.

Cheque Log for 1010 Bank Chequing Account from Apr 15, 2016 to Apr 30, 2016

Cheque No.	Che... Type	Payee	Amount	Cheque Date	Times Prin...	Entered... system	JE#	JE Date
2515	Payment	NAS Business Forms	333.00	Apr 15, 2016	0	Yes	J3	Apr 15, 2016
2516	Payment	Lanting Speciality Toys	3,403.56	Apr 18, 2016	0	Yes	J6	Apr 18, 2016
2517	Payment	Jason's Transport Service	1,356.00	Apr 18, 2016	0	Yes	J7	Apr 18, 2016
2518	Payment	City Office Supplies	154.57	Apr 18, 2016	0	Yes	J8	Apr 18, 2016
2519	Payment	Alan Cohen & Associates	465.56	Apr 19, 2016	0	Yes	J9	Apr 19, 2016
2520	Payment	Jerry Tyson	900.00	Apr 20, 2016	0	Yes	J11	Apr 20, 2016
2522	Payment	A-Your Name Toy Parts	109.89	Apr 26, 2016	0	Yes	J14	Apr 26, 2016
2523	Payment	Receiver General HST	1,088.11	Apr 29, 2016	0	Yes	J17	Apr 29, 2016
2524	Payment	Meadowvale Insurance Br...	1,296.00	Apr 29, 2016	0	Yes	J18	Apr 29, 2016
2525	Payment	Visa Credit	152.55	Apr 30, 2016	0	Yes	J21	Apr 30, 2016

The cheque log (from Chapter 3A) is shown next:

Cheque No.	Che... Type	Payee	Amount	Cheque Date	Times Prin...	Entered... system	JE#	JE Date

Cheque Log for 1010 Bank Account from Mar 31, 2016 to Apr 15, 2016

Cheque No.	Che... Type	Payee	Amount	Cheque Date	Times Prin...	Entered... system	JE#	JE Date
2511	Payment	Willowdale Mall Ltd.	2,260.00	Apr 07, 2016	0	Reversed	J3	Apr 07, 2016
2512	Payment	Willowdale Mall Ltd.	2,373.00	Apr 07, 2016	0	Yes	J7	Apr 07, 2016
2513	Payment	Lanting Speciality Toys	718.68	Apr 07, 2016	0	Yes	J10	Apr 07, 2016
2514	Payment	Thompson Toy Makers	2,745.55	Apr 15, 2016	2	Yes	J11	Apr 15, 2016

This report displays the cheque numbers, amounts and dates the entries were recorded. As noted early in the chapter, in order to conserve paper you would not print cheques, unless your instructor requires you to do so.

In the Chapter 3A report above, cheque 2511 was recorded and reversed. Cheque 2512 was printed. In a job situation, the **Times prin...** (Times Printed**)** column would indicate a **1** (for cheques printed) and perhaps **2** if there was a printer jam and the cheque had to be reprinted. The report would ensure that management knew the number of times cheques were printed in order to prevent fraud (the same cheque printed more than once). The manager would want to see all damaged cheques and make sure that they were voided and unusable.

5 ➤ Compare your printed reports to the reports for Tyson's Toys in the data files from your instructor.

Viewing Graphs

WWW You may find information on using the graph feature (pie and bar charts) for PAYABLES comparisons in Appendix 2015 K, *Graphs Feature* by opening your course materials at www.nelson.com/student.

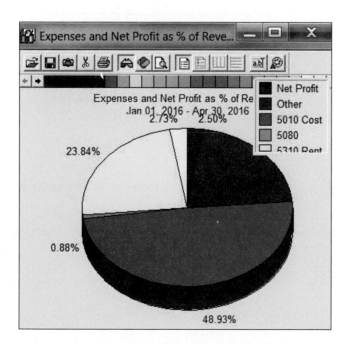

Summary, Part B

Here is a summary of tasks and transactions in Chapter 3B.

Transaction	Journal/Ledger	Remarks
Prepayment	Purchase Orders	Record a Vendor prepayment with a Purchase Order.
New Vendor (Supplier)	Vendors Ledger	At the Taxes tab, change the Tax Exempt status for HST, GST or PST where necessary and select the appropriate tax code. Select an appropriate default expense account.
Drawings	Payments	Create owner's Vendor record. Use Make Other Payment option to record a memo and a cheque together.
HST Remittance	Payments	Create Receiver General as a Vendor. Use Make Other Payment option to record a memo and a cheque together.
		Determine balance of HST Charged On Sales and HST Paid on Purchase accounts to be paid. Enter a negative amount to HST paid on Purchases account.

Review **Slideshows 3A** and **3B** now. They will help you better understand the next chapter on **Setting Up a Company**.

Before Moving On ... Part B

Read the following questions and make sure you know the answers to them; otherwise, read the corresponding part in the chapter before moving on.

1. When journalizing non-merchandise purchases with HST, how is **HST** recorded?

2. Give the journal entry for a purchase return of $300.00 plus HST of $39.00:

   a) for merchandise for resale.

   b) for merchandise not for resale, plus $39.00 HST (non-purchase items - office supplies).

3. Describe briefly the steps in recording a payment of an invoice when taking a cash discount, using as the base the cost before taxes:

   a) for merchandise for resale.

   b) for merchandise not for resale (Office Supplies).

4. Give the journal entry for a prepayment of $100.00 to a vendor. How is it entered in Sage 50 Accounting?

5. Describe briefly how the HST remittance is calculated.

6. What happens when you post journal transactions in the PAYABLES module?

7. When journalizing non-merchandise purchases with HST, what amount is the **HST** based on?

8. What would a manager look for when reviewing the cheque log?

Relevant Appendices, Part B

WWW   The following appendices are available by opening your course materials at www.nelson.com/student.

Appendix 2015 D	**Printing/Filing a Tax (HST) Report**
Appendix 2015 G	**Updating Inventory and COGS Balances for Companies Using Periodic Inventory System**
Appendix 2015 K	**Graphs Feature**
Appendix 2015 V1	**Perpetual Mini-Guide Receivables—Payables** (in Excel)

Challenge Exercise 03 C3B-1, Network
(PAYABLES and GENERAL Ledger)

1 ➤ Refer to Exercise 1-1b to unzip the **03 C3B-1 Network.exe** file.

2 ➤ Open the **03 C3B-1 Network** file and enter **PAYABLES** transactions for Mar for a company that sells various computer parts. Apply HST of 13% when needed. Network Company does *not* print cheques.

The business is open every day. You worked on March 5, 12, 19, 26, and March 31.

3 ➤ **Record** and **Post** the following transactions:

Mar 2   Ordered on PO# 651, 28 Ethernet network cards for $75.00 each, plus HST, from PC Cards Company. Shipping date to be Mar 12. Terms 2/10, net 30 days. PO total $2,373.00.

Mar 3   A $300.00 cheque is issued to Umax Cables as a prepayment for a special order of 80 RJ45 cables at $21.50 each, plus HST. Total cost $1,720.00, plus HST. Issue next PO. These cables are required by Mar 28. Terms are 2/10, net 30.

Mar 9   Purchased from new vendor, Your Last Name (surname) Supplies, various store supplies for $145.00, plus HST. Goods arrived and were stored. Invoice #8261, terms 2/10, net 30, calculate discounts before tax. The default Expense Account field in the Vendor Setup, Options tab window, can be an Asset or other account type. Select an appropriate account for this field.

Mar 10 Next cheque issued to J.D. Long for 2 Network Hubs at $40.50 each, plus HST, invoice #10005 received.

Mar 12 Received 28 Ethernet network cards from PC Cards Company ordered on PO# 651. Invoice #6638 was received totalling $2,373.00. Terms 2/10, net 30 days.

Mar 15 Issued cheque to the Receiver General for the HST owing at the end of February. Note that the Trial Balance HST amounts at February month-end are correct.

Mar 16 Returned 1 Ethernet network card to PC Cards Company because it is damaged. PC Cards accepted the return with a credit note 6638RT.

Mar 19 Issued cheque to Your Last Name (surname) Supplies, for invoice #8261.

Mar 22 Issued cheque to PC Cards Company as payment in full for invoice #6638, after return.

Mar 28 80 RJ45 cables arrived with invoice #8964 from Umax Cables Company (P.O. #652). Each cable cost $21.50, plus HST. Terms on the order are 2%10, net 30.

Mar 30 Bank statement as of March 29 arrived with debit note that the bank charge for the period ending March 29 is $19.35. No HST.

4 ➤ When you have recorded the above entries, **print** the following:

  a) Vendor Aged Detail all vendors with terms at Mar 31
  b) All Journal Entries for the monthly activity with ✓. Show Corrections.
  c) General Journal Entries for the monthly activity with ✓. Show Corrections.
  d) Purchase Journal Entries for March
  e) Payment Journal Entries for March
  f) Income Statement for the year to date
  g) Cheque log for the month

Challenge Exercise 03 C3B-2, China
(GENERAL, PAYABLES, RECEIVABLES, and INVENTORY & SERVICES Modules)

1 ➤   Refer to Exercise 1-1b to unzip the **03 C3B-2 China.exe** file.

This exercise is a review of the 4 modules (GENERAL, PAYABLES, RECEIVABLES, and INVENTORY & SERVICES).

2 ➤   Open the **03 C3B-2 China** file.

The China Company sells various kinds and sizes of china for everyday use and for special occasions. Apply 13% HST to sales. Terms for non-retail sale customers are 2/10, net 30. Vendor invoices normally have terms of 2/10, net 30, except where additional information is given.

All sales invoices and cheques are issued in numerical order. China Company does not print invoices or cheques. The company does not use the **Shipped** field in Purchase Invoices. Cash discounts when appropriate are calculated on the cost price before HST. You normally work on March 5, 12, 19, 26 and March 31. You advance the session date when you open the data file.

3 ➤   **Record** and **Post** the following transactions:

Ignore phone and fax numbers for new customers and vendors.

Mar 1	Issued Purchase order #106 to BNS Printing Ltd. for new invoices with a revised logo. Delivery date is Mar 5. Cost of the new invoices will be $100.00, plus HST, with terms 2/10, net 30.
Mar 1	Advertisement in today's issue of Yourtown Newspaper, a new vendor, 5569 Ace Avenue, Yourtown, Ontario L5N 1X6, contact Stanley Faria. Invoice #1099 received for $200.00, plus HST. Terms Net 15 days. Use an appropriate account for the default Expense field.
Mar 2	Purchased 30 dinner plates, code DP-01, at $25.00 each, plus HST, from Specialty Manufacturer Ltd. All plates were received in good condition. Invoice #361 dated today with terms of 2/10, net 30.
Mar 3	Sold on invoice #5270, one Luncheon Service, code LSS-01, to a new customer, **Your Actual Name**, 85 Lake Avenue, Rockton, Ontario L6N1B9. The selling price is $1,000.00, plus HST. **Your Actual Name** will pay the net amount in 15 days. Credit limit $3,000.00.
Mar 5	The new invoices from BNS Printing ordered on PO#106 are received in good condition with invoice #875 dated today.
Mar 5	We returned 4 plates from the Mar 2 order from Specialty Manufacturer Ltd., because the pattern is not centred. Original cost of the plates was $25.00 each, plus HST.
Mar 6	Sold 1 dozen soup bowls, SB-01, at $15.00 per bowl, plus HST, to Plates and More. Normal terms.
Mar 6	Issued cheque to pay Receiver General the HST owing at the end of February.

Mar 7   Plates and More returned 5 of the soup bowls because they arrived damaged. We have called the shipping company to determine what happened. Plates and More have requested a reduction to their account. We accepted the returned bowls by issuing a credit note with the original Invoice number as a reference.

Mar 8   Issued an $800.00 cheque to Mary Opal, owner, based on a memo received. The money is for personal expenses.

Mar 12   Issued cheque to Specialty Manufacturer Ltd. to pay only for dinner plates purchased, after returns, on invoice #361.

Mar 15   Issued cheque to pay BNS Printing Ltd. for invoice #875.

Mar 16   Received $116.55 cheque #789 from Plates and More re: invoice #5271.

Mar 16   Issued cheque to Yourtown Newspaper for outstanding invoice #1099.

Mar 19   Received cheque #788 from Your Actual Name for invoice #5270.

4 ➤ Print the following reports:

   a) Income Statement, year-to-date
   b) All Journal Entries for Mar 1 to Mar 19
   c) General Journal Entries for Mar 1 to Mar 19
   d) Customer Aged Detail, all customers, with terms at Mar 19
   e) Vendor Aged Detail, all vendors, with terms at Mar 19
   f) Cash Flow Projection (detail) for the next 30 days

Challenge Exercise 03 C3B-3, Dance Studio
(GENERAL, PAYABLES, RECEIVABLES, and INVENTORY & SERVICES Modules)

1 ➤   Refer to Exercise 1-1b to unzip the **03 C3B-3 Dance.exe** file.

2 ➤   Open the **03 C3B-3 Dance** file and enter transactions for Mar.

The Dance Studio is a service business that instructs students in various types of dance classes (Tap, Scottish, Irish, Ballet, etc.). Dance lessons are taxable at 13% HST.

Terms for customers are net 5 days with a few customers being given 2/10, net 30. Vendor invoices normally have terms of 2/10, net 30, except where additional information is given. Discounts for paying vendor invoices early are charged to Cleaning and Repairs Expense. All sales invoices and cheques are issued in numerical order. Dance Studio Company does not print invoices or cheques. Ignore Shipped By field. HST is 13%.

You work on a weekly basis, Mar 5, 12, 19, 26 and 31, therefore, advance the date as needed. Ignore phone and fax numbers for new customers and vendors.

3 ➤   Enter the following transactions:

Mar 1   Received from new vendor, Speciality Services (create vendor with any address information and ✓calculate discounts before tax) purchase invoice #748 with terms 2/10, net 15 days for 10 boxes of wax at $32.00 each, plus HST. Charge to Cleaning & Repairs Expense as the wax will be used in the next two weeks on the new dance practice studio floor.

Mar 2   Issued cheque #897 to pay for invoice #1962 owing to Quinton Cleaning Services.

Mar 5   Sold on invoice #426, dance lessons, for the week, $40.00, plus HST, to **Your Actual Name**. You paid with a Universal credit card.

Mar 5   Returned 1 box of the wax to Speciality Services. Credit note #748RT received.

Mar 8   The owner, Rajwinder Opuku, issued a memo requesting an $800.00 cheque to cover personal expenses. Cheque #898 is issued.

Mar 14   Purchased 1 box of sales invoices from NAJ Printing Ltd. Invoice #875, $100.00, plus HST. Terms, net 20 days.

Mar 15   Paid Speciality Services with cheque #899, for invoice #748 after taking off the return.

Mar 19   Sold on invoice #427, dance lessons, for the week, $40.00, plus HST to **Your Actual Name**. You paid with your cheque #158.

Mar 26   The bank advised by $428.00 debit memo dated today that the bank interest on the loan was $28.00 and the loan payment was $400.00.

Mar 29   Sold on invoice #428 dance lessons for the week $55.00, plus HST, to Ying Zhu. Ying paid cash for the invoice.

Mar 30   Received invoice #456 in the amount of $80.00, plus HST, for cleaning of classroom from Quinton Cleaning Services. Terms 2/10, net 20.

Mar 30   Received insurance bill #A4589 for $175.00, plus HI (8% portion of HST) from Metro Insurance (any address information) for the month of March. Bill to be paid in 5 days.

4 ➤ Advance the date to **Mar 30** and **print** the following:
   a)   Income Statement, year-to-date
   b)   All Journal Entries for Mar 1 to Mar 30
   c)   General Journal Entries for Mar 1 to Mar 30
   d)   Customer Aged Detail, all customers, with terms, at Mar 1 to Mar 30
   e)   Vendor Aged Detail, all vendors, with terms, at Mar 1 to Mar 30

Challenge Exercise 03 C3B-4, Chairs
This exercise is a review of 4 modules—COMPANY, PAYABLES, RECEIVABLES, and INVENTORY & SERVICES

1 ➤   Refer to Exercise 1-1b to unzip the Chairs.exe file and Chairs document file that is appropriate for your province or territory located in your course materials at www.nelson.com/student: **Chapter Data files\Chairs-Provincial Data Files.**   **www**

Chairs-Alberta.exe   Chairs-Nova Scotia.exe
Chairs-British Columbia.exe   Chairs-Ontario.exe
Chairs-Manitoba.exe   Chairs-Prince Edward Island.exe
Chairs-New Brunswick.exe   Chairs-Quebec.exe
Chairs-Newfoundland.exe   Chairs-Saskatchewan.exe
Chairs-North West Territories.exe   Chairs-Yukon.exe

2 ➤   Open the appropriate **Chairs** file.

3 ➤   **Print** the appropriate **Chairs Adobe PDF file** for your province or territory.

If you do not have Adobe Reader on your computer, go directly to: http://get.adobe.com/reader/ to download.

Each data file has the HST, GST, or PST rates appropriate for that province or territory. See Fig. 3B-29 below.

The HST rate of 13% is used in this text and reflected in the solutions. This rate, however, may have changed since the publication date. When on the job be sure to use the appropriate HST, GST, or PST rates.

4 ➤   **Record** the transactions listed in the PDF document.

5 ➤   **Print** the reports required in step 3 of the PDF document.

		HST	GST	PST/QST	Total
NS	Nova Scotia	15.0	-	-	15.0
QC	Quebec	-	5.0	9.975	14.975
PE	Prince Edward Island	14.0			14.0
MB	Manitoba	-	5.0	8.0	13.0
NB	New Brunswick	13.0	-	-	13.0
NL	Newfoundland & Labrador	13.0	-	-	13.0
ON	Ontario	13.0	-	-	13.0
BC	British Columbia	-	5.0	7.0	12.0
SK	Saskatchewan	-	5.0	5.0	10.0
AB	Alberta	-	5.0	-	5.0
NT	North West Territories	-	5.0	-	5.0
YT	Yukon	-	5.0	-	5.0

Fig. 3B-29: Provincial and Territory tax rates (at July 1, 2015).

Mini-Guide for Chapters 3A and 3B

Mini-guide for Perpetual transactions in Sage 50 Premium Accounting 2015****
***Not all types of transactions listed here.
***Study Suggestion—Add additional transactions from your chapters.

Purchase Events	Entry	Module	Journal	Comments	You fill in the Text Ref
You ask vendor for price quote	No entry	PAYABLE	Purchases, Orders & Quotes	No Purchase; you are asking for prices	
You confirm quote & place order for later delivery	No entry	PAYABLE	Purchases, Orders & Quotes	No Purchase; price confirmed for future delivery	
Purchase of merchandise	Inventory HST on Purchases Accounts Payable	PAYABLE	Purchases, Orders & Quotes	May be preceded by purchase quote May be preceded by purchase order May be a purchase without prior quote or order	
Purchase Rtn of Merchandise	Accounts Payable Inventory HST on Purchases	PAYABLE	Purchases, Orders & Quotes	Add "Rt" to invoice number If credit memo received, then add "CMxx"	
Payment (no discount)	Accounts Payable Cash	PAYABLE	Payment	Can be partial or full payment Can be after a return	
Payment, with discount	Accounts Payable Purchase Discount Cash	PAYABLE	Payment	Full payment Can be after a return	

www * Appendix 2015 V1, *Perpetual Mini-Guide for Receivables—Payables (in Excel)* in your course materials at www.nelson.com/student.

Chapter 4A

Setting Up a New Company

Sarah's Kitchen Stores

Learning Objectives

After completing this chapter you will be able to:

- ☐ Set up a company from scratch.
- ☐ Set up User Preference and System defaults.
- ☐ Add account names with specific account types for displaying reports.
- ☐ Modify and delete accounts as required.
- ☐ Set up links from modules to the General Ledger.
- ☐ Set up Tax Classes, Codes and Rates.
- ☐ Record opening balances for General Ledger accounts.
- ☐ Set up Receivable and Payable accounts and balances.
- ☐ Turn the modules to READY mode.
- ☐ Display and Print reports.

In this chapter you will create (SET UP) a company's data file from scratch. You will convert a manual set of accounting records to a computerized accounting system.

Before you can use Sage 50 Accounting software to process company transactions, you will need to create the data file; add accounts, customers, vendors, and balances; enter defaults and various settings; and set the module to READY. It is important to prepare the system carefully, to avoid problems when you start processing transactions.

This chapter explains the typical procedure in setting up a company in Sage 50 Accounting. Since every company is different, some of these requirements may vary. To help you learn the setup procedures, we will guide you in setting up the COMPANY, PAYABLES, and RECEIVABLES modules for **Sarah's Kitchen Stores**, a business that buys and sells kitchen cabinets and accessories.

The contents of this chapter are as follows:

Run **Slideshow 4—Setting Up a New Company**. This will give you a good idea of what is involved in setting up a new company from scratch and how to link the various modules.

Step 1: Creating Company Files

Creating Sage 50 Accounting Files

A company data file must be created in Sage 50 Accounting for Sarah's Kitchen Stores that is the same as the existing company's manual system. This is known as the **CONVERSION** process. Sage 50 Accounting provides a selection of sample companies, with General Ledger Chart of Accounts already set up (called templates). One of these company templates may be copied to a new Sage 50 Accounting company folder to save the time required to enter the G/L accounts. You would select a company that has a chart of accounts most similar to your own company. A template chart of accounts for the Retail Company contains 165 G/L accounts. You will see the template companies in Exercise 4A-1, Fig. 4A-7.

Using the template, you would have to delete accounts you do not need, such as 1920 Goodwill, 1930 Incorporation Costs and others. You would then modify account names to match your own Chart of Accounts, such as 1060 Chequing Bank Account to 1060 Nova Scotia Bank Account and others. You would add accounts that are not on the list, such as 4510 Handling Fee for processing clients' NSF cheques.

The text will show you how to set up a company from scratch. This structure will start with one account, 3600 Current Earnings, which will allow for the transfer of the Net Income or Loss from the Income Statement to the Balance Sheet Equity section.

 Starting a company from a template is covered in Appendix 2015 L, *Setting Up a New Company File Using a Sage 50 Premium Accounting Template* in your course materials at www.nelson.com/student.

 As you are going through this chapter, remember to save at regular intervals.

Account Number Structure

It is important that you understand how the Sage 50 Accounting account numbering structure works to make sure that the program processes transactions properly.

Sage 50 Accounting uses an Account Number Range (shown next) to identify the type of account and how to process each accordingly.

Study the next example regarding the position of account numbering in Sage 50 Accounting:

Account Type	Account # Range	Normal Balance	Amount Entered
Assets	1000—1999	Debit	positive
Liabilities	2000—2999	Credit	positive
Equity	3000—3999	Credit	positive
Revenue	4000—4999	Credit	positive
Expense *	5000—5999	Debit	positive

* Includes **Cost of Goods Sold** and **Expenses**.

Sage 50 Accounting will allow account numbers up to 8 digits. This text uses 4 digits in account numbers; therefore, you cannot use an account number outside this structure, i.e., a number lower than 1000 or higher than 5999.

Account Types

If you use a template to create your company file, print the chart of accounts before you make changes to the structure.

View the structure of the Current Assets section shown below. The complete financial statements with account codes (HASGT) are shown in Fig. 4A-37b. The displayed or printed Chart of Accounts shows only the account code.

Look carefully at the type of account and where it is located in the statement structure; i.e., column 1, the first dollar value on the left (coded as **A** "Subgroup **A**ccount" [values that accumulate]), or column 2, the second dollar value column, which is on the right (coded as **S** "**S**ubgroup Total," **G** "**G**roup Account," or **T** "**G**roup **T**otal").

Acct #	Description	Type	Code	Column 1 Amount	Column 2 Amount
1000	Current Assets	Group Heading	H		
1005	Petty Cash	Subgroup Account	A	100.00	
1010	Bank Account Chequing	Subgroup Account	A	17,106.00	
1011	Bank Account Credit Card	Subgroup Account	A	0.00	
1080	**Cash Total (subtotal)**	**Subgroup Total**	**S**		17,206.00
1200	Accounts Receivable	Subgroup Account	A	12,848.10	
1210	Allowance for Bad Debts	Subgroup Account	A	-550.00	
1219	**Net Accounts Receivable**	**Subgroup Total**	**S**		12,298.10
1240	Inventory of Goods	Group Account	G		102,500.00
1260	Store/Office Supplies/Prepaid	Group Account	G		400.00
1299	**Total Current Assets**	**Group Total**	**T**		132,404.10

It is very important that you understand the use of the Sage 50 Accounting type of accounts:

Group **H**eadings   Group Headings start each section. They provide descriptions of section account types, are **not postable** and have no balances.

Acct #	Description	Type	Code	Amount	Amount
1000	Current Assets	Group Heading	H		

Other Examples:

1400   Capital Assets
2000   Current Liabilities
2300   Long Term Liabilities

Subgroup **A**ccount	**Postable** accounts. Subgroup **A**ccounts are used when you need to add accounts together to get a subtotal. **A** accounts can have opening balances and are updated whenever debits and credits from journal entries are posted to them. They are not in Debit or Credit columns. They are printed in the left column of the appropriate group on the financial statement.
Subgroup Total (Accumulates **A** accounts)	**S**ubgroup Total accounts are used when you want to subtotal **A** accounts. **S** type of accounts are **not postable** and create a subtotal of **A** accounts above the **S**. **S** accounts are printed in the right column of the appropriate group on the financial statement. This makes your financial statement easier to understand.

Study the example below regarding the position of the **A**, **S** accounts.

Example:

Acct #	Description	Type	Code	Amount	Amount
1005	Petty Cash	Subgroup Account	A	100.00	
1010	Bank Account Chequing	Subgroup Account	A	17,106.00	
1011	Bank Account Credit Card	Subgroup Account	A	0.00	
1080	**Cash Total (subtotal)**	**Subgroup Total**	**S**		17,206.00

The **A** type of accounts **are postable** and their balances are printed in the left column of the appropriate group on the financial statement. **A** type of accounts require an **S** type of account to subtotal the amounts.

The **S** account **1080 Total Cash**, is the subtotal of the **A** type of accounts (#'s 1005, 1010 and 1011) and it is printed in the right column of the appropriate group on the financial statement.

Another example:

Acct #	Description	Type	Code	Amount	Amount
1200	Accounts Receivable	Subgroup Account	A	12,848.10	
1210	Allowance for Bad Debts	Subgroup Account	A	-550.00	
1219	**Net Accounts Receivable**	**Subgroup Total**	**S**		12,298.10

Group Account	**Postable** accounts. **Group** accounts are used when there are no **A** accounts to be subtotalled. These accounts are in the right column and can have an opening balance and are updated with debits and credits from journal entries posted to them.

Study the example below regarding the position of the **G** accounts.

Acct #	Description	Type	Code	Amount	Amount
1240	Inventory of Goods	Group Account	G		102,500.00
1260	Store/Office Supplies/Prepaid	Group Account	G		400.00

Notice that the amounts for the **G** accounts 1240 and 1260 are placed at the right column, whereas amounts for the **A** accounts were placed in the left column.

Group **T**otal — Used to end each section. They are **not postable**, and will subtotal all the **G** and **S** accounts in the section above it. They are descriptions only of the previous sections.

Acct #	Description	Type	Code	Amount	Amount
1299	Total Current Assets	Group Total	T		132,404.10

Other examples of **T**otals are:

1499	Net Capital Assets
2299	Total Current Liabilities
2399	Total Long Term Liabilities

Important things to remember:

1) Each section must begin with an **H** (Heading) and end with a **T** (Total account). You cannot have 2 Hs or 2 Ts together.

2) **A** (Subgroup accounts) and **G** (Group accounts) are the only postable account types.

3) **A** (Subgroup accounts) must be followed by an **S** (Subgroup Total) account—**Always**.

4) The Group Total **T** account adds all **G** (Group accounts) and **S** (Subgroup Total accounts) between the **H** (Heading; e.g., 1000 Current Assets) and the **T** (Total account; e.g., 1299 Total Current Assets).

End of Important section.

Current Earnings **X** — **Not Postable**. The **X** account is like the manual accounting INCOME SUMMARY account. It is used only to move dollar values from the Income Statement to the Balance Sheet.

Sage 50 Accounting assigns the number 3600 **Current Earnings** to the **X** account. **This cannot be changed**. It automatically adds the **Net Revenue Earned** and subtracts the **Cost of Goods Sold** and **Expenses**. The difference, the **Net Profit or Loss**, is carried forward to the Balance Sheet in the Equity Section.

Setting Up a New Company File from Scratch

You will now set up the company file for Sarah's Kitchen Stores using the Scratch method.

Exercise 4A-1—Setting Up a New Company File from Scratch

This exercise will demonstrate the creation of a new company data file from scratch. If you want to use a template, refer to Appendix 2015 L, *Setting Up a New Company File Using a Sage 50 Accounting Template,* in your course materials at www.nelson.com/student, in case you need to use one in the future.

1 ➤ Start **Sage 50 Accounting** the normal way.

Fig. 4A-1: What do you wish to do window.

Note: You may not see [⊙ Open the last company you worked on:] at the bottom.

2 ➤   Click the **Create a new company** button, then **OK**.

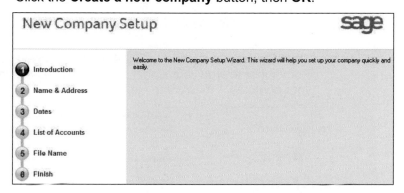

Fig. 4A-2a: New Company Setup Wizard using School Edition.

This window informs you that the wizard will help in setting up the new company, and that changes may be made to any options chosen. If you click the Help button, you will see a checklist of steps to complete when setting up a new company from scratch.

If you are using the **Student** version that came with the text, you will see Fig. 4A-2b. As noted in Appendix 2, *Sage 50 Premium Accounting 2015.0 Student Version Installation Instructions*, at the back of the book, the links shown, Customer Support and Accounting expert, are not available for students. The links require an upgrade to the retail version.

Fig. 4A-2b: New Company Setup Wizard using Student Edition.

3 ➤ Click **Next >**.

Fig. 4A-3: Company Name and information.

4 ➤ **Type the information** from Fig. 4A-3 into the fields in your window. Remember to type your actual name, in place of Student's Name, to identify your printouts. When complete, click **Next >**.

If your computer has been set up to display dates as DD/MM/YYYY, then the dates would appear as follows:
Start   01/01/2022
Earliest   31/08/2022
Year End 31/12/2022

Fig. 4A-4: Dates window. (See side note box.)

5 ➤ Sarah's Kitchen Stores, a single-owner business, has a calendar fiscal year ending Dec 31 of each year. Enter the dates shown in Fig. 4A-4. You will see the setting for changing the dates display to show the month name in Exercise 4A-3, step 31. The default setting for dates when starting a company is **Short Dates** (01/01/2022).

Fiscal Year Start	**01/01/2022**	(Jan 1, **Start date** of the fiscal year.)
Earliest Transaction	**08/31/2022**	(Aug 31, this is the last date the accounting records were completed manually, or were completed on another computer system, or the day the records were converted to Sage 50 Accounting. This may also be called a **conversion date**. The records are being created in Sage 50 Accounting as of this date.)
Fiscal Year End	**12/31/2022**	(Dec 31, **End date** of the fiscal year.)

6 ➤ When complete, click **Next >**.

Fig. 4A-5: Setup Method.

> ⦿ Have Sage 50 create a list of accounts based on your business type.
> (Recommended)

a) With this option, Sage 50 Accounting will create a company with approximately 165 General Ledger accounts that would be used by similar businesses. Using a template may save time in setting up a company; however, if you have a small company, using a template may take more time because you have to modify, delete and/or add new accounts and change the default settings using **Setup, Settings** window. Refer to Appendix 2015 L, *Setting Up a New Company File Using a Sage 50 Accounting Template* in your course materials at www.nelson.comstudent.

www

> ⦿ Have Sage 50 create a list of accounts from an export file.
> Select this option if you are switching from QuickBooks®, Quicken®, or MYOB®.

b) Using this option, Sage 50 Accounting will create a list of General Ledger accounts *from Quickbooks®, Quicken®, MYOB® export file* ® (or other accounting software programs). This means that Sage 50 Accounting will convert the data from the export file to a Sage 50 Accounting data file structure.

> ⦿ Let me build the list of accounts myself after the company is created.

c) Using this method, Sage 50 Accounting will create a company with only one General Ledger account (i.e., **3600 Current Earnings)** in the chart of accounts. You would create (add) accounts into each section as needed. In the author's view, this is the best way for students to create a company, as you will build each section containing the H A S G T accounts.

This is the method you will be using in this chapter.

7 ➤ Click method **c) Let me build the list of accounts myself after the company is created**, then **Next >**.

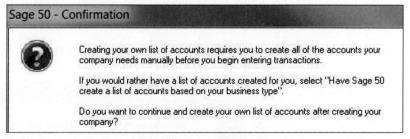

Fig. 4A-6: Warning Message.

8 ➤ This window informs you that you have chosen to create your own list of accounts method. Click **Yes**.

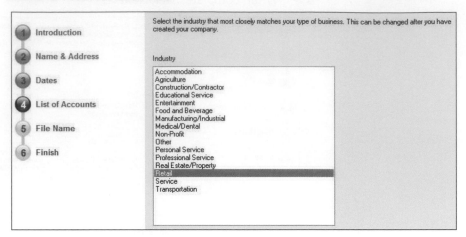

Fig. 4A-7: Type of Business window (Choose a Template).

This window lists a number of different types of businesses.

9 ➤ Select the **Retail** Industry (type of business). Click **Next >**.

Fig. 4A-8: Enter the name of company file window.

10 ➤ **Type the information** from Fig. 4A-8 into the fields in your window (see caution box).

Do NOT type your name here as part of the company file name. If you type your name here, it will become part of the company data file name, e.g., Sarah's Kitchen Stores Guida Marisa.SAI

Change the **C:** to your drive letter. The rest of the information in the field should be: [your drive letter]:\Sage 50 Data 2015\Sarah's Kitchen Stores. Delete any information and space to the right, some of which may be hidden.

11 ➤ When Fig. 4A-8 is complete, click **Next >**. You may not see this Confirmation window. Go to step 12.

C:\Sage 50 Data 2015\ Sarah's Kitchen Stores means that Sage 50 Accounting will create on the **C:** drive, inside the Sage 50 Data 2015 folder, a folder named **Sarah's Kitchen Stores.SAJ**, and will create the **Sarah's Kitchen Stores.SAI** file in the Kitchen folder.

.SAI may be lower case, as in **.sai.**

12 ➤ Sage 50 Accounting informs you that the folder and file do not exist in the location you have specified. Verify the location and when correct, click **Yes** and Sage 50 Accounting will create the folder and file. (See side note box.)

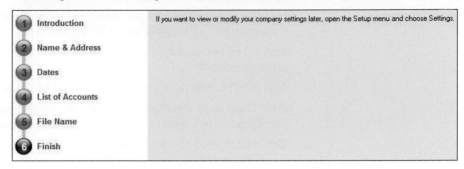

13 ➤ The above display informs you that in order to view or modify settings after continuing, you need to change settings. Click **Finish** to have Sage 50 Accounting set up the files for the company.

After you click Finish, a message box will appear to advise you, ***Creating new database***, similar to the following.

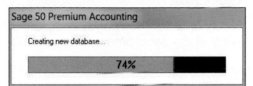

The creating database procedure can take up to *3 minutes or more*, depending on the type of computer system you are using—it might look as if the computer has stalled at the 74% or other point. Closing the Sage 50 Accounting program or shutting the computer off can cause a major problem in the data file and you will have to redo the setup procedure again. Moreover, it is possible that the file will not be able to be deleted from your storage space. **Wait until the system has set up the data file before proceeding.**

When Sage 50 Accounting has created the data files, the program will display the next window.

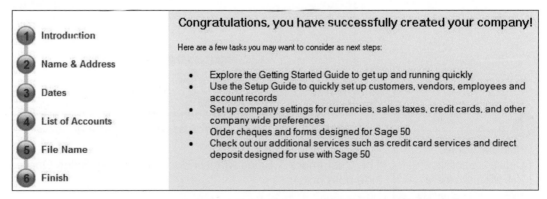

Fig. 4A-9: Successfully created the company data file.

This window lists some of the tasks that may be needed to finish setting up the company data file.

a.   Explore the Getting Started Guide to view tutorials that are available.

b.   Modify the company settings to those needed by the company (Exercise 4A-2a, 4A-2b, and 4A-3).

c.   Use the Setup Guide to add and link General Ledger accounts with open balances (Exercise 4A-4 to 4A-10 inclusive).

d.   Add list of vendors and record unpaid invoices (Exercise 4A-12). Note the text adds vendors first.

e.   Add list of customers and record unpaid invoices (Exercise 4A-13).

f.   If required, add inventory items and services, with quantities. Sarah's Kitchen Stores does not require the INVENTORY module at this time.

g.   Get customized cheques, quotes, orders, and invoices from a printer.

14 ➤ Click **Close**.

15 ➤ You should then see the Getting Started window. If you do not see it, check the bottom taskbar for the Getting Started icon. Click on the icon. Click on ☐ Show this window on start up to remove the ✓ and not display the window. Click **Close**.

IT IS IMPORTANT that you complete this step to ensure you can access all fields in the setup process through to the end of this chapter.

Fig. 4A-10: Sarah's Kitchen Stores Home window (see side note box).

> **ⓘ**
> Note that Quotes and Orders are not shown. You will make these selections in Exercise 4A-3, step 12.

The Customers & Sales window does not display Sales Quotes or Sales Orders. (See side note box.)

The Suppliers & Purchases window does not display Purchase Quotes or Purchase Orders.

The following modules display the History symbol (quill pen): Customers & Sales, Suppliers & Purchases, Inventory & Services, Employees & Payroll, and Company.

16 ➤ You can view the Chart of Accounts created from scratch, using two methods:

a) Click the **Report Centre**, **Accounts**, **Chart of Accounts**, click **Display**.

b) Click the **COMPANY** module, click the **Chart of Accounts** icon.

Use method **a)** to view the **Chart of Accounts**.

Fig. 4A-11: Chart of Accounts from scratch.

The Chart of Accounts structure is created with the five main financial statement categories and the X account **3600 Current Earnings**. You will be adding accounts to this structure to create Sarah's Kitchen Stores Chart of Accounts before linking accounts. Remember, if you had used the template, you would have to remove (delete) the accounts you don't need, change (modify) the names of accounts to those that your firm would use, and add other accounts that are not listed. If you decide to use a template, you should print the default Chart of Accounts to determine which accounts to keep, delete, modify, or add. (See side note box.)

> If you had used the template option, **www** (see Appendix 2015 L, *Setting Up a New Company File Using a Sage 50 Premium Accounting Template* in your course materials at: www/nelson.com/student) Sage 50 Accounting would have created a set of standard default General Ledger accounts (165 or more) for the company and created the linked accounts.

Congratulations! You have successfully set up the files for a company from scratch in your data location!

At the end of this chapter, after setting up the company, you will be shown how to turn the COMPANY, PAYABLES, and RECEIVABLES modules to READY.

You will also set up the linked accounts to the General Ledger that will be used by the PAYABLES and RECEIVABLES modules. This will be explained in Exercise 4A-8.

17 ➤ Click X and **Close** to return to the Home window.

Step 2: Setting User Preferences Defaults

A **default** is a pre-selected option that is automatically set until you choose a different option. Each of the next windows will allow you to either accept the defaults or select new options to set as defaults for various windows and reports.

Exercise 4A-2a—Setting User Preferences–View Defaults

We are going to hide the modules that we will not use in this chapter. The procedure can be reversed later to reveal the modules as you need them.

1 ➤ To hide modules, click **Setup**, **User Preferences**.

2 ➤ In the left pane click on the **View** item.

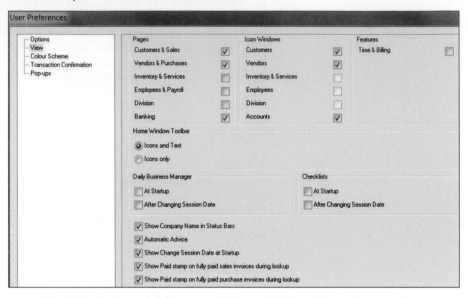

Fig. 4A-12: User Preferences View window (after changes).

This window (Fig. 4A-12) will allow you to choose the modules you plan to use for your company. Unclick a Pages item (e.g., Division ✓), and the corresponding Icon Windows ✓ is unchecked as well.

Customers & Sales	Allows you to keep track of your Accounts Receivable.
Vendors & Purchases	Allows you to keep track of your Accounts Payable.
Inventory & Services **WWW**	Allows you to maintain individual records using the perpetual inventory system. (Shown in Appendix 2015 H, *INVENTORY & SERVICES Module Setup Perpetual Inventory for Sarah's Kitchen Stores (4B)* in your course materials at www.nelson.com/student and in Chapter 8.)
Employees & Payroll	Allows you to record employee paycheques with payroll deductions and prepare government reports (T-4s). (Shown in Chapter 7.)
Division	This option allows you to maintain records of cost centres (projects, jobs, departments, etc.) for sale of goods and/or sale of services you provide to others. (Shown in Chapter 11.)
Banking	Allows you to Receive Payments (Receipts from Chapters 2A and 2B), make Deposits, Pay various bills (Payments Chapter 3A and 3B), Transfer funds between Company bank accounts and Reconcile accounts (Chapter 12).
Features column, Time & Billing **WWW**	Used with Customers & Sales, Employees & Payroll. Allows you to maintain time for employees and use the information to bill the customer. Shown in Appendix 2015 S, *Time & Billing Journal* in your course materials at www.nelson.com/student.

3 ➤	**Pages**	Remove the ✓ at **Inventory & Services, Employees & Payroll** and **Division**. This will hide the modules in the Home window.
4 ➤	**Features**	Remove the ✓ at **Time & Billing**.

Home Window Toolbar

Leave the selection as 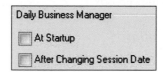. If you select Icons only, the home window icons will display without wording.

Daily Business Manager

The default setting is to display the Daily Business Manager ✓ **After Changing the Session Date**.

5 ➤ Click ✓ **After Changing the Session Date** to NOT display the Daily Business Manager. The ✓ has been removed.

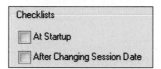

Checklists

WWW You can find information on Checklists in Appendix 2015 I, *Checklists for Task Completion* in your course materials at www.nelson.com/student.

The default setting is to display the **Checklists, After Changing the Session Date**.

6 ➤ To change the Checklists to not display, click on ✓ **After Changing Session Date**. The ✓ has been removed.

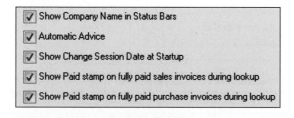

Checklists will not display unless you repeat the procedure.

Lower section

☑ Show Company Name in Status Bars
☑ Automatic Advice
☑ Show Change Session Date at Startup
☑ Show Paid stamp on fully paid sales invoices during lookup
☑ Show Paid stamp on fully paid purchase invoices during lookup

☑ Show Company Name in Status Bars Do NOT change. The default is to have the company name displayed at the bottom of each journal.

☑ Automatic Advice Do NOT change. This will provide advice on the Help menu if requested.

7 ➤ ☑ Show Change Session Date at Startup Click this field to place a ✓. This will provide the change session date window when you open a company data file.

☑ Show Paid stamp on fully paid sales invoices during lookup
☑ Show Paid stamp on fully paid purchase invoices during lookup Do NOT change. This will display the Paid stamp on fully paid invoices during lookup.

Colour scheme

8 ➤ In the left pane, click on the **Colour scheme** item. You will see the current colours used in journal windows. Sage 50 Accounting allows the user to change the background colour of the Journals.

The network system at your school may not allow you to change the background colour settings. You can change the colour background (appearance) of any window (from the default) by clicking the ▼ to see the various choices available from the list. Many of the default windows already have different colour backgrounds. There is no exercise for changing the settings. (See side note box.)

Many businesses use different background colours for quotes, orders and invoices. It is easier to see and know that you are in the correct window by the colour of the window.

Transaction Confirmation

9 ➤ In the left pane, click on the **Transaction Confirmation**.

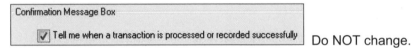

Confirmation Message Box
☑ Tell me when a transaction is processed or recorded successfully Do NOT change.

This choice will provide a window advising you the entry was posted or recorded. You may uncheck this box if you do not want to see the advice window.

Pop-ups

10 ➤ In the left pane, click on the **Pop-ups**.

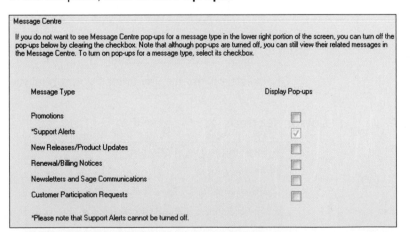

11 ➤ Remove the checkmarks as shown. Note: Messages are not available for students.

Exercise 4A-2b—Setting User Preferences–Options Defaults

---

1 ➤ In the left pane, click **Options** to move to the Options window.

Changing Preferences Settings

Use the following procedure to customize the options for your data file. If a row or rows of information are not discussed, leave the default unchanged.

Terminology

Fig. 4A-13: Terminology window.

2 ➤ Click **Use Accounting Terms** button. This will allow you to display familiar accounting terms.

Microsoft Excel Language

Do NOT change from English.

Print Button

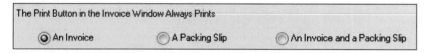

3 ➤ Leave the choice as **An Invoice**.

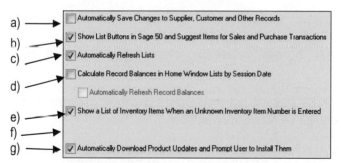

4 ➤ Change the settings as shown next.

a) [✓] Automatically Save Changes to Supplier, Customer and Other Records **Check** this box ✓ to automatically save changes to these records.

b) [ ] Show List Buttons in Sage 50 and Suggest Items for Sales and Purchase Transactions
The box should be **Unchecked**. Many businesses do not want to see the List buttons [___🔍] (magnifying glass) in journal fields. The author has removed the ✓ to not show List buttons in all journal columns.

c) [ ] Automatically Refresh Lists **Uncheck** the box. This is used with the Network version of Sage 50 Accounting when two or more employees are entering information and changing various lists of information.

d) [✓] Calculate Record Balances in Home Window Lists by Session Date
[ ] Automatically Refresh Record Balances
Click on the 2nd box, you will see this confirmation.

Click **Yes**. A second checkmark appears.

e) ☐ Show a List of Inventory Items When an Unknown Inventory Item Number is Entered   The box should be **Unchecked.** This choice would be checked when you are using Perpetual Inventory & Services. Discussed in Appendix H 2015, *INVENTORY & SERVICES Module Setup Perpetual Inventory for Sarah's Kitchen Stores (4B)* in your course materials at www.nelson.com/student and in Chapter 8.

WWW

f) ☐ Always Apply Allocation to Entire Transaction   Note: You may not see this selection. Do NOT change. This choice is with the DIVISION module.

g) ☐ Automatically Download Product Updates and Prompt User to Install Them   **Uncheck** the box. Product updates are not available in the Student version. It is only available for retail versions.

5 ➤ Click **OK** to return to the Home window.

Fig. 4A-14: Sarah's Kitchen Stores Receivable Payable display before Update Exercise 4A-3. (See Fig 4A-26 after changes.)

The program, based on your choices earlier, has amended the scratch company data file and displays the RECEIVABLES, PAYABLES, BANKING, COMPANY, and LEARNING CENTRE modules.

Since you did not use a template, you will need to add accounts and link appropriate accounts for the COMPANY, PAYABLES, and RECEIVABLES modules. This window does not display the INVENTORY & SERVICES, EMPLOYEES & PAYROLL, DIVISION or TIME AND BILLING modules, because you removed the ✓ in Exercise 4A-2a, step 3. See View item information Fig. 4A-12, User Preferences View window.

Step 3: Changing System Defaults

In this section, you will be confirming and/or changing some of the system settings defaults. If you need to change any settings in the future (e.g., comments to appear on sales quotes, orders, or invoices), this section is where you would come to make the change.

In this section, you will be looking at new settings that were not shown in Exercises 4A-1, 4A-2a and 4A-2b.

Exercise 4A-3—Changing System Defaults

---

1 ➤   Related Tasks   From the Home window, bottom area, click on **Settings**.

Information

2 ➤   In the left pane, click the ⊞ at Company. Click on **Information**.

3 ➤   Business No.   Type **R4675 2567**. [Tab]. Some companies have one registration number for both HST and Employee payroll. This number is issued by Canada Revenue Agency (CRA) [formerly called Canada Customs and Revenue Agency (CCRA)] and needs to be printed on Sales invoices and T4 slips.

Industry Type

Fig. 4A-15: Business Number window.

4 ➤   Click the ▼ to view the choices available. *Note*: These are the same choices available in Fig. 4A-7. Select **Other**.

System

5 ➤   In the left pane, click on **System**. You will see the following confirmation.

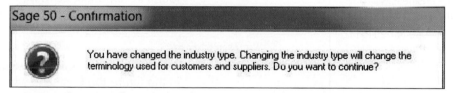

6 ➤   Click **No** to return to the Retail setting. You do not want to change the Industry type settings. In the left pane, click on **System**.

Fig. 4A-16a: Cash Basis Accounting Settings window—System.

Cash-Basis Accounting   Recognizes revenue when cash is received and recognizes expenses when cash is paid. The cash basis of accounting is used by farmers and fishermen and is *NOT* covered in this text.

Sarah's Kitchen Stores uses **Accrual Based** accounting. Do NOT click the box.

> ☑ Use Cheque No. as the source code for cash purchases and sales
> ☑ Do not allow transactions dated before: 08/31/2022   📅
> ☐ Allow transactions in the future (beyond the session date)
>   ☐ Warn if transactions are   days in the future
>   ☐ Allow General Journal and payroll transactions for the next fiscal year or calendar year
>   Note: Since payroll transactions must be recorded in the appropriate tax year, payroll transactions are only allowed until December 31 of
>   the next calendar year even if the fiscal year extends beyond that date.

Fig. 4A-16b: Other System defaults Settings window.

☑ Use Cheque No. as the source code for cash purchases and sales — Do NOT change this field. It should be ✓. When using the Reconciliation and Deposits journal, it is useful to know the cheque number for a cash purchase or sale. Checking this option results in Sage 50 Accounting using the cheque number as the source code rather than the invoice number.

☑ Do not allow transactions dated before: 08/31/2016   📅 — Check this box. This feature NOT will allow you to post transactions from previous months (e.g., May, August, or previous years). When you check this box ✓, the date field and box will be available to change. Sarah's Kitchen Stores wants to ensure no prior transactions are recorded.

---

a) If transactions are allowed in the future, you would check the first field to permit them and then set the second field with a time limit on how far into the future the business will allow these transactions.

b) Appendix 2015 M, *Post-Dated Cheques,* uses this option and is appropriate for businesses that accept and handle post-dated cheques.

---

7 ➤ ☑ Allow transactions in the future (beyond the session date) — Uncheck this box. (See side note box.) This feature would allow you to record transactions in the future (e.g., post-dated cheques). At this time Sarah's Kitchen Stores does not want to allow future postings. Information can be found in Appendix 2015 M, *Post-Dated Cheques* in your course materials at www.nelson.com/student.

www

☐ Warn if transactions are   days in the future — This box should be unchecked. If you checked the box, you would be able to indicate how far in the future the business will allow transactions. Uncheck this box. Sarah's Kitchen Stores will not allow future entries.

☐ Allow General Journal and payroll transactions for the next fiscal year or calendar year
Note: Since payroll transactions must be recorded in the appropriate tax year, payroll transactions are only allowed until December 31 of the next calendar year even if the fiscal year extends beyond that date.

This box should be unchecked. Sage 50 Accounting will allow General Journal entries and Payroll entries to be recorded in the next fiscal or calendar year. Sarah's Kitchen Stores will not allow future entries.

☐ Warn if accounts are not balanced when entering a new month — Do NOT change. This feature will allow the user to buy and install the software and immediately start to record transactions before putting in the previous month's General Ledger balances and CUSTOMERS and PAYABLES invoice details called **History**. If you record transactions in a new month, a warning message will appear to advise you that the subledger(s) do not balance with the General Ledger. Do NOT change the settings.

Backup

8 ➤   In the left pane, click on **Backup**.

Display a backup reminder when session date changes	Daily ▼
☑ Display a backup reminder when closing this company	
Compact data before backing up to save disk space	
☑ Verify backup file after back up completion	

Scheduled Backup

☐ Automatically back up this file   Every Monday ▼   To   C:\Users\Public\Documents\Sage Softwar   Browse...

when the file is first closed for the day

☐ Remove the oldest backup file when the total number of files exceeds

Fig. 4A-17: Backup window.

This feature assumes you are backing up as shown in Exercise 1-24.

9 ➤   Change the settings as shown in Fig. 4A-17.

If you are using a different backup procedure (e.g., creating backups outside Sage 50 Accounting), then these settings would not be required.

☐ Display a backup reminder when session date changes   Daily ▼

Uncheck this item. When you advance the date, this feature would display a backup reminder window.

In a business setting, this item could be used, but in a classroom environment it is not required.

☑ Display a backup reminder when closing this company   Do NOT change. When closing the company (exiting), you will be reminded to back up before exiting. Discuss a backup procedure with your instructor.

The authors recommend that daily backups be completed, and a copy of the data on a USB storage device, CD or other media be taken off-site to ensure safety of the material. There are many cases where a business has suffered losses due to fire, etc., and has recovered because the accounting records were backed up and stored away from the business location. See Exercise 1-24.

☐ Compact data before backing up to save disk space   Do NOT change. In a classroom environment there is no need to Compact Data when exiting. In a business environment when the file contains thousands of entries, there would be a need to compact the data file.

☑ Verify backup file after back up completion   Do NOT change. When using any backup procedure, it is recommended that you maintain a setting to verify the backup data.

Scheduled Backup

10 ➤   ☐ Automatically back up this file   **Uncheck** this item. In a classroom environment, there is no need to schedule backups. In a business environment, it is recommended that you schedule backups daily.

Features

11 ➤   In the left pane, click on **Features**.

Sarah has decided that she will not use Purchase Quotes for vendors/suppliers. She will use only Purchase Orders to confirm orders placed with vendors. She will use customer Quotes and Orders and will not use Packing Slips.

Fig. 4A-18: Orders, Quotes, and Packing Slips.

12 ➤ Change the selections as shown in Fig. 4A-18.

Language

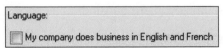

Do NOT change. Sarah's Kitchen Stores does not have any customers using French.

Credit Cards and Sales Taxes

The following items in the left pane will be left for a later exercise as they need account number information to proceed. **Sales Taxes** (Exercise 4A-9) **Credit Cards** (Exercise 4A-11).

Currency

13 ➤ In the left-hand pane, click on **Currency**.

The Home Currency is Canadian dollars. You will notice that the window has a column for Foreign Currency, but you cannot enter information unless you click the ☐ I want to enter transactions using Foreign Currencies .

Click the **I want to enter transactions using Foreign Currencies** box; a ✓ appears. The ☐ I want to enter transactions using Foreign Currencies account field is not greyed out.

14 ➤ **Foreign Currency** **Double-click** on the column to see a list of foreign currencies available in Sage 50 Accounting. You could select a foreign currency or click **Cancel**.

15 ➤ Click **Cancel** in the Select Foreign Currency list window. Sarah's Kitchen Stores does not plan to sell to the U.S. or any other country at the present time. See Chapter 14 for information on Foreign Currency.

16 ➤ ☐ I want to enter transactions using Foreign Currencies Click the box again to remove the ✓ in.

Forms

17 ➤ In the left pane, click on **Forms**.

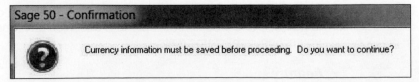

Sage 50 Accounting needs to save currency information, even though you changed the setting back to the original default setting.

18 ➤ Click **Yes**. The next window is Forms.

	Next Form Number	Verify Number Sequence	Confirm Printing/E-mail	Print Company Address on	Print in Batches	Check for Duplicates
Customers & Sales						
Invoices:	1	☑	☐	☑	☐	☐
Sales Quotes:	1	☑	☐	☑	☐	--
Sales Orders:	1	☑	☐	☑	☐	--
Receipts:	1	☑	☐	☑	☐	☐
Statements:	--	--	--	☑	--	--
Customers Deposits:	1	☑	--	--	--	--
Suppliers & Purchases						
Purchase Orders:	1	☑	☐	☑	☐	--
Banking						
Cheques:	--	☑	☐	☐	☐	
Direct Deposit Stubs:						
Supplier:	1	☑	☐		☐	
Pre-Authorized Debit:	1	☑	--	--	--	--
Deposit Slips:	--	☑	☐			

Fig. 4A-19: Settings—Forms tab (see side note box).

> **ℹ** There is no box for Cheque Number. The next cheque number will be entered when you set up bank accounts (see Exercise 4A-7, step 6).

Next Form Number — The number entered in these fields is the next number that will print on the appropriate form. Sage 50 Accounting has the capability to print any number from 1 to 200,000,000 on all forms.

19 ➤ **Invoices:** This number is the invoice number that will print on the next sales invoice to be issued by Sarah's Kitchen Stores. Type **922**, Tab.

20 ➤ **Sales Quotes:** This number is the next number that will print on sales quotes to be given to customers. Leave at **1**, Tab. Sarah's Kitchen Stores will start to use this feature.

21 ➤ **Sales Orders:** This number is the next number that will print on sales orders to be given to customers. Leave at **1**, Tab.

22 ➤ **Receipts:** Delete **1** from this field. A blank field in the receipts journal will allow you to record the cheque number received from your customer, Tab.

23 ➤ **Customer Deposits:** Delete **1** from this field, Tab. If your company issued numbered printed receipts for deposits, you can assign that number to customer deposits in the Receipts Journal. Sarah's Kitchen Stores does not issue receipts for deposits at this time.

Suppliers & Purchases

24 ➤ **Purchase Orders:** This number is the next number that will print on purchase orders given to vendors. Leave at **1** (Sarah's Kitchen Stores will start using purchase orders in the near future), Tab.

Banking

25 ➤ | Cheques: | Click on the **Confirm Printing/E-mail** box on this line. When printing cheques, you will receive a warning confirmation that the cheque has not been printed.

Direct Deposit Stubs

26 ➤ | Supplier: | Delete **1** from this field. [Tab] This number would be used when a business makes electronic payments for Payables and Payroll. Sarah's Kitchen Stores does not use this feature at this time. There is a bank fee for this service.

You may need to scroll down to see the next information.

| Pre-Authorized Debit: | Delete **1** from this field. [Tab] The field would be used when a business received electronic receipts from customers for Sales. It is shown as Pre-Authorized Debit (PAD) in the Receipts Journal. Sarah's Kitchen Stores does not receive receipts for deposits at this time. There is a bank fee for this service.

27 ➤ | Deposit Slips: | This field would be a sequence number allocated by Sage 50 Accounting for deposits.

28 ➤ **Verify Number Sequence**   **Uncheck** Deposit slips and Do NOT change the rest.

This will make sure the numbers of forms identified increase by 1 each time you use the next form.

Confirm Printing/ E-mail   Do NOT change. In business, you check the boxes to confirm that you want to print or e-mail a client. For classroom use, leave the boxes unchecked.

Print Company Address on   Do NOT change. When this option is ✓, the company name and address (as set up in the Company Information window) will print on forms. Note: This field is ✓ for classroom/lab use to identify students' work. In a business setting the business name and address would be on the pre-printed document.

Print in Batches   Do NOT change. You can enter many invoices during a day and then print them at one time. For classroom use, leave the boxes unchecked so you can print individual forms, as required. Refer to Appendix 2015 AB, *Printing in Batches* in your course materials at www.nelson.com/student.

WWW

> ⓘ
> If you click on the bottom computer link, "Order cheques and forms" you would be taken to a Sage 50 Accounting Business Services window with more information about buying customized forms.

29 ➤ **Check for Duplicates**   Click the **Invoice** box ✓. This will verify that duplicate numbers are not used on invoices. (See side note box.)

E-mail

30 ➤ In the left pane, click the **E-mail** item.

Fig. 4A-20: Settings—E-mail.

Do NOT change. This text does not have an exercise to send or receive e-mail. Sarah's Kitchen Stores will not be e-mailing documents to customers or vendors. Click each of the forms and notice the wording in the message box. This wording can be changed when the form is being e-mailed.

Date format

31 ➤   Click the **Date Format** item.

Select the choices as shown. The dates will display and print in words (e.g., Aug instead of 08).

Shippers

32 ➤   Click the **Shippers** item.

Sarah's Kitchen Stores is not going to record Shipper information at this time. You can return here at a later date and add information as required.

Logo

33 ➤   Click the **Logo** item.

Sarah's Kitchen Stores is not going to use a logo on forms. There is no exercise to use this feature.

Names

34 ➤   Click the **Names** item.

 Do NOT change. Refer to Appendix 2015 Q, *Names Fields* in your course materials at www.nelson.com/student.

General Accounts

35 ➤   Click the **+** at General (Accounts), the list is expanded.

Budget

36 ➤   Click the **Budget** item.

You can find information on using Budgets in Appendix 2015 E *Budgets—General Ledger* in your course materials at www.nelson.com/student.

WWW

Budget revenue and expense accounts

You would record budgeted amounts for reporting and control purposes. You can select the frequency of the budget period from a drop-down list. If this option is checked, each Revenue and Expense account can be modified to include budgeted amounts by budget period. (See side note box.)

The Income Statement can then be displayed with a comparison of actual to budget for the period.

At this time, Sarah's Kitchen Stores is not planning to set up a budget. Do NOT change. **Leave** the box **unchecked**. This default can be changed at a later date, if desired.

Numbering

37 ➤ Click **Numbering**. Do NOT change.

Fig. 4A-21: Numbering.

Show account numbers in reports	Do NOT change. If you select this option, account numbers (e.g., 5330 for Telephone Expense) will not appear in the General Ledger printouts.
38 ➤ **Number of digits in account number**	Click the ▼. You can extend the account number up to 8 digits. **Change** to 8 digits. **Change** back to 4 digits. This text will use only 4 digits in all account numbers. Do NOT change.

Departments

39 ➤ Click **Departments**.

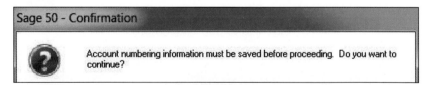

40 ➤ This confirmation is aware that you clicked the ▼, and assumes that you changed a setting. Click **Yes** to continue.

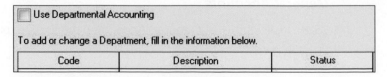

Fig. 4A-22: Departmental Accounting.

41 ➤ Click **Use Departmental Accounting**; the following warning appears.

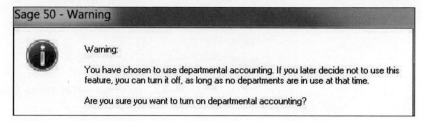

42 ➤ Select **Cancel**. Sarah's Kitchen Stores has decided not to use Departmental Accounting at this time.

Names

43 ➤ Click the **Names** item and the following warning message appears.

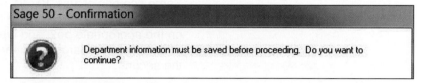

This message appears because you changed a setting in Departments and changed it back to the default. Click **Yes** to continue without creating Departments. Sage 50 Accounting does not realize there is no change.

 A list of 5 Field Names appears. Do NOT change. See Appendix 2015 Q, *Names Fields,* in your course materials at www.nelson.com/student for discussion of this topic.

Linked Accounts

44 ➤ Click the **Linked Accounts** item.

You will return here after entering the General Ledger accounts.

Payables

45 ➤ In the left pane, click on **+** at **Payables**; the list is expanded.

Address

46 ➤ Click the **Address** item.

47 ➤ **Change** the information as shown. This default information will appear when you add new suppliers (vendors).

Options

48 ➤ Click the **Options** item.

Fig. 4A-23: Settings—Payables Options.

Aging	Do NOT change. Aging is a process of sorting Accounts Payable transactions in the Vendor Aged reports using predefined categories; e.g., 30, 60, or 90 days based on the current session date. Aging enables you to easily see which invoices are due within the time periods.
	Some companies use 10, 30, and/or 60 days as the aging periods. If you wish to change the aging period, you would click on the appropriate box, and type in the new setting. The second number must be larger than the first, and the third larger than the second.
49 ➤ Early Payment Terms	Click the **Calculate discounts before tax for one-time suppliers** field. A ✓ appears. This will allow cash discounts for early payments to be taken from One-time Suppliers (when appropriate) on the value of goods purchased before HST was added to the invoice value.

Duty

50 ➤ Click **Duty**.

Do NOT change. Sarah's Kitchen Stores does not plan on importing merchandise at this time.

Names

www   Ignore Additional Info Titles at this time. See Appendix 2015 Q, *Names Fields,* in your course materials at www.nelson.com/student for discussion on this topic.

Terminology				
Vendors:	Vendors	Invoices:	Invoices	
Purchases:	Purchases	Payments:	Payments	
Orders:	Orders	Quotes:	Quotes	

51 ➤ Click **Names**. Click each of the ▼ to see the various choices. Change the settings as shown.

Linked Accounts

You will return here after entering the General Ledger accounts.

Receivables

52 ➤ You may need to scroll down in the left-hand pane to see Receivables. Click the **+** at **Receivables**. The list is expanded.

Address

53 ➤ Click the **Address** item.

Enter default address information for new customers.

City:	Hamilton
Province:	Ontario
Country:	

54 ➤ Change the information as shown. This default information will appear when you add new customers.

Options

55 ➤ Click the **Options** item.

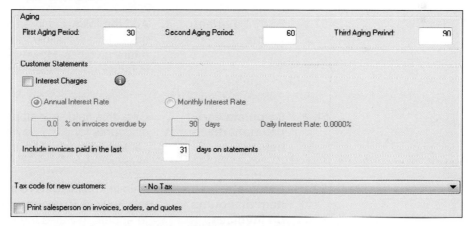

Fig. 4A-24: Settings—Receivables Options.

Aging	Do NOT change (see Payables Aging).
Interest Charges	Do NOT change. Interest on overdue invoices can be calculated by checking this box. If desired, you may enter an interest rate and the number of days the invoice is overdue before interest applies. The interest charges will appear on the customer statement. When this is used, Sage 50 Accounting shows only the amount on the statement. It does not automatically post it as an interest charge to the account. Leave the default blank.
WWW	See Appendix 2015 AF, *Calculating Interest on Overdue Receivable Balances*, in your course materials at www.nelson.com/student for instructions on using the feature to calculate the compound interest on Receivables.
Include invoices paid in the last 31 days on statements	Do NOT change. You can print details of paid invoices with receipts on customer statements for the selected number of days with this option. If you have cleared paid invoices from the system, no paid invoices will be printed.

| Tax code for new customers | You are unable to change this field as you have not set up individual tax codes. You will set up Sales Tax codes in Exercise 4A-9. |

☐ Print salesperson on invoices, orders, and quotes Refer to Appendix 2015 N, *Adding a Salesperson's Name to an Invoice,* in your course materials at www.nelson.com/student.

www

Discount

56 ➤ Click on **Discount**.

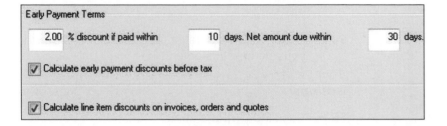

57 ➤ Early Payment Terms   Add the following in each box: **2**%, **10** days, net **30** days. This will allow these terms to be applied to all future invoices. However, the default can be changed in individual invoices, if desired.

58 ➤ Calculate early payment discounts before tax   Click this field. A ✓ appears. This will allow cash discounts for early payment to be taken on the value of goods sold before HST is added to the invoice value.

59 ➤ Calculate line item discounts on invoices, orders & quotes   This field should have a ✓. If there is no ✓, click this field. A ✓ appears. This will allow a Discount % to appear in Sales Invoices. See Fig. 2A-7a (Discount column) in Chapter 2A.

Comments

60 ➤ Click the **Comments** item.

Fill in the boxes below to add a standard comment to sales invoices, sales orders, and sales quotes. You can change the comment text in individual transactions.

Comments

Sales Invoices:	Thank you for your order
Sales Orders:	Thank you for your order, it will be shipped as quoted.
Sales Quotes:	Thank you for allowing us to quote on your order

Fig. 4A-25: Settings—Comment tab.

61 ➤ Type the comments as shown in Fig. 4A-25. They will appear on the appropriate form when recording quotes, orders, and invoices.

Names

62 ➤ Click the **Names** item. Do NOT change. Click each of the ▾ to see the various choices.

Ignore Additional Info Titles at this time. See Appendix 2015 Q, *Names Fields*, in your course materials at www.nelson.com/strudent, for discussion on this topic.

Linked Accounts

You will return here after entering the General Ledger accounts.

63 ➤ Click **OK** to accept the setting changes and return to the revised Home window, shown next.

Study the Home window in Fig. 4A-26. Modules CUSTOMERS & SALES, and VENDORS & PURCHASES are changed to RECEIVABLES and PAYABLES. The following modules are hidden: INVENTORY & SERVICES, EMPLOYEES & PAYROLL and DIVISIONS. The middle Tasks diagram displays the Sales and Purchase icons.

Fig. 4A-26: Revised Sarah's Kitchen Stores Home window after changes. See Fig. 4A-14, before changes.

64 ➤ Click the PAYABLES module. Notice the icon **Purchase Quotes** is not displayed, as a result of the setting made in step 12, Fig. 4A-18 to not use Quotes.

Step 4: Conversion Process with Accounts

The next step is to enter accounting data, such as accounts and account balances, from the manual records of the company. This is required not only for Sarah's Kitchen Stores, but also for any company converting to Sage 50 Accounting.

Conversion, in this chapter, means changing from one accounting system to another. There are two types of conversions:

1. Changing from a manual system to a computerized system.
2. Changing from one computerized system to another computerized system.

When a company buys the Sage 50 Accounting software program it has two choices:

a) After setting up the Chart of Accounts, the company can record transactions immediately without entering previous history balances in the General Ledger, and Customer and/or Vendor subledgers. They would add previous history during the next month(s), but before a year-end.

b) The company can set up the Chart of Accounts, then record their previous history balances at a specific time, normally from the end of a month. This is done when all accounting records from the original accounting system have been updated, and the Trial Balance and financial statements have been prepared.

It is possible to have more than one conversion date. A company may decide to use a computerized GENERAL LEDGER on one date; e.g., January 1, and could start to use the computerized RECEIVABLE subledger on another date; e.g., March 1. In either case, the accounts and balances for the manual system and computer system must be the same on the dates when information is converted.

Regardless of the method the company chooses, the new computerized Chart of Accounts should accurately reflect the company's Chart of Accounts. Then the Trial Balance amounts, and customers' and vendors' balances are entered in the computer records.

At this time, both the manual and computer records should agree. This specific time is called the **Conversion Date**. Sage 50 Accounting refers to it as the **Earliest Transaction Date**. When all information and dollar values have been entered in Sage 50 Accounting and they agree with the old records, you will change the system from a HISTORY mode to a READY mode. After this date, the company would stop using the manual records and start to enter transactions using the Sage 50 Accounting system. (See side note box.)

Sarah's Kitchen Stores has decided to use method **b**. They will take the time to set up the completed company records, namely COMPANY, ACCOUNTS PAYABLE, and ACCOUNTS RECEIVABLE modules, before recording new transactions.

The Chart of Accounts

Part of the conversion process is to ensure that the General Ledger accounts are the same for the manual system and the computerized system. The G/L accounts for Sarah's Kitchen Stores need to be set up.

Using the COMPANY module of Sage 50 Accounting, you can add, change, or delete the G/L accounts. Before making any changes, it is important to understand how Sage 50 Accounting sets up the chart of accounts.

The following is a summary of the information provided at the beginning of this chapter: Step 1: Account Number Structure.

Account Numbering System in Sage 50 Accounting

The account numbering system for this company and all companies in this text starts with 1000 and ends with 5999. Each section of a classified statement must always:

- start with an **H** account (Group Heading), and
- end with a **T** (Group Total) account.

Postable accounts that require a subtotal are shown in the first dollar value column on the left as an **A** (subgroup Account).

The **S** subtotal account, **Subgroup Total**, adds the **A** type of accounts and is shown in the second dollar column.

Postable accounts that do not require a subtotal are shown in the second dollar value column on the right as a **G** (group account).

Leave spaces between account numbers for adding accounts in the future without having to make new account groups to accommodate the new accounts. For example, if you start **Cash In Bank** at 1050, and the next account is Accounts Receivables, assign Accounts Receivable number 1060 so that if you need to insert other bank accounts in the future, you can assign them numbers close to the first bank account.

You will now start setting up Sarah's Kitchen Stores, Chart of Accounts. You will be starting with the scratch Chart of Accounts, which Sage 50 Accounting sets up when you select the option to start the Chart of Accounts from scratch (shown next). You will add accounts under each account category. Refer to Fig. 4A-32 (Chart of Accounts) to see the accounts and structure that you will be setting up.

Exercise 4A-4—Setting Up (Adding) the Chart of Accounts

To Add an Account

For illustrative purposes, you will add three accounts:

> **1000 Current Assets**
> **1005 Petty Cash**
> **1010 Bank Account Chequing**

There are three ways to enter new accounts:

Chart of
Accounts

a. From the Home window, click on the **COMPANY** module, then click the ▼ at Chart of Accounts to view the four choices. The blue quill pen icon (History) means this module is still in History mode. Select **Add Account** to display Fig. 4A-27a.

b. From the Home window, click the **Company** module, then the **Chart of Accounts** icon to open the Accounts window; click the **Create** 🔲 icon. The General Ledger window (Fig. 4A-27a) will be displayed. This method will be shown for information purposes for Exercise 4A-4.

c. Click **Setup, Setup Guide**, click on **Accounts** to open new window, Fig 4-27b.

1 ➤ Use method **B** to display the General Ledger window.

Fig. 4A-27a: New Account window. *Note the red * indicating a Required Field.*

2 ➤ **Account**   Notice that there are three tabs. Type **1000**, a number within the Asset section. Notice that three new tabs appear:
Reconciliation & Deposits, Related Historical Accounts and Notes. The Reconciliation & Deposits tab is covered in Chapter 12.

The Related Historical Accounts tab information is created by Sage 50 Accounting when you move into a new fiscal year. The information for this tab is available only when you have recorded transactions in Sage 50 Accounting in a previous fiscal year.

Notes Using this feature will display and print Notes on Financial Statements. See Appendix 2015 U, *Adding Notes/Footers to Statements,* in your course materials at www.nelson.com/student for more information.

Tab to move to the next field, which is the Account Name field. Type **Current Assets**, Tab.

3 ➤ **Type**   Click ⊙ Group Heading. Current Assets is the heading (H) for the Current Assets section on the Balance Sheet.

You will see that some of the options (under GIFI Code) are now hidden. The options will be seen and explained in step 6 (Information section).

Information

GIFI Code: Do NOT change. This field is used for electronic filing of Corporate Tax Returns. Sarah's Kitchen Stores is not a corporation.

4 ➤ Click on Class Options tabs.

There are no Class Options for accounts which are used as a Group Heading, Subgroup Total, or Group Total.

5 ➤ Click on the [Additional Info] tab. You can add up to five additional lines of description about this account (e.g., the manager or assistant manager responsible for the account). See Appendix 2015 Q, *Names Fields,* in your course materials at www.nelson.com/student for information about these fields.

WWW

6 ➤ Click on the [Reconciliation & Deposits] tab.

> Account Reconciliation cannot be performed on Group Heading, Subgroup Total, Group Total, and most linked accounts.

The Options are available only for **postable** type accounts (**A** and **G**).

7 ➤ Click on the [Related Historical Accounts] tab.

> There are no Related Historical Accounts for accounts which are used as a Group Heading, Subgroup Total, or Group Total.

8 ➤ Click on the [Notes] tab. As mentioned in step 2, you can add notes to display and print on Financial statements.

9 ➤ Click once again on [Account] tab. Click **Save and Close**, **X** to return to the Home window.

10 ➤ From the menu bar, click **Setup**, **Setup Guide**, **Accounts** to display the Accounts window (Fig. 4A-27b).

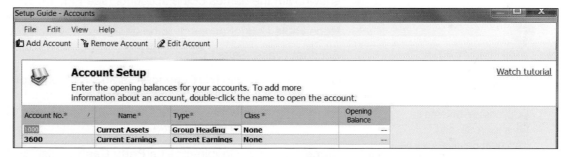

Fig. 4A-27b: New Account Setup window. *Note the red * Asterisk for Required Fields.*

Note that Account 1000 is displayed from the previous steps.

> The author has used a minimum number of account class options in the setup of accounts to allow you to understand the basic setup of the account classes without spending too much time on it.
>
> Account classes can be changed at a later time if the business needs to break down the accounts into specific groupings.

11 ➤ Account Below account 3600 Type **1005**, [Tab].

12 ➤ Name Type **Petty Cash**, [Tab].

13 ➤ Type Click the [▼]. Select **Subgroup Account** because this account will require a subtotal. [Tab].

Remember: If you use a **Subgroup Account (A)**, then you must also use a **Subgroup Total (S)** after the last A in a group.

14 ➤ Class Click the [▼]. A list of account classes displays. They can be used for sorting and filtering reports in later versions of the Sage 50 Accounting program. Enter the classes as indicated. (See side note box.)

Not all classes are discussed as follows. (See side note box.)

Asset:	All Items owned by a company.
Cash:	Amount of cash on hand.
Bank:	A bank account (chequing or savings).
Credit Card Receivable:	Amount owed by credit card company to you for sales made to customers.
Accounts Receivable:	Amount that is owed to you for goods and services sold on credit.
Other Receivable:	Amount that is owed to you that is not a normal sale of goods and services (e.g., sale of old office equipment).
Inventory:	Goods on hand for sale to customers.
Current Asset:	Assets that will be replaced/or used up within a year (e.g., Prepaid Items, Investments).
Capital Asset:	An asset that will be used for a long period of time (e.g., Building, Computer Equipment).
Other Asset:	An asset that does not fit into any of the other categories.

15 ➤ Sarah has decided to keep a minimum number of classes of accounts, as shown with the names of the accounts (see Fig. 4A-32). Sage 50 Accounting requires certain types with specific accounts, such as the Accounts Receivable Ledger account, to be an Accounts Receivable Option type.

Account Class, Select **Cash**. `Tab`.

Opening Balance	Do NOT change. Sarah's Kitchen Stores has decided to add all the accounts and the account structure (**H A S G T**) before adding the account balances in Exercise 4A-10. (See side note box.)

> You may also add each account's balance as you create the account. Accounts and Class Options are entered in this exercise, and Account Balances will be entered in Exercise 4A-10. When you become more comfortable with account types and contra balances, you may try to add the account balances as you create the accounts.

16 ➤ **Name**   Double-click on **Petty Cash** to display the General Ledger window.

Information Section

GIFI Code	Do NOT change.
Omit from Financial Statements if Balance is Zero	Do NOT change. If you click this box and the account has a zero balance, it will not show when viewing or printing the financial statements. Sarah's Kitchen Stores has decided to show all accounts when viewing or printing statements.
Allow Division Allocation	Do NOT change. Sarah's Kitchen Stores will not use the DIVISION module. The DIVISION or PROJECT module will be discussed in Chapter 11. Leave blank.

Class Options Tab

17 ➤ | Next Deposit No.: [   ] | Sarah's Kitchen Stores will not keep track of receipts by deposit numbers. Remove **1**, `Tab`.

To see information about the different types of classes, on the menu bar click **Help**, **Contents,** in the top right search field, type **classes**, then press `Enter`. You will see a list of categories below classes. Click on any one that you would like information about. **Exit** the Help window. Click `Save and Close`.

18 ➤   Create account **1010 Bank Account Chequing**, with **Subgroup Account** type and with a **Class Option of Bank**. Double-click on **Bank Account Chequing**, and click the **Class Options** tab.

You may see the following window.

19 ➤   **Save Changes:** Accept the selection to always save changes.

20 ➤   **Institution:**   Click on ▼ and you will see a list of banks that allow electronic transfer of funds using Sage 50 Accounting. Select **Other**.

Do NOT change the Branch Name, Transit Number, and Account Number fields.

21 ➤   Sarah's Kitchen Stores will not keep track of receipts by deposit numbers. Remove **1**, ⬚Tab .

Fig. 4A-28: Bank Class Options window.

If you choose the Account Class Option, Cash, then you will be able to record the Next Cheque No. in Exercise 4A-7, step 6, as well as being able to assign the Principal Bank Account as shown in Linking the Modules Exercise 4A-8, Fig. 4A-34 and Fig. 4A-35.

If you choose an Account Class Option other than Cash or Bank (e.g., Asset, Current Asset) you will not be able to link the Principal Bank Account in Linking the Modules, Exercise 4A-8, Fig. 4A-34 and Fig. 4A-35.

You will also see the following Confirmation window, indicating that you cannot post a transaction.

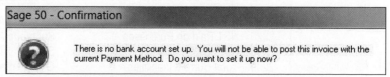

Fig. 4A-29: Bank Confirmation window.

22 ➤ With a selection of **Bank** Account Class, click Save and Close to add the account.

23 ➤ After reviewing the possible warning messages next, create the remaining accounts from the lists.

Note: If you attempt to add an account number that has already been set up, you should see the following message; click **OK** to continue.

> **Sage 50 - Duplicate Entry**
>
> You have entered a number that has been assigned to another Account. You cannot have two Accounts with the same number.

Click **OK**. Remember that the account number has already been entered/created.

Note: Sage 50 Accounting may not allow you to enter more accounts after entering the first screen or later. If this happens, click Close. You will see an error message about "accounts are not in logical order or the accounts are not balanced." Click **Continue** to be returned to the Setup Guide. Click **Accounts** and continue entering accounts.

Some users prefer **HEADING** and **TOTAL** names in all capital letters, while others capitalize only the first letter (**Heading** and **Total**). Sarah's Kitchen Stores uses the latter format.

* When you create account 1080 Cash Total, select type Subgroup Total account **S**.

To **delete** an account set up in error, see Exercise 4A-5. To **modify** an account, see Exercise 4A-6.

(See three side note boxes.)

Acct #	Account Name	Type of Account	Code	Class
1011	Bank Account Credit Card Receivable	Subgroup Account	A	Credit Card Receivables (no other changes)
1080	Cash Total	Subgroup Total	S*	(See side note box.)
1200	Accounts Receivable	Subgroup Account	A	Accounts Receivable
1210	Allowance for Bad Debts	Subgroup Account	A	Allowance for Bad Debts
1219	Net Accounts Receivable	Subgroup Total	S	
1240	Inventory of Good	Group Account	G	Inventory
1260	Store/Office Supplies/Prepaid	Group Account	G	Current Assets
1299	Total Current Assets	Group Total	T	
1400	Capital Assets	Group Heading	H	
1410	Display Equipment	Subgroup Account	A	Capital Asset
1415	Accumulated Deprec. Display Eq	Subgroup Account	A	Accum. Amort. & Depreciation
1419	Display Equipment: Net Value	Subgroup Total	S	
1420	Office Furniture/Equipment	Subgroup Account	A	Capital Asset
1425	Accumulated Deprec. Office Fur/Eq	Subgroup Account	A	Accum. Amort. & Depreciation
1429	Office Furniture/Equipment: Net Val	Subgroup Total	S	
1499	Net Capital Assets	Group Total	T	

The **Liability** section heading is automatically put in by the program. Create the Liability accounts as shown next:

2000	Current Liabilities	Group Heading	H	
2010	Accounts Payable	Group Account	G	Accounts Payable
2030	Visa Credit Card Payable	Group Account	G	Credit Card Payable*

* DO NOT CHANGE other fields in the Class Options tab for this account.

2210	HST Charged on Sales	Subgroup Account	A	Sales Tax Payable
2220	HST Paid on Purchases	Subgroup Account	A	Sales Tax Payable
2230	Net HST Owing/Receivable	Subgroup Total	S	
2299	Total Current Liabilities	Group Total	T	
2300	Long Term Liabilities	Group Heading	H	
2310	Bank Loan Payable	Group Account	G	Long Term Debt
2399	Total Long Term Liabilities	Group Total	T	

The **Equity** section heading is automatically put in by the program. Create the Equity accounts as shown next:

3000	Owner's Equity	Group Heading	H	
3020	Capital Beginning Sarah Kafa	Subgroup Account	A	Retained Earnings
3030	Capital Additional Investments	Subgroup Account	A	Equity
3040	Drawings Sarah Kafa	Subgroup Account	A	Equity
3050	Net Capital before Current Earnings	Subgroup Total	S	
3699	Total Owner's Equity	Group Total	T	

Notice that the full details of the Statement of Owner's Equity have been built into the equity section of the Balance Sheet (including the Current Earnings account #3600).

The **Revenue** section heading is automatically put in by the program. Create the following Revenue accounts:

4000	Sales Revenue	Group Heading	H	
4010	Sales Kitchen Cabinets	Subgroup Account	A	Revenue
4020	Sales Kitchen Sinks	Subgroup Account	A	Revenue
4030	Sales Kitchen Accessories	Subgroup Account	A	Revenue
4099	Sales Total	Subgroup Total	S	
4210	Sales Returns	Subgroup Account	A	Revenue
4220	Sales Discounts	Subgroup Account	A	Revenue
4229	Sales Deductions Total	Subgroup Total	S	
4399	Sales Net	Group Total	T	
4500	Other Revenue	Group Heading	H	
4510	Handling Fee	Group Account	G	Revenue
4520	Total Other Revenue	Group Total	T	

The **Expense** section heading is automatically put in by the program. Create the Cost of Goods Sold and Expense accounts next.

5000	Cost of Goods Sold	Group Heading	H	
5020	Cost of Goods Sold	Group Account	G	Cost of Goods Sold
5050	Purchase Discounts	Group Account	G	Cost of Goods Sold
5060	Inventory Adjustments	Group Account	G	Cost of Goods Sold
5099	Total Cost of Goods Sold	Group Total	T	

5300	Store Expenses	Group Heading	H	
5310	Rent Expense	Group Account	G	Expense
5320	Store Salaries Expense	Group Account	G	Expense
5330	Telephone Expense	Group Account	G	Expense
5340	Advertising Expense	Group Account	G	Expense
5350	Depreciation Expense-All	Group Account	G	Expense
5360	Delivery Costs to Customers	Group Account	G	Expense
5370	Bad Debts Expense	Group Account	G	Expense
5380	Utilities (Hydro/Water) Expense	Group Account	G	Expense
5399	Total Store Expenses	Group Total	T	
5500	Other Expenses	Group Heading	H	
5510	Bank Charges Expense	Group Account	G	Expense
5520	Credit Card Charges	Group Account	G	Expense
5530	Bank Interest on Loan	Group Account	G	Expense
5599	Total Other Expenses	Group Total	T	

ⓘ

You will not be able to view the Income Statement or Balance Sheet until all sections are set up.

If you place an account in a wrong section, refer to Appendix 2015 X, *Removing an Account from a Wrong Section,* in your course materials at www.nelson.com/student to correct the account.

www

You should be aware that there are many different ways to number and structure accounts. Some companies would subtotal accounts 5510 and 5520 to show bank costs before Interest on loans. (See side note box.)

24 ➤ When you have entered all the accounts, click on the **Validate** button. If everything is okay, you will see Fig. 4A-30. If your accounts are not in logical order, Exercise 4A-5 will provide some insight as to what needs to be done to resolve these issues.

Deleting an Account

To delete an account, complete the following steps:

Exercise 4A-5—Deleting an Account

This exercise is used to show you the steps involved in removing an account.

1 ➤ Click on account **5530 Bank Interest on Loan**, to highlight the account in blue.

2 ➤ Click 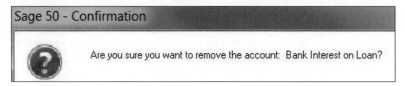 icon, and the following message box will request confirmation that you want to remove the account.

3 ➤ Click **No**. If you wanted to remove the account, you would click **Yes** and the account would be removed. The account has to have a zero balance and no recorded or posted transactions before it can be deleted.

Review and Check Account Coding Changes Made

There are three ways to verify that the account structure you added is correct.

a) Use the Validate button.

b) Display an Income Statement or Balance Sheet to indicate that the structure is correct.

c) From the Home page, click on the Chart of Accounts icon, and click the validity of accounts icon.

4 ➤ Click the **Validate** button. If there are no errors you will see the message box Fig. 4A-30. The Validate button may be greyed out if there were no changes since the last time you clicked the Validate button in Exercise 4A-4, step 24.

Sage 50 - Information

The accounts are in logical order.

Fig. 4A-30: Accounts in order.

5 ➤ Click **OK** to return to the Home window.

6 ➤ **Display** an Income Statement or Balance Sheet. If there are any errors in your account coding (accounts not in logical order) the message box shown

in Fig. 4A-31 will advise you where the account coding error has occurred. If there are a number of coding errors, you may see a similar message box a number of times.

Fig. 4A-31: Example of an Account Coding Error window.

It may be helpful to display or print the Chart of Accounts and check your structure near the account number given. You would then change the account coded in error and try again.

You may need to do this a number of times due to an incorrect **H A S G T** structure.

7 ➤ You may need to repeat steps 4, 5, and 6 a number of times until the **H A S G T** account structure is validated as "logical."

Modifying an Account

Sarah has decided that she wants to change the name of account 3600 Current Earnings, using a different way from the Setup guide.

Exercise 4A-6—Modifying an Account

1 ➤ From the Account Setup window, locate and double-click the **3600 Current Earnings** Account No. or Name column.

The General Ledger window similar to Fig. 4A-27a will appear.

2 ➤ Account Change the name to: **Net Income from Income Statement**, Tab .

As explained earlier, this account will transfer the balance of the Net Income from the Income Statement to the Owner's Equity section of the Balance Sheet.

The Account with no Type coding cannot be changed. If you clicked the Class Options tab, you will see the greyed-out Account Class as Current Earnings.

(See side note box.)

> **ℹ** Other types of accounts could be changed; however, the Current Earning **X** account cannot be changed.

3 ➤ GIFI Code Remove **3620**. Tab .A single-owner non-incorporated business does not use GIFI codes.

4 ➤ Click the ▶ or ◀ to save the changes. On the last account to be modified use the **Save and Close** button.

All the accounts have been added. Refer to Fig. 4A-32.

5 ➤ Exit to the Home window.

Sarah's Kitchen Stores—Student's Name
Chart of Accounts

ASSET

1000 Current Assets..................................H
  1005 Petty Cash ....A Cash
  1010 Bank Account Chequing ....A Bank
  1011 Bank Account Credit Card Receivable ......A Credit Card Receivable
  1080 Cash Total.......................................S
  1200 Accounts Receivable ....A Accounts Receivable
  1210 Allowance for Bad Debts ....A Allowance for Bad Debts
  1219 Net Accounts Receivable.................S
  1240 Inventory of Goods ....G Inventory
  1260 Store/Office Supplies/Prepaid ....G Current Asset
1299 Total Current Assets...........................T

1400 Capital Assets....................................H
  1410 Display Equipment...........................A Capital Asset
  1415 Accumulated Deprec. Display Eq.............A Accum. Amort & Depre
  1419 Display Equipment: Net Value..............S
  1420 Office Furniture/Equipment..................A Capital Asset
  1425 Accumulated Deprec. Office Fur/Eq.........A Accum. Amort & Depre
  1429 Office Furniture/Equipment Net Val.........S
1499 Net Capital Assets..............................T

LIABILITY

2000 Current Liabilities.............................H
  2010 Accounts Payable ....G Accounts Payable
  2030 Visa Credit Card Payable ....G Credit Card Payable
  2210 HST Charged on Sales....................A Sales Tax Payable
  2220 HST Paid on Purchases ....A Sales Tax Payable
  2230 Net HST Owing/Receivable..............S
2299 Total Current Liabilities ....T

2300 Long Term Liabilities ....H
  2310 Bank Loan Payable........................G Long Term Debt
2399 Total Long Term Liabilities ....T

EQUITY

3000 Owner's Equity ....H
  3020 Capital Beginning Sarah Kafa ....A Retained Earnings
  3030 Capital Additional Investments.............A Equity
  3040 Drawings Sarah Kafa......................A Equity
  3050 Net Capital before Current Earnings ....S
  3600 Net Income from Income Statement...........X Current Earnings
3699 Total Owner's Equity ....T

REVENUE

4000 Sales Revenue ....H
  4010 Sales Kitchen Cabinets ....A Revenue
  4020 Sales Kitchen Sinks.......................A Revenue
  4030 Sales Kitchen Accessories.................A Revenue
  4099 Sales Total.................................S
  4210 Sales Returns ....A Revenue
  4220 Sales Discounts ....A Revenue
  4229 Sales Deductions Total ....S
4399 Sales Net..T

4500 Other Revenue ....H
  4510 Handling Fee ....G Revenue
4520 Total Other Revenue ....T

EXPENSE

5000 Cost of Goods Sold ....H
  5020 Cost of Goods Sold ....G Cost of Goods Sold
  5050 Purchase Discounts ....G Cost of Goods Sold
  5060 Inventory Adjustments...................G Cost of Goods Sold
5099 Total Cost of Goods Sold ....T

5300 Store Expenses................................H
  5310 Rent Expense ....G Expense
  5320 Store Salaries Expense..................G Expense
  5330 Telephone Expense ....G Expense
  5340 Advertising Expense.....................G Expense
  5350 Depreciation Expense-All................G Expense
  5360 Delivery Costs to Customers.............G Expense
  5370 Bad Debts Expense......................G Expense
  5380 Utilities (Hydro/Water) Expense..........G Expense
5399 Total Store Expenses ....T

5500 Other Expenses ....H
  5510 Bank Charges Expense..................G Expense
  5520 Credit Card Charges ....G Expense
  5530 Bank Interest on Loan ....G Expense
5599 Total Other Expenses........................T

> H = Group Heading
> A = Subgroup Account
> S = Subgroup Total
> G = Group Account
> T = Group Total

Fig. 4A-32: Sarah's Kitchen Stores Chart of Accounts before linking accounts.

Exercise 4A-7—Changing Next Cheque Number & Settings

You were not able to change the Payment Cheque Information links in Exercise 4A-3, because the bank accounts were not set up at that time. The bank accounts are now set up and you can update the next cheque number.

1 ➤ Click **Setup, Reports & Forms,** in the left pane click **Cheques**, in the right pane click 1010 Bank Account Chequing. The window contains the default settings for Payment Cheque, Payroll Cheque, and Cheque Settings.

Payment Cheque Settings

2 ➤ In the right pane ensure the selection is .

3 ➤ At Form Type select the following to conform to the Canadian Payments Association guidelines for cheques. Information on the guidelines can be seen at Exercise 3A-13, step 8.

Payroll Cheque Settings

4 ➤ In the right pane ensure the selection is .

5 ➤ At Form Type there are two Easy-Align form types available to conform to the Canadian Payments Association guidelines for cheques.

a) 8½ × 11 in. (two stub) - Easy Align

b) 8½ × 11 in. (long single stub with YTD) - Easy Align

Select **b**, with 1 stub.

Cheque Settings

Cheque Settings	
Next Cheque No:	642

6 ➤ Type **642** for the next cheque number.

7 ➤ Click **OK** to return to the Home window.

8 ➤ Now that your structure is correct, *this is a good time to do a **backup***. Use a folder name for your backup similar to **Sarah's Kitchen Stores_with_accts**.

The next step is to link the accounts before entering the $ values to the accounts from the Trial Balance.

Step 5: Linking Modules/Accounts

The Sage 50 Accounting program allows you to copy information (Debits and Credits) from the RECEIVABLES and/or the PAYABLES modules to the General Ledger. This process, called **Linking**, permits the modules to talk to each other to ensure information is up to date across the modules.

Remember that earlier in the RECEIVABLES and PAYABLES modules you entered only one side of an entry; e.g., when you entered a SALES amount for a sales transaction on credit, Sage 50 Accounting automatically debited ACCOUNTS RECEIVABLE and credited HST ON SALES. This is because these accounts have been linked from the RECEIVABLES module (see linked windows in this exercise). The person setting up the linked accounts determines which account data needs to be copied to General Ledger linked accounts.

One thing to remember: you can change the account structure and links **before** setting the module to **Ready**.

If you have to change the account structure and the links after setting the module to READY, you need to be very careful as you adjust the links. If you had posted transactions to a Sales Discount account and then had to change the account number, you will also need to change the links.

You can change the links between General Ledger accounts at any time.

When a General Ledger account is linked, it is impossible to delete the account without deactivating the link of the accounts. A General Ledger account cannot be deleted if it contains posted transactions.

If you had used a template to create a company, Sage 50 Accounting would have created a set of linked accounts for you.

When using a template, there are two ways to set up or change the links:

1. Remove the links before changing the accounts.
2. Change the accounts while using the default links.

The author believes it is easier to use method 1. Remove the links, then change the default chart of accounts to the company's needs. Then you would return and link the appropriate accounts.

Changes or deletions to the linked accounts are made by using the **Setup** options from the menu bar. A link to a General Ledger account can be deactivated or changed. A deactivated linked account cannot be deleted if the Ledger account contains posted transactions.

You now need to set up your own linked accounts because you have not used a template. This will allow you to better understand the process of linking accounts.

Linking the Modules

The next step in the setup process is to make the modules "talk" to each other. Before transactions can be entered in the appropriate subledger modules, links to General Ledger accounts must be specified. This procedure can also be called **Integration**.

Exercise 4A-8—Linking the Modules

COMPANY Module Links

1 ➤ From the Home window Related Tasks area, click **Settings**, click on **General** (**Accounts**); in the right pane select **Linked Accounts**, and a window similar to the following is displayed.

Fig. 4A-33: COMPANY Linked Accounts window.

2 ➤ **Retained Earnings:**   In a single-owner business, the proper account name is Capital (account 3020). Sage 50 Accounting will not allow you to change the program heading **Retained Earnings**.

Account 3020 accumulates the profits of the firm from prior years. It is automatically updated by the program when a new accounting year is started.

When you start a new fiscal year (see side note box), the program closes the prior year's accounting records and transfers the balance in the Net Income from the Income Statement or Current Earnings (account 3600) to the identified Retained Earnings account.

Refer to Chapter 10 for the start of a new fiscal year and the changes to the Current Earnings **X** account and the Retained Earnings account.

3 ➤   Select **3020 Capital Beginning Sarah Kafa**, `Tab` .

You cannot change the program heading **Retained Earnings**.

Do NOT click Record opening balances in my Retained Earnings account, as it will update the account automatically. You want to record your own balance.

Current Earnings: The program transfers the year-to-date Net Income or Loss from the Income Statement, and adds the value to the Equity section of the Balance Sheet.

4 ➤   Move to the PAYABLES module as shown next.

PAYABLES Module Links

1 ➤   In the left pane click **Payables,** in the right pane select **Linked Accounts**, to display the Payables Linked Accounts window.

When you process invoices or payments, these accounts are used as needed.	
Principal Bank Account:	1010 Bank Account Chequing ▼
Accounts Payable:	2010 Accounts Payable ▼
Freight Expense:	▼
Early Payment Purchase Discount:	5050 Purchase Discounts ▼
Prepayments and Prepaid Orders:	2010 Accounts Payable ▼

Fig. 4A-34: Payables Linked Accounts window.

2 ➤   Select the accounts shown above.

Principal Bank Account   **1010 Bank Account Chequing**. This will allow the program to credit the bank account in the General Ledger when you record a cheque being issued in the PAYABLES module.

Accounts Payable   **2010 Accounts Payable**. This will allow the program to credit ACCOUNTS PAYABLE in the General Ledger when you purchase goods or services on credit. It will also debit ACCOUNTS PAYABLE when you return goods and issue cheques.

Freight Expense	Leave this field blank. This account is used for freight costs that cannot be included in purchases. Sarah's Kitchen Stores does not use this account.
Early Payment Purchase Discount	**5050 Purchase Discounts**. This is the account Sage 50 Accounting will credit when a purchase discount is taken on an invoice for merchandise purchased for resale.
Prepayments and Prepaid Orders	**2010 Accounts Payable**. This is the account Sage 50 Accounting will debit when a prepayment is made on a purchase order.

3 ➤ In the left pane, click **Receivables**. In the right pane, select **Linked Accounts** to display the Receivables Linked Accounts window.

RECEIVABLES Module Links

When you process invoices or receipts, these accounts are used as needed.

Principal Bank Account:	1010 Bank Account Chequing ▼
Accounts Receivable:	1200 Accounts Receivable ▼
Default Revenue:	4010 Sales Kitchen Cabinets ▼
Freight Revenue:	▼
Early Payment Sales Discount:	4220 Sales Discounts ▼
Deposits and Prepaid Orders:	1200 Accounts Receivable ▼

Fig. 4A-35: RECEIVABLES Linked Accounts window.

4 ➤ Select the accounts shown above.

Principal Bank Account	**1010 Bank Account Chequing**. Receipts from customers entered in the Receipts journal will be debited to this account in the General Ledger.
Accounts Receivable	**1200 Accounts Receivable**. This account will be automatically debited and credited when entering sales transactions for customers.
Default Revenue	**4010 Sales Kitchen Cabinets.** This account will be automatically set up when creating new customers.
Freight Revenue	Leave this field blank. This account is used for **freight** revenue that is not part of sales. Sarah's Kitchen Stores does not use this account.
Early Payment Sales Discount	**4220 Sales Discount,** for paying early (within discount terms), is taken off a sales invoice.
Deposits and Prepaid Orders	**1200 Accounts Receivable**. This is the account Sage 50 Accounting will automatically credit when a deposit is received on a Sales Order.

5 ➤ Click **OK** and you are returned to the Home window.

Step 6: Setting Up Tax Classes, Codes, Rates & Customization

In this section, you will enter the appropriate taxes (HST) with the corresponding linked accounts. You will also set up abbreviated tax codes for each tax class.

Exercise 4A-9—Setting Up Tax Classes, Codes, Rates & Customization

Taxes

1 ➤ Click **Setup**, **Settings**, in the left pane click ⊞ at **Company**, click ⊞ at **Sales Taxes**, click **Taxes** and enter the information shown in Fig. 4A-36.

To add a tax, enter the tax name on a new line in the Tax column.						
Tax	Tax ID Included on Forms	Exempt from this tax?	Is this Tax taxable?	Acct. to track tax paid on purchases	Acct. to track tax charged on sales	Report on taxes
HST	R4675 2567	No	No	2220 HST Paid on Purchase	2210 HST Charged on Sales	Yes

Fig. 4A-36: Sales Tax Information window.

Tax	**HST**.
Tax ID Included on Forms	**R4675 2567** (the Business registration number), [Tab].
Exempt from this tax?	**No**. The business must **collect** HST on Sales and **pay** HST on Purchases.
Is this Tax taxable?	**No**. In the province of Ontario, you do not pay tax on HST.
Acct. to track tax paid on purchases	Double-click in the field and scroll down and select **2220 HST Paid on Purchases.**
Acct. to track tax charged on sales	Double-click in the field and scroll down and select **2210 HST Charged on Sales**.
Report on taxes	Press the **spacebar**, or click on the field to change it to **Yes** for HST. (See side note box.)

Using the Report on Taxes feature (Yes) will take up a lot of memory space on the drive. Some firms would use the procedure shown in Exercise 3B-31 to determine the amount of HST to pay.

Report on taxes:
This field will accumulate the HST to be included in an HST Report. You will find information on *Printing/Filing a Tax (HST) Report* in Appendix 2015 D in your course materials at www.nelson.com/student

www

Tax Codes

2 ➤ In the left pane, click on **Tax Codes** and enter the information shown.

To add a tax code, enter in a code and description.		
To see tax code details, double-click on a tax code or description.		
Code	Description	Use In
	No Tax	All journals
HS	Harmonized Tax at 13%	All journals
HI	Harmonized Tax at 8% Insurance	All journals
		All journals

Code	An abbreviation for the tax code (2 digits).
Description	A description of the tax being collected.
Use In	Select All Journals.

3 ➤   Code   Double-click the **HS** field and the Tax Code Details window appears. **Type** the information as shown. The tax code HS is shown first, as it is the one that will be used in the majority of transactions. (See side note box.)

> When entering the tax rate (e.g., **13.0**, the **.0** does not show). If the rate does not have a decimal point, the .0 does not display even if you type it in.
>
> The **Is Refundable** column (for HST) is set to **Yes** because the HST **collected** is deducted from the HST **paid** and the difference can be recovered (receive a refund) from the Federal Government.

Tax Code: HS - Harmonized Tax at 13%

To add a tax to the Tax code, on a blank line, double-click in the Tax field and select the tax.

Tax	Status	Rate	Included In Price	Is Refundable
HST	Taxable	13	No	Yes

4 ➤   Click **OK** to accept the information, codes, and rates.

5 ➤   Repeat **steps 3** and **4** to enter the information for the HI code as follows:

Code **HI**   Set up HST (for insurance) as shown.

Tax	Status	Rate	Included In Price	Is Refundable
HST	Taxable	8	No	No

6 ➤   Click **OK** and return to the Home window.

Changing Settings for Item Number and Allocations

The Journal columns are not set the way we are used to. The Journal columns may not resemble what you have used in previous chapters. We are going to change some of the column fields (Allocation or Division).

1 ➤   Click the **Company** module, click the **General Journal** icon. Click on the ⌹ **Customize Journal** icon. In the left pane, click on **Columns**. In the right pane click on **Allocations**, to insert a ✓ to NOT display this item.

Purchase Invoices

2 ➤   In the left pane near the top, click **+** at **Purchase Invoices** and **Columns**. **Repeat step 1** to not display Division.

Purchase Orders

No changes are needed.

Pay Purchase Invoices

No changes are needed.

Make Other Payment

3 ➤   Click on the **Make Other Payment** and **Columns**. **Repeat step 1** to NOT display Allocations.

Sales Invoices

4 ➤   Click on the **Sales Invoices**, then **Columns**, click on **Division,** to insert a ✓ to NOT display this item. You will use the Division column in Chapter 11.

Sales Orders

5 ➤   In the left pane, click **+** at **Sales Orders** and **Columns**. **Repeat step 1** to NOT display Division.

Sales Quotes

No changes are needed.

Receipts

No changes are needed.

The Invoice window columns will now resemble the ones you used previously. Note, you may have to repeat Exercise 2A-5 to Customize columns to widths that you want.

6 ➤ Click **OK** to return to the General Journal window. Click ☒ to return to the Home window.

Step 7: Entering Opening G/L Account Balances (History)

Important: Back up your data before proceeding.

You have now set up the chart of accounts, but the ledger accounts do not have the current manual record dollar balances. We need to enter the August 31, 2022 Trial Balance so that the starting point in the computerized system is the ending point of the manual records.

As you have learned before, Sage 50 Accounting structures G/L accounts into five categories (or groups):

1. Assets
2. Liabilities
3. Equity
4. Revenue
5. Expense

Sage 50 Accounting also breaks up the previous categories into subgroups (class options) as seen in Exercise 4A-4, step 14. How does Sage 50 Accounting know whether an amount entered is a debit or a credit? The answer is based on the **normal balance** of the account.

If the account has a normal **debit balance** (e.g., asset—OFFICE SUPPLIES), then a **positive** amount entered is a **debit** and a negative amount, for a contra account, is entered for a **credit**.

Similarly, if the account has a normal **credit balance** (e.g., SALES) then a **positive** value entered is a **credit** and a **negative** amount, for a contra account, is entered for a **debit**.

VERY IMPORTANT:

To enter a **contra balance** (a decrease) to an Asset account (normal debit balance) you enter the amounts with a **negative**. For example, DRAWINGS is an Equity section contra account. **Equity** normally has a credit balance. When you enter the Drawings amount with a **negative** sign it will cause Sage 50 Accounting to **debit** it.

To enter a **Sales Return** or a **Purchase Return** (inventory**),** you would enter the amount with a **negative** sign. As SALES RETURNS is a contra (decrease) balance to SALES (with a normal credit balance), entering a negative amount will cause Sage 50 Accounting to **debit** it. Inventory returns is a negative to Cost of Goods Inventory account and a credit entry.

Here are the rules for entering debits or credits to accounts:

#	Category/ Group	Normal Balance	Normal Balance to Be Entered	Contra Balance to Be Entered
1	Asset	Debit	Positive	Negative (Credit)
2	Liability	Credit	Positive	Negative (Debit)
3	Equity	Credit	Positive	Negative (Debit)
4	Revenue	Credit	Positive	Negative (Debit)
5	Cost of Goods and/or Expenses	Debit	Positive	Negative (Credit)

Sarah's Kitchen Stores, Student's Name
Trial Balance As At Aug 31, 2022

		Debits	Credits
1005	Petty Cash	100.00	-
1010	Bank Account Chequing	17,106.00	-
1011	Bank Account Credit Card Receivable	0.00	-
1200	Accounts Receivable	12,848.10	-
1210	Allowance for Bad Debts	-	550.00
1240	Inventory of Goods	102,500.00	-
1260	Store/Office Supplies/Prepaid	400.00	-
1410	Display Equipment	30,700.00	-
1415	Accumulated Deprec. Display Eq	-	11,000.00
1420	Office Furniture/Equipment	8,125.00	-
1425	Accumulated Deprec. Office Fur/Eq	-	3,450.00
2010	Accounts Payable	-	12,134.25
2030	Visa Credit Card Payable	-	0.00
2210	HST Charged on Sales	-	3,517.50
2220	HST Paid on Purchases	1,410.00	-
2310	Bank Loan Payable	-	51,256.00
3020	Capital Beginning Sarah Kafa	-	83,496.35
3030	Capital Additional Investments	-	0.00
3040	Drawings Sarah Kafa	16,900.00	-
4010	Sales Kitchen Cabinets	-	338,165.00
4020	Sales Kitchen Sinks	-	22,560.00
4030	Sales Kitchen Accessories	-	53,289.00
4210	Sales Returns	6,200.00	-
4220	Sales Discounts	5,731.00	-
4510	Handling Fee		0.00
5020	Cost of Goods Sold	285,386.00	-
5050	Purchase Discounts	-	7,212.00
5060	Inventory Adjustments	0.00	-
5310	Rent Expense	16,800.00	-
5320	Store Salaries Expense	46,980.00	-
5330	Telephone Expense	3,216.00	-
5340	Advertising Expense	7,468.00	-
5350	Depreciation Expense-All	0.00	-
5360	Delivery Costs to Customers	9,645.00	-
5370	Bad Debts Expense	0.00	-
5380	Utilities (Hydro/Water) Expense	1,796.00	-
5510	Bank Charges Expense	743.00	-
5520	Credit Card Charges	9,842.00	-
5530	Bank Interest on Loan	2,734.00	-
		586,630.10	586,630.10

Fig. 4A-37a: Sarah's Kitchen Stores Trial Balance.

Sarah's Kitchen Stores, Student's Name
BALANCE SHEET As at Aug 31, 2022

ASSET		Column 1 Subgroup	Column 2 Group Subtotal Total
Current Assets	H		
Petty Cash	A	100.00	
Bank Account Chequing	A	17,106.00	
Bank Account Credit Card Receivable	A	0.00	
Cash Total	S		17,206.00
Accounts Receivable	A	12,848.10	
Allowance for Bad Debts	A	-550.00	
Net Accounts Receivable	S		12,298.10
Inventory of Goods	G		102,500.00
Store/Office Supplies/Prepaid	G		400.00
Total Current Assets	T		132,404.10
Capital Assets	H		
Display Equipment	A	30,700.00	
Accumulated Deprec. Display/Eq.	A	-11,000.00	
Display Equipment: Net Value	S		19,700.00
Office Furniture/Equipment	A	8,125.00	
Accumulated Deprec Office Fur/Eq	A	-3,450.00	
Office Furniture/Equipment: Net Val	S		4,675.00
Net Capital Assets	T		24,375.00
TOTAL ASSETS			156,779.10
LIABILITY			
Current Liabilities	H		
Accounts Payable	G		12,134.25
Visa Credit Card Payable	G		0.00
HST Charged on Sales	A	3,517.50	
HST Paid on Purchases	A	-1,410.00	
Net HST Owing/Receivable	S		2,107.50
Total Current Liabilities	T		14,241.75
Long Term Liabilities	H		
Bank Loan Payable	G		51,256.00
Total Long Term Liabilities	T		51,256.00
TOTAL LIABILITIES			65,497.75
EQUITY			
Owner's Equity	H		
Capital Beginning Sarah Kafa	A	83,496.35	
Capital Additional Investments	A	0.00	
Drawings Sarah Kafa	A	-16,900.00	
Net Capital before Current Earnings	S		66,596.35
Net Income from Income Statement	X		24,685.00
Total Owner's Equity	T		91,281.35
TOTAL EQUITY			91,281.35
LIABILITIES AND EQUITY			156,779.10

Sarah's Kitchen Stores, Student's Name
INCOME STATEMENT Jan 01, 2022 to Aug 31, 2022

REVENUE		Column 1 Subgroup	Column 2 Group Subtotal Total
Sales Revenue	H		
Sales Kitchen Cabinets	A	338,165.00	
Sales Kitchen Sinks	A	22,560.00	
Sales Kitchen Accessories	A	53,289.00	
Sales Total	S		414,014.00
Sales Returns	A	-6,200.00	
Sales Discounts	A	-5,731.00	
Sales Deductions Total	S		-11,931.00
Sales Net	T		402,083.00
Other Revenue	H		
Handling Fee	G		0.00
Total Other Revenue	T		0.00
TOTAL REVENUE			402,083.00
EXPENSE			
Cost of Goods Sold	H		
Cost of Goods Sold	G		285,386.00
Purchase Discounts	G		-7,212.00
Inventory Adjustments	G		0.00
Total Cost of Goods Sold	T		278,174.00
Store Expenses	H		
Rent Expense	G		16,800.00
Store Salaries Expense	G		46,980.00
Telephone Expense	G		3,216.00
Advertising Expense	G		7,468.00
Depreciation Expense-All	G		0.00
Delivery Costs to Customers	G		9,645.00
Bad Debts Expense	G		0.00
Utilities (Hydro/Water) Expense	G		1,796.00
Total Store Expenses	T		85,905.00
Other Expenses	H		
Bank Charges Expense	G		743.00
Credit Card Charges	G		9,842.00
Bank Interest on Loan	G		2,734.00
Total Other Expenses	T		13,319.00
TOTAL EXPENSE			377,398.00
NET INCOME			24,685.00

Fig. 4A-37b: Balance Sheet and Income Statement after changes (with codes).

Note: The Trial Balance information will be recorded in Exercise 4A-10.

Account names with boxes around them, | ASSET | | TOTAL REVENUE | and others, are automatically put in by the computer program. You cannot delete or change them.

Exercise 4A-10—Entering Opening G/L Balances (History)

One **VERY IMPORTANT thing to remember:** You may change the balances you have entered for G/L accounts up until you set the modules to **Ready** (ready to record transactions). Once the modules are **Ready**, balances can be changed only by making journal entries. Setting modules to **Ready** is covered in Exercise 4A-14.

1 ➤ From the menu bar, click **Setup, Setup Guide, Accounts**.

Group Heading (H) type of accounts (non-postable accounts) do not have amounts associated with them.

Subgroup Accounts (A) and **Group Accounts (G)** accounts have amounts posted to them.

Subgroup Total (S) and **Group Totals (T)** and the **Current Earnings (X)** account balances are non-postable accounts, but have amounts that are calculated by Sage 50 Accounting based on the balances you enter for the corresponding postable accounts.

---

2 ➤ Click on the **Opening Balance** field for **1005 Petty Cash** (from Fig. 4A-37a).

3 ➤ **Opening Balance** Type **100** `Tab`. Sage 50 Accounting puts in .00 to input 100.00.

(See side note box.)

> You can also press the down arrow key ▼ to move to the next amount field.

If you make a mistake in entering the dollar amount or you forgot to press the negative (minus) key for an opposite balance, you can return to the field and correct the amount. The new amounts will replace the incorrect values you entered before.

4 ➤ Move down the **Opening Balance column**, where the 0.00 fields are, and **continue entering balances** from the Trial Balance (Fig. 4A-37a), subject to the Contra Account Balance notes in the next section. If the account does *not* have a 0.00 displayed, it is a non-postable account like an H (Group Heading), S (Subgroup Total), or T (Group Total).

5 ➤ See steps 6 and 7 for entering a contra account balance.

Contra Account Balance

As you have learned earlier, **Contra** means **opposite**. For example, a **contra asset account** (e.g., ACCUMULATED DEPRECIATION of an asset account such as a truck or computers) is placed in the Asset section, but since it **decreases** the value of the asset, it is entered with a **negative** sign, causing Sage 50 Accounting to **credit** this account, instead of the normal debit entry for Assets.

Other examples of Contra accounts are:

Section	*Contra Account Name*
Asset	Allowance for Bad Debts
	Accumulated Depreciation Display Eq
	Accumulated Depreciation Office Fur/Eq
Liability	HST Paid on Purchases

Equity	Owner's Withdrawals (**Drawings** in a sole proprietorship)
	Dividends Declared (used in a corporation)
Revenue	Sales Returns & Allowances
	Sales Discounts
Cost of Goods Sold	Purchase Returns & Allowances
	Purchase Discounts
	Ending Inventory

6 ➤ Click on the **0.00** field, for the **Allowance for Bad Debts** account.

7 ➤ **Opening Balance**   Type **-550 (negative)**, ⌨Tab . The -550.00 shows up in the Accounts window in the Debit column with a negative -550.00. If you display a Trial Balance, you will see the amount in the Credit column.

Continue entering the **other accounts**.

Only **postable** accounts [Subgroup (**A**) and Group (**G**)] have balances.

Subgroup totals and Group Totals are calculated automatically. The **X** account balance is calculated automatically based on the total of revenues less expenses (net income).

If you do not enter all the account balances during one session and you need to quit, or if you have an error in the amounts you entered, you will receive a warning message window with two choices:

Choice 1: Will allow you to return and check your information, or

Choice 2: Will save the opening balances and record the difference in the Retained Earnings account.

8 ➤ If you select the 1st choice, you can check the amounts entered. *Note*: Verify that you have recorded the Contra accounts with negative amounts. Go to step 9 for the treatment of the difference caused by amounts not yet inputted.

9 ➤ If you select the 2nd choice, the window will allocate the amount difference to the 3020 Capital Beginning Sara Kafa (Retained Earning account) The "Cannot undo" means you can't undo the balance at this time. You can amend amounts later before turning the system to Ready.

10 ➤ Click **Close**. **Print** a Trial Balance and check that the amounts agree with the amounts in Fig. 4A-37a.

11 ➤ Return to the Setup Guide and correct the Opening Balance amounts.

You can take your time to locate the error(s). When the account with the error is found (e.g., Sales discount entered as a positive amount but should have been a negative amount), return to the Setup Guide and update the accounts that have the errors.

12 ➤ When all corrected account balances have been entered, click **Close** and you are returned to the Setup Guide window, without the error message from step 7. Click **Close** to return to the Home window.

Displaying the Trial Balance

13 ➤ Display the **Trial Balance**. Check that the amounts agree with the Trial Balance in Fig. 4A-37a and make corrections if necessary.

14 ➤ It would be a good idea to print the Trial Balance, Income Statement, and Balance Sheet. Compare them to Fig. 4A-37a and Fig. 4A-37b. This would be done in an office setting to prove that the starting computer General Ledger accounts agree with the manual General Ledger.

15 ➤ Back up your data before moving on. Identify the backup with a name similar to Sarah's Kitchen Stores_B4_Ready. You are returned to the Home window when the backup is complete. Make a note in your logbook similar to **Starting balances**, **not ready**. If you make a major mistake and want to start back at this point, it will be easy with a backup data file.

Step 8: Adding Credit Card Information

To process credit card transactions, you must set up the information for the specific credit card company that your firm accepts.

Exercise 4A-11—Adding Credit Card Information

The following procedure is used to add credit card information:

1 ➤ At the bottom, Related Tasks, click **Settings,** click ⊞ at **Company,** click **Credit Cards**.

Credit Cards Used

2 ➤ In the right pane, click **Used**. The blank Settings window for **Credit Cards Used** appears.

Enter the credit cards you use to make purchases.			
Under Payable Acct, enter the account that tracks the amount you owe the credit card company.			
Under Expense Acct, enter the account you want to charge any fees, such as interest charges and annual fees, against.			
Credit Card Name	Payable Acct	Expense Acct	
Visa	2030 Visa Credit Card Payable	5520 Credit Card Charges	

Fig. 4A-38: Credit Cards used window.

Sarah's Kitchen Stores uses a business credit card from the Visa Credit Card Company for their purchases.

3 ➤ Type the information as shown in Fig. 4A-38.

Credit Card Name	**Visa**. Sarah will use this card to make purchases for the business. She may apply for other business credit cards later.
Payable Acct	**2030 Visa Credit Card Payable** is the account where the amounts owing to the credit card company will be charged.
Expense Acct	**5520 Credit Card Charges** is the account where the amounts that the credit card company charges the business for annual fees, etc., will be recorded. This is the same account to which the discount fee on customer credit card sales is charged. Sarah's Kitchen Stores has decided to use one account for all credit card fees and charges.

Credit Cards Accepted

4 ➤ In the left pane, click the **Credit Cards Accepted** item.

Enter the credit cards you accept from customers.

Under Asset Acct, enter the account that tracks the amount the credit card company owes you.

Under Discount Fee, enter the % fee the credit card company charges on transactions.

Under Expense Acct, enter the account you want to charge the discount fee against.

Credit Card Name	Currency	Asset Acct	Discount Fee %	Expense Acct
Visa	CAD	1011 Bank Account Cre	3.50	5520 Credit Card Charge

Fig. 4A-39: Credit cards accepted window.

5 ➤ Type the information as shown in Fig. 4A-39.

Credit Card Name	**Visa** (maximum 13 characters). Sarah has decided to accept only the Visa Credit Card for use by her customers. Other credit cards may be added later.
Currency	A business may have two or three credit cards with different currencies; for example, Canadian (CAD) and United States (USD).
Asset Acct	**1011 Bank Account Credit Card Receivable** is the asset account where the receivable (cash) amount from the credit card company will be charged.
Discount Fee %	When you entered the Visa name above, a 0.00 appeared in this column. The rate would be the discount fee the credit card company charges the business for using the credit card. The Visa credit company charges a fee of **3.5%** on the sales value including taxes; e.g., Sale 100.00, plus $13.00 HST = $113.00. The discount fee would be $3.96 (3.5% of $113.00).
Expense Acct	**5520 Credit Card Charges** is the account where the discount fee will be charged as an expense.

Sage Payment Solutions

6 ➤ Click on **Processing Service**. This feature can be used to accept credit card payments. This feature is not shown in the text, as it requires a fee for service.

7 ➤ Click **OK** to Exit.

VERY IMPORTANT: Back up your data before proceeding.

Step 9a: Setting Up Subledgers—Vendors

Another part of the conversion process is to enter **vendors** and **vendor history** into the Vendors subledgers. The subledgers in Sage 50 Accounting have the same purpose as those in a manual accounting system.

Detailed vendor balances in the Vendors subledger are compared in total to the balance of the ACCOUNTS PAYABLE account in the G/L.

Before setting up Vendors & Customers it is strongly recommended that you review Appendix 2015 Y, *Cancel a History Invoice* in your course materials at www.nelson.com/student, as this is a common mistake in Setting up invoices.

The following are the vendor details for Sarah's Kitchen Stores at Aug 31, 2022.

Exercise 4A-12—Setting Up Vendor Subledgers

Entering the Vendor Accounts

Create an account for each vendor as follows:

1 ➤ From the Home window, click **Setup**, **Setup Guide**, **Vendors**. You are in the Vendor Setup window.

2 ➤ Create the first vendor, with the following information:

Vendor	Office Stationery Plus
Contact	Owen Cliff
Telephone	905-675-6628
Street 1	987 Emerson Street
City	Hamilton
Province	Ontario
Postal Code	L8S 4W3

3 ➤ Before entering Balance Owing amounts, you will enter other Vendor information. Double-click the **Vendor**, **Office Stationery Plus**. This is using the same procedure as discussed in Chapter 3A, Exercise 3A-9 after step 6 information section, *To Enter a New Vendor Account*.

4 ➤ Click the **Options** tab. Enter the information shown next. Remember to click the ☑ **Calculate Discounts before Tax** button when amounts are in the 2.00% discount, 10 day fields.

5 ➤ Click the **Taxes** tab. Tax **HST**, Tax Exempt **No**, choose tax code **HS**.

Direct Deposit

Sarah's Kitchen Stores will not use this feature as a user fee.

6 ➤ Click the **Historical Transactions** tab.

7 ➤ Click the **Invoices** button. The Historical Invoices window is displayed.

Historical Invoices

Vendor:	Office Stationery Plus
Invoice No.:	5628
Date:	Aug 25, 2016
Terms:	2.00 % 10 Days, Net 30 Days
Pre-tax Amount:	278.27
Tax:	36.18
Invoice Total:	314.45

Fig. 4A-40: Historical Invoices window.

8 ➤ Type the information from Fig. 4A-40 into the fields in your window.

Pre-tax Amount This field and the Tax field will not display if the vendor does not have Calculate Discounts before Tax field ✓. (See Exercise 4A-12, step 4.) Only an amount field will display.

Amount:

If there is no discount available, the program does not need a breakdown in the amount.

Tax You would type the amount of the tax, HST, where applicable. Note: the cost of the office goods purchased was 278.27. The 36.18 tax cost is HST.

9 ➤ When your window resembles Fig. 4A-40, click the **Record** button.

There are no other invoices to be entered for Office Stationery Plus.

> To *Cancel a History Invoice*, refer to Appendix 2015 Y in your course materials at www.nelson.com/student.
>
> **www**

10 ➤ **Close** Click on the **Close** button when finished.

At the bottom of the window the vendor Balance Owing 314.45 now shows 314.45 for Office Stationery Plus. (See side note box.)

11 ➤ Click X to Exit.

12 ➤ Enter the other vendors' information and outstanding balances (referred to as **History**).

Vendor	Custom Cabinets Ltd.	Kitchen Gadgets Inc.	Your Name Landlord
Contact	Toby Aharonhi	Sarah Ditlove	Carol Smith
Street 1	3890 Barton Street	200 Lakeshore Blvd	16 Main Street West
City	Hamilton	Hamilton	Hamilton
Province	Ontario	Ontario	Ontario
Postal Code	L8E 8Q2	L2X 4C3	L8S 4J1
Telephone	905-819-4751	905-623-3926	905-569-2863
Expense	Leave blank*	Leave Blank*	5310
Terms	(See Fig 4A-42)	(See Fig 4A-42)	Net 3 days
Discounts	✓	✓	No
HST	Exempt No	Exempt No	Exempt No
Tax code	HS	HS	HS

Fig. 4A-41: Vendor Names and Addresses.

* The account number for Inventory items comes from the Inventory item.

Accounts Payable Outstanding Balances - August 31, 2022

Vendor	Inv. #	Date	Terms	Pre-Tax Amount	HS Tax Amount	Invoice Total
Custom Cabinets Ltd.	3620	Aug 16, 2022	2/10, net 30	7,810.00	1,015.30	8,825.30
Kitchen Gadgets Inc.	600	Aug 20, 2022	2/10, net 30	2,650.00	344.50	2,994.50
Office Stationery Plus	5628	Aug 25, 2022	2/10, net 30	278.27	36.18	314.45

* entered in Exercise 4A-12   <u>$ 12,134.25</u>

Fig. 4A-42: Vendor Names and History.

History for vendors can be entered in detail by entering individual invoices and payments, or entered as one balance carried forward. The detail method provides an accurate aging of the payable balance.

Expense Account. See information at Fig. 4A-41.

 Remember to record the terms and ✓ the Calculate Discounts before Tax box for vendors that allow discounts to be taken on the purchase price of the goods before HST.

 When you add the invoice details for an invoice that has no discount for paying early, the Pre-tax Amount box does not show. Record the full amount of the invoice owing.

www Do NOT change any information for other fields. You may find information on what goes in the **Additional Info** tab in Appendix 2015 Q, *Names Fields,* in your course materials at www.nelson.com/student.

13 ➤ When all vendors have been entered, you should see the following at the bottom of the Vendor Setup Guide. The amounts agree.

> Accounts Payable Balance: $12,134.25   equals   ⓘ   Total Balance Owing: $12,134.25

14 ➤ Close the Setup Guide and return to the Home window.

 Depending on the configuration of your computer, the Home window Vendors Opening Balance amounts may not be updated. You may have to backdate the Session date and return it to the correct date to update the vendor amounts.

15 ➤ It would be a good idea to print the Vendor Aged Detail report and compare vendor totals. Using the **Report Centre**, **Payables**, display the **Vendor Aged Detail, Modify this report**, all vendors should be **selected**, click **Include Terms, OK** to display the aged vendor balances. ($12,134.25 to G/L ACCOUNTS PAYABLE account 2010.) The amounts must be the same ($12,134.25**)**. This is done to prove that the starting PAYABLES module agrees with the COMPANY module (General Ledger).

Vendor Aged Detail As at Aug 31, 2022

Source	Date	Terms	Transaction Type	Total	Current
Custom Cabinets Ltd.					
3620	Aug 16, 2022	2%/10, Net 30	Invoice	8,825.30	8,825.30
Total outstanding:				8,825.30	8,825.30
Kitchen Gadgets Inc.					
600	Aug 20, 2022	2%/10, Net 30	Invoice	2,994.50	2,994.50
Total outstanding:				2,994.50	2,994.50
Office Stationery Plus					
5628	Aug 25, 2022	2%/10, Net 30	Invoice	314.45	314.45
Total outstanding:				314.45	314.45
Total unpaid invoices:				12,134.25	12,134.25
Total prepayments/prepaid order:				-	-
Total outstanding:				12,134.25	12,134.25

Fig. 4A-43: Vendor Aged Detail Aug 31, 2022.

16 ➤ **Exit** the Vendor Aged Detail window.

17 ➤ **Exit** the Report Centre window.

The history for the PAYABLES module is now complete.

18 ➤ **Back up** (save) your work before proceeding.

When the Vendor Ledger Does Not Agree with the General Ledger

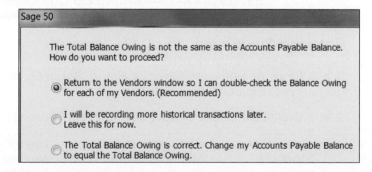

What would you do if the Vendor Aged Detail total does not agree with the General Ledger ACCOUNTS PAYABLE account 2010? Sage 50 Accounting will not allow you to change from History to **Ready**. You would then take steps to find the error(s).

Errors could be caused by:

a) one or more missing vendor information records.
b) one or more incorrect outstanding balances in the payable detail.
c) an error in the manual General Ledger (posting error).

Most companies would like to get the Sage 50 Accounting system working as soon as possible. In the event that an error occurred, the business may enter an **UNKNOWN VENDOR** account for the difference between the Vendor Aged Detail total and the ACCOUNTS PAYABLE account.

www

If you see the window below step 18, select the 2ⁿᵈ choice. **I will be recording more historical transactions later**. This will allow you to print the Aged Detail report and compare it to the manual records. You would then return to the Vendors area and add the missing amount(s) or correct an amount. See Appendix 2015 Y, *Cancel a History Invoice,* in your course materials at www.nelson.com/student.

Difference	General Ledger Balance	Accounts Payable Detail	Difference To GL	Difference	Unknown Vendor Adjustment required
Short	$12,134.25	$11,924.25	$-210.00	Short	Positive Invoice
Over	$12,134.25	$12,449.25	$ 315.00	Over	Negative Invoice

The UNKNOWN VENDOR would be entered with an invoice number as:

a) **Unknown**, or
b) ? ? ? or
c) 9999999 or something similar to indicate an unknown invoice number.

You can get the Sage 50 Accounting program working with the subledgers balanced; meanwhile, you will have time to find and correct the error. The error may be found when a vendor calls for payment, a missing vendor card is located, a posting error is corrected, etc.

Step 9b: Setting Up Subledger—Customers

Follow the same procedure that you used in Exercise 4A-12 to create the Customer Ledger and enter Customer balances to add the dollar value to each customer's history.

Exercise 4A-13—Setting Up Customer Subledgers

Entering Customers

1 ➤ From the Home window, click **Setup**, **Setup Guide**, **Customers.** You are in the Customer Setup window.

2 ➤ Create the following customers, with the following information.

Customer	Chaiken's Home Depot	Lee's Department Store
Contact	Marion Chaiken	Michael Lee
Street 1	268 Grandview Street	2075 Heron Road
City	Kitchener	Ottawa
Province	Ontario	Ontario
Postal Code	N2B 2B9	K1N 2A4
Telephone	519-745-1481	613-748-6358

3 ➤ Before entering Balance Owing amounts, you will enter another customer's information. Double-click **Chaiken's Home Depot**. Refer to Exercise 2A-23 for steps and fields to be completed when setting up a customer subledger.

	Chaiken's Home Depot	*Lee's Department Store*
Options tab		
Revenue Account	4010	4010
Terms	2/10, net 30	2/10, net 30
Taxes tab		
HST	Tax Exempt, No	Tax Exempt, No
Tax code	HS	HS
Statistics tab		
Credit Limit	15,000.00	15,000.00

Customer	*Inv. #*	*Date*	*Terms*	*Pre-tax Amount*	*HST Tax Amount*	*Invoice Total*
Chaiken's Home Depot	598	Aug 23, 2022	2/10, n30	4,760.00	618.80	5,378.80
Lee's Department Store	613	Aug 28, 2022	2/10, n30	6,510.00	846.30	7,356.30

						$12,735.10

Fig. 4A-44: Customer Outstanding Invoices.

Entering Customer Balances (History)

4 ➤ Click the **Historical Transactions** tab.

5 ➤ Click the **Invoices** button. The Historical Invoices window is displayed. Enter the invoice information in Fig. 4A-44 for each customer. When complete, click **Record** and **Close** for each customer.

6 ➤ When you have entered both customers' historical transactions, **exit** the RECEIVABLES Ledger.

At the bottom of the Customer Setup window you will see:

Accounts Receivable Balance: $12,848.10   does not equal ⑦ Total Balance Owing: $12,735.10

You will notice that the total of the Customer Aged Detail report (Total Balance Owing) is $12,735.10 and **does not balance with** the $12,848.10 balance of the G/L ACCOUNTS RECEIVABLE Balance account 1200.

7 ➤ Click **Close** to exit to the Home window.

8 ➤ Click the 2nd choice as you will return to record another customer, and exit to the Home window.

9 ➤ From the top menu, click **Reports, Receivables, Customer Aged, Detail.**
Both customers should be selected, **Include Terms, OK** to display the aged
customer balances.

Customer Aged Detail As at Aug 31, 2022					
Source	Date	Terms	Transaction Type	Total	Current
Chaiken's Home Depot					
598	Aug 23, 2022	2%/10, Net 30	Invoice	5,378.80	5,378.80
Total outstanding:				5,378.80	5,378.80
Lee's Department Store					
613	Aug 28, 2022	2%/10, Net 30	Invoice	7,356.30	7,356.30
Total outstanding:				7,356.30	7,356.30
Total unpaid invoices:				12,735.10	12,735.10
Total deposits/prepaid order:				-	-
Total outstanding:				12,735.10	12,735.10

Fig. 4A-45: Customer Aged Detail—not balanced.

Difference	General Ledger Balance	Accounts Receivable	Difference Detail	Difference To GL	Unknown Customer Adjustment Required
Short	$12,848.10	$12,735.10	$-113.00	Short	Positive Invoice

As discussed in the vendor section, you may create an UNKNOWN CUSTOMER
account to record the missing balance. This will allow the module to be turned to
Ready and will give you time to locate the missing invoice.

A search of invoices issued has located all invoices except 615. Invoices 613, 614 and
616 were issued on Aug. 28, 2022; therefore, invoice 615 would have been issued on
the same day. The Sales Journal on Aug. 28, 2022 has an entry for $100.00, plus 13%
HST, for Kitchen Accessories for a total invoice of $113.00. However, the customer's
name was not recorded, and the staff cannot remember to whom the sale was made.

The above invoice (615) was recorded correctly in the General Ledger.

You will enter the sales invoice information you have and try to locate the missing invoice.

You may not be able to locate information about the missing invoice(s) before
turning the module to **Ready**. A suggested solution is to add an **Unknown
Customer**, similar to step 8, with an unknown invoice number or other code,
for the missing amount.

10 ➤ Add a customer ledger for **Unknown Customer,** with **no address
information**, Ship to Address is the **same as mailing address**; leave
Revenue Account field blank as you do not know what Revenue account this
customer normally uses. Terms **2/10, net 30** given to all customers. Click the
Taxes tab, HST **No**, Tax Code **HS**. Click the **Statistic** tab, Credit Limit
$113.00.

11 ➤ Add historical invoice number #**615** with the following: Date **August 28, 2022**,
Pre-tax Amount **$100.00**, Tax **13.00**, Invoice total **113.00**. If the invoice
number is not known, use a code similar to **Unknown, ? ? ?,** or **999999**, etc.,
as discussed in Exercise 4A-12 after step 18.

12 ➤ After entering the Unknown Customer, **exit** the Receivable Ledger. At the bottom of the Customer Setup window you will see:

Accounts Receivable Balance: $12,848.10	equals ⓘ	Total Balance Owing: $12,848.10

The subledger now agrees to the General ledger balance. Click **Close** and **Exit** to the Home window.

13 ➤ Display the **Customer Aged Detail** report as shown:

Customer Aged Detail As at Aug 31, 2022

Source	Date	Terms	Transaction Type	Total	Current
Chaiken's Home Depot					
598	Aug 23, 2022	2%/10, Net 30	Invoice	5,378.80	5,378.80
Total outstanding:				5,378.80	5,378.80
Lee's Department Store					
613	Aug 28, 2022	2%/10, Net 30	Invoice	7,356.30	7,356.30
Total outstanding:				7,356.30	7,356.30
Unknown Customer					
615	Aug 28, 2022	2%/10, Net 30	Invoice	113.00	113.00
Total outstanding:				113.00	113.00
Total unpaid invoices:				12,848.10	12,848.10
Total deposits/prepaid order:				-	-
Total outstanding:				12,848.10	12,848.10

Fig. 4A-46: Customer Aged Detail—after correction.

Compare the Customer Aged Detail $12,848.10 to the General Ledger again to prove that the starting CUSTOMERS module agrees with the General Ledger.

14 ➤ **Exit** to the Home window.

The history for the CUSTOMERS module is now complete.

Step 10: Setting Modules to Ready

The final step in the setup process is to set the modules to **Ready** (change from History). The journals can be used for transaction entries from September 1, 2022 onwards. The modules that are being used for Sarah's Kitchen Stores are COMPANY, PAYABLES, and RECEIVABLES.

Here's a last-minute checklist:

1. All sections in the Chart of Accounts must begin with an **H** and end with a **T**.

2. All **A** type accounts must be followed by an **S**.

3. All Accounts must be in logical order.

4. All Linked accounts needed should have been set up. You may change or modify the linked accounts at any time in the future, as the need arises.

5. Before the system can be made **Ready**, all subledger module balances must agree with the associated Linked account balances in the General Ledger. They now agree.

6. It is best to print a Trial Balance, Income Statement, Balance Sheet, Schedules of Accounts Payable and Accounts Receivable, and verify that the balances agree.

Mistakes made in entering History **cannot** be changed once the module is set to **Ready**. Corrections can be made by journal entry.

Back up your data and use the backup to correct History errors. Once the errors are corrected, another backup must be made before setting to Ready.

Remember, **BACK UP** before proceeding. Make *TWO* backup copies of your data. *THIS IS VERY IMPORTANT.* In Chapter 5, Sarah's Kitchen Stores is used to enter transactions. An extra backup, *before setting the modules to Ready*, could be vital. It should be kept in case you have to start Chapter 4A again, or fix errors when entering transactions.

If the above conditions are met, you can turn the modules to **Ready**.

Setting the System to READY

The following procedure will turn the COMPANY, RECEIVABLES, and PAYABLES modules to **Ready**, and the quill pens (History icons), will disappear from the window.

Exercise 4A-14—Setting the System to READY

1 ➤ On the menu bar, click on **History**, and then **Finish Entering History**.

If the PAYABLES or RECEIVABLES do not balance with the General Ledger, you will receive an error message similar to the following:

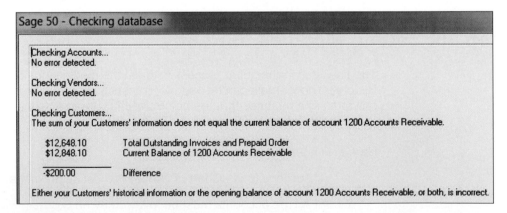

The Sage 50 Accounting database verifies that all modules displayed are error-free. If errors exist, the program identifies the area where the error occurred (see above).

You will need to go back to the module that is not balanced and correct the error.

If you have not set up the Chart of Accounts in a logical order, an error message similar to the following is displayed, preventing you from changing to Ready and continuing. The error must be fixed before you can turn the modules to Ready.

> Your accounts are not in logical order. The reason is: there is a missing Subgroup Total before account '2299 Total Current Liabilities'.
>
> Until this issue is resolved, you cannot open some of your reports.

When the subledger balances agree with the G/L, you will see the following window and warning message to back up your data files:

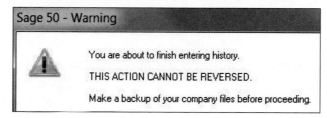

Sage 50 - Warning

You are about to finish entering history.

THIS ACTION CANNOT BE REVERSED.

Make a backup of your company files before proceeding.

2 ➤   Click **Proceed**.

The screen will flicker and the quill pens will disappear. The RECEIVABLES, PAYABLES, BANKING, and COMPANY modules, with all historical data, are now in READY mode.

CONGRATULATIONS! The Journals in RECEIVABLES (Sales Quotes, Sales Orders, Sales Invoices and Receipts), PAYABLES (Purchase Orders, Purchase Invoices, and Payments), COMPANY (Chart of Accounts and General Journal) and BANKING (Reconcile Accounts) are ready to use without Perpetual Inventory. To complete Chapter 5 Recording business transactions, with Perpetual Inventory, you need to review the instructions in Appendix 2015 H, *INVENTORY & SERVICES Module Setup Perpetual Inventory for Sarah's Kitchen Stores (4B),* in your course materials at www.nelson.com/student. If you wish to use other modules, you must complete the conversion process before making the module **Ready**. The Setup for other modules is covered later in this book.

WWW

3 ➤   **Exit** Sage 50 Accounting.

Chapter 5 continues to use the Sarah's Kitchen Stores data file, and will provide a review of journalizing transactions in the COMPANY, PAYABLES, and RECEIVABLES modules using simulated source documents.

In future exercises refer to **Slideshow 4—Setting Up a New Company** when creating a new G/L account for a new vendor or a new customer.

Before Moving On ...

Read the following questions and make sure you know the answers to them; otherwise, read the corresponding part in the chapter before moving on.

1. Explain the differences between the following dates: **Fiscal Start**, **Fiscal End**, **Earliest Transaction**, **Session**, **Latest Transaction**, and **Historical Transactions**.

2. Before assigning account numbers, why is it important to know what accounts go with each account group number; e.g., 1000, 2000, 3000, 4000, or 5000?

3. What is the difference between **postable** and **non-postable** accounts? How do you designate a postable account?

4. Assume that mistakes have been made in entering the history balances and the system has been changed to **Ready**. What are two ways to correct this problem?

5. What does setting a module to **Ready** mean?

6. What is a **Linked** account?

7. Briefly explain each category of the account types **H A S G T** and **X**.

8. What is the purpose of the **X** account in the chart of accounts?

9. Would you enter the history balance of HST Paid on Purchases account as a positive or a negative number? Explain why.

10. Briefly explain what is meant by Class Options in Accounts.

Challenge Exercise 04 C4-1, Balloons Store
Conversion to Sage 50 Accounting (G/L, A/R & A/P)

1 ➤ Use the **Wizard** to create a new company from scratch.

The trial balance provided shows only postable accounts. It is expected that you will use the techniques shown in Sarah's Kitchen Stores (Chapter 4A) to:

a) Add Headings (**H**), Postable accounts (**A** and **G**) with Subtotal (**S**) accounts and Total (**T**) accounts. You should have a minimum of 3 **S**-type accounts.
b) Create **Linked accounts** for the COMPANY, PAYABLES, and RECEIVABLES modules.
c) Select **Class Options** required.
d) Add **Vendor** and **Customer** invoice information.

Balloons Store is assumed to be a sole proprietorship business. It sells various kinds of party balloons.

This review assignment does not use all accounts that may be used by a typical business—it uses only the RECEIVABLES (Customers), PAYABLES (Vendors), and COMPANY modules. Balloons Store does not use the budget feature, credit cards, or shippers. When all data has been entered, turn the related modules to **Ready**.

A) The business using a calendar fiscal year has the following important dates:
Opened for business   **Sep 12, 1997**
Year-end this year   **Dec 31, 2022**
Year-end last year   **Dec 31, 2021**
Manual books stopped   **Apr 30, 2022**   This will be the conversion date the manual accounting records will be transferred to Sage 50 Accounting.

B) The business is: Balloons Store, Your Name, 936 Alfred St., Sarnia, Ontario N7V 3K7.

> *Remember, your name must appear on all reports.*

C) Business Type is Retail and Business number is Z345.

D) Forms use the next number on:
Invoices (342)
Cheques (384)
All other forms start at **1**, except for:
    Receipts (# blank)
    Customer Deposits (# blank)
    Direct Deposit Stubs (# blank)

E) Discounts are calculated **before tax** for both customer and vendor invoices, with Customer early payment terms **2/10 net 30**.

F) The computer financial statements should be set up with the following sections:

Current Assets	Owner's Equity
Capital Assets	Revenue
Current Liabilities	Cost of Goods Sold
Long Term Liabilities	Store Expenses

The **normal** account balances from the Apr 30, 2022 Balloons Store Trial Balance are listed below. Use appropriate **account classes** in setting up your accounts.

Account Names	Balance	Class	Other
Bank Account	$ 3,187	Bank	Cheque #384
Accounts Receivable	6,780	Accounts Receivable	
Inventory of Goods	61,360		
Supplies Store & Office	800		
Store Furniture	34,400		
Accumulated Depreciation	6,100		
Accounts Payable	9,718	Accounts Payable	
HST on Sales	2,463		
HST on Purchases	900		
Bank Loan Payable	24,600	Long Term Debt	8 year loan
Capital Your actual name	26,504		
Capital Additional Investments	0		
Drawings Your actual name	6,500		
Sales Revenue	186,000		
Sales Returns	3,046		
Sales Discounts	312		
Cost of Goods Sold	122,640		
Purchase Discounts	2,086		
Rent Expense	16,221		
Advertising Expense	1,325		
Depreciation Expense	0		

G) Tax Classes, Codes and Rates:

   HST rate is 13%, HST registration # R1234, and HST is refundable.

   HS   code is HST at 13%
   HI   code is HST at 8%

H) Customize the Journals as shown in Exercise 4A-9.

I) Set up Customers and Vendors:

   Accounts Receivable Customers
   Belair Hospital (balloons for rooms & patients)
   Contact: Jordan Royes
   85 Colborne Road
   Sarnia, Ontario, N7V 5B3
   Phone: (519) 826-7520, Fax –None
   Terms: 2/10, net 30. Credit Limit $10,000.
   Revenue Account: Sales Revenue
   Price List: Regular
   Invoice #340 April 26, 2022 $6,000;
   HST $780. Total invoice $6,780
   Tax Code HS

   Accounts Payable Vendors
   "Your Last Name Here" Balloon Supply
   Contact: Kylie Lunn
   289 Talford Street
   Sarnia, Ontario, N7T 6L4
   Phone: (519) 726-6722, Fax –None
   Terms: 2/10, net 30.
   Invoice #349 April 25, 2022, $8,500
   HST $1,105. Total invoice: $9,605.
   Expense Account: Leave Blank
   Tax Code HS

J) Set the related modules, accounts, vendors and customers to **Ready** mode.

2 ➤ Print the following reports.

As of Apr 30, 2022

    a) Income Statement Jan 1-Apr 30
    b) Balance Sheet
    c) Customer Aged Detail report
    d) Vendor Aged Detail report
    e) Trial Balance at Apr 30

3 ➤ Record and **post** the next transaction.

May 2   Your Name completed a $2,000 bank transfer investment from their personal account to the business bank account.

4 ➤ Print the following reports.

As of May 2, 2022

    a) Income Statement Jan 1-May 2
    b) Balance Sheet
    c) Customer Aged Detail, all customers, with terms at May 2
    d) Vendor Aged Detail, all vendors, with terms at May 2
    e) All Journal Entries
    f) Chart of Accounts

Challenge Exercise 04 C4-2, Kojokaro
(Setup of a company file, using G/L, A/R & A/P)

1 ➤ Refer to Exercise 1-1b, to unzip the **04 C4-2 Kojokaro.exe** file.

2 ➤ Open the **04 C4-2 Kojokaro** file with a date of Feb. 01.

This exercise is a review of the setup of a company file.

The account structure—Chart of Accounts, with many errors, was created by an employee of Kojokaro. Account classes have not been shown in the information below. As a consultant hired to help with the setup of the company, you will:

1 ➤ Identify the errors.

2 ➤ Add, modify, and delete accounts, necessary to fix the account structure.

3 ➤ Print the Balance Sheet.

4 ➤ Print the Income Statement.

5 ➤ Print the Chart of Accounts.

Chart of Accounts

ASSET

1000 Current Assets	**H**
1001 Cash in Bank	A
1030 Total Cash	S
1050 Accounts Receivable	A
1059 Accounts Receivable Net	S
1100 Store Supplies	A
1299 Total Current Liabilities	S

1400 Capital Assets	**H**
1410 Equipment	A

LIABILITY

2000 Current Liabilities	**H**
2005 Accum Depreciation	G
2100 Accounts Payable	G
2200 Drawings by Owner	G
2500 Long Term Liabilities	**H**
2530 Bank Loan - Mortgage	G

EQUITY

3010 Owner's Equity	A
3020 Inventory	A
3030 Capital	A
3600 Current Earnings	X

REVENUE

4010 Sales	**H**
4020 Sales -All	A
4040 Sales Discounts	A
4050 Sales Returns	G
4060 Inventory Adjustments	G
4100 HST on Sales	G
4110 Capital Additional Investments	G

EXPENSE

5000 Cost of Goods Sold	**H**
5020 Cost of Goods Sold	A
5030 Purchase Discounts	A
5050 HST on Purchases/Service	A
5300 Rent Expense	G
5310 Depreciation Expense	G
5325 Telephone Expense	A
5390 Other Expenses	S

Challenge Exercise 04 C4-3, Skates Stores
Conversion to Sage 50 Accounting, using G/L, A/R & A/P

1 ➤ Use the **Wizard** to create a new company from scratch.

The trial balance provided shows only postable accounts in alphabetical order. It is expected that you will use the techniques shown in Sarah's Kitchen Stores (Chapter 4A) to:

a) Add Headings (**H**), Postable accounts (**A** and **G**) with Subtotal (**S**) accounts and Total (**T**) accounts. You should have a minimum of 3 **S**-type of accounts.
b) Use a **Difference at Startup** account.
c) Create **Linked accounts** for the COMPANY, PAYABLES, and RECEIVABLES modules.
d) Select **Class Options** required.
e) Add **Vendor** and **Customer** invoice information.

Skates Stores is assumed to be a sole proprietorship business. It sells figure skates and hockey skates.

This review assignment does not use all accounts that may be used by a business, and uses only the COMPANY, PAYABLES (Vendors), and RECEIVABLES (Customers) modules. Skates Stores does not use the budget feature, credit cards, or shippers. When all data has been entered, turn the related modules to **Ready**.

A) The business using a calendar fiscal year has the following important dates:

Opened for business	**Feb 15, 1996**	
Year-end this year	**Dec 31, 2022**	
Year-end last year	**Dec 31, 2021**	
Manual books stopped	**May 31, 2022**	This will be the conversion date when the manual accounting records will be transferred to Sage 50 Accounting.

B) The business Is: Skates Stores, Your Name, 514 Canon Avenue, Your Town, Ontario, L0N 1B0.

> *Remember, your name must appear on all reports.*

C) Business Type is Retail and Business Registration # R1176.

D) Forms: use the next number on:

Invoices (#983)
Cheques (#468)
All other forms start at **1**, except:
    Receipts (# blank)
    Customer Deposits (# blank).

E) Discounts are calculated **before tax** for both customer and vendor invoices, with Customer early payment terms **2/10 net 30**.

F) The computer financial statements should be set up with the following sections:

Current Assets	Owner's Equity
Capital Assets	Revenue
Current Liabilities	Cost of Goods Sold
Long Term Liabilities	Store Expenses

The normal account balances from the May 31, 2022, Skates Stores. Trial Balance in alphabetical order are:

Account Name	Balance	Class	Other
Accounts Payable	$ 1,356.00	Accounts Payable	
Accounts Receivable	1,243.00	Accounts Receivable	
Accumulated Depreciation	4,100.00		
Depreciation Expense All	0.00		
Capital Additional Investments	0.00		
Capital Your last name	9,240.00		
Cash in Bank	424.00	Bank	Cheque #468
Cost of Goods Sold	13,185.00		
Drawings Your last name	1,000.00		
HST on Sales	252.00		
HST Paid on Purchases	136.00		
Inventory on hand	6,100.00		
Notes Payable (Long Term)	21,400.00		
Purchase Discounts	125.00		
Rent Expense	3,200.00		
Sales Discounts	300.00		
Sales Returns	350.00		
Sales Revenue	14,165.00		
Store Equipment	23,700.00		
Store Supplies	200.00		
Telephone Expense	800.00		

G) Tax Classes, Codes and Rates:

   HST rate is 13%, HST registration # R1234, and HST is refundable.
   HS code is 13%.
   HI code is 8%.

H) Customize the Journals as shown in Exercise 4A-9.

I) Set up Customers and Vendors:

Accounts Receivable customers:

Elvis Skates Corp., Contact Elvis Schafer
2 Huron Street
Woodstock, Ontario, N4S 1A5
Phone 519-546-8588 - Fax: none
Terms 2/10, net 30
Invoice #980, date May 24, 2022
Invoice amount $1,243.00 (including $143.00 HST)
Revenue Account: Sales Revenue
Tax: HS

Credit Limit: $5,000.00

Accounts Payable vendors:

Skates Supply Ltd., Contact Greg Johnson
43 McKay Avenue
Windsor, Ontario, N9B 1A4
Phone: 519-675-8940
Terms 2% 10, net 30
Fax: 416-675-8930
Invoice # 6512, date May 10, 2022
Invoice amount $791.00 (including $91.00 HST)
Expense Account: Leave Blank
Tax: HS

Manufacture Supply Inc., Contact Jessie Grant
645 Bancroft Drive
Sudbury, Ontario, P3B 8T4
Phone: 705-672-4860 - Fax: 705-672-4860
Terms 2% 10, net 30
Invoice # 1431, date May 28, 2022
Invoice amount $565.00 (including $65.00 HST)
Expense Account: Leave Blank
Tax: HS

2 ➤ Turn the system to **Ready**.

3 ➤ **Record** and Post the next transaction.

Jun 1 Issued cheque #468 to purchased new shelving (Store Equipment) $800.00, plus HST, on invoice #5609 from one-time vendor Jason Notela.

4 ➤ After the transaction has been posted, **print** the following reports:
   a) Income Statement, year-to-date
   b) Balance Sheet
   c) Vendor Aged Detail, all vendors, with terms at Jun 1
   d) Customer Detail, all customers, with terms at Jun 1
   e) All Journal Entries for Jan 1 to Jun 1
   f) Chart of Accounts

Back up your file regularly.

Challenge Exercise 04 C4-4, R. Park Uniforms
(Conversion to Sage 50 Accounting Accounting, using the G/L)

1 ➤ Refer to Exercise 1-1b to unzip the **04 C4-4 Uniforms.exe** file.

2 ➤ Open the Sage 50 Accounting file **04 C4-4 Uniforms**. This file contains only the account 3600 Current Earnings account. See Fig. 4A-11 as a reference.

Mr. Roland Park has asked for your assistance in setting up the General Ledger in Sage 50 Accounting. The manual paper records are not in the proper order, but he knows that the Trial Balance, which he cannot find now, was balanced.

The bookkeeper will not be back for a week. The individual Accounts Receivable customer and Payable vendor pages are in her car. She will need your help with the PAYABLES and RECEIVABLES modules when she returns.

3 ➤ Set up the General Ledger accounts with balances using appropriate H A S G T account classes.

Other information:

The business opened	Jun 01, 2001
Year-end this year	Dec 31, 2022
Year-end last year	Dec 31, 2021
Manual books stopped	Oct 31, 2022

Business Name is R. Park Uniforms, any address (file created with Ontario)
Business type is Retail and Business number is R56-B37
HST rate is 13%, registration #R1234 and HST is refundable
HS   code is 13%
HI   code is 8%
Next Cheque # and all Forms start at 1
Discounts are all 2/10, net 30

R. Park Uniforms: List of accounts (not in order) at October 31, 2022

HST Charged on Sales	7,124
Bank	27,868
Inventory Asset	39,900
Cost of Goods Sold	92,510
HST Paid on Purchases/Services	1,846
Salaries Expense	78,600
Prepaid Insurance	750
Accounts Payable	7,910
Advertising Expense	9,000
Capital R. Park	11,000
Mortgage Payable (Due March 2020)	31,020
Rent Expense	19,500
Sales Revenue	226,960
Accounts Receivable	9,040
Drawings R. Park	0
Sales Discounts	5,000
Purchase Discounts	0
Capital Additional Investments	0

4 ➤ Print the following:
   a) Trial Balance as at October 31
   b) Income Statement, year-to-date
   c) Balance Sheet as at October 31
   d) Chart of Accounts

Chapter 4B

INVENTORY & SERVICES Module
Setup Perpetual Inventory for Sarah's Kitchen Stores (4B)

www

> You can complete Appendix 2015 H, *INVENTORY & SERVICES Module Setup Perpetual Inventory for Sarah's Kitchen Stores (4B)* in your course materials at www.nelson.com/student, after you finish Chapter 4A and before you complete Chapter 5. (Your instructor may provide this Appendix to you.) This will allow you to complete Sarah's Kitchen Stores with Perpetual Inventory.

Relevant Appendices

www The following appendices are available in your course materials at www.nelson.com/student.

Appendix 2015 D	**Printing/Filing a Tax (HST) Report**
Appendix 2015 E	**Budgets—General Ledger**
Appendix 2015 H	**INVENTORY & SERVICES Module Setup Perpetual Inventory for Sarah's Kitchen Stores (4B)**
Appendix 2015 I	**Checklists for Task Completion**
Appendix 2015 L	**Setting Up a New Company File Using a Sage 50 Premium Accounting Template**
Appendix 2015 M	**Post-Dated Cheques**
Appendix 2015 N	**Adding a Salesperson's Name to an Invoice**
Appendix 2015 Q	**Names Fields**
Appendix 2015 S	**Time & Billing Journal**
Appendix 2015 U	**Adding Notes/Footers to Statements**
Appendix 2015 X	**Removing an Account from a Wrong Section**
Appendix 2015 Y	**Cancel a History Invoice**
Appendix 2015 AB	**Printing in Batches**
Appendix 2015 AF	**Calculating Interest on Overdue Receivable Balances**
Appendix 2 (in textbook)	**Sage 50 Premium Accounting 2015.0 Student Version Installation Instructions**

Chapter 5

Review of COMPANY, PAYABLES and RECEIVABLES Modules

Sarah's Kitchen Stores

Learning Objectives

After completing this chapter you will be able to:

☐ Use the data file created in Chapter 4A.
☐ Record transactions from source documents, in the COMPANY, ACCOUNTS RECEIVABLE, and ACCOUNTS PAYABLE modules.
☐ Display and print various reports and journals.

This chapter contains transactions that will allow you to review the concepts and procedures you have learned so far. You will be presented with source documents, and will need to determine what type of transaction each of them represents, and which module to use to process them. After processing the transactions, you will be required to print financial statements and reports.

The setup of the COMPANY, PAYABLES, and RECEIVABLES modules for Sarah's Kitchen Stores was covered in Chapter 4A.

Students have the following options to complete Chapter 5.

Option A

Use the 05 Kitchen2 data file to complete the entries. (This option, and data file, is available at the discretion of your instructor.)

Option B

Starting with your solution for Chapter 4A, complete Appendix 2015 H, *INVENTORY & SERVICES Module Setup Perpetual Inventory for Sarah's Kitchen Stores (4B)* in your course materials at www.nelson.com/student, and then complete the entries.

WWW

Sarah's Kitchen Stores Profile

Before starting work in this chapter, display the Sarah's Kitchen Stores Balance Sheet and Income Statement and be sure that they are the same as those shown in Fig. 4A-37b in Chapter 4A. If you have any differences, check with your instructor.

1 ➤ The following source document transactions should be recorded using appropriate modules with dates in September 2022. If you are not sure which module to use, look back to Chapters 1, 2A, 2B, 3A, and 3B, or ask your instructor for assistance. Begin recording the transactions assuming you work only 1 day a week, starting on September 2, 2022. Advance your Session Date appropriately.

Note: **SD** refers to Source Document.

Some important points to note are as follows:

- Make sure that you enter appropriate descriptions, and invoice credit or debit note numbers with proper codes where required.
- You may have to create new vendors, customers, and G/L accounts.
- Discounts for paying early are calculated on pre-tax amounts.
- There is no HST on discounts.
- Discount on Office Supplies should be charged to the Office Supplies account.
- Late payment amounts on Utilities should be charged to the Utilities account.
- Remember that the HST remittance is calculated from the difference between the HST CHARGED ON SALES account and the balance of HST PAID ON PURCHASES account in previous months.

2 ➤ When you have finished, **print** the following reports:

- Trial Balance as of	Sep 30
- Income Statement for	Sep 01 to 30
- Vendor Detail, all vendors, with terms at	Sep 30
- Customer Detail, all customers, with terms at	Sep 30
- All Journal Entries	Sep 01 to 30
- General Ledger from	Sep 01 to 30
- Cash Projections (Detail) as of	Sep 30
- Inventory Summary, Latest Transactions at	Sep 30

Compare your reports to those given in the Solutions Manual provided to your instructor. If you have any differences, try to find out which transaction(s) caused the difference. To correct any errors, you must enter adjusting (or correcting) entries. You cannot change the existing entries once they have been posted. Refer to Chapters 1, 2A, 2B, 3A, and 3B, or 13 for correcting errors.

Inventory Details

Description	Item Code	Minimum	Cost	Selling Price	In Stock	Total Cost
Cabinets M612	M612	5	2,385.00	4,770.00	22	52.470.00
Cabinets ML45	ML45	5	1,837.50	3,675.00	18	33,075.00
Cutting Gadgets	CG01	10	4.98	9.95	200	995.00
Food Pro Blades	FB02	5	6.00	12.00	95	570.00
Kitchen Gadgets	KG11	20	4.48	8.95	200	895.00
Knives	K01	5	18.38	36.75	80	1,470.00
Sink Model D256	D256	10	150.00	300.00	50	7,500.00
Special Drawers	SD01	5	162.50	325.00	34	5,525.00
					Total	102,500.00

Transactions

Transactions are recorded using the original date of the document to ensure that our records match the records of our suppliers and customers for discount periods, etc. (e.g., a 2%/10, net 30 day purchase invoice dated September 23, received on September 24, and approved on September 25, would be recorded as a purchase using the September 23 date, as this is the date the discount starts.)

SD-1

Sarah's Kitchen Stores   339 Hudson Court, Hamilton ON L9C 6B3

Quote

To: Chaiken's Home Depot
268 Grandview Street
Kitchener ON N2B 2B9

Ship To:
(Same)

Quote NO.	DATE
1	Sep 01, 2022

Item	Qty.	Order	Back Order	Description	Base Price	Disc. %	Price	Tax	Amount
ML45		1		Cabinets ML45	$3,675.00		$3,675.00	HS	3,675.00
D256		1		Sink Model D256	300.00		300.00	HS	300.00
SD01		1		Special Drawers	325.00		325.00	HS	325.00

	Subtotal	4,300.00
HST #R4675 2567	HST 13%	559.00

TOTAL DUE
$ 4,859.00

Shipping Date: Sep 07, 2022
Terms: 2%/10, Net 30 days

SD-2

RECEIVED   Sep 02 2022

FOR DEPOSIT ONLY

Chaiken's Home Depot
268 Grandview Street
Kitchener, ON N2B 2B9

CHEQUE NO.   **791**

DATE   0 1 0 9 2 0 2 2
D D M M Y Y Y Y

PAY   Five Thousand Two Hundred Eighty Three and 60/100 $**5,283.60
To The
Order Of   Sarah's Kitchen Stores

Bank of Nova Scotia
936 Grandview Street
Kitchener, ON N2B 2D3

Chaiken's Home Depot
Marion Chaiken

⑈79⑈⑈   ⑈02890⑈006⑈   116⑈93351⑈2

DETACH BEFORE CASHING

Chaiken's Home Depot		CHEQUE NO. **791**
Date	**Description**	**Amount**
Sep 01, 2022	#598	$ 5,283.60

SD-3

Sarah's Kitchen Stores	CHEQUE NO. **642**
339 Hudson Court, Hamilton ON L9C 6B3	**DATE** 0 1 0 9 2 0 2 2
	D D M M Y Y Y Y

PAY   Two Thousand Three Hundred Seventy Three and 00/100 $\$**2,373.00$

To   Your Name Landlord
The   16 Main Street West
Order   Hamilton ON L8S 4J1

Toronto Dominion Bank   **Sarah's Kitchen Stores**
2 Palace Rd.
Hamilton, Ontario L3X 1T3   *S. Kafa*

⑈642⑈ ⑈26 14⑈007⑈ 192⑈991 2⑈

Please Detach Before Cashing

Sarah's Kitchen Stores	CHEQUE NO. **642**
Your Name Landlord	Sep. 01, 2022
	$2,373.00

Note: Change the name of Your Name Landlord to be Your Actual Name Landlord.
Note: Rent $2,100, plus 13% HST payment for month based on lease.

SD-4

Sarah's Kitchen Stores	**Order**
339 Hudson Court, Hamilton ON L9C 6B3	

To: Chaiken's Home Depot   Ship To:
      268 Grandview Street   (Same)
      Kitchener ON N2B 2B9

Quote NO.	DATE
1	Sep 02, 2022

Item	Qty.	Order	Back Order	Description	Base Price	Disc. %	Price	Tax	Amount
ML45		1		Cabinets ML45	$3,675.00		$3,675.00	HS	3,675.00
D256		1		Sink Model D256	300.00		300.00	HS	300.00
SD01		1		Special Drawers	325.00		325.00	HS	325.00
							Subtotal		4,300.00
				HST #R4675 2567			HST 13%		559.00
							TOTAL DUE		
									$ 4,859.00

Shipping Date: Sep 07, 2022
Terms: 2%/10, Net 30 days

SD-5

Sarah's
Kitchen Stores
339 Hudson Court, Hamilton ON L9C 6B3

CHEQUE NO.   **643**

DATE   0 2 0 9 2 0 2 2
       D D M M Y Y Y Y

PAY   Three Hundred eight and 88/100 $**308.88

To   Office Stationery Plus
The   987 Emerson Street
Order   Hamilton ON L8S 4W3

Toronto Dominion Bank
2 Palace Rd.
Hamilton, Ontario L3X 1T3

Sarah's Kitchen Stores

S. Kafa

⑆643⑈ ⑆261400 7⑆ 192 991 2⑈

- -

Please Detach Before Cashing

Sarah's Kitchen Stores
Office Stationery Plus

Discount
Inv. 5628   5.57

Cheque No.   **643**
Sep. 02, 2022
$308.88

SD-6

Jack Daly
614 Manley Street
Hamilton, ON L9K 3A5

CHEQUE NO.   **501**

DATE   0 6 0 9 2 0 2 2
       D D M M Y Y Y Y

PAY One Hundred Eleven and 00/100 $**111.00

To The   Sarah's Kitchen Stores
Order   339 Hudson Court
Of   Hamilton, ON L9C 6B3

Central Bank
601 Main St.
Hamilton, ON L9Z 1M2

J. Daly

⑆050 1⑈ ⑆11330501⑈ 91   8901⑈

RECEIVED   Sep 06, 2022   **FOR DEPOSIT ONLY**

Note: This is the cheque from the missing customer. Change the name and customer information to Mr. Daly and increase credit limit to $200.00.

SD-7

FOR DEPOSIT ONLY
RECEIVED   Sep. 07, 2022

LEE'S Department Stores	CHEQUE NO. **4680**
2075 Heron Road	
Ottawa, ON K1N 2A4	D A T E 0 6 0 9 2 0 2 2
	D D M M Y Y Y Y

To the
Order Of _____Sarah's Kitchen Stores_____ $**7,226.10

PAY _Seven Thousand two hundred twenty six_ -----------------------------------10/100 DOLLARS

Bank of Montreal   LEE'S Department Stores
618 Main St.
Erinvale, ON N0Z 1Z0   *M. Lee*
                                                         _____

⑆4680⑈   ⑈0003⑈012⑈   180232⑈5

DETACH BEFORE CASHING

Date	*Description*	*Amount*	*Discount*	CHEQUE NO. **4680**
Sep 06, 2022	Payment re: 613	$7,226.10	130.20	LEE'S Department Stores

SD-8

Sarah's
Kitchen Stores   339 Hudson Court, Hamilton ON L9C 6B3

INVOICE

To: Chaiken's Home Depot   Ship To:
268 Grandview Street   (Same)
Kitchener ON N2B 2B9

Invoice No.	DATE
922	Sep 07, 2022

Item	Qty.	Order	Back Order	Description	Base Price	Disc. %	Price	Tax	Amount
ML45	1			Cabinets ML45	$3,675.00		$3,675.00	HS	3,675.00
D256	1			Sink Model D256	300.00		300.00	HS	300.00
SD01	1			Special Drawers	325.00		325.00	HS	325.00
							Subtotal		4,300.00
			HST #R4675 2567				HST 13%		559.00

Reference: Sales Order 1
Shipped: Sep 07, 2022
Terms: 2%/10, Net 30 days

TOTAL DUE
$ 4,859.00

SD-9

Sarah's Kitchen Stores
339 Hudson Court, Hamilton ON L9C 6B3

Order

To: Connoisseur Gadgets Ltd.
896 Shaw Park Road
Belfountain ON L0N 1B3

Ship To:
Sarah's Kitchen Stores
339 Hutson Court
Hamilton ON L9C 6B3

Quote NO.	DATE
1	Sep 07, 2022

Item	Qty.	Order	Back Order	Description	Base Price	Disc. %	Price	Tax	Amount
K01		10		Knives	$18.40		$18.40	HS	184.00
CG01		8		Cutting Gadgets	5.00		5.00	HS	40.00
FB02		9		Food Pro Blades	6.00		6.00	HS	54.00

HST #R4675 2567

Subtotal	278.00
HST 13%	36.14

TOTAL DUE
$ 314.14

Shipping Date: Sep 08, 2022
Terms: 2%/10, Net 30 days

SD-10

- CREDIT MEMO -

Sarah's Kitchen Stores
339 Hudson Court, Hamilton ON L9C 6B3

To: Chaiken's Home Depot
268 Grandview Street
Kitchener ON N2B 2B9

Ship To:
(Same)

Invoice No.	DATE
922Rt	Sep 08, 2022

Item	Qty.	Order	Back Order	Description	Base Price	Disc. %	Price	Tax	Amount
D256	-1			Sink Model D256	$300.00		$300.00	HS	-300.00

HST #R4675 2567

Subtotal	-300.00
HST 13%	-39.00

TOTAL CREDIT
$ -339.00

SD-11

<table>
<tr><td rowspan="4"> Connoisseur Gadgets Ltd.
896 Shaw Park Road,
Belfountain ON L0N 1B3

HST# 118 112 113</td><td><h2>Invoice # 15838</h2>

TO:
Sarah's Kitchen Stores
339 Hudson Court
Hamilton ON L9C 6B3</td></tr>
</table>

DATE	CUSTOMER #	TERMS	P.O. #
Sep 08, 2022	4040	2/10 n30	1

ITEM	QTY	UNIT	BACK ORDERED	DESCRIPTION	UNIT PRICE	TOTAL
K01	10	each		Knives	18.40	184.00
CG01	7	each	1	Cutting Gadgets	5.00	35.00
FB02	8	each	1	Food Pro Blades	6.00	48.00
					Subtotal	267.00
					HST	34.71
					TOTAL	$ 301.71

SD-12

Sarah's Kitchen Stores
339 Hudson Court, Hamilton ON L9C 6B3

CHEQUE NO. **644**

DATE 0 8 0 9 2 0 2 2
      D D M M Y Y Y Y

PAY   One Hundred Thirteen and 00/100 $**113.00

To
The   Auto-Rite Mechanics
Order   6589 Rexford Drive
        Hamilton ON L8W 7P3

Toronto Dominion Bank
2 Palace Rd.
Hamilton, Ontario L3X 1T3

Sarah's Kitchen Stores

S. Kafa

⑈644⑈ ⑈2614⑈007⑈ 192⑈991 2⑈

Please Detach Before Cashing

Sarah's Kitchen Stores
  Auto-Rite Mechanics
  Re: Invoice 3396 ($100.00 +HST $13.00
     maintenance husband's personal car)

Cheque No. **644**
Sep. 08, 2022
$113.00

SD-13

Connoisseur Gadgets Ltd.

▸ **CREDIT MEMO** ◂

896 Shaw Park Road,
Belfountain, ON L0N 1B3

HST# 118 112 113

TO:
Sarah's Kitchen Stores
339 Hudson Court
Hamilton ON L9C 6B3

▸ **DEBIT MEMO** ◂

DATE	CUSTOMER #	TERMS	INVOICE #
Sept. 10, 2022	*4040*	*2/8, n 28*	*15838Rt*

ITEM	QTY	UNIT	BACK ORDERED	DESCRIPTION	UNIT PRICE	TOTAL
FB02	*-3*	*each*		*Food Pro Blades returned*	*6.00*	*-18.00*
				- Original Invoice 15838		
					Subtotal	*-18.00*
					HST	*-2.34*
					TOTAL	*$- 20.34*

SD-14

INVOICE

Sarah's Kitchen Stores 339 Hudson Court, Hamilton ON L9C 6B3

To: Kurpreet Gilbert
Visa Credit Card

Ship To:
Pickup

Invoice No.	DATE
923	Sep 11, 2022

Item	Qty.	Order	Back Order	Description	Base Price	Disc. %	Price	Tax	Amount
KG11	8			Kitchen Gadgets	$8.95		$8.95	HS	71.60
							Subtotal		71.60
				HST #R4675 2567			HST 13%		9.31
							TOTAL DUE		
									$ 80.91

Shipped: Sep 11, 2022

SD-15

Metro Hydro

55223 Electric Drive, Hamilton ON L6Y 3B3

Sarah's Kitchen Stores 339 Hudson Court Hamilton ON L9C 6B3	Phone Date:	(905) 448-6320 Sept 13, 2022

Service to Sept. 8	$212.39	
HST. R142887665	27.61	
Current charges including tax.	**$240.00**	DUE BY SEPT. 20
If paid after DUE DATE	**$250.00**	

APPROVAL Date <u>Sep 14, 2022</u> Acct. <u># Utilities</u> Approved *SW*	RECEIVED Sep. 14, 2022

**Note: Record $240.00 amount. It is anticipated that we can pay this invoice by the due date.

SD-16

Sarah's **Kitchen Stores**	CHEQUE NO. **645**
339 Hudson Court, Hamilton ON L9C 6B3	DATE 1 5 0 9 2 0 2 2 D D M M Y Y Y Y

PAY   Two Thousand One Hundred Seven and 50/100 $**2,107.50

To   Receiver General
The   875 Heron Road
Order Ottawa ON K1A 1A3

Toronto Dominion Bank   Sarah's Kitchen Stores
2 Palace Rd.
Hamilton, Ontario L3X 1T3   *S. Kafa*

⑆645⑈   ⑆2614⑈007⑆   192⑉991⑈ 2⑆

Please Detach Before Cashing

Sarah's Kitchen Stores Receiver General Re: HST at end of Aug 31, 2022	CHEQUE NO. **645** Sep 15, 2022 $2,107.50

SD-17

INVOICE

Sarah's
Kitchen Stores   339 Hudson Court, Hamilton ON L9C 6B3

To: Mr. Lennie Bercovitch   Ship To:
    Visa Credit Card   (Same)

Invoice No.	DATE
924	Sep 15, 2022

Item	Qty.	Order	Back Order	Description	Base Price	Disc. %	Price	Tax	Amount
M612	1			Cabinets M612	$4,770.00	10	$4,293.00	HS	4,293.00

HST #R4675 2567

Subtotal	4,293.00
HST 13%	558.09
TOTAL DUE	**$ 4,851.09**

Shipped: Sep 15, 2022

* 10% Senior Discount

SD-18

Sarah's
Kitchen Stores
339 Hudson Court, Hamilton ON L9C 6B3

CHEQUE NO.   **646**

DATE 1 6 0 9 2 0 2 2
         D D M M Y Y Y Y

PAY   Two Hundred Seventy Six and 39/100 $**276.39

To   Connoisseur Gadgets Ltd.
The   896 Shaw Park Road
Order Belfountain ON L0N 1B3

Toronto Dominion Bank
2 Palace Rd.
Hamilton, Ontario L3X 1T3

Sarah's Kitchen Stores

S. Kafa

⑆646⑈ ⑆2614⑈007⑈ 192⑆991 2⑈

- -
Please Detach Before Cashing

Sarah's Kitchen Stores
  Connoisseur Gadgets Ltd.
  Re: Invoice 15838, 15838Rt

CHEQUE NO.   **646**
Sep. 16, 2022
$276.39

SD-19

Sarah's Kitchen Stores
339 Hudson Court, Hamilton ON L9C 6B3

CHEQUE NO.   **647**

DATE   3 0 0 9 2 0 2 2
        D D M M Y Y Y Y

PAY   Two Hundred Fifty and 00/100 $**250.00

To The Order   Metro Hydro
          55223 Electric Dr.
          Hamilton ON L6Y 3B3

Toronto Dominion Bank
2 Palace Rd.
Hamilton, Ontario L3X 1T3

Sarah's Kitchen Stores

S. Kafa

⑆647⑈   ⑈2614⑈007⑉   192⑆991 2⑈

Please Detach Before Cashing

Sarah's Kitchen Stores
   Metro Hydro
   Re: Sep. 13 bill. Includes late payment $10 (Utility Expense)

CHEQUE NO.   **647**
Sep. 30, 2022
$250.00

SD-20

Smith & Sons Tool Company
SCO – 06-6168
159 Main Street, North York ON M6W 4X6

Date: Sep. 30, 2022   Inv. # 515807
Time: 11:10 am   By: Al
Type: Visa

281-8275   Various tools $83.00   B

------------------------SUBTOTAL ----------------------   83.00
HST: 13.00%   10.79

-----------------------------TOTAL ------------------------   93.79

============AMOUNT(S) TENDERED===============

VISA   93.79

===================SOLD TO ===================
Sarah's Kitchen Stores
339 Hudson Court,
Hamilton ON L9C 6B3
VISA Account: Z320-011-007
Exp.Date: 02/26

S. Kafa
Customer's Signature

> **Note:** Students should make a new account:
> #5390 Tools Expense
> Type: G
> Class Option: Expense

Chapter 6

Challenge COMPANY, RECEIVABLES, PAYABLES Setup and Transactions

Shirts & Ties

Learning Objectives
After completing this chapter you will be able to:

Option A
- ☐ Record transactions from source documents, in the COMPANY, RECEIVABLES, PAYABLES, and INVENTORY & SERVICES modules where necessary.
- ☐ Display and print various reports and journals.

Option B
- ☐ Create a new data file using knowledge gained from Chapter 4A and Appendix 2015 H, *INVENTORY & SERVICES Module Setup Perpetual Inventory for Sarah's Kitchen Stores (4B)*.
- ☐ Record transactions from source documents, in the COMPANY, RECEIVABLES, PAYABLES, and INVENTORY & SERVICES modules.
- ☐ Display and print various reports and journals.

This chapter provides an option for the student:

Option A

Use the **06 Shirts** data file to record the transactions in the source documents. (This option, and data file, is available at the discretion of your instructor.)

Option B

A challenge for you is to set up the COMPANY, RECEIVABLES, PAYABLES, and INVENTORY & SERVICES modules for the company, and process transactions in the appropriate modules using the source documents.

This challenge is appropriate if you have completed Appendix 2015 H, *INVENTORY & SERVICES Module Setup Perpetual Inventory for Sarah's Kitchen Stores (4B)* located in your
WWW course materials at www.nelson.com/student, before starting this chapter. (Your instructor may change some of the accounts and/or starting dollar values in the Trial Balance.)

Study the information for the company and set up the various modules. Use your last name followed by Shirts & Ties as the company name (e.g., Smith Shirts & Ties) with the following address: 8 Shirt Drive, Ottawa, ON K2Z 1Z1. Supply all other missing details.

Analyze and process the source documents that follow.

(Your Last Name) Shirts & Ties: Company Profile

(Your Last Name) Shirts & Ties (business number R133922445) sells special shirts and ties to other businesses. The company has recently experienced rapid growth both in sales dollars and in sales volume, forcing management to look into another more efficient accounting system. The company books, up to this point, had been kept manually by your friend, but the increased size of the company has forced the business to computerize the accounting records. You are to convert this manual system to Sage 50 Accounting, and help your friend with the first month of computerized operation (August 2022).

The company follows a **calendar fiscal year** and would like to convert after business closed on July 31, 2022.

The July 31, 2022 Trial Balance and details of Accounts Receivable and Accounts Payable are shown on the next two pages.

Some points to remember:

- Suggested company data file name is Shirts.

- The Trial Balance provided shows only postable accounts. You will have to create headings, subtotals, and total accounts so that the appropriate financial statements can be printed.

- The Discount Fee percentage for credit cards accepted is 3.5%.

- Add Tax codes HS at 13% and HI at 8%.

- Remember to make a backup before setting the modules to Ready.

- Remember to enter appropriate invoice numbers, cheque numbers, descriptions, etc., for the transactions (audit trail).

- When you allocate account numbers for your system, always leave a gap of at least 5 to 10 numbers to allow for future accounts to be inserted. Here is an example of why this is so important:

  Assume your number sequencing is similar to:

        2010 Accounts Payable
        2020 HST Charged on Sales
        2030 HST Paid on Purchases

  You discover after turning the system to **Ready** mode that you missed adding the "Universal Credit Card Payable" account into your chart of accounts.

  You will be able to easily insert Universal Credit Card Payable account number 2015 or any number between 2011 and 2019.

> If you had numbered the above three accounts as:
>
>   2010 Accounts Payable
>   2011 HST Charged on Sales
>   2012 HST Paid on Purchases
>
> You would have a lot of work to do to fix all four of the accounts.

(Your Last Name) Shirts and Ties
Trial Balance Jul 31, 2022

	Debits	Credits
Bank Account Chequing	21,434.00	-
Accounts Receivable	15,350.32	-
Credit Card Receivables	0.00	-
Inventory	21,261.00	-
Prepaid Expenses	1,420.00	-
Warehouse Equipment	63,650.00	-
Accumulated Deprec Warehouse Equip	-	21,300.00
Office Equipment	25,800.00	-
Accumulated Deprec Office Equip	-	10,350.00
Accounts Payable	-	6,751.75
Universal Credit Card Payable	-	0.00
HST Charged on Sales	-	3,100.00
HST Paid on Purchases	950.00	-
Bank Loan Payable (Long Term)	-	75,000.00
Capital (Your Last Name)	-	13,847.57
Drawings (Your Last Name)	7,000.00	-
Sales	-	269,385.00
Sales Returns	2,650.00	-
Sales Discounts	2,800.00	-
Cost of Goods Sold	102,735.00	
Purchase Discounts	-	1,628.00
Inventory Adjustments	0.00	
Wages Expense	98,030.00	-
Warehouse/Office Supplies Expense	1,790.00	-
Other Office Expenses	1,850.00	-
Travel & Entertainment Expense	2,630.00	-
Utilities Expense	2,800.00	-
Telephone Expense	2,400.00	-
Legal Expenses	1,600.00	-
Depreciation Expense-All	2,900.00	-
Rent Expense	14,000.00	-
Credit Card Charges	7,512.00	-
Insurance Expense	800.00	-
	----------------	----------------
	401,362.32	401,362.32
	==========	==========

Leave spaces between account numbers for adding accounts in the future without having to make new account groups to accommodate the new accounts. For example, if you start **Bank Account Chequing** at 1050, and the next account is Accounts Receivables, assign Accounts Receivable number 1060 so that if you need to insert other bank accounts in the future, you can assign them numbers close to the first bank account.

Accounts Receivable Details   [Credit limit - all customers $15,000.00]
Jul 31, 2022

	Tax Code	Invoice Number	Invoice Date	Amount	Taxes	Inv. Amt.	Terms
Flight Airways Inc. 2983 Somerset Street W Ottawa ON K2P 3W2 (613) 889-8855 Contact: John Stammers	HS	5686	Jul 30, 2022	4,184.35	543.97	$ 4,728.32	Net 30
McBurger Chain 903 Wheeler Street Ottawa ON K2J 5J3 (613) 554-2236 Contact: Jim Muir	HS	5681	Jul 26, 2022	2,400.00	312.00	$ 2,712.20	2/10, net 30
Radisser Hotels Inc. 3865 Pickford Drive Ottawa ON K2J 5Z6 (613) 554-8833 Contact: Sandra Wilson	HS	5683	Jul 30, 2022	7,000.00	910.00	$ 7,910.00	2/10, net 30
					Total	$15,350.32	

Accounts Payable Details
Jul 31, 2022

	Tax Code	Invoice Number	Invoice Date	Amount	Taxes	Inv. Amt.	Terms
Arrow Clothing Centre 2830 Appollo Way Ottawa ON K4A 6N8 (613) 938-4220 Contact: Legoria Simmons	HS	2531	Jul 24, 2022	3,975.00	516.75	$ 4,491.75	2/10, net 30
Polo Accessories 36 Canter Blvd Ottawa ON K2G 4L7 (613) 338-4322 Contact: Kiran Kenth	HS	6528	Jul 27, 2022	2,000.00	260.00	$ 2,260.00	2/10, net 30
					Total	$ 6,751.75	

Inventory Details

Description	Item code	Minimum	Cost Price	Selling Price	Items In stock	Item Cost
Shirt	NS01	20	21.00	42.00	206	4,326.00
Shirt	NS02	20	20.00	40.00	230	4,600.00
Shirt	Mod 42	10		49.50	0	0.00
Shirt	FA-6	20	10.50	21.00	250	2,625.00
Shirt	Mod 36	10	10.00	20.00	271	2,710.00
Ties	MC31	20	15.00	30.00	200	3,000.00
Ties	VA-Mac	20	16.00	32.00	250	4,000.00
					Total	$21,261.00

Transactions

Transactions are recorded using the original date of the document to ensure that our records match the records of our suppliers and customers for discount periods, etc. (e.g., a 2%/10, net 30 day purchase invoice dated August 23, received on August 24, and approved on August 25, would be recorded as a purchase using the August 23 date, as this is the date the discount starts.)

1 ➤ The following transactions took place in August 2022. Enter them in the appropriate journals.

SD-1

Shirts & Ties	CHEQUE NO. **5001**
8 Shirt Drive	DATE 0 1 0 8 2 0 2 2
Ottawa ON K2Z 1Z1	D D M M Y Y Y Y

PAY One Thousand Eight Hundred Fifty three   and 20/100 $**1,853.20

To The Order Of McTavish Building Management
80 Scott Street
Ottawa ON K4Z 1K9

Shirts & Ties

Bank of Central Ontario
601 Duke St.
Ottawa, ON K0Z 1Z2

Per _____ *YST*
Authorized Signature

⑈00500⑈" "⑈113305 01⑈ 9⑈⑈1055⑈"

- -

Shirts & Ties Inc.   *Please Detach Before Cashing*   CHEQUE NO.   **5001**

Aug 1, 2022   Re: Lease ($1,640.00 plus HST) $1,853.20

SD-2

Shirts & Ties	CHEQUE NO. **5002**
8 Shirt Drive	DATE 0 2 0 8 2 0 2 2
Ottawa ON K2Z 1Z1	D D M M Y Y Y Y

PAY Four Thousand Four Hundred twelve ----------------25/100 $**4,412.25

To The Order Of Arrow Clothing Centre
2830 Appollo Way
Ottawa ON K4A 6N8

Shirts & Ties

Bank of Central Ontario
601 Duke St.
Ottawa, ON K0Z 1Z2

Per _____ *YST*
Authorized Signature

⑈00500 2⑈" "⑈113305 01⑈ 9⑈⑈1055⑈"

- -

Shirts & Ties Inc.   *Please Detach Before Cashing*   CHEQUE NO.   **5002**

Aug 2, 2022   Paid #2531   Discount $79.50 $4,412.25

SD-3

Shirts & Ties

INVOICE

8 Shirt Drive
Ottawa ON K2Z 1Z1
Phone: (613) 927-3838

Sold:	Flight Airways Inc.	Ship To:
To	2983 Somerset St. West	(Same)
	Ottawa ON K2P 3W2	

INVOICE NO.	DATE
5694	Aug 04, 2022

Item	Qty.	Order	Back Order	Description	Base Price	Disc. %	Price	Tax	Amount
FA-6	250			Shirt FA-6	$21.00		$21.00	HS	$5,250.00

	Subtotal	5,250.00
R133922445	HST 13%	682.50

TOTAL DUE
$5,932.50

Shipping Date: Aug 04, 2022
Terms: Net 30 days

SD-4

Ottawa Hydro Company

55223 Electric Drive, Ottawa ON K6Y 3I3

Shirts & Ties   Phone: (613) 445-8875
8 Shirt Drive   Date: Aug 04, 2022
Ottawa ON K2Z 1Z1

Service to July 29	$403.54
H.S.T. R142887665	52.46

Note...
Record 456.00 amount owing. If payment is late, the additional cost is charged to Other Office Expenses.

Current charges including tax **$456.00**

If paid after August 19 pay   **$466.00**

APPROVAL	
Date Aug 5, 2022	
Acct. # Utilities	
Approved *GK*	

RECEIVED   Aug 05, 2022

SD-5

Shirts & Ties

8 Shirt Drive
Ottawa ON K2Z 1Z1
Phone: (613) 927-3838

PURCHASE ORDER
1

To:	Arrow Clothing Centre	Ship:	
	2830 Appollo Way	To:	(Same)
	Ottawa ON K4A 6N8		

Date	Aug. 9, 2022
Ship Date	Aug. 15, 2022

Item	Qty.	Order	Back Order	Description	Unit Price	Unit	Tax	Amount
Mod 42		200		Shirt Mod 42	$24.75	Each	HS	$4,950.00
						Subtotal		4,950.00
					R133922445	HST 13%		643.50
							TOTAL DUE	
				Terms: 2/10, net 30				$5,593.50

SD-6

Springman & Associates

6990 Winston Churchill Road
Caledon ON L0P 1P6
519-927-8885
GST Number: R222444666
Anne Springman

PURCHASE ORDER
 # 2180

Date: Aug 9, 2022
Ship Date: Aug 11, 2022

To: Shirts & Ties
8 Shirt Drive
Ottawa ON K2Z 1Z1

Ship To: Springman & Associates
6990 Winston Churchill Road
Caledon ON L0P 1P6

Item	Order	Description	Unit Price	Unit	Tax	Total
Mod 36	38	Shirts Mod 36	$20.00	Each	HS	$ 760.00
VA-Mac	38	Ties VA-Mac	$32.00	Each	HS	1,216.00
					Subtotal	$ 1,976.00
					HST	256.88
		Terms: 2/10, net 30			**TOTAL**	$ 2,232.88

SD-7

Radisser Hotels Inc.
3865 Pickford Drive
Ottawa ON K2J 5Z6

CHEQUE NO.   **93288**

DATE   0 9 0 8 2 0 2 2
D D M M Y Y Y Y

| PAY | Seven Thousand Seven Hundred Seventy and 00/100 | $**7,770.00 |

| To The Order Of | Shirts & Ties
8 Shirt Drive
Ottawa ON. K2Z 1Z1 |

Canadiania Bank
19 Moore Avenue
Nepean ON K4C 2A1

B J Radisser

⑆93288⑈   ⑈042⑉1⑈004⑉   112⑈181 8⑈

DETACH BEFORE CASHING

Radisser Hotels Inc.   **93288**

DATE	DESCRIPTION	AMOUNT
Aug 09,2022	RE: Payment of Invoice #5683, less $140.00 discount	$ 7,770.00

RECEIVED   Aug 09, 2022
For Deposit Only

SD-8

Shirts & Ties

8 Shirt Drive
Ottawa ON K2Z 1Z1
Phone: (613) 927-3838

INVOICE

Sold: To	Springman & Associates 6990 Winston Churchill Road Caledon ON L0P 1P6	Ship To: (Same)

INVOICE NO.	DATE
5695	Aug 13, 2022

Item	Qty.	Order	Back Order	Description	Base Price	Disc. %	Price	Tax	Amount
Mod 36	38			Shirts Mod 36	$20.00		$20.00	HS	$ 760.00
VA-Mac	38			Ties, VA-Mac	32.00		32.00	HS	1,216.00

		Subtotal	1,976.00
R133922445		HST 13%	256.88

TOTAL DUE
$2,232.88

PO 2180 Attn: Anne Springman
Shipping Date: Aug 13, 2022
Terms: 2%10, Net 30 days

SD-9

Arrow Clothing Centre

2830 Appollo Way
Ottawa ON K4A 6N8
Phone: (613) 938-4220
   HST# 53842

I N V O I C E 2689

Sold: To	Shirts and Ties 8 Shirt Drive Ottawa ON K2Z 1Z1	Ship To: (Same)

P. O.	DATE
1	Aug 15, 2022

Item	Qty.	Order	Back Ordered	Description	Base Price	Unit	Price	Tax	Amount
Mod 42	170		30	Shirts Model 42	$24.75	Each	$24.75	HS	$4,207.50

	Subtotal	4,207.50
	HST 13%	546.98

Shipping Date: Sept 01, 2022

Terms: 2/10, net 30

TOTAL DUE
$ 4,754.48

SD-10

Shirts & Ties

8 Shirt Drive
Ottawa ON K2Z 1Z1
Phone: (613) 927-3838

I N V O I C E
– Credit Memo –

Sold: To	Springman & Associates 6990 Winston Churchill Road Caledon ON L0P 1P6	Ship To: (Same)

INVOICE NO.	DATE
5695Rt	Aug 15, 2022

Item	Qty.	Order	Back Order	Description	Base Price	Disc. %	Price	Tax	Amount
Mod 36	-2			Shirts Mod 36	$20.00		$20.00	HS	$ -40.00

	Subtotal	-40.00
R133922445	HST 13%	-5.20

PO 2180 Attn: Anne Springman
Shipping Date: Aug 15, 2022
Terms: 2% 8, Net 28 days

TOTAL DUE
$ -45.20

SD-11

Shirts & Ties

8 Shirt Drive
Ottawa ON K2Z 1Z1

CHEQUE NO.   **5003**

DATE   1 5 0 8 2 0 2 2
        D D M M Y Y Y Y

PAY Two Thousand One Hundred Fifty and 00/100 $**2,150.00

To The Order Of	Receiver General 875 Heron Road Ottawa ON K1A 1A3

Shirts & Ties

Bank of Central Ontario
601 Duke St.
Ottawa, ON K0Z 1Z2

Per _____ *YST* _____
Authorized Signature

⑆005003⑆ ⑈113050⑈ 91⑈1055⑆

Shirts & Ties Inc.   *Please Detach Before Cashing*   **CHEQUE NO.   5003**

Aug 15, 2022   Re: HST to July 31 $2,150.00

SD-12

M E M O

Shirts & Ties

August 19, 2022

To: Your Name

From: Robert Amber, Manager

Issue cheque #5004 today to pay the August 4, 2022 Ottawa Hydro (utilities) bill. This must be paid today to save $10.00.

Robert

SD-13

Arrow Clothing Centre

2830 Appollo Way
Ottawa ON K4A 6N8
Phone: (613)938-4220
   HST# 53842

INVOICE
RETURN

Sold: Shirts & Ties
To   8 Shirt Drive
      Ottawa ON K2Z 1Z1

Ship To:
(Same)

INVOICE NO.	DATE
2689Rt	Aug 19 2022

Item	Qty.	Order	Back Order	Description	Base Price	Unit	Price	Tax	Amount
Mod 42	-2			Shirts Mod 42	$24.75	Each	$24.75	HS	$ -49.50

Subtotal	-49.50
HST 13%	- 6.44

Right sleeve defective
Shipping Date: Aug 19, 2022
Terms: 2%6, net 26

TOTAL	
	$ -55.94

SD-14

Springman & Associates
6990 Winston Churchill Rd.
Caledon, ON L0P 1P6

CHEQUE NO.   **556**

DATE 2 3 0 8 2 0 2 2
          D D M M Y Y Y Y

To the order of

> Shirts & Ties
> 8 Shirt Drive
> Ottawa ON K2Z 1Z1

Pay: Two Thousand One Hundred Forty-eight and 96/100- - - - - - - - - - - - - - $**2,148.96

Canadian City Bank
125 Mavis Dr., Ottawa, ON K3Y 2M9

S Springman

⑆00556⑆ ⑈2500 2080⑈ 89662⑈

- -

Springman & Associates   CHEQUE NO. 556

DATE	INV.NO.		AMOUNT
Aug 23, 2022	#5695, 5695Rt	Paid order less return, discount	$2,148.96

RECEIVED   **August 24, 2022**

For Deposit Only

SD-15

Shirts & Ties

8 Shirt Drive
Ottawa ON K2Z 1Z1

CHEQUE NO.   **5005**

DATE 3 1 0 8 2 0 2 2
D D M M Y Y Y Y

PAY One Thousand Four Hundred Seventy-four and 20/100 $**1,474.20

To The	Meadows Insurance Brokers Inc.
Order	197 Larange Avenue, Suite 125
Of	Ottawa ON K8Z 4R9

Shirts & Ties

Bank of Central Ontario
601 Duke St.
Ottawa, ON K0Z 1Z2

Per _____ *YST* _____
Authorized Signature

⑆005005⑈ ⑈113305⑇⑆ 91⑆1055⑈

Shirts & Ties Inc.   *Please Detach Before Cashing*   CHEQUE NO.   5005

Aug 31, 2022   Re: Insurance Renewal Aug. 1, 2022 through Jul. 31, 2023
                        $1,365.00 plus HST $1,474.20

SD-16

Shirts & Ties

M E M O

Aug 31, 2022

To: Your Name

From: Robert Amber, Manager

Please enter the following in the data file.

- Andrea Mosely, the new bank accounting clerk, completed the bank reconciliation to August 23 and advised that there are 2 items (Bank Charges $100.00 and Bank Interest Expense $500.00 on our loan) that have not been recorded. Please create 2 new accounts to record these 2 charges.

Robert

2 ➤   At the end of the month, **print** the following:

• Income Statement	Jan 01 to Aug 31
• Balance Sheet at	Aug 31
• Vendor Aged Detail, all vendors, with terms at	Aug 31
• Customer Aged Detail, all customers, with terms at	Aug 31
• All Journal Entries	Aug 01 - Aug 31
• General Journal Entries	Aug 01 - Aug 31
• Pending Purchase Order report	Aug 31
• Inventory Summary report	Aug 31
• Chart of Accounts	

Chapter 7

EMPLOYEES & PAYROLL Module Setup and Processing

Creative Wallpaper

Learning Objectives

After completing this chapter you will be able to:

☐ Set up a company's Payroll defaults and linking accounts.
☐ Create and modify employee accounts with specific payroll information.
☐ Record opening employee balances before turning the module to Ready.
☐ Turn the module to Ready.
☐ Record payroll transactions, using cheque run or individual cheques.
☐ Reverse a payroll cheque issued in error.
☐ Record Payroll loans and reimbursements.
☐ Record Payroll remittance for source deductions.
☐ Record Payroll vacation pay.
☐ Display and Print appropriate Payroll reports and journals.

This chapter allows you to set up the Employees ledger in the EMPLOYEES & PAYROLL module for **Creative Wallpaper**, and record some payroll transactions for the month (January 2019).

Important: This chapter was written using the Sage 50 Premium Accounting 2015.0 Version software. If you use a different version you may receive different payroll solutions.

The **Student Edition** of the software included with this textbook is the same software with restrictions. See Appendix 2, *Installation Instructions*, located at the back of this textbook.

Businesses must purchase a Payroll ID code to activate the Automatic payroll calculations for taxes. The student edition does not require a Payroll activation code.

The payroll taxes are effective from July 1, 2014. If you are using a different Sage 50 Accounting version (see information symbol note above) and, therefore, a different edition of the tax tables, which covers a different time period, the instructions still apply, but there may be a slight difference between your net pay amounts and those in the solution.

The following topics are covered:

Instructions in this chapter assume that you have some knowledge of the basic principles of payroll accounting. If you are unsure of some of the accounting entries for payroll or government regulations, you should research these areas before starting the chapter. Refer to your accounting textbook for more information.

Accrual for wages owed for a short period of time, at the beginning of the month and at month-end, will be discussed in this chapter.

Slideshow 7A—Setting Up the PAYROLL Module explains in detail the important steps in setting the module to **Ready**. Run this slideshow before proceeding.

EMPLOYEES & PAYROLL Module

The EMPLOYEES & PAYROLL module is used to record money earned by employees in a company during a calendar year. The EMPLOYEES Ledger is used to record employees' personal information and payroll information such as hourly rates of pay and additional deductions. The **Paycheques** and **Payroll Cheque Run** journals calculate the gross pay, and subtract government deductions (CPP, EI, Income Tax) and other deductions; e.g., safety shoes, insurance, dental plans, charitable donations and other benefits to arrive at Net Pay.

The Sage 50 Accounting program contains tax tables and deduction formulas for all earnings amounts. Sage 50 Accounting updates these tables and formulas on a regular basis, based on information received from the Canada Revenue Agency (CRA). There is a fee for these updates.

The COMPANY, RECEIVABLES, and PAYABLES modules have been set up and are **Ready** to use.

To set the EMPLOYEES & PAYROLL module to **Ready**, the following needs to be completed:

1. Make payroll-related adjustments.
2. Set the PAYROLL module default settings.
3. Set the PAYROLL module Linked accounts.
4. Create an employee record for each employee in the EMPLOYEES Ledger. Each record will contain the employee's name, address, and other basic personal information, pay rates, deductions, etc.

Sage 50 Accounting EMPLOYEES & PAYROLL module follows similar procedures to setting the default linked accounts in Chapter 4A, and creating customer and vendor records in the RECEIVABLES and PAYABLES modules.

After the employee information is entered in the Employees Ledger, the total of the individual balances must balance with the General Ledger PAYROLL–related accounts.

Sage 50 Accounting can print T4s (summary of each employee's earnings and deductions), an employee payroll summary, and Detail reports whenever required.

Creative Wallpaper data files will be used to record payroll transactions for the month of January 2019. The instructions in this chapter are based on Sage 50 Premium Accounting Version 2015.0 version for Windows issued in December 2014.

Your instructor will advise you which of the two Wallpaper data files to use in Exercise 7-1.

If you use the 07 Wallpaper file:

Data file **07 Wallpaper** follows the text exercises in the following sequence:

1. recording the reversing accrual entry
2. setting defaults
3. linking the appropriate accounts to the General Ledger
4. entering each employee's data
5. turning the EMPLOYEES & PAYROLL module to Ready
6. recording paycheques and payments—to the end of the chapter

If you use the 07 Wallpaper2 file:

Data file **07 Wallpaper2** has the EMPLOYEES & PAYROLL module set to **Ready** (Steps 1 through 5 above have been completed for you). If you use it, start at

Exercise 7-8 (Creating a New Employee Ledger). Assume you have been hired to be the new payroll clerk and the EMPLOYEES & PAYROLL module was set up by your supervisor, Mrs. Singh.

If you use 07 Wallpaper2, you may want to review the steps that were completed, to have the module ready to use by reading through the steps shown in Exercises 7-1 to 7-7.

Difference between Manual Accounting and Sage 50 Accounting Payroll

The following illustrates the difference in processing payroll in a manual system and Sage 50 Accounting. The entries assume an employee's basic Wage is $1,000.00 ($12.50 per hour × 80 hours) plus 4% Vacation Pay ($40.00) per two-week pay period.

Manual Accounting

1.	**Payroll journal entry from payroll register as printed on employee pay-stub.**		
	Wages Expense	$1,040.00	$
	Bank Account Chequing		766.80
	Vacation Payable		40.00
	EI Payable		18.80
	CPP Payable		42.84
	Income Tax Payable		87.56
	Union Dues Payable		20.00
	Pension Plan Payable		40.00
	Medical Plan Payable		24.00
	Record payroll cheque information		
2.	**Payroll: deduction expense entry (expense for company)**		
	EI Expense	26.32	
	CPP Expense	42.84	
	EI Payable		26.32
	CPP Payable		42.84
	Record payroll benefit costs		
3.	**Payroll: other expenses (expense for company)**		
	WSIB Expense	4.10	
	WSIB Payable		4.10
	Record other benefit costs		

Fig. 7-1a: Manual Payroll.

Sage 50 Accounting Payroll

Sage 50 Accounting generates the following combined journal entry (parts 1, 2, and 3).

Sage 50 Accounting - payroll entry: combines parts 1, 2, 3		
Wages Expense	1,040.00	
EI Expense	26.32	
CPP Expense	42.84	
WSIB Expense	4.10	
Bank Account Chequing		766.80
Vacation Payable		40.00
EI Payable		45.12
CPP Payable		85.68
Income Tax Payable		87.56
Union Dues Payable		20.00
Pension Plan Payable		40.00
Medical Plan Payable		24.00
WSIB Payable		4.10

Fig. 7-1b: Sage 50 Accounting Payroll.

Creative Wallpaper: Company Profile

Creative Wallpaper sells wallpapers, from many manufacturers, and related materials (tools, cutters, glue, cleaning solvents, and other accessories). Information about the company's payroll is shown below.

- Hourly employees are paid bi-weekly (26 times a year).

- Commission employees are paid bi-weekly (26 times a year).

- Salaried employees are paid twice a month (bi-monthly), 24 times a year.

- Overtime is paid at the rate of time and one-half. (Regular pay plus ½ regular pay.)

- Vacation pay (4%) is retained for hourly and commission employees until the employee takes holidays. Vacation pay is not calculated or retained for salaried employees.

- The Employment Insurance (EI) rate (federal regulations) for the company is 1.4 times that which the employees have deducted from their paycheques.

- WCB or Workers' Safety and Insurance Board (WSIB Ontario) rate for the company is 0.41%.

- The Employer Health Tax (EHT—Ontario) expense is based on payroll costs. Effective January 1, 2014, employers with payrolls of less than $450,000 are exempt from this tax. The payroll example that follows assumes the payroll costs for Creative Wallpaper will be less than $450,000 and, therefore, the payroll entries will not indicate this expense. See the "Information Only" section at the end of the chapter for an example of a payroll entry that contains the EHT expense and EHT payable.

- Each payday, union dues of **$20.00** (before tax) are deducted from the wages of each of the hourly and commission employees.

- A company policy is that, in extenuating circumstances, employees may receive a loan of up to $600.00. The loan is repayable by regular payroll installments. *Hourly* workers repay **$30.00** and *Salaried* employees repay **$45.00** each pay date. Mrs. Singh, store supervisor, approves loans.

- Full-time employees contribute **4%** of their wages or salary, not including vacation pay, to a pension plan. Contributions are sent to the pension plan quarterly.

Study the Trial Balance of Creative Wallpaper shown next.

Creative Wallpaper, Student's Name
Trial Balance As At Jan 01, 2019

		Debits	Credits
1010	Bank Account Chequing	16,800.00	-
1200	Accounts Receivable	15,142.00	-
1241	Loans Receivable	90.00	-
1260	Inventory of Goods	75,325.00	-
1280	Store/Office Supplies/Prepaid	600.00	-
1520	Equipment & Shelving	67,800.00	-
1540	Office Furniture & Fixtures	15,628.00	-
1620	Accumulated Depreciation Equipment	-	21,200.00
1640	Accumulated Deprec: Office Furn/Fixt	-	3,420.00
2200	Accounts Payable	-	16,611.00
2210	Accrued Payroll Payable	-	512.00
2300	Vacation Payable	-	900.00
2310	EI Payable	-	512.00
2320	CPP Payable	-	497.00
2330	Income Tax Payable	-	2,345.00
2390	United Way Donations Payable	-	260.00
2420	Union Dues Payable	-	220.00
2430	Pension Plan Payable	-	480.00
2440	Medical Plan Payable	-	200.00
2450	Safety Shoes Payable	94.00	-
2460	WSIB Payable	-	450.00
2650	HST Charged On Sales	-	1,432.00
2670	HST Paid On Purchases	1,050.00	-
3100	Capital M. Storoschuk	-	143,490.00
3580	Drawings M. Storoschuk	-	0.00
4010	Sales	-	0.00
4210	Sales Returns	-	0.00
4220	Sales Discounts	-	0.00
5020	Cost of Goods Sold	0.00	-
5050	Purchase Discounts	0.00	-
5060	Inventory Adjustment	0.00	
5120	Advertising Expense	0.00	-
5140	Bank Charges and Interest Expense	0.00	-
5160	Insurance Expense	0.00	-
5180	Office Supplies Expense	0.00	-
5200	Telephone Expense	0.00	-
5220	Utilities Expense	0.00	-
5240	Bad Debts Expense	0.00	-
5300	Wages Expense	0.00	-
5302	Salaries Expense	0.00	-
5304	Commissions Expense	0.00	-
5308	Wages-Overtime Expense	0.00	-
5310	EI Expense	0.00	-
5320	CPP Expense	0.00	-
5330	WSIB Expense	0.00	-
5395	Reimbursement Payroll Suspense	0.00	-
		192,529.00	**192,529.00**

> ℹ️ $94.00 Debit balance is from the safety shoes payment, by the company, to the Safety Shoe Company. This balance will decrease as deductions are made from the employee's pay.

Fig. 7-2: Creative Wallpaper, Opening Trial Balance.

Exercise 7-1—Making the EMPLOYEES & PAYROLL Module Visible

1 ➤ Refer to Exercise 1-1b, to open the appropriate Wallpaper data folder as shown below.

   If you are using **07 Wallpaper**, open the data file and **continue with step 2 in this exercise**.

   If you are using **07 Wallpaper2**, open the data file and **continue with Exercise 7-8**.

2 ➤ Advance the date to **Jan 2, 2019** (the business was closed for New Year's Day). The year 2019 beginning data year file is used for the exercises in this chapter. It will demonstrate the use of two payroll accruals, **January 1** (reverse prior year December 2018 accrual) and the setup of a **January 31, 2019** month-end accrual.

3 ➤ The EMPLOYEES & PAYROLL module is not visible and, therefore, not available for use. To make the EMPLOYEES & PAYROLL module available, click **Setup**, **User Preferences**, in the left panel click **View**, in the right panel, **Pages** section, at EMPLOYEES & PAYROLL, click the box. Two ✓ appear (one in the Icon Windows section). Click **OK** and the EMPLOYEES & PAYROLL module in History mode is displayed for use.

4 ➤ Study the Trial Balance in Fig. 7-2. You will notice that account numbers 2210 to 2460 are payable accounts, which are directly affected by Payroll and Payroll Accrual Adjustment transactions.

The normal pay date at the end of December 2018, based on Friday paydays, would have been Friday, December 28. To match revenue with expenses, you would have recorded an accrual for wages owed to employees who work on any of the 3 days December 29, 30 and/or 31. Notice the greyed-out dates on the calendar below.

As of **December 31, 2018**, there were accrued salaries/wages of $512.00 owing to hourly and commission employees. This December 31 accrual will need to be reversed at January 2, 2019. This topic will be discussed in more detail in Chapter 9, **Month-End/Year-End Processing**, and Chapter 10, **Year-End Closing**.

The hourly and commission employees will be paid on Friday, January 11, 2019. (See calendar below.)

At the end of January 2019, the normal pay date for hourly and commission employees would be Friday, January 25. An accrual would be recorded for the wages owed for the period Saturday, January 26 to Thursday, January 31 (see Exercise 7-19). Employees would be paid on Friday, February 8.

December 2018							January 2019						
S	**M**	**T**	**W**	**T**	**F**	**S**	**S**	**M**	**T**	**W**	**T**	**F**	**S**
						1							
2	3	4	5	6	7	8			1	2	3	**4**	5
9	**10**	**11**	**12**	**13**	**14**	**15**	6	7	8	9	10	11	12
16	**17**	**18**	**19**	**20**	**21**	**22**	13	14	15	16	17	18	19
23	24	25	26	27	28	29	20	21	22	23	24	25	26
30	31						27	28	29	30	31		

The days that Doreen David and Jordan Currie worked were recorded in the month of December 2018 as shown next, based on a memo from Mrs. Singh, as an accrued wages and commission expense. (See Trial Balance, Fig. 7-2, account #2210 Accrued Payroll Payable.)

Study the memo below:

M E M O

From: Gurjeet Singh
Date: December 31, 2018
To: Accounting

Please record a payroll accrual for the following employees.

Doreen: 3 days (Dec 29, 30, 31) (8 hours each) at $14.00 per hour $336.00
Jordan: Commission for 2 days (Dec. 28, 30), estimated $176.00

                                Total accrued wages owed $512.00

Please remember to reverse this accrual in January 2019, before you record the cheques being issued on January 10, 2019.

The entry that was recorded on December 31, 2018 for the accrued wages is shown below:

Dec. 31, 2018

Dr **5300 Wages Expense**	336.00	
Dr **5304 Commission Expense**	176.00	
Cr **2210 Accrued Payroll Payable**		512.00

Accrued wages @ Dec. 31, 2018 per calculation

Accruals do not include EI, CPP, and Income Tax Payable amounts because they are recorded when they are actually deducted from each employee on each pay date.

Doreen and Jordan will not get paid for the period December 29 to 31 until January 11, 2019, which is the end of a bi-weekly pay period.

The accounting records on January 2, 2019 should reverse the payroll accrual.

The General Ledger data, accounts, and balances have been entered as of January 1, 2019. Payroll liability accounts remain active because the amounts are payable to the Federal Government, and other agencies, for payroll deductions collected up to December 31, 2018. Employee deduction history information for 2018 is used in the year 2018 T4 slips, and is not entered in the 2019 data file information. Year 2019 employee deduction history will be zero (0.00).

After the EMPLOYEES & PAYROLL system is turned to **Ready**, you will see how your payroll entries affect the General Ledger accounts and financial statements.

Making a Payroll-Related Adjusting Entry

As discussed earlier, a payroll accrual adjusting entry was recorded at December 31, 2018 for wages owed to employees who worked on any of the 3 days at the end of December. On January 2, 2019, a reversing entry will be recorded and its purpose is twofold:

a) To ensure expenses are matched to revenues correctly in each of 2018 and 2019, and

b) To keep payroll processing straightforward and simple by removing the need to adjust the paycheques for the amount of the December accrual.

When the actual paycheques for the individuals who had accrued wages are paid, their paycheque amounts for December would be properly accounted for.

Exercise 7-2—Recording Reversing Entry

1 ➤ From the Company module, **record** and **post** a January 2 entry to reverse the December 31, 2018 General Journal accrual entry based on the memo. Use the Recurring entry "**Reverse prior month wages accrual**" to **Post** a January 2 entry to reverse the December 31, 2018 General Journal accrual. Change the information as needed. The entry should be similar to the following:

General Journal Entry Jan 02, 2019 (J1)			
Account Number	Account Description	Debits	Credits
2210	Accrued Payroll Payable	512.00	-
5300	Wages Expense	-	336.00
5304	Commissions Expense	-	176.00
Additional Date:	Additional Field:		
		512.00	512.00

2 ➤ **Update** the Recurring entry.

3 ➤ **Exit** the General Journal window.

Step 1: Setting EMPLOYEES & PAYROLL Module Defaults

You will now set the EMPLOYEES & PAYROLL module defaults that give information about the way the employees are paid.

Exercise 7-3—Setting EMPLOYEES & PAYROLL Module Defaults

Names—Payroll

1 ➤ From the Home window, click **Setup**, click **Settings**, in the left pane, click ⊞ at **Payroll**, click ⊞ at **Names,** click **Incomes and Deductions** to display the fields.

Sage 50 Accounting allows you to change the names of the default fields:

Income fields, 1 to 20 (Linked accounts)	Income codes 1 through 20 are descriptions for the type of payroll paid to employees by a company in addition to regular wages. Income codes 4 through 20 are not used by Creative Wallpaper.

2 ➤ Income 3   Change Income Name field to **Reimburse**, Tab . This field would be used to pay an employee for money they spent on behalf of the business.

Deduction   Sage 50 Accounting provides up to 20 linked
fields, 1 to 20   accounts that can be used for deductions because some companies have many deductions from employees' earnings.

3 ➤ Deduction 1-4   Change Deduction Name fields to the Names listed below.

The default names for 1 through 4 are typical of the deductions that exist in many companies.

Income	Name		Deduction	Name	
Advances	Advances		Deduction 1	Pension	
Loans	Loans		Deduction 2	Union Dues	
Benefits	Benefits		Deduction 3	Medical	
Benef. (Que)	Benef. (Que)		Deduction 4	Safety Shoes	
Vac. Earned	Vac. Earned		Deduction 5	Deduction 5	
Vac. Paid	Vac. Paid		Deduction 6	Deduction 6	
Regular	Regular		Deduction 7	Deduction 7	
Overtime 1	Overtime 1		Deduction 8	Deduction 8	
Overtime 2	Overtime 2		Deduction 9	Deduction 9	
Income 1	Salary		Deduction 10	Deduction 10	
Income 2	Commission		Deduction 11	Deduction 11	
Income 3	Reimburse		Deduction 12	Deduction 12	

In this exercise we are not removing the additional unused names for Income or Deductions. If you want to remove the Income or Deduction names from the Names column you would click on the name (e.g., Income 20 or, Deduction 11), press Delete and Tab . The wording will no longer display in journal windows. You may receive a warning confirmation message.

4 ➤ Prov. Tax   In the left pane, click **Additional Payroll**. Remove **(Que)**, at **Prov Tax** Tab . This field would be used to name a provincial payroll tax not collected by the Federal Government. Certain provinces have such a tax. Ontario does not. Leave the box blank.

5 ➤ Worker's Comp   Click ▼ and select **WSIB** (Workplace Safety and Insurance Board) as the appropriate code for Ontario. Tab . Other provinces have different codes.

6 ➤ When your Names Income & Deductions window and Additional Payroll windows resemble the above, click **OK** to accept changes and return to the Home window. (See side note box.)

Printers

> You may not be allowed to change settings in your network system. Check with your instructor. If not, skip this section—read for information only.

The next step is to define printer settings.

1 ➤ From the Home window, click **Setup**, **Reports & Forms,** in the left pane click **Cheques** and in the right pane click on ‹1010 Bank Account Chequing› to display the Reports & Forms Options window.

2 ➤   This window allows setting changes for both the Payment Cheque and Payroll Cheque. The Next cheque number should be as shown.

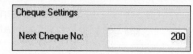

The printer, form type, font, and margin spacing are displayed in the Printer Forms Settings fields. No changes are necessary; however, check with your instructor to make sure that the settings are appropriate.

3 ➤   Click on the **+** at **Government Forms**.

Vendors	Used to print T5018 forms for subcontractors payroll information.
Federal Payroll	Used to print Record of Employment, T4 Slips, and T4 Summary forms.
Quebec Payroll	Used to print Relevé 1 slips.

No changes are necessary. You can identify various printers (if available) for various reports.

In order to conserve paper, you will not be required to print payroll or payment cheques or T4/Relevé 1 slips in this chapter.

4 ➤   Click **OK**, to return to the Home window.

Payroll Settings

1 ➤   From the Home window, click **Setup, Settings**, click on the **+** at **Payroll** and click on **Incomes** to display the settings window. The option changes are shown as follows:

2 ➤   At Income **Regular**, in the column Type, triple-click the **Hourly Rate** and you will see two choices. Do NOT change.

Hourly Rate	The rate the employee earns per hour for regular work.
Differential Rate	Extra rate the employee earns per hour for working shifts, higher job classifications, etc.

3 ➤   Click **Cancel**, and at Income **Salary**, in the column Type, double-click **Income** and you will see seven choices. Do NOT change.

Income	Used to pay employees for regular work.
Benefit	Used for taxable employee benefits such as car allowance; paying employees for using their own vehicle (car, van, truck) for the business, or life insurance, etc., where the company pays the cost on the employee's behalf. Creative Wallpaper does not pay for these types of items.
Benefit (Que)	Used for taxable employee benefits in Quebec. Creative Wallpaper does not have employees in Quebec.
Reimbursement	Used when an employee is being repaid for money they paid out for the company (e.g., travelling expenses). Using the PAYROLL module method will allow you to charge only one account for the reimbursement. In most situations, there are two accounts being charged, the Expense or Purchase account and an HST Paid account. Many companies use the

PAYABLES module (Make Other Payment option) to reimburse the employee.

WWW   See Appendix 2015 T, *Reimbursement (Payroll)* in your course materials at www.nelson.com/student.

Hourly Rate   Information is the same as in Step 2.

Piece Rate   Employees can be paid based on the number of items (pieces) they can produce during the time they work. If the Piece Rate was chosen, then the Unit of Measure column would change to item.

Differential Rate Information is the same as in Step 2.

4 ➤   Click **Cancel** to leave the Salary line choice as **Income**.

Income	Type	Unit of Measure	Calc. Tax	Calc.	Calc. EI	Calc. Ins. Hours	Calc. CPP/QPP	Calc. EHT	Calc. QHSF	Calc. Vac.	Calc. QPIP	Calc. VRSP
Advances	System	Period	✓	✓	✓		✓	✓	✓	✓	✓	✓
Loans	System	Period										
Benefits	System	Period	✓				✓	✓				
Benef. (Que)	System	Period		✓			✓		✓	✓		✓
Vac. Earned	System	Period										
Vac. Paid	System	Period	✓	✓	✓	✓	✓	✓	✓		✓	✓
Regular	Hourly Rate	Hour	✓	✓	✓	✓	✓	✓	✓	✓	✓	✓
Overtime 1	Hourly Rate	Hour	✓	✓	✓	✓	✓	✓	✓	✓	✓	
Overtime 2	Hourly Rate	Hour	✓	✓	✓	✓	✓	✓	✓	✓	✓	
Salary	Income	Period	✓	✓	✓	✓	✓	✓	✓	✓	✓	✓
Commission	Income	Period	✓	✓	✓	✓	✓	✓	✓	✓	✓	✓
Reimburse	Income	Period	✓	✓	✓	✓	✓	✓	✓	✓	✓	✓

Fig. 7-3: Payroll Incomes window after changes.

You will not be able to change any settings in the top blue section (System Type items).

The column is ✓ checked if you calculate the Income type **before** the column deductions.
The column is   unchecked if you calculate the Income type **after** the column deductions.
The column is left checked ✓ as you may need the column calculations at a later time.

At the **Commission** line, leave the choice as **Income**.

Calc.   This column is for Quebec. Leave the ✓ in the column even though Creative Wallpaper currently does not have any employees in Quebec.

Calc. EHT   Leave the ✓ in the column even though Creative Wallpaper is currently exempt from the (EHT) Employer Health Tax in Ontario.

5 ➤ Reimburse   At Reimburse, triple-click the **Income**, select **Reimbursement**. It will remove the ✓ marks from the Reimburse line. Reimbursement is not subject to any taxes, deductions or Vacation Pay.

6 ➤   For all other line items use the following instructions.

Calc. QHSF   Leave the ✓ in the Quebec Health Services Fund column even though Creative Wallpaper currently does not have employees in Quebec.

Calc. Vac.	There is no vacation pay on reimbursements. Leave the column unchecked.
Calc. QPIP	Leave the ✓ in the column Quebec Parental Insurance Plan. Creative Wallpaper currently does not have any employees in Quebec.
Calc. VRSP	Leave the ✓ in the column Quebec Voluntary Retirement Savings Plan. Creative Wallpaper currently does not have any employees in Quebec.
Track Quebec Tips	Do NOT change. Creative Wallpaper currently has no Quebec employees.

Payroll Deductions

1 ➤ Click the **Deductions** item in the left pane.

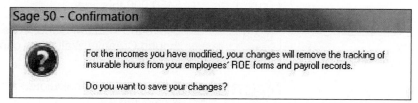

2 ➤ You will see the above confirmation window that confirms that the changes affect only the Reimbursement line that you changed and no others. Click **Yes.**

The column is ✓ checked if you calculate the deduction **after** calculating Tax.
The column is   unchecked if you calculate the deduction **before** calculating Tax.

Deduction	Deduct By	Deduct After Tax	Deduct After	Deduct After EI	Deduct After CPP/QPP	Deduct After EHT	Deduct After QHSF	Deduct After Vacation	Deduct After QPIP
Pension	Percent of Gr		✓	✓	✓	✓	✓	✓	✓
Union Dues	Amount		✓	✓	✓	✓	✓	✓	✓
Medical	Amount	✓	✓	✓	✓	✓	✓	✓	✓
Safety Shoes	Amount	✓	✓	✓	✓	✓	✓	✓	✓

Fig. 7-4: Payroll Deductions window after changes.

Deduct After Tax	Means that the Income Tax calculations are based on the amount of income an employee earns each pay period, less deductions allowed for Income Tax purposes.

3 ➤
Deduct After Tax	**Pension:** Triple-click on the **Amount** in the **Deduct by** column and select **Percent of Gross,** `Tab`. Pension can be a set amount per week (e.g., $65.00 per pay period) or a percentage of the employee's gross pay.

Uncheck the column beside **Pension** and **Union Dues** to be blank because these deductions are calculated before calculating Income Tax. Income tax is calculated on the Earned Income after these amounts are deducted.

Leave the ✓ in the columns beside **Medical** and **Safety Shoes.** Medical benefit cost and Safety Shoes are not allowable deductions for Income Tax purposes and are calculated and deducted after calculating Income Tax.

 This column is for Quebec. Leave the ✓ in the column even though Creative Wallpaper currently does not have any employees in Quebec.

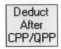 The deduction is calculated after the Employment Insurance amount is calculated.

 The deduction is calculated after the Canada Pension Plan/Quebec Pension Plan deduction amount is calculated.

 Employee Health Tax. Leave ✓ in column. Creative Wallpaper is currently exempt from this tax, as the Payroll will not exceed $450,000 this year.

 Leave the ✓ in the Quebec Health Services Fund column even though Creative Wallpaper currently does not have employees in Quebec.

 The deduction is calculated after the Vacation Pay amount is calculated.

Leave the ✓ in the column Quebec Parental Insurance Plan even though Creative Wallpaper currently does not have any employees in Quebec.

Payroll Taxes

1 ➤ In the left pane, click the **Taxes** item. Change the fields as shown.

EI Factor for new employees:	1.4
WSIB Rate for new employees:	0.41
EHT Factor:	0.0
QHSF Factor:	0.0

EI Factor — Current Federal Government law requires Creative Wallpaper, the employer, to contribute to EI based on an employee's EI payroll deduction times the factor **1.4**.

2 ➤ WSIB Rate — Workplace Safety and Insurance Board. Type **0.41** (zero dot 41). Premiums are paid by Creative Wallpaper based on a percentage of employees' gross earnings. Various industries pay various rates.

EHT Factor — Employee Health Tax. Do NOT change. Creative Wallpaper is exempt from this tax as the Payroll will not exceed $450,000 this year.

QHSF Factor — Do NOT change. Creative Wallpaper currently has no Quebec employees.

Payroll Entitlements

1 ➤ Click the **Entitlements** item in the left pane.

The number of hours in the work day:	8.00		
Default Entitlements:			
Name	Track Using % Hours Worked	Maximum Days	Clear Days at Year-end
Days 1	0.00	0.00	No
Days 2	0.00	0.00	No
Days 3	0.00	0.00	No
Days 4	0.00	0.00	No
Days 5	0.00	0.00	No

Note: You can change the entitlements for individual employees in their records.

Fig. 7-5: Payroll Ledger—Entitlements tab.

Some firms allow employees to accumulate sick days or leaves of absence based on the number of hours/days they have worked. The more hours worked, the more accumulated sick days or leaves of absence employees can have off with pay. Creative Wallpaper does not accumulate entitlement days. There is no exercise in the text for entitlements. Do NOT change.

Remittance (Payroll)

Payroll Remittance is being skipped at this time. You will return to Payroll Remittance in Exercise 7-5, after the linked accounts are selected.

This feature allows the software to calculate the amount of the remittance to the Receiver General for the previous month.

Job Categories

1 ➤ Click the **Job Category** item in the left pane.

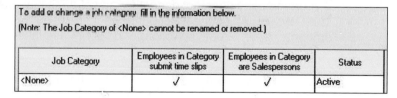

Job Category	Employees in Category submit time slips	Employees in Category are Salespersons	Status
<None>	✓	✓	Active

To add or change a job category fill in the information below.
(Note: The Job Category of <None> cannot be renamed or removed.)

www Job Categories would be used with the *Time & Billing Journal* (see Appendix 2015 S, *Time & Billing Journal* in your course materials at www.nelson.com/student) or when you want to classify employees working in various types of jobs. Wallpaper does not use this feature.

2 ➤ Click **OK** to save any changes in the Settings window and return to the Home window. You will return to the Settings window to set up the linked accounts in the next step.

Step 2: Setting Up Linked Accounts

The next step in the setup process is to select the **linked** accounts for the PAYROLL module. These accounts are the G/L accounts for which the entries will be automatically updated when entering data in the PAYROLL module. To link accounts, follow the procedure in the next exercise.

Exercise 7-4—Linking Accounts with PAYROLL

---

1 ➤ From the Home window, click **Setup, Settings,** in the left pane, click the ⊞ at **Payroll**. Then in the left pane, click the ⊞ at **Linked Accounts**, in the left pane click **Incomes** to display the Payroll Linked Accounts window.

2 ➤ **Set up** the Payroll Linked Accounts as shown in Fig. 7-6, click **Deductions** for Fig. 7-7, and click **Taxes** for Fig. 7-8.

When you process payroll transactions, these accounts are used as needed.

Principal Bank:	1010 Bank Account Chequing ▼	Advances & Loans:	1241 Loans Receivable ▼
Vac. Owed:	2300 Vacation Payable ▼		

Income	Linked Accounts	
Vac. Earned	5300 Wages Expense	
Regular	5300 Wages Expense	
Overtime 1	5308 Wages-Overtime Expense	
Overtime 2		
Salary	5302 Salaries Expense	
Commission	5304 Commissions Expense	
Reimburse	5395 Reimbursement Payroll Suspense	

Fig. 7-6: Payroll Linked Accounts—Incomes window.

Payroll cheques will be credited from the bank account defined at the top of the window, and employee loans (if any) will be applied against the LOANS RECEIVABLE account. Note: Creative Wallpaper has only temporary loans to employees, not advances on payroll.

Deduction	Linked Accounts	Payment Adjustment Account
Pension	2430 Pension Plan Payable	
Union Dues	2420 Union Dues Payable	
Medical	2440 Medical Plan Payable	
Safety Shoes	2450 Safety Shoes Payable	

Fig. 7-7: Payroll Linked Accounts—Deductions window.

If your company does not deduct for any of the items, the field should be left blank. The Payment Adjustment Accounts would be used for minor discrepancies in amounts. *Note*: Creative Wallpaper does not use these accounts.

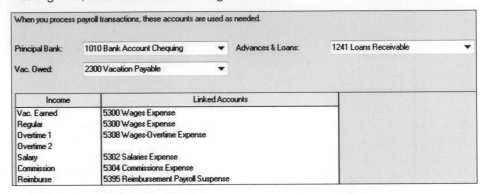

Fig. 7-8: Payroll Linked Accounts—Taxes window.

The **Payables** section contains the Balance Sheet accounts that employee deductions are posted to, which in turn, must be remitted on the employee's behalf to the Federal Government (EI, CPP, Tax), union, WCB (WSIB in Ontario), etc.

The **Expense** section contains the Income Statement expense accounts to which the company-related payroll expenses are charged.

The Payments Adjustments account for EI is not used in this chapter.

Notice that there are no Linked accounts for the Quebec Payables and Quebec Expenses, as the company currently has no Quebec employees.

Payroll User-Defined Expenses

Fig. 7-9: Payroll Linked Accounts—User-Defined Expenses window.

The User-Defined Expenses and Payable accounts would be used when the company pays for various benefits (insurance, dental benefits, etc.) and/or any payment adjustment. Creative Wallpaper does not use this feature.

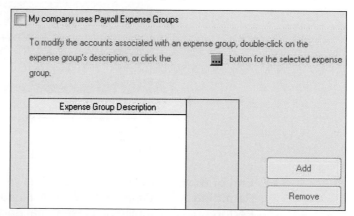

Fig. 7-10: Payroll Linked Accounts—Expense Groups window.

The Payroll Expense Groups would be used when you want to report the same employees' payroll expenses at different locations, job categories, different administration departments, etc. There is no exercise for this feature.

3 ➤ Click **OK** when complete to exit to the Home window.

The next step in the setup process is to select the **Payroll Remittance Linked accounts** for the EMPLOYEES & PAYROLL module. These accounts are the G/L accounts for which the entries will be automatically updated when entering data in the EMPLOYEES & PAYROLL module. To link remittance accounts, follow the procedure in the next exercise.

Exercise 7-5—Linking PAYROLL Remittance Accounts

1 ➤ From the Home window, click **Setup, Settings,** click the **+** at **Payroll,** and click **Remittance**. Set up the Remittance as shown.

For each remittance, select the remittance vendor receiving your payment and how often the payments are remitted. You also need to enter the last day of your next remitting period which will be updated based on the remitting frequency.

Remittance	Remittance Vendor	Remitting Frequency	End of Next Remitting Period
EI	Receiver General - Payroll Taxes	Monthly	Jan 01, 2019
CPP	Receiver General - Payroll Taxes	Monthly	Jan 01, 2019
Tax	Receiver General - Payroll Taxes	Monthly	Jan 01, 2019
WSIB	Workplace Safety & Insurance Boa	Monthly	Jan 01, 2019
Pension	Accredited Pension Agency	Monthly	Jan 01, 2019
Union Dues	Union Local #569	Monthly	Jan 01, 2019
Medical	London Medical Group	Monthly	Jan 01, 2019
Safety Shoes			

2 ➤ EI Double-click the **Remittance Vendor** item in the column.

3 ➤ Remittance Vendor Double-click the column, and select the Vendors as shown. *Note:* Do NOT set up Safety Shoes as a Remittance Vendor, as Safety Shoes are paid for by the company and the company is reimbursed by the employee. The Payroll Liability amounts are collected from the employees (and employer for EI, CPP, and Income Tax) and are remitted to the appropriate authority. See Exercise 7-13 Recording Withholdings Payment.

4 ➤ Remitting Frequency Double-click in the column, and select the frequency as shown. It is assumed that Creative Wallpaper remits payments monthly.

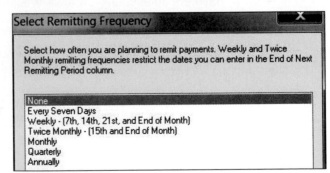

5 ➤ End of Next Remitting Period Select the date as shown. In January 2019, Creative Wallpaper will remit various December 31, 2018 remittances (see Trial Balance for amounts). The end of the previous period Dec 31, 2018 cannot be accessed.

Note: There is no Remittance Vendor for Safety Shoes. The deduction for Safety shoes is used to reduce General Ledger account 2450 Safety Shoes Payable.

You will use this feature and amounts in Exercise 7-13, when you are remitting Payroll amounts to the Receiver General. (See side note box.)

> Care must be taken if you are going to have cheques issued on End of Next Remitting Period Date. The amounts recorded are the amounts in the converted Trial Balance before any payroll entries.

The PAYROLL module defaults are complete.

6 ➤ Click **OK** to return to the **Home** window.

	This would be a good time to do a backup.

Payroll Conversion

Conversion in this chapter means changing from a manual payroll system to a system using the Sage 50 Accounting program. It can also mean converting from another computerized software to Sage 50 Accounting. All personnel records at a given time, usually after month-end, will be added to the PAYROLL module.

The Payroll Department must balance all payroll earnings, deductions, and liability accounts in the manual General Ledger system with the Sage 50 Accounting personnel data information. When all the records have been entered and balanced, the PAYROLL module can be turned to **Ready** and payroll transactions can be entered.

1 ➤ Click the **EMPLOYEES & PAYROLL** module, click the **Paycheques** icon before turning the PAYROLL module to **Ready**. You will then receive this warning message.

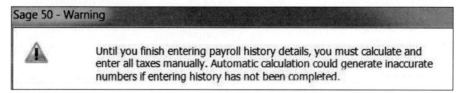

Sage 50 - Warning

> Until you finish entering payroll history details, you must calculate and enter all taxes manually. Automatic calculation could generate inaccurate numbers if entering history has not been completed.

2 ➤ Click **OK**.

3 ➤ The icons (9th from left) *Calculate taxes automatically* and (10th from left) *Enter taxes manually* are greyed out and cannot be activated. **(No employee information has been entered; therefore, these options are not available at this time.)**

4 ➤ Click the X button to cancel the Payroll Journal and return to the Home window.

Step 3: Entering Employee Payroll Information

Employee names, personal information, payroll balance, and amounts deducted from employees during the current year will be entered next.

Creative Wallpaper is converting at January 1, the beginning of a calendar year, and all employee balances of CPP, EI, Income Tax, Taxable Benefits, etc., except for vacation pay owed, would be 0 (nil). This will allow payroll transaction information to be accumulated and used in preparing T4 slips at the end of 2019.

An example of the employee payroll information that would be entered if the conversion took place at June 30 is shown at the end of the chapter.

Before the EMPLOYEES & PAYROLL module can be used, employee personal information must be set up, and payroll account dollar value information added by using the **History** option.

Exercise 7-6—Entering Employee PAYROLL Information

You can also type **David, Doreen** and Sage 50 Accounting will print the last name (DAVID) in capitals on the T4s as long as there is a comma between the names.

Creating Individual Employee Ledgers

1 ➤ From the Home window, **click Setup, Setup Guide, Employees** and enter the following information.

   Employee   DAVID, Doreen

   Enter Employee surname first (last name in CAPITAL letters); i.e., **DAVID,** then a comma, then the first name **Doreen**. (See side note box.)

Last name first in CAPITAL letters (required by Canada Revenue Agency [CRA]). The program prints the Last Name (Surname) in CAPITAL letters on the T4 slip.

---

* If you have difficulty entering date information as needed (your system data settings display day, month, and year), enter date information in step 3. Double-click the **birth dates** and **hire dates** before you return to the setup guide to add the next employee.

Birth date*	Apr 26, 1957
Tax Table	Ontario
Pay periods per year	26
SIN	456 812 635
Hire Date*	Mar 14, 1998
Street 1	17 Huron Street
City	London
Province	Ontario
Postal	N5Y 1Z5

2 ➤ Double-click on the **Employee Name** to display the Employees window. This window is similar to the Vendors and Customers windows.

3 ➤ Enter the Phone 1 information shown in Fig. 7-11, **Personal** Information.

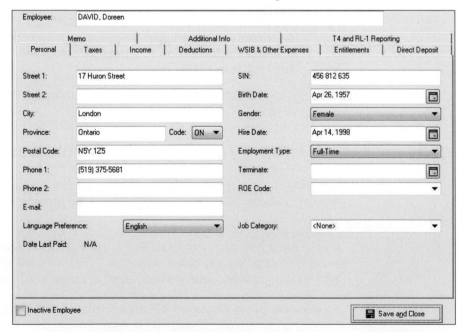

Fig. 7-11: Payroll Ledger window—Personal tab completed.

SIN   An Invalid Entry warning box will appear if you type an invalid SIN number, when you click Close or Save and Close.

Birth Date	This field is used by Sage 50 Accounting to deduct CPP if the employee is 18 years or older. It is faster if you type the date (e.g., **042657**, 04/26/1957 or apr26 57). Using the calendar feature, you could click on the **calendar**, click on **January**, and a drop-down menu appears. Select the appropriate month. Click on **2019**; a 📅 appears. Click the up or down button to move to the appropriate year, and select the appropriate day. Using the calendar feature to go back years takes a little more time.
Gender	There are 3 choices. Unknown, Female or Male. Select **Female**.
Hire Date	Type **Apr 14, 1998**.
Employment Type	Full-Time or Part-time. Select **Full-Time**.
Terminate	Leave blank. This date field would be used when the employee leaves the company.
ROE Code	Do NOT change. If you click the ▾ a list of Record of Employment termination codes appears.
Job Category	Leave blank. This field would be used to identify job categories identified by management. Employees could be sorted for various reports. Creative Wallpaper does not use this feature.
Date Last Paid	On the bottom left side of the Payroll ledger window you will see Date Last Paid N/A . The area to the right will automatically show date information after each pay is issued.
Inactive Employee	The ☐ Inactive Employee box would be checked (✓) if you have an employee who has temporarily left the firm (because of layoff, leave of absence, vacation, etc.) or has left the firm and is not expected to return.

4 ➤ When your window resembles Fig. 7-11, click the **Taxes** tab.

Taxes

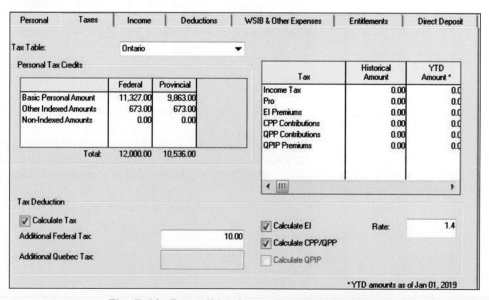

Fig. 7-12: Payroll Ledger—Taxes completed.

5 ➤ Complete the fields as indicated in Fig. 7-12.

Tax Table	Click the ▾ arrow to see the other choices. Do NOT change. (Doreen works and is taxed in Ontario.)

Personal Tax Credits

Basic Personal Amount	Federal column **11,327.00** (amount from their TD-1 Personal Tax Credits Return form). This is the amount of income for the year that a person does not need to pay Federal Income Tax on. This allows the program to determine the income tax to be deducted from each employee.
Other Indexed Amounts	Federal Claim **673.00**. This is the amount of additional Federal Tax Credits that can be claimed by this person. This amount may be different from the Basic Federal claim. This will not be discussed in this text.
Provincial Amount	**9,863.00** The amount from TD1ON (Ontario). This is the amount of income for the year that a person does not need to pay Provincial Income Tax on. Ontario has its own tax rates for the Provincial Income Tax calculation.
Other Indexed Amounts	Provincial claim **673.00**. This is the amount of the additional Provincial Tax credits that can be claimed by this person.
Non-Indexed Amounts	Additional amounts that may be claimed by an individual. This will not be discussed in this text.
Calculate Tax	If you have employees whose total income will be less than their total claim amount on their TD-1, you can turn off the tax calculation in their employment record (remove the ✓). None of the employees will earn less than the TD-1 amount, therefore leave the box ✓.
Additional Federal Tax	This field will allow the firm to deduct extra income tax based on requests from employees. Doreen David has an extra **$10.00** for income tax deducted each pay period.
Calculate EI	✓ indicates that Doreen is eligible for Employment Insurance benefits.
Rate	Current Federal Government law requires Creative Wallpaper, the employer, to contribute to EI based on an employee's EI payroll deduction times the factor **1.4**.
Calculate CPP/QPP	The ✓ would be removed if the employee was receiving a disability pension and works on a full- or part-time basis. It also applies to employees who are receiving Canada Pension. Effective Jan 01, 2012, individuals may also contribute to the Canada Pension Plan (CPP) while they are collecting CPP benefits.
*YTD amounts as of Jan 01, 2019	This will be discussed at the end of step 7.

6 ➤ When your window resembles Fig. 7-12, click the **Income** tab.

Income

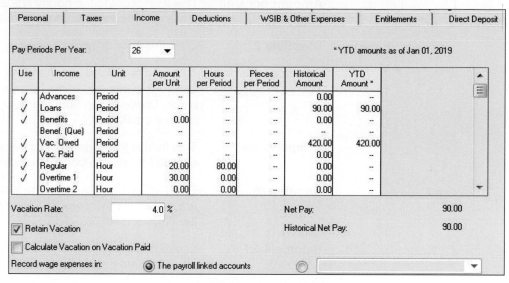

> *i* All Historical and YTD amounts—Taxes, Income, and Deductions—will be 0.00, except for Loans 90.00 and Vacation Pay Owed 420.00, which are recorded at step 7. (The conversion of payroll information for Creative Wallpaper takes place at the beginning of the calendar year.)

Fig. 7-13: Income tab completed.

7 ➤ Complete the fields as indicated in Fig. 7-13. (See side note box.)

Pay Periods Per Year	**26** Doreen is paid bi-weekly.
Use	A ✓ would be in the field when the Income line is used.
Loans Historical Amount	**90.00** The amount that remains to be repaid by an employee for a payroll loan. When you enter 90.00 in the field, the YTD * amount changes and cannot be amended unless the Historical amount is changed.
Benefits	Do NOT change. $ value benefits; e.g., additional life insurance, are given to employees in addition to wages. There are no such benefits for Creative Wallpaper employees.
Benef. (Que)	This field would be for taxable benefits for Quebec employees. The company has no employees in Quebec.
Historical Amount **Vac. Owed**	**420.00** The accumulated amount of Vacation Pay owed to the employee for vacation from previous calendar year 2018. The YTD * amount changes and cannot be amended unless the Historical amount is changed.
Vac. Paid	Do NOT change. This would be the amount the employee has received in vacation pay this current calendar year.
Regular Amount Per Unit	**20.00** This field records the hourly wage rate that is paid to the employee in the current calendar year. This number will show up as a default when you enter the PAYROLL module to pay the employee.
Regular Hours Per Period	**80.00** This field records the normal weekly hours (two week period) that the employee works in the current calendar year. This number will show up as a default when you enter the PAYROLL module to pay the employee. (See side note box.)

> *i* **Hours Per Period** for employees is used for Employment Insurance eligibility and the Record of Employment form.

Overtime 1 Amount per Unit	**30.00**. You may need to scroll down to see this field. This field records the hourly wage rate that is paid to the employee for each hour of overtime.
Overtime 2	Overtime 2 fields are not used by Creative Wallpaper.
Salary per period	This field is lower down in the window. Use the down slider ▼ to see additional Income fields. Leave this field blank. Doreen is an hourly employee and does not receive a salary.
Commission	This field is lower down in the window. Shows the income earned for commission in the current calendar year.
Reimburse	This field is lower down in the window. Shows the amount of reimbursement the employee has received in the current calendar year.
Income 4-20	Leave this field blank. Creative Wallpaper does not use other Income categories.
Vacation Rate % field	Type **4.0**, [Tab].
Retain Vacation	The box would be (✓) to accumulate vacation pay. Doreen's vacation pay is 4% of her gross pay, and it accumulates week by week until she takes a vacation. Vacation paid to an employee will be shown in Exercise 7-15. If you uncheck the **Retain** field, the vacation pay will be added to each paycheque. The employee would receive no vacation pay when going on vacation. The employee would have received it on a continual basis. Do NOT uncheck.
Calculate Vacation on Vacation paid	Do NOT change the default as Ontario does not calculate vacation pay on vacation pay amounts paid to employees.
Record wage expenses in	Do NOT change the default. The button to the right of the Payroll linked accounts would be clicked if the wages for an employee were to be charged to an account that was not identified on the Linked accounts—Incomes window (see Fig. 7-13). All employees use the Payroll Linked account button.
Net Pay	This field, calculated automatically by Sage 50 Accounting, is the gross pay minus deductions. The 90.00 displayed is the outstanding payroll loan. You cannot change this field.
Historical Net Pay	This field, calculated automatically by Sage 50 Accounting, is the gross pay minus deductions. The 90.00 displayed is the outstanding payroll loan. You cannot change this field.
*YTD amounts as of Jan 01, 2019	This * refers to the column YTD * Amount. The date will advance as the session changes. (e.g., *YTD amounts as of Jan 01, 2019).

8 ➤ When your window resembles Fig. 7-13, click the **Deductions** tab.

Deductions

Personal	Taxes	Income	Deductions	WSIB & Other Expenses	Entitlements	Direct Deposit

Use	Deduction	Amount per Pay Period	Percentage per Pay Period	Historical Amount	YTD Amount *		▲
✓	Pension	--	4.0000	0.00	--		≣
✓	Union Dues	20.00	--	0.00	--		
✓	Medical	24.00	--	0.00	--		
✓	Safety Shoes	16.00	--	0.00	--		

Fig. 7-14: Payroll Ledger—Deductions tab.

9 ➤ Complete the fields as indicated in Fig. 7-14.

Amounts entered in this window will be used by Sage 50 Accounting to calculate net pay for each pay date. If necessary, the amounts may be edited on the paycheque at the time the pay is entered.

Pension	**4.0000** Full-time employees contribute 4% of gross salary, wages and/or commission to a registered pension plan.
Union Dues	**20.00** The amount taken from employees', bi-weekly pay for Union dues. It is a set amount that does not fluctuate based on income.
Medical	**24.00** The amount the employee pays, which is 100% of the cost for an extended medical and dental plan.
Safety Shoes	**16.00** Effective January 2, the amount Doreen will have deducted from each bi-weekly pay, to pay back $94.00 for new safety shoes. The shoes have been ordered.
Deductions 5-20	Do NOT change. Creative Wallpaper does not use these fields. These fields could be used for other deductions the employee and the firm agree upon; e.g., United Way, other charitable donations.
Historical Amount	There are no Historical amounts to be recorded.

10 ➤ When your window resembles Fig. 7-14, click **WSIB & Other Expenses** tab.

WSIB & User-Defined Expenses

Personal	Taxes	Income	Deductions	WSIB & Other Expenses	Entitlements	Direct Deposit

WSIB

WSIB Rate: 0.41 %

User-Defined Expenses

Expense	Amt. per Period	Historical Amount	YTD Amount *
User Exp 1	0.00	0.00	0.0

🛈 When a new employee is created, the WSIB current default rate is entered by Sage 50 Accounting. When the WSIB rate changes, you must change the rate in every employee's ledger to the new rate.

WSIB Rate	As shown before, the rate is 0.41 (see side note box).
User-Defined Expenses	As shown previously, these fields are not used by Creative Wallpaper.

Entitlements

11 ➤ Click **Entitlements** tab.

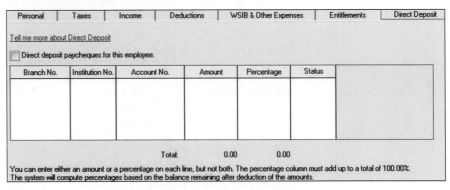

This window is similar to Fig. 7-5, but it now contains Historical Days & Net Days Accrued (Net days Accrued column partially hidden). No changes required.

Direct Deposit

12 ➤ Click **Direct Deposit** tab.

Personal	Taxes	Income	Deductions	WSIB & Other Expenses	Entitlements	Direct Deposit

Tell me more about Direct Deposit

☐ Direct deposit paycheques for this employee.

Branch No.	Institution No.	Account No.	Amount	Percentage	Status	

Total: 0.00   0.00

You can enter either an amount or a percentage on each line, but not both. The percentage column must add up to a total of 100.00%. The system will compute percentages based on the balance remaining after deduction of the amounts.

Fig. 7-15: Payroll Ledger—Direct Deposit tab.

To use this feature, you must arrange with your bank to allow direct deposits of employees' net pay to one or more employee bank accounts. The bank charges for this feature.

Creative Wallpaper gives each employee a cheque for their pay and does not use this feature.

Memo

13 ➤ Click the **Memo** tab.

You may enter any personal information you may want to record about the employee, such as name and number to call in case of an emergency. See step 14 for additional fields. The memo notes can also display in the Daily Business Manager. Do NOT change.

Additional Information

14 ➤ Click the **Additional Info** tab. These fields can be used to keep personal information about the employee, similar to what was discussed at step 13. Some of the fields could be used to record wage increase dates, performance review date, etc. Refer to Appendix 2015 Q, *Names Fields* in your course materials at www.nelson.com/student.

www

15 ➤ **Field 1:** Type **Payroll Loan $30.00** and click (✓) the Display Info box on the right. When the employee is chosen for a payroll transaction, an information window will appear. Click the **T4 & RL-1 Reporting** tab.

T4 & RL-1 Reporting

Memo	Additional Info	T4 and RL-1 Reporting
	Current Year: 2019	Historical Amounts
EI Ins. Earnings:	0.00	0.00
Pensionable Earnings:	0.00	0.00
QPIP Ins. Earnings:	0.00	0.00
RPP/DPSP Reg. No:	589896	
Pension Adjustment:	0.00	
T4 Emp. Code:	▼	
E-file Information	Current Year: 2019	
T4 E-file Submission ID:		
T4 Date of Transmission:		
RL-1 E-file Slip No.:		
RL-1 Date of Transmission:		

	EI Ins. Earnings (Historical)	This field would record EI Insurable Earnings when employee records are being converted during the year.
	Pensionable Earnings (Historical)	This field reports the Pensionable earnings that are recorded under the CPP plan for the current year.
16 ➤	**RPP/DPSP Reg. No.**	Type **589896**. This is the Registered Pension Plan number registered with the Federal Government.
	Pension Adjustment	This field would contain a value for a Pension adjustment that reduces the RRSP deduction limit of persons who are in a company-sponsored registered pension plan. This topic is not discussed in this text.
	E-file Information	These fields would contain information if the company sent T4 and/or Quebec RL-1E forms over the Internet to the government. Do NOT change.

17 ➤   Click the $\boxed{\text{Save and Close}}$ button to save the Payroll Ledger information for Doreen David.

18 ➤   Use the same method as above to **enter employee payroll information for the other active employees**, MCINTYRE, Sharon, SINGH, Gurjeet, and CURRIE, Jordan as shown in Fig. 7-16 which follows.

When you finish making changes to the individual employee's historical data, and the balances in the Employee Ledger balance with the General Ledger, you may receive this message:

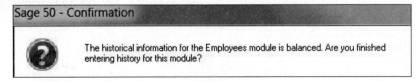

> **Sage 50 - Confirmation**
>
> The historical information for the Employees module is balanced. Are you finished entering history for this module?

19 ➤   If you see this Confirmation, click **No** and $\boxed{\text{X}}$ to exit to the Employees window.

20 ➤   When you are finished entering all the employees, the Gross YTD and Deductions YTD should all be 0.00 because you have not paid the employees in the current calendar year. The Net YTD displays $90 for Doreen David, as this is the outstanding Payroll Loan she received (see Exercise 7-6, Fig. 7-13).

21 ➤   When finished, **Exit** to the Home window.

Employee	SINGH, Gurjeet	MCINTYRE, Sharon	CURRIE, Jordan *
Birth Date	Apr 02, 1952	May 20, 1966	Dec 11, 1953
Tax Table	Ontario	Ontario	Ontario
Pay Periods per year	24	24	26
SIN (No spaces)	445 678 907	623 148 392	719 983 256
Hire Date	Aug 18, 1997	Aug 06, 1990	Feb 12, 1989
Street 1	6342 Fanshawe Park Rd	753 Regent Street	2132 Maitland Street
City	London	London	London
Province	Ontario	Ontario	Ontario
Postal	N6G 2T6	N5Y 7P6	N5Y 6B7
Personal Tab			
Phone 1	519 555-1212	519 826-2566	519 355-1269
Gender	Female	Female	Female
Employment Type	Full-Time	Full-Time	Full-Time
Taxes Tab			
Tax Table	Ontario	Ontario	Ontario
Personal Tax Credits			
Basic Federal	11,327.00	11,327.00	11,327.00
Other Indexed Amounts	173.00	250.00	1,036.00
Basic Provincial	9,863.00	9,863.00	9,863.00
Other Indexed Amounts	173.00	250.00	1,036.00
Additional Fed Tax	0.00	0.00	0.00
Calculate EI Rate	✓ 1.4	✓ 1.4	✓ 1.4
Calculate CPP/QPP	✓	✓	✓
Income Tab			
Historical Loan	0.00	0.00	0.00
Benefits	0.00	0.00	0.00
Vacation Owed	0.00	0.00	480.00
Regular Amount per unit *			0.00
Hours per period			0.00
Overtime 1 (per hour)			0.00
Salary	2,500.00, Hours 80	2,000.00, Hours 80	
Commission			0.00 Hours 0.00
Pay periods	24	24	26
Retain Vacation	No	No	✓ 4.0
Deductions Tab			
Pension	4.0	4.0	4.0
Union Dues			20.00
Medical	24.00	24.00	24.00
Safety Shoes	0.00	0.00	0.00
WSIB Tab			
WSIB Rate	0.41	0.41	0.41
T-4 Reporting			
RPP/DPSP Reg. No.	589896	589896	589896

Fig. 7-16: Creative Wallpaper Employees PAYROLL Information.

* Note: CURRIE, Jordan is a commission sales person and does not receive an hourly wage.

Reviewing Related Payroll—G/L Balances

The history values entered for all employees must be equal to certain accounts in the General Ledger.

1 ➤ **Display or print the Trial Balance as at January 2, 2019**. This should agree with Fig. 7-2 except for the reversing entry for Wages Expense and Commissions Expense, which now have a credit balance, and Accrued Payroll Payable is 0.00.

Review the balances for the following payable accounts:

> **2300 Vacation Payable**
> **2310 EI Payable**
> **2320 CPP Payable**
> **2330 Income Tax Payable**
> **2420 Union Dues Payable**
> **2460 WSIB Payable**

These accounts represent the employee deductions during December 2018 and the company portion of the same costs, where applicable (required by law), during the month of December 2018.

The asset 1241 LOANS RECEIVABLE is $90.00, which is equal to Doreen David's outstanding balance, and will reduce until repaid. A company policy is to lend individual employees up to $600.00 for emergencies. The amount must be repaid with $30.00 or $45.00 installments each payday.

2 ➤ **Display the Balance Sheet at January 2, 2019** to verify the asset and payable amounts.

Step 4: Setting the PAYROLL Module to Ready

The last step is to set the module to **Ready**. It is important to back up your data files before setting a module to Ready. Once the modules are made **Ready**, you cannot go back to make changes to historical information.

Are you ready to make PAYROLL Ready?

Exercise 7-7—Setting PAYROLL to Ready

1 ➤ **Back up** your data files now. Update your logbook, too.

2 ➤ From the menu bar, click **History**, **Enter Historical Information** ▶ and click ✓ **Payroll**.

This is an example of a warning message (see side note box).

ⓘ A warning message will be displayed if the balances of the Employees Ledger do not match the G/L linked accounts Vacation Payable and Loans Receivable. No warning message is displayed for the other linked accounts should any balances be different. You must review the balances carefully yourself.

Sage 50 - Checking database

Checking Employees...
Your Employees' vacation pay owed does not equal the current balance of account 2300 Vacation Payable.
$420.00	Total Vacation Owed to Employees
$900.00	Current Balance of 2300 Vacation Payable
-$480.00	Difference

Either your Employees' historical information or the opening balance of account 2300 Vacation Payable, or both, is incorrect.

If the linked accounts balances are correct, you will receive a standard message to back up data files before proceeding.

Remember to **Backup** before clicking Proceed to turn the PAYROLL module to **Ready**.

3 ➤ Click **Proceed**.

The PAYROLL module is ready to use for January 2019 and future transactions. Payroll Journal icons may now be selected.

Start here if your instructor suggests that you use the data file **Wallpaper2**.

Slideshow 7B—Processing PAYROLL Transactions will help you better understand the tasks relating to PAYROLL transactions. Run it now.

Entering EMPLOYEE Transactions

The rule in setting the Session Date in the PAYROLL module is different from other modules. The PAYROLL module will record the session date as the processing date regardless of the Period Ending date you record. Sage 50 Accounting uses the Session Date to determine which tax table to use.

The tax tables change according to government regulations (Sage 50 Accounting provides software updates). As mentioned above, you may enter a Period ending date that is different from the Session Date, but the session date is posted. The limitation is the fiscal year. It is possible to back-date cheques in the PAYROLL module to previous months and also to a previous year if a system setting is changed. However, the Session Date is still considered the date of posting.

For the PAYROLL module, therefore, advance the Session Date for each work session.

The Creative Wallpaper store and office were closed for New Year celebrations and did not reopen until January 2.

Entering a New Employee

Jan 02, 2019 You will now enter your own personal information as a new employee who will work part-time for the first 3 months.

Exercise 7-8—Creating a New Employee Ledger

---

1 ➤ Enter a new employee account (see Exercise 7-6 for reference), using your name. In order to keep the window displays of existing employees and cheque numbers in proper sequence, **type your name with an A- before your actual last name** (e.g., A-BROWN, Wakina). Enter the rest of the profile as follows:

Personal

Employee Name	A-YOUR LAST NAME, First Name
Birth Date	Jul 08, 1976
Tax Table	Ontario
Pay Periods	26
SIN	712 336 106
Hire Date	Jan 02, 2019
Street 1	690 Barker Street
City	London
Province	Ontario
Postal code	N5Y 8P3
Phone 1	519 841-5045
Gender	Select your gender
Employment Type	Part-Time

Taxes

Tax Table	Ontario
Personal Tax Credits Basic Federal	11,327.00
Other Indexed Amounts	1,010.00
Personal Tax Credits Basic Provincial	9,863.00
Other Indexed Amounts	1,010.00
Calculate EI, Rate	✓ 1.4
Calculate CPP/QPP	✓

Income

Regular Per Hour	14.00	40 hours
Overtime Per Hour	0.00	0
Retain Vacation	✓ 4.0	

Deductions

Pension*	0.00	*only full-time staff belong to
Union	20.00	the Pension Plan and have
Medical*	0.00	medical benefits.

WSIB & Other

WSIB Rate	0.41

Fig. 7-17: YOUR Name Information.

2 ➤ Click **Save** to return to the Home window.

Payroll for Pay Period Ending Jan 11, 2019

1 ➤ Advance the Session date to **Jan 11, 2019**.

The payroll data may be entered in two different ways:

a) You may use the **Paycheques** icon to pay one employee at a time.

b) You may use the **Payroll Cheque Run** icon to pay multiple employees at the same time.

In Exercise 7-9, you will use the **Payroll Cheque Run**, method **b**, to pay employees.

In Exercise 7-10, you will use method **a**, to pay one employee at a time.

Issuing Paycheques

At payroll preparation time, you would receive information from the manager or supervisor on memos or time cards similar to the following:

EMPLOYEE TIME SHEET   200

Date:___Jan. 11, 2019_____   Cheque No.

Employee Name:___A-Your LAST NAME, First Name___   Employee #___5___

Regular Hours	Overtime Hours	Commission Hours	Commission Amount	Deductions		Other Information
26	None	None		Pension	No	
				Union Dues	$20.00	

Hint: Net Pay $325.81

Approved by:_ *G. S.* _

EMPLOYEE TIME SHEET   201

Date:___Jan. 11, 2019_____   Cheque No.

Employee Name:_____Doreen David_____   Employee #___2__

Regular Hours	Overtime Hours	Commission Hours	Commission Amount	Deductions		Other Information
80	2	None		Pension	$ 66.40	Loan Repaid $30.00
				Union Dues	20.00	
				Medical	24.00	
				Safety Shoes	16.00	

Hint: Net Pay $1,170.41

Approved by:_ *G. S.* _

Jordan Currie's Employee Time sheet is not available at this time. A cheque will be issued later.

Exercise 7-9—Issuing Paycheques (Payroll Cheque Run)

To reduce paper usage, you do NOT need to print paycheques for any exercise in this chapter. An example of what will print on the preprinted cheques appears in Fig. 7-19.

1 ➤ To issue bi-weekly paycheques to Doreen David and yourself, click the **Payroll Cheque Run** icon. A Payroll Run Journal window, similar to the following, will appear.

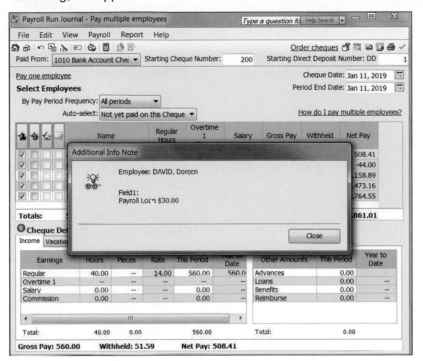

Fig. 7-18: Payroll Cheque Run Journal, before changes.

2 ➤ The Additional Info box advising you of the loan to be repaid by Doreen is seen in the middle of the window. Click **Close**.

Your A-LAST NAME, First name will show as the first employee in the Employee column.

Starting Cheque Number: 200 Payroll and vendor cheques to be issued will start with this number. (See side note box.) Do NOT change.

Starting Direct Deposit Number: DD   Do NOT change. Creative Wallpaper does not use the Direct Deposit feature of Sage 50 Accounting.

Pay one employee If only one employee is to be paid on this cheque run, you could use this option to move to the Payroll Journal. See Exercise 7-10.

Cheque Date   The payroll is being paid today, Jan 11. Do NOT change. This is the date that will be printed on the cheque and the date the payroll entry will get posted to the General Ledger. Sage 50 Accounting will allow you to issue pre- and post-dated cheques. Creative Wallpaper does not use this feature.

If there were an error printing the cheques, you could use this icon to renumber the cheques, and a message box would inform you that the summary report and cheques will need to be reprinted.

Period End date	The employees are being paid to this date. Do NOT change.
	Note that a ✓ is shown for all employees to be paid on this pay date.

3 ➤   By Pay Period   Click the ▼ select **26**, [Tab] to **Auto-Select**.
        Frequency   (Note that only 3 employees are being paid on this pay
                           date). MCINTYRE and SINGH are not ✓, as they are paid
                           twice a month. Do NOT change the ✓ for Jordan Currie.
                           This will be explained later.

                           You may see the following confirmation.

Auto-select

4 ➤ [Not yet paid on this Cheque Date ▼] This option would be
used for a group who are paid 52, 24, 26 times per year,
etc. Although individual paycheques could be paid from the
Payroll Cheque Run, Creative Wallpaper uses the Payroll
Journal to pay individual paycheques. See Exercise 7-10.

[All for this Cheque Date ▼] This option would be
used when all employees are paid on this pay period
frequency.

[All Employees ▼] This option would be used
when you select all employees regardless of the pay period
frequency. You can select individual employees to be paid.

5 ➤ Move your mouse pointer and position it above [⊞⊞⊞⊞]. Look at the
Payroll Run Journal status bar as you move your mouse.

   Allows you to choose which employee is to be paid this pay date.

   Allows you to choose which employee cheque will be printed in
        this cheque run.

   Allows you to choose which employee payroll information will be e-
        mailed on this cheque run. Creative Wallpaper does not use this
        feature.

   Allows you to identify which employee will be paid by Direct Deposit.
        Creative Wallpaper does not use this feature. (See side note box.)

6 ➤ Select [Not yet paid on this Cheque Date ▼] .

> **ℹ️** A PAYROLL Direct Deposit Business Service is included with the Premium software that will deposit the net pay directly to the employee's bank account. There would be a setup and additional bank charges for using this module. This text does not have an exercise for using this special feature.

The Payroll Cheque Run feature assumes that default employee hours recorded in
the Income tab window (Fig. 7-18) are correct. If an employee has worked overtime
or has reduced hours, then the hourly Income fields need to be updated.

You are going to change the hours for A-Your LAST NAME, First name from 40 Regular hours to 26 as follows:

7 ➤   Regular Hours   In the top section for A-YOUR LAST NAME, First name, change 40.00 to **26.00**, [Tab]. The Gross Pay field will change to 364.00, and the Net Pay will change to 325.81.

The bottom Payroll Detail Income tab window displays as shown next.

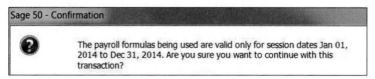

Cheque Details - A-YOUR LAST NAME, First Name

Income | Vacation | Deductions | Taxes | Entitlements

Earnings	Hours	Pieces	Rate	This Period	Year to Date	Other Amounts	This Period	Year to Date
Regular	26.00	--	14.00	364.00	364.00	Advances	0.00	--
Overtime 1	--	--	--	--	--	Loans	0.00	--
Salary	0.00	--	--	0.00	--	Benefits	0.00	--
Commission	0.00	--	--	0.00	--	Reimburse	0.00	--
Total:	26.00	0.00		364.00		Total:	0.00	

Gross Pay: 364.00   **Withheld: 38.19**   **Net Pay: 325.81**

8 ➤   Click on the **Name** column line for DAVID, Doreen.

Overtime 1, Hours column, type **2**, [Tab]. The Net Pay changes to 1,200.41

9 ➤   This Period   In the lower section right side, at Loans, type **-30.00** (negative) to reduce the loan [Tab]. Notice the 60.00 Year to Date amount remaining to be paid on the loan.

Other Amounts	This Period	Year to Date
Advances	0.00	--
Loans	-30.00	60.00

The Net Pay changes to 1,170.41.

10 ➤   Click **Report**, on the menu bar. Three different reports are listed.

11 ➤   Click **Print Payroll Cheque Run Summary**, the following message box appears.

Sage 50 - Confirmation

(?)   The payroll formulas being used are valid only for session dates Jan 01, 2014 to Dec 31, 2014. Are you sure you want to continue with this transaction?

This message advises you that the tax tables used in this module to create paycheques are valid for dates between Jan 1, 2014 to Dec 31, 2014.

If you do not use the same Sage 50 Accounting software, version 2015 version 1, then the tax tables for the period (e.g., Jan 1, 2014 to Dec 31, 2014), may calculate different amounts from the solutions provided with this text for Canada Pension (CPP), Employment Insurance (EI) and Income Tax.

12 ➤   Although we are using a 2019 data file, click **Yes** to accept the formulas. The dates in the previous confirmation window should be the same.

Payroll journal entries are part of one entry (e.g., J2) for display purposes. Each entry will be posted separately.

CURRIE, Jordan will not display in the Payroll Cheque Summary report as the amount is a debit (negative pay) to the BANK account and cannot be posted.

A new warning message appears:

> **Sage 50 - Confirmation**
>
> Negative cheques will not be posted. Do you want to continue printing the direct deposit stub summary?

This message informs you that an employee (Jordan) has a negative net pay (deductions but no income recorded) and cannot be posted in the Payroll Cheque Run. As discussed earlier, you will issue a paycheque to Jordan later in Exercise 7-10. (See side note box.)

13 ➤ Click **NO** to continue. The Summary report would print a copy of the cheque stubs (pay stubs) that the employees will receive. You and/or a supervisor would review the payroll amounts to verify that they are reasonable and approve the payment. You will verify this to the display. *Hint*: Boxes in the Employee's Time Sheet will advise you of the net pay amounts that are considered correct for the 2015 Release 0 of the Payroll formulas.

14 ➤ Click **Report, Display Payroll Journal Entry**; the journal entry for 3 employees will display.

15 ➤ **Exit** from the Payroll Run Journal Entry window.

If a paycheque was printed, the printout on plain paper would be similar to Fig. 7-19. If the cheque was damaged while printing, or there is a serious error on the cheque (e.g., wrong amount), changes could be made and the cheque printed again with a new number (see Exercise 7-10). The payroll records and General Ledger are not updated until the entry is posted.

16 ➤ **Post** the payroll entry. You will see the same payroll date warning message throughout this chapter. Click **Yes** to continue.

You will see the negative pay warning message mentioning CURRIE, Jordan's name.

> **Sage 50 - Confirmation**
>
> CURRIE, Jordan has a negative net pay amount and cannot be processed through the Payroll Cheque Run Journal. Employees with negative net pay amounts need to be processed through the Payroll Journal. Do you want to continue with this payroll run, omitting this employee?

17 ➤ Click **Yes** to process the pay omitting Jordan in this transaction.

When you click **Yes**, a message box will appear briefly with a message, "Selected employee payroll transactions are being processed" and you will see the number of employees decrease to 0. You will then see the following confirmation window.

> **Sage 50 - Transaction Confirmation**
>
> The transaction was posted successfully.
>
> 2 Journal Entries: J2 to J3.

Click **OK**. You will be returned to the Payroll Run Journal window.

18 ➤ **Exit** the Payroll Run Journal.

Creative Wallpaper, Student's Name
3106 Ambleside Drive
London, Ontario N3G 1V9

CHEQUE NO.		201
DATE		1 1 0 1 2 0 1 9
		D D M M Y Y Y Y

One Thousand One Hundred seventy and 41/100 $1,170.41

   DAVID, Doreen
   17 Huron Street
   London, Ontario N5Y 1Z5

Creative Wallpaper, Student's Name

DAVID, Doreen   Jan 11, 2019   For Pay Period   Jan 11, 2019   201

Period		**Period**		**Period**	
Regular	1,600.00	CPP	75.51	Gross	1,660.00
Overtime	60.00	EI	31.21	Withheld	-459.59
		Tax	226.47	Loan Paid	-30.00
Gross	1,660.00	Pension	66.40		
		Union Dues	20.00	Net	1,170.41
		Medical	24.00		
		Safety Shoes	16.00	Day 1 ....0.00	
				Day 2 ....0.00	
		Withheld	459.59	Day 3 ....0.00	
				Day 4 ....0.00	
				Day 5 ....0.00	

Regular: 80.00 Hours @20.00
Overtime 2:00 Hours @30.00

Fig. 7-19: Paycheque information printed on two stub Easy Align cheques.

Jordan Currie arrives late and submits an Employee Time Sheet shown in Exercise 7-10. Jordan informed you that she was late due to her car not starting. The service station repair will cost $849.00 and she has asked for a $600.00 payroll loan to help pay for her car repairs. Mrs. Singh approved the loan based on Mrs. Currie's employment history.

Study the following payroll information for recording individual paycheques.

The PAYROLL Journal

When you need to issue a single paycheque, you can use the Paycheques icon as shown in the next exercise.

Exercise 7-10—Issuing a Single Paycheque

---

1 ➤ Click the ▼ at the **Paycheques** icon, select **Create Paycheque**. The Payroll Journal window is displayed.

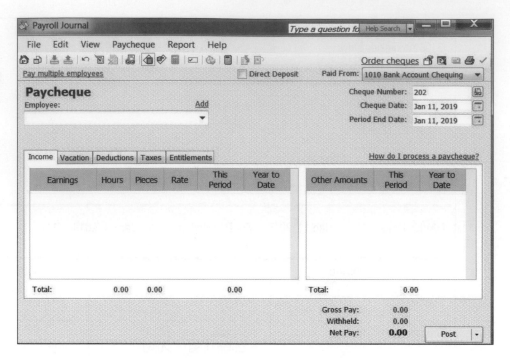

Fig. 7-20: Payroll Journal window.

The journal is intended to look like a payroll cheque with advice. You fill in the appropriate fields to complete the advice.

The Paycheque item on the paycheque menu bar is similar to other menus with drop-down lists. Many items are not available until after cheques have been processed.

Study the following icons on the toolbar:

 Adjust Paycheque: A previously posted payroll cheque (using the same pay period) can be recalled and corrected with the Adjust Cheque icon. If you are not adjusting the most recent paycheque for employees who have reached the maximum deduction for EI, CPP or WSIB, then errors in government deductions in the reversal amounts can occur. You can also adjust a cheque from the Home page, Paycheques icon, Adjust Paycheque. (See image in side note box.)

This is also not a good choice if the tax tables have been updated and you are adjusting a paycheque that used a previous tax table, or adjusting a payroll entry from an earlier period (which used the current tax table), because the taxable income amounts may not be correct. You may see the following warning message.

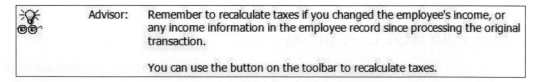

Advisor:	Remember to recalculate taxes if you changed the employee's income, or any income information in the employee record since processing the original transaction. You can use the button on the toolbar to recalculate taxes.

To reverse a paycheque in these circumstances, see Making PAYROLL Corrections (Exercises 7-16a and 7-16b).

Make sure the cheque date falls into the range of dates for the pay period that the cheque covers. This ensures that taxes are calculated properly for the revised cheque.

 You have seen this icon in previous chapters; it is used to reverse a paycheque before issuing a correct paycheque. See Making PAYROLL Corrections (Exercises 7-16a and 7-16b).

Calculate Taxes Automatically: The program will calculate EI, CPP, and Income tax automatically, based on defaults previously entered.

 Enter Taxes Manually: You will enter the EI, CPP, and Income tax manually. This is used when reversing (cancelling) a cheque.

 Recalculate Taxes: When used, Sage 50 Accounting will recalculate the taxes if amounts entered have been changed.

EMPLOYEE TIME SHEET　　　202

Date: ___Jan. 11, 2019_____　　　　Cheque No.

Employee Name: ___Jordan Currie_____　　　Employee # __1___

Regular Hours	Overtime Hours	Commission Hours	Commission Amount	Deductions		Other Information
None	None	77	$1,385.00	Pension	$ 55.40	Salary loan $600.00
				Union Dues	20.00	
				Medical	24.00	

Hint: Net Pay $1,640.18

Approved by: *G. S.*

---

2 ➤ Employee　　Select **CURRIE, Jordan** and [Tab]. The employee name and address are displayed and will be printed on the payroll cheque. [Tab].

Cheque Number 202 is the correct next cheque number.

Cheque Date　Jan 11, 2019.

> **Regular** and **Overtime 1** do not have a field available (--) for entering data. When Jordan was set up earlier, on commission, you indicated that she did not have an hourly rate for regular or overtime pay.
>
> Some fields are not available because they are not defaults (e.g., Pieces).

3 ➤ Period End Date　　Click the **calendar** icon. You are able to change the period ending date if the date displayed is not correct. [Tab] twice to accept Jan 11, 2019. This is Jordan Currie's pay for the week ended Jan 11, 2019. This is the date that the entry will be posted to the General Ledger.

(See side note box.)

Salary　　These fields are for salaried employees only. Jordan is paid on a commission basis; therefore there is nothing to record.

4 ➤ Commission Hours　　This field is for the number of commission hours worked. Type **77**, [Tab].

5 ➤ Commission This Period　　This field is the dollar amount of commissions earned by Jordan. Type **1385.00**. [Tab]. The Gross Pay and Net Pay amounts at the bottom of the window change.

If you cannot see the Net Pay at the bottom of the window, drag the Payroll Journal title bar up a bit. The bar should now be seen, or you can maximize this window.

Most firms would issue a separate cheque for a loan, advance, or reimbursement. This ensures that the payroll records are separate from other types of disbursements to employees.

6 ➤ Advances   Jordan has no advances this period Tab.

7 ➤ Loans   Type **600.00**, Tab. The amount of any payroll loan issued or repaid would be recorded here. (See side note box.) To reduce a payroll loan, you would enter a negative amount. The Net Pay field changes again to include the loan amount.

8 ➤ Benefits   This field is for taxable employee benefits such as car allowance, or life insurance, for which the company pays the cost on the employee's behalf. Creative Wallpaper does not pay for this type of item, Tab.

If any amounts are entered, the program adds this amount to the gross pay before calculating the taxes.

Reimburse   There are no reimbursements for Jordan this period.

9 ➤   Your Income tab should look like the following, Tab.

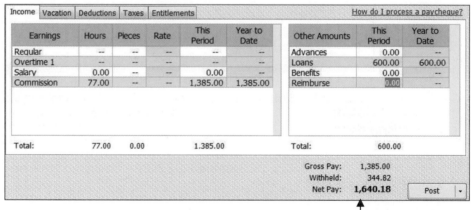

Fig. 7-21: Pay Window Income tab.

> The Net Pay amount includes the loan of $600.00

10 ➤ Vacation Earned This Period   See Fig 7-22a. The amount of vacation pay earned this pay period. **$1,385.00 commission × 4% = $55.40**. This field is calculated from the default information entered previously.

If the amount is incorrect, it can be changed. Tab.

Vacation Earned Year To Date   This field will show the accumulated vacation pay (535.40) retained by the company for the employee. The $55.40 will be added to account: **2300 VACATION PAYABLE**.

Vacation Paid   Leave blank. This field is used to give some or all of the vacation pay retained by the company to the employee. This means that Jordan will not be paid the vacation pay earned.

Vacation Owed   This field shows the amount of vacation pay that is owed, not paid to the employee.

Fig. 7-22a: Pay Window Vacation tab.

11 ➤ [Tab] The window changes to the Deductions tab.

Deductions

This window will display the default amounts that were entered when you set up the employee. The **Pension** field cannot be changed because this field is calculated by Sage 50 Accounting. **Safety Shoes** does not have an amount because Jordan does not owe any money for safety shoes.

Fig. 7-22b: Pay Window Deductions tab.

 If the amounts for **Union Dues** and **Medical** do not correspond to the text, check to see if you entered the deductions incorrectly when setting up the Employee Ledger.

12 ➤ Click the **Taxes** tab.

Taxes

You cannot change these fields because Sage 50 Accounting calculates these amounts. The program will add the employee's EI, CPP, and Tax amounts, together with the business benefit cost of EI and CPP, to the liability (Payable) accounts.

The business will remit these amounts (employee's deductions and business expense) at regular intervals to Canada Revenue Agency (Receiver General). This is explained in Exercise 7-13.

The Taxes tab window should resemble Fig. 7-23.

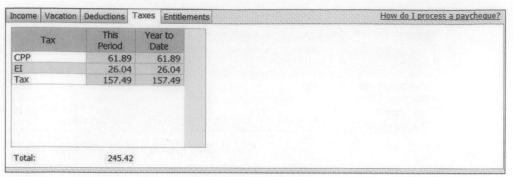

Fig. 7-23: Taxes tab.

13 ➤ Display the journal entry by clicking **Report** from the top menu, then **Display Payroll Journal Entry**.

The entry should be similar to the display in Fig. 7-24. If you upgraded from Sage 50 Accounting 2015 Release 1, your amounts may be different.

Payroll Journal Entry Jan 11, 2019 (J4)

Account Number	Account Description	Debits	Credits
1241	Loans Receivable	600.00	-
5300	Wages Expense	55.40	-
5304	Commissions Expense	1,385.00	-
5310	EI Expense	36.46	-
5320	CPP Expense	61.89	-
5330	WSIB Expense	5.68	-
1010	Bank Account Chequing	-	1,640.18
2300	Vacation Payable	-	55.40
2310	EI Payable	-	62.50
2320	CPP Payable	-	123.78
2330	Income Tax Payable	-	157.49
2420	Union Dues Payable	-	20.00
2430	Pension Plan Payable	-	55.40
2440	Medical Plan Payable	-	24.00
2460	WSIB Payable	-	5.68
Additional Date:	Additional Field:		
		2,144.43	2,144.43

Fig. 7-24: Payroll Journal Entry window.

The vacation pay portion of the commission earned by Jordan is charged to the default link Wages Expense #5300 account. Management has decided not to separate the vacation pay between regular pay and commission pay.

14 ➤ **Exit** from the Payroll Journal Entry window.

15 ➤ Click the **Post** button to post this payroll transaction.

16 ➤ You will see the date warning message. Click **Yes** to proceed, and **Exit** from the Payroll journal.

17 ➤ Click the **Employees** icon, double-click on **CURRIE Jordan** and click on the **Additional Info** tab. In Field 1, type **Payroll Loan $30.00** and click **Display this** ☑ . Click Save and Close .

18 ➤ Exit to the Home window.

Reviewing PAYROLL Entries After Posting

Exercise 7-11—Reviewing PAYROLL Entries

Review the entry for Doreen David as follows:

1 ➤ From the Home window, click the **Employees** icon to display the Employees window.

2 ➤ Click **Reports**, **Employee** and the Employee Report—Modify Report, window is displayed. Change the information as shown in Fig. 7-25a and 7-25b.

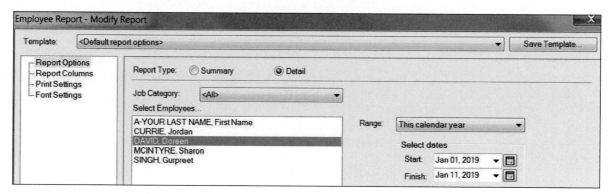

Fig. 7-25a: Employee Report Options window.

Do NOT change the start and finish dates, as they are appropriate for this exercise.

If you click Summary, the **Select dates** options are hidden.

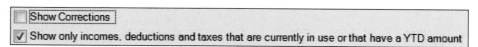

Fig. 7-25b: Employee Report Options window lower portion.

Note: The Advances Paid column appears, even though the balance is 0.00, as it is directly related to the Loans Paid column.

3 ➤ By clicking the lower box (Fig. 7-25b) payroll columns with no posted amounts will not display. Click **OK**. The report will display. (See side note box.) If you repeated this step, but did not click the lower box, three additional columns QPIP, QPP, and Prov. Tax would display with 0.00 amounts.

4 ➤ **Exit** from the report. The next step will allow you to customize the columns.

5 ➤ Repeat step 2, but this time in the left pane click **Report Columns**.

6 ➤ Click the ⦿ Custom report column settings button and you will see the columns on the right side of the window that are currently shown in the report.

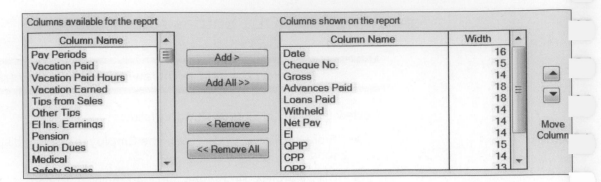

You have two choices:

Method a)   Click <<Remove All to move all the right column items to the left
            column. Then you can pick and choose the ones you want to see on the
            report by clicking an item and choosing   Add> .

Method b)   In the right pane, click the items you do not want to see on the report
            and click on   <Remove .

            There are over 50 items available to choose from and we want to create
            a small report. The author has used choice **a**.

7 ➤   Click **<<Remove All** to move all items to the left.

8 ➤   In the left column, click on each in the order that is shown below, and choose
       Add> . Other columns could have been chosen.

Columns shown on the report	
Column Name	**Width**
Date	16
Cheque No.	15
Pay Periods	4
Gross	14
Withheld	14
Net Pay	14
Loans Paid	18
Advances Paid	18
EI	14

9 ➤   Click **OK** to display the report.

       If you had customized by moving any of the other columns, the report would
       display, but you would need to use the slider button to see the other columns
       and, depending on the columns chosen, it may print on two pages. You
       would have to remove some columns if you wanted this report to print on one
       page or make the font size smaller, but then it will be more difficult to read.

       A portion of the report is shown next. (See side note box.)

The column P 26 refers
to a bi-weekly pay
period.

Employee Detail Jan 01, 2019 to Jan 11, 2019								
Date	Cheque No.	P	Gross	Withheld	Net Pay	Loans Paid	Advances Paid	EI
DAVID, Doreen								
Jan 11, 2019	201	26	1,660.00	459.59	1,170.41	-30.00	0.00	31.21
Total			1,660.00	459.59	1,170.41	-30.00	0.00	31.21

10 ➤   Click **X** to return to the Employees window.

11 ➤ You can also see the YTD (Year-to-Date) payroll amounts. You may have to scroll to the right to see Net YTD. Double-click on **DAVID, Doreen**.

12 ➤ Click the **Income** tab. In the YTD* amount column, the amounts displayed are the amounts as of Jan 11, 2019. The YTD * column amounts will increase with the posted payroll amounts. The Loan 60.00 is the amount remaining to be repaid.

13 ➤ **Exit** to the Employees window.

You can also display and/or print the Employee Summary.

14 ➤ Click **Reports, Employee**, select **Summary. DAVID, Doreen** should be selected. Make sure a ✓ is in the Show only Incomes, deductions and taxes box. This will display fields that are in use at this time.

15 ➤ Click **OK**.

> **ⓘ**
>
> Net Pay refers to the normal net pay considering $90 Loans issued. Net Pay $1,260.41.
>
> If payroll cheques are not printed by Sage 50 Accounting (money deposited by the Direct Deposit feature or other cheques issued), the print cheque feature is still available. The advice portion of the cheque can be given to employees for their records.

Employee Summary for 2019

DAVID, Doreen		SIN _____ 456 812 635	Birthdate _____ Apr 26, 1957
Tax Table _____ Ontario	Regular _____ 1,600.00	EI _____ 31.21	
Federal Claim _____ 12,000.00/yr	Overtime _____ 60.00	CPP _____ 75.51	
Provincial Claim _____ 10,536.00/yr	Salary _____ 0.00	Tax _____ 226.47	
Pay Periods _____ 26/yr	Commission _____ 0.00	Pension _____ 66.40	
WSIB Rate _____ 0.41%	Advances Paid _____ 0.00	Union Dues _____ 20.00	
Insurable _____ Yes	Benefits _____ 0.00	Medical _____ 24.00	
Pensionable _____ Yes	Vacation Paid _____ 0.00	Safety Shoes _____ 16.00	
EI Factor _____ 1.40			
Vacation _____ 4.00%	Gross Pay _____ 1,660.00		
Retained _____ Yes	Less Benefits _____ 0.00		
Vacation on Vacation Paid _____ No	Loans Owing _____ 60.00	Withheld _____ 459.59	
Regular _____ 20.00/Hour	Reimburse _____ 0.00	Net Pay _____ 1,260.41	
Overtime _____ 30.00/Hour			
Salary _____ 0.00/Period	Gross Paid _____ 1,720.00		
Commission _____ 0.00/Period			
Reimburse _____ 0.00/Period	Advances Owing _____ 0.00		
Benefits _____ 0.00/Period	Vacation Owed _____ 486.40		
Additional Federal Tax _____ 10.00/Period	EI Ins. Earnings _____ 1,660.00		
	Pens. Earnings _____ 1,660.00		
	Pension Adjust... _____ 0.00		
	RPP/DPSP Re _____ 589896		
Days 1 _____ 0.00	Days 2 _____ 0.00	Days 3 _____ 0.00	
Days 4 _____ 0.00	Days 5 _____ 0.00		

Fig. 7-26: Employee Summary window. (See side note box.)

16 ➤ Click **X** and return to the Home window.

Payroll for Pay Period Ending Jan 15, 2019

Exercise 7-12—Entering PAYROLL for Salaried Employees

1 ➤ Advance the Session date to **Jan 15, 2019**.

2 ➤ Process the salaried employees' pay from the following time sheets using the **Payroll Cheque Run** option.

3 ➤ Close the **Additional Info notes** for Doreen and Jordan, as they are not needed at this time.

4 ➤ **By Pay Period Frequency** Change to **24**. Two ✓ appear on the left of the window.

EMPLOYEE TIME SHEET   203

Date: Jan. 15, 2019   Cheque No.

Employee Name: Sharon McIntyre   Employee # 3

Salary	Deductions	Other Information
$ 2,000.00	Medical $24.00	Pension $80.00

Hint: Net Pay $1,473.16

Approved by *: G. S.*

EMPLOYEE TIME SHEET   204

Date: Jan. 15, 2019   Cheque No.

Employee Name: Gurjeet Singh   Employee # 4

Salary	Other Deductions	Information
$ 2,500.00	Medical $24.00	Pension $100.00

Hint: Net Pay $1,764.55

Approved by *: G. S.*

---

5 ➤ Display the **Payroll Run Journal** **E**ntry.

You will notice that salaried employees' pay is charged to #5302 SALARIES EXPENSE. Some businesses charge hourly employees' and salaried employees' earnings to the same account and do not split the expenses between accounts.

6 ➤ **Exit** the entry window and **Post** when correct.

7 ➤ **Exit** to the Home window.

Paying Receiver General Pay Withholdings

You are required to send the payroll deductions (CPP, EI, and Income Tax) to the Receiver General on a regular basis. These are referred to as **source deductions**.

Depending on the procedures established in your company, your manager may or may not remind you to do this task. If it is your responsibility to make the payments, be sure to know the schedule for payments. The month's source deductions are usually due on the 15th day of the next month (e.g., January's deductions are due to be paid by February 15).

When you use this exercise (Pay Remittance feature) to issue the Receiver General Payroll Remittance cheque, please note that you can use the Reverse or Adjust a Cheque icons feature as shown in previous chapters.

Note: When posting the entry, Sage 50 Accounting automatically creates two journal entries for the remittance. Journal #7 dated Jan 1, transfers the EI, CPP, and Income Tax amounts from the G/L accounts (at the end of the remittance period) and moves the balances to Accounts Payable. This entry updates the G/L balances at the beginning of the remittance period and allows the G/L to show only new amounts owing for the new remittance period. The second entry, Journal #8, dated Jan 15, records the remittance payment and reduces Accounts Payable with cheque #205.

Exercise 7-13—Recording Withholdings Payment

Study the next memo:

M E M O

205
Cheque No.

From: Gurjeet Singh
Date: Jan. 15, 2019
To: Accounting

To pay the Receiver General—Payroll Taxes, the EI, CPP and Income Tax amounts owing at December 31, 2018.

> *Hint: Review the Jan 01, 2019 Trial Balance for appropriate amounts.*

> *Hint: Cheque amount = $3,354.00*

This exercise is similar to the procedure to pay the Receiver General for HST OWING (Exercises 3B-31 and 3B-32), except we are paying the Payroll deductions owing at the end of the previous month. This exercise will be using the Sage 50 Accounting feature Remittance payment selection as shown next.

Creative Wallpaper has the following payroll payable accounts that need to be remitted to the Receiver General:

2310	EI Payable
2320	CPP Payable
2330	Income Tax Payable

Check the previous month's Trial Balance (on January 1, 2019, you would view the December 31, 2018 Trial Balance amounts). You could also check the Balance Sheet for the same date. The amounts to be paid are the amounts collected from the employees, plus the company's portion of the deductions where applicable by law. These amounts are recorded in the appropriate PAYABLE accounts.

1 ➤   From the Home page, Employee's and Payroll module, click on the **Pay Remittance** icon, select **Receiver General-Payroll Taxes,** the End of Remitting period date should be Jan 01, 2019.

2 ➤   **Payment Amount**   Click in the **Payment Amount** column for each **EI**, **CPP**, and **Tax**, to update the total to 3,354.00.

In future months you would select the last day of the previous month.

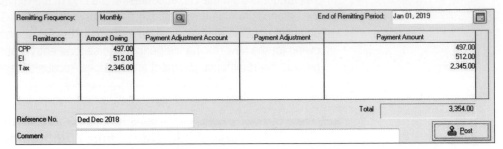

3 ➤   **Reference No.**   An appropriate reference would be **Ded Dec 2018**, or Dec Pay Ded, or something similar to identify what is being paid.

4 ➤   Remember to **view** the entry before posting. You cannot set this up as a recurring entry as the Store and Recall icons are greyed out.

Payments Journal Entry

		Account Number	Account Description	Debits	Credits
Jan 01, 2019	(J7)		Ded Dec 2018, Receiver General - Payroll Taxes		
		2310	EI Payable	512.00	-
		2320	CPP Payable	497.00	-
		2330	Income Tax Payable	2,345.00	-
		2200	Accounts Payable	-	3,354.00
Jan 15, 2019	(J8)		205, Receiver General - Payroll Taxes		
		2200	Accounts Payable	3,354.00	-
		1010	Bank Account Chequing	-	3,354.00
Additional Date:		Additional Field:			
				6,708.00	6,708.00

5 ➤   Click **Post**.

6 ➤   Return to the Home window.

Note for Audit trail purposes J7 moves the amounts from the Payroll Liability accounts to the Accounts Payable account. J8 records the payment of the payroll remittance amounts.

Exercise 7-14—More PAYROLL Transactions

Payroll for January 25, 2019

1 ➤   Advance the date to **January 25, 2019**.

2 ➤ **Record** the bi-weekly payroll, using the **Payroll Cheque Run**, for the following employees based on the following time sheets. Click **Close** for both Additional Info Note windows.

EMPLOYEE TIME SHEET   206

Date:___Jan. 25, 2019_____   Cheque No.

Employee Name: A-Your LAST NAME, First Name   Employee # ___5___

Regular Hours	Overtime Hours	Commission Hours	Commission Amount	Deductions		Other Information
40	None			Pension		No
				Union Dues	$20.00	

Hint: Net Pay $508.41

Approved by*: G. S.*

EMPLOYEE TIME SHEET   207

Date:___Jan. 25, 2019_____   Cheque No.

Employee Name:_____Jordan Currie_____   Employee # ___1___

Regular Hours	Overtime Hours	Commission Hours	Commission Amount	Deductions		Other Information	
None	None	79	$1,560.00	Pension	$ 62.40	Loan Repaid	$30.00
				Union Dues	20.00		
				Medical	24.00		

Hint: Net Pay $1,129.36

Approved by*: G. S.*   *Hint: Use the lower portion to enter the payroll hours and commission amount*

EMPLOYEE TIME SHEET   208

Date:___Jan. 25, 2019_____   Cheque No.

Employee Name:___Doreen David_____   Employee # ___2___

Regular Hours	Overtime Hours	Commission Hours	Commission Amount	Deductions		Other Information	
80	4	None		Pension	$ 68.80	Loan Repaid	$30.00
				Union Dues	20.00		
				Medical	24.00		
				Safety Shoes	16.00		

Hint: Net Pay $ 1,210.82

Approved by*: G S.*

3 ➤   **Post** when correct and **Exit** to the Home window. Remember to close the
Additional Info boxes.

Processing Vacation Pay

In the late afternoon of January 25, Jordan Currie receives a phone call about her
parents suddenly taking ill, and she has requested one week off to help them. She
wishes to collect her vacation pay, which has been retained by the company. A memo
approving the request is received from Gurjeet Singh as shown next. To issue a
cheque for vacation pay, follow the procedure in the next exercise.

M E M O   **209**
                                                                         Cheque No.

From: Gurjeet Singh   Date: January 25, 2019
To: Accounting

Please issue vacation pay owing to Jordan Currie. Please adjust the time
period to allow for appropriate Income Tax to be deducted. Do not take any
loan repayments on vacation pay. Pension is $23.91.

Hint: Net Pay $472.57

Exercise 7-15—Processing Vacation Pay

Jordan is paid commission bi-weekly. Jordan will receive her vacation pay for one
week, and when she comes back she will receive a pay for one week. She will,
therefore, receive two paycheques in a two-week period (vacation pay and regular
commission).

By taking all vacation pay for a one-week period (during a bi-weekly pay period),
Sage 50 Accounting will not take off enough Federal Income Tax or CPP from the
total pay. To avoid this problem, the number of pay periods in the year can be
increased from 26 (bi-weekly) to 52 (weekly) temporarily. Once the vacation
paycheque and her one-week pay for commission, when she returns, have been
posted, the pay periods must be switched back to 26 per year.

The next pay period will be February 8. You will need to remember to issue a
separate commission paycheque for Jordan with the 52-week setting. After her
February 7 pay is paid, you will change the setting back to 26 and you can resume
paying Jordan in the Payroll Cheque Run window.

1 ➤   From the Home window, click the **Employees** icon.

2 ➤   Double-click the icon for **CURRIE Jordan** to display the Payroll Ledger
window for Jordan.

3 ➤ Click the **Income** tab and change the Pay Periods Per Year from 26 to **52** (press ⌨Tab to accept the change). Click 🔲**Save & Close**🔳.

4 ➤ **Exit** to the Home window.

5 ➤ Click the **Paycheques** icon.

6 ➤ Select **CURRIE, Jordan**, ⌨Tab. **Close** the Additional Info Note.

7 ➤ Jordan is not receiving commission; therefore, do NOT enter any amount.

Vacation tab

8 ➤ Click the **Vacation tab**. The accumulated vacation pay retained by the company $597.80 for Jordan can be found in the YTD Amount column.

Vacation Earned	--	0.00	--	597.80

You want to pay this amount to Jordan. In This Period Hours, type 40, ⌨Tab.

In This Period Amount column type **597.80**.

Vacation Paid *	40.00	597.80	40.00	--

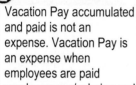

9 ➤ ⌨Tab.Click the **Vacation** tab. You will see that the Vacation Owed Amount changes to - - and the Year to Date amount changes to - -.

10 ➤ Click the **Deductions** tab.

11 ➤ **Union Medical:** Press the 🔲*Delete*🔳 key to remove Union and Medical amounts in this window. These deductions are paid on weekly commissions, which included vacation pay owed and, therefore, should not be deducted again.

> Vacation Pay accumulated and paid is not an expense. Vacation Pay is an expense when employees are paid regular wages/salaries and commissions.
>
> EI, CPP, and WSIB expenses are calculated on actual amounts paid to employees. They are not calculated on vacation pay accumulated each pay period.

12 ➤ View the Payroll entry. (See side note box.)

Payroll Journal Entry Jan 25, 2019 (J12)

Account Number	Account Description	Debits	Credits
2300	Vacation Payable	597.80	-
5310	EI Expense	15.74	-
5320	CPP Expense	26.26	-
5330	WSIB Expense	2.45	-
1010	Bank Account Chequing	-	472.57
2310	EI Payable	-	26.98
2320	CPP Payable	-	52.52
2330	Income Tax Payable	-	63.82
2430	Pension Plan Payable	-	23.91
2460	WSIB Payable	-	2.45
Additional Date:	Additional Field:		
		642.25	642.25

Fig. 7-27: Payroll Entry.

13 ➤ **Exit** the entry window and **post** when correct.

14 ➤ **Exit** from the Payroll Journal and return to the Home window.

Making Payroll Corrections

After the cheques were issued, Doreen brought to Mrs. Singh's attention that she had taken Tuesday off last week as an unpaid leave of absence and, therefore, should not have been paid for the day.

There are two ways to correct this problem.

At the Paycheques icon, click the 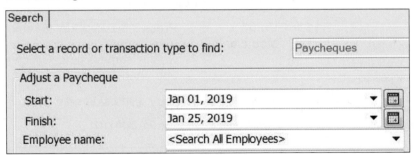, select Adjust Paycheque and follow steps 1 through 6 and make changes required, including the cheque number. However, this will work only if the paycheque being corrected is from a recent paycheque date (e.g., Jan 25) and not a prior pay period (e.g., Jan 11).

When adjusting/correcting paycheques from prior pay periods (before the most recent pay period), please note the following:

- Income taxes have to be re-calculated, AND
- extra precaution must be taken to ensure the revised cheque correctly includes all deductions, AND
- double-check to ensure Gross Pay and YTD figures are correct.

- THEREFORE, it is strongly recommended that every effort be made to make corrections for a pay period BEFORE processing the next pay period's entries.

Exercise 7-16a—Making PAYROLL Corrections- Reverse Cheque

Step 1: Reverse Original Entry

1 ➤ At the Paycheques icon, click the 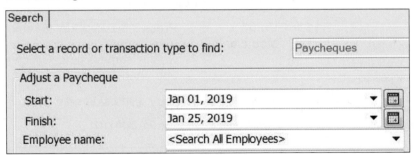, select **Adjust Paycheque**, you will see the following:

Search	
Select a record or transaction type to find:	Paycheques
Adjust a Paycheque	
Start:	Jan 01, 2019
Finish:	Jan 25, 2019
Employee name:	<Search All Employees>

2 ➤ Do NOT change the settings. Click **OK** to see the next window.

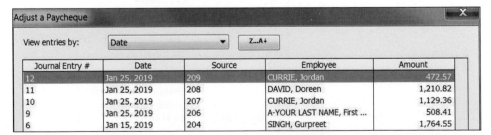

Adjust a Paycheque

View entries by: Date   Z...A↓

Journal Entry #	Date	Source	Employee	Amount
12	Jan 25, 2019	209	CURRIE, Jordan	472.57
11	Jan 25, 2019	208	DAVID, Doreen	1,210.82
10	Jan 25, 2019	207	CURRIE, Jordan	1,129.36
9	Jan 25, 2019	206	A-YOUR LAST NAME, First ...	508.41
6	Jan 15, 2019	204	SINGH, Gurpreet	1,764.55

3 ➤ Only a partial window is shown here. Click the appropriate Journal Entry # (**11**), and click **Select**.

	Advisor:	Remember to recalculate taxes if you changed the employee's income, or any income information in the employee record since processing the original transaction.
		You can use the button on the toolbar to recalculate taxes.

4 ➤ Click to **close** this window. You are in the Payroll Journal - Adjusting Cheque 208 | Tab |.

5 ➤ You may see the **Additional Info Note** window. If not move to step 6.
Click **Close**.

6 ➤ Click 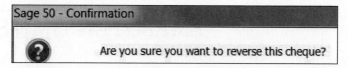 **Reverse paycheque** icon.

Sage 50 - Confirmation
❓   Are you sure you want to reverse this cheque?

7 ➤ When you are sure that this is the correct cheque you want to reverse, click
Yes. You will see the confirmation window.

Sage 50 - Transaction Confirmation
ⓘ   This transaction was reversed successfully.

8 ➤ Click **OK**. You are returned to a blank Payroll Journal window. The original
journal entry #11 for DAVID, Doreen has been reversed (cancelled) by
Journal entry #13.

9 ➤ Click **X** to return to the Home window.

10 ➤ Click **Report Centre**, click **Financials**, click **All Journal Entries**, click
Modify this report, click on **Journal Number**, change the Start and Finish
fields to **13**. Click **Corrections**, and click **OK**.

All Journal Entries J13 to J13				
	Account Number	Account Description	Debits	Credits
Jan 25, 2019 J13	ADJ208, Rev. of J11. Corr. is J13.			
	1010	Bank Account Chequing	1,210.82	-
	1241	Loans Receivable	30.00	-
	2300	Vacation Payable	68.80	-
	2310	EI Payable	77.62	-
	2320	CPP Payable	156.96	-
	2330	Income Tax Payable	239.56	-
	2420	Union Dues Payable	20.00	-
	2430	Pension Plan Payable	68.80	-
	2440	Medical Plan Payable	24.00	-
	2450	Safety Shoes Payable	16.00	-
	2460	WSIB Payable	7.05	-
	5300	Wages Expense	-	1,668.80
	5308	Wages-Overtime Expense	-	120.00
	5310	EI Expense	-	45.28
	5320	CPP Expense	-	78.48
	5330	WSIB Expense	-	7.05
			1,919.61	1,919.61

Fig. 7-28: Payroll Reversing Journal Entry for J11.

The entry will display with the following wording error. ADJ208, Rev. of J11. Corr. is J13.

J13 is actually the reversing entry and not the correction entry. The correcting
entry will be shown in the next exercise.

11 ➤ Click **X** twice to return to the Home window.

Exercise 7-16b—Making PAYROLL Corrections–Issue New Cheque

Step 2: Record the Correct Entry and Issue a New Cheque

EMPLOYEE TIME SHEET   210

Date: Jan. 25, 2019   Cheque No.

Employee Name: Doreen David   Employee #   2

Regular Hours	Overtime Hours	Commission Hours	Commission Amount	Deductions		Other Information
76	None	None	None	Pension	$ 60.80	1 day leave of absence
				Union Dues	20.00	Loan Repaid $30.00
				Medical	24.00	
				Safety Shoes	16.00	

Hint: Net Pay $1,074.34

Approved by: *G. S. (revised)*

---

12 ➤   Click on the **Paycheques** icon.

13 ➤   **Employee**   Select **DAVID, Doreen,** Tab . **Close** the Additional Info Note.

14 ➤   Change the Regular hours from 80 to **76** for the correct hours. (Doreen David took an unpaid leave of absence, therefore, 80 hours - 8 plus 4 = 76 regular hours with no overtime.) The correct net pay should be **$1,074.34**.

(See side note box.)

15 ➤   **Post** when correct.

16 ➤   Click X to return to the Home.

> Most companies pay overtime only if an employee has worked more than the normal regular hours, based on the company's regular hours. Regular business hours typically range from 70 to 80 hours per bi-weekly pay.

Exercise 7-17—PAYROLL for Pay Period Ending Jan 31, 2019

1 ➤   Advance the Session date to **Jan 31, 2019**.

Issue cheques to salaried employees Sharon McIntyre and Gurjeet Singh, based on time sheets 211 and 212.

For salaried employees use:

2 ➤   **Starting Cheque Number**   211

3 ➤   **Cheque Date**   Jan 31, 2019

4 ➤   **Period End Date**   Jan 31, 2019

5 ➤   **By Pay Period Frequency**   24

6 ➤   **Auto Select**   Auto-select: Not yet paid on this Cheque Date   ▼

7 ➤ **Record** and **post** the following salaried employee time sheets.

EMPLOYEE TIME SHEET   211

Date: Jan. 31, 2019   Cheque No.

Employee Name: Sharon McIntyre   Employee #   3

Salary	*Deductions*		*Other Information*	
$ 2,000.00	Medical	$24.00	Pension	$ 80.00

Hint: Net Pay $1,473.16

Approved by *:*   *G. S.*

EMPLOYEE TIME SHEET   212

Date: Jan. 31, 2019   Cheque No.

Employee Name: Gurjeet Singh   Employee #   4

Salary	*Deductions*		*Other Information*	
$ 2,500.00	Medical	$24.00	Pension	$ 100.00

Hint: Net Pay $1,764.55

Approved by *:*   *G. S.*

Jordan Currie has advised Mrs. Singh that she will be returning on Monday, February 3. There is no setting to change for her until after she gets paid on the 7th.

8 ➤ Click ☒ to return to the Home window, and click **Close** to close the Additional Info Notes.

Additional Transaction

During the month, the Payroll department must remit money collected from employees or on behalf of employees to appropriate vendors. Examples of these would be union dues payable to the local union branch, pension plan payable amount to the pension fund trustee, and WSIB payment to the provincial association. There can be many others.

Exercise 7-18—Remittances for PAYROLL Deductions

---

1 ➤ Click on **Pay Remittance** and select the appropriate Payroll Authority to process each of the next two transactions.

M E M O   **213**
                                                                   Cheque No.

From: Gurjeet Singh
Date: Jan. 31, 2019
To: Accounting

Please remit the funds at January 1, in account 2460 WSIB Payable, to the WSIB office. Reference our file #2589-B-X304.

> *Hint: Review the Jan 01, 2019 Trial Balance for appropriate amounts.*

> *Hint: Cheque amount = $450.00*

Sage 50 - Transaction Confirmation

The transaction was posted successfully.

2 Journal Entries: J17 to J18.

Note: As noted at the Receiver General payment Exercise 7-13, there are two entries.

M E M O   **214**
                                                                   Cheque No.

From: Gurjeet Singh
Date: Jan. 31, 2019
To: Accounting

Please remit the funds at January 1, in account 2420 Union Dues Payable, to the Local Union office. Reference our file #569-2018-12.

> *Hint: Review the Jan 01, 2019 Trial Balance for appropriate amounts.*

> *Hint: Cheque amount = $220.00*

Ignore message | Advisor: Your chequing account is overdrawn. See the Advice topic "Managing Your Cash Flow" for suggestions. | .

The owner has made arrangements at the bank to cover overdrafts.

2 ➤ Return to the Home window.

Recording Payroll Accrued Wages

Study the calendar for the last week of January 2019 and the first week of February 2019. You pay employees every second Friday; therefore the next pay date for hourly paid employees is Friday, February 8.

January 2019								February 2019						
S	M	T	W	T	F	S		S	M	T	W	T	F	S
20	21	22	23	24	25	26							1	2
27	28	29	30	31				3	4	5	6	7	8	9

To record January expenses properly according to GAAP, a payroll expense accrual for the period Saturday, January 26 to Thursday, January 31 must be recorded. Payroll accruals are recorded in the General Journal.

Mrs. Singh has checked the time cards for the employees and, as per her memo, calculated the following:

DAVID, Doreen   5 days at 8 hours per day at $20.00 per hour 800.00
A-YOUR LAST NAME, First Name 5 days at 8 hours per day at $14.00 per hour 560.00
                                                                    Total Accrual $1,360.00

Exercise 7-19—Recording PAYROLL Accruals

1 ➤ Click the **COMPANY** module, click the **General Journal** icon.

2 ➤ Click the **Recall Recurring** icon.

3 ➤ Select **Setup Wages accrual for month end**.

4 ➤ Enter the accrual as shown in Fig. 7-29. Your General Journal window should resemble the following:

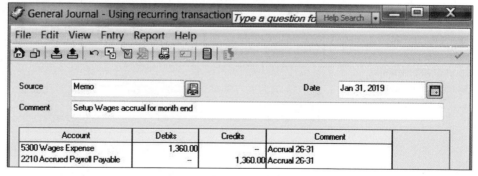

Fig 7-29: Payroll Accrual.

5 ➤ **Post** when correct and **Exit** to the Home window.

Processing T4 Slips (or Relevé 1)

T4s and Relevé 1 slips must be completed at the end of a calendar year after the payroll for the entire year has been processed. They are completed on special forms created by using Sage 50 Accounting Reports & Forms setting of Plain-paper laser & Inkjet form, or creating them on similar forms provided by Canada Revenue Agency or the Quebec government. To save paper, do NOT print T4s or Relevé 1 slips. Study a sample T4 in Fig. 7-30.

Your instructor will have the printouts of all the T4 employees to date. It is possible to print regular T4s on plain paper, but the Report and Forms setting would need to change. There is no exercise for this procedure. Your instructor will have the setting for printing. Printing T4s uses a lot of paper.

At year-end, you will need to back up your data and keep a copy in a locked cabinet to ensure that you always have a backup in case the original payroll data is lost or corrupt. If the data were to become lost or corrupt, the firm would need someone to manually create T4s for all employees. Once you advance the Session date to a new calendar year, Sage 50 Accounting resets all the T4 or Relevé 1 information to zero to start the new calendar year.

Before you proceed, back up your data. It is very important that you are able to print T4s again in case of errors. Without a separate backup, T4s could not be printed again.

Also, once you advance the Session date to a new calendar year, the T4 data is placed in the previous year.

In future, if you wish to print T4s or other payroll forms, you would follow the procedure below. You do not need to do it now.

From the Home window, click Reports, Payroll, then select the appropriate item(s) required and options.

Fig. 7-30: A sample T4 form.

There is no exercise for this procedure. (See side note box.)

Printing Month-End Employee-Related Reports

All of the transactions for the Creative Wallpaper PAYROLL module for January have been completed. As part of the normal month-end procedures for any company, you should print reports for the month's transactions.

Exercise 7-20—Printing Month-End Employee-Related Reports

The Payroll Journal report lists only payroll transactions. The payroll transactions are also contained in the All Journal Entries report.

Printing the PAYROLL Journal

1 ➤ Click **Report Centre,** click **Employees & Payroll,** click **Payroll Journal Entries,** click **Modify this report,** click **Show Corrections.** (See side note box.) Dates should be: Start date **Jan 01, 2019,** Finish date **Jan 31, 2019,** click **OK.**

(See side note box.)

Entries #1 and #21 are General Journal entries and are listed in the All Journal Entries report. Entry #7, #8, #17, #18, #19, and #20 (cheques #205, #213 and #214) are not payroll transactions and are listed in the All Journal Entries and or Payments reports.

To Print an Income Statement for Jan 1 to Jan 31, 2019

Refer to instructions shown in previous chapters.

Review the balances in the accounts shown. The Wages Expense is the total of the regular pay and vacation pay the employees earned. Salary, commission, and overtime pay are recorded separately.

The other expenses (EI, CPP, and WSIB) are benefit costs of hiring employees and are normally referred to as payroll or benefit expenses.

Companies will normally group these expenses together and calculate a percentage of the benefits compared to gross payroll expenses (Wages, Salaries, Commissions, Wages-OT). Creative Wallpaper's cost of benefits is 7.32%.

To Print the Balance Sheet as at Jan 31, 2019

To print the Balance Sheet, refer to instructions as shown in previous chapters.

Review the balances for the payroll-related G/L accounts:

- LOANS RECEIVABLE is owed to the company by employee(s).

- VACATION PAYABLE is owed to the employees for accrued vacation.

- EI PAYABLE, CPP PAYABLE, and INCOME TAX PAYABLE are owed to the Federal Government (Receiver General) and are normally paid monthly.

- United Way Donations Payable records the amounts collected from employees during a recent campaign and is not deducted from paycheques. This money will be sent to the United Way in February.

- UNION DUES PAYABLE are owed to the union to which the employees belong.

- WSIB (WCB) PAYABLE is owed to the provincial Workplace Safety and Insurance Board and is normally paid monthly.

You do not need to print the following reports at this time. Use the information for future reference. These reports are normally used by management to verify information regarding employees.

To Display a Cheque Log for Jan 1 to Jan 31, 2019

1 ➤ **Display** a Cheque Log for cheques issued from January 1, 2019 to January 31, 2019. Refer to Exercise 3B-37. You do NOT need to print this report at this time. The report (partial) shown next, indicates that cheque #208 was reversed.

(See side note box.)

208	Payroll	DAVID, Doreen	1,210.82	Jan 25, 2019	0	Reversed	J11	Jan 25, 2019
209	Payroll	CURRIE, Jordan	472.57	Jan 25, 2019	0	Yes	J12	Jan 25, 2019
210	Payroll	DAVID, Doreen	1,074.34	Jan 25, 2019	0	Yes	J14	Jan 25, 2019

To Print the Employee Detail Report

The Employee Detail Report is a list of the employees' payroll information for the current year. The information is listed by pay period, and can be displayed and/or printed for one date or a range of dates.

You do NOT need to print this report at this time. You would print this report, however, if you need to verify employee payroll details. If you were to print this report, you would do the following from the Home window:

- Click Reports, Payroll, Employee.
- Click Detail, set the range of dates, Start Jan 01, 2019 to Finish Jan 31, 2019.
- Select DAVID, Doreen or Select All to include all employees.
- Check the Show only incomes, deductions, and taxes that are currently in use, or that have a YTD amount item.
- Click OK. You may need to scroll down or click the full window icon to see the balance of the report.

The program will keep these default boxes for all employees until you change them.

To Print the Employee YTD (Year-To-Date) Report

The Employee YTD Report is a list of the employees' YTD payroll information for the current year. The information is listed in summary for the Year-to-Current Session date.

You do NOT print this report for this exercise.

Click Reports, Payroll, Employee.

Click Summary.

Select a specific employee, or Select All to include all employees, OK.

You may need to maximize the window, or scroll down to see other employees.

Compare your printouts to those in the Creative Wallpaper section of the instructor's Solutions Manual. Remember, the payroll entries and amounts may be slightly different if you are using a version of Sage 50 Accounting that is different from Premium Accounting 2015 version 1.

The following section is **FOR INFORMATION ONLY**. Use it for future reference.

Payroll Entry with EHT (Employer Health Tax)

Payroll Journal Entry Jan 31, 2019 (J22)

Account Number	Account Description	Debits	Credits
5300	Wages Expense	1,040.00	-
5310	EI Expense	26.32	-
5320	CPP Expense	42.84	-
5330	WSIB Expense	4.10	-
5360	EHT Expense	9.80	-
1010	Bank Account Chequing	-	738.20
2300	Vacation Payable	-	40.00
2310	EI Payable	-	45.12
2320	CPP Payable	-	85.68
2330	Income Tax Payable	-	100.16
2395	EHT Payable	-	9.80
2420	Union Dues Payable	-	20.00
2430	Pension Plan Payable	-	40.00
2440	Medical Plan Payable	-	24.00
2450	Safety Shoes Payable	-	16.00
2460	WSIB Payable	-	4.10
Additional Date:	Additional Field:		
		1,123.06	1,123.06

Converting During the Year

Do NOT enter the next example. If payroll conversion takes place during a calendar year (e.g., June 30), Historical employee deductions for EI, CPP, Income tax, and other payroll deductions would be entered as of June 30. The payroll information for the conversion (January 1 to June 30) and payroll information entered for the months of July–December are accumulated by the program, and will be used in preparing T4 slips for the complete year. See Fig. 7-31.

Employee data, converted at June 30

Personal
Employee name and information

Historical Income

Regular Wages:	12,800.00
Overtime Wages 1:	395.00
Taxable Benefits:	250.00
Vac Pay Paid:	177.80
Vac Pay Owed:	350.00
EI Earnings:	12,760.00
Net Pay:	9,165.22

Historical Deductions

Pension:	527.80
Union:	260.00
Medical:	312.00

Historical Taxes

Income Tax:	2,399.54
EI Premiums:	396.89
CPP Premiums:	311.35

Fig. 7-31: Conversion information during the year.

Garnishee and Reimbursement

Information on *Payroll Garnishment* (Appendix 2015 P) and *Reimbursement (Payroll)* (Appendix 2015 T) can be found in your course materials at www.nelson.com/student.

End of the Information section.

Relevant Appendices

www The following appendices are available in your course materials at www.nelson.com/student.

Appendix 2015 P	**Payroll Garnishment**
Appendix 2015 Q	**Names Fields**
Appendix 2015 S	**Time & Billing Journal**
Appendix 2015 T	**Reimbursement (Payroll)**

Before Moving On ...

Read the following questions and make sure you know the answers to them; otherwise, read the corresponding part in the chapter before moving on:

1. Briefly describe how the Sage 50 Accounting EMPLOYEE & PAYROLL module works:

   - its purpose.

   - the records or forms it can automatically produce.

   - built-in tables and formulas.

2. After entering the employee payroll for January 2019, the total of year-to-date employees' gross pay plus vacation pay owed must equal the balance of which G/L accounts?

3. Why is the session date particularly important to consider when processing in the Sage 50 Accounting PAYROLL module? If you set a particular session date, what restrictions are set by Sage 50 Accounting?

4. Why is it particularly important to back up your data before printing Tax slips for employees and/or CRA at December 31?

5. What is the procedure for correcting an error in posting a paycheque in the PAYROLL module?

Challenge Exercise 07 C7-1, Carpets 4Home
(PAYROLL and PAYABLES Modules)

This exercise is a review of the PAYROLL and PAYABLES modules.

1 ➤   Refer to Exercise 1-1b to unzip the **07 C7-1 Carpets.exe** file.

2 ➤   Open the **07 C7-1 Carpets** file.

Payroll information:

- All employees are paid bi-weekly.

- Overtime is paid at time and a half (regular pay, plus ½ regular pay).

- Vacation pay (4%) is retained from hourly and commission employees until the employee takes a vacation. Vacation pay is not calculated or retained for salaried employees.

- The EI rate is 1.4% times the employee deductions.

- It is assumed that the employer is exempt from the Employee Health Tax (EHT).

- Union dues are deducted from hourly and commission employees' paycheques.

- The company does not have a pension plan.

- The company allows employees to receive a payroll loan up to $700.00 for extenuating circumstances. The loan is repayable by all employees at $20.00 per pay. Hardeep Singh has a $500.00 loan owing at January 1.

- Commission employee Vibeke Ipanaque is on a medical leave of absence and is expected back to work by the middle of January.

3 ➤   **Record** and **Post** the following transactions for January:

Jan 2   Change employee "A-YOUR ACTUAL LAST, First Name" to your own name before processing payroll transactions.

Jan 2   Memo 1-YM received from Owner, to reverse the Accrued Payroll Payable entry created in the previous year. See the January 1 Trial Balance. (There was no accrual for commission employees.)

Jan 4   Pay by Payroll Cheque Run, pay period effective today:

Hardeep Singh	80 hours, she is repaying her loan by $20.00 per pay
Herve Lions	80 hours and 1 hour overtime
A-YOUR ACTUAL LAST, First Name	salary (80 hours per period)

Jan 4   Hardeep Singh (normally paid bi-weekly) will go on a one-week vacation starting today. She will return on January 13. As discussed in the chapter, change the pay periods to 52 and then issue a vacation paycheque $650.00 of the amount accrued. Use the Paycheques icon to pay the Vacation Pay. Union dues and/or loan repayments are not deducted on vacation pay.

Jan 4   Manager called Herve Lions to advise him his cheque was incorrect. He had been 2 hours late for work on January 2, and the cheque should have been for 79 hours at his regular wage rate. Received and reversed original cheque. Issued a corrected cheque.

Jan 14   Vibeke Ipanaque and Hardeep Singh both returned to work today. They will each be working just one week in this pay period (ending Jan. 18). Make sure their employee setup reflects this (Income tab) to ensure taxes will be deducted properly. Return Vibeke Ipanaque to "Active Employee" status.

Jan 14   Canada Revenue Agency (CRA) payroll auditor arrived today to do an audit on the previous year's payroll records.

Jan 15   The payroll auditor verified that the previous year's files and records were in order. The manager approved issuing the next cheque to the Receiver General, for December 31, amount owing for PAYROLL amounts (Trial Balance amounts at January 1).

Jan 18   Pay by **Payroll Cheque Run**, pay period effective today.

Singh, Hardeep	for 40 hours. She is repaying her loan by $20.00 per pay
Ipanaque, Vibeke	for $912.00 commission for 40 hours
Lions, Herve	for 80 hours and 1 hour overtime
A-YOUR ACTUAL Last, First Name	salary (80 hours per period)

After the payroll cheque run is completed, return Vibeke and Hardeep to 26 pay periods per year.

Jan 21   The owner has given you a memo to update the accounting records by recording a payroll accrual for $976.00 salary and $350.00 commission, for the period ending today. The owner needs the reports, listed below, for a meeting with the bank.

4 ➤ Print the following reports for the manager for his meeting with the bank manager.
   a) Balance Sheet
   b) Income Statement (All amounts will be zero, except for payroll)
   c) Payroll Journal Entries, with corrections, to January 21
   d) All Journal Entries, with corrections, for the same period
   e) General Journal Entries for the same period
   f) Cheque log for January 1 to January 21

Challenge Exercise 07 C7-2, Glass
(PAYROLL and PAYABLES Modules)

The company sells assorted glasses and glassware products to both wholesale and retail customers.

This exercise is a review of the PAYROLL and PAYABLES modules.

1 ➤ Refer to Exercise 1-1b to unzip the **07 C7-2 Glass.exe** file.

2 ➤ Open the **07 7C-2 Glass** file.

Payroll information:

- All employees are paid as noted in the information below.

- Overtime is paid at time and a half (regular pay plus ½ regular pay).

- Vacation pay (4%) is retained from hourly and commission employees, until the employee takes a vacation. Vacation pay is not calculated for salaried employees.

- The EI rate is 1.4% times the employee deductions.

- It is assumed that the employee is exempt from the Employee Health Tax (EHT).

- Union Dues are deducted from hourly and commission employees' paycheques.

- The company has a pension plan.

- The Company allows employees to receive a payroll loan up to $700.00 for extenuating circumstances. The loan is repayable by all employees at $20.00 per pay. There are no outstanding loans.

January Pay Dates:	Hourly and commission employees are paid weekly. Salaried employees are paid bi-weekly (4th and 18th).

Weekly:
January 4th
January 11th
January 18th
January 25th

Bi-Weekly:
January 4th
January 18th

Deductions per pay period:	Medical	Pension	Union Dues	Safety Shoes
Hourly employees:	✓	✓	✓	✓
Commission employees:	✓	✓	✓	
Salary employees:	✓	✓		

3 ➤ **Record** and **Post** the following transactions for January.

Change employee "A-YOUR ACTUAL LAST, First Name" to your own name before processing.

Jan 2   Received "Memo Sal-Rev" from the owner to reverse the December 31st payroll accrual in the amount of $1,500 for <u>all</u> employees. (The total accrual for wages and salaries was accrued in Salaries Expense at Dec 31, 2018.)

Jan 4   Process a payroll cheque run for ALL pay periods.
Note: A-YOUR ACTUAL LAST, First Name worked 40 hours + 4 hours overtime, and Valerie Kott worked 40 hours and earned $450 in commissions.

Jan 7   Valerie Kott phoned this morning requesting one week off for personal reasons and asked for her vacation pay. Released total vacation pay owing as of January 4th. Did not deduct for medical plan or union dues.

Jan 11   *Non-salaried* payroll for the week ending January 11th is recorded as follows:

A-YOUR ACTUAL LAST, First Name worked 40 regular hours plus 2 overtime hours. Issued a cheque for the net pay.

Jan 14   A-YOUR ACTUAL LAST, First Name stopped by the payroll office today. It was confirmed there was an error with the Jan. 11th paycheque. In addition to 40 regular hours, First Name should have been paid for 5 overtime hours. They returned the payroll cheque to the office. Prepare the necessary reversing and correcting entries. (Use the approach presented in your textbook.) Issue a replacement cheque (next available cheque number) for the correct amount to A-YOUR ACTUAL LAST, First Name.

January Pay Dates:

Weekly:
January 4th
January 11th
January 18th
January 25th

Bi-Weekly:
January 4th
January 18th

Jan 14   Valerie Kott returned to work today. She was approved for a staff loan of $600.00 as her furnace motor needs repairs. Issue next cheque.

Jan 18   Process a payroll cheque run for ALL pay periods. Valerie Kott worked 40 hours this week and earned $575 in commissions, and A-YOUR ACTUAL LAST, First Name worked 40 hours, plus + 1 overtime hour.

Jan 21   Issued next cheque to the Receiver General for the EI, CPP, and Income Tax payable balances outstanding at January 1, 2019.

Jan 25   Valerie worked 40 hours this week and earned $500 commission.
A-YOUR ACTUAL, LAST, First name worked 40 hours, no overtime.

4 ➤   Print the reports indicated below after you have inputted the transactions.

a)   Journal Entries All (**No corrections)** for the period of the entries.
b)   Payroll Journal Entries, **with Corrections** to Jan 25.
c)   Balance Sheet at Jan 25.
d)   Income Statement.
e)   Employee Detail (all employees for month of January).
f)   Cheque log to Jan 25.

Challenge Exercise 07 C7-3, Tool Shed Company
(PAYROLL and PAYABLES Modules)

The company sells assorted tools and saw blades to both wholesale and retail customers.

This exercise is a review of the PAYROLL and PAYABLES modules.

1 ➤ Refer to Exercise 1-1b to unzip the **07 7C-3 Tool Shed.exe** file.

2 ➤ Open the **07 7C-3 Tool Shed** file.

Payroll information:

- All employees are paid as noted in the information below.

- Overtime is paid at time and a half (regular pay plus ½ regular pay).

- Vacation pay (4%) is retained from hourly and commission employees, until the employee takes a vacation. Vacation pay is not calculated for salaried employees.

- The EI rate is 1.4% times the employee deductions.

- It is assumed that the employee is exempt from the Employee Health Tax (EHT).

- Union Dues are deducted from hourly and commission employees' paycheques.

- The company has a pension plan.

- The Company allows employees to receive a payroll loan up to $500.00 for extenuating circumstances. The loan is repayable by all employees at $30.00 per pay. There are no outstanding loans

January Pay Dates:	
Weekly: January 4th January 11th January 18th January 25th	
Bi-Monthly: January 15th January 31st	

Hourly and commission employees are paid weekly on Friday.

Salaried employees are paid bi-monthly (15th and 31st).

Deductions per pay period:	Medical	Pension	Union Dues	Safety Shoes
Hourly employees:	✓	✓	✓	✓
Commission employees:	✓	✓	✓	
Salary employees:	✓	✓		

3 ➤ **Record** and **Post** the following transactions for January.

Change employee "A-LAST NAME, First Name" to your own name before processing.

Jan 2   Received "Memo Sal-Rev" from the owner to reverse the December 31st payroll accrual in the amount of $1,500 for <u>all</u> employees. (The total accrual for wages and salaries was accrued in Salaries Expense at Dec 31, 2018.)

Jan 4   Process a payroll cheque run for 1st payroll of month.

   Note: A-LAST NAME, First Name worked 40 hours + 4 hours overtime, and
        Canon, Marisa worked 40 hours and earned $450 in commissions.

Jan 7   Canon, Marisa phoned this morning requesting one week off for personal reasons and asked for her vacation pay. Released total vacation pay owing as of January 4th. Did not deduct for medical plan or union dues.

Jan 8   A-LAST NAME, First Name brought his paycheque to the office. It was confirmed there was an error with the paycheque. In addition to 40 regular hours First Name should have been paid for 5 overtime hours. Prepare the necessary reversing and correcting entries. (Use the approach presented in your textbook.) Issue a replacement cheque (next available cheque number) for the correct amount to YOUR ACTUAL LAST, First Name.

Jan 11   Hourly payroll for the week ending January 11th is recorded. A-LAST NAME, First Name worked 40 regular hours.

Jan 14   Canon, Marisa returned to work today. She was approved for a staff loan of $500.00 as her car motor needed repairs. Issue next cheque.

Jan 14   Issued next cheque to the Receiver General for the EI, CPP, and Income Tax payable balances outstanding at January 1st, 2019.

Jan 15   *Bi-monthly* salary payroll for January 15th is recorded.

Jan 18   Process a payroll cheque run for the weekly pay period:

> A-LAST NAME, First Name worked 40 regular hours plus 2 overtime hours.
> Canon, Marisa worked 32 hours and earned commission of $623.

January Pay Dates:

Weekly:
January 4th
January 11th
January 18th
January 25th

Bi-Monthly:
January 15th
January 31st

Jan 25   Process a payroll cheque run for the weekly pay period:

> A-LAST NAME, First name worked 40 hours, no overtime.
> Canon, Marisa worked 40 hours this week and earned $500 commission.

Jan 31   *Salary* payroll for January 31 is recorded.

Jan 31   Prepare a Payroll accrual adjustment:

> A-LAST NAME, First Name worked 32 regular hours.
> Canon, Marisa worked 36 hours for $580 commission.

4 ➤ **Print the reports** indicated below after you have inputted the transactions.

    a)   Journal Entries All (**No corrections)** for the period of the entries.
    b)   Payroll Journal Entries, **with Corrections** to Jan 31.
    c)   Balance Sheet at Jan 31.
    d)   Income Statement.
    e)   Employee Detail (all employees for month of January).
    f)   Cheque Log at Jan 31.

Chapter 8

INVENTORY & SERVICES Module Setup and Transactions Review: G/L, A/P, A/R

Printers Company

Learning Objectives

After completing this chapter you will be able to:

☐ Create and modify inventory and service item information.
☐ Set up the module defaults and Linking accounts.
☐ Turn the module to Ready.
☐ Record transactions (Sales and Purchases) using Perpetual Inventory items.
☐ Display and print appropriate inventory reports and journals.

This chapter reviews the setup procedures for the INVENTORY & SERVICES module and provides practice in processing inventory transactions using the **Printers Company** files. The COMPANY, PAYABLES, and RECEIVABLES modules are also used. Refer to Fig. 2A-1a and Fig. 2A-1b, **Comparison of Periodic** and **Perpetual Inventory Systems**.

This chapter assumes that you have some knowledge of Perpetual Inventory accounting. If you are unsure of the procedures, you should research the topic before starting this chapter.

The contents of this chapter are as follows:

INVENTORY & SERVICES Module Overview

The INVENTORY & SERVICES module is used to keep track of the quantity and cost of a company's inventory items (i.e., goods for sale) and services (e.g., veterinary services, repairs to equipment, office visits). This chapter illustrates the use of the **Perpetual Inventory Ledger**, where detailed records of purchases and sales of each item of inventory are kept. The quantity and cost are increased by each purchase and decreased by each sale.

Companies that use the INVENTORY & SERVICES module charge the cost of inventory **purchased for resale** (e.g., printers, ink, cables) to a **G/L asset inventory** account (e.g., INVENTORY INKJET PRINTERS) rather than the PURCHASES account.

When goods are sold:

a) The asset Inventory account (in the Balance sheet) is reduced ↓ by the cost of the goods.

b) The Cost of Goods Sold account in the Income Statement is increased ↑ by the cost of the goods.

The Sage 50 Accounting INVENTORY & SERVICES module keeps track of inventory at **Average Cost** or **First In, First Out** (**FIFO**) methods. The average cost method takes the total cost of the individual goods divided by the number of items in stock.

Example: Inventory item: **Laser Black Cartridge** = $1,056.00. Divide by 16, (the number of items in stock) = average cost of $66.00. If you buy 10 more cartridges for $645.00 = $1,701.00 total cost for 26 total cartridges. The new average cost = $65.42 (1,701.00/26). Refer to your accounting textbook for further explanation. This is also illustrated in Exercise 8-11.

Sage 50 Accounting will allow you to change from the Average Cost method to the FIFO method. Sage 50 Accounting does not allow the use of the Last In, First Out (LIFO) costing method.

When goods are purchased, the transactions are recorded in the PAYABLES module, and the INVENTORY & SERVICES module records (cost and quantity) are increased ⬆.

When goods are sold, the transactions are recorded in the RECEIVABLES module, and the INVENTORY & SERVICES module records (cost and quantity) are decreased ⬇.

Sage 50 Accounting allows you to have regular and preferred pricing for customers. Preferred pricing, which is a reduction in the selling price, would be given to customers who buy a large amount (quantity) of merchandise and/or services. See Exercises 8-7 and 8-9.

Before the INVENTORY & SERVICES module can be used, the COMPANY, PAYABLES, and RECEIVABLES modules must be set to **Ready**. Inventory items must be added to the INVENTORY module, and the quantities and cost of the goods must be entered as of the conversion date.

Run **Slideshow 8A—Setting Up the INVENTORY & SERVICES Module** now. It explains the various steps required to set the INVENTORY & SERVICES module to **Ready**.

Printers Company: Company Profile

Printers Company is in the business of buying and selling computer printers, black ink cartridges, and printer cables. The company carries only two types of printers, related ink cartridges, and printer cables. The company is planning to sell colour cartridges at a later date. Printers Company sells to other companies that sell directly to the public, and does not normally sell retail.

The management of Printers Company has hired you to set up the INVENTORY & SERVICES module and use it to process transactions.

INVENTORY Policies and Procedures

Sales invoices and purchase payment cheques are prepared manually and are entered in the computer on a weekly basis. In the workplace, the same documents can be printed using the Sage 50 Accounting program on special preprinted form paper.

CASH DISCOUNTS are allowed to all customers based on the selling price of the items sold before taxes.

The company does not use the Additional Information fields.

Printers Company, Student's Name
Trial Balance As At Jan 01, 2019

		Debits	Credits
1020	Bank Account	8,131.00	-
1200	Accounts Receivable	15,068.55	-
1250	Inventory InkJet Printers	7,950.00	-
1260	Inventory Laser Printers	5,800.00	-
1270	Inventory Ink Cartridges InkJet	800.00	-
1280	Inventory Ink Cartridges Laser	1,056.00	-
1290	Inventory Printer Cables	350.00	-
1330	Prepaid Store Supplies	800.00	-
1510	Equipment	53,146.00	-
1515	Accum Deprec Equipment	-	26,000.00
1520	Office, Warehouse Furniture	28,560.00	-
1525	Accum. Deprec Office/Warehouse	-	13,490.00
2200	Accounts Payable	-	15,992.73
2650	HST Charged on Sales	-	400.25
2670	HST Paid on Purchases	210.56	-
2710	Bank Loan Payable	-	0.00
3100	Capital Gavin Mosely	-	65,989.13
3230	Drawings Gavin Mosely	-	0.00
4100	Sales InkJets	-	0.00
4110	Sales Lasers	-	0.00
4120	Sales Cables	-	0.00
4150	Sales Discount	-	0.00
4200	Sales Returns & Allowances	-	0.00
4510	Handling Fee		0.00
5010	Cost of Goods Sold- InkJets	0.00	-
5020	Cost of Goods Sold- Lasers	0.00	-
5030	Cost of Goods Sold- Cables	0.00	-
5040	Purchase Discounts	0.00	-
5050	Inventory Adjustments	0.00	-
5310	Wages Expense	0.00	-
5400	Rent Expense	0.00	-
5410	Advertising Expense	0.00	-
5420	Bank Charges & Interest	0.00	-
5430	Insurance Expense	0.00	-
5440	Office/Store Supplies Expense	0.00	-
5450	Telephone Expense	0.00	-
5460	Utility Expense	0.00	-
5470	Bad Debts Expense	0.00	-
		121,872.11	121,872.11

Fig. 8-1: Printers Company Trial Balance as at Jan 01, 2019.

Customer Aged Detail As at Jan 01, 2019

Source	Date	Transaction Type	Total	Current	31 to 60
Computers and More					
11568	Dec 14, 2018	Invoice	5,520.05	5,520.05	-
Total outstanding:			5,520.05	5,520.05	-
Davis Computers					
11571	Dec 14, 2018	Invoice	6,158.50	6,158.50	-
Total outstanding:			6,158.50	6,158.50	-
Do-It Yourself Inc.					
11575	Dec 24, 2018	Invoice	3,390.00	3,390.00	-
Total outstanding:			3,390.00	3,390.00	-
Total unpaid invoices:			15,068.55	15,068.55	-
Total deposits/prepaid order:			-	-	-
Total outstanding:			15,068.55	15,068.55	-

Fig. 8-2: Printers Company Customer Aged Detail report.

Vendor Aged Detail As at Jan 01, 2019

Source	Date	Transaction Type	Total	Current	31 to 60
Cables and Accessories					
2998	Dec 17, 2018	Invoice	316.40	316.40	-
Total outstanding:			316.40	316.40	-
H-Printers Company					
3689501	Dec 31, 2018	Invoice	9,944.00	9,944.00	-
Total outstanding:			9,944.00	9,944.00	-
Laser Products Ltd.					
3625	Dec 24, 2018	Invoice	5,732.33	5,732.33	-
Total outstanding:			5,732.33	5,732.33	-
Total unpaid invoices:			15,992.73	15,992.73	-
Total prepayments/prepaid order:			-	-	-
Total outstanding:			15,992.73	15,992.73	-

Fig. 8-3: Printers Company Vendor Aged Detail report.

Conversion

As in other modules, when a conversion is made from a manual to a computerized system or from one computerized system to another, the General Ledger, RECEIVABLES, PAYABLES, and INVENTORY balances in the new system should match the old system.

www There are two files in your course materials at www.nelson.com/student that refer to **Printers Company**: **08 Printers** and **08 Printers2**, which can be used to record INVENTORY & SERVICES transactions for this chapter. Your instructor will advise you which of the two **Printers** data files you are to use.

If you use the 08 Printers data file:

You need to use the data file **08 Printers** to do all the chapter exercises, which cover the following topics:

1. Setting defaults
2. Linking the appropriate accounts to the General Ledger
3. Creating individual Inventory Item ledgers
4. Setting the INVENTORY & SERVICES module to Ready
5. Recording Perpetual Inventory transactions

If you use 08 Printers2 data file:

In data file **08 Printers2,** the INVENTORY & SERVICES module was set up by your supervisor and has been set to **Ready**. It is, therefore, ready for processing transactions. You have been hired to be the new accounting clerk. If you wish to review the steps that your supervisor completed to have the module ready to use, read the instructions for Exercises 8-1 to 8-6.

Step 1: Starting the INVENTORY & SERVICES Module

Exercise 8-1—Starting the INVENTORY & SERVICES Module
---

1 ➤   Refer to Exercise 1-1b, to unzip the appropriate **08 Printers,** or **08 Printers2** file.

2 ➤   Start **Sage 50 Accounting** and open the appropriate **08 Printers** or **08 Printers2** data file.

If you are using 08 Printers2, proceed to Exercise 8-7.

If you are using the **08 Printers** file, proceed to step 3.

3 ➤   Accept the Session date of **Jan 01, 2019**. The Printers Company Home window is displayed.

4 ➤   To view and update the INVENTORY & SERVICES module, from the top menu click **Setup, User Preferences**, click **View**, in the Pages area, click the **Inventory & Services** box, and both the Pages and Icon Window boxes now have a ✓.

5 ➤   Click **OK**. The INVENTORY & SERVICES module is displayed on the left side of the Home window.

6 ➤   Click the **INVENTORY & SERVICES** module. The appropriate icons are now displayed and the module is available to update.

The Inventory and Services icons are described below.

The Inventory & Services Journals

| **Inventory & Services** | This journal is used to view, add, modify, or remove an Inventory & Service item. Only items with no item count and no dollar value information can be removed. |

| **Build from Bill of Materials** | This journal can be used on a regular basis for the transfer of several items into one finished item. When an item icon is highlighted, the journal automatically inserts **item code, description, unit of measure**, and **cost**. See Exercise 8-21. |

| **Build from Item Assembly** | This journal is used on a random basis for the transfer of several items into one finished item. When an item icon is highlighted, the journal automatically inserts **item code, description, unit of measure**, and **cost**. See Information Only section at the end of Exercise 8-21. |

| **Adjust Inventory** | This journal is used for recording adjustments to item quantity or cost. When an item icon is highlighted, the Adjustments journal automatically inserts **item code**, **description**, **unit of measure**, and **cost**. |

| **Transfer Inventory** | You use this icon to transfer inventory from one location (warehouse or store) to another location. This feature is not shown in the text. |

7 ➤ Remember that Printers Company uses the **Perpetual** Inventory system. In this step we will include fields to permit inventory items to be used in Purchase and Sales invoices, quotes, and orders. We will also remove fields that pertain to the Projects module, which is not in use for this company.

(i) Click the **PAYABLES** module on the left, click the **Purchase Invoices** icon. Click the **Customize Journal** icon 🖳. In the left pane, the Purchase Invoices selection should be shown with a ⊟. If a ⊞ is displayed at **Purchase Invoices**, click the ⊞ then click **Columns**. You need to remove the ☑ in the **Item Number** field.

(ii) Repeat the ⊞ procedure for the following column items: **Purchase Orders, Sales Invoices, Sales Orders, Sales Quotes**.

(iii) Repeat the ⊞ procedure for the column items. **Adjustments and Make Other Payment**, but instead, place a ☑ in the **Allocations** field. (See side note box.)

> ℹ️ Failure to remove the ✓ from the 5 column items as indicated will not allow you to record the perpetual inventory purchases and sales properly.

8 ➤ Click **OK**. The item column is now available for use.

9 ➤ *Note:* You may have to move column widths < or > to see information.

10 ➤ **Exit** to the Home window.

11 ➤ **Display** the Chart of Accounts. Click **Report Centre, Accounts, Chart of Accounts**, click **Modify this report**. The Current Year (2019) is in blue, click **OK**. Notice that inventory accounts #1250 to 1290 are **Inventory** class, and accounts #5010 to 5050 are **Cost of Goods Sold** class. For the INVENTORY module to work, you must have the Inventory and Cost of Goods Sold class accounts identified. Click ⊠ to close the report. Return to the Home window.

Step 2: Setting the INVENTORY & SERVICES Module Defaults

Exercise 8-2—Setting INVENTORY & SERVICES Module Defaults
---

1 ➤ From the top menu click **Setup, Settings,** click the ⊞ at **Inventory & Services**, click **Options**.

Inventory Costing Method

As discussed at the beginning of this chapter (Overview), Sage 50 Accounting can record inventory using the methods shown. This chapter will use the Average Cost method. Do NOT change the default **Average Cost**.

Profit Evaluation Method

The default shows the method used by Sage 50 Accounting to calculate the Gross Profit percentage. **Markup** or **Margin** is the difference between the inventory items, selling price and average cost. **Gross profit** is displayed using 1 of 2 methods:

Markup % = (Selling Price - Cost)/Cost

Margin % = (Selling Price - Cost)/Selling Price

Do NOT change the default **Margin**.

Sort Inventory & Services by

○ Number   ● Description

Inventory items in this ledger can be sorted by **Number** or by **item description**. **Description** should be selected.

Allow inventory levels to go below zero

☐ Allow inventory levels to go below zero

Do NOT change. Printers Company does not allow inventory levels to go below zero.

2 ➤ In the left pane, click **Price List** to display the default price list names. This will be explained in Exercise 8-4. Do NOT change.

3 ➤ In the left pane, click **Locations**. The user can identify various locations where inventory is stored (warehouse, in another city, etc.). There is no exercise for this feature. Do NOT change.

4 ➤ In the left pane, click **Categories** to display the heading and note as shown next. If the business had thousands of similar items in stock with various inventory codes, the user could identify the items as part of a category (e.g., printers or print cartridges) and the report would display the category items. There is no exercise for this feature. Do NOT change.

☐ My company uses Categories for inventory and service items

Use categories to group related inventory and service items together.
To add a new category, enter a category name on a new line.

Names   Additional information about items of inventory would display when the item of inventory is used in a sale or purchase. This feature is not used by Sarah's Kitchen.

Leave this window open for the next exercise.

Step 3: Setting Up INVENTORY & SERVICES Linked Accounts

The next step in the setup process is to define the **linked** accounts in order to update the INVENTORY module when relevant journal information (Journal transaction) is entered in the PAYABLES and RECEIVABLES modules.

Sales invoices for inventory items are recorded in the RECEIVABLES module.

Purchase invoices for inventory items are recorded in the PAYABLES module.

Purchase and Sales invoices include inventory descriptions, quantities bought or sold, and prices.

Exercise 8-3—Setting Up INVENTORY & SERVICES Linked Accounts

The INVENTORY & SERVICES Linked accounts are set up as follows:

1 ➤ In the left pane click **Linked Accounts**.

When you process inventory adjustments or assemble items with Item Assembly, these accounts are used as needed.

Item Assembly Costs:

Adjustment Write-off:

Item Assembly Costs	Do NOT change. (Leave the field blank.) This would be used when a business takes a number of parts and makes them (assembles them) into a product for sale (e.g., a number of different computer parts are made into a saleable computer system). Printers Company does not assemble new printers; therefore, the company does not use this feature.
Adjustment Write-Off	There are various ways for a firm to keep track of inventory differences.

Some companies use an account, Inventory Adjustments, when the computer inventory records need to be updated to the actual goods on hand due to theft, damage, shrinkage, overage, etc.

Some firms may also use an account, Damaged Goods, when goods for sale are damaged and cannot be sold. Printers Company does not use a Damaged Goods account.

These accounts would be in the Cost of Goods section of the Income Statement.

There are many other accounts that could be used to record differences. Each firm would use account names that would best represent what has happened to the inventory.

> Many companies do not keep a separate account for adjustments/changes to inventory. Adjustments, therefore, would be posted to a **Cost of Goods Sold** (Cost of Sales) account.

2 ➤ **Adjustment Write-Off**   Type **5050**, `Tab` for **Inventory Adjustments**. If adjustments have to be made to inventory costs, they will be posted to this G/L expense account.

Adjustment Write-off: 5050 Inventory Adjustments

3 ➤ Click the **OK** button to save changes and **Exit** to the Home window. (See side note box.)

The Linked accounts for INVENTORY & SERVICES are now set up. The Linked accounts for the other modules have been set up for you earlier.

Step 4: Creating Inventory Item Ledgers

In order to keep track of increases and decreases for each INVENTORY item, you need to create individual Inventory or Service item ledgers. You cannot use the Setup Guide to enter inventory items. The procedure is very similar to creating individual customer and vendor ledgers.

___

Exercise 8-4—Creating INVENTORY & SERVICES Item Ledgers

Inventory & Services

1 ➤ From the Home window, click the **INVENTORY & SERVICES** module, click the **Inventory & Services** icon.

The Inventory & Services window is similar to previous windows used to create the Customers, Vendors and Employees lists. The difference is in the **Journal** option on the menu bar.

Journal	Reports	Help
Bill of Materials & Item Assembly Journal		
Inventory Adjustments Journal		

The toolbar has icons ⚓ ⚖ for the same journals.

2 ➤ From the **Inventory & Services** window, click the 📄 Create icon to display the **Inventory Ledger** window. The Quantities tab displays.

Inventory Information

Study this chart. The first inventory item (first line in Fig. 8-4) will be set up through the completion of steps 3 to 12. Step 13 will return you to this figure to set up the rest of the inventory items. (Do NOT include an asterisk when setting up InkJet Printer 5 in 1.)

| Quantities | | | Units | Pricing | | | Linked | | | History | |
| Tab | | | Tab | Tab | | | Tab | | | Tab | |
Inventory Name	Inventory Item #	Minimum Level	Stocking Unit of Measure	Regular	Preferred	Web Price	Asset	Revenue	C.O.G.S.	Opening Quantity	Opening Value
InkJet Black Cartridge	IBC-01	26	Each	38.50	37.50	0.00	1270	4100	5010	40	800
InkJet Printer 5 in 1*	IP-001	30	Each	245.00	235.00	0.00	1250	4100	5010	53	7,950
Laser Black Cartridge	LBC-01	10	Each	99.00	98.00	0.00	1280	4110	5020	16	1,056
Laser Printer 20P	LP001	12	Each	400.00	385.00	0.00	1260	4110	5020	20	5,800
Printer Cable USB	C-01	20	Each	15.00	14.50	0.00	1290	4120	5030	50	350
											15,956

* Printer, copier, scanner, fax, PC fax.

Fig. 8-4: Summary of Fig. 8-5 and 8a and 8b Inventory items and values.

You will be entering the information for the first line from Fig. 8-4 in steps 3 through 13.

Quantities

3 ➤ Complete Fig. 8-5 as shown below with the information for the quantities tab.

Fig. 8-5: Inventory & Services Ledger Quantities.

Item Description	Description of the item.
Item Number	Management has decided to use a combination of numbers and letters for the internal company numbering system.

Sage 50 Accounting will allow a combination of 14 numbers and/or letters for item number. The letter codes **I** and **L** identify the item as an InkJet or Laser. The other numbers are in a numerical sequence increasing for future items that may be sold. The codes *IBC* and *LBC* refer to: InkJet **B**lack **C**artridge and **L**aser **B**lack **C**artridge. The red * will disappear when information is entered in a required field.

Type	Do NOT change the Inventory default. Printers Company sells items of inventory. Service items will be shown later in this chapter.
Show Quantities In	This is a unit of measure of how goods are sold. Some companies may sell items in boxes, packages, etc.
On Hand	These fields are shaded because the information has not been entered in the other tab fields.
Pending Orders	These fields are shaded because the information has not been entered in the other tab fields.
Reorder Quantities	Minimum level is the lowest number of items that should be on hand before ordering new items. Sage 50 Accounting will provide a warning message when the inventory item falls below the reorder point. View the Inventory & Service Quantity report. The **To Order** column will indicate the quantity that is below the reorder point. See Exercise 8-8.

Units

4 ➤ Click the **Units** tab.

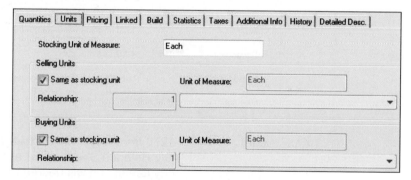

Stocking Unit of Measure	Do NOT change. As noted on the previous window, this field can indicate **each**, **boxes**, etc.
Selling Units	Do NOT change. If the selling unit is different from the stocking unit you would remove the ✓ and change the appropriate fields (e.g., you stock units by the box, and sell individual items).
Buying Units	Do NOT change. If the buying unit is different from the stocking unit, you would remove the ✓ and change the appropriate fields (e.g., you stock units by items and buy by the box).

Pricing

5 ➤ Click the **Pricing** tab and enter the information shown next:

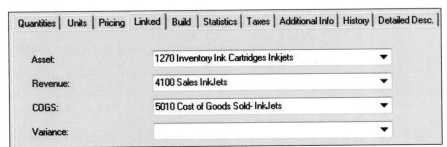

As you input the first amount, the same price amount is recorded for all Selling units.

Sage 50 Premium Accounting allows up to 100 different price lists.

(See side note boxes.)

Price List	Price per Selling Unit
Regular	38.5000
Preferred	37.5000
Web Price	0.0000

Regular Price   This is the normal selling price of the item.

Preferred Price   This is the price at which you will sell this item to customers who buy a large quantity of goods from your firm. The manager has decided to give only one customer this preferred status. This will be shown in Exercise 8-7.

Web Price   Change to 0, then **Tab**. The amount changes to 0.0000. (See side note box at step 13 for information about Sage 50 Accounting removing all 0.0000 amounts in the Price per Selling Unit.) Printers Company does not have a Web-based Store.

Linked

6 ➤ Click the **Linked** tab, and **enter** the information shown next:

Asset	1270 Inventory Ink Cartridges Inkjets	▼
Revenue:	4100 Sales InkJets	▼
COGS:	5010 Cost of Goods Sold- InkJets	▼
Variance:		▼

Asset   **1270 Inventory Ink Cartridges Inkjets**. This field contains the G/L Balance Sheet linked account that will increase when you buy items, and will decrease when you sell items.

Revenue   **4100 Sales InkJets**. This field contains the G/L Income Statement linked account that will increase when you sell items and will decrease when items previously sold are returned.

C.O.G.S.   **5010 Cost of Goods Sold- InkJets**. This field contains the G/L Income Statement linked account that will increase by the cost of the items sold and will decrease when items previously sold are returned.

Variance   Leave blank. This field would be used when you allow negative inventory levels. Printers Company does not allow negative inventory. This topic is not discussed in this text.

Build

7 ➤ Click the **Build** tab.

Build   Do NOT change. Management has decided to use this feature when they create packages for sale (printers, ink, and cables). You will see how this works in Exercise 8-21 as you cannot create a build without inventory items.

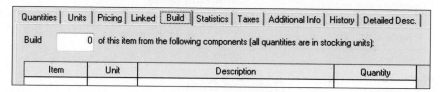

Statistics

8 ➤ Click the **Statistics** tab.

Year To Date   Do NOT change. When the module is turned to Ready, information about previous sales will be available for statistical analysis.

Date of Last Sale   Do NOT change. When the module is turned to Ready, this field will show the last sales transaction date.

Last Year   Do NOT change. Printers Company has decided not to research previous sale information and will track statistical information starting from the conversion date of the INVENTORY module.

Taxes

9 ➤ Click the **Taxes** tab. Do NOT change.

Tax	Tax Exempt		
HST	No		

Additional Info

10 ➤ Click the **Additional Info** tab. Do NOT change. These fields, together with the Detailed Desc. fields, can describe the item. The fields could display the companies we are able to buy the inventory item from. See Appendix 2015 Q, *Names Fields,* in your course materials at www.nelson.com/student.

WWW

History

11 ➤ Click the **History** tab and **enter** the appropriate information from summary Fig. 8-4.

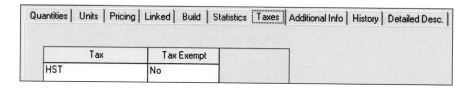

Stocking Units
On Hand   The number of items you currently have in stock.
Opening Quantity   (See Fig. 8-4, also Fig. 8-6, 8-7 and 8-8a and 8-8b.)

Stocking Units
On Hand   The total cost value of the items in stock.
Opening Value   (See Fig.8-4, also Fig. 8-6, 8-8a and 8-8b.)

(See side note box.)

> Opening value divided by Opening Quantity = Average cost.

Detailed Desc.

12 ➤ Click the **Detailed Desc**. tab. Do NOT change. You could use these fields and picture for a longer description of the item. Technical information could be provided to customers for details such as dots per inch, pages per minute, etc.

> After you finish recording the inventory item, click Create Another or Save and Close. Sage 50 Accounting will remove the 0.0000 amounts from any Selling Unit.
>
> Return to the Pricing tab (step 5) to see the 0.0000 removed in the Web Price field.

13 ➤ Click ⟨ **Create Another** ⟩ to save this item. Return to Fig. 8-4 to input the rest of the inventory items using previous steps 2 to 12. (See side note box.)

Add Additional Inventory Items

14 ➤ When you have finished entering the last item with the dollar quantities and values, the software may (or may not) advise you, with the message box shown next, that the total dollar value of the inventory asset accounts is equal to the totals of the individual inventory items you have just entered.

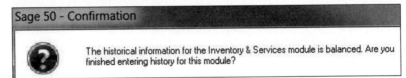

Sage 50 - Confirmation

The historical information for the Inventory & Services module is balanced. Are you finished entering history for this module?

15 ➤ If you see the Confirmation message box, click **No**. If you click Yes, Sage 50 Accounting will turn the INVENTORY module to **Ready**, and you do not want to do that at this point.

The best thing to do at this time is to display and print out the reports in Exercise 8-5 to verify what you have entered so far. If the information printed matches the information in Figures 8-6, 8-7 and 8-8b, then you can proceed. You should make a backup after Exercise 8-5 before proceeding.

16 ➤ Click on the **Display by** icon ⬚. This display does not provide the user with any Quantity or Value information.

17 ➤ Click **Display by name** icon ⬚. Your inventory window should resemble Fig. 8-6 with five inventory items and Quantity and Total Value Information.

Balances are as of the latest transaction date	Quantity	Total Value
InkJet Black Cartridge IBC-01	40	800.00
InkJet Printer 5 in 1 IP-001	53	7,950.00
Laser Black Cartridge LBC-01	16	1,056.00
Laser Printer 20P LP001	20	5,800.00
Printer Cable USB C-01	50	350.00

Fig. 8-6: Inventory window.

Displaying Inventory Details

Exercise 8-5—Displaying Inventory Details

To review the information entered, use the following steps:

1 ➤ Click the **Select a Report** icon 🖩. Click the 🔽 to display a list of available reports, select **Quantity**, **Select**, the Asset accounts should be highlighted in blue, or click Select All if they are not in blue, **OK**.

The window display (Fig. 8-7) shows the items on order and items to order that are below minimum stock. (See Exercise 8-8 for an example or information in the To Order column.) Note: The displayed and printed report will not indicate any date. **Exit** this window.

Inventory Quantity

Description	▲	Item No.	Unit	Quantity	Minimum	On Purc...	On Sale...	To Order
InkJet Black Cartridge		IBC-01	Each	40	26	0	0	-
InkJet Printer 5 in 1		IP-001	Each	53	30	0	0	-
Laser Black Cartridge		LBC-01	Each	16	10	0	0	-
Laser Printer 20P		LP001	Each	20	12	0	0	-
Printer Cable USB		C-01	Each	50	20	0	0	-

Fig. 8-7: Printers Company Inventory Quantity.

2 ➤ Click the **Select a Report** icon. Click the 🔽 to display a list of available reports. Select **Summary**, **Select**. All inventory items should be highlighted in blue, or otherwise click Select All.

At the bottom left of the window you have two choices of displaying/printing the report.

The default selection is As at.

3 ➤ Latest Transaction   The report can be displayed only after the latest transaction. Click **Latest Transaction** button. The As at date line is greyed out. Click **OK**.

Inventory Summary Jan 01, 2019

Description	▲	Item No.	Unit	Price	Quantity	Cost	Value	Margin %
InkJet Black Cartridge		IBC-01	Each	38.50	40	20.00	800.00	48.05
InkJet Printer 5 in 1		IP-001	Each	245.00	53	150.00	7,950.00	38.78
Laser Black Cartridge		LBC-01	Each	99.00	16	66.00	1,056.00	33.33
Laser Printer 20P		LP001	Each	400.00	20	290.00	5,800.00	27.50
Printer Cable USB		C-01	Each	15.00	50	7.00	350.00	53.33
							15,956.00	

Fig. 8-8a: Printers Company Inventory Summary with Margin (%).

This report displays the Margin % of profit earned on the sale of individual items (average inventory cost).

4 ➤   Click **Modify, Report Options**. Click **As at**. The selection is available.

5 ➤   ⦿ As at: | Today   ▼ | Date: | Jan 01, 2019 ▼ | 🗓

As At   Click the ▼ to display the various time periods that are available
               during a fiscal year. Do NOT change the date. Click **OK**. This
               report does not display the Margin %.

Inventory Summary As at Jan 01, 2019					
Description	Item No.	Unit	Quantity	Cost	Value
InkJet Black Cartridge	IBC-01	Each	40	20.00	800.00
InkJet Printer 5 in 1	IP-001	Each	53	150.00	7,950.00
Laser Black Cartridge	LBC-01	Each	16	66.00	1,056.00
Laser Printer 20P	LP001	Each	20	290.00	5,800.00
Printer Cable USB	C-01	Each	50	7.00	350.00
					15,956.00

Fig. 8-8b: Printers Company Inventory Summary (without Margin %).

Look at these two reports to notice that some of the information is the same and some
is different. The displays are the result of the input you just completed. The Summary
As At date report cannot display the Selling price and/or Margin %, as the selling price
of items could have changed during the period and, therefore, the Margin % cannot be
calculated.

The authors believe the Summary report with Margin % is more important to
management, as it identifies which inventory items are making less of a profit for the
business. Users must be aware that the percentage may be low due to a temporary
reduction in the sales price.

6 ➤   Exit the **Summary** report, and click the **Select a Report** icon. Click **Select** to
       accept the **Display Inventory and Services list**, the window changes, click
       OK. Compare the displayed information to the Summary chart, Fig. 8-4, to
       verify your input. Note: Ignore the Uncategorized column.

7 ➤   **Exit** this window and return to the Home window.

Make a backup before proceeding. Name your backup similar to:
Printers_B4_Ready.

The conversion process is now complete.

Step 5: Setting the INVENTORY & SERVICES Module to READY

The INVENTORY & SERVICES module is ready to change from History to **Ready**
mode. The COMPANY, PAYABLES, and RECEIVABLES modules have been set to
Ready for you. Only the INVENTORY & SERVICES module needs to be set to **Ready**
at this point.

1 ➤   Double-check that the total cost of the inventory on hand, as entered in the
       Inventory Ledger, is equal to the balance of the Inventory accounts 1250 to
       1290 in the G/L. If the balances are not equal, return to the **Inventory &
       Services Ledger**, and correct where necessary.

Before making the module Ready, it is important to back up your data files. Once the
modules are made Ready, you cannot go back to make changes.

2 ➤ If you did not back up your files before, do it now.

Back up your files before proceeding and record details in your logbook.

Exercise 8-6—Setting INVENTORY & SERVICES Module to READY

Set the INVENTORY & SERVICES module to **Ready** as follows:

1 ➤ From the Home window, click **History, Enter Historical Information** ▶,
Inventory & Services.

A warning message is displayed if the inventory account balances do not balance with
the General Ledger inventory accounts.

The normal warning message box shown next is seen when inventory details are
balanced to the G/L. Make sure you have a backup.

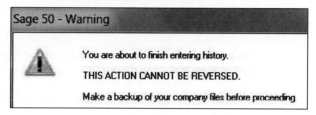

2 ➤ Click **Proceed** to continue. The Quill pen is removed, because history
information has been entered and is complete.

Slideshow **8B—Journalizing INVENTORY-Related Transactions** demonstrates how
the INVENTORY & SERVICES module works and the accounting principles related to
the various inventory-related tasks. Run it now.

Step 6: Journalizing Inventory-Related Sales

Start here from Exercise 8-1 if your instructor suggested that you use the data file
Printers2.

Exercise 8-7—Journalizing Inventory-Related Sales

---

1 ➤ Advance the Session date to **Jan 07, 2019**.

2 ➤ Click the **RECEIVABLES** module, and click the **Sales Invoice**s icon. Notice
the Sales Invoice window does *not* indicate a preferred status field. **Exit** to
the Home window.

Preferred Pricing

Study this transaction:

Jan 07, 2019   **The manager has finalized plans to extend preferred pricing
only to customer More Computers Ltd. effective today, as they
normally buy a large quantity of merchandise from the firm.**

To have More Computers Ltd. receive preferred pricing, complete the next three steps.

1 ➤ Click the **Customers** icon, and double-click **More Computers Ltd**.

2 ➤ Click the **Options** Tab, at Price List, click the ⏷, select **Preferred**, [Tab].

3 ➤ Click [Save & Close] and [X] to return to the Home window.

Inventory-Related Sale on Credit

Study this transaction:

> **Jan 07, 2019**   **The following inventory items are sold plus HST to More Computers Ltd. (a preferred customer) on invoice #11592 dated today with terms 2/10, net 30 days.**
>
> | | | |
> |---|---|---|
> | 15 InkJet Printer 5 in 1 at | $ | 235.00 ea. plus HST |
> | 15 InkJet Black Cartridge at | $ | 37.50 ea. plus HST |
> | 15 Printer Cable USB at | $ | 14.50 ea. plus HST |
> | Invoice total = | $ | 4,864.66 |

This transaction is a normal inventory-related sale on credit and is entered in the RECEIVABLES module as follows:

1 ➤ From the Home window, click the **Sales Invoices** icon.

The procedures to record the credit sale are similar to Exercise 2A-15, in RECEIVABLES (Chapter 2A).

Enter the invoice as indicated below:

ⓘ In many situations, the branch office orders the goods, and the invoices are sent to Head Office for payment, or vice versa.

2 ➤	**Customer**	Select **More Computers Ltd.**, [Tab].
	Shipping Address	Do NOT change. (See side note box.)
	Invoice No.	Do NOT change. This is the next invoice to be issued.
	Order/Quote No.	Printers Company does not use sales orders or quotes at this time. Leave blank.

ⓘ There is no indication in the Sales Invoice window that preferred pricing is being used for this customer. The reference, as noted, is in the Customer Ledger window.

3 ➤ **Item Number**   Press [Enter] (or double-click in the first line of the Item column) to display a list of inventory items. Before Selecting, notice that the display shows the quantity of each item in stock. Select **InkJet Printer 5 in 1**. Automatically the Item number, Unit, Item Description, Base Price, Price, Tax code, and G/L account for Sales InkJets are displayed in the first row of the invoice. This information is retrieved from the Inventory Ledger as you enter the item. (See side note box.)

4 ➤ **Quantity**   Type **15** (items sold), [Tab] to **Base Price**.

5 ➤ **Base Price**   [Tab] to accept the price of **235.00**. This price can be changed by typing the new price if the actual selling price is different from the regular or preferred price.

6 ➤ **Discount %**   [Tab] to move to Price. This client has previously been given a preferred selling price.

7 ➤ **Price**   <u>Tab</u> to accept the amount of **235.00**.

8 ➤ **Amount**   <u>Tab</u> to accept the amount of **3,525.00**. The Amount field is automatically calculated as **quantity** times **price**.

9 ➤ **Tax**   HS, <u>Tab</u>. The goods are being purchased, plus HST.

10 ➤ **Account**   <u>Tab</u> to accept the G/L account number **4100 Sales InkJets**. This field can be changed as needed (e.g., returns).

The cursor moves to the second row of the invoice.

Using the mouse, resize the columns to approximate Fig. 8-9.

11 ➤ **Enter** the other sales items on the next two rows by using the above procedure. The G/L sales account is different for the cable items.

    Terms   Do NOT change.

(See side note box.)

The Sales Invoice should display like Fig. 8-9.

> **ℹ** Printers Company does not charge for delivery. If the customer is charged for delivery, a linked account in the RECEIVABLES module for Freight Revenue needs to be added. Then you would enter an amount in the **Freight** field.

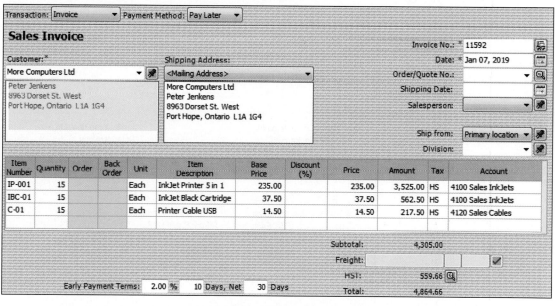

Fig. 8-9: Sales Invoice window.

12 ➤ Display the **Sales Journal Entry**. The entry should be as follows:

Sales Journal Entry Jan 07, 2019 (J1)

Account Number	Account Description	Debits	Credits
1200	Accounts Receivable	4,864.66	-
5010	Cost of Goods Sold- InkJets	2,550.00	-
5030	Cost of Goods Sold -Cables	105.00	-
1250	Inventory Inkjet Printers	-	2,250.00
1270	Inventory Ink Cartridges Inkjets	-	300.00
1290	Inventory Printer Cables	-	105.00
2650	HST Charged on Sales	-	559.66
4100	Sales InkJets	-	4,087.50
4120	Sales Cables	-	217.50
Additional Date:	Additional Field:		
		7,519.66	7,519.66

Fig. 8-10: Sales Journal Entry.

13 ➤ **Exit** from the entry window.

Sage 50 Accounting combines two journal entries into one entry when an inventory sale is recorded.

1.   *The Sales entry:*

	DR	CR
Accounts Receivable	4,864.66	
HST Charged on Sales		559.66
Sales InkJets		4,087.50
Sales Cables		217.50

2.   *The Cost of Goods Sold entry:*

	DR	CR
Cost of Goods Sold- InkJets	2,550.00	
Cost of Goods Sold- Cables	105.00	
Inventory InkJet Printers		2,250.00
Inventory Ink Cartridges InkJet		300.00
Inventory Printer Cables		105.00

The credits to the **Sales** accounts (Section 1) are based on the **selling price** of the items.

Printers Company , Student's Name						11592
1075 Aberdeen Avenue						
Vaughan, Ontario L4L 8V7						Jan 07, 2019
						1 of 1

More Computers Ltd.	More Computers Ltd.
Peter Jenkens	Peter Jenkens
8963 Dorset St. West	8963 Dorset St. West
Port Hope, ON L1A 1G4	Port Hope, ON L1A 1G4

IP-001	15	Each	InkJet Printer 5 in1	HS	235.00	3,525.00
IBC-01	15	Each	InkJet Black Cartridge	HS	37.50	562.50
C-01	15	Each	Printer Cable USB	HS	14.50	217.50

Sub-total: 4,305.00

HS- HST added at 13%

HST   559.66

Terms: 2%/10, Net 30. Due Feb 06, 2019

Printers Company , Student's Name HST: #Rx25693

Terms: 2%10, Net 30. Due Feb 06, 2019

Thank you for your order.   4,864.66

Fig. 8-11: Invoice details printed on plain paper.

The debits to the **Cost of Goods Sold** accounts and the credits to **Inventory** accounts (Section 2) are based on the **average cost** of the items in inventory.

Refer to Fig. 8-11 to see the invoice details that will print on preprinted forms.

14 ➤ **Post** when correct.

A message window should appear advising you that an item quantity has fallen below the minimum level (reorder point).

<table>
<tr><td></td><td>Advisor:</td><td>Entries just processed caused one or more inventory items to drop below the reorder point. Print the Inventory Item Quantity report to see which items to reorder.</td></tr>
</table>

[Click here to close.]

15 ➤ **Click** anywhere in the box.

16 ➤ **Exit** from the Sales Journal window.

Back up your files regularly and update your logbook.

Determining Inventory Items to Order

You should check the number of items in stock on a regular basis to determine if there are stock items that need reordering. In Exercise 8-7, step 14, a message window advised you that one or more items have dropped below the reorder point. You may view and/or print a report that will show you all the items that need reordering.

Exercise 8-8—Determining What Items to Order

In this exercise, you will view the Inventory Quantity report that will show you what items need reordering.

1 ➤ Follow the procedures in Exercise 8-5 to display an Inventory **Quantity** report for all Inventory items. Alternatively, from the Home window, click **Reports** and then click **Inventory & Services**, **Quantity**. On the right, ensure your screen shows **Inventory by Asset** and **Stocking units** selected and all inventory items are highlighted in blue. Click **OK**.

Description	Number	Unit	Quantity	Minimum	On Pur Order	On Sal Order	To Order
InkJet Black Cartridge	IBC-01	Each	25	26	0	0	1

The 1 listed in the **To Order** column means that the InkJet Black Cartridge is one below the minimum quantity; therefore, an order to purchase should be placed.

2 ➤ **Exit** to the Home window.

Recording a New Item

There are two ways to add a new item to the INVENTORY listing:

a) Click the Inventory & Services icon and create the new item as you learned earlier.

b) Add the new inventory item as you record the Purchase Order.

Using method **b**, follow the steps in Exercise 8-9 to record a Purchase Order and to add a new inventory item.

Exercise 8-9—Recording a New Inventory Item

Jan 07 2019   After many requests from customers for colour InkJet
              cartridges, the manager ordered from InkJet Cartridges Ltd.,
              the following on Purchase Order #65:

     50 InkJet Colour Cartridges at $27.00 each plus HST
     60 InkJet Black   Cartridges at $20.00 each plus HST

Terms are 2/10, n30, with a shipping date of Jan 09, 2019. Total Purchase
Order is $2,881.50.

To record the Purchase Order, follow these steps:

1 ➤ Click the **PAYABLES** module, click the **Purchase Orders** icon.

    Transaction   Leave selection as Order.

2 ➤ **Vendor**   Select **InkJet Cartridges Ltd.**, `Tab`.

    Order No.   The next PO is 65.

3 ➤ **Date**   **Jan 07, 2019,** `Tab` `Tab`.

4 ➤ **Shipping Date**   **Jan 09, 2019,** `Tab`.

5 ➤ **Item Number**   Press `Enter` and the Select Inventory/Service window appears
     with the first line as:

          <Add new inventory/service>

6 ➤ Click **Select**.

    Enter the inventory item and details as shown next:

> The **On Hand Quantity,**
> **Pending Purchase**
> **Order**, **Sales Order**, and
> **Value** fields are not
> available, as this is a
> new item. These fields
> are updated when a
> purchase or a sale is
> completed.

(See side note box.)

7 ➤ **Minimum Level**:**10**, `Tab`. Click the **Pricing** tab.

Pricing

8 ➤ Enter the pricing as follows.

Price List	Price per Selling Unit
Regular	44.0000
Preferred	43.0000
Web Price	0.0000

9 ➤ Click the **Linked** tab, and set the linked accounts (**1270** [Asset], **4100** [Revenue] and **5010** [COGS] which are the same as the InkJet Black Cartridges).

Taxes

10 ➤ Click the **Taxes** tab. Do NOT change. We do not know which of our customers can buy inventory items HST-Exempt.

11 ➤ Click Save & Close.

After item #ICC-01 has been added to the inventory list, enter the Purchase Order as shown next:

12 ➤ **Item** Tab to accept ICC-01, InkJet Colour Cartridge.

13 ➤ **Order** Type **50**, Tab .

14 ➤ **Back Order** Tab to accept 50. Tab to Price.

15 ➤ **Price** Type **27.00**, Tab . (See side note box.)

16 ➤ **Tax** Tab to accept **HS**.

17 ➤ **HST** Tab to accept 175.50.

18 ➤ **Amount** Tab to accept **$1,350.00** in the Amount column.

Account The account number should be 1270 (the linked account for InkJet Cartridges) and the total Purchase Order amount is 1,525.50.

> The price field in the Purchase Order is blank because this is the first time a cost is being entered for this item.
>
> When the invoice is received and posted, the average cost shown for this item will be $27.00. It will change after each purchase, if the cost price changes.

19 ➤ **Enter** the order for **60** InkJet Black Cartridges using the same procedure.

Terms **2/10, n/30**.

The Purchase Order should be as shown in Fig. 8-12.

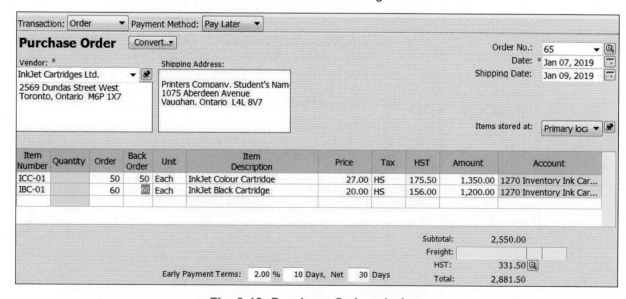

Fig. 8-12: Purchase Order window.

20 ➤ Record when correct. **Exit** to the Home window.

Exercise 8-10—Displaying the Pending Purchases Report

Study the next transaction and record as follows:

Displaying the Pending Purchases Report

If you selected Vendor Detail you would be able to view details about Item, Description, Unit, and Back Ordered Quantities.

1 ➤ From the main menu, click **Reports, Payables, Pending Purchase Orders, By Vendor, Summary,** if all items are not highlighted in blue, click **Select All,** change the date to **Jan 09, 2019, OK.** The report as shown next will display outstanding Purchase Orders. If you want to see the details of the Purchase Order, drill down by double-clicking on any item on the line. (See side note box.)

Pending Purchase Orders Summary by Vendor As at Jan 09, 2019

Purchase Order Number	Purchase Order Date	Ship Date	Amount Original Order
InkJet Cartridges Ltd.			
65	Jan 07, 2019	Jan 09, 2019	2,881.50
			2,881.50
			2,881.50

2 ➤ **Exit** to the Home window.

Other Transactions

1 ➤ **Record** and **Post** this transaction.

This transaction is a normal cash receipt from a customer. Use the Receipts journal with a deposit date of Jan 07, 2019 to record this transaction.

> **Jan 07, 2019 Received cheque #998 in the amount of $3,330.00 from Do-It Yourself Inc. in payment of Invoice 11575.**
>
> **The Discount Available column indicates 0.00. A discount of $60.00 for paying within 10 days will be allowed (Discount Taken column), due to the volume of mail delivery during the holiday season.**
>
> **The envelope was dated and postmarked December 31.**

Your window should appear as follows:

Invoice Date	Invoice or Deposit	Original Amount	Amount Owing	Discount Available	Discount Taken	Amount Received
Dec 24, 2018	11575	3,390.00	3,390.00	0.00	60.00	3,330.00

2 ➤ Advance the Session date to **Jan 08, 2019.**

3 ➤ **Record** and **Post** this transaction.

Jan 08, 2019 **Sold to Davis Computers, for immediate shipment today, the following items at regular price plus HST:**

        7 Laser Printers 20P
        7 Laser Black Cartridges
        7 Printer Cable USB

Terms 2/10, n30. Invoice 11593, total $4,065.74.

A low inventory warning message should appear.

4 ➤ Click anywhere in the box to **close** the window. **Return** to the Home window.

5 ➤ Display the **Inventory Quantity** report. You may have to expand the column to see the heading wording.

The report indicates that:

On Purchase Order	Under this column, opposite the black and colour InkJet cartridges are the quantities on order for these items.
To Order	1 item below the minimum quantity for the Laser Black Cartridge. This item should be ordered.
	1 Item above the minimum quantity for the Laser Printer 20P.

6 ➤ **Exit** to the Home window.

7 ➤ **Record** the following Purchase Order:

Jan 08, 2019 **The manager asked you to issue Purchase Order #66 to Laser Products Ltd. for the following items plus HST.**

    25 Laser Printer 20P   **at $290.00 each**
    25 Laser Black Cartridges   **at $ 66.00 each**

Terms 2/10, net 30 and ship by Jan 09, 2019.

Total Purchase Order $10,057.00.

---

8 ➤ **Exit** to the Home window.

9 ➤ Advance the Session date to **Jan 09, 2019**.

Journalizing Inventory Purchases

Notice that items purchased under the **Perpetual** method do not go to the PURCHASES account, but rather go to the INVENTORY account on the Balance Sheet. When the items are sold, the cost of the inventory is taken out of the INVENTORY account and charged to COST OF SALES.

Exercise 8-11—Journalizing Inventory Purchases

Study the next transaction and record as follows:

INKJET CARTRIDGES LTD.
2569 Dundas Street West
Toronto, Ontario, M6P 1X7

INVOICE # 25831

Date: Jan. 9, 2019
Your P.O. 65
Terms: 2/10, n 30

-We sell Quality Products -

SOLD TO:
Printers Company, Student's Name
1075 Aberdeen Avenue
Vaughan, ON
L4L 8V7

HST # 332 445 667

ITEM	QTY	ORDER	B/O	UNIT	DESCRIPTION	HST	UNIT PRICE	AMOUNT
ICC-01	50			Each	InkJet Colour Cartridges	HS	27.00	1,350.00
IBC-01	50		10	Each	InkJet Black Cartridges	HS	19.50	975.00
							Sub Total	2,325.00
							HST	302.25

Total Invoice Amount	$2,627.25

> **Received the above invoice with a note from the vendor's manager that effective Jan 07, 2019 a price decrease to $19.50 each was given on the InkJet Black Cartridges. The note also stated that 10 InkJet Black Cartridges are back ordered and should be shipped by Jan 14, 2019.**

This transaction is a purchase of inventory items from a Purchase Order.

1 ➤ From the Home window, click the **Purchase Invoices** icon.

    Transaction   **Invoice**.

    Payment Method **Pay later**.

2 ➤ **Order No.**   Click the **Finder** icon and the Select Order or Quote appears. Select **PO 65**. Automatically, details from Purchase Order 65 are retrieved and displayed in the invoice.

3 ➤ **Invoice**   Type **25831**, Tab .

4 ➤ **Quantity**   For colour cartridges, type **50,** Tab .

5 ➤ **Back Order**   Tab to accept a blank field.

    Price   The 27.00 unit price displayed is the cost of the individual inventory items on the PURCHASE ORDER.

    Tab to Quantity on the next line.

The cursor does not allow entry to the **Account** field because this account is the default linked account. To change the account number, you would have to reassign the specific linked account.

6 ➤ **Quantity**   For black cartridges, type **50,** [Tab].

7 ➤ **Back Order**   Notice that 10 cartridges are back ordered. [Tab] to Price.

8 ➤ **Price**   Type **19.50**. This is the new price of the cartridges. As a result of this price change, the average cost of the InkJet Black Cartridge will decrease to $19.6667 each. This will be explained later. [Tab] to accept.

9 ➤ Display the Purchases Journal Entry.

Purchases Journal Entry Jan 09, 2019 (J4)

Account Number	Account Description	Debits	Credits
1270	Inventory Ink Cartridges Inkjets	2,325.00	-
2670	HST Paid On Purchases	302.25	-
2200	Accounts Payable	-	2,627.25
Additional Date:	Additional Field:		
		2,627.25	2,627.25

10 ➤ **Exit** from the Journal Entry. **Post** when correct and **Exit** to the Home window.

11 ➤ Display the **INVENTORY Summary** report, with **Latest Transaction** selected.

Inventory Summary Jan 09, 2019

Description	Item No.	Unit	Price	Quantity	Cost	Value	Margin %
InkJet Black Cartridge	IBC-01	Each	38.50	75	19.6667	1,475.00	48.92
InkJet Colour Cartridge	ICC-01	Each	44.00	50	27.00	1,350.00	38.64
InkJet Printer 5 in 1	IP-001	Each	245.00	38	150.00	5,700.00	38.78
Laser Black Cartridge	LBC-01	Each	99.00	9	66.00	594.00	33.33
Laser Printer 20P	LP001	Each	400.00	13	290.00	3,770.00	27.50
Printer Cable USB	C-01	Each	15.00	28	7.00	196.00	53.33
						13,085.00	

Note that the InkJet Black Cartridge average cost per unit has changed due to the reduction in the purchase price of the last order. Sage 50 Accounting calculates the cost of inventory on hand using the **Average Cost** method.

25 items on hand	@ $20.00 each = $ 500.00
50 items purchased	@ $19.50 each = $ 975.00
75 items total cost	= $1,475.00

ℹ

Sage 50 Accounting calculates AVERAGE COST to 4 decimal places.

The average cost of each InkJet Black Cartridge is:

$1,475.00 / 75 items = $19.6667 (See side note box.)

The gross margin has increased from an average of 48.05% to 48.92%. The manager has decided not to decrease the selling price of the InkJet cartridges at this time.

12 ➤ **Exit** the Summary window.

Another Transaction

1 ➤ **Record** the following transaction. Select the purchase order number, then enter the invoice number and verify the date, click the **Fill Backordered quantities** 🔲 icon and the **Quantity** column will fill with the items ordered.

The Fill Backordered quantities icon can be useful when you have ordered many items on a Purchase Order and the complete order has been filled. You would still have to verify all received items with the invoice total.

Jan 09, 2019 Received Invoice #3661 dated today from Laser Products Ltd. for the goods ordered on Purchase Order #66, and 5 extra printers ordered yesterday by the manager without changing the Purchase Order. Terms 2/10, net 30.

30 Laser Printers 20P	**$ 8,700.00**
25 Laser Black Cartridges	**1,650.00**
HST	**1,345.50**
Total	**$ 11,695.50**

Notice that the Back Order column amounts are removed because the purchase order request has been received in full.

2 ➤ Change the Laser Printer 20P quantity to **30,** Tab .

3 ➤ **Post** when correct. A message box will appear advising you that the Purchase Order has been filled, because there are no items on back order.

4 ➤ Click **OK** and **Exit** to the Home window.

5 ➤ Advance the Session date to **Jan 15, 2019**.

Journalizing a Cash on Delivery (COD) Sale

Normally a COD (Cash on Delivery) sale is processed as a **cash** sale. However, if you are giving the customer a sales discount, you would process the transaction a bit differently than a normal cash sale.

In this particular case, you are not sure if this customer will purchase again in the future; therefore, the customer's information will be added to the customer list, but will be given a 0.00 (nil) credit limit.

Exercise 8-12—Journalizing a Cash on Delivery (COD) Sale

This customer has applied for credit, and the credit application is being processed. In the meantime, you will give the customer a sales discount of 2%, which you usually provide for regular customers for early payment.

1 ➤ Study the following transaction:

Jan 13, 2019   Sold the following goods to a new customer, McPherson's Computers Co., terms COD, on our invoice #11594 dated today. Sale is made with 13% HST.

A 2% discount for paying for the goods at time of sale is given to McPherson's Computers Co. Cheque #1362 in the amount of $1,681.65 (not certified) was received.

Create a customer ledger with the following information:

McPherson's Computers Co.
310 Kendalwood Road
Whitby, Ontario, L1N 2G3
905 430-2830

Contact: **Mrs. Diane van Ingen**
Revenue Account: **Select 4100 Sales InkJets**.
Terms: **Leave blank**.
Taxes: **HS**
Credit Limit: **0.00**
Memo: **Credit check requested Jan 13, 2019 by our manager**.

To-Do Date: **Jan 24, 2019**
Check ☑ **Display this memo in the Daily Business Manager**

2 InkJet Black Cartridges	$ 38.50 each
2 InkJet Colour Cartridges	44.00 each
2 InkJet Printer 5 in 1	245.00 each
2 Laser Printers 20P	400.00 each
4 Printer Cables USB	15.00 each

Total (including HST) before discount   **1,711.95**

---

2 ➤   From the Home window, click the **RECEIVABLES** module, click the **Sales Invoices** icon to display the Sales Journal window.

Transaction	Invoice

3 ➤   **Payment method**   Select **Cheque**, `Tab` `Tab` to Cheque.

4 ➤   **Cheque No.**   Type **1362**, `Tab` to Customer.

5 ➤   **Customer**   Type **McPherson's Computers Co.**, `Tab`, select **Full Add**. Enter the appropriate information (see the above transaction information box). Select Save and Close. `Tab`.

6 ➤   **Date**   Select **Jan 13, 2019**. `Tab`.

7 ➤   **Details**   Enter the rest of the invoice with inventory items from the transaction information box. You may have to drag the bottom of the window down to see the five items in the window. You could also maximize the window.

8 ➤   **Message**   Change to: **Thank you for your order. COD paid by cheque** (this will show on the invoice that this is a cash sale and the invoice has been paid), `Tab`.

9 ➤ Early Payment Discount Type **2**, Tab . The box to the right of % will display: 30.30 , which is the discount for paying early.

The Cheque Amount should be as follows:

Cheque Amount: 1,681.65

(The invoice Total $1,711.95 less $30.30 discount equals the cheque amount). Tab .

10 ➤ Display the journal entry (see side note box). It should be as follows:

ℹ️ BANK ACCOUNT is debited, and not ACCOUNTS RECEIVABLE, since this is a cash sale. The entry shows the **sales discount** amount.

Sales Journal Entry Jan 13, 2019 (J6)

Account Number	Account Description	Debits	Credits
1020	Bank Account	1,681.65	-
4150	Sales Discount	30.30	-
5010	Cost of Goods Sold- InkJets	393.33	-
5020	Cost of Goods Sold -Lasers	580.00	-
5030	Cost of Goods Sold -Cables	28.00	-
1250	Inventory Inkjet Printers	-	300.00
1260	Inventory Laser Printers	-	580.00
1270	Inventory Ink Cartridges Inkjets	-	93.33
1290	Inventory Printer Cables	-	28.00
2650	HST Charged on Sales	-	196.95
4100	Sales InkJets	-	655.00
4110	Sales Lasers	-	800.00
4120	Sales Cables	-	60.00
Additional Date:	Additional Field:		
		2,713.28	2,713.28

11 ➤ Exit the entry window, **Post** when correct and **Exit** to the Home window.

Another Transaction

1 ➤ Record and **post** this transaction.

> **Jan 13, 2019**   Purchase from new vendor, **Rotex Printing Ltd., 212 Caster Avenue, Vaughan, Ont. L4L 7U9, Phone 905-675-6629, Invoice #4012 for $200.00 plus HST for 1 box of new sales invoices. Terms N20 days, Invoice total $226.00.**

The default expense account for these sales invoices is **1330 Prepaid Store Supplies**. This is a purchase of supplies for store use and is not a purchase of inventory for resale; therefore, when recording the invoice you:

a) Do NOT use the Item column in the Purchases Invoice window.
b) Do NOT add this to the inventory listing of goods for sale.

Item Number	Quantity	Order	Back Order	Unit	Item Description	Price	Tax	HST	Amount	Account
	1			box	New sales invoices	200.00	HS	26.00	200.00	1330 Prepaid Store S...

2 ➤ Exit to the Home window.

Journalizing an Inventory Sales Return

Goods returned must be entered in the RECEIVABLES module as a **negative** sale. A Sales Return in a business using the Perpetual Method of accounting for inventory records the return of goods to the INVENTORY & SERVICES module at the cost value.

Exercise 8-13—Journalizing an Inventory Sales Return

Study this transaction:

> **Jan 14, 2019**   **Received cheque #720 in the amount of $5,068.05 from Computers & More, re invoice #11568 with a letter from Larry Richards, Operations Manager, asking why they have not received a credit memo in the amount of $452.00 for the return of 1 Laser printer 20P on Jan 3, 2019. You have checked and found that the printer was received on Jan 3, but the paperwork did not get to Accounting.**

You will issue **Credit Memo 11568Rt CM61**, referenced back to the original invoice for the returned item, and adjust your Accounts Receivable and Inventory accounts accordingly.

This transaction with Computers & More must be recorded in two steps:

     a.   Enter the goods returned.
     b.   Record the cash receipt.

Step 1: Record the Sales Return

1 ➤   Click the **RECEIVABLES** module, click the **Sales Invoices** icon from the Home window.

2 ➤   **Enter the return** as shown in Fig. 8-13.

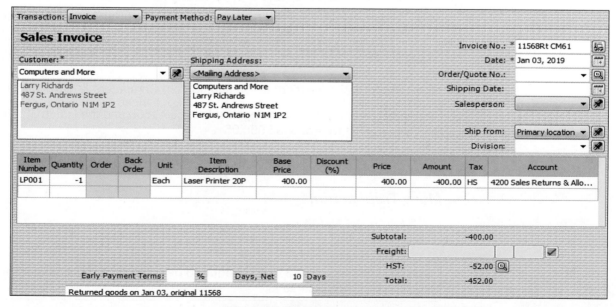

Fig. 8-13: Sales Invoice showing return.

Transaction	Invoice (**Sales** and **Sales Returns** use the same window).	
Date	The date the return should have been recorded in the accounting records. There is no effect on a discount and the Message field also records the actual date received.	
Shipping Date	This date records the actual date the goods were returned.	
Quantity	**-1**. The minus sign will result in items being added to the inventory quantity and reduce the ACCOUNTS RECEIVABLE subledger for Computers & More.	
Base Price	You may have to retype the price amount if the customer received a special or different price. The original 11568 sales invoice price was **400.00**.	
Account	**4200 Sales Returns and Allowances**. The entry results in a **debit** to Sales Returns and Allowances, and a **credit** to Accounts Receivable (see side note box).	
Message	Add appropriate information (see Fig. 8-13).	
Terms	We are receiving payment for the invoice less the return and the terms would have no effect on the payment. Change the Net Days to 10.	

> Printers Company does not use separate accounts for the different types of returns and records them in account 4200 Sales Returns & Allowances.
>
> Some companies may not use a Sales Returns account and would record sales returns as **negative** sales.

3 ➤ **Display** the Sales Journal entry. It should display as follows:

Sales Journal Entry Jan 03, 2019 (J8)

Account Number	Account Description	Debits	Credits
1260	Inventory Laser Printers	290.00	-
2650	HST Charged on Sales	52.00	-
4200	Sales Returns & Allowances	400.00	-
1200	Accounts Receivable	-	452.00
5020	Cost of Goods Sold -Lasers	-	290.00
Additional Date:	Additional Field:		
		742.00	742.00

The Inventory asset account and Sales Returns account are debited, and the Cost of Goods Sold account is credited using the **average** cost of the inventory.

4 ➤ **Exit** the entry window. **Post** when correct, and **Exit** to the Home window.

Step 2: Record the Cash Receipt from Computers & More

5 ➤ **Record** cheque **#720** for **$5,068.05** from Computers & More on Jan. 14.

Remember to apply the receipt against Invoice 11568 and the Return 11568Rt CM61, resulting in a net receipt of $5,068.05.

6 ➤ **Post** when correct, and **Exit** from the Receipts Journal.

More Transactions

1 ➤ **Record** and **post** the following transactions:

> **Jan 14, 2019 Issue a $316.40 cheque to pay Cables and Accessories for invoice 2998.**

> **Jan 14, 2019 Received cheque #1012 from More Computers Ltd. in the amount of $4,778.56 for invoice #11592.**

> **Jan 15, 2019 Received cheque #712 in the amount of $10,152.28 from Davis Computers in payment of invoices #11571 and #11593.**

2 ➤   Return to the **Home** window.

3 ➤   Advance the Session date to **January 18, 2019**.

Journalizing an Inventory Purchase Return

Returned goods must be removed from the INVENTORY ledger by entering a **negative** purchase.

Exercise 8-14—Journalizing an Inventory Purchase Return

Study the next transaction:

> **Jan 18, 2019 You received a memo from your Sales Manager that one Laser Printer 20P in inventory is damaged. It is from the shipment from Laser Products Ltd. on invoice #3661.**
>
> **Laser Products Ltd. agreed you could return the printer for credit. They faxed a credit memo to you (#C103) dated today for $327.70 including HST. The printer was returned.**

You will process the return of the printer in this exercise. In the next exercise, you will pay the invoice with a cash discount.

1 ➤   Click the **PAYABLES** module, click the **Purchase Invoices** icon from the Home window.

>   **Transaction   Invoice.**
>
>   **Payment Method Pay later**.

2 ➤   **Vendor**   Select **Laser Products Ltd.**, [Tab].

3 ➤   **Invoice**   **3661Rt C103,** [Tab].

>   **Date**   **Jan 18, 2019.**

4 ➤   **Item Number**   Select **LP001 Laser Printer 20P.**

5 ➤   **Quantity**   **-1**. A minus will result in items being reduced from INVENTORY and will reduce the Accounts Payable subledger for Laser Products Ltd., [Tab].

Price	**290.00** is the original purchase price for these printers and is the amount of the credit memo issued by Laser Products Ltd. If the price was different, you would change it here. `Tab` .
Tax	HS, the original code used when the printer was purchased.
Account	The cursor does not stop at Account as the account shown is the linked account for inventory. Using the **Perpetual Inventory system** for purchases, costs of goods bought and sold are charged to Asset Inventory accounts. Goods returned are charged to the INVENTORY account and not to a Purchase Returns account. In this exercise the cost of the returned printer is charged to the asset 1260 INVENTORY LASER PRINTERS account.

6 ➤ **Terms**   Refer to original invoice. Date of invoice Jan 09, 2019 with terms of 2/10, net 30. The return is subject to the same terms as the original invoice. The terms should be:

2%/1 day, Net 21 days.

7 ➤ **Display** the Purchases Journal Entry. The entry should be as follows:

Purchases Journal Entry Jan 18, 2019 (J13)

Account Number	Account Description	Debits	Credits
2200	Accounts Payable	327.70	-
1260	Inventory Laser Printers	-	290.00
2670	HST Paid On Purchases	-	37.70
Additional Date:	Additional Field:		
		327.70	327.70

8 ➤ **Post** when correct, and return to the **Home** window.

Recording a Payment with Cash Discount

When goods are purchased using the Perpetual INVENTORY module, the INVENTORY asset account increases.

In the transaction that follows, you will pay the invoice related to the purchase return you posted in the last exercise, and take a cash discount. To allocate the cash discount to INVENTORY, you have to break down the discount based on the purchase price of each item. However, on invoices with many items, this technique is not practical.

The discount is not charged to the INVENTORY asset account, but is charged to the PURCHASES DISCOUNT account in the COST OF GOODS SOLD section.

Exercise 8-15—Recording an Inventory Payment with Cash Discount

---

Study the following transaction:

Jan 18, 2019	**Paid Laser Products Ltd. for invoices #3625, 3661 and 3661Rt C103, with the next cheque, in the amount of $16,898.93 taking advantage of a 2% cash discount on Invoice #3661 less the return on invoice #3661Rt C103.**

Record the transaction as follows:

1 ➤ From the Home window, click **Payments**.

2 ➤ **Pay To** Select **Laser Products Ltd.**, [Tab].

　　　　 Date **Jan 18, 2019**.

3 ➤ **Invoice/Pre-pmt** Click 3625. [Tab] [Tab] [Tab] to accept Payment Amount of **$5,732.33** for invoice #3625.

4 ➤ **Disc. Taken** The cursor should be in the **Disc. Taken** column for Invoice **#3661**. [Tab] [Tab] to accept **$207.00** Discount Taken and Payment Amount **$11,488.50**.

5 ➤ **Disc. Taken** The cursor should be in the Disc. Taken column for invoice **#3661Rt C103**. [Tab] [Tab] to accept **-5.80** Discount Taken and Payment Amount **$-321.90**.

The Total payment will be **$16,898.93**.

	Merchandise	HST	*Total*
3661	$ 10,350.00	$ 1,345.50	$11,695.50
3661Rt C103	$　-290.00	$　- 37.70	$　-327.70
Net Purchase	$ 10,060.00	$ 1,307.80	$11,367.80

2% discount based on **$10,060.00** (net purchase) equals **$201.20**.

Discount Taken shown in window	$ 207.00
less	$　-5.80
equals	$ 201.20

Due Date	Invoice or Prepayment	Original Amount	Amount Owing	Discount Available	Discount Taken	Payment Amount
Jan 23, 2019	3625	5,732.33	5,732.33	0.00		5,732.33
Feb 08, 2019	3661	11,695.50	11,695.50	207.00	207.00	11,488.50
	3661Rt C103	-327.70	-327.70	-5.80	-5.80	-321.90
					Total	16,898.93

Fig. 8-14: Payment with discount.

Payments Journal Entry Jan 18, 2019 (J14)

Account Number	Account Description	Debits	Credits
2200	Accounts Payable	17,100.13	-
1020	Bank Account	-	16,898.93
5040	Purchase Discounts	-	201.20
Additional Date:	Additional Field:		
		17,100.13	17,100.13

6 ➤ **Post** when correct and return to the Home window.

7 ➤ Advance the Session date to **January 22, 2019**.

New Services Provided

A number of customers and individuals who live in the area have asked your firm to repair printers that are out of warranty. The manager agreed to provide this service, with a 30-day warranty for repairs, and asked you to create new General Ledger accounts and Service items.

In this exercise you will create new General Ledger accounts for repair revenue and Inventory & Service items for repairs of InkJet and Laser Printers.

Exercise 8-16—Creating Ledger Accounts & Service Items

Create New Ledger Accounts

1 ➤ From the Home page, click the **COMPANY** module.

2 ➤ Click the **Chart of Accounts** icon. Click **Create** icon.

3 ➤ **Account**   Type **4310**, [Tab] type **Repairs InkJet Printers**, [Tab].

4 ➤ **Type**   Select **Group** Account, if it is not already selected.

5 ➤ **Allow Division**   Remove the ✓.
     Allocations

Class Options Tab

6 ➤ Click the **Class Options** Tab and select **Revenue** [Tab].

7 ➤ Click Create Another.

8 ➤ Repeat steps 3 to 6 to create account **4320 Repairs Laser Printers**, with the same settings. Click Save & Close.

9 ➤ **Exit** to the Home window.

Create New Service Items

1 ➤ From the Home window, click the **INVENTORY & SERVICES** module. Click the **Inventory & Services** icon.

2 ➤ Click the **Create** icon.

3 ➤ **Description**   Type **Repair InkJet Out of Warranty**.

4 ➤ **Number**   **OWI-01 (O**ut of **W**arranty **I**nkJets).

5 ➤ **Type**   Click the **Service** option button.

Unit Tab

6 ➤ **Unit of**   Change to **20 minutes**.
     Measure

Pricing Tab

7 ➤ Click the **Pricing** tab, and record as follows. (The unit price will be for each 20 minutes of service.)

Price List	Price per Selling Unit
Regular	20.0000
Preferred	19.0000
Web Price	0.0000

Linked Tab

> **ℹ** With Service Items there are 2 linked accounts, whereas with Inventory Items there are 4 linked accounts.

8 ➤ Click the **Linked** tab. (See side note box.)

9 ➤ **Revenue**   Select **4310 Repairs InkJet Printers**.

      Expense   Do NOT change. There is no associated expense account with this service. Leave this field blank. The manager assumes that if parts are required, they would be ordered specifically for each service call.

10 ➤ Click Create Another .

11 ➤ Repeat steps 3 to 8 to create service item **Repair Laser Out of Warranty**, with code **OWL-01**, same unit of measure, same pricing and link account **4320**. Click Save & Close .

12 ➤ **Exit** to the Home window.

Exercise 8-17—Journalizing an Invoice for Warranty Repairs

The Manager has decided that each warranty repair will be set up with the name of the customer with a name code that begins with W- and the customer name. (W- to represent the warranty work.) The customer file will contain the customer's address with a memo note stating the warranty dates.

> **Jan 22, 2019** Mrs. Judy Marsh, on the recommendation of Computers and More, brought in her older model Laser Printer (out of warranty), that was not printing properly. One of your technicians worked on the printer for approximately 40 minutes. Bill Mrs. Marsh for 2 units of service, plus HST. Invoice total $45.20. Mrs. Marsh paid with her cheque #653.

1 ➤ From the Home window, click the **RECEIVABLES** module. Click the **Sales Invoice** icon.

2 ➤ **Payment Method** Change to **Cheque,** [Tab] twice.

3 ➤ **Cheque**   Type **653**. [Tab].

4 ➤ **Customer**   Create a customer account (Full Add) for Mrs. Marsh, with a name code of **W-Marsh Judy**; address, **635 Sonoma Blvd, Vaughan, Ontario, L4H 6P8**; Phone **905 897-8632**; Options tab, link **4320 Repairs Laser Printers,** remove

the terms; Taxes tab, select **HS**; Statistics tab, Credit limit field type **0.00**; Memo tab, type **Laser Out of Warranty repair Jan 22 to expire Feb 21 (30 days)**; Save and Close.

5 ➤ **Item Number**   Double-click and select **Repair Laser Out of Warranty (OWL-01)**.

6 ➤ **Quantity**   Type **2** (2 units of 20 minutes). Tab.

       Tax   This service is a retail sale and requires HST to be charged.

7 ➤ **Message**   Change to: **Warranty for 30 days**.

The journal entry should be as follows:

Sales Journal Entry Jan 22, 2019 (J15)			
Account Number	Account Description	Debits	Credits
1020	Bank Account	45.20	-
2650	HST Charged on Sales	-	5.20
4320	Repairs Laser Printers	-	40.00
Additional Date:	Additional Field:		
		45.20	45.20

8 ➤ **Post** when correct, and **Exit** to the Home window.

Changing Selling Prices

You may increase or decrease the selling price of goods when the purchase price changes. Some companies change the selling price only when the lower-cost goods are sold.

In the next exercise, you will **reduce** the selling price of an INVENTORY item. The same procedure would be used to **increase** a selling price.

Exercise 8-18—Changing the Selling Price

1 ➤ Advance the Session date to **Jan 28, 2019**.

> **Jan 27, 2019 The Manager noted that other wholesalers in your area have reduced the price of the 5 in 1 Inkjet Printers by $15.00. He advised you to reduce the selling price of IP-001 to $230.00 for regular customers and to $220.00 for preferred customers on all future sales.**

2 ➤ Click the **INVENTORY & SERVICES** module. Click the **Inventory & Services** icon.

3 ➤ Double-click **InkJet Printer 5 in 1 IP-001**.

4 ➤ Click the **Pricing** tab, and **change the prices** as noted previously.

5 ➤ Click Save and Close and return to the Home window.

More Transactions

1 ➤ **Record** the following transactions:

Jan 27, 2019 Do-It-Yourself Inc. requested a Sales price quote (#1) on the following goods (retail sale), plus HST. Requested shipping date is Jan 28, 2019 and terms are 2% 10 days, net 30 days.

2 InkJet Printer 5 in 1 at	$ 230.00 each
2 InkJet Black Cartridges at	38.50 each
2 InkJet Colour Cartridges at	44.00 each
2 Printer Cable USB at	15.00 each
Total quote including taxes	$740.15

Jan 28, 2019 The manager of Do-it-Yourself Inc. agreed to the price quote of Jan 27, 2019. Record the sale from Sales Quote #1.

The journal entry should look like this:

Sales Journal Entry Jan 28, 2019 (J16)			
Account Number	Account Description	Debits	Credits
1200	Accounts Receivable	740.15	-
5010	Cost of Goods Sold- InkJets	393.33	-
5030	Cost of Goods Sold -Cables	14.00	-
1250	Inventory Inkjet Printers	-	300.00
1270	Inventory Ink Cartridges Inkjets	-	93.33
1290	Inventory Printer Cables	-	14.00
2650	HST Charged on Sales	-	85.15
4100	Sales InkJets	-	625.00
4120	Sales Cables	-	30.00
Additional Date:	Additional Field:		
		1,147.48	1,147.48

2 ➤ **Post** when correct. You may see an Inventory Advisor window. Return to the Home window.

3 ➤ Advance the Session date to **Jan 29, 2019**.

Correcting Wrong Price after Posting

There are three ways to make a correction for an invoice containing an incorrect price or quantity.

a) Use the Adjust Invoice icon (refer to Exercise 2B-26b or Chapter 13, *Correcting Transaction Errors After Posting*), and issue a corrected invoice by correcting the price of the printer. All items on the original invoice would be shown.

b) Correct the item(s) (assuming one or two items) in a new invoice. This method makes it easier for the customer to see that the price change has taken place. The customer would receive two invoices (original and correction).

c) Reverse (Cancel) the original invoice (refer to Exercise 2A-21), then issue a correct invoice. If the invoice contains many items, this method takes too long and is a waste of an employee's time. The customer would receive two invoices (original and correction).

Method **b** will be shown as follows:

Exercise 8-19—Correcting Invoice Price After Posting

> **Jan 29, 2019** Do-It-Yourself Inc. advised you, by fax, that the items shipped on the 28th were received in good condition, but the 2 InkJet printers were priced at $230.00 each, which was $5.00 higher than what your manager quoted. Mrs. Davis confirmed her verbal agreement with Do-it-Yourself Inc. Mrs. Davis forgot to inform you of the change to $225.00 and, therefore, requested that you change the selling price for this invoice.

You will be preparing a net negative invoice:

1 ➤ Click the **Sales Invoices** icon from the Home window.

    Transaction   **Invoice**.

    Payment Method **Pay later**.

2 ➤ **Customer**   Select **Do-It Yourself Inc.**, Tab .

3 ➤ **Invoice**   **11596Co** (Co for correction), Tab .

    Date   **Jan 29, 2019**.

Removing the Incorrect Item

4 ➤ **Item Number**   **InkJet Printer 5 in 1**.

5 ➤ **Quantity**   **-2**, Tab . The minus sign will result in items being added back to the inventory quantity, and the customer's account will be reduced by the amount of the negative sale.

Item Number	Quantity	Order	Back Order	Unit	Item Description	Base Price	Discount (%)	Price	Amount	Tax	Account
IP-001	-2			Each	InkJet Printer 5 in 1	230.00		230.00	-460.00	HS	4100 Sales InkJets

6 ➤ Tab across the invoice fields.

    Base Price   Accept $230.00 (the original price).

    Amount   -460.00 (this is a negative amount since it is a reduction in the amount owed by the customer).

    Tax   Accept HS.

    Account   To accept 4100 Sales. (This is a price adjustment, not a sales return.)

Insert the Item with the Correct Sales Amount

7 ➤ **Item Number**   **InkJet Printer 5 in 1**, Tab .

8 ➤ Quantity   **2**, [Tab] to Base Price.

| IP-001 | 2 | | Each | InkJet Printer 5 in 1 | 225.00 | 225.00 | 450.00 | HS | 4100 Sales InkJets |

9 ➤ Base Price   **225.00**. This is the correct selling price as agreed upon.

Amount   Accept **450.00**.

10 ➤ Terms   **2.00**%, **9** Days, Net **29** days.

11 ➤ Message   Type **To correct invoice #11596 re error in price**. [Tab].
The net invoice total should be $-11.30.

Item Number	Quantity	Order	Back Order	Unit	Item Description	Base Price	Discount (%)	Price	Amount	Tax	Account
IP-001	-2			Each	InkJet Printer 5 in 1	230.00		230.00	-460.00	HS	4100 Sales InkJets
IP-001	2			Each	InkJet Printer 5 in 1	225.00		225.00	450.00	HS	4100 Sales InkJets

Subtotal: -10.00
Freight:
HST: -1.30
Total: -11.30

Early Payment Terms: 2.00 % 9 Days, Net 29 Days

Message: To correct invoice 11596 re error in price

Post

The journal entry should be as follows:

Sales Journal Entry Jan 29, 2019 (J17)

Account Number	Account Description	Debits	Credits
2650	HST Charged on Sales	1.30	-
4100	Sales InkJets	10.00	-
1200	Accounts Receivable	-	11.30
Additional Date:	Additional Field:		
		11.30	11.30

12 ➤ **Post** when correct, and **Exit** to the Home window.

13 ➤ Advance the Session date to **Jan 30, 2019**.

Making Inventory Adjustments

Sage 50 Accounting allows the user to use the Adjustments journal for two types of adjustments:

a. Adjustment to cost only.
b. Adjustment to quantity only.

For an adjustment to cost only (e.g., if you wish to increase or decrease the cost of an item without adjusting the quantity on hand), then leave the **Qty.** field blank and enter the adjustment amount into the **Amount** field.

For an adjustment to quantity only (e.g., if you wish to increase or decrease quantity without adjusting the total cost of the item) enter the quantity change into the **Qty.** field but leave the **Amount** field blank.

Exercise 8-20—Recording the INVENTORY Adjustments

Study the following scenario:

> **Jan 30, 2019   The accountant suggested that an inventory count be completed by staff to verify goods available for sale.**

1 ➤   Print the Inventory Quantity report (refer to Exercise 8-5).

The inventory report should be as follows:

Inventory Quantity

Description		Item No.	Unit	Quantity	Minimum	On Pu...	On Sal...	To Order
InkJet Black Cartridge	▲	IBC-01	Each	71	26	10	0	-
InkJet Colour Cartridge		ICC-01	Each	46	10	0	0	-
InkJet Printer 5 in 1		IP-001	Each	34	30	0	0	-
Laser Black Cartridge		LBC-01	Each	34	10	0	0	-
Laser Printer 20P		LP001	Each	41	12	0	0	-
Printer Cable USB		C-01	Each	22	20	0	0	-

This report would be printed and a copy of the first two columns, **Description** and **Number**, showing items the firm sells, would be given to the clerks counting the inventory. The actual counted report would be compared to the computer report above, and any variances or discrepancies adjusted.

It is not normal to give the counting staff the complete report, including the **Quantity** column, because it may cause them to count inaccurately.

The following counted inventory report was returned from the supervisor: The shortage of both types of InkJet cartridges was noted and a recount was completed. The missing inkjet cartridges were not located and an extra printer cable was found.

INVENTORY REPORT

Printers Company , Your Name

Date ___Jan 30, 2019___

Signed: ___*JED*___

Description	Number	Unit
InkJet Black Cartridge	IBC-01	69 each
InkJet Colour Cartridge	ICC-01	45 each
InkJet Printer 5 in 1	IP-001	33 each
Laser Black Cartridge	LBC-01	34 each
Laser Printer 20P	LP001	41 each
Printer Cable-USB	C-01	23 each

Note: One 5 in 1 printer damaged and removed from inventory. The Repair Department reports that it is damaged beyond repair. Not saleable.

The IP-001 printer fell from the display shelf. See note on count at the bottom of the inventory report.

As a result, the manager has ordered new, stronger display shelf brackets and a lockable display cabinet to hold the InkJet cartridges for safekeeping.

The missing ink cartridges and the broken printer must be written off to various accounts. Some companies may write off damaged goods that cannot be sold to a DAMAGED GOODS account in the expense section of the Income Statement. Other companies may record the above changes to the **Adjustments** account in the Cost of Goods Sold section of the Income Statement.

The management of Printers Company has decided to record this type of change to the **Adjustment** account. If the dollar value became a larger amount, then management may decide to use two or three accounts to record INVENTORY changes.

2 ➤ From the Home window, click the **INVENTORY & SERVICES** module, then click the **Adjust Inventory** Journal icon.

This journal is used to record only adjustments to inventory quantity and value due to loss, damage, etc.

Many of the drop-down menus and icons have been discussed previously. The Adjustment menu item will allow the entry to be Stored, Recalled, Allocated, and/or Posted.

3 ➤ **Record** the Adjustment as shown below. Note: You may have to expand the Acct column.

Item	Qty	Unit	Description	Unit Cost	Amount	Acct
IBC-01	-2	Each	InkJet Black Cartridge	19.6669	-39.33	5050
ICC-01	-1	Each	InkJet Colour Cartridge	27.00	-27.00	5050
IP-001	-1	Each	InkJet Printer 5 in 1	150.00	-150.00	5050
C-01	1	Each	Printer Cable USB	7.00	7.00	5050

Inventory Adjustments — At Location: Primary location
Source: Inv-Adj-JCD   Date: Jan 30, 2019
Comment: Adjust inventory to actual count

Total: -209.33

Fig. 8-15: Inventory Adjustments Journal window.

Source	**Inv-Adj-JCD** For Inventory Adjustment, memo with approval received from manager (initials JCD).
Qty	**-2**, Negative amounts indicate that items are to be removed from inventory because they are missing (probably theft). Positive amounts indicate that items are to be added to inventory when more items are counted as being in stock compared to the Sage 50 Accounting Quantity listing.
Unit Cost	The average unit cost of this item is **19.6668**. Do Not change for this entry.
Amount	Quantity (Qty) times Unit Cost.
Acct	The G/L account 5050 for INVENTORY ADJUSTMENTS was set up as the **Integration** account. See Exercise 8-3, step 2.

4 ➤ Display the Adjustments Journal entry (select **Report** and then **Display Inventory Adjustments Journal Entry**). The entry should be as follows:

Inventory Adjustments Journal Entry Jan 30, 2019 (J18)			
Account Number	Account Description	Debits	Credits
1290	Inventory Printer Cables	7.00	-
5050	Inventory Adjustments	209.33	-
1250	Inventory Inkjet Printers	-	150.00
1270	Inventory Ink Cartridges Inkjets	-	66.33
Additional Date:	Additional Field:		
		216.33	216.33

5 ➤ The inventory quantity and inventory value will be reduced and/or increased by this adjustment. **Exit** from the entry window.

6 ➤ New in 2015, **Select Report**, then **Display Inventory Adjustments Detail** report. This report also shows the increases and decreases to inventory. **Exit** from the entry window.

7 ➤ **Post** when correct and **Exit** to the Home window.

(See side note box.)

> ℹ To correct or cancel an Inventory adjustment, refer to Chapter 13.

Correcting Inventory Errors

Errors that originate from entries posted in the Sales or Purchases journal should be corrected using **the same** journal. As with other modules, the best way is to reverse the original entry for both **quantity** and **cost** and then enter a new entry.

The Adjustments journal is used to correct inventory errors (damaged goods, theft, or obsolescence) as shown in Exercise 8-20. Errors in the average cost and/or quantity may also be made using the Adjustments journal.

Build from Bill of Materials and/or Build from Item Assembly Journal

Sometimes a company may decide to group inventory items as a package for special promotions or transfer inventory (and costs) from one item to another item; for example, when individual parts are used to make (assemble) a smoke detector.

A new inventory number must be set up that will combine all the inventory items into the new item.

The **Build from Bill of Materials Journal** is used when you are building packages of items that you normally build or assemble (on a regular basis) and then sell.

The **Build from Item Assembly Journal** can be used to build the same packages or special order packages that do not occur on a regular basis.

Exercise 8-21—Using the Build from Bill of Materials Journal

1 ➤ Advance the Session date to **Jan 31, 2019**.

> Jan 31, 2019 **A number of customers have requested buying a package consisting of a printer, ink cartridges, and printer cable for a special price. The manager has decided that the firm will sell an InkJet package deal on a regular basis. The manager has moved 5 InkJet printers, 5 black cartridges, 5 colour cartridges, and 5 printer cables to the front of the store for this special deal.**

Printers Company will use the Build from Bill of Materials Journal feature to have the software create and record the special package deal.

2 ➤ Create a new General Ledger account **#1292 Inventory InkJet Package Deal**. Select **Subgroup Account**, Class Options **Inventory**.

3 ➤ Create a new inventory item with the following information:

Item Description	**InkJet Package Deal**
Item number	**IJP-01**
Type	Select **Inventory**

Quantities tab

Minimum Level	**2** (if we sell 3 units, we will need to make more packages).

Pricing tab

Pricing	**Regular price $294.00** (Normal selling price of all components is $327.50.) The Package Sales price is $33.50 less than the regular price (an approximate 10% savings).
	The Preferred Pricing will be $284.00, and the Web Pricing will be 0.00.

Linked tab

Linked Accounts	**1292 (Asset), 4100 (Revenue)** and **5010 (COGS)**.

Build tab

Enter the following information:

Quantities	Units	Pricing	Linked	**Build**	Statistics	Taxes	Additional Info	Detailed Desc.

Build ___1___ of this item from the following components (all quantities are in stocking units):

Item	Unit	Description	Quantity
IP-001	Each	InkJet Printer 5 in 1	1
IBC-01	Each	InkJet Black Cartridge	1
ICC-01	Each	InkJet Colour Cartridge	1
C-01	Each	Printer Cable USB	1

Additional Costs: ___0.00___   Record additional costs in: _____ ▼

You will be using one of each component to build one promotion package (see step 5).

See Appendix 2015 AD, *Using the Build from Bill of Materials with Additional Costs* in your course materials at www.nelson.com/student **www**

Additional Costs	This field would be used for any additional costs such as labour or freight expenses. Printers Company does not have additional costs associated with building these packages. (See side note box.)
Record additional costs in	To use this field, you would need to create an Income Statement account such as Wages Expense Transfer, which must be specified when defining the Linked accounts for the INVENTORY module. There is no exercise for this feature. (See side note box.)

4 ➤ Click **Save and Close** and **Exit** to Home window.

5 ➤ Click the **Build from Bill of Materials** icon. Input the information shown in Fig. 8-16.

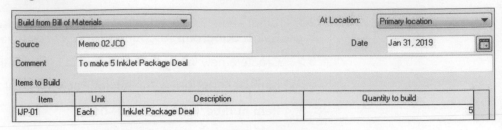

Build from Bill of Materials ▼				At Location:	Primary location ▼
Source	Memo 02 JCD			Date	Jan 31, 2019
Comment	To make 5 InkJet Package Deal				
Items to Build					

Item	Unit	Description	Quantity to build
IJP-01	Each	InkJet Package Deal	5

Fig. 8-16: Build from Bill of Materials Journal.

6 ➤ View the entry. The cost of the components has been moved from the individual inventory accounts to the new #1292 account.

Bill of Materials & Item Assembly Journal Entry Jan 31, 2019 (J19)

Account Number	Account Description	Debits	Credits
1292	Inventory InkJet Package Deal	1,018.33	-
1250	Inventory Inkjet Printers	-	750.00
1270	Inventory Ink Cartridges Inkjets	-	233.33
1290	Inventory Printer Cables	-	35.00
Additional Date:	Additional Field:		
		1,018.33	1,018.33

	Individual *Cost*	*5 units* *Total cost*
5 in 1 Printer	$150.00	750.00
Black cartridge	19.6669	98.33 (rounded)
Colour cartridge	27.00	135.00
USB cable	7.00	35.00
Total for one unit	203.67 (rounded)	1,018.33

7 ➤ **Exit** the Journal entry, **Post**. Sage 50 Accounting will create the 5 package deals.

The following warning message appears:

> Advisor: Entries just processed caused one or more inventory items to drop below the reorder point. Print the Inventory Item Quantity report to see which items to reorder.

This message informs the user that even though the inventory has not been sold, some of the individual items are below the reorder point. If the package deals sell, new inventory will need to be ordered. Click anywhere in the grey box to close the warning message.

The Build from Bill of Materials and Build from Item Assembly Journal entry can be reversed (negative amount) to cancel the promotion and return the unsold items to normal inventory status.

If you make a package deal such as this, it may cause one or more of the individual parts quantities to fall below the reorder point. The manager and staff will have to review the Inventory Quantity report to monitor the inventory.

To correct or cancel an Inventory Assembly Journal entry, refer to Chapter 13.

8 ➤ **Close** the Advisor and **Exit** to the Home window.

9 ➤ On the Home page, Inventory section, you will see

▼	InkJet Package Deal IJP-01	5	$1,018.33

(See side note boxes.)

Information only

If you were to use the Build from Item Assembly Journal to make the packages, the window would look similar to the following. If the top window does not show all the items, click the bottom right of the window, and drag (move) to the right until all items show. The completed Assembly Journal is shown in Fig. 8-17.

Fig. 8-17: Build from Item Assembly Journal.

Assembly Components

This section contains the components that will make up the new product or item.

Unit Cost   (This is the average cost of each item being moved.)

Amount   (This is the total cost of individual items being moved.)

Additional Costs

Discussed in Exercise 8-21 and Appendix 2015 AD, *Using the Build from Bill of Materials with Additional Costs,* which can be found in your course materials at www.nelson.com/student.

If you TAB past the Unit Cost field and enter the total cost (1,018.33) in the Amount field, Sage 50 Accounting will calculate the Unit cost for you.

Assembled Items

This section contains the item(s) that have been made up to sell as one unit.

Unit Cost   This is the average cost of the items being made (total cost of all parts used/divided by the number of items, $1,018.33/5 = **$203.666**). (See side note box.)

Amount $1,018.33 (this is the total cost of the items being made). ***Note***: You may have to adjust the Unit Cost to make the amount agree with the Assembly Components Amount due to rounding of fractions of a cent.

The Build from Item Assembly Journal can be reversed to cancel the promotion and return the unsold items to normal inventory status.

End of Information section.

Inventory Reports

There are a number of inventory reports available. Study each one, so you will know what to print when the need arises.

Exercise 8-22—Viewing INVENTORY Reports

In this exercise, from the Home window (bottom right, Inventory Reports section) you will print 3 reports (steps 1 and 2). In steps 3 through 5 you will view others, without printing to save paper.

1a ➤ **Quantity Report** Print this report. At Reports, click ▼ , select **Inventory Quantity**, click **Display**. This report (similar to Fig. 8-7) lists items that need to be ordered—low inventory.

1b ➤ **Summary Report** Print this report. At Reports, click ▼ , select **Inventory Summary**, click **Display**, click **Modify**, **Report Options**, select **Latest Transaction,** click **OK**. This report (similar to Fig. 8-8a) lists details of cost, total cost margin %, etc.

2 ➤ **Statistics Report** Print this report. At Reports, click ▼ , select **Inventory and Services Statistics**, click **Display**. This report will help management see which items have not sold during the period, or have not been sold recently.

3 ➤ **Inventory and Services List** Display. **Do NOT print.** At Reports, click ▼ , select **Inventory and Services List,** click **Display**. This will display a list of all inventory items on hand, with the Average Cost value. Ignore the Category column. Study the report, then exit.

4 ➤ **Sales Report** Display. **Do NOT print.** At Reports, click ▼ , select **Inventory and Services Sales Summary (or Detail)**, click **Display**. This will display a Y-T-D report (summary or detail) of dollar revenue, and cost of goods sold including dollar profits and margin %.

5 ➤ **Transaction Report** Display. **Do NOT print.** At Reports, click ▼ , select **Inventory and Services Transaction Summary (or Detail),** click **Display**. Click **Modify**, **Report Options**. You can print the report with or without Bill of Materials and/or Adjustments & Transfers. This will display a Y-T-D report of Quantity In (Purchase) and Quantity Out (Sales) with dollar amounts for each listing.

Other Reports

6 ➤ **Print** the following reports:

    a) Customer Aged Detail report as at Jan 31, 2019
    b) Vendor Aged Detail report as at Jan 31, 2019
    c) All Journal Entries for the month of January 2019
    d) Income Statement for the month of January 2019
    e) Balance Sheet as of Jan 31, 2019
    f) Cheque Log

7 ➤ Compare your printouts to the Printers Company solutions with your instructor.

Before Moving On ...

Read the following questions and make sure you know the answers to them; otherwise, read the corresponding part in the chapter before moving on.

1. Explain the difference between the **Margin** and **Markup** methods of calculating gross profit.

2. Which journal is used to process:

    Sales returns of inventory items?

    Purchase of inventory items?

3. State at least one benefit of using the **Minimum** field in the INVENTORY ledger window.

4. When are adjustments made on inventory items? What types of adjustments can be made?

5. What inventory valuation methods are used by Sage 50 Accounting?

6. What is the difference between the Bill of Materials Journal and the Item Assembly Journal?

7. How do you make corrections for posting errors related to inventory purchases and sales?

8. What is preferred pricing?

 Review **Slideshows 8A** and **8B** before doing the challenge exercise(s) assigned to you.

Relevant Appendix

WWW The following appendices are available in your course materials at www.nelson.com/student.

Appendix 2015 Q   **Names Fields**

Appendix 2015 AD   **Using the Build from Bill of Materials with Additional Costs**.

Appendix 2015 AE   **Recording Chapter 1 Transactions with Perpetual Service Items**

Challenge Exercise 08 C8-1, Stain Company (Your Name)
COMPANY, RECEIVABLES, PAYABLES, INVENTORY & SERVICES

1 ➤ Refer to Exercise 1-1b to unzip the **08 C8-1 Stain.exe** file.

2 ➤ Open the **08 C8-1 Stain** file and enter transactions for January.

You are the new accounting clerk for the **Stain Company Your Name** (Your name is the student's name).

Company Accounting Policies:

- Terms of 2/10, net 30 are applied to credit sales and purchases unless other information is provided.
- All cash discounts are calculated on price before tax.
- Sales invoices and cheques are assumed to be in numerical order.
- HST at 13% is used for Sales and Purchases.
- HST at 13% is used for Retail Sales and Purchases of goods for own use.
- Tax codes HS and HI can be used in this challenge case.
- This company does not use Purchase Orders.
- Ignore Shipped by field.
- Address information is not important.

Note: Accounts Receivable Subsidiary customer balances are nil.
Accounts Payable   Subsidiary vendor   balances are nil.

3 ➤ Record and **Post** the transactions in the appropriate module.

Jan 2   Based on special requests from customers, we received a new stain, as indicated below, on invoice #9873 from new vendor Kevin Paint Supply (address not important) terms 2/10, net 30. Tax code HS, Expense Account - you decide.

Item Description	Stain—Indoor-Better
Item Number	ST-I-BQ
Received	20 items at $11.10 each plus HST.
Selling price	$21.00 each
Minimum is	5 items, as this is the first time we will carry this type of stain.

Jan 3   New Retail customer, Mrs. Pottery, purchased 4 Stain - ST-I-GD at 10.60 each, plus HST paid by Universal Credit Card.

Jan 3   Sold the following goods to Paint Plus with HST. The sale is with normal terms of 2/10, net 30:

Quantity	Item	Unit	Description	Selling Price Plus HST
20	ST-O-BE	each	Stain - Outdoor-Better	$ 12.50
30	ST-O-E	each	Stain - Outdoor-Excellent	$ reduced to $12.90

Note: Ignore "inventory low" message if seen.

Jan 4   Purchased from Canada Paint Ltd. 50 Stain - Indoor-GD at $5.30 each, plus HST. Invoice #5512 with terms 2/10, net 30.

Jan 4   Purchased store supplies from Office Supplies Company on Invoice #825, terms 2/10, net 30, with the following information:

> 10 rolls of special wrapping material at $15.00 each, plus HST.

Jan 5   Retail sale to Bayview Terrace of the following items. Terms 2/10, net 30.

Quantity	Item	Unit	Description	Selling Price
20	ST-I-E	each	Stain - Indoor E	$11.00 plus HST
5	BR-Ex	each	Brushes-Excellent	$ 7.00 plus HST

Jan 7   Received from Painters Supplies, per their invoice #4912, twenty (20) each of Stain - Indoor GD at $5.30 each plus HST, terms 2/10, net 30.

Jan 9   The manager noticed that 3 of the Stain - Indoor GD purchased on invoice #4912 have a small leak and must be returned for replacement. Returned the 3 containers, for full credit, to Painters Supplies.

Jan 10 A display cabinet shelf broke and 5 Stain - Outdoor Better paint cans were damaged. The manager issued a memo to write off these items.

Jan 11 Paid insurance agent, Marshall Insurance, $240.00 plus HST, for a one-year policy #5689B effective January 1. Charge the January cost of insurance to expense.

Jan 11 The owner, A-Your Name (First and Surname) withdrew $1,205.00 for a monthly draw. **Note**: Use A- before your name.

Jan 12 Received cheque #362 from Paint Plus for amount owing.

Jan 14 Prepayment of $250.00 issued to Canada Paint Ltd. for a future order of paint. A Purchase Order was not issued.

Jan 14 Paid Office Supplies Company for Invoice #825.

Jan 16 Paid Receiver General for HST owing at Jan 1.

Jan 18 A purchase order received from retail customer, Bayview Terrace, for 10 Stain-Indoor E at $11.00 each plus HST, to be delivered on January 21. Issued Sales Order # 125, terms 2/10, n30.

4 ➤ Print the following reports:

   a) Income Statement, year-to-date
   b) Customer Aged Detail, all customers, with terms at Jan 18
   c) Vendor Aged Detail, all vendors, with terms at Jan 18
   d) All Journal Entries Jan 1 to Jan 18
   e) (Inventory & Services) Summary for all items of inventory
   f) (Inventory & Services) Quantity for all items of inventory
   g) Pending Sales Order Detail by Customers Jan 21

Challenge Exercise 08 C8-2, Charlie's Hair Styling
COMPANY, RECEIVABLES, PAYABLES, INVENTORY & SERVICES

Charlie's Hair Styling cuts ladies' and men's hair and sells hair products. *Note*: All haircuts and products are subject to 13% HST. Ignore the Shipped By field.

1 ➤ Refer to Exercise 1-1b to unzip the **08 C8-2 Hair.exe** file.

2 ➤ Open the **08 C8-2 Hair** file.

3 ➤ **Record** and **Post** the following transactions for March:

Mar 1   Change the customer name "Your Actual First and Last Name" to your own name before recording transactions.

Mar 1   Issued next cheque to pay $600.00 rent, plus HST at 13%, to Mega Mall Ltd.

Mar 2   Ms. Rodrigues paid by Universal Credit Card for 1 lady's haircut at $30.00 plus taxes, and 1 bottle of regular shampoo (SG01) at $12.00, plus HST.

Mar 3   Mr. Miguel Santos paid by cheque #569 for a man's haircut at $20.00 and a child's haircut at $10.00, plus HST.

Mar 3   Cash sale of 2 bottles shampoo (SB01) $13.00 each and 2 bottles conditioner (CB01) $14.50 each, plus HST, to Mrs. Kiran Kenth.

Mar 5   Your First and Last Name ordered a new style hair dryer on sales order #16 at $40.00, plus HST, terms leave blank. Item will be delivered March 13. Create the new item with the following information:

Description	New Style Hair Dryer #23
Number	HD-23
Selling Price	$40.00
Link	Sales Other
Minimum Quantity	0

Mar 5   Issued Purchase Order #19 to Hair Products International for 3 new style hair dryer #23 at $28.00 each, plus HST. Delivery date, Mar 7. This is a new item described on March 5. Terms 2/10, net 30.

Mar 6   Mrs. Chen purchased 2 bottles of mousse (MB01) at $18.00 each, plus HST. Cheque #126 received in full payment.

Mar 7   Issued cheque to new vendor Flooring Specialty (address not important) for 2 gallons (6 months supply) of Heavy Duty Floor Cleaner at $125.00 per gallon, plus HST. Invoice #9682. Charge to Store Supplies.

Mar 7   Two new hair dryers were delivered by Hair Products International on invoice #6589 at price agreed on Purchase Order #19. The remaining dryer is back ordered and will be available in 6 days.

Mar 8   The manager called Your First and Last Name to tell them that the hair dryer arrived. Received their cheque #257 to pay for the hair dryer on invoice #236. (Sales Order # 16.)

Mar 10   Mrs. Del Rosario had a haircut $30.00, and purchased 1 each of shampoo (SB01) $13.00, conditioner (CB20) $16.00 and mousse (MB01) $18.00, plus HST. She paid with her Universal Credit Card.

Mar 10   Mrs. Del Rosario returned the mousse because she decided she did not want the product at this time. Process a credit card adjustment to accept the return.

4 ➤ **Print** the following reports:

    a) Income Statement, year-to-date
    b) Balance Sheet to March 10
    c) All Journal Entries to March 10
    d) Pending Purchase Orders Detail by Vendor at Mar 10
    e) (Inventory & Services) Summary at Mar 10
    f) (Inventory & Services) Quantity at Mar 10

Challenge Exercise 08 C8-3, Vet Services
COMPANY, RECEIVABLES, PAYABLES, INVENTORY& SERVICES

This exercise provides practice in recording transactions for a business that combines service revenue and sales of goods (to keep track of the quantity and cost of a company's inventory items). The data file for **Vet Services** has been set up to use the COMPANY, PAYABLES, RECEIVABLES, and INVENTORY & SERVICES modules.

1 ➤ Refer to Exercise 1-1b to unzip the **08 C8-3 Vet.exe** file.

2 ➤ Open the **08 C8-3 Vet** file.

Company Accounting Policies:

- Vet Services provides services for dogs and cats and is owned by Dr. Katherine DiGenova.
- Each client is charged for an office visit (**0-1 Office Visit**).
- Fiscal year is January 1 to December 31.
- The staff uses the memo tab record to include the name of the pet, breed name, sex, and other relevant information.
- Full payments from clients for goods and services are required after the veterinarian has seen the pet.
- A 10% discount will be given to seniors for office visits and lab tests. Seniors will pay regular prices for medication. The only senior client at this time is Mr. Jason Alexander.
- Cheques are issued when necessary for purchases of goods and services. Vendor purchase and/or service invoices are normally with terms of 2/10, n30 days, unless other information is provided.
- HST at 13% is used for all services. Tax code HS is set up as a default because most services and medications are sold with HST.
- The office does not use Purchase Orders.
- Ignore Shipped by field.
- Address information is not important.
- Universal Credit Card is accepted for services and medication. Occasionally clients do not have a credit card and cannot pay cash.
- One client, Mrs. Wakenna Zia, has an outstanding account.

Inventory Summary Jan 01, 2017

Item No. △	Description	Unit	Price	Quantity	Cost	Value	Margin %
Meds-1	Medicine Antibiotic	Each	20.00	40	10.00	400.00	50.00
Meds-2	Medicine-pain	Each	12.00	100	6.00	600.00	50.00
Meds-3	Flea Treatment plan	Each	47.00	15	20.00	300.00	57.45
Meds-4	Rabies Needle	Each	15.00	0	0.00	0.00	100.00
						1,300.00	

Vet Services Inventory Summary.

3 ➤ Advance the date on a daily basis after **January 3,** and **record** the following transactions. The Daily Business Manager has been set up to advise Katherine of clients who need to be contacted to bring their pets in for various reasons.

Jan 3   Mrs. Helen Tyson brought her cat for an examination. The veterinarian examined the cat and prescribed one antibiotic medication, which was supplied by the vet. Mrs. Tyson paid the $62.09 invoice by Universal Credit Card.

Jan 4   Mrs. Eileen Rosen brought in her dog for a consultation. She asked the veterinarian to clip the dog's nails. Katherine decided that since she has been asked to do this procedure many times, she will now start charging for this service. Katherine provided a regular checkup and prescribed a flea program for the dog. The total invoice amount is $101.64, paid by Universal Credit Card.

Create a new Service item, Description: Nail Clipping Dog with Item Number: S-5, Unit of Measure should be: Each, Pricing Regular Price 8.00, Preferred Price 7.20, Web Price 0.00, Linked tab, 4330 Veterinary fees - Other, Expense: There is no associated expense account with this service, Taxes tab. Tax HS.

Jan 4   Received from Medical Supplies Inc. 25 Rabies Needles at $7.00 each, plus HST. A purchase order was not issued. Invoice #3280 for $197.75. Terms 2/10, net 30.

Jan 5   A new client, Your Actual First and Last Name, Contact: **Dalmatian Male: Salem, 3 Ann Street, Guelph, Ontario, N1H 2Z4**; Ship-to-Address tab: Same as mailing address; Options tab: Revenue Account **4310, no terms**; Taxes tab: **HS**; Statistics tab: Credit Limit **0.00**; Memo tab: **Dalmatian Male: Salem, born Oct 3, 2009. Jan 05, 2017 special blood tests ordered. Patient to return on Monday, Jan 9, 2017 at 4:00 PM**; To-Do-Date: **Jan 07, 2017**. The vet ordered special blood tests (the clinic charges a $10.00 laboratory test fee plus HST) and the results will be back from the lab on Friday. Your Actual First and Last Name has been scheduled for a return visit as noted on the Memo tab. Prepare an office visit and lab fee invoice. Total fee $50.79 paid by cash.

Jan 7   Issue a cheque to pay Medical Supplies Inc., invoice #265.

Jan 7   Mrs. Carol Wright brought in her cat for her rabies needle. Bill her for the office visit (annual check-up) and the regular price for 1 rabies needle. Total invoice $56.44 paid by Universal Credit Card. After posting the transaction, change the To-Do date to Jan 08, 2018 in Mrs. Wright's memo file.

Jan 7   The Ontario Lab Testing results for Your Actual First and Last Name pet arrived, Invoice #7763 in amount of $6.78 (lab test $6.00 and HST $.78). Record this invoice, terms n10. (*Note*: Charge 5345 Laboratory fees. Do NOT use lab item.)

Jan 9   Your Actual First and Last Name brought in Salem and the vet informs her that the lab tests show Salem has an infection that requires antibiotic medication.

Issue an invoice $62.09, for an office visit and one antibiotic medication paid by personal cheque #442. The vet informs Your Actual First and Last Name that a follow-up visit (at no charge) is required within 2 weeks to see if the medication has cleared the problem. Add a notation to Your Actual First and Last Name memo file: vet needs to see Salem on Jan 23, for a special office visit (checkup) at no charge.

Jan 11   Cheque #634 in the amount of $58.25 received from Mrs. Zia.

Jan 11   Mr. Nathan brought his cat in for an office visit and checkup. The vet prescribed the flea medication plan. Invoice of $92.60 paid by personal cheque #813. Change the To-Do Date to Jan 11, 2018.

Jan 11   Mr. Alexander brought his dog in as she was in a fight. The vet prescribed one antibiotic and one pain medication. Mr. Alexander receives a 10% seniors discount on office visits and paid with a Universal Credit Card. Invoice total $71.71. Mr. Alexander's follow-up visit is scheduled for Jan 18.

4 ➤   **Print** the following reports:

   a) All Journal Entries Jan 1 to Jan 11
   b) Income Statement, year-to-date
   c) (Inventory & Services) Summary at Jan 11
   d) (Inventory & Services) Quantity at Jan 11

Challenge Exercise 08 C8-4, Bears
Perpetual Inventory Average Cost and First In First Out (FIFO)

This Challenge Exercise will allow you to record transactions in both Perpetual Inventory systems: Average Cost and First In First Out (FIFO) and compare results for both Cost of Goods Sold and Balance Sheet Inventory.

The Bears Company is a new company started by Jessica Jordan that will sell teddy bears to toy stores. She is not sure which Perpetual Inventory system to use and will record the first few entries in both data files for comparison. She plans to sell only 1 type of teddy bear for the first few weeks.

A college student has created 2 data files for this company, which will open for business on Jan 2.

Note: Both data files **08_C8-4_Bears-PI-1-Avg** and **08_C8-4_Bears-PI-2-FIFO** are identical.
You will change data file PI-2 to use the FIFO method.

1 ➤ Unzip and open the **08_C8-4_Bears-PI-1-Avg** data file.

2 ➤ Click **Setup, Settings, ⊞ at Inventory & Services, Options**. The Inventory Costing method: Average Cost should be selected. Click **Cancel** to return to the Home page.

Note: To assist in learning the difference between the 2 methods, **taxes** are *ignored* in the following transactions.

After each transaction, record the appropriate amount in the tables in Exercise C8-4D.

Exercise C8-4A—Record Transactions using the Average Cost Method

---

3 ➤ Record the following transactions, using the Average Cost method.

a) After the input of each transaction, fill in the appropriate table in Exercise C8-4D.

b) After the completion of all transactions, complete Exercise C8-4E.

Jan 2   Received from David Morris Company, 60 Bears at $10.00 each on Invoice #67888, dated today, terms 2% 10 days, net 30 days. They will sell for $20.00 each.

Jan 3   40 bears are sold to Ditlove Toys Inc. for $20.00 each on invoice #1, terms 2% 10 days, net 30 days. Before posting the entry, display the Journal entry.

Jan 4   Received from David Morris Company, 50 bears at $12.00 each on invoice #67897, terms 2/10, net 30. The selling price is not changed, as another store in the area sells similar bears for the same price.

Jan 5   Sold 30 bears to Jen Milton Toys for $20.00 each, on the next invoice.

Jan 6   Received from David Morris Company, 20 more bears at $12.50 each on Invoice #68002, with terms of 2/10, net 30. The selling price is not changed, as another warehouse store in the area sells similar bears for the same price.

Jan 7   Sold 35 bears to Ditlove Toys Inc. for $20.00 each, on the next invoice, terms 2% 10 days, net 30 days.

Exercise C8-4B—Change Inventory Costing Method to the First In First Out (FIFO) Method

1 ➤ Unzip and open the **08 C8-4 Bears –PI -2 (FIFO)** data file.

2 ➤ Click **Setup, Settings, click ⊞ at Inventory & Services,** click **Options**. The Average Cost Inventory Costing Method is selected. Select **First In, First Out (FIFO)**. Click **OK**.

The following warning message appears.

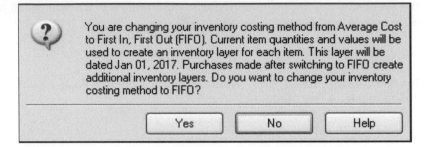

3 ➤ Click **Yes** to change to FIFO, and return to the Home page.

Exercise C8-4C—Record Transactions Using the First In First Out (FIFO) Method

1 ➤ Record the same transactions from Exercise C8-4A and record the information in the tables.

Exercise C8-4D—Record Information in the Following Tables

Cost of Purchases (Average Cost)

Date	Items Purchased	$ Cost
Jan 02	60	
Jan 04	50	
Jan 06	20	
Total	130	$

Cost of Purchases (FIFO)

Date	Items Purchased	$ Cost
Jan 02	60	
Jan 04	50	
Jan 06	20	
Total	130	$

Cost of Goods Sold (Average Cost)

Date	Items Sold	$ CGS
Jan 03	40	
Jan 05	30	
Jan 07	35	
Total	105	$

Cost of Goods Sold (FIFO)

Date	Items Sold	$ CGS
Jan 03	40	
Jan 05	30	
Jan 07	35	
Total	105	$

Exercise C8-4E—For Both Methods, Print the Following and Record Information in the Following Tables

1 ➤ From the ACCOUNTS PAYABLE module window, what is the total cost of the bears purchased from David Morris Company?

$_____

2 ➤ For both methods, print the Income Statement and Balance Sheet and record information below:

a) **Income Statement** (Compare Cost of Goods Sold amounts)

Cost of Goods Sold – (Average Cost)	Cost of Goods Sold – (First In First Out)
$	$

b) **Balance Sheet** (Compare Inventory amounts)

Inventory Average Cost	Inventory First In First Out
$	$

3 ➤ Print the Inventory & Services, Summary Report at Jan 07, and record information.

Inventory Summary – Average Cost

Jan 07 ____items at $_____ = $_____

4 ➤ Print the Inventory & Services, FIFO Costing Report at Jan 07, and record information.

Jan 04 _____ items at $_____ $

Jan 06_____ items at $_____ $_____
                    Total $____0

                                        Average Cost (FIFO) $_____

5 ➤ Comparison of both methods:

Average Cost		FIFO	
Cost of Goods Sold:	$	Cost of Goods Sold:	$
Balance Sheet Inventory _____		Balance Sheet Inventory	_____
Total inventory values $_____		Total inventory values	$_____

Chapter 9

Month-End/Year-End Processing

Kafa Sweaters

Learning Objectives

After completing this chapter you will be able to:

- ☐ Record various month-end adjusting entries in the General Journal.
- ☐ Record Inventory adjustment entry using the Adjust Inventory Journal.
- ☐ Add new General Ledger accounts as required.
- ☐ Display and print various reports and journals.

This chapter reviews recording adjusting entries at month-end or year-end and starting a new fiscal year. Reversing entries is discussed.

The instructions assume that you are familiar with manual accounting, processing month-end and year-end adjustments, and closing a year for a company. Procedures vary from company to company, depending upon the Sage 50 Accounting modules used and the nature of the business; e.g., merchandise versus service.

The chapter contains the following:

Kafa Sweaters: Company Profile

Kafa Sweaters has been in business for five years and sells a selection of sweaters to both retail and wholesale customers. All transactions for the year have been entered into the accounting records, except for the year-end adjusting entries. Mr. Kafa has hired you to assist in recording the December month-end adjustments and closing the books (shown in Chapter 10) for the year.

The COMPANY module is used to record the normal month-end and year-end adjustments. Some of these adjustments will be reversed in the new year.

The Adjust Inventory Journal in the INVENTORY & SERVICES module is used to record any adjustments to the ending inventory.

Kafa Sweaters does not use **recurring entries** or the **Track Additional Transaction Details** feature.

Reviewing Existing Accounting Data

1 ➤ Refer to Exercise 1-1b, to **unzip** the **09 Kafa**.exe file.

(*Do NOT use the 10 Kafa2 data file.*)

2 ➤ Start Sage 50 Accounting and open the **09 Kafa** data file.

3 ➤ Accept the Session Date of December 31, 2018 (the fiscal year-end of the firm).

Trial Balance for Kafa Sweaters

> Most companies will have printed a Trial Balance and a General Journal before adjustments are made. The accountant or manager would review the accounts and $ values to see if the $ values need changing.

4 ➤ **Display** and compare the Trial Balance at December 31, 2018 to Fig. 9-1. All previous entries have been cleared. Only the adjusting entries will display when reviewing your work in this chapter.

(See side note box.)

Entering Month-End (Period-End) Adjustments

Adjustments are made after all the regular monthly transactions have been entered. Most of the adjustments shown in this chapter are typical monthly entries. Some entries (Accrued Revenue and Expense) are reversed in the next month.

All of the adjustments shown in this chapter should be entered in the COMPANY module, except for the Adjusting Inventory Journal (using the Inventory & Services module) with a date of December 31, 2018.

Usually one of the accounting clerks would be responsible for recording all adjustments at month-end. The manager has decided you are the individual to record all accrued entries at December 2018.

Kafa Sweaters, Student's Name
Trial Balance As At Dec 31, 2018

		Debits	Credits
1100	Bank Chequing Account	9,725.00	-
1200	Accounts Receivable	13,889.00	-
1210	Allowance for Doubtful Accounts		400.00
1260	Inventory of Goods	60,320.00	-
1270	Prepaid Office Supplies on Hand	500.00	-
1300	Prepaid Insurance	1,200.00	-
1420	Equipment	88,129.00	-
1440	Furniture	31,020.00	-
1520	Accum. Deprec. Equipment	-	35,252.00
1540	Accum. Deprec. Furniture	-	12,408.00
2200	Accounts Payable	-	13,545.00
2231	Accrued Liabilities	-	0.00
2310	EI Payable	-	589.00
2320	CPP Payable	-	523.00
2330	Income Tax Payable	-	3,233.00
2350	HST Charged on Sales	-	3,561.00
2360	HST Paid on Purchases	1,841.00	-
2710	Bank Loan Payable	-	21,000.00
3120	Capital Nathan Kafa	-	86,274.00
3140	Drawings Nathan Kafa	10,000.00	-
4010	Sales-All	-	327,600.00
4210	Sales Returns	3,980.00	-
4220	Sales Discounts	5,725.00	-
4510	Handling Fee		0.00
5010	Cost of Goods Sold	123,470.00	-
5050	Purchase Discounts	-	1,942.00
5070	Inventory Adjustments	-	
5110	Rent Expense	24,000.00	-
5120	Wages Expense	86,300.00	-
5122	EI Expense	3,452.00	-
5124	CPP Expense	3,193.00	-
5260	Office Supplies Expense	2,040.00	-
5330	Telephone Expense	3,720.00	-
5340	Advertising Expense	15,137.00	-
5350	Depreciation Expense-All	0.00	-
5360	Bad Debts Expense	2,438.00	-
5410	Water/Hydro Expense	4,568.00	-
5510	Bank Charges Expense	1,380.00	-
5530	Bank Interest on Loan Expense	1,540.00	-
5540	Insurance Expense	2,100.00	-
5550	Automobile Expense	2,810.00	-
5560	Automobile Lease	3,840.00	-
		----------------	----------------
		506,327.00	506,327.00
		==========	==========

Fig. 9-1: Trial Balance for Kafa Sweaters.

It is important to understand what and how you do month-end and year-end adjustments, and why you need to do them. Also focus on the effects of the adjustments to the various financial statements you need to produce at period-end. Run **Slideshow 9—Month & Year-End Processing** now.

Exercise 9-1—Entering Period-End Adjustments

Bank Reconciliation: Expense Entries

At month-end, differences between the company's bank statement and accounting records must be reconciled. Bank charges and deductions from your company's bank account must be recorded in your company's accounting system. You have not yet learned how to do bank reconciliations using Sage 50 Accounting, but it will be covered in detail in Chapter 12.

All bank adjustments are processed in the COMPANY module, General Journal.

The bank statement for December for Kafa Sweaters would not be received until some time in the middle of January. During each month, the manager of Kafa Sweaters would receive debit and/or credit memos from the bank to alert the company to any changes made to the bank account. Examples of these entries include NSF cheques and regular service charges. This also makes the company aware of entries that occur regularly, such as lease payments or normal bank charges.

Kafa Sweaters' bank normally charges bank service fees at the end of the month. The bank has not sent the normal Debit memo for bank service fees.

Mr. Kafa sent you a note to prepare an entry to the bank account for estimated bank service charges of $33.00. (See side note box.)

This adjusting entry will be reversed on the first day of the next period.

> If the company has access to the bank account using the Internet, then the manager can locate the actual bank charges. If the actual amount is being used, then the Chapter 10 reversal for bank charges does not need to be reversed.

1 ➤ From the Home window, **COMPANY** module, click the **General Journal** icon.

2 ➤ **Source**:   **Dec-Adj-1** (code December adjustment #1).

3 ➤ **Date**:   **Dec 31, 2018**

4 ➤ **Comment** line: **Estimated Bank Service Fees per N. Kafa**.

The entry should be recorded as follows:

5510	Bank Charges Expense	33.00	
2231	Accrued Liabilities		33.00

> This entry is recorded on a monthly basis. If desired, you could set it up as a Recurring Transaction entry. Remember that the Recurring Entry feature is optional. It is designed to help save you time in making repetitive entries and to minimize chances of making errors.

5 ➤ **Comment** column for: 5510 **Estimated Bank Service Fees**.
                                     2231 **Estimated Bank Service Fees**.
                                     (See side note box.)

6 ➤ **Post** after verifying accuracy.

Prepaid Expense Adjustment: Office Supplies

Most companies charge office supplies purchased to an asset account, similar to Prepaid Office Supplies On Hand. At month-end, the asset is adjusted for the amount of supplies consumed (used) during the period. The consumed supplies are normally charged to an expense account similar to Supplies Expense.

Study the following memo:

Kafa Sweaters

Memorandum

Date: *December 31, 2018*

To: *Jordan Royes, Accounting Department*

From: *Nathan Kafa, General Manager*

The office staff has determined, by counting and calculating the cost price, that we have $120.00 worth of Office Supplies on Hand.

Prepare an entry to record the supplies used.

> *Hint: General Ledger #1270 Prepaid Office Supplies on Hand $500.00, less $120.00 at December 31 = $380.00 used.*

Fig. 9-2: Memo on Prepaid Office Supplies.

1 ➤ **Record** and **Post** the following journal entry **Dec-Adj-2**:

Comment line   **Office Supplies Used**

5260	Office Supplies Expense	380.00	
1270	Prepaid Office Supplies on Hand		380.00

Comment column for: 5260 - **Office Supplies Used**
                           1270 - **Office Supplies Used**

Use appropriate Comments for remaining adjustments.

Prepaid Expense Adjustment: Prepaid Insurance

The two Prepaid Expense adjustments (Prepaid Insurance and Prepaid Office Supplies On Hand), are examples of proper matching of revenues earned with expenses incurred. This results in a more accurate financial statement for Kafa Sweaters. If the adjustments were not made, the profits of the company would be higher than the true profits for 2017 and lower for 2018.

Kafa Sweaters

Memorandum

Date: *December 31, 2018*

To: *Jordan Royes, Accounting Department*

From: *Nathan Kafa, General Manager*

Re: *Insurance policy FT2786-09*

The 6 month FT (Fire/Theft) Insurance Policy purchased on November 15, 2018 for $1,200.00 expires in 4-1/2 months (May 14, 2019).

Prepare an entry to record the insurance used from November 15 to December 31.

Fig. 9-3: Memo on Prepaid Insurance Expense.

> **(i)** Proper matching results from recording the prepaid insurance premiums as an expense as the policy expires.

You need to reduce the ledger account **1300 Prepaid Insurance** to show that only 4-1/2 months of insurance remain in effect after the year-end.

$1,200.00/6 months = $200.00 per month.

1-1/2 months used up = $300.00. This will leave $900.00 in the PREPAID INSURANCE account for the following year. (See side note box.)

1 ➤ **Record** and **Post** the following journal entry **Dec-Adj-3**:

5540	Insurance Expense	300.00	
1300	Prepaid Insurance		300.00

This expense adjustment occurs each month and could be set up as a recurring entry for $200.00.

Accrued Expenses

GAAP **Matching Principle** requires that all expenses incurred to earn revenues must be reported in the same time period as the corresponding revenues. The revenues are to be "matched" with the expenses incurred to earn them. Expenses incurred but not yet paid for are referred to as accrued expenses. Proper matching of revenues **earned** and expenses **incurred**, **separated from the related cash flows**, results in an accurate accounting of net income or loss.

In this section you will match the expenses recorded in December with the corresponding revenues earned by Kafa Sweaters in the same month.

Study the following memo:

Kafa Sweaters

Memorandum

Date: *December 31, 2018*

To: *Jordan Royes, Accounting Department*

From: *Gus Hollin, Accounting Supervisor*

In reviewing the trial balance, we noticed the following expense bills have not been received or entered. Would you please process an accrual entry.

	Amount Subject to Tax	*HST Amount*
Telephone	*$260.00*	*33.80*
Electricity	*340.00*	*44.20*
Automobile Gas	*90.00*	*11.70*
Totals	*$690.00*	*89.70*

Fig. 9-4: Memo on Accrued Expense.

5330	Telephone Expense	260.00	
5410	Water/Hydro Expense	340.00	
5550	Automobile Expense	90.00	
2360	HST Paid On Purchases	89.70	
2231	Accrued Liabilities		779.70

1 ➤   **Record** and **Post** the following journal entry **Dec-Adj-4**:

Remember to view the transaction before posting.

Entries similar to this will occur each month; however, it should **not** be set up as a recurring entry, as the expense accounts may be very different each month.

When you click the **Post** icon you will see a confirmation window.

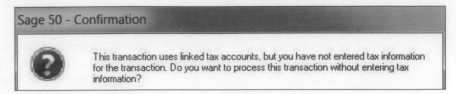

In Chapter 1 the General Journal was used to record entries without HST.

In Chapters 3A and 3B, when you recorded entries in the Purchases Journal, you identified the purchase amount before HST was added. Sage 50 Accounting then allocated taxes based on the tax codes and rates that were previously set up.

In the General Journal when you record an entry affecting the Taxes account (HST), the program requires the pre-tax amounts.

2 ➤ Click **No** to process the transaction entering the tax information. If you click Yes (entering without tax information), you would have to manually adjust the Sage 50 Accounting HST report when submitting the report to the Receiver General.

> You entered an HS tax code for HST at 13%. $690.00 appears in the Amount Subject to Tax column.
>
> Sage 50 Accounting divides the HST amount entered in the HST Paid on Purchases account #2360 ($89.70) by .13 (the HST rate) to determine the amount subject to HST tax ($690.00).

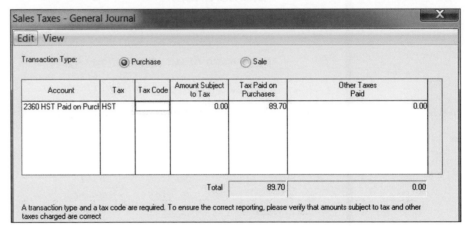

3 ➤ **Tax Code**   Type **HS** or select HS, [Tab]. (See side note box.)

4 ➤ **Other Taxes Paid**   See side note box. [Tab].

> The $0.00 (Other Taxes Paid) column would be used when PST is applicable. As of June 30, 2010, Ontario no longer collects PST.

5 ➤ Click **OK**.

The Sales Tax button now has a blue ✓ indicating Tax information is being recorded.

(See side note box.)

6 ➤ You need to click the **Post** icon again to post the entry.

Accrued Interest Expense

This entry is very similar to the previous entry for ACCRUED EXPENSES.

Kafa Sweaters

Memorandum

Date: *December 31, 2018*

To: *Jordan Royes, Accounting Department*

From: *Nathan Kafa, General Manager*

The loan interest for December is due on January 1, 2019. Would you please accrue, to account #2231 Accrued Liabilities, the loan interest as of December 31, 2018.

The loan balance is $21,000.00; the loan interest rate is 8% per year. The monthly interest cost is $140.00.

Fig. 9-5: Memo on Accrued Interest.

$21,000.00 x 8% /12 months = $140.00 per month.

(See side note box.)

1 ➤ **Record** and **Post** the following journal entry **Dec-Adj-5**:

5530	Bank Interest on Loan Expense	140.00	
2231	Accrued Liabilities		140.00

This entry will occur each month as the interest expense accrues on the loan, and could be set up as a recurring monthly entry.

Remember to view the transaction before posting.

(See side note box.)

Accrued Wages Expense

This scenario occurs at the end of some months during the year depending on when employees are paid. This adjustment could be set up, therefore, as a monthly recurring entry.

Kafa Sweaters

Memorandum

Date:	*December 31, 2018*
To:	*Jordan Royes, Accounting Department*
From:	*Nathan Kafa, General Manager*

The payroll department has advised me that we need to accrue $1,809.00 in wages for December 31. Employees were last paid up to and including December 25, 2018.

Ignore employee benefits for this period. The benefit accrual is not material in amount.

Open a new account for WAGES PAYABLE.

Fig. 9-6: Memo on Accrued Wages Payable.

1 ➤ Before this transaction can be recorded, add a new G/L account **#2220 Wages Payable**. Select **Group Account** and **Other Payable** on the Class Options tab.

2 ➤ **Record** and **Post** the following journal entry **Dec-Adj-6**:

5120	Wages Expense	1,809.00	
2220	Wages Payable		1,809.00

Depreciation Expense

Depreciation represents the reduction of the value of a **capital asset** such as machinery, equipment, or building. The cost minus the expected salvage value is divided by the estimated life of the asset. This amount would be the Depreciation cost per year.

Kafa Sweaters

Memorandum

Date: *December 31, 2018*

To: *Jordan Royes, Accounting Department*

From: *Nathan Kafa, General Manager*

We have determined, based on the depreciation schedules, that we need to record yearly depreciation in the amounts of:

Equipment	*$ 8,813.00*
Furniture	*$ 3,102.00*

Please make a note to record Depreciation next year on a monthly basis.

Fig. 9-7: Memo on Depreciation.

1 ➤ Record and **Post** the following journal entry **Dec-Adj-7:**

5350	Depreciation Expense – All	11,915.00	
1520	Accum. Deprec. Equipment		8,813.00
1540	Accum. Deprec. Furniture		3,102.00

Remember to view the journal entry before posting.

A monthly depreciation expense entry totalling $992.92 ($734.42 Accum. Deprec. Equipment; $258.50 Accum. Deprec. Furniture) will occur each month as the capital assets are used up and could be set up as a monthly recurring entry.

Bad Debt Expense/Allowance for Doubtful Accounts

The amount of the Accounts Receivable accounts that will not be collected is difficult to calculate correctly.

At the end of each accounting period (monthly, quarterly, or annually) an estimated amount of the accounts receivable that will not be collected (Bad Debts Expense) is calculated and recorded.

Kafa Sweaters

Memorandum

Date: December 31, 2018

To: Jordan Royes, Accounting Department

From: Nathan Kafa, General Manager

The manager and accountant have determined that an industry-wide Bad Debt calculation is currently at 10% of the balances outstanding.

The balance of account #1200 is $13,899.00 at 10% is an estimated $1,390.00 of Bad Debts

However, West-Mart Shopping Centre store is overdue in payments of 91 days and may not be collected.

The manager and accountant have decided to increase the amount of Bad Debts Expense for the period ending December 31 to cover the outstanding balance of the amount of West-Mart Shopping Centre

Balance of West-Mart Shopping Centre	$3,955.00
Balance of account #1210 Allowance for Doubtful Accounts	400.00
Balance needed to cover the amount	$3,555.00

Please increase the balance of the Allowance for Doubtful Accounts as per the calculation above.

Fig. 9-8: Memo on Bad Debt Expense.

1 ➤ **Record** and **Post** the following journal entry **Dec-Adj-8**:

5360	Bad Debts Expense	3,555.00	
1210	Allowance for Doubtful Accounts		3,555.00

Remember to view the journal entry before posting.

Inventory Adjustments

During the year, inventory amounts are checked on a regular basis. It is important that the ending inventory be as accurate as possible to provide an Income Statement for the accounting period.

At the close of business on December 31, the staff were given the following report and counted the sweaters before they left.

Item No. ⌂	Description
LSC01	Ladies Sweaters Cardigan
LSR01	Ladies Sweaters Regular
LST01	Ladies Sweaters High Neck
MSC01	Men's Sweaters Cardigan
MSR01	Men's Sweaters Regular
MST01	Men's Sweaters High Neck

The following counts were determined as being on hand and are considered accurate.

LSC01	Ladies Sweaters Cardigan	786
LSR01	Ladies Sweaters Regular	870
LST01	Ladies Sweaters High Neck	840
MSC01	Men's Sweaters Cardigan	640
MSR01	Men's Sweaters Regular	1,045
MST01	Men's Sweaters High Neck	758

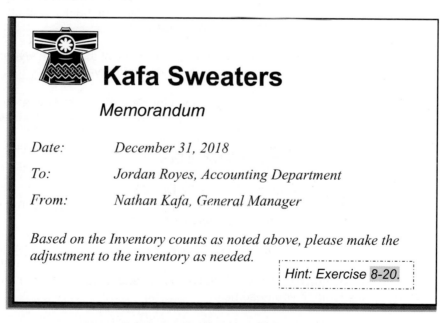

Kafa Sweaters

Memorandum

Date: *December 31, 2018*

To: *Jordan Royes, Accounting Department*

From: *Nathan Kafa, General Manager*

Based on the Inventory counts as noted above, please make the adjustment to the inventory as needed.

Hint: Exercise 8-20.

Fig. 9-9: Memo on the Inventory.

1 ➤ **Record** and **Post** the following journal entry **Dec-Adj-9**:

5070	Inventory Adjustments	60.00	
1260	Inventory of Goods		60.00

Remember to view the journal entry before posting.

All of the month-end/year-end adjustments and accruals have now been made.

Backing Up the Data Files

After all adjustments have been made, make a backup copy of the data files for Kafa Sweaters. This is very important for a number of reasons:

- Once the Session Date is advanced to a new fiscal year, no more entries should be entered in the year ended December 31, 2018, except for the fiscal year-end adjusting entries from the accountant.

- The company's accountant will review the accounting data and may make adjustments, including Audit adjustments, after the fiscal year is completed. The backup copy can then be used to make the adjustments and print revised final financial statements that agree with the audited statement.

- Data loss may occur (very rarely, but it could happen) during the Sage 50 Accounting year-end closing procedures, by using another program for the backup.

Back up your data now and record details in your logbook.

Printing Month-End and Year-End Reports

Month-End/Year-End reports are made available for review by management, accountants, and in some cases shareholders, banks, and other parties that have a major financial interest in the company.

It is also good practice to keep a hard copy of the month's/year's activity, just in case computer data is lost. Back up at regular intervals.

1 ➤ **Print** the following reports for Kafa Sweaters at year-end and retain for future use. There would be other reports printed if other modules were used.

a) Trial Balance as at Dec 31
b) Balance Sheet as at Dec 31
c) Income Statement year-to-date
d) All Journal Entries for Dec 31
e) General Ledger Listing (all G/L account activity in detail) for Dec 31
f) Inventory Summary as at Dec 31

2 ➤ **Compare** your results with those in the Instructor's Solutions Manual.

If you find differences, make adjusting entries to correct the problems. See your instructor if you need help.

Summary

The adjustments and accruals entered for Kafa Sweaters' month-end/year-end processing are typical month-end and year-end entries.

Entries could be stored and recalled at future month-ends as a time-saving feature.

Financial statements and reports are printed at period-end.

The Year-End close is performed by advancing the Session Date into the new fiscal year. See Chapter 10.

Before Moving On ...

Read the following questions and make sure you know the answers to them; otherwise, read the corresponding part in the chapter before moving on.

1. Explain the concept of matching revenues with expenses in a specific accounting period.

2. What kind of adjustment is required to Prepaid Expenses at the end of an accounting period?

3. What are accrued expenses? Give at least two examples.

4. What is accrued interest? Why is it necessary to make an adjustment to this account at the end of the accounting period?

5. Name two major reasons for backing up data files before doing the year-end closing in Sage 50 Accounting.

6. What is the benefit of using recurring entries?

Chapter 10

Year-End Closing

Kafa2 Sweaters

Learning Objectives

After completing this chapter you will be able to:

- ☐ Close the previous year's financial records (year-end).
- ☐ Record appropriate reversing entries.
- ☐ Display and print various reports and journals.

This chapter continues with Kafa Sweaters data, from Chapter 9, after all adjusting entries have been entered. The balances in each account are the final balances before year-end closing entries. You will be using the **Kafa2** company files for **Kafa2 Sweaters**. The files are in your course materials at www.nelson.com/student.

How do you close the fiscal year at year-end? What do you need to do at the end of the year, after year-end adjustments are posted? How do they affect the financial statements? These are the questions that **Slideshow 10—Year-End Closing** will answer. Run it now.

To Close the Books (Fiscal Year-End)

The final step for Kafa Sweaters' year-end processing is to close off the fiscal year.

In a manual system:

To close the books at year-end, you would do the following:

For a sole proprietorship:
a) Prepare and post a Journal entry to transfer the Revenue and Expense accounts to the CAPITAL account.
b) Close the DRAWINGS account to the CAPITAL account.

For a corporation:
a) Prepare and post a Journal entry to transfer the Revenue and Expense accounts to the RETAINED EARNINGS account.
b) Close the DIVIDENDS DECLARED account to the RETAINED EARNINGS account.

In the Sage 50 Accounting system:

a) Make backups of your data before proceeding and put the backups in a safe place. Start the new fiscal year with new backup storage devices.
b) In Sage 50 Accounting you would advance the Session Date to the first day of the new fiscal year.
c) Sage 50 Accounting automatically records and posts the closing entry (after giving you a warning) which effectively closes the Revenue and Expense accounts and then transfers the net profit or loss to the default Capital or Retained Earnings account. Note: Sage 50 Accounting does not make or prepare a closing journal entry.
d) In addition, Sage 50 Accounting clears journal entries and resets journal numbers to 1. PROJECT/DIVISION detail is accumulated as one balance forward amount (removing the detail; therefore, you need printouts and backups before period-end processing).

Kafa2 Sweaters: Company Profile

The Fiscal Start date becomes the first day of the new fiscal year (for Kafa2 Sweaters, it is January 1, 2019), and the Fiscal End date is the last day of the new fiscal year (December 31, 2019).

Study the following Trial Balance of **Kafa2 Sweaters** as at Dec 31, 2018. This will be the basis of the closing entries.

 Make sure you have a backup before proceeding!

Kafa2 Sweaters, Student's Name
Trial Balance As At Dec 31, 2018

		Debits	Credits
1100	Bank Chequing Account	9,725.00	-
1200	Accounts Receivable	13,899.00	-
1210	Allowance for Doubtful Accounts		3,955.00
1260	Inventory of Goods	60,260.00	-
1270	Prepaid Office Supplies on Hand	120.00	-
1300	Prepaid Insurance	900.00	-
1420	Equipment	88,129.00	-
1440	Furniture	31,020.00	-
1520	Accum. Deprec. Equipment	-	44,065.00
1540	Accum. Deprec. Furniture	-	15,510.00
2200	Accounts Payable	-	13,545.00
2220	Wages Payable	-	1,809.00
2231	Accrued Liabilities	-	952.70
2310	EI Payable	-	589.00
2320	CPP Payable	-	523.00
2330	Income Tax Payable	-	3,233.00
2350	HST Charged on Sales	-	3,561.00
2360	HST Paid On Purchases	1,930.70	-
2710	Bank Loan Payable	-	21,000.00
3120	Capital Nathan Kafa	-	86,274.00
3140	Drawings Nathan Kafa	10,000.00	-
4010	Sales-All	-	327,600.00
4210	Sales Returns	3,980.00	-
4220	Sales Discounts	5,725.00	-
4510	Handling Fee		-
5010	Cost of Goods Sold	123,470.00	-
5050	Purchase Discounts	-	1,942.00
5070	Inventory Adjustments	60.00	-
5110	Rent Expense	24,000.00	-
5120	Wages Expense	88,109.00	-
5122	EI Expense	3,452.00	-
5124	CPP Expense	3,193.00	-
5260	Office Supplies Expense	2,420.00	-
5330	Telephone Expense	3,980.00	-
5340	Advertising Expense	15,137.00	-
5350	Depreciation Expense-All	11,915.00	-
5360	Bad Debts Expense	5,993.00	-
5410	Water/Hydro Expense	4,908.00	-
5510	Bank Charges Expense	1,413.00	-
5530	Bank Interest on Loan Expense	1,680.00	-
5540	Insurance Expense	2,400.00	-
5550	Automobile Expense	2,900.00	-
5560	Automobile Lease	3,840.00	-
		524,558.70	524,558.70

Fig. 10-1: Kafa2 Trial Balance as of December 31, 2018.

Exercise 10-1—Closing the Fiscal Year

 WWW   1 ➤   Unzip the **10 Kafa2.exe** file found in your course materials at
www.nelson.com/student.

2 ➤   Start Sage 50 Accounting and select **10 Kafa2** as the company file.

3 ➤   Accept Session Date of **Dec 31, 2018, OK**.

4 ➤   **Display** and **Print** the Balance Sheet at December 31, 2018 and note the
dollar values of the Equity accounts. File for Audit Trail.

Owner's Equity	
Capital Nathan Kafa	86,274.00
Drawings Nathan Kafa	-10,000.00
Current Earnings	20,967.00
Total Owner's Equity	**97,241.00**

In this exercise you are
not required to back up;
however, in a real-life
business year-end
situation, you should
create backups at every
step of the year-end
closing process in case
you need to restore
your data.

5 ➤   **Display** and **Print** the Income Statement **for the fiscal year** to view the
Revenue, Expenses, and Net Income. File for Audit Trail.

6 ➤   Return to the Home window.

7 ➤   **Session Date**   Click the **Calendar**. Click the and select **Jan 01, 2019**,
click **OK**.

(See side note box.)

The following message window appears:

Sage 50 - New Fiscal and Calendar Year

> You have entered both a new calendar and a new fiscal year. If you proceed, the
> program will move the current year's data into last year, close all revenue and
> expense account balances into the Retained Earnings linked account, and set the
> new fiscal year's dates. Print all employee reports and make a backup before
> proceeding.
>
> If you have chosen to keep financial history for a certain number of years, you can
> still see financial reports for those years.
>
> Do you want the program to back up your data before beginning the new fiscal and
> calendar year?

◉ Yes   ○ No

You are using a 2018
data file. In a real
business setting, the file
can also contain 2017
prior year data.

Study the whole message before proceeding. It is assumed that you are
now in the year 2019. This is a warning that four things will happen:

1a. The year 2018 data (currently in Sage 50 Accounting) will be **deleted**.

1b. The 2018 year's data is **moved** into the previous year's storage area.

2. The previous year's data (2018) revenue and expense account balances will be **closed** (changed to zero) and the balance will be transferred to the **Retained Earnings** linked account. The Retained Earnings linked account can be one of the following:

   a. Capital Account (Sole Proprietorship)
   b. Retained Earnings (Corporation)
   c. Net Profit Holding account (Partnership) for later allocation to the partners.

3. The new fiscal year's (2019) dates will be set.

4. All journal entry records will be cleared, and Journal entry numbers for 2019 are reset to 1. All employee data for 2019 will start at 0.

8 ➤ Click the **No** button regarding backing up your data. In this exercise there is no need to back up. When ready, click **OK**.

9 ➤ Click **OK**.

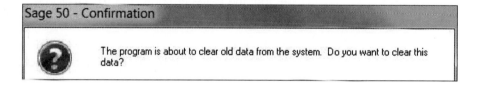

10 ➤ This message refers to item 1a in step 7 in this Exercise. Any previous data in the storage area (e.g., 2017) will be deleted from the system.

The current 2018 year data will move to the storage area and the 2019 year data fields will be created and will remain in the system. Click **Yes**.

The screen will flicker and you will see the following message window:

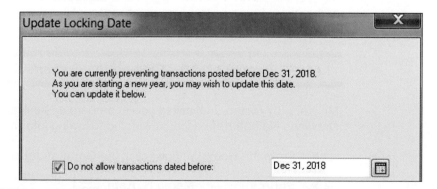

This window would allow you to post transactions to a previous year data file. You have moved the 2018 data and will not be posting any information to 2018. You should update this field to Jan 01, 2019. This will prevent posting entries to the previous 2018 year. This field could be changed later in the Setup, System Settings, Setting window. See Year-End Entry Missing Information only, after Before Moving On.

11 ➤ In the Update Locking Date box, change the date to **Jan 01, 2019**, and click **OK**.

You return to the Home window. Continue with the next exercise.

Starting a New Fiscal Year

As you start a new fiscal year, you need to:

1. View the 2019 Statements to make sure the Income Statement accounts have zero balances.

2. Record entries in the General Journal to:
    a) Close the Owner's Drawing Account.
    b) Reverse the prior year-end accrued entries.
    c) For a Periodic Inventory system, update the Inventory accounts.

Exercise 10-2—Viewing the New Year's Statements

You should be at the Kafa2 Home window.

1 ➤ To verify that the year-end procedure was done correctly, repeat the steps to view the Current Year Income Statement.

You will see that the dates are now **Jan 01, 2019** (1st day of **new fiscal year**) and all Revenue and Expense accounts are zero (0).

2 ➤ View the Balance Sheet and you will see that the balance of the CAPITAL account has increased by the amount of the net income (Current Earning) from 2018.

Owner's Equity	
Capital Nathan Kafa	107,241.00
Drawings Nathan Kafa	-10,000.00
Current Earnings	0.00
Total Owner's Equity	**97,241.00**

The data file is now ready to record transactions in 2019. The first entry should be to transfer the balance of Drawing for a sole proprietorship, or Dividends Declared for a corporation, to the appropriate equity account.

Exercise 10-3—Closing the Owner's Drawing Account

Mr. Kafa, by memo, has asked you to prepare a General Journal entry to close the Drawings Nathan Kafa account with the following information:

1 ➤ From the Home window, click the **General Journal** icon.

2 ➤ Source: **Memo N. Kafa, [Tab]**.

     Date: **Jan 01, 2019**.

3 ➤ Comment: **Close the Owner's Drawing account.**

4 ➤   **Record** and **Post** the following journal entry:

3120	Capital Nathan Kafa	10,000.00	
3140	Drawings Nathan Kafa		10,000.00

In a corporation to close the DIVIDENDS DECLARED account, the entry would be similar to:

3120	Retained Earnings	xx,xxx.00	
3140	Dividends Declared		xx,xxx.00

Exercise 10-4—Reversing Prior-Year Accrued Entries

The next step is to reverse any accrued revenues and expenses recorded in the previous year (2018). You will not be able to use the Reverse entry icon for previous fiscal year entries.

Accrued expenses and accrued revenues that were recorded in the previous year (for matching purposes) must be reversed in the current year. The reversing entry amounts are opposite to the original entry(ies) made in December 2018.

Accruals are amounts that have been estimated or based on source documents that have not yet been received from suppliers, or invoices that have not yet been issued by our firm in time to process at year-end. When the vendor documents arrive or Kafa2 issues the corresponding invoices, they will be processed as usual in the RECEIVABLES or PAYABLES module.

If reversing entries are not made for accrued items, the amounts will have been recorded twice, once in the previous year (2018) and again in the current year (2019). The accrued payable account will also not be correct.

The accountant would need to review the entries that were made at year-end to determine which entries need to be reversed.

The adjusting entries that need to be made at year-end, and why they need to be reversed or not reversed, are shown next.

Bank Service Charge

As discussed in Chapter 9, Exercise 9-1, it is possible to record an actual bank charge if the business has access to Internet banking. If you recorded an actual bank charge, then you do not need to reverse the entry.

The estimated bank service charge needs reversing, because the correct service charge will be recorded when the December bank reconciliation is completed in January. (See side note box.)

The General Journal should still be opened. To reverse the accrual, the following is the suggested wording for each field:

1 ➤   **Source**   **Yr-End-Reversal**.

Date   **Jan 01, 2019**.

2 ➤   **Comment**   **Reverse Estimated December bank fees**. (A better comment line would include the original December Journal entry number to cross-reference for audit trail purposes.)

3 ➤ Comment column   Record the information shown below. The comment column includes information about the entry number Adj-1 (from 2018) to cross-reference the entry (2019 year) for audit trail purposes.

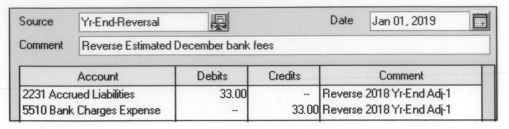

Source	Yr-End-Reversal		Date	Jan 01, 2019
Comment	Reverse Estimated December bank fees			

Account	Debits	Credits	Comment
2231 Accrued Liabilities	33.00	--	Reverse 2018 Yr-End Adj-1
5510 Bank Charges Expense	--	33.00	Reverse 2018 Yr-End Adj-1

4 ➤ Post when correct to reverse the original accrual made December 31.

Office Supplies

Does not need a reversal; the correct cost of supplies used in December was recorded in December.

Prepaid Insurance

Does not need a reversal; the correct cost of insurance used in December was recorded in December.

Accrued Expenses

The accruals for the Telephone, Electricity, and Automobile expenses in 2018 were estimated and, therefore, need to be reversed. The actual December invoices will be recorded as an expense in January.

1 ➤ Click the **General Journal** and reverse the entry as shown below.

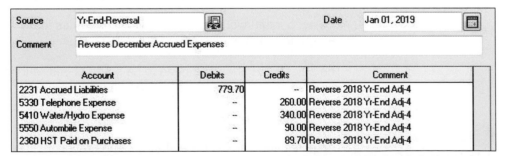

Source	Yr-End-Reversal		Date	Jan 01, 2019
Comment	Reverse December Accrued Expenses			

Account	Debits	Credits	Comment
2231 Accrued Liabilities	779.70	--	Reverse 2018 Yr-End Adj-4
5330 Telephone Expense	--	260.00	Reverse 2018 Yr-End Adj-4
5410 Water/Hydro Expense	--	340.00	Reverse 2018 Yr-End Adj-4
5550 Autombile Expense	--	90.00	Reverse 2018 Yr-End Adj-4
2360 HST Paid on Purchases	--	89.70	Reverse 2018 Yr-End Adj-4

Notice that the amounts are opposite to the original entry made on December 31, 2018.

2 ➤ Post when correct and you will see the Tax Linked confirmation window.

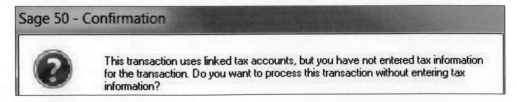

Sage 50 - Confirmation

This transaction uses linked tax accounts, but you have not entered tax information for the transaction. Do you want to process this transaction without entering tax information?

3 ➤ Click **No** to continue.

4 ➤ **Enter** the Tax Code and `Tab`. The information should be as shown (with negatives). This is opposite to what was recorded in Chapter 9.

5 ➤ Click **OK**. A blue ✓ appears in the Sales Tax button to indicate sales taxes were recorded.

6 ➤ **Post** the entry.

Accrued Interest Expense

1 ➤ **Record** and **Post** the following journal entry:

Accrued Wages Expense

This needs to be reversed; otherwise, the full amount of the actual payroll cheques will be recorded in January as an expense. The January debit expense for the payroll will be reduced by the January reversal credit entry. When reversed, the payroll expense for the first pay period in the current year would be January 1 to January 6.

1 ➤ **Record** and **Post** the following journal entry:

Depreciation Expense

Does not need a reversal; the correct cost of depreciation expense used in the year 2018 was recorded in December 2018.

Bad Debts Expense

Does not need a reversal at this time. If the West-Mart Shopping Centre account is partially or fully collected, the Bad Debts Expense entry can be adjusted at that time.

Updating Inventory Accounts

When you displayed the new Income Statement, you should have noticed that all Revenue and Expense accounts were closed, including the three Cost of Goods Sold accounts.

(See side note box.)

The **Jan. 1, 2019** Trial Balance, therefore, contains the following values:

		DR	CR
ASSET	1260 Inventory of Goods	$60,260.00	
*COGS	5010 Cost of Goods Sold	0.00	
*COGS	5050 Purchase Discounts	0.00	
*COGS	5070 Inventory Adjustments	0.00	

*COGS = Cost of Goods Sold

> **Kafa Sweaters uses the Perpetual Inventory system to record purchases of merchandise for resale. The inventory account is used to record all purchases and is changed when goods are sold.**

On the first day of the new fiscal year; i.e., January 1, 2019, in this example, the Beginning Inventory (last year's Ending Inventory) is $60,260.00.

The Cost of Goods Sold in the Income Statement accounts is currently $0.

There is no need to create a Cost of Goods Sold adjustment, as the Asset account #1260 is at the correct value

Printing Reports

1 ➤ Print the following reports.

    a) All Journal Entries at Jan 01, 2019.
    b) Income Statement at Jan 01, 2019.
    c) Balance Sheet at Jan 01, 2019.
    d) Trial Balance at Jan 01, 2019.
    e) Inventory Summary as at Jan 01, 2019

The Kafa2 Sweaters company file is now set up for you to record transactions for January 2019.

Summary

The year-end close is performed by advancing the Session date into the new fiscal year. Reports are displayed to see the result of closing of Income Statement accounts to the Capital for a Sole Proprietorship or Retained Earnings for a Corporation.

Using the January 1, 2019 date:

- Drawings accounts or Dividends Declared are closed.
- Reversing entries are made to avoid recording of revenues and expenses to the next accounting period.

Review **Slideshows 9** and **10** and make sure you understand the GAAPs related to month- and year-end adjustments. Also focus on the effects of the adjustments on both the Balance Sheet and the Income Statement.

Before Moving On ...

Read the following questions and make sure you know the answers to them; otherwise, read the corresponding part in this chapter before moving on.

1. Why is it necessary to enter reversing entries for accruals after closing the year?

2. What steps are involved in closing the current year in a manual system? How is this done in Sage 50 Accounting?

3. What are two reasons you would back up the data files before doing the year-end closing in Sage 50 Accounting?

Year-End Entry Missing

The following section is **For Information only**.

What if you've started a new fiscal year, posted reversing entries, posted 200 entries for the new 2019 fiscal year and realize an entry from the accountant's adjustments for 2018 was not recorded?

> Do you: Restore your backup.
> Make the correction.
> Start the new fiscal year and record the 200 entries again.

The answer is NO. What you would do is the following:

1. Go back to the System file window, **Setup, Settings, System**.

2. **Change the date** to: 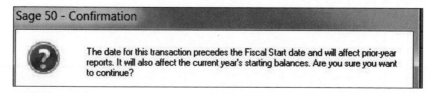 or the date of the adjustment, click **OK**.

3. From the Home window, select the module that requires adjusting. Assume the General Journal.

4. **Record** the adjustment (assume Dec 31, 2018) and **Post**. You will see the following window.

> **Sage 50 - Confirmation**
>
> ❓ The date for this transaction precedes the Fiscal Start date and will affect prior-year reports. It will also affect the current year's starting balances. Are you sure you want to continue?

5. Click **Yes**. The current year 2019 Capital Account has been adjusted. Remember to return the Reports Fiscal Year to 2019 in your reports.

End of Information section

Challenge Exercise 10 C10-1 (Chapters 9-10), Rama Magazines
Month-End Procedures Review

This exercise is a review of month-end procedures.

1 ➤   Refer to Exercise 1-1b to unzip the **10 C10-1 Magazines.exe** file.

2 ➤   Open the **10 C10-1 Magazines** file.

3 ➤   Record January 31 month-end adjustments for Rama Magazines, a company that supplies various magazines, candy, and small toys to businesses. Rama Magazines is using the COMPANY, PAYABLES, RECEIVABLES, and INVENTORY & SERVICES modules and does not use the Account Reconciliation journal.

Rama Magazines has the following adjustments for the January month-end:

a) Bank service charges for the month are estimated to be $43.50.

b) The Prepaid insurance account balance represents 4 months' insurance that has not been used as of January 1. Adjust the account accordingly.

c) A part-time employee (use YOUR ACTUAL NAME as the part-time employee's name in the comment line) did not submit his time sheet and was not paid $158.00, the regular wages for the pay period ending January 28. (Magazine Sales charges all salaries and wages to Salaries Staff Account #5290.) Accrue the wages for the period (ignore CPP and EI).

d) The value of the Store Supplies on hand was counted, and is $358.00.

e) Depreciation of Store Equipment is $1,500.00 for the year ($125.00 per month).

f) The long-term bank loan arranged on December 31, 2016 with the Canadian Bank is for a 5-year period at an interest rate at 9% (per annum effective monthly rate of 0.7207%). Monthly payments of $998.26 are due at the end of each month. The January 31 automatic bank payment of $998.26 (including interest of $291.07) has not been made or recorded.

g) A new vendor, Snowgone Services, submitted a January snow removal invoice (#5631) dated today, for $140.00 plus HST, net 30 days (Maintenance Expense).

h) The inventory count found that 10 Puzzle magazines are missing. Adjust inventory. (*Hint*: Chapter 8, Exercise 8-20.)

4 ➤   Print **All Journal Entries** for the entries above.

5 ➤   Print a **Trial Balance** as at January 31.

6 ➤   **Back up** your data before moving on.

Your instructor may require you to:

i) advance the date to February 1.

j) reverse the appropriate accruals on February 1.

7 ➤   If required, print All Journal Entries for the February reversing entries above.

Challenge Exercise 10 C10-2 (Chapters 9-10), City Gravel
Month-End Procedures Review

This exercise is a review of month-end procedures and year-end procedures.

1 ➤ Refer to Exercise 1-1b to unzip the **10 C10-2 Gravel.exe** file.

2 ➤ Open the **10 C10-2 Gravel** file.

3 ➤ Record the following December 31, month-end adjustments for City Gravel. City Gravel uses the COMPANY, PAYABLES, RECEIVABLES, and INVENTORY & SERVICES modules and does not use the Account Reconciliation journal.

  a) Bank service charges for the month are estimated to be $37.90.

  b) The Prepaid insurance account balance represents 3 months' insurance that has not been used as of December 1. Adjust the account accordingly.

  c) The value of the Office Supplies on hand was counted, and is $266.00.

  d) Depreciation of Equipment is estimated at $8,760.00 for the year and has been recorded for 11 months.

  e) Depreciation of Office Furniture is estimated at $3,120.00 for the year and has been recorded for 11 months.

  f) The manager forgot to create an invoice for 40 cubic yards of medium gravel at $186.00 per cubic yard, plus HST, to a new customer, Your Name Builders. Your actual first and last name must appear as a customer, credit limit $10,000.00. Address is not important. Create an invoice for this customer dated December 31, with credit terms 2/10 net 30 days.

  g) The long-term bank loan arranged on November 30, 2016 with the Bank of Montreal is for a 5-year period at an interest rate at 8% (effective monthly rate of 0.6434%). The December 31, $236.10, monthly payment (including interest of $75.31) has not been made or recorded.

  h) Keith Barrett is a part-time employee. The manager made an error in Mr. Barrett's time-sheet and Mr. Barrett was underpaid by $58.00 for the period ending December 31. City Gravel charges all salaries and wages to Pit Crew Wages Expense #5310. The $58.00 will be paid with the next paycheque. Accrue the wages for the December period (ignore CPP and EI).

4 ➤ Print **All Journal Entries** for the entries above.

5 ➤ Print a **Trial Balance** as at December 31.

6 ➤ **Back up** your data before moving on.

Your instructor may require you to:

  i) advance the date to January 1 to close the current year and move into 2018. (Do not allow transactions dated before Jan 01, 2018.)

  j) advance the date to January 2 and reverse the appropriate accruals on January 2.

7 ➤ If required, print All Journal Entries for the January reversing entries above.

Chapter 11

PROJECTS* Module
Setup and Transactions

HotTubs Company Ltd.

Learning Objectives

After completing this chapter you will be able to:

☐ Set up a company's Project Title name.
☐ Set up a company's Individual Project names.
☐ Record regular transactions, using the Perpetual Inventory system, and allocate revenues and costs to individual Projects.
☐ Record regular transactions using the Perpetual Inventory system and Project costs. Adjust Inventory and Cost of Sales with allocations to individual Projects.
☐ Display and print appropriate Projects reports and journals.

* The name of the PROJECTS module can also be called Job Sites, Divisions, Crops, Properties, etc., depending on the type of business you operate.

This chapter reviews the setup of the Sage 50 Accounting PROJECT module, and then provides practice on transaction processing using **HotTubs Company** to record related transactions for a month using the COMPANY, RECEIVABLES, PAYABLES, EMPLOYEES & PAYROLL, INVENTORY & SERVICES, and PROJECTS modules, using the Perpetual Inventory system where appropriate.

The contents of this chapter are as follows:

The PROJECTS Module

PROJECTS (or Job Sites, Divisions, Crops, Properties, etc.) refers to a group of accounts where costs and revenues are allocated and accumulated for particular business activities. A Project is a job or activity (e.g., building a house, assembling a computer) or a cost centre (e.g., department of a company).

The PROJECTS module is used to record revenue and expenses, including employees' wages from the PAYROLL module, and allocate them to one or more Projects. For example, you may allocate RENT, ADVERTISING, SUPPLIES, etc. to various Projects. Similarly, if a company has several salespeople and they are paid according to sales volume, the company needs to keep track of sales (and expenses) for each salesperson's territory. Each territory may be specified as a separate project or other appropriate name.

Run **Slideshow 11A—Setting Up the PROJECTS Module** to get a good understanding of how the PROJECTS module works before you do the practice exercises in setting the module to **Ready**.

HotTubs Company: Profile

HotTubs Company Ltd. has been in business for five years. The business sells four models of hot tubs, and chemicals, and arranges for the installation and service of the hot tubs. The fiscal year will end on December 31, 2019.

The manager has decided to use the Sage 50 Accounting PROJECTS module to track revenues and expenses for the following Projects:

- hot tubs—all models
- all chemicals

The company has just completed the conversion of the manual accounting records to Sage 50 Accounting at June 30, 2019. The COMPANY, RECEIVABLES, PAYABLES, EMPLOYEES & PAYROLL, and INVENTORY & SERVICES modules have been set up and set to **Ready**. You will display the PROJECTS module and set up the individual Projects. The manager has decided to use the **Perpetual** Inventory system (INVENTORY module), and the **Track Additional Transaction Details** is not being used.

The manager, Mrs. Shortt, would like to allocate Revenue and Expenses to the various models of hot tubs and chemicals being sold to determine the profitability of each type of hot tub and the chemical sales. Each staff member was asked, as of July 2, to keep a record of the time he or she spends on selling each model, including talking to customers, writing up sales orders, and making sure the hot tubs are delivered and installed correctly.

Project Title

Mrs. Shortt has decided to use the Project title name of **Tubs/Chemic**, into which you will enter the names of six individual projects that will be tracked. Project revenues and expenses are tracked only from the day the PROJECTS module names are set up and used.

Invoices and cheques will be prepared manually and recorded in Sage 50 Accounting, and will not be printed by the computer program.

Financial Reports and Other Information

The following financial information is available:

Employee Details: Two employees, **Hillary Buchanan** and **Vivian Shortt**, have been set up in the PAYROLL module.

Hillary Buchanan   Wages per hour: $20.00
Vivian Shortt   Wages per hour: $25.00

The company uses a 26 pay-period system. **WSIB, EHT,** and **Vacation Pay** are not shown in this chapter to make it easier to illustrate the salary allocation.

The Employment Insurance (EI) rate is: **1.4**

Accounts Payable Details

The following vendors have been set up in the company's PAYABLES module. Purchase orders were issued manually to these companies and are not set up in Sage 50 Accounting.

Acrylic Tubs Inc.	Terms: 2/10, net 30
Eco Tubs Canada Ltd.	Terms: 2/10, net 30
George Kouretsoes & Associates*	Terms: Due on Receipt
Markham Lumber	Terms: 2/10, net 30

*George Kouretsoes & Associates delivers and installs all hot tubs.

Outstanding Vendor Invoices:

Acrylic Tubs Inc.
Invoice #7530 dated: Jul 25, 2019, Amount $2,260.00, Terms 2/10, net 30.

Other Vendor:

Receiver General for Canada—used for payroll remittances.

Accounts Receivable Details

The company has received orders from the following customers:

Carol's Bed & Breakfast	Terms: 2/10, net 30
Mrs. Faygie Noble	Terms: net 3 days

Outstanding Sales Invoices:

Carol's Bed & Breakfast
Invoice #640 dated Jul 30, 2019, amount $5,650.00, Terms 2/10, net 30.

The majority of the transactions in this chapter will affect accounts that have been shaded in Fig. 11-1.

Inventory Details

Inventory Item	Quantity	Total
▼ Chemicals - Bulk Chem - Bulk	1222	$6,415.50
▼ Chemicals - Individual Chem Indi...	325	$2,073.50
▼ HotTubs 1.0 HP 72" x 72" H 1.0	3	$6,945.00
▼ HotTubs 4.0 HP 84" x 84" H 4.0	2	$5,580.00
▼ HotTubs 4.4 HP 84" Gazebo H 4.4	3	$10,200.00
▼ HotTubs 4.6 HP 84" Enclosed H 4.6	1	$3,950.00

HotTubs Company Ltd., Student's Name
Trial Balance As At Jul 31, 2019

		Debits	Credits
1020	Bank Account	21,000.00	-
1200	Accounts Receivable	5,650.00	-
1310	Inventory-Hot Tubs	26,675.00	-
1350	Inventory-Chemical	8,489.00	-
1370	Display Hot Tub-models	12,455.00	-
1380	Prepaid Store Supplies, etc.	250.00	-
1510	Display Fixtures/Cabinets	22,800.00	-
1515	Accum. Deprec Display Fixtures/Cabi	-	6,600.00
1520	Office, Warehouse Furniture	24,200.00	-
1525	Accum. Deprec Office/Ware Equipment	-	6,672.00
2200	Accounts Payable	-	2,260.00
2205	Payroll Accrual	-	0.00
2220	EI Payable	-	181.66
2225	CPP Payable	-	163.55
2230	Income Tax Payable	-	873.98
2650	HST Charged on Sales	-	3,084.00
2670	HST Paid On Purchases/Services	2,010.00	-
3100	Common Stock	-	1,000.00
3201	Retained Earnings	-	71,474.81
3230	Dividends Declared	2,000.00	-
4100	Sales-Hot Tubs	-	216,800.00
4110	Sales-Hot Tubs Allowances	400.00	-
4200	Sales-Chemicals	-	8,620.00
4210	Sales Returns-Chemicals	100.00	-
4310	Sales - Discount	1,200.00	-
4510	Handling Fee		0.00
5010	Cost Of Sales-HotTubs	80,364.00	-
5040	Cost Of Sales-Outside Labour	28,236.00	-
5060	Cost Of Sales-Chemicals	4,310.00	-
5070	Purchase Discounts	-	1,412.00
5080	Inventory Adjustments	0.00	-
5310	Wages Expense	28,000.00	-
5320	EI Expense	1,124.00	-
5330	CPP Expense	840.00	-
5410	Advertising Expense	22,090.00	-
5420	Bank Charges & Interest	620.00	-
5430	Insurance Expense	11,400.00	-
5450	Credit Card Expense	3,535.00	-
5540	Office/Warehouse Supplies Expense	2,850.00	-
5550	Telephone Expense	1,109.00	-
5560	Utility Expense	825.00	-
5570	Truck Expenses-gas, repairs	1,810.00	-
5580	Truck Lease Expense	2,700.00	-
5590	Legal Expense	2,100.00	-
5600	Depreciation Expense – All	0.00	-
		---------------	---------------
		319,142.00	319,142.00

Fig. 11-1: HotTubs Trial Balance.

Starting Sage 50 Accounting

1 ➤ Refer to Exercise 1-1b, to unzip the **11 HotTubs** file.

2 ➤ Open the **11 HotTubs** data file.

3 ➤ Advance the Session Date to **Aug 01, 2019**. The HotTubs Company Ltd.'s home window is displayed. Remember to **add your name** to the Company Name.

Setting Up the PROJECTS Module

The following exercises will show you how to use the PROJECTS module. To get the PROJECTS module to work, you need to go through the following steps:

- Display the PROJECTS module.
- Set up the PROJECTS module settings.
- Set up the Project Title Name default.
- Set up the Project Names.
- Enter the Balance Forward.

You will then be ready to process transactions, allocating expenses/revenues and/or payroll to the specific Projects.

Step 1: Displaying the PROJECTS module

Exercise 11-1—Displaying the PROJECT Module

1 ➤ From the top menu, click **Setup, User Preferences, View**, at **Pages** click the **DIVISION** box (2 ✓appear), **OK**.

The **DIVISIONS** module now displays and is available to modify in the Home window. Management has decided to call the module PROJECTS. See Exercise 11-2.

Step 2: Setting Up PROJECTS Settings

The following steps refer to setting up the default PROJECTS module settings.

Exercise 11-2—Setting Up PROJECTS Settings

1 ➤ From the top menu click **Setup, Settings**; in the left pane, click the ➕ at **DIVISIONS**, click **Names**.

The Project Title determines the title of the icon and the Project window.

2 ➤ **Project Title**: Change to Project Title: Tubs/Chemic .

Do NOT change the Title field names.

3 ➤ In the left pane, click on **Budget**.

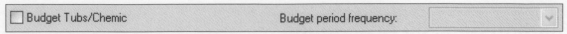

Fig. 11-2a: Budget Settings window.

Budget: Do NOT change. Management has decided to defer
                            (hold off) the budget process until they have a new
                            financial plan in place.

Allocation

4 ➤ In the left pane, click on **Allocation**, and select the options shown in
     Fig. 11-2b.

Fig. 11-2b: Allocation Settings window.

Allocate refers to the way that expenses and revenues are divided (split) among
Projects. The allocation could be a set amount, or an amount based on a
percentage, or by employee hours.

Allocate Payroll Transactions by	The default setting for distributions is by Percent rather than by Hours. HotTubs' management has decided to distribute payroll by **hours** spent on each model and chemical sales. Employee hours are averaged to the nearest one-quarter (.25) of an hour.
Allocate Other Transactions by	Do NOT change.
Warn if allocation is not complete	The box should be ✓ so that if an amount is not fully distributed a warning message will appear.
Allow access to Allocate field using the Tab key	The box should be ✓ to allow you to tab to the Allocate field, instead of using the mouse.

5 ➤ Click **OK** to accept the changes. You will see the following window.

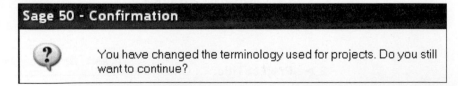

6 ➤ The term "Projects" is a default term and cannot be changed in this
     window. Click **Yes** to continue and return to the Home window.

     The module column now displays the new name Tubs/Chemic.

Step 3: Setting Up a Project Name/Balance Forward

Project Names are the names of the individual projects within the **Project Title**.

1 ➤ From the Home window, click the **Tubs/Chemic** icon to display the Tubs/Chemic window; click the **Create** icon and enter the information as shown in Fig. 11-3.

Fig. 11-3: Tubs/Chemic Ledger.

Tubs/Chemic	This field will contain the name of the particular project, job, or department for which you want revenues and expenses tracked.
Start Date	This field will contain the date the Project is expected to start.
End Date	This field will contain the date the Project is expected to end.
Balance Forward	These fields (Revenue and Expense) record Project values that are being converted (moved) to Sage 50 Accounting.

You could enter Project revenue and expense totals brought forward from the previous year or previous accounting system. However, in the case of HotTubs Company Ltd., the staff does not have any records of their time before this date, and sales and expenses were not allocated to the various models or chemicals. You will, therefore, start recording project information in Sage 50 Accounting as of Aug 01, 2019.

Status	There are 4 choices, select **In Progress**.

Pending:	Project may start in the near future.
In Progress:	Project currently in use.
Cancelled:	Project cancelled, not started.
Completed:	Project finished.

Step 4: Entering Other Projects

1 ➤ Click Create Another button to add the other project names.

2 ➤ Repeat the procedure, adding the five remaining project names (see Fig. 11-4), all with a Start Date of **Aug 01, 2019** and Status: In Progress.

Status column:
The display may cut off the right-hand side of the word Progress.

	Start date	End date	Status
Chemicals-Bulk	Aug 01, 2019	–	In Progress
Chemicals-Individual	Aug 01, 2019	–	In Progress
HT 1.0 HP 72" x 72"	Aug 01, 2019	–	In Progress
HT 4.0 HP 84" x 84"	Aug 01, 2019	–	In Progress
HT 4.4 HP 84" Gazebo	Aug 01, 2019	–	In Progress
HT 4.6 HP 84" Enclosed	Aug 01, 2019	–	In Progress

Fig. 11-4: Project names (see side note box).

3 ➤ Click Save and Close to Exit to the Tubs/Chemic window.

The display window is using the **Display by Name** icon.

The codes in the names mean the following:

HT	Hot tub
1.0 HP	Power of the motor
72" x 72"	Size of hot tub

4 ➤ **Exit** to the Home window.

The ledgers in the RECEIVABLES, PAYABLES, EMPLOYEES & PAYROLL, and COMPANY modules were previously set to **Ready**.

The PROJECTS module is automatically set to **Ready**.

> ▶ **Slideshow 11B—Processing Transactions in the PROJECTS Module** helps you do the various allocations in the PROJECTS module. Run it now.

Processing Transactions in the PROJECTS Module

You are now able to process transactions in the PROJECTS, HotTubs/Chemic module.

HotTubs Company Ltd. uses **Perpetual** Inventory records. Account #1310 Inventory HotTubs are the new tubs ready for sale. Account #1350 Inventory Chemicals are the various chemicals ready for sale, Account #1370 Display Hot-Tub models are the tubs that are on display that are not for sale at this time and are not in Inventory account #1310. The display models will go on sale in September when new models are available.

There are two ways to record Sales Quotes and Sales Orders using Sage 50 Accounting.

1. Click the RECEIVABLES module, click on Sales Quotes or Sales Orders and continue.

2. Click the TUBS/CHEMIC module, click Sales Invoices, at Transaction, click ▾ select the appropriate journal and continue.

Exercise 11-3—Processing Transactions

---

1 ➤ **Record** the following transaction using either method.

Aug 01, 2019	**Mrs. Vivian Shortt sent you a memo to issue Sales Order #423 ($36,230.63) to a new customer, Radisser Hotels Inc., contact Alvina Cassiani, 3890 Glen Erin Street, Mississauga, Ontario, L6X 3B9, phone number 905 841-3363, Revenue Account 4100, Standard Discount 5.00%. Terms 2/10, net 30, Tax Code HS, Credit Limit $40,000. The tubs are to be installed and working by Friday, August 16. The Salesperson field cannot be used in this order, as both Mrs. Shortt and Mrs. Buchanan worked together on this order. Sales Order total $36,230.63.**

Order	Description	Price
1	HT 1.0 HP 72" x 72"	**$4,630.00 each, less 5% discount plus HST**
4	HT 4.0 HP 84" x 84"	**$5,580.00 each, less 5% discount plus HST**
1	HT 4.4 HP 84" Gazebo	**$6,800.00 each, less 5% discount plus HST**

You cannot allocate a sales or purchase order. You will allocate a sales invoice as shown in Exercise 11-5 and a Purchase Invoice-by cheque in Exercise 11-4.

The *Salesperson* field will not be used on individual sales invoices, or sales orders.

There are two ways to record Purchase Quotes and Purchase Orders using Sage 50 Accounting.

a. Click the PAYABLES module, click on Purchase Quotes or Purchase Orders and continue.

b. Click the TUBS/CHEMIC module, click Purchase Invoices, at Transaction, click ▼ select the appropriate journal and continue.

You do not have enough HT 4.0 84" × 84" in stock to fill this order. Issue next purchase order to Eco Tubs Canada Ltd, for 5 HT 4.0 84" × 84" tubs. Shipping date should be August 05, with terms 2/10, net 30 days. This entry does not use revenue or expense accounts, and would not be recorded as a Tubs/Chemic entry.

1 ➤ **Record** the following transaction using either method.

Aug 01, 2019   Issue Purchase Order #28 to Eco Tubs Canada Ltd. to buy:

Order	Description	Price
5	HotTubs 4.0 HP 84" x 84"	$2,790.00 each plus HST

Terms 2/10, net 30. Total PO amount including HST was $15,763.50. Shipping date was noted as Monday, Aug 05.

This entry does not use revenue or expense accounts and would not be recorded as a Tubs/Chemic entry.

Aug 01, 2019	**Issue cheque today, to arrive by August 05, to pay Acrylic Tubs Inc. for Invoice #7530. The manager of Acrylic Tubs Inc. has agreed to give you the discount, if the cheque arrives on Monday the 5th.**

1 ➤   Advance Session date to **Aug 05, 2019**.

2 ➤   **Record** and **post** the following transaction:

Aug 05, 2019	**Received the complete order from PO #28, in good condition, from Eco Tubs Canada Ltd. on Invoice #36781, dated today, $15,763.50.**

This entry does not use revenue or expense accounts, and would not be recorded as a Tubs/Chemic entry.

Allocating a Purchase to a Project(s)

HotTubs does not charge all expenses or revenues to Projects. Only expenses and revenues directly related to hot tubs or chemical sales are charged to Projects. However, some companies allocate all revenue and expense accounts to Projects. This procedure ensures that all expense and revenue items are accounted for, resulting in much better cost control. When Project costs and revenues are totalled, the totals match the corresponding revenue and expense accounts on the Income Statement.

1 ➤   Advance the Session date to **Aug 08, 2019**.

Exercise 11-4—Allocating a Purchase to a Project(s)

To allocate a purchase to various Projects means to divide the purchase price among various Projects.

Aug 08, 2019	**Paid George Kouretsoes & Associates $800.00 plus HST, re their invoice #465 for partial installation of tubs at Radisser Hotels. Terms: Payment upon receipt. Per instructions, his invoice allocated 32 hours as follows:**

HT 1.0 HP 72″ x 72″	**12.5%**
HT 4.0 HP 84″ x 84″	**66.5%**
HT 4.4 HP 84″ Gazebo	**21.0%**

To allocate this vendor invoice to the Tubs Project, follow these instructions:

1 ➤   Click the **Payments** icon.

2 ➤   **Pay Purchase**   Click ▼ select **Make Other Payment**.
      Invoices

3 ➤	**To the Order of**	Select **George Kouretsoes & Associates**, [Tab] .
	Acct.	The default account **5040 Cost of Sales-Outside Labour** is shown. This account is used to record all work done by non-employees; i.e., businesses or individuals hired to work on the hot tubs but who are not employees. If you want a different account, double-click the account shown and select an account from the list.
4 ➤	**Description**	Type **Time on Hot Tubs at Radisser Hotels**, [Tab] .
5 ➤	**Amount**	Type **800.00**, [Tab] .
6 ➤	**Tax**	[Tab] to accept code HS.
7 ➤	**HST**	[Tab] to accept **104.00**.
8 ➤	**Allo**	Click the **Allo** column to display the **Tubs/Chemic Allocation - Payments Journal** window or click the allocate icon ✓ on the toolbar.

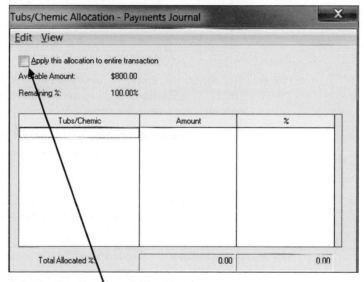

On the top left of window is the **$800.00** amount to be allocated.

☐ Apply this allocation to entire transaction   The box would be ✓ if there was more than 1 item on the sales or purchase invoice with the same % to be allocated. This will be shown in Exercise 11-5.

9 ➤	**Tubs/Chemic**	Press [Enter] to display the chemical and hot tubs Projects.
		Select **HT 1.0 HP 72" × 72"**; the cursor jumps to the % column with an amount of 100%.
10 ➤	**%**	Change the 100% to **12.5**. (This represents 12.5% of George Kouretsoes & Associates' time spent on preparing this model for sale.) Press [Tab] . The Amount field changes to $100.00; the cursor moves to the next line. Note at top that the Remaining % changes to 87.50%.

11 ➤ Tubs/Chemic   Press **Enter**, then select **HT 4.0 HP 84" × 84"**. Change the % to **66.5**, [Tab] .

12 ➤ Tubs/Chemic   Press **Enter**, then select **HT 4.4 HP 84" Gazebo**, [Tab] to accept **21.00%**.

The Tubs/Chemic Allocation - Payments Journal window should appear as follows:

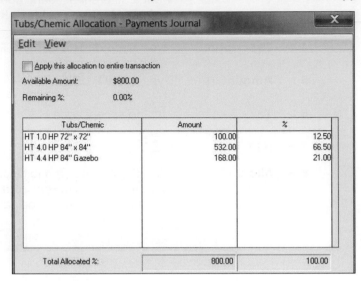

13 ➤ The Amount column Total should be **800.00** and the % column should be **100%**. The Remaining % to be allocated is 0.00%, therefore, the $800.00 amount has been allocated.

Mr. Kouretsoes did not do any work on Model 4.6 HP 84" Enclosed; therefore, there is no allocation.

14 ➤ Click **OK** to accept the distribution.

The window changes back to the Payments Journal, and you will notice the **Allo** column has a ✓ indicating that the allocation has taken place.

15 ➤ Invoice/Ref.   Type **465** [Tab] . (Invoice 465.)

The bottom portion of the Payments Journal window should resemble the following:

Acct	Description	Amount	Tax	HST	Allo
5040 Cost Of Sales-Outside Labour	Time on Hot Tubs at Radisser Hotels	800.00	HS	104.00	✓

Subtotal	800.00
Tax	104.00
Total	904.00

Invoice/Ref.   465

Comment

Post

16 ➤ Display the Payments Journal Entry.

Payments Journal Entry Aug 08, 2019 (J3)					
Account Number	Account Description	Tubs/Chemic	Debits	Credits	Tubs/Che...
2670	HST Paid On Purchases/Services		104.00	-	
5040	Cost Of Sales-Outside Labour		800.00	-	
		- HT 1.0 HP 72" x 72"			100.00
		- HT 4.0 HP 84" x 84"			532.00
		- HT 4.4 HP 84" Gazebo			168.00
1020	Bank Account		-	904.00	
Additional Date:	Additional Field:				
			904.00	904.00	

If your entry screen does not have the Tubs/Chemic allocation on the right, you forgot to allocate the costs, or you may have to expand the window to see the allocation.

17 ➤ **Exit** from the Journal Entry window and **Post** when correct, and **Exit** to the Home window.

Allocating Cash Sales to a Project(s)

1 ➤ Advance the Session date to **Aug 12, 2019**.

Exercise 11-5—Allocating Cash Sales to a Project(s)

Record and post the following transaction:

Aug 12, 2019	Record a cash sales invoice to cash customers for the following chemicals:

Ship	Unit	Description	Price	Amount	Tax
40	each	Chemicals-Individual	12.76	510.40	HS
320	each	Chemicals-Bulk	10.50	3,360.00	HS
		Total Sales invoice amount is		$4,373.55	

1 ➤ Click the **RECEIVABLES** module, **Sales Invoices** icon.

> **Transaction** **Invoice**.

2 ➤ **Payment Method** Select **Cash**, Tab .

> **Invoice** #642

3 ➤ **Customer** Type **Various Cash Customers**, Tab , select **Full Add** to add the name to the file, click the **Options** tab, Revenue Account select **4200 Sales-Chemicals** and remove the early payment terms. The terms should all be blank. Click the **Taxes** tab. The Tax code should be **HS**. Click the **Statistics** tab. Leave the Credit Limit blank. Click Save and Close . Tab . On future cash sales, the default fields will display in the Invoice.

4 ➤ **Item Number** Select **Chemicals-Individual**.

5 ➤ **Quantity** Type **40**, Tab to **Item Description**.

6 ➤ **Item Description** You may want to amend the Item Description to suit the situation. Tab .

Use the drop-down menu items feature only when the whole invoice is to be allocated to one Project.

7 ➤ **Base Price**   `Tab` to accept 12.76. `Tab` to Amount.

8 ➤ **Amount**   `Tab` to accept 510.40.

9 ➤ **Tax**   `Tab` to accept HS.

10 ➤ **Account**   `Tab` to accept 4200 Sales-Chemicals.

11 ➤ **Tubs/Chemic**   Above the column, `Tubs/Chemic:` [▼] [⊠].

Click the ▼ arrow to select **Chemicals-Individual,** `Tab` , and the `C.☑` image appears in the column. (See side note box.)

> In step 11, when you select one of the choices, Sage 50 Accounting will allocate all the items on the invoice to the entire transaction, but the allocation for each sales item (line) should be separate. This error is to show you how this feature works. It will be corrected in step 16.

12 ➤ Click the ☑. A ☑ appears in [☑ Apply this allocation to entire transaction].

Click **OK** to accept. The 100% allocation will be applied to both Sales items. `Tab`.

13 ➤ **Repeat** from step 4 to 10 to enter the Chemical-Bulk sales to the invoice. The same Ch…or C…appears in the Tubs/Chemic column as a result of the selection.

14 ➤ The lower portion of the Sales window should appear as follows:

Item Number	Quantity	Order	Back Order	Unit	Item Description	Base Price	Discount (%)	Price	Amount	Tax	Account	Tubs/Chemic
Chem Individual	40			Each	Chemicals - Individual	12.76		12.76	510.40	HS	4200 Sales-...	Chemical...
Chem - Bulk	320			Each	Chemicals - Bulk	10.50		10.50	3,360.00	HS	4200 Sales-...	Chemical...
												☑

15 ➤ **Display** the Sales Journal entry. You will see that both sales amounts have been allocated to the Chemicals-Individual Project, which is not correct.

4200	Sales-Chemicals		-	3,870.40
	- Chemicals-Individual			3,870.40

✓ You will now enter the correct allocation Project.

16 ➤ **Exit** the entry. At `Tubs/Chemic:` [Chemicals-indivi ▼] [⊠], click the ▼. Select the blank space above Chemicals-Bulk. This will clear the ☑ from the [☑ Apply this allocation to entire transaction].

17 ➤ **Tubs/Chemic** column   Click the Tubs/Chemic line for Chemicals-Individual. Click the ☑.

18 ➤ **Tub/Chemic** column   Double-click and select **Chemicals-Individual**.

19 ➤ **%**   `Tab` to accept 100.00, click **OK**.

The image changes to `Tubs/Chemic:` [[By Line] ▼] [⊠].

20 ➤ Tub/Chemic Column   Click the Tubs/Chemic line for Chemicals-Bulk, click on the the ✔. Double-click and select **Chemicals-Bulk**.

21 ➤ %   `Tab` to accept 100.00, click **OK**.

You are returned to the Sales Invoice window. You will notice that the lower portion has changed.

22 ➤ Display the Sales Journal entry. The entry now allocates the sales to the two Projects.

4200	Sales-Chemicals	-	3,870.40	
	- Chemicals-Individual			510.40
	- Chemicals-Bulk			3,360.00

23 ➤ Exit the entry and return to the Sales Invoice window.

The ☑ Apply this allocation to entire transaction would be used only when all sales lines on an invoice apply to one project. An example of this would be if sales invoices were prepared for each customer, with individual sales items listed on the invoice that apply to one project.

24 ➤ Post when correct and **Exit** to the Home window.

25 ➤ Advance the Session date to **Aug 16, 2019**.

Allocating Payroll to a Project(s)

To allocate Payroll to various Projects, you would process the allocation in the PAYROLL module. Allocation is based on hours spent by particular employees on specific Projects.

Exercise 11-6—Allocating Payroll to a Project(s)

You may allocate 100% or any percentage of the payroll to a specific Project(s) (see step 12).

In this exercise you will be allocating payroll costs using the PAYROLL module.

> **Aug 16, 2019**   **Issued the company payroll, Payroll Cheque Run, based on the allocations prepared by each of the employees. Vivian and Hillary worked 80 hours each from Friday, August 2nd to Friday, August 16[th.]**
>
> Hours are estimated for Friday, August 16. Allocated hours will be shown in Fig. 11-5, Payroll Run Journal.

1 ➤ From the Home window click the **EMPLOYEES & PAYROLL** module, then the **Payroll Cheque Run**.

2 ➤ Pay Period Frequency Click ▼ and select **26**, Tab.

Cheque Number   863.

Direct Deposit   Do NOT change. HotTubs Company Ltd. does
Number   DD   not use this feature.

Cheque Date   Accept Aug 16, 2019.

Pay Period End Date Accept Aug 16, 2019.

In the column 🖼 to the left of both employees' names, make sure a ✓ appears in the column.

   Regular Hours   You will see that Hillary and Vivian both have 80.00 in the Regular Hours column.

3 ➤ Click **Report, Display Payroll Journal Entry**. The total of the expense account numbers 5310, 5320, and 5330 is:

   Hillary $1,714.65
   Vivian $2,144.98

Some or all of the total expense amounts can be expensed in the allocation. Vivian also works on administrative duties that will not be allocated to a Project. The bottom total is **$3,859.63**.

4 ➤ **Exit** from the Journal entry window.

5 ➤ Select the Line for **Buchanan, Hillary** and click on the **Tubs/Chemic** field or click the ✓ on the top-right corner of the window beside the printer icon.

6 ➤ **Tubs/Chemic**   Below the blue shaded area, **double-click**, or press Enter.

7 ➤ Enter the Allocation (Regular hours column) shown in Fig. 11-5.

Tubs/Chemic Allocation By Hours - Payroll Run Journal - Pay multiple employees

Edit   View

Allocate available paycheque hours to Tubs/Chemic.

☐ Apply this allocation to entire transaction

Tubs/Chemic	Total	%	Regular	Overtime 1	Overtime 2
Available Hours	80.00	100.00	80.00	--	--
Remaining Hours	--	--	--	--	--
Chemicals-Bulk	5.00	6.25	5.00	--	--
Chemicals-Individual	2.25	2.81	2.25	--	--
HT 1.0 HP 72" x 72"	4.75	5.94	4.75	--	--
HT 4.0 HP 84" x 84"	18.25	22.81	18.25	--	--
HT 4.4 HP 84" Gazebo	47.75	59.69	47.75	--	--
HT 4.6 HP 84" Enclos...	2.00	2.50	2.00	--	--
Total Allocated Hours:	80.00	100.00	80.00	0.00	0.00

Fig. 11-5: Payroll Run Journal—Allocation for Hillary Buchanan.

8 ➤ Click **OK** when correct.

9 ➤ Click **Report, Display Payroll Journal Entry**.

The window portion for Hillary is shown next. Note that the entry shows the detail split of payroll expense $1,714.65 among the Tubs/Chemic Projects.

Payroll Run Journal Entry Aug 16, 2019 (J5)

Account Number	Account Description	Tubs/Chemic	Debits	Credits	Tubs/Che...
BUCHANAN, Hillary					
5310	Wages Expense		1,600.00	-	
		- Chemicals-Bulk			100.00
		- Chemicals-Individual			45.00
		- HT 1.0 HP 72" x 72"			95.00
		- HT 4.0 HP 84" x 84"			365.00
		- HT 4.4 HP 84" Gazebo			955.00
		- HT 4.6 HP 84" Enclosed			40.00
5320	EI Expense		42.11	-	
		- Chemicals-Bulk			2.63
		- Chemicals-Individual			1.18
		- HT 1.0 HP 72" x 72"			2.50
		- HT 4.0 HP 84" x 84"			9.61
		- HT 4.4 HP 84" Gazebo			25.13
		- HT 4.6 HP 84" Enclosed			1.05
5330	CPP Expense		72.54	-	
		- Chemicals-Bulk			4.53
		- Chemicals-Individual			2.04
		- HT 1.0 HP 72" x 72"			4.31
		- HT 4.0 HP 84" x 84"			16.55
		- HT 4.4 HP 84" Gazebo			43.30
		- HT 4.6 HP 84" Enclosed			1.81
1020	Bank Account		-	1,267.47	
2220	EI Payable		-	72.19	
2225	CPP Payable		-	145.08	
2230	Income Tax Payable		-	229.91	
Additional Date:	Additional Field:				
			1,714.65	1,714.65	

10 ➤ **Exit** from the window.

11 ➤ Continue with Vivian's allocation as follows; no overtime:

Chemicals-Bulk	**8.00 hours**
Chemicals-Individual	**1.00 hours**
HT 1.0 HP 72" x 72"	**4.75 hours**
HT 4.0 HP 84" x 84"	**19.50 hours**
HT 4.4 HP 84" Gazebo	**38.75 hours**
	72.00 hours

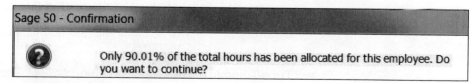

Total Allocated Hours:	72.00	90.01	72.00	0.00	0.00

72 hours only are allocated to Projects. The other 8 hours were spent on management duties and are not allocated. 72 hours divided by 80 hours equals 90.00%. Due to rounding of individual %, the % allocation is 90.01% of the total.

12 ➤ Click **OK** to continue. A Confirmation window will appear.

Sage 50 - Confirmation

❓ Only 90.01% of the total hours has been allocated for this employee. Do you want to continue?

13 ➤ Click **Yes** to continue.

14 ➤ Display the **Payroll Journal Entry**. Note the bottom totals. Vivian's total expense is $2,144.98 and the total of the Debit and Credit columns is $3,859.63. Note also that there is no total for the allocated Tubs/Chemic column.

The net pay for Hillary is $1,267.47 and for Vivian is $1,521.11.

15 ➤ **Exit** from the Payroll Journal entry.

16 ➤ **Post** the **Payroll Cheque Run** entry when correct. A Confirmation window will appear.

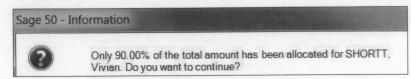

Sage 50 - Information

Only 90.00% of the total amount has been allocated for SHORTT, Vivian. Do you want to continue?

17 ➤ This confirmation % is slightly different from the step 12 confirmation % window. This is an allocation calculation error. Click **Yes** to Continue.

18 ➤ Click **Yes** to the warning message about the payroll dates needing to be between Jan 01, 2014 and Dec 31, 2014.

19 ➤ **Exit** to the Home window.

To Allocate Credit Sales to a Project(s)

Unlike allocating PAYROLL, you would allocate credit sales to a Project(s) based on percentage of the amount for each item. Sage 50 Accounting will automatically calculate the specific amount based on the percentage you enter.

Exercise 11-7—Allocating Credit Sales to a Project(s)

In this exercise, you will be allocating credit sales invoices to specific Projects, similar to what you did in Exercise 11-5 for a Cash Sale.

Aug 16 2019	**Issue sales invoice #643 to Radisser Hotels for the hot tubs based on Sales Order #423.**

1 ➤ In the **TUBS/CHEMIC** module, click the **Sales Invoices icon**.

Transaction	**Invoice**
Paid by	**Pay later**

2 ➤ **Order/Quote No**   Click the 🔍 and select **423**. The window fills with the information from the Sales Order.

3 ➤ All items ordered have been installed and are working to the satisfaction of the Hotel Assistant Manager. Click the **Fill Backordered quantities** icon.

     Quantity   The fields fill with the quantities ordered. Invoice total is $36,230.63.

4 ➤ **Tubs/Chemic**   Click in the column, click ☑. The Tubs/Chemic Allocation - Sales Journal, Creating an Invoice window is displayed. Click the ☑ box for Apply this allocation to entire transaction to remove the ☑. You will then see the following information box. Click **OK**.

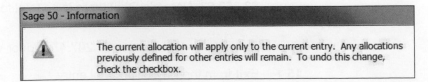

Sage 50 - Information

⚠   The current allocation will apply only to the current entry. Any allocations previously defined for other entries will remain. To undo this change, check the checkbox.

5 ➤ Allocate each line on the invoice 100% to the appropriate Project. Click **OK** to accept the distribution.

6 ➤ **Display** the Sales Journal Entry. It should be as follows:

Account Number	Account Description	Tubs/Chemic	Debits	Credits	Tubs/Che...
Sales Journal Entry Aug 16, 2019 (J7)					
1200	Accounts Receivable		36,230.63	-	
5010	Cost Of Sales HotTubs		16,875.00	-	
		- HT 1.0 HP 72" x 72"			2,315.00
		- HT 4.0 HP 84" x 84"			11,160.00
		- HT 4.4 HP 84" Gazebo			3,400.00
1310	Inventory HotTubs		-	16,875.00	
2650	HST Charged On Sales		-	4,168.13	
4100	Sales -Hot Tubs		-	32,062.50	
		- HT 1.0 HP 72" x 72"			4,398.50
		- HT 4.0 HP 84" x 84"			21,204.00
		- HT 4.4 HP 84" Gazebo			6,460.00
Additional Date:	Additional Field:				
			53,105.63	53,105.63	

7 ➤ **Exit** from the entry window. Click **POST**. You will see the sales order has been removed from the system window. Click **OK**.

8 ➤ Click **OK** for Journal Entry J7.

> Advisor: Entries just processed caused one or more inventory items to drop below the reorder point. Print the Inventory Item Quantity report to see which items to reorder.

9 ➤ Click inside the **Advisor** box to close and **Exit** to the **Home** window.

10 ➤ Click **Reports, Inventory & Services, Quantity, OK**.

Inventory Quantity

Description	Item No.	Unit	Quantity	Minimum	On Purc...	On Sale...	To Order
Chemicals - Bulk	Chem - Bulk	Each	902	40	0	0	-
Chemicals - Individual	Chem Indiv...	Each	285	40	0	0	-
HotTubs 1.0 HP 72" x 72"	H 1.0	Each	2	2	0	0	-
HotTubs 4.0 HP 84" x 84"	H 4.0	Each	3	2	0	0	-
HotTubs 4.4 HP 84" x 84" Gazebo	H 4.4	Each	2	2	0	0	-
HotTubs 4.6 HP 84" Enclosed	H 4.6	Each	1	1	0	0	-

There is an error in this report. No item of inventory is below the reorder point.

11 ➤ **Exit** from the report and return to the Home window.

Allocating Sales Returns to a Project(s)

In Exercise 11-5 you recorded sales to various customers and allocated the sale amounts 100% to each Project. When sales are returned, the return should be allocated back to the same Project(s).

Exercise 11-8—Allocating Sales Returns to a Project(s)
---

1 ➤ Advance the Session date to **Aug 17, 2019**.

> **Aug 17, 2019**   A cash customer, Mr. John Stammers, from the Chemicals-Individual summary sales records on Aug 12, 2019, (our invoice #642) returned 2 bottles of chemicals at $12.76 each, plus HST, due to leaking containers. Vivian Shortt checked the remaining stock and found that 3 additional Chemicals-Individual containers were leaking.
>
> The manufacturer's representative will be replacing the stock of this item.
>
> **Total Invoice = $ -28.84**

Mr. Stammers is interested in purchasing an accessory for his hot tub and wants to have this return credited to an account in his name. Mrs. Shortt is looking into ordering this new accessory.

Create an account for Mr. Stammers and issue a credit refund for the returned chemicals as shown in this exercise. **Do NOT forget to allocate the return to the Project**.

2 ➤ Click the **Sales Invoices** icon to:

> - Set up a customer account.
> - Issue a credit refund.

Transaction	**Invoice**.
Paid by	**Pay Later**.

3 ➤ **Customer**   Type **Mr. John Stammers**, Tab , click Full Add , record with any address information. Terms **net 10 days**, leave revenue account blank, Tax code **HS**, credit limit **$500.00** and click Save and Close .

4 ➤ **Invoice**   Type **642Rt Cash**, Tab .

5 ➤ **Record** the return as shown in the next window portion:

Item Number	Quantity	Order	Back Order	Unit	Item Description	Base Price	Discount (%)	Price	Amount	Tax	Account	Tubs/Chemic
Chem Individual	-2			Ea...	Chemicals - Individual	12.76		12.76	-25.52	HS	4210 Sales Return...	
												✔

Subtotal:	-25.52	
Freight		✔
HST:	-3.32	

Early Payment Terms: ____ % Days, Net 10 Days   Total: -28.84

Returned accepted - leaking containers

6 ➤ **Tubs/Chemic**   Click ✔.

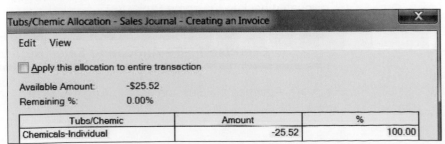

Tubs/Chemic	Amount	%
Chemicals-Individual	-25.52	100.00

7 ➤ Tubs/Chemic   Double-click, select **Chemicals-Individual**.

8 ➤ %   ⟨Tab⟩ to accept **100%,** and allocate the -25.52 return to the Project. Click **OK** to return to the Sales Journal. Notice that the box above Tubs/Chemic displays Tubs/Chemic: [By Line] ▼ 🖈 .

9 ➤ Display the entry.

Sales Journal Entry Aug 17, 2019 (J8)					
Account Number	Account Description	Tubs/Chemic	Debits	Credits	Tubs/Che...
1350	Inventory-Chemicals		12.76	-	
2650	HST Charged On Sales		3.32	-	
4210	Sales Returns -Chemicals		25.52	-	
		- Chemicals-Individual			-25.52
1200	Accounts Receivable		-	28.84	
5060	Cost of Sales-Chemicals		-	12.76	
		- Chemicals-Individual			-12.76
Additional Date:	Additional Field:				
			41.60	41.60	

10 ➤ Exit the window, **Post** when correct and **Exit** to the Home window.

11 ➤ Record and **post** the following entry:

Aug 17, 2019   **Received George Kouretsoes & Associates' invoice #468 dated Aug 16, 2019 for $2,150.00, plus HST for time spent on completing the delivery and installation of hot tubs at Radisser Hotel. Total invoice $2,429.50. Terms: Payment upon receipt. Cheque issued. Allocation of his staff time of 172 hours is as follows:**

       HT 1.0 HP 72" x 72"   12.5%
       HT 4.0 HP 84" x 84"   66.5%
       HT 4.4 HP 84" Gazebo 21.0%

Hint: Use **Make Other Payment**

---

12 ➤ Return to the **Home** window. Advance the Session date to **Aug 23, 2019**.

Correcting PROJECT Errors

It is common to make errors in allocations to Projects. For example, the wrong Project could be selected, the wrong percentage may be used, or the Project allocation forgotten. As with other modules, to correct the error, you can reverse the entry and then enter a new transaction to record the correct entry, or you can make an adjusting entry to correct the item(s) that need correcting.

The reversal should be made in the originating module (TUBS/CHEMIC, RECEIVABLES, PAYABLES, or EMPLOYEES & PAYROLL). The reversal must be the exact original amount. As mentioned, the correction can be entered using the **Reverse** invoice icon or **Adjust** icon. The corrections are the same as those covered in previous chapters, except that the allocation must be reversed as well.

The Payroll Accrual

Although PAYROLL allocation can be allocated by hours, the PAYROLL accrual must be allocated by percent, because Sage 50 Accounting will not allow Payroll accruals to be allocated by hours (see Fig. 11-2b).

Exercise 11-9—Recording Payroll Accrual to a Project(s)

Aug 23, 2019 The owner has asked you to prepare a Project report as of the end of business today. The staff has prepared the information below to assist you in updating all Project records:

Salary accrual report for five days is allocated as follows:

	Vivian Shortt Hours	Hillary Buchanan Hours	Total Hours	Total Percent
Chemicals-Bulk	5.00	2.50	7.50	9.40%
Chemicals-Individual	3.75	4.25	8.00	10.00%
1.0 HP 72" x 72"	10.50	9.50	20.00	25.00%
4.0 HP 84" x 84"	16.75	21.75	38.50	48.10%
4.4 HP 84" Gazebo	2.00	1.25	3.25	4.00%
4.6 HP 84" Enclosed	2.00	0.75	2.75	3.50%
Totals	40.00	40.00	80.00	100.00%

	Hours	Rate	Amount
Vivian Shortt	40.00	$25.00	1,000.00
Hillary Buchanan	40.00	$20.00	800.00
			1,800.00

Fig. 11-6: Salary Accrual Report.

Follow the steps below to record the information.

1 ➤ Click the **COMPANY** module, click the **General Journal** icon.

2 ➤ **Source**   Type **Payroll Accrual**, [Tab] to Comment line.

3 ➤ **Comment**   Type **Payroll Accrual August 16 – 22**, [Tab].

4 ➤ **Account**   Select **5310 Wages Expense**.

5 ➤ **Debits**   Type **1,800.00** (40 hours at $25.00 per hour and 40 hours at $20.00 per hour). [Tab].

6 ➤ **Comment**   Type **Payroll Accrual**, [Tab].

7 ➤ **Allo**   Press enter or click the column at the **5310 Wages Expense** line.

8 ➤ Enter the percentages from the Salary Accrual report in Fig. 11-6 and click **OK** when complete. | Total Allocated %: | 1,800.00 | 100.00 | [Tab] to move to the Account column.

9 ➤ **Account**   Select **2205 Payroll Accrual**.

10 ➤ **Credits**   to accept 1,800.00.

The payroll accrual allocation journal entry should resemble the following:

General Journal Entry Aug 23, 2019 (J10)					
Account Number	Account Description	Tubs/Chemic	Debits	Credits	Tubs/Che...
5310	Wages Expense		1,800.00	-	
	Payroll Accrual				
		- Chemicals-Bulk			169.20
		- Chemicals-Individual			180.00
		- HT 1.0 HP 72" x 72"			450.00
		- HT 4.0 HP 84" x 84"			865.80
		- HT 4.4 HP 84" Gazebo			72.00
		- HT 4.6 HP 84" Enclosed			63.00
2205	Payroll Accrual		-	1,800.00	
Additional Date:	Additional Field:				
			1,800.00	1,800.00	

The PAYROLL accrual, as a General Journal entry, would be allocated to Tubs/Chemic Projects in the same manner as when the payroll cheques are issued. The payroll accrual does not normally record EI and CPP Expense, because they are expensed only when actually paid.

11 ➤ **Post** when correct and return to the Home window.

The payroll accrual, including the allocation, would be reversed before the next actual paycheques are issued. This will allow the cheque entry for actual pay on August 30 to be allocated without being adjusted for accruals.

Another Transaction

1 ➤ **Record** and **post** the transaction that follows. Ignore the message about low inventory for now. Chemicals-Individual are below the minimum reorder point.

Aug 23, 2019	Made the following cash sales from Aug 13, 2019 to Aug 23, 2019.
	Do not forget to allocate the sales to the corresponding Projects!

Quantity	Unit	Description	Price	Amount	Tax	Total
23	each	Chemicals-Bulk	10.50	241.50	HST	
251	each	Chemicals-Individual	12.76	3,202.76	HST	
		Total cash sales				**$3,892.02**

Adjusting INVENTORY and Cost of Sales

As discussed in Chapter 8, the dollar value of goods on hand inventory (e.g., Hot tubs and chemicals) at the end of a period should be adjusted (reduced) to show the actual cost of material used during the month. The corresponding adjustment (increase) is shown in the Cost of Goods Sold during the period.

Exercise 11-10—Adjusting INVENTORY and Cost of Sales

The INVENTORY of all tubs and chemicals on hand was counted and verified to determine the actual cost of all products sold. There are 3 containers of bulk chemicals missing. It is not known where they are. Charge the cost to Inventory Adjustment.

1 ➤ **Journalize** an **Inventory Adjustment entry** as shown in Fig. 11-7.

Source	Inventory count						Date	Aug 23, 2019	
Comment	Inventory count today, missing containers								

Item	Qty	Unit	Description	Unit Cost	Amount	Acct	Allo
Chem - Bulk	-3	Each	Chemicals - Bulk	5.25	-15.75	5080 Inventory Adjustments	✓

Fig. 11-7: Inventory Adjustment—Inventory.

2 ➤ **Allocate** the costs to the appropriate Inventory.

Inventory Adjustments Journal Entry Aug 23, 2019 (J12)

Account Number	Account Description	Tubs/Chemic	Debits	Credits	Tubs/Che...
5080	Inventory Adjustments		15.75	-	
		- Chemicals-Bulk			15.75
1350	Inventory-Chemicals		-	15.75	
Additional Date:	Additional Field:				
			15.75	15.75	

Fig. 11-8: Inventory Adjustment Journal entry.

3 ➤ **Exit** from the window and **post** when correct.

Printing Month-End PROJECTS Reports

There are no other transactions to be recorded for this exercise. Reports should be printed as part of the normal month-end procedures.

Exercise 11-11—Printing PROJECTS-Related Reports

1 ➤ From the Home window, click **Reports**, move to **Tubs/Chemic**, and select **Income** to display the Tubs/Chemic Income Report Options window.

Fig. 11-9: Tubs/Chemic Income Report window.

The Tubs/Chemic Income Reports are based upon Revenue and Expense accounts only, and the Projects can be selected for display.

2 ➤　Select the options as shown in Fig. 11-9. (**Detail**, **Start** and **Finish** dates.)

3 ➤ **Select**　　　If the project names are not blue, click **Select All**.
Tubs/Chemic　They turn blue.

4 ➤ **Select**　　　If the account names (Revenue and Expense accounts)
Accounts　　are not blue, click **Select All**. They turn blue.

　　　　　　　　Note: The report may be printed for one or more revenue or
　　　　　　　　expense accounts.

5 ➤ **Balance**　　Check ✓ the 🔲, **OK**. This will produce a complete
Forward　　Income Statement for each HotTubs Project with the
　　　　　　　　balance forward from previous periods. The balance
　　　　　　　　forward amount is 0.00 since we have no previous period
　　　　　　　　information. Notice the details for revenue and expenses
　　　　　　　　shown in the report.

6 ➤　Maximize the report to fill the screen.

　　　Depending on the size of the font used, the report may be six pages long. To
　　　see each project on a separate page, from the menu bar, click:

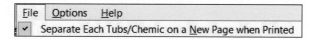

7 ➤　You may want to print only one or two Project reports. This will show you
　　　the detail available in the reports. **Repeat** the procedure above and choose
　　　any individual Project report(s) that you would like to see.

8 ➤　Click **File, Print** to print the Project reports you requested.

The **Summary** report, like a financial statement, will show the balance of each
Revenue and Expense account only. If you need more detail, you can drill down to
the line or lines on which you need more detail, or you could print the complete
Detail report.

9 ➤　Return to the Home window.

Journal Entries

1 ➤ Print **All Journal Entries** transactions for the period **Aug 01, 2019** to **Aug 23, 2019**.

Don't forget to ✓ ☑ Tubs/Chemic Allocations in the Modify Report Options. If you forget, the **Project Distributions** detail will not print on the report.

 This report in default mode (Arial size 8 font) will print on 3 pages. As shown in Exercise 11-11 step 6, you can print the report with an Income Statement on each page. You could also print the report in Landscape format (Change Print Settings, Setup, Landscape), but you will have to remember to change it back to Portrait for the other reports, otherwise all reports will print in Landscape mode.

Income Statement

2 ➤ Print the Income Statement for the period **Aug 01, 2019** to **Aug 23, 2019**.

Note that the Income Statement cannot be printed with Project detail.

Balance Sheet

3 ➤ **Print** the Balance Sheet for **Aug 23, 2019**.

4 ➤ **Compare** your printouts to those in the instructor's Solutions Manual.

 Review **Slideshows 11A** and **11B** before proceeding.

Before Moving On ...

Read the following questions and make sure you know the answers to them; otherwise, read the corresponding part in the chapter before moving on.

1. Explain briefly the use of the PROJECTS module.

2. Explain briefly how the RECEIVABLES, PAYABLES, and EMPLOYEES & PAYROLL modules may be used effectively with the PROJECTS module in producing a detailed picture of a company's financial position.

3. What options are available for allocation of the dollar value of Projects?

4. Why would most companies that use the PROJECTS module allocate 100% of revenues and expenses to Projects? (To assist with this answer, compare the total of the Project reports to the Income Statement.)

5. How should you correct an error in allocating amounts to Projects?

Chapter 12

BANKING Module
Reconciliation & Deposits

Wedding Flowers Company

Learning Objectives

After completing this chapter you will be able to:

☐ Set up the BANKING module, Reconciliation & Deposits, Linked accounts.
☐ Prepare the Reconciliation & Deposits with Outstanding Bank Items.
☐ Turn the module to Ready.
☐ Reconcile the bank account by identifying cleared items and various other items such as outstanding deposit(s) or cheque errors.
☐ Display and print appropriate reports and journals.

This chapter illustrates the Sage 50 Accounting BANKING module feature using the **Reconciliation & Deposits Journal**.

The chapter assumes you have some knowledge of bank reconciliation and the types of items that require reconciling. If you are unsure of bank reconciliation theory and/or procedures, refer to your accounting textbook.

Topics in this chapter include:

The Accounting and Sage 50 Accounting Terminology has been deliberately placed at the beginning of this chapter in order to help you better understand account (bank) reconciliation concepts and principles. Read this section carefully before you proceed with the exercises.

Accounting and Sage 50 Accounting Terminology

Bank: A basic definition used in the context of this text; a financial institution that holds amounts of money for personal or commercial use.

Bank Reconciliation: The process of determining and processing the differences in the company bank account(s) as shown in the company's records, and the balance as shown on the bank statement.

Cancelled Cheque: A client's cheque that has been cashed by the bank and deducted from the client's bank account.

Cash: In business terms, this refers to actual cash, cheque, or credit card payment.

NSF: **N**ot **S**ufficient **F**unds. The customer did not have enough money in the bank account to allow the bank to pay the cheque.

Outstanding cheque: Cheque issued by the company and recorded in the General Ledger, but has not been cashed by the bank by the statement date.

Outstanding deposits: Deposits recorded in the company General Ledger that have not been deposited (credited) by the bank into the customer's account by the statement date. This could be due to a deposit being taken to the bank late in the day and the bank recording the deposit on the next day, or a deposit processed in the books but not yet taken to the bank.

Reconciliation: See *Bank Reconciliation*.

Unresolved Balance: The difference between the bank statement and the General Ledger bank account. The difference may be from bank errors or from errors in processing transactions in Sage 50 Accounting.

Banking Codes

A (Adjustment) for transactions posted as adjustments to a bank account.

C (Cleared) items (matched deposits with depositor cheques) that are recorded in your General Ledger bank account and that have been processed by the bank (on the bank statement).

D (Deposit Error) is used for deposits that are recorded in your General Ledger bank account but which differ from the bank statement. The difference must be recorded with a journal entry and assigned the Deposit Error code. When both D codes are entered, they can be cleared with the C code. The original deposit coded as a D and the error correction coded as a D can be cleared together with a C (cleared) code.

N (NSF) Means **N**ot **S**ufficient **F**unds. Cheques returned by the bank to the depositor when there is not enough money in the customer's bank account.

P (Payment Error) is used for cheques that are recorded in your General Ledger bank account but which differ from the bank statement. The difference must be recorded with a journal entry and assigned the Payment Error code. When both P codes are entered, they can be cleared with the C code. The original cheque, coded as a P, and the error correction, coded as a P, can be cleared together with a C (Cleared) code.

R (Reversed) When a cheque is received by the bank as a deposit, it is entered as a credit on the depositor's bank statement. When the cheque is cancelled (usually because of NSF), the entry in the depositor's bank statement is reversed, so the entry is assigned the **R** (Reversed) code. The reversing entry is normally recorded in the company's Sales Journal. A reversing entry is required and is then assigned the **A** (Adjustment) code.

V (Void) is used to identify cheques that were cancelled because they were issued incorrectly. A reversing entry is required and is then assigned the **A** (Adjustment) code.

Slideshow 12—The BANKING Module is designed to help you relate the RECONCILIATION & DEPOSITS Module to manual bank reconciliation. Run it before you proceed.

BANKING Module

The Reconciliation & Deposits Journal

The **Reconciliation & Deposits** journal is where all BANK (cash) transactions are tracked by the Sage 50 Accounting program for selected bank accounts. At month-end or period-end, when the bank reconciliation is performed, the Reconciliation & Deposits Journal is used to identify items (cheques or deposits, etc.) that are not shown on the bank statements. Items on the bank statement that have not been recorded in the company files must be journalized in the Accounts RECEIVABLE, PAYABLE, or General Journal, as required.

Receive Payments

This icon is the same as the RECEIVABLES module journal used to record receipts from customers. Either journal can be used. This journal is not used in this chapter.

Make Deposit

This journal can be used to record deposits that consist of a number of customer receipts. This feature is not used in this text.

Transfer Funds

This journal is used to transfer funds between different business bank accounts. This feature is shown in Appendix 2015 W, *Transfer Funds—Transfer Money Between Bank Accounts* in your course materials at www.nelson.com/student. It could have been used in Chapters 2A, 2B, 3A, or 3B to transfer funds between a regular bank account and a credit card bank account. **WWW**

Pay Bills ▼

This icon is the same as the PAYABLES module journal used to record payments to Vendors. Either journal can be used. This journal is not used in this chapter.

Reconcile Accounts

This journal (**Reconciliation & Deposits)** is used to reconcile bank accounts. It will be used in Exercise 12-2.

The **Wedding Flowers Company** has been preparing reconciliations manually, and now intends to use the Reconciliation & Deposits journal in Sage 50 Accounting. The last bank reconciliation was completed for the period ending April 30, 2019.

The Reconciliation & Deposits journal must be set up before it can be used. Wedding Flowers Company is currently using the COMPANY, RECEIVABLES, PAYABLES, and INVENTORY & SERVICES modules, and all transactions have been recorded up to May 31, 2019.

Wedding Flowers Company

The company records include cheque and deposit information from May 1, 2019, to May 31, 2019. You will now use the Reconciliation & Deposits journal to perform a reconciliation between account 1060 CASH IN BANK and the May 31 bank statement.

It would be helpful for you to do a manual bank reconciliation before attempting to use the Sage 50 Accounting BANKING module. This will enable you to understand what you are processing in the Reconciliation & Deposits journal.

You will use Fig. 12-1, Fig. 12-2, and Fig. 12-5 to complete a manual bank reconciliation.

General Ledger Report May 01, 2019 to May 31, 2019
Sorted by: Transaction Number

Date	Comment	Source #	JE#	Debits	Credits	Balance
1060	**Cash in Bank**					1,185.00 Dr
May 02, 2019	Etobicoke Newspaper	623	J1	-	113.00	1,072.00 Dr
May 06, 2019	D. Wadkins	801	J2	222.00	-	1,294.00 Dr
May 08, 2019	Receiver General for Canada	624	J3	-	885.00	409.00 Dr
May 16, 2019	Judy Johnson, Payroll	625	J4	-	400.00	9.00 Dr
May 13, 2019	Rowena's Wedding Boutique	256	J5	1,260.00	-	1,269.00 Dr
May 20, 2019	Etobicoke Hydro	626	J6	-	113.00	1,156.00 Dr
May 20, 2019	Better Built Builders	627	J7	-	500.00	656.00 Dr
May 20, 2019	246, Shierel Hampton	Cash	J8	226.00	-	882.00 Dr
May 31, 2019	247, Soung Tran	Cash	J9	79.10	-	961.10 Dr
				1,787.10	2,011.00	

Fig. 12-1: Cash in Bank Report.

Fig. 12-2 shows the manual reconciliation that was completed for the April 30 bank statement. The unrecorded service charge item on the reconciliation has been recorded in the General Ledger at April 30.

Wedding Flowers Company
Bank Reconciliation at April 30, 2019

Balance per Bank Statement April 30, 2019	$ 1,185.00
Add: Outstanding Deposits	None
Less: Outstanding Cheques	None
(All previous cheques have been cashed)	
Adjusted Bank Balance	$ 1,185.00
Balance per General Ledger April 30, 2019	$ 1,203.00
Add: Interest earned on account not recorded	None
Less: Service Charges* not previously recorded	-18.00 (negative)
Adjusted Bank Balance	$ 1,185.00

Fig. 12-2: Bank Reconciliation.

*The service charges were recorded in the General Ledger before the trial balance at April 30, 2019.

The first time the Reconciliation & Deposits journal is used, you must enter background information about the **linked accounts** you want to use. This is done only once for each bank account.

Background information includes:

1. The starting and ending dates of the month(s) you want to reconcile the bank (cash) account from the General Ledger.

2. The beginning and ending dates on the bank statement that you are going to reconcile.

3. Transactions that were posted to the bank account before you started to use the Reconciliation & Deposits journal.

Setting Up the Reconciliation & Deposits Journal

You will now set up the linked accounts for the Reconciliation & Deposits journal. Follow the steps in the exercise that follows:

Exercise 12-1—Setting Up the Reconciliation & Deposits Journal

---

WWW **1 ➤** Unzip the **12 Weddings.exe** file from your course materials at www.nelson.com/student.

2 ➤ Start Sage 50 Accounting and open the **12 Weddings** data file.

3 ➤ Session Date will be **May 31, 2019**.

This will allow you to enter all bank reconciliation information into **History** for the period. Sage 50 Accounting will gather cheque and deposit information previously entered and make it available for use in the Reconciliation & Deposits journal.

To Set Up Linked Accounts

1 ➤ From the Home window, click the **COMPANY** module, then click the **Chart of Accounts** icon, to display the Accounts windows.

2 ➤ Double-click **1060 Cash in Bank** to display the General Ledger window.

3 ➤ Click the **Reconciliation & Deposits** tab.

Reconciliation & Deposits

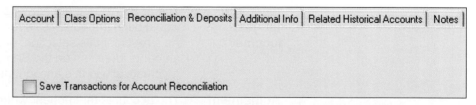

Fig. 12-3: General Ledger—Reconciliation & Deposits tab.

In the future, if you decide not to use the RECONCILIATION & DEPOSITS Journal to assist with the bank reconciliation, uncheck the **Save Transactions for Reconciliation** box. If you do NOT uncheck the box, the program will continue to accumulate bank data, using storage space unnecessarily.

4 ➤ Click the **Save Transactions for Account Reconciliation** box. The **Set Up** button appears near the bottom on the right side. (See side note box.)

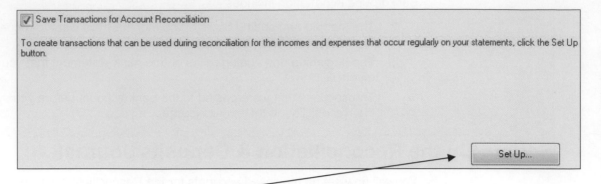

5 ➤   Click the **Set Up** button. The Account Reconciliation Linked Accounts window appears.

6 ➤   **Change** the fields to those shown in Fig. 12-4.

Fig. 12-4: Linked Accounts window.

Income 1 Interest Income	The accounts that appear when you click the ▾ would be in the 4000-4999 range (Revenue accounts). As a result of this selection, unrecorded Interest Income amounts identified on the Bank Statement can be posted automatically to this account number.
Adjustment Unresolved	The accounts that appear when you click the ▾ would be in the 4000 to 5999 range (Revenue and Expense accounts). As a result of this selection, unresolved amounts will be posted to this account. You will take steps to locate information that will allow this item to be resolved.
Expense 1 Bank Charges	The accounts that appear when you click the ▾ would be in the 5000-5999 range (Expense accounts). As a result of this selection, unrecorded bank charge amounts identified on the Bank Statement can be set to be posted automatically to this account number.

Expense 3	The accounts that appear when you click the ▼	
Interest	would be in the 5000-5999 range (Expense accounts).	
Expense	As a result of this selection, unrecorded bank loan interest, identified on the Bank Statement, can be posted automatically to this account.	

7 ➤ Click **OK** to save the changes and return to the **General Ledger** window for account 1060.

The Reconciliation & Deposits journal default names and Linked accounts have now been set up.

A company can have several bank reconciliation accounts (i.e., U.S. dollar accounts, several local chequing accounts, etc.). However, you will be using only one bank account for bank reconciliation purposes in this chapter.

8 ➤ Click X twice to return to the **Home** window.

Reconciling Bank Accounts in Sage 50 Accounting

Sage 50 Accounting may now be used for bank reconciliation. The next reconciliation date is May 31, 2019. The May 31, 2019 bank statement is received and the reconciliation can be completed.

Commercial Bank of Canada
1234 Main Street Toronto, Ontario L5X 2Y9

Wedding Flowers Company
3896 Lakeview Terrace
Mississauga, ON L5N 3M3

                              Account Number: 256-589-4   May 31, 2019

(OD = Overdrawn)

Date	Information	Cheques	Deposits	Balance
May 01	Balance Forward			1,185.00
May 03	Cheque 623	113.00		1,072.00
May 06	Deposit		222.00	1,294.00
May 14	Cheque 624	885.00		409.00
May 14	Deposit		1,260.00	1,669.00
May 16	Cheque 625	400.00		1,269.00
May 20	NSF item	1,260.00		9.00
May 20	Cheque 626	113.00		-104.00 OD
May 27	Deposit Interest		1.40	-102.60 OD
May 28	Service Charge	10.00		-112.60 OD
May 28	Loan Interest	100.00		-212.60 OD

Fig. 12-5: Bank Statement. (See side note box.)

> ⓘ **OD** means Overdrawn or Overdraft. The May 28 service charge is for Overdraft protection.

Before attempting the Sage 50 Accounting Reconciliation & Deposits for the first time, prepare a manual reconciliation first. This will help you understand what you are updating in the Reconciliation & Deposits journal.

Steps to Complete a Bank Reconciliation in Sage 50 Accounting

There are five basic steps in completing a bank reconciliation in Sage 50 Accounting:

1. Compare the deposits and withdrawals on the bank statement to the debits and credits (General Ledger bank account transactions) that are processed by Sage 50 Accounting. Enter the appropriate codes as shown below:

C	Cleared (the two sources match)	**R**	Reverse
D	Deposit error	**V**	Void
P	Payment error	**A**	Adjustment
N	Not Sufficient Funds	**O**	Outstanding (The item is in the General Ledger but NOT on the bank statement or vice versa.)

2. Using the designated Income and Expense Fields, enter the Interest Earned and Service Charges as shown on the bank statement.

3. After displaying the bank reconciliation, the "unresolved" amount(s) if any, need to be investigated.

4. Journal entries to clear any unresolved amounts should be made. Return to the Reconciliation & Deposits process to complete the codes for the resolved items.

5. Print the General Ledger bank account to confirm that the entries have been made and the ledger amounts have been updated.

Using the Reconciliation & Deposits Journal

Exercise 12-2—Using the Reconciliation & Deposits Journal

---

1 ➤ Click the **BANKING** module, click **Reconcile Accounts** icon. Fill in the fields in the Reconciliation & Deposits Journal as follows:

Account	Click the ▾ and select **1060 Cash in Bank**. The Statement Start, End and Reconciliation Dates are automatically filled in.
Statement Opening Balance	Type **1185.00**, ⌷Tab⌷. This is the May 1 Balance forward from the bank statement Fig 12-5.
Statement End Balance	Type **–212.60**, ⌷Tab⌷. This is the ending balance from the bank statement dated May 31. (See side note box.)
Comment	Type **Reconciliation at May 31, 2019.**

The **Statement End Balance** amount is the Bank Statement balance.

Read the important information on the Transactions tab.

2 ➤ Click on the | **Add Prior Outstanding** | button.

A message box to save the changes to the Journal appears.

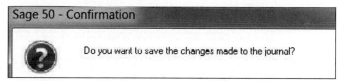

3 ➤ Click **Yes** to save the date and amount changes. The Add Outstanding Transactions window appears.

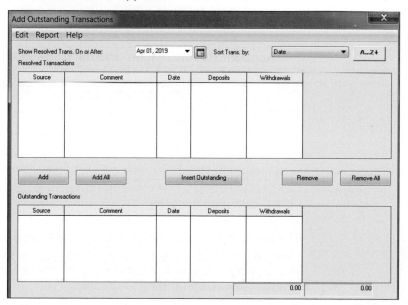

This window allows you to add in previous Resolved and Outstanding transactions.

4 ➤ The Bank Reconciliation (Fig. 12-2), prepared on April 30, 2019, for Wedding Flowers Company had no outstanding transactions (cheques or deposits) and the bank service charge was recorded in the month of April.

Show Resolved   Click ▾ select **Apr 30, 2019**, click **OK**.
Trans. On or After

The Reconciliation & Deposits Journal appears showing the Outstanding items for May. You may have to drag the bottom-right corner to the right to see the window below.

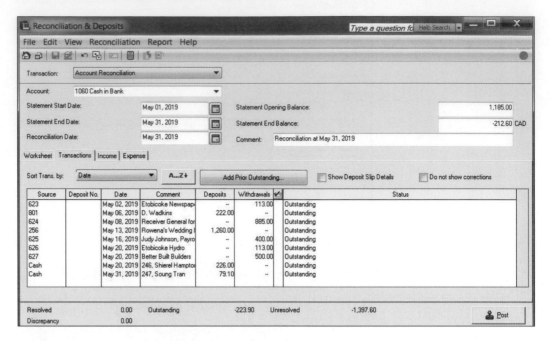

The unresolved balance should be **-1,397.60**. This represents the amount that has to be reconciled.

Show Deposit Slip Details   This feature is not used with Wedding Flowers Company. If a business identified individual cheques as being part of a single deposit, then the details of the deposit made could be shown.

5 ➤   Do NOT Post. Click **Report, Display Account Reconciliation Journal Entry**.

Account Reconciliation Journal Entry May 31, 2019

	Account Number	Account Description	Debits	Credits
May 31, 2019	Account Rec., Reconciliation at May 31, 2019			
	1060	Cash in Bank	-	1,397.60
	5380	Bank Rec Unresolved (Unknown)	1,397.60	-
Additional Date:	Additional Field:			
			1,397.60	1,397.60

6 ➤   **Exit** from the entry.

The transactions that have cleared the bank, as indicated by the bank statement, must be identified in the journal by clicking under the ☑ column icon next to the Withdrawals column. A ✓ will identify the item as cleared, and the Status column changes from **Outstanding** to **Cleared**.

If the item appears as the same dollar amount on the bank statement as it is recorded in the General Ledger, identify the item as (**C**) **cleared**. If the dollar amount is not the same, accept the appropriate code (shown in the Banking Codes section) at the beginning of this chapter.

7 ➤ Mark the following transactions as **cleared** (both the General Ledger transaction and the bank item agree as to the amount):

Source	Date	Vendor	Debit	Credit
623	May 02, 2019	Etobicoke Newspaper		113.00
801	May 06, 2019	D. Wadkins	222.00	
624	May 08, 2019	Receiver General for Canada		885.00
256	May 13, 2019	Rowena's Wedding Boutique	1,260.00	
625	May 16, 2019	Judy Johnson, Payroll		400.00
626	May 20, 2019	Etobicoke Hydro		113.00

The lower portion of the window should resemble the following:

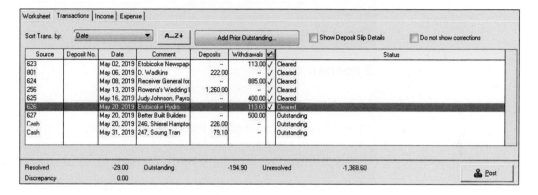

8 ➤ View (**Display Account Reconciliation Journal Entry**) created by the above changes. The unresolved amount has changed to -$1,368.60.

Account Reconciliation Journal Entry May 31, 2019

	Account Number	Account Description	Debits	Credits
May 31, 2019		Account Rec., Reconciliation at May 31, 2019		
	1060	Cash in Bank	-	1,368.60
	5380	Bank Rec Unresolved (Unknown)	1,368.60	-
Additional Date:	Additional Field:			
			1,368.60	1,368.60

9 ➤ **Exit** the entry.

Income tab

10 ➤ Click the **Income** tab, and on the Interest Income line, update the information as follows:

Source No.   Type **Bank Statement**, `Tab`.

Date   Change the date to **May 27, 2019** (the date the interest was deposited to the bank account). `Tab` to Amount.

Amount   Type **1.40**, `Tab`. The Unresolved amount changes to -$1,370.00.

Name	Source No.	Date	Comment	Acct	Amount
Interest Income	Bank Stateme	May 27, 2019	Interest Income	4210 Interest	1.40
NOT USED		May 31, 20	NOT USED		–
NOT USED		May 31, 2019	NOT USED		–

11 ➤ View the journal entry created by the previous changes.

Account Reconciliation Journal Entry May 31, 2019				
	Account Number	Account Description	Debits	Credits
May 27, 2019	Bank Statement, Interest Income			
	1060	Cash in Bank	1.40	-
	4210	Interest Income	-	1.40
May 31, 2019	Account Rec., Reconciliation at May 31, 2019			
	1060	Cash in Bank	-	1,370.00
	5380	Bank Rec Unresolved (Unknown)	1,370.00	-
Additional Date:	Additional Field:			
			1,371.40	1,371.40

12 ➤ Exit the entry.

Expense tab

13 ➤ Click the **Expense** tab.

14 ➤ On the Bank Charges line, change the information as follows:

Source No.	Type **Bank Statement**, Tab .
Date	Change the date to **May 28, 2019** (the date the charges were taken out of the account), Tab .
Comment	Change to **Service Charges**. Tab to Amount.
Amount	Type **10.00**, Tab .

On the Interest Expense line, change the information as follows:

Source No.	Type **Bank Interest,** Tab .
Date	Change the date to **May 28, 2019** (the date the charges were taken out of the account). Tab .
Comment	Change to **Loan Interest**. Tab to Amount.
Amount	Type **100.00**, Tab .

The lower portion of the window appears as follows and the Unresolved amount changes to -$1,260.00.

Name	Source No.	Date	Comment	Acct	Amount
Bank Charges	Bank Stateme	May 28, 2019	Service Charges	5342 Bank C	10.00
NOT USED		May 31, 2019	NOT USED		–
Interest Expense	Bank Interest	May 28, 2019	Loan Interest	5345 Bank L	100.00

15 ➤ View the journal entry created by the additional activity.

Account Reconciliation Journal Entry May 31, 2019

	Account Number	Account Description	Debits	Credits
May 27, 2019	Bank Statement, Interest Income			
	1060	Cash in Bank	1.40	-
	4210	Interest Income	-	1.40
May 28, 2019	Bank Statement, Service Charges			
	1060	Cash in Bank	-	10.00
	5342	Bank Charges Expense	10.00	-
May 28, 2019	Bank Interest, Loan Interest			
	1060	Cash in Bank	-	100.00
	5345	Bank Loan Interest	100.00	-
May 31, 2019	Account Rec., Reconciliation at May 31, 2019			
	1060	Cash in Bank	-	1,260.00
	5380	Bank Rec Unresolved (Unknown)	1,260.00	-
Additional Date:	Additional Field:			
			1,371.40	1,371.40

Fig. 12-6: Reconciliation & Deposits Journal entry.

16 ➤ Exit the entry.

Sage 50 Accounting has created entries for the linked items identified earlier and for the -$1,260.00 unresolved balance, which is the same as the NSF item on May 18.

Do NOT Post yet.

In the manual bank reconciliation shown in Fig. 12-7, the items that have been reconciled so far are shaded. The only cheque that has not cleared the bank (been cashed by the bank) is cheque #627 for $500.00. This cheque has the Outstanding status. Deposits 226.00 and 79.10 are also outstanding.

There is still an unresolved amount of **-1,260.00**, which is the NSF item from Rowena's Wedding Boutique. This will be adjusted in Exercise 12-3.

Wedding Flowers Company
Bank Reconciliation at May 31, 2019

Balance per Bank Statement			($ -212.60)	Overdrawn
Add: Outstanding Deposits	May 31	226.00		
	May 31	79.10	305.10	
	Subtotal		92.50	
Less: Outstanding cheque #627			500.00	
Adjusted Bank Balance			($ 407.50)	Overdrawn
Balance per General Ledger			$ 961.10	
Add: Deposit interest			1.40	
	Subtotal		962.50	
Less: Bank Charges		10.00		
Loan Interest		100.00		
NSF cheque -				
Rowena's Wedding Boutique		1,260.00	1,370.00	
Adjusted Bank Balance			($ 407.50)	Overdrawn

Fig. 12-7: Manual Bank Reconciliation.

17 ➤   **Post** when correct. All of the entries in Fig. 12-6 will be posted, including the one for the unresolved amount of -$1,260.00.

A warning message advising the fourth entry in Fig. 12-6 will be posted.

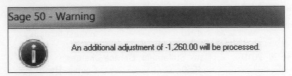

18 ➤   Click **OK** to accept.

The Select Adjustment Account window requires you to identify the account where the unresolved adjustment amount is to be posted.

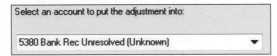

19 ➤   Click the ▼. A selection of accounts that can be used for the adjustment are displayed. With the default 5380 account selection, click **OK**.

20 ➤   When posting, 4 Journal Entries: J10 to J13. , the Sage 50 Accounting Advisor reports that the chequing account (1060 Cash in Bank) is overdrawn. **Click in the box** to proceed. Arrangements have been made to cover overdrafts up to $5,000.00.

After posting the entry, the Reconciliation & Deposits journal has been updated (the reconciled items have been deleted from the Reconciliation & Deposits data base).

21 ➤   **Account**   Click the ▼ and select **1060 Cash in Bank**. The **Statement Start Date** has been updated to June 01, 2019. Outstanding cheque **#627** is shown as carried forward, as well as the two outstanding deposits. The window now reflects the balance forward for the next period (June). (July dates would be changed to June 30 when preparing the next reconciliation.)

Fig. 12-8: Reconciliation & Deposits Journal.

22 ➤   **Do NOT Post**. If you Post, you will update the June Bank Reconciliation, which you do not want to do. **Exit** to the Home window.

23 ➤   Display the Income Statement and locate the Expense account **5380 Bank Rec Unresolved (Unknown)**. The balance is $1,260.00. We need to enter the NSF cheque information in the CUSTOMERS module, to charge the customer with the amount they owe the business. Their cheque to pay invoice #221 was not valid. If the customer is not charged for the NSF cheque, the amount will be an expense to the business and the account reconciliation will NOT be complete.

24 ➤   **Exit** to the Home window.

Exercise 12-3—To Clear the Unresolved by Recording the NSF Cheque

1 ➤ Using the **Sales Invoice Journal**, record NSF cheque #256 from Rowena's Wedding Boutique original invoice 221, following procedures learned in Chapter 2B. Terms fields should be blank. Use account **5380 Bank Rec Unresolved (Unknown)**. There are no bank charges for the NSF cheque. Wedding Company charges a $15.00 Handling Fee for NSF cheques.

The May 20 entry (date the cheque became NSF in our account) to update Rowena's Receivable account will be:

Sales Journal Entry May 20, 2019 (J14)

Account Number	Account Description	Debits	Credits
1200	Accounts Receivable	1,275.00	-
4510	Handling Fee	-	15.00
5380	Bank Rec Unresolved (Unkno...	-	1,260.00
Additional Date:	Additional Field:		
		1,275.00	1,275.00

The CREDIT entry will be to **5380 Bank Rec Unresolved (Unknown)**, not 1060 BANK.

2 ➤ **Exit** the entry, **Post** when correct, and **Exit** to the Home window. The Customers section (top right) displays the $1,275.00 balance for Rowena's account.

Some banks charge a fee to the company or individual depositing an NSF cheque. Some banks do not charge a fee for this type of transaction. If the bank charges a fee for this type of entry, the entry remains the same except that the bank fee should be added to the NSF cheque amount and Handling Fee. The customer should pay this fee.

If the bank charged a service fee of $20.00, and the business charged a handling fee of $15.00, the entry to Rowena's account would be:

		Debit	Credit
Dr	1200 Accounts Receivable	1,295.00	
Cr	5380 Bank Rec. Unresolved (Unknown)		1,280.00
Cr	4510 Handling fee		15.00

End of Information section.

3 ➤ **Display** the Income Statement and locate account **5380 Bank Rec. Unresolved (Unknown)** account. After the NSF Adjustment, the account balance should be 0.00.

Printing Reconciliation & Deposits Reports

Exercise 12-4—Printing Reconciliation & Deposits Reports

---

1 ➤ From the Home page, click **BANKING** module, click **Report Centre**, click **Banking, Reconciliation Transactions Detail,** click **Display**. The report for Account 1060 Cash in Bank is displayed. *Note:* A vertical line on the display will indicate it will display/print on 2 pages (see arrow).

Reconciliation Transactions Detail Report Jan 01, 2019 to Jul 01, 2019

Account: 1060 Cash in Bank

Date	JE#	Comment	Source	Deposits	Withdrawals	Deposit No.	C	Status
May 02, 2019	J1	Etobicoke Newspaper	623	-	113.00		Y	Cleared
May 06, 2019	J2	D. Wadkins	801	222.00	-		Y	Cleared
May 08, 2019	J3	Receiver General for Canada	624	-	885.00		Y	Cleared
May 16, 2019	J4	Judy Johnson, Payroll	625	-	400.00		Y	Cleared
May 13, 2019	J5	Rowena's Wedding Boutique	256	1,260.00	-		Y	Cleared
May 20, 2019	J6	Etobicoke Hydro	626	-	113.00		Y	Cleared
May 20, 2019	J7	Better Built Builders	627	-	500.00		N	Outstanding
May 20, 2019	J8	246, Shierel Hampton	Cash	226.00	-		N	Outstanding
May 31, 2019	J9	247, Soung Tran	Cash	79.10	-		N	Outstanding
				1,787.10	2,011.00			

Fig. 12-9: Reconciliation Transactions Detail Report.

2 ➤ To display/print the report on one page, click the **Modify ▾** icon, then **Report Options**. In the left pane, click **Report Columns**; in the right pane, click **Custom report columns settings.** In the Columns shown in the report pane, change four columns:

Journal Number, from 10 to **5**
Comment,   from 35 to **30**
Source Number, from 18 to **10**
Deposit Number, from 15 to **10**

3 ➤ Click **OK**, to display the report.

The report should resemble Fig. 12-9, and will display/print on one page.

4 ➤ **Exit** to the Home window.

General Journal

1 ➤ From the Home page, click **Report Centre,** click **Banking** (if not selected) click **Account Reconciliation Journal Entries**. Click **Display**.

The report should resemble Fig. 12-6, except that each entry has a Journal Entry number.

(See side note box.)

> The entry for Rowena's NSF cheque does not show in the Reconciliation & Deposits journal entries, because it was prepared in the Sales, Invoice Journal as an entry for an NSF cheque.

2 ➤ **Print** the Report. **Exit** to Report Centre window.

3 ➤ Click **Financials,** click **All Journal Entries**, click **Display** to see Rowena's NSF adjustment entry (J14).

4 ➤ **Exit** to the Report Centre window.

General Ledger—1060 BANK ACCOUNT

Display the report as follows:

1 ➤ At **Financials,** click **General Ledger**, click **Modify this report**, Start date   **May 01, 2019**, Finish date **May 31, 2019**, select **Account 1060, Sort by Date, OK**. Notice that the **J13 May 31, 2019** entry is done automatically by Sage 50 Accounting. The report should resemble Fig. 12-10.

General Ledger Report May 01, 2019 to May 31, 2019
Sorted by: Date

Date	Comment	Source #	JE#	Debits	Credits	Balance
1060	**Cash in Bank**					1,185.00 Dr
May 02, 2019	Etobicoke Newspaper	623	J1	-	113.00	1,072.00 Dr
May 06, 2019	D. Wadkins	801	J2	222.00	-	1,294.00 Dr
May 08, 2019	Receiver General for Canada	624	J3	-	885.00	409.00 Dr
May 13, 2019	Rowena's Wedding Boutique	256	J5	1,260.00	-	1,669.00 Dr
May 16, 2019	Judy Johnson, Payroll	625	J4	-	400.00	1,269.00 Dr
May 20, 2019	Etobicoke Hydro	626	J6	-	113.00	1,156.00 Dr
May 20, 2019	Better Built Builders	627	J7	-	500.00	656.00 Dr
May 20, 2019	246, Shierel Hampton	Cash	J8	226.00	-	882.00 Dr
May 27, 2019	Interest Income	Bank Statement	J10	1.40	-	883.40 Dr
May 28, 2019	Service Charges	Bank Statement	J11	-	10.00	873.40 Dr
May 28, 2019	Loan Interest	Bank Interest	J12	-	100.00	773.40 Dr
May 31, 2019	247, Soung Tran	Cash	J9	79.10	-	852.50 Dr
May 31, 2019	Reconciliation at May 31, 2019	Account Rec.	J13	-	1,260.00	407.50 Cr
				1,788.50	3,381.00	

Fig. 12-10: General Ledger Report.

Notice that the ending Cash in Bank balance of 407.50 Cr is equal to the Manual Bank Reconciliation Adjusted Bank Balance of ($407.50) shown in Fig. 12-7.

2 ➤ Return to the Report Centre window.

General Ledger—5380 BANK REC UNRESOLVED (Unknown)

1 ➤ At **Financials,** click **General Ledger**, click **Modify this report**:

Start date   **May 01, 2019**.

Finish date **May 31, 2019**.

Select **5380 Bank Rec Unresolved (Unknown), Sort by Date, OK**.

The report should resemble Fig. 12-11.

General Ledger Report May 01, 2019 to May 31, 2019
Sorted by: Date

Date	Comment	Source #	JE#	Debits	Credits	Balance
5380	**Bank Rec Unresolved (Unknown)**					- Dr
May 20, 2019	Rowena's Wedding Boutique	221NS Ck256	J14	-	1,260.00	1,260.00 Cr
May 31, 2019	Reconciliation at May 31, 2019	Account Rec.	J13	1,260.00	-	- Dr
				1,260.00	1,260.00	

Fig. 12-11: General Ledger Report on Account 5380 Bank Rec Unresolved (Unknown).

2 ➤ Return to the **Home** window.

Other Reconciliation & Deposits Features

There are some other features of the Reconciliation & Deposits journal that are not covered in this chapter. They are as follows:

a) A deposit slip containing numerous receipts can be entered into the Transactions display of the journal. If each receipt is identified with the deposit slip number, then the status of all the receipts can be changed to "Cleared" in one step by clicking the button at the top of the check mark column.

b) The button in the Transactions display can be used to change the status of **all** items to "Cleared."

c) The "Clear Account Rec. Data" option under the Maintenance menu is used to clear selective data from the reconciliation for space reasons. Transactions that cannot be cleared are Outstanding items.

Summary

The BANKING module, Reconciliation & Deposits journal, can be activated, then set up for a company with information from the most recent manual bank reconciliation. The Reconciliation & Deposits Journal will maintain a running record of all transactions affecting the bank accounts specified.

The Sage 50 Accounting program will allow you to:

- identify normal recurring items; e.g., bank interest.
- identify all bank statement items as cleared or error items.
- record entries to update client files for NSF cheques, etc., which will update the Reconciliation & Deposits journal.

This next section is **FOR INFORMATION ONLY**. Do NOT follow the instructions, use them for future reference.

Reconciliation Errors

This should be done only after the previous work in the chapter has been completed.

1. Click the **Reconcile Accounts** icon.

2. **Account**   Select the **1060 Cash in Bank** account.

3. **column**   For source cheque #627 click in the column to change the blank to a ✓ and the status will change to "Cleared."

4. Triple-click in the **Status column**, and the Select Transaction Status window appears as shown next. A list of alternatives for the status of the transaction are displayed.

An explanation for each of the status options is as follows:

Cleared
The default status for a normal transaction that has cleared the bank and matches the amount recorded in the General Ledger.

Deposit Error
To identify a deposit on the bank statement that is different from the General Ledger amount due to a recording error. The error difference must be recorded with a journal entry and assigned the Deposit Error (D) status also. The original deposit coded as a D and the error correction coded as a D can be cleared together with a C (cleared) code.

Payment Error
To identify a payment on the bank statement that is different from the General Ledger amount due to a recording error. The error difference must be recorded with a journal entry, and assigned the Payment Error (P) status code. The original payment coded as a P and the error correction coded as a P can be cleared together with a C (cleared) code.

NSF
To identify customer deposit cheques that were returned by the bank to you because there was not enough money in the customer's bank account to cover the cheque. An adjusting entry (to record the NSF cheque and the bank charges) must be made in the Sales Journal. If the Sales Journal is not ready for use, then the NSF cheque and bank charges would be recorded in the General Journal.

The adjustment must then be assigned the **A (Adjustment)** status (explained later).

Reversed
To identify cheques that the firm has cancelled by recording a reversing entry to the bank. The reversing entry is normally made in the Sales or Purchases Journal. A reversing entry is required and is then assigned the A (Adjustment) code.

Void
For a cheque that has not been used or has been cancelled. A reversing entry is required for a cancelled cheque and is then assigned the A (Adjustment) code.

Adjustment
For transactions posted as adjustments in other journals as described above.

5. Select the **Adjustment** as an example. You are returned to the Reconciliation window. Notice that the Status has now changed to ✓ Adjustment.

The above procedure is to show you how you can change the status to fit the situation.

6. Click the **X** to cancel the above procedure.

7. At the message box, click **NO** to cancel the changes.

End of Information section.

Reviewing **Slideshow 12** will help you make sense of the reconciliation procedure in Sage 50 Accounting.

Before Moving On ...

1. What are the steps required to activate and set up a Reconciliation & Deposits Journal?

2. Explain the term "Unresolved Balance."

3. If a deposit does not match figures/entries on the bank statement, what possible causes could there be for the difference?

4. If a cheque does not match entries on the bank statement, what possible causes could there be for the difference?

Relevant Appendix

WWW The following appendix is available in your course materials at www.nelson.com/student.

Appendix 2015 W   **Transfer Funds—Transfer Money Between Bank Accounts**

Challenge Exercise 12 C12-1, China
COMPANY, RECEIVABLES, PAYABLES, INVENTORY & SERVICES and BANKING (Reconciliation)

This challenge exercise is using the Challenge Exercise **03 C3B-2** solution file from Chapter 3B.

1 ➤ Open the **China solution** file. Change the company name to **China Co Bank Rec**, **Your Name**.

2 ➤ Add a new GL account **#5380 Bank Rec Unresolved**, with a Class type of **Expense**.

3 ➤ From the **General Ledger #1010 Bank Account**, click on **Reconciliation & Deposits** tab and follow the steps outlined in the chapter to set up the linked accounts for: **Adjustment** Bank Rec Unresolved and **Expense 1** Bank Charges and Interest.

Note: The company does not have any Bank Income earned on investments, nor do they have any Bank Loan Payable amounts.

Note: The bank reconciliation was completed last month (Feb) and there were no outstanding cheques. Bank service charges were recorded in Feb.

As noted in the Challenge Exercise in Chapter 3B, on March 19 the bank manager asked the owner to provide financial statements. The bank provided the following interim bank statement.

Commercial Bank of Canada
2008 Victoria Street West, Alliston ON L9R 6P2

China Company
1012 Victoria Street East
Alliston ON L9R 3Z4

Account Number: 158-2591-3   Mar 19, 2018

(OD = Overdrawn)

Date	Information	Cheques	Deposits	Balance
Mar 01	Balance Forward			3,120.00
Mar 09	Cheque 625	800.00		2,320.00
Mar 10	Cheque 624	700.00		1,620.00
Mar 14	Cheque 626	721.50		898.50
Mar 17	Cheque 627	111.00		787.50
Mar 17	Deposit		116.55	904.05
Mar 19	NSF item Plates & More	116.55		787.50
Mar 19	Service Charge	9.10		778.40

OD means Overdrawn or Overdraft. The Mar 19 service charge is for regular bank charges.

4 ➤ From the **BANKING** module, click on **Reconciliation Accounts** and complete the bank reconciliation noting the following dates: Statement Start Date: **Mar 1, 2018**, Statement End Date: **Mar 19, 2018** and Reconciliation Date: **Mar 19, 2018**.

5 ➤ **Reconcile** the bank account in Sage 50 Accounting and make the appropriate journal entries to update the Financial Statements. *Note*: Refer to the original deposit entry to see if there was a discount on the receipt.

6 ➤ **Prepare** the following revised reports:
   a) Income Statement year-to-date
   b) Customer Aged Detail, all customers, at Mar 19
   c) All Journal Entries to Mar 19
   d) Bank Reconciliation Transaction Detail report Mar 1 to Mar 19

Chapter 13

Correcting Transaction Errors After Posting

Learning Objectives

After completing this chapter, you will be able to:

☐ Reverse and adjust posted entries or other information (quotes or orders).

The contents are as follows:

No one is perfect, and we all make mistakes from time to time. This chapter will help you correct errors in invoices, quotes, orders, and/or journal entries after you have posted your transactions.

You can avoid having to do these corrective steps if you view each entry before posting. See Exercise 1-8 if you wish to review the procedure.

Errors in vendor, customer, employee, number of items shipped, description of item being sold, general ledger account number, etc., may all be corrected. Remember, that it is **very** important to document any corrections you make. Write a memo explaining the original error, including the posting entry number (e.g., J125), how the entry was corrected, including the new posting entry number (e.g., J147). This memo notation is part of what is called an **Audit trail**. This trail helps someone else trace or track what has happened in accounting records.

Always use codes to identify corrections made to entries. See Exercise 2A-16 for a sample listing of invoice codes. Companies may use many other codes to identify corrections. The secret of effective use of these codes is **consistency**.

There are three ways to correct entries:

a)   You may use the ⊞ Lookup icon to locate the entry that needs correcting. The window changes and the header will be similar to:

Sales Journal – looking up invoice 2310. You would then click on ▣ Adjust icon and the header changes to: Sales Journal – Adjusting Invoice No. 2310. You make the necessary changes and post when correct.

Using this method, the original and reversing entries **do NOT** show in the Customer or Vendor aged detail listings. Only the corrected invoice will show in the report.

When you display journal entries (with corrections) that have been corrected and posted, you will see the reversing entry with a source field similar to: ADJ2310, Reversing J3, Correction is J5. The correcting entry will have a source field based on the changes that you have made.

b)   If you want to see the original, reversal, and correcting entries in the Customer or Vendor aged detail reports, you will need to record and post:

  i.   A reversing entry with a code similar to 2310Rv (2310 Reversed). In the reversing entry, accounts that were originally debited are credited, and accounts that were credited originally are now debited.

  ii. The correct entry, new invoice 2314 (assumed new invoice number), will display the way it should have been recorded.

The Aged Detail report will show the original 2310, 2310Rv, and 2314.

c)   If you want to reverse an entry (cancel) because the entry was in error and there is no correction (new entry not needed), you may use the ▣ Reverse icon.

The Adjustment icon method (a) and Reverse an entry icon will be shown in this chapter. You will see:

1.   information about the original entry
2.   a screen display of the original entry
3.   a screen display of the original posted journal entry
4.   correcting screen display
5.   correcting screen display of the revised entry

Remember to **view** the reversing entry before posting. This will allow you to verify that the reversing entry you are making is correct; otherwise, you will complicate the problem even further.

WWW

1 ➤ Refer to Exercise 1-1b to unzip the **13 Corrections.exe** file in your course materials at www.nelson.com/student.

2 ➤ Open the **Corrections** file and accept the date of **Jan 04, 2021**.

The **Corrections Prizes Company** sells various games and prizes for home and office party loot bags.

The Corrections Prizes Company was closed for the holiday period and reopened on January 4, 2021. Unfortunately, the bookkeeper made many mistakes. He was going to correct the errors, but was called out of town. You were called in to print the entries that he made and correct them.

You will be shown how to correct each type of error using the Adjustment icon and/ or Reversing icon.

Exercise 13-1—Printing General Journal Entries

The first thing you need to do is to print the **ALL Journal Entries** to identify the entries that need to be corrected.

1 ➤ **Print** All Journal Entries for January 4, 2021.

Correcting General Journal Entries

Jan 04, 2021	The bank faxed the debit memo for printing new cheques. Information on the fax was New cheques $43.00, HST $5.59, total debit to the account $48.59.

The General Journal entry recorded in error was:

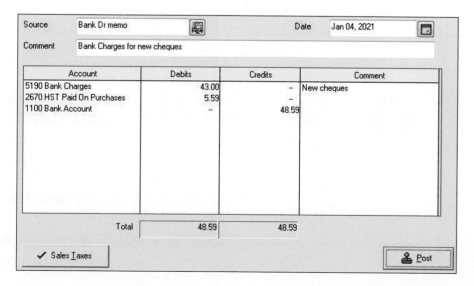

Source	Bank Dr memo				Date	Jan 04, 2021	
Comment	Bank Charges for new cheques						

Account	Debits	Credits	Comment
5190 Bank Charges	43.00	--	New cheques
2670 HST Paid On Purchases	5.59	--	
1100 Bank Account	--	48.59	
Total	48.59	48.59	

✓ Sales Taxes   🖉 Post

New cheques are normally charged to a Prepaid Office Supplies account and expensed as they are used. In this situation the cost of printing the cheques is not a large amount (immaterial amount) and is charged to Office Supplies Expense account. Cheques are normally not charged to Bank Charges.

In Chapter 1 (Photos Company), there were no taxes (HST) recorded when using the General Journal. The following correction entry will show you how Sales taxes are recorded in the General Journal.

Exercise 13-2—Correcting General Journal Entries

1 ➤ To correct this entry, click the **COMPANY** module, then click the **General Journal** icon.

2 ➤ Click the [icon] **Adjust a previously posted entry** icon.

3 ➤ At the Search window, do NOT change dates, click **OK**.

4 ➤ At the Select Entry to Adjust window, select **Journal #1**, with a description of Bank charges for new cheques. Notice that only General Journal entries recorded show in this display.

5 ➤ Change the **accounts, amounts, and comments** to reflect the journal shown next. The bank withdrew the money on January 4.

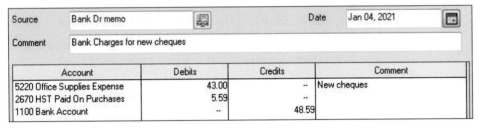

Source	Bank Dr memo			Date	Jan 04, 2021	
Comment	Bank Charges for new cheques					

Account	Debits	Credits	Comment
5220 Office Supplies Expense	43.00	--	New cheques
2670 HST Paid On Purchases	5.59	--	
1100 Bank Account	--	48.59	

6 ➤ **View** the entry before posting.

General Journal Entry Jan 04, 2021 (J10)

Account Number	Account Description	Debits	Credits
5220	Office Supplies Expense	43.00	-
	New cheques		
2670	HST Paid On Purchases	5.59	-
1100	Bank Account	-	48.59
Additional Date:	Additional Field:		
		48.59	48.59

As discussed in Exercise 1-14, all adjusting entry numbers will be increased due to the automatic reversing entry; therefore, after posting, J9 would be the reversing entry and J10 would be the correction.

Jan 04, 2021	J9	ADJBank Dr memo, Rev. of J1. Corr. is J10.

7 ➤ Exit the Journal entry window. Click the **Sales Tax** button (with the blue ✓). See the information field after step 8.

8 ➤ The Sales Taxes- General Journal—Adjusting Bank Dr Memo window displays.

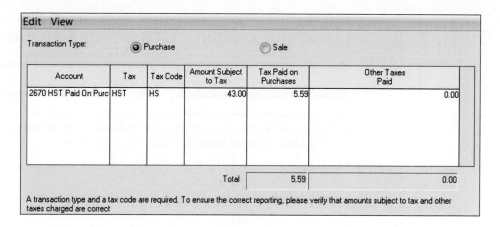

The window records amounts affecting linked tax accounts. In order for the HST Tax report to be correct, the cost of the cheques and taxes must be recorded properly.

If the original entry did not use the sales taxes button and, therefore, the linked tax accounts were not recorded properly, you would see the following window.

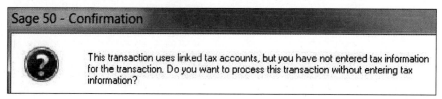

You should click **No**, to record taxes properly. The tax information window appears and should be filled in as noted in step 8.

End of Information section.

HS Tax Code would be the appropriate code for this transaction.

The **Amount Subject to Tax** and **Other Taxes Paid** column amounts appear as shown.

Sage 50 Accounting divides the HST amount (Tax Paid on Purchases) $5.59 by .13 (the HST rate) to determine the amount subject to HST tax ($43.00).

9 ➤ Click **OK** to continue. The Sales Tax button has the blue ✓ to indicate that Sales Tax (purchase taxes) information will be updated for the report.

10 ➤ **Post** when correct.

11 ➤ Return to the Home window.

Correcting or Cancelling Sales Orders or Quotes

Exercise 13-3—Correcting a Sales Order or Quote

> The bookkeeper recorded a Sales Quote for 10 Prizes Adults- metal (P20).
> This should have been a quote for 15 prizes.

Sales Quote Recorded in Error

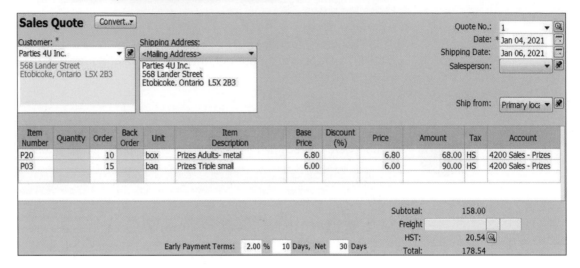

To Change a Sales Order or Quote

1 ➤ Click the **RECEIVABLES module**, click the **Sales Quotes** icon.

2 ➤ **Quote No.**   Ignore the 2 in the field. Click the ▾, select **1** and [Tab].   The original Quote is displayed.

3 ➤ Click on 🖾 **Adjust quote** icon and change the order for P20 Prizes Adults-metal to **15** [Tab].

4 ➤ The new total is $216.96. **Record** when correct, click **OK**, then return to the Home window.

To Cancel (Remove) a Sales Order or Quote

1 ➤ Click the **Sales Quotes** icon.

2 ➤ **Quote No.**   Click the ▾, select **1,** [Tab]. The revised quote is displayed.

3 ➤ Click on 🗑 **Remove sales order or sales quote** icon.

4 ➤ You will be asked: Are you sure you want to remove this Quote? Click **No** to leave the Sales Quote with 15 units of each item ordered, and Return to the Home window.

Correcting Sales Journal Entry for Merchandise

There are two scenarios shown below, illustrating different ways to adjust or reverse a Sales journal entry for goods for resale.

Scenario: Invoice with errors has *not* been sent to the customer.

Method One

To correct

Use the Sage 50 Accounting **Adjust Invoice** feature that will allow you to change the item(s) that are in error, and post. This will reverse the original customer's invoice and prepare a correct invoice.

Method Two

Use the **Reverse** icon feature to cancel the original entry if there are many errors. This will allow you to create a new invoice with the correct amounts.

As discussed earlier, methods one and two do not provide an audit trail for the customer, because the original and reversing entries will not show in the customer's ledger record. Only the new corrected invoice will appear in the All Journals Entries report.

Method Three

Scenario: Invoice with errors has been sent to the customer.

If the invoice has been sent to the customer, methods one and two are not appropriate because the original and reversing entries will not show in the customer's ledger record. Only the new corrected invoice will appear. This discrepancy between your company records and those of the customer could present a problem later.

There are two ways to resolve the problem:

a) **Assuming there are a few items on the invoice**.

    i.   Reverse the original invoice entry to cancel the original invoice (Method 2).
    ii.   Record a correct invoice with appropriate comments to reference the original invoice.

b) **Assuming there are many items on the invoice**.

Record an invoice reversing only the item with the error. This, in effect, is cancelling the sale of those items with the error. On the next line, record the **correct** item with the correct information. This is similar to Exercise 8-19.

An example of b) is shown in Exercise 13-4.

Exercise 13-4—Correcting a Sales Invoice

> The original sales entry (invoice #11505) was recorded to the Rideau Social Club. Their manager called, stating that the price given by our manager for the Prizes Adults- metal should be $6.70. Your manager confirmed the price. You will create an invoice adjustment for the Prizes Adults-metal item.

Original Sales Journal

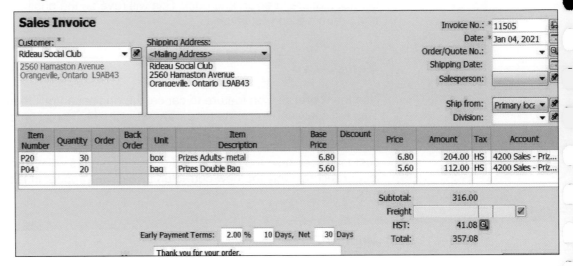

Sales Invoice

Customer: * Rideau Social Club — 2560 Hamaston Avenue, Orangeville, Ontario L9AB43

Shipping Address: <Mailing Address> — Rideau Social Club, 2560 Hamaston Avenue, Orangeville, Ontario L9AB43

Invoice No.: * 11505
Date: * Jan 04, 2021
Order/Quote No.:
Shipping Date:
Salesperson:
Ship from: Primary loca
Division:

Item Number	Quantity	Order	Back Order	Unit	Item Description	Base Price	Discount	Price	Amount	Tax	Account
P20	30			box	Prizes Adults- metal	6.80		6.80	204.00	HS	4200 Sales - Priz...
P04	20			bag	Prizes Double Bag	5.60		5.60	112.00	HS	4200 Sales - Priz...

Subtotal: 316.00
Freight: ☑
HST: 41.08
Total: 357.08

Early Payment Terms: 2.00 % 10 Days, Net 30 Days

Thank you for your order.

Original Sales Journal Entry

Sales Journal Entry Jan 04, 2021 (J6)

Account Number	Account Description	Debits	Credits
1200	Accounts Receivable	357.08	-
5080	Cost Of Sales - Prizes	159.08	-
1280	Inventory -Prizes	-	159.08
2650	HST Charged On Sales	-	41.08
4200	Sales - Prizes	-	316.00
Additional Date:	Additional Field:		
		516.16	516.16

1 ➤ Click the **Sales Invoices** icon.

2 ➤ Create a **Partial Revised** Sales invoice #11505 as shown next. Invoice number code **PtCo** refers to **Part correction**. The Comments section can also contain relevant information.

Revised Sales Invoice

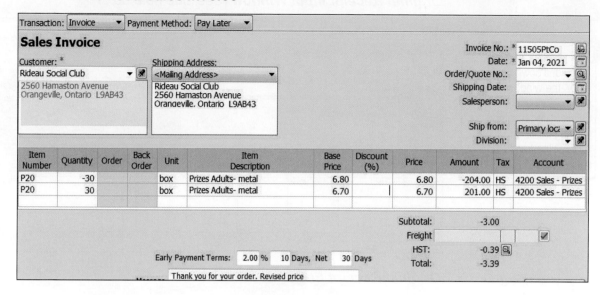

Revised Sales Invoice Journal Entry

Sales Journal Entry Jan 04, 2021 (J11)

Account Number	Account Description	Debits	Credits
2650	HST Charged On Sales	0.39	-
4200	Sales - Prizes	3.00	-
1200	Accounts Receivable	-	3.39
Additional Date:	Additional Field:		
		3.39	3.39

3 ➤ Post when correct. Return to the Home window.

Correcting Sales Receipt Entry

Exercise 13-5—Correcting a Sales Receipt Entry

Before correcting this Receipt for Parties 4U Inc., note that the Customers area displays an outstanding balance of $7.20. Sage 50 Accounting has converted the $7.20 Discount Available in the Original Receipt window (next), to an Outstanding Receivable balance of $7.20.

The clerk forgot to record the $7.20 discount.

The original receipt for Parties 4U Inc. of $399.60 was recorded as shown next.

Original Receipt Input Window *(See side note box.)*

If you drill down on this entry, the window you will see will be slightly different because you are viewing the window AFTER the transaction was posted.

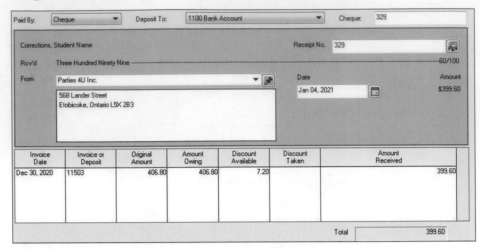

Original Receipt Entry

Receipts Journal Entry Jan 04, 2021 (J8)

Account Number	Account Description	Debits	Credits
1100	Bank Account	399.60	-
1200	Accounts Receivable	-	399.60
Additional Date:	Additional Field:		
		399.60	399.60

To Reverse the Original Entry

1 ➤ Click the **Receipts** icon.

2 ➤ Click the 🖳 **Lookup a receipt** icon.

3 ➤ At the Search window, do NOT change dates, click **OK**.

4 ➤ At the Select a Receipt window, select **Journal #8**, with customer Parties 4U Inc.

5 ➤ Click on the **Reverse receipt** 📇 icon. You will see the following window.

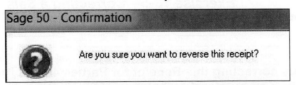

6 ➤ You want to reverse this receipt. Click **Yes**. You are returned to a blank Receipts Journal. The original receipt has been reversed as shown next.

Jan 04, 2021	J12	ADJ329, Parties 4U Inc.: Rev. of J8. Corr. is J12.		
		1200 Accounts Receivable	399.60	-
		1100 Bank Account	-	399.60

You will notice that the debit entry is to Accounts Receivable.

7 ➤ **Rec'd From**   Select **Parties 4U Inc**. in the Receipts window. You will now record the proper cheque amount with a cheque number of **329Co** as shown next.

Correct Receipts Window

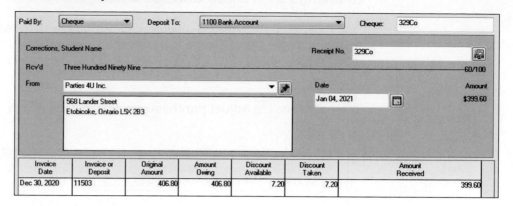

Correct Receipts Entry

Receipts Journal Entry Jan 04, 2021 (J13)

Account Number	Account Description	Debits	Credits
1100	Bank Account	399.60	-
4290	Sales Discounts, all items	7.20	-
1200	Accounts Receivable	-	406.80
Additional Date:	Additional Field:		
		406.80	406.80

8 ➤ **Post** when correct. Return to the Home window.

Cancelling or Correcting Purchase Orders or Quotes

Exercise 13-6—Cancelling or Correcting Purchase Orders or Quotes

A Purchase order issued for 55 boxes of Games Wooden Medium size 1 was recorded as 50 boxes in error, as shown next.

You will be adjusting the quantity ordered in this exercise.

Original Purchase Order Window

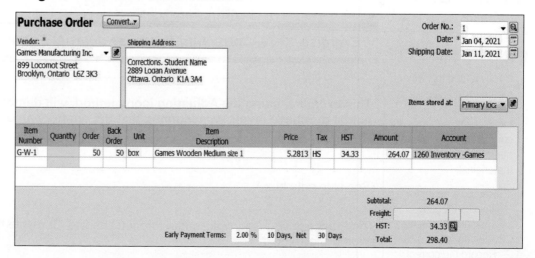

To Change a Purchase Order or Quote

1 ➤ Click the **PAYABLES** module, click **Purchase Orders** icon.

2 ➤ **Order No.**   Click ▼, select 1 ⌈Tab⌋. The original Purchase order is displayed.

3 ➤ Click on **Adjust purchase order** icon and change the order quantity to **55**. ⌈Tab⌋.

Item Number	Quantity	Order	Back Order	Unit	Item Description	Price	Tax	HST	Amount	Account
G-W-1		55	55	box	Games Wooden Medium size 1	5.2813	HS	37.76	290.47	1260 Inventory...

4 ➤ The new total is $328.23. **Record** when correct.

5 ➤ Return to the Home window.

To Cancel (Remove) a Purchase Order or Quote

Click the **Purchase Orders** icon.

Order No.   Click ▼, select **1**, ⌈Tab⌋. The original Purchase order is displayed.

Click on 🔒 **Remove purchase order** icon.

You will be asked: | ❓ Are you sure you want to remove this order? |

Click **No** to leave Purchase Order 1 with 55 items ordered.

Return to the Home window.

End of Information section.

Correcting Purchase Journal Entries for Goods for Resale (Merchandise)

Exercise 13-7—Correcting Purchase Journal Entries for Merchandise

If you wanted the vendor record to show the original incorrect entry, the reversal, and the correction entry, you will need 2 entries to correct the original:

1. Record a negative invoice (negative quantity) to reverse the original invoice.
2. Record the correct entry.

This exercise, using the Adjusting icon method, will demonstrate how to adjust purchase invoices, assuming that the quantity amount should have been 35.

(See side note box.)

The Purchase Journal Invoice entry for merchandise for resale that was recorded in error is shown next.

Original Purchase Invoice Entry

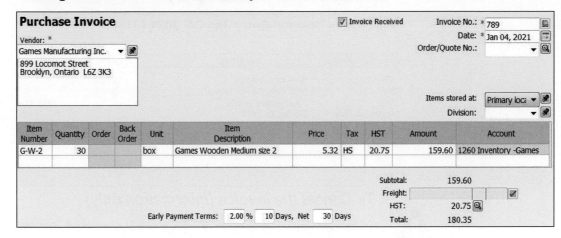

Purchase Journal Entry

Purchases Journal Entry Jan 04, 2021 (J2)

Account Number	Account Description	Debits	Credits
1260	Inventory -Games	159.60	-
2670	HST Paid On Purchases	20.75	-
2200	Accounts Payable	-	180.35
Additional Date:	Additional Field:		
		180.35	180.35

1 ➤ Click on **Purchase Invoices** icon.

2 ➤ Click on ![] **Lookup an invoice** icon.

3 ➤ At the Search window, do NOT change dates, click **OK**. Outstanding invoices are listed. Select **Games Manufacturing Inc.** entry dated **Jan 04, 2021** (invoice **789**) in the amount of $180.35.

4 ➤ Click on the **Adjust invoice** icon and change the Quantity amount to **35**, `Tab`. The invoice total changes to 210.41.

Purchase Journal Adjusted

Item Number	Quantity	Order	Back Order	Unit	Item Description	Price	Tax	HST	Amount	Account
G-W-2	35			box	Games Wooden Medium size 2	5.32	HS	24.21	186.20	1260 Inventory -Games

Subtotal:	186.20
Freight:	
HST:	24.21
Total:	210.41

Early Payment Terms: 2.00 % 10 Days, Net 30 Days

Purchase Journal Adjusted Entry

Purchases Journal Entry Jan 04, 2021 (J15)

Account Number	Account Description	Debits	Credits
1260	Inventory -Games	186.20	-
2670	HST Paid On Purchases	24.21	-
2200	Accounts Payable	-	210.41
Additional Date:	Additional Field:		
		210.41	210.41

5 ➤ **Post** when correct. Return to the Home window.

To Cancel the Invoice (Information only)

To cancel the invoice completely, click on Lookup icon, and select the invoice to be reversed.

Click on 🖾 Reverse icon.

> ❓   Are you sure you want to discard this transaction?

Click Yes, if this is the correct invoice to cancel. Do not reverse the above entry.

The entry is reversed (Cancelled).

End of Information section.

Correcting Purchase Journal Entries for Non-Merchandise

Exercise 13-8—Correcting Purchase Journal Entries for Non-Merchandise

> **This exercise assumes the wrong price of 300.00 was recorded. The price should have been 200.00.**

Purchase Journal (non-merchandise) entry that was recorded in error.

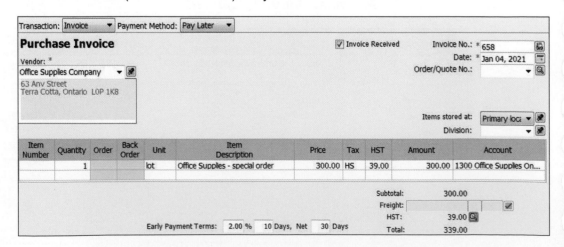

Purchases Journal Entry Jan 04, 2021 (J3)

Account Number	Account Description	Debits	Credits
1300	Office Supplies On Hand	300.00	-
2670	HST Paid On Purchases	39.00	-
2200	Accounts Payable	-	339.00
Additional Date:	Additional Field:		
		339.00	339.00

1 ➤ Click the **Purchase Invoices** icon.

2 ➤ Click the 🖼 **Lookup an invoice** icon.

3 ➤ At the Search window, do NOT change dates, click **OK**. Outstanding invoices are listed.

4 ➤ Select **Office Supplies Company** entry **#3**, dated **Jan 04, 2021** (invoice **658**) in the amount of $339.00.

5 ➤ Click on the **Adjust invoice** icon and change the Price amount to **200.00**, [Tab] . The invoice total changes to 226.00.

Purchase Journal Adjusting Invoice

Item Number	Quantity	Order	Back Order	Unit	Item Description	Price	Tax	HST	Amount	Account
	1			lot	Office Supplies - special order	200.00	HS	26.00	200.00	1300 Office Supplies On...

Subtotal:	200.00
Freight:	☑
HST:	26.00
Total:	226.00

Early Payment Terms: 2.00 % 10 Days, Net 30 Days

Purchase Journal Entry

Purchases Journal Entry Jan 04, 2021 (J17)

Account Number	Account Description	Debits	Credits
1300	Office Supplies On Hand	200.00	-
2670	HST Paid On Purchases	26.00	-
2200	Accounts Payable	-	226.00
Additional Date:	Additional Field:		
		226.00	226.00

6 ➤ **Post** when correct. Return to the Home window.

Correcting Vendor Payments

Exercise 13-9—Correcting Vendor Payments

The clerk issued a cheque to Games Manufacturing to pay invoice #731, but he entered $621.00 in the Payment field. He did not accept the discount amount of $11.00 that Sage 50 Accounting was showing.

You will cancel (Reverse) the original payment (with the error) and record a correct payment.

Original Payment Input Window (See side note box.)

ⓘ If you drill down on this entry, the window you will see will be slightly different because you are viewing the window AFTER the transaction was posted.

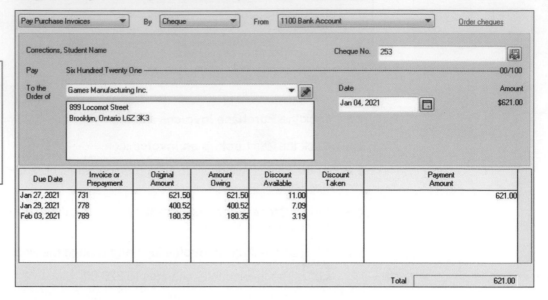

Original Payment Entry

Payments Journal Entry Jan 04, 2021 (J5)

Account Number	Account Description	Debits	Credits
2200	Accounts Payable	621.00	-
1100	Bank Account	-	621.00
Additional Date:	Additional Field:		
		621.00	621.00

1 ➤ Click the **Payments** icon.

2 ➤ Click the 📇 **Lookup a payment** icon.

3 ➤ At the Search window, do NOT change dates, click **OK**, journal entry payment #5 is listed.

4 ➤ Select **Games Manufacturing Inc.**, entry **#5,** dated **Jan 04, 2021** in the amount of $621.00.

5 ➤ Click on **Reverse payment** 📄 icon. You will see the following:

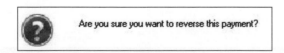

6 ➤ You want to reverse this payment. Click **Yes**. Return to a blank Payments journal window.

Record the Correct Payment

7 ➤ **Record** a correct payment to Games Manufacturing Inc. Issue replacement **cheque #254** as shown next.

Due Date	Invoice or Prepayment	Original Amount	Amount Owing	Discount Available	Discount Taken	Payment Amount
Jan 27, 2021	731	621.50	621.50	11.00	11.00	610.50
Jan 29, 2021	778	400.52	400.52	7.09		
Feb 03, 2021	789	210.41	210.41	3.72		
					Total	610.50

Correct Payment Entry

Payments Journal Entry Jan 04, 2021 (J19)

Account Number	Account Description	Debits	Credits
2200	Accounts Payable	621.50	-
1100	Bank Account	-	610.50
5090	Purchase Discounts	-	11.00
Additional Date:	Additional Field:		
		621.50	621.50

8 ➤ Post when correct. Return to the Home window.

Correcting Payments (Make Other Payment)

Exercise 13-10 —Correcting Payments (Make Other Payment)

In this exercise, the HST on Sales and HST on Purchases amounts on a payment entry, to the Receiver General for Canada, were not recorded correctly. Fortunately, the cheque has not been mailed. Reverse original cheque 252, and issue a new cheque for the correct amounts.

Original Payment

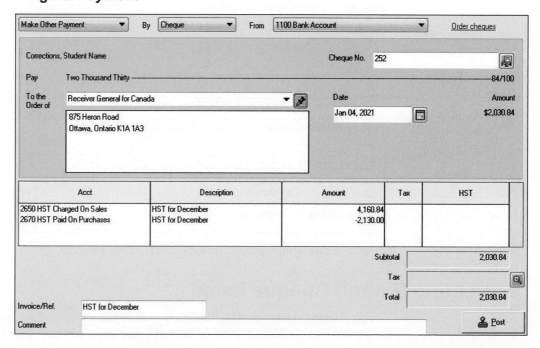

Payment Journal Entry

Payments Journal Entry Jan 04, 2021 (J4)

Account Number	Account Description	Debits	Credits
2650	HST Charged On Sales	4,160.84	-
1100	Bank Account	-	2,030.84
2670	HST Paid On Purchases	-	2,130.00
Additional Date:	Additional Field:		
		4,160.84	4,160.84

1 ➤ Click the **Payments** icon.

2 ➤ **Pay Purchase**   Select **Make Other Payment**.
Invoices

3 ➤ Click the **Lookup** icon.

4 ➤ At the Search window, do NOT change dates, click **OK**. Payments are listed.

5 ➤ Select **entry #4 dated Jan 04, 2021** (cheque 252) in the amount of $2,030.84.

6 ➤ Click on 🗎 **Reverse other payment** icon. You will see:

> ❓ Are you sure you want to reverse this payment?

7 ➤ You want to reverse this payment. Click **Yes**. Return to a blank Payments journal window.

Record the Correct Payment

8 ➤ **Record** a correct Receiver General payment, cheque number **255**, as shown next.

Payment Correction

Acct	Description	Amount	Tax	HST
2650 HST Charged On Sales	HST for December	4,152.84		
2670 HST Paid On Purchases	HST for December	-2,113.22		

	Subtotal	2,039.62
	Tax	🔍
	Total	2,039.62

Invoice/Ref.	HST for December

Payment Correction Entry

Payments Journal Entry Jan 04, 2021 (J21)

Account Number	Account Description	Debits	Credits
2650	HST Charged On Sales	4,152.84	-
1100	Bank Account	-	2,039.62
2670	HST Paid On Purchases	-	2,113.22
Additional Date:	Additional Field:		
		4,152.84	4,152.84

9 ➤ **Post** when correct. Return to the Home window.

Correcting Payroll Cheque Items

You **CANNOT** use the Payroll Cheque Run journal to correct payroll cheques. You must use the Paycheques journal to cancel (reverse) a cheque. See Exercise 7-16a and 16b.

Correcting Inventory Adjustments Journal Entries

There is no Adjust icon in the Inventory Adjustments Journal.

There are two ways to adjust INVENTORY adjustment errors:
1. Reverse the original entry, then record the correct entry.
2. Reverse and correct the entry in one step (shown below).

Exercise 13-11—Correcting Inventory Adjustments

This adjustment assumes method 2 will be used to correct the error in one step.

The manager's memo stated that the Prizes Double bag should be reduced by 15 units. In error, the Prizes Single was reduced by 5 units.

Incorrect Inventory Adjustment

	Inventory Adjustments ▼				At Location:	Primary location ▼	

Source	Mgr memo-1				Date	Jan 04, 2021	📅
Comment	Missing inventory per memo						

Item	Qty	Unit	Description	Unit Cost	Amount	Acct
P01	-5	bag	Prizes Single	2.5073	-12.54	5120 Inventory Adjustments

Incorrect Inventory Adjustment Journal Entry

Inventory Adjustments Journal Entry Jan 04, 2021 (J7)

Account Number	Account Description	Debits	Credits
5120	Inventory Adjustments	12.54	-
1280	Inventory -Prizes	-	12.54
Additional Date:	Additional Field:		
		12.54	12.54

You need to record a correction entry as shown next:

1 ➤ Click the **INVENTORY & SERVICES** module, click the **Adjust Inventory** icon.

2 ➤ Enter the **correct** entry shown as follows:

Source	Correct J7				Date	Jan 04, 2021	📅
Comment	Correction of missing inventory per memo						

Item	Qty	Unit	Description	Unit Cost	Amount	Acct
P01	5	bag	Prizes Single	2.5073	12.54	5120 Inventory Adjustments
P04	-15	bag	Prizes Double Bag	2.8056	-42.08	5120 Inventory Adjustments

Correcting Entry

Inventory Adjustments Journal Entry Jan 04, 2021 (J22)

Account Number	Account Description	Debits	Credits
1280	Inventory -Prizes	-	29.54
5120	Inventory Adjustments	29.54	-
Additional Date:	Additional Field:		
		29.54	29.54

3 ➤ **Post** when correct. Return to the Home window.

Correcting Build from Inventory Assembly Journal Entries

Exercise 13-12—Correcting Build from Inventory Assembly

The manager sent a memo to set up 10 Games Loot Bag #1 as a promotional sales item using the Bill of Materials Journal.

This adjustment assumes the bookkeeper used the Build from Item Assembly Journal. This procedure may also be used to set up or cancel inventory items that do not occur on a regular basis.

The clerk set up the promotional Games Loot Bag 1, using the Item Assembly Journal; however, the manager wants to use the Bill of Materials Journal instead.

There is no Adjust icon, and you cannot display a posted Item Assembly Journal.

To use the Bill of Materials Journal, as the manager requested, you need to reverse the original Build from Item Assembly Journal process, then set up the Build from Bill of Materials as shown.

Original Item Assembly Journal

Build from Item Assembly ▼					At Location:	Primary location ▼
Source	Mgr Memo-2				**Date**	Jan 04, 2021 📅
Comment	Set up Games Loot Bags					

Assembly Components

Item	Qty	Unit	Description	Unit Cost	Amount
G-W-1	10	box	Games Wooden Medium size 1	5.2813	52.81
G-P-1	10	box	Games-Plastic Medium size 1	5.50	55.00
G-M1	10	box	Games-Metal Spring	6.5205	65.21

Additional Costs	
Total	173.02

Assembled Items

Item	Qty	Unit	Description	Unit Cost	Amount
GLB-1	10	Each	Games Loot Bag 1	17.302	173.02

Total	173.02

Original Item Assembly Entry

Bill of Materials & Item Assembly Journal Entry Jan 04, 2021 (J8)

Account Number	Account Description	Debits	Credits
There is no data to report.			

It appears that journal entry #8 with no amounts is created when the original entry is posted, but entry #8 is not created.

 Inventory quantities will be updated but no journal entry will be created for this build because the net change to each affected account is zero.

It is a transfer within the INVENTORY module. The Games Loot Bags use the same General Ledger linked accounts as the individual games items and there is no Journal entry created.

To Reverse an Item Assembly

1 ➤ Click the **Build from Item Assembly** icon. Leave the choice as **Build from Item Assembly**.

2 ➤ To **reverse** the setup of the Games Loot Bag, type the following information into the Item Assembly Journal as shown next.

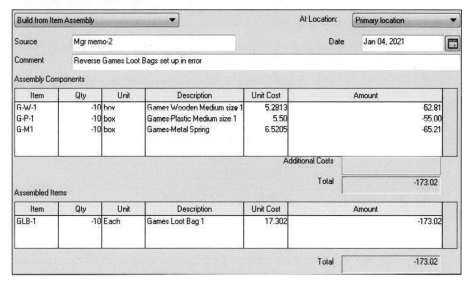

If you display the Journal, you will see:

Bill of Materials & Item Assembly Journal Entry Jan 04, 2021 (J23)

Account Number	Account Description	Debits	Credits
There is no data to report.			

3 ➤ **Post** the entry when correct.

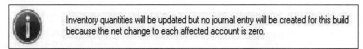 Inventory quantities will be updated but no journal entry will be created for this build because the net change to each affected account is zero.

4 ➤ Click **OK** to continue. Click **OK** again. You will see an Inventory Low report.

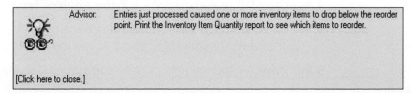

Advisor: Entries just processed caused one or more inventory items to drop below the reorder point. Print the Inventory Item Quantity report to see which items to reorder.

[Click here to close.]

5 ➤ Ignore this report for this exercise. Click in the **box** to continue. **Return** to the Home window.

To set up the proper 10 Games Loot Bag #1 as a promotional sales item using the Bill of Materials Journal, complete the following steps. Refer to Exercise 8-21.

To set up the Build from Bill of Materials Loot Bag Build Information

1 ➤ Click the **Inventory & Services** icon (in Tasks area).

2 ➤ Locate and double-click **Games Loot Bag 1 GLB-1** icon.

3 ➤ Click on the **Build** tab.

4 ➤ Type the information as shown.

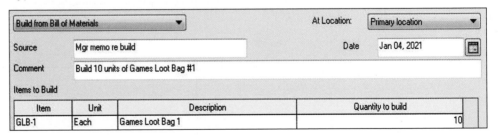

5 ➤ Click the Save and Close button. **Exit** to return to the Home window.

To Create the Loot Bag Using the Build from Bill of Materials Journal

1 ➤ Click the **Build from Bill of Materials** icon.

2 ➤ Type the information shown next.

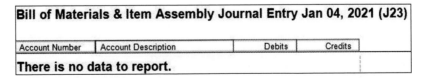

If you display the Journal, you will see:

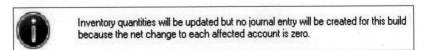

3 ➤ **Post** the entry when correct.

> ℹ️ Inventory quantities will be updated but no journal entry will be created for this build because the net change to each affected account is zero.

4 ➤ Click **OK** to continue. Click in the **Advisor box** to close. **Exit** to the Home window.

5 ➤ To confirm that the 10 units have been built, display the **Inventory Summary** or **Inventory Quantity report** to see the 10 units created.

6 ➤ **Print** All Journal entries (with corrections) for January 04, 2021.

Chapter 14

Foreign Currency

Saddles Company

Learning Objectives

After completing this chapter you will be able to:

☐ Use the Foreign Currency feature.
☐ Create a U.S. bank account and transfer funds.
☐ Record a Sale to a U.S. Customer.
☐ Record a Receipt from a U.S. Customer.
☐ Display Reports.

The contents of this chapter are as follows:

Slideshow 14—Foreign Currency will demonstrate how easy, yet powerful, this Sage 50 Accounting feature is. Run it now.

Foreign Currency Overview

There have been many requests from customers for saddles to be shipped to the United States. The business will be able to receive U.S. dollars for sales receipts and pay in U.S. dollars for a number of different saddle cleaners that can be purchased in the United States.

The Saddles Company business manager has decided to transfer Canadian funds, in order to open a new U.S. bank account, due to future receipts and payments being received and paid in U.S. funds.

www

1 ➤ Refer to Exercise 1-1b, to **unzip** the **14 Saddles exe** file, from the course materials at www.nelson.com/student.

2 ➤ Start **Sage 50 Accounting** and open the **Saddles** file.

3 ➤ Accept the session date of **Feb 01, 2017**.

Exercise 14-1—Turning on the Foreign-Currency Feature

Sage 50 Accounting needs to know that you want the system to work with U.S. dollars (currency). The Premium version can work with as many different currencies as you need.

1 ➤ Click **Setup, Settings**, in the left pane, click ⊞ at **Company**, click **Currency**. This window shows that the currency to be used is Canadian (Sage 50 Accounting calls this the Home Currency).

☐ I want to enter transactions using Foreign Currencies

Enter information about your home currency.

Home Currency:	Canadian Dollar ▼	Merchant Account:	▼
Currency Code:	CAD	Thousands Separator:	,
Symbol:	$	Decimal Separator:	.
Symbol Position:	Leading ▼	Decimal Places:	2 ▼
Format:	$999,999.99	Denomination:	Canadian Dollars ▼
Track Exchange and Rounding Differences in:		▼	

Add or modify foreign currency(s) used. Each merchant account can be linked to multiple currencies.

Foreign Currency	Code	Merchant Account	Symbol	Symbol Position	Thousand Separator	Decimals Separator	Decimal Places	Format

Home Currency   Do NOT change. If you click the ▼ you can see the selection of currencies available and the Home Currency could change. You want to leave it as Canadian.

Currency Code Do NOT change from CAD.

Symbol   Do NOT change. Different currencies in the world use different symbols to represent their money.

Symbol Position Do NOT change. Most currencies have the symbol at the beginning of the amount, similar to what we do in Canada. Some currencies have the symbol at the end of the amount.

Format   This is a display of the currency amounts (codes) above.

Merchant Account If you click the ⏷ there is no linked account set up. This field will be available after you select a Foreign currency, and you have received an account with Sage Payment Solutions. There is a fee for this service and the text does not use this feature.

Thousands Separator Do NOT change. Some currencies use a space, instead of a comma as we do in Canada. If you change any of the settings, then the Format displayed below changes. Remember to change the settings back to a comma.

Decimal Separator Do NOT change. Some currencies use a comma instead of a dot, similar to what we do in Canada.

Decimal Places Do NOT change. Some currencies only use 1 decimal place.

Denomination   Do NOT change. If you click the ⏷ you can see a selection of currency wording available.

2 ➤ At the top, click on ☐ I want to enter transactions using Foreign Currencies . A ✓ appears and the "Track Exchange and Rounding Differences in" field is now available (not greyed out).

3 ➤ Track Exchange Click the ⏷, select **5400 US Exchange Gains/ Losses**, [Tab] .
and Rounding Saddles has decided to record exchange differences
Differences in in this account. This account could also have been set up in the Revenue section of the chart of accounts.

4 ➤ Foreign Double-click and select **United States Dollars**. The USD
Currency currency code, symbols, and other fields to the right are filled in. You will have to scroll to the right to see more columns.

The Currency Information window should appear as follows:

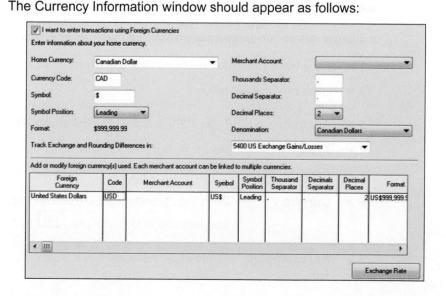

5 ➤ Click the Exchange Rate button.

Display a reminder if the exchange rate is:	Do NOT change. You do not need to be notified if the rate is old. If you click the ▼ you will see other choices.
Currency Exchange Web Site:	Leave blank. Do NOT change. You could enter an Internet URL (Uniform Resource Locater) web site where daily exchange rates are updated.

Exchange Rate Table

6 ➤ **Date**   Type **Feb 01, 2017**, [Tab] .

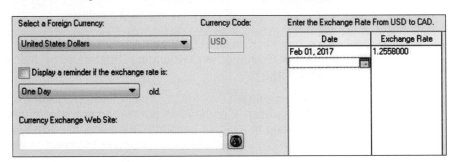
Note: 1.2558 was the actual exchange rate for May 22, 2015.

7 ➤ **Exchange Rate** Type **1.2558**, [Tab] . This would be the U.S. dollar exchange rate to Canadian for this date. (See side note box). The rate can change many times during the day. Sage 50 Accounting adds the extra 3 zeros.

In business there are two rates for each of purchasing and selling U.S. dollars, one rate for under $1,000 and one rate for over $1,000. For this exercise we will use only one rate per day, because most businesses would use only one rate for the daily activity.

Your Exchange Rate tab should look like the following:

Select a Foreign Currency:	Currency Code:	Enter the Exchange Rate From USD to CAD.	
United States Dollars ▼	USD	Date	Exchange Rate
☐ Display a reminder if the exchange rate is:		Feb 01, 2017	1.2558000
One Day ▼ old.			
Currency Exchange Web Site:			

8 ➤ Click **OK** when correct. You are returned to the Setting window. Click **OK** to return to the Home window.

Exercise 14-2—Creating a U.S. Dollar Bank Account

---

1 ➤ Click the **COMPANY** module, click the **Chart of Accounts** icon.

2 ➤ Click on the **Create** icon.

3 ➤ **Account**   Type **1080**, [Tab] , **U.S. Chequing Account**, [Tab] .

4 ➤ **Type**   Select **Subgroup Account**.

5 ➤ Click the **Class Options** tab. Click the ▼ and select **Bank**.

6 ➤ **Currency**   Click the ▼ and select **USD**. The account will record transactions in U.S. dollars. [Tab] to Next Deposit No.

7 ➤ **Next Deposit No.**   Remove 1 and leave blank, [Tab] .

Do NOT click on ⌜Change the Next Cheque Number⌝. If you click this selection, you will see the following:

 Changes have been made to this account but they have not been saved. Save your changes if you want to change the next cheque number for this account.

Click **OK** to return to the General Ledger window.

---

8 ➤ Click ⌜**Save and Close**⌝ to create the account.

You will notice that the U.S. Chequing account is under the Canadian bank account. You should also notice that a new column, Foreign Balance, now shows the U.S. Chequing account with a U.S. $0.00 balance.

Balances are as of the latest transaction date	Type	CAD Balance	Foreign Balance
ASSETS			
🔷 **1000 CURRENT ASSETS**	H		
🔷 1060 Cash In Bank	A	3,120.00	
🔷 1080 U.S. Chequing Account	A	0.00	US$0.00

You should also notice that both #1200 Accounts Receivable and #2200 Accounts Payable show Canadian dollars and Foreign Balances in United States dollars (US$0.00).

Balances are as of the latest transaction date	Type	CAD Balance	Foreign Balance
📖 1200 Accounts Receivable	G		
Canadian Dollar		2,712.00	
United States Dollars		0.00	US$0.00
Total		2,712.00	
📖 2200 Accounts Payable	G		
Canadian Dollar		5,989.00	
United States Dollars		0.00	US$0.00
Total		5,989.00	

There are two ways to enter the next cheque number for this account.

Method 8a) Follow the steps starting at step 9.

Method 8b) From the Home window, click **Setup**, **Reports & Forms**, in the left pane click the ➕ at Cheques, click **1080 U.S. Chequing Account**. You will be taken to the Reports & Forms Options window. In the right pane, follow step 11 to enter the cheque number.

9 ➤ Using method **8a**, double-click **1080 U.S. Chequing Account**, click **Class Options** tab.

10 ➤ Click ⌜Change the Next Cheque Number⌝. You will be taken to the Report & Form Options window as noted in method **8b**.

11 ➤ Next Cheque No. At the bottom type **101**, ⌜Tab⌝. Special cheques with the wording "Pay in U.S. funds" should be purchased.

Click **OK**. You are returned to the General Ledger Accounts window.

Do NOT change the other fields for this exercise.

Notice at the bottom right the new information.

| Current Balance in | CAD | 0.00 |
| Current Balance in | USD | 0.00 |

12 ➤ Click ⊠ to return to the Accounts window. Return to the Home window.

Exercise 14-3—Setting Up Linked Accounts

1 ➤ From the Home window, click on **Setup**, **Settings**, in the left pane, click the ⊞ at Payables, click **Linked Accounts**. The right pane shows the Linked Accounts. Change as shown next.

When you process invoices or payments, these accounts are used as needed.

Select default bank accounts for currencies

Currency	Bank account to use	
Canadian Dollar	1060 Cash In Bank	
United States Dollars		

Accounts Payable:	2200 Accounts Payable ▼
Freight Expense:	▼
Early Payment Purchase Discount:	5120 Purchase Discounts ▼
Prepayments and Prepaid Orders:	2200 Accounts Payable ▼

2 ➤ Bank account to use   Double-click on the **United States Dollars** line and select **1080 U.S. Chequing Account**.

Select default bank accounts for currencies

Currency	Bank account to use
Canadian Dollar	1060 Cash In Bank
United States Dollars	1080 U.S. Chequing Account

3 ➤ In the left pane, click the ⊞ at **Receivable**; if it is not selected, click **Linked Accounts** and repeat step 2.

4 ➤ Click **OK** to return to the Home window.

Exercise 14-4—Creating a U.S. Customer

1 ➤ Click the **RECEIVABLES**, click the **Customers** icon, and click the **Create** icon.

2 ➤ Customer   Type **Saddle Barn Inc.**, and type the Address tab information as shown next:

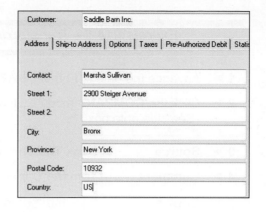

Ship-to-Address tab

3 ➤ **Ship-to address** leave the selection as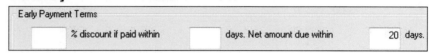

Options tab

4 ➤ Change the items indicated.

Revenue Account   **4010 Sales Saddles**
Currency   **USD**

Early Payment Terms		
___ % discount if paid within	___ days. Net amount due within	20 days.

The bottom-right display now shows:

Balance Owing in CAD	0.00
Balance Owing in USD	0.00

The balance in the account will display both Canadian and U.S. dollars.

Taxes tab

5 ➤ **Tax Exempt**   Click to make Tax Exempt HST column **Yes**.
When goods are shipped to the U.S., there are no taxes.

   Tax Code   Select - **No Tax** as the Tax Code.

Statistics tab

6 ➤ **Credit Limit**   Type CAD **6,000.00**   USD **4,700.00**.

7 ➤ Click **Save and Close** to create the account.

   Customers Window   The Balances for this customer are shown in U.S. dollars.

Balances are as of the latest transaction date	Balance Owing	YTD Sales	Credit Limit
Saddle Barn Inc.	US$0.00	US$0.00	US$4,700.00

8 ➤ Return to the Home window.

Exercise 14-5—Transferring Money to a U.S. Account

An alternative method is to use the BANKING module, Transfer Funds feature. However, you will not be able to display the entry before posting.

See Appendix 2015 W, *Transfer Funds — Transfer Money Between Bank Accounts* in your course materials at www.nelson.com/ student.

www

1 ➤ Advance the date to **Feb 02, 2017**.

2 ➤ Click the **COMPANY** module, click the **General Journal** icon. (See side note box.)

3 ➤ **Source**   **Bank Transfer,** to Comment.

4 ➤ **Comment**   **Transfer Canadian funds to open U.S. account**.

5 ➤ **Currency**   Click the ▾ and select **USD**.

6 ➤ **Exchange Rate** The rate (1.2558) entered in Exercise 14-1, step 7 is displayed as 1.2558000.

7 ➤ Enter the information shown in the next figure.

The amount entered is in U.S. dollars (currency).
If you do not select USD, account 1080 will not display in the Account field.

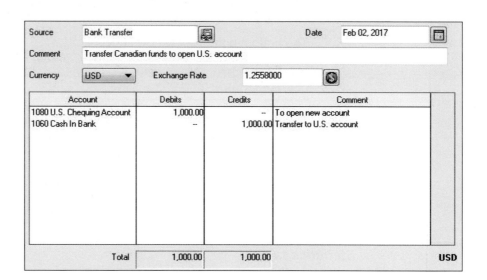

8 ➤ Display the General Journal entry. It should resemble the following:

Account Number	Account Description	Foreign A...	Debits	Credits
1080	U.S. Chequing Account	US$1,000.00	1,255.80	-
	To open new account			
1060	Cash In Bank	US$1,000.00	-	1,255.80
	Transfer to U.S. account			
1 United States Dollars equals 1.2558000 Canadian Dollar				
Additional Date:	Additional Field:			
			1,255.80	1,255.80

General Journal Entry Feb 02, 2017 (J1)

Notice: It required 1,255.80 Canadian dollars to buy 1,000.00 U.S. dollars.

9 ➤ **Exit** the General Journal Entry and **Post** when correct.

10 ➤ **Exit** to the Home window.

Exercise 14-6—Recording a Sale to a U.S. Customer

1 ➤ Advance the date to **Feb 03, 2017**.

Feb 03, 2017   Shipped 1 #501 saddle at $1,000.00 U.S. to
Saddle Barn Inc. (U.S. customer). Invoice $1,000.00 USD.
Terms Net 20 Days.

---

2 ➤ Click **RECEIVABLES** icon, click on the **Sales Invoices** icon.

3 ➤ **Sold To**   Select **Saddle Barn Inc**. Note that the Exchange Rate field now displays. `Tab`.

4 ➤ **Exchange Rate** Change the rate to **1.2551**, `Tab`.

Note: The actual rates may be very different when you do these entries. This is an example of how to record entries.

5 ➤ **Item Number**   Double-click and select **501** `Tab`.

6 ➤ **Quantity**   Type **1**, `Tab`.

Unit   Each, Do NOT change.

Description   Saddle Model 501. Do NOT change.

7 ➤ **Base Price**   Change 796.7493 to **1,000.00** (the amount in U.S. funds).

Disc %   There is no discount at this time.

Amount   1,000.00.

Tax   As noted previously, when goods are shipped to the U.S., there are no taxes (HST).

8 ➤ **Account**   Leave as 4010 Sales Saddles. Some companies may want to have different sales accounts for foreign currencies. Saddles Company is using only one Sales account.

The Sales Invoice window should resemble the following:

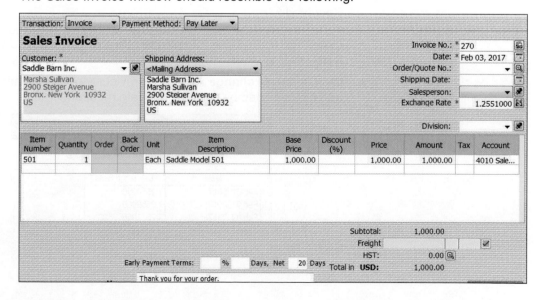

The Total in box | Total in **USD:**   1,000.00 | .

9 ➤ Display the Sales Journal Entry. It should resemble the following:

Sales Journal Entry Feb 03, 2017 (J2)

Account Number	Account Description	Foreign A...	Debits	Credits
1200	Accounts Receivable	US$1,000.00	1,255.10	-
5010	Cost of Goods Sold		550.00	-
1260	Inventory		-	550.00
4010	Sales Saddles	US$1,000.00	-	1,255.10
1 United States Dollars equals 1.2551000 Canadian Dollar				
Additional Date:	Additional Field:			
			1,805.10	1,805.10

10 ➤ **Exit** the Sales Journal Entry and **Post** when correct.

11 ➤ **Exit** to the Home window.

Exercise 14-7—Recording a Receipt from a U.S. Customer

1 ➤ Advance the date to **Feb 23, 2017**.

> **Feb 23, 2017**   Received cheque #867 in the U.S. amount of $600.00 from
> Saddle Barn Inc. as partial payment on our invoice #270.

2 ➤ Click the **Receipts** icon.

3 ➤ **From**   Click the ▾ and select **Saddle Barn Inc**. The "Deposit to" field
changes to the 1080 U.S. Chequing Account. This is
automatically set because you linked the U.S. dollar account in
Exercise 14-3. Note that the Exchange Rate field displays. [Tab]

4 ➤ **Cheque**   Type **867**.

5 ➤ **Receipt No.**   Type **867**, [Tab] to Amount Received.

6 ➤ **Amount**   Type **600.00**. [Tab].
     Received

7 ➤ **Exchange**   Type **1.2496** (the rate changes daily), [Tab].
     Rate

8 ➤ Click on the **Exchange** icon [icon]. Previously used exchange rates are listed
and may be used by selecting the rate required.

Exchange Rate

Enter a new exchange rate or select an existing one

Date	Exchange Rate	
Feb 01, 2017	1.2558000	
Feb 02, 2017	1.2558000	
Feb 03, 2017	1.2551000	

9 ➤ Click **Cancel**.

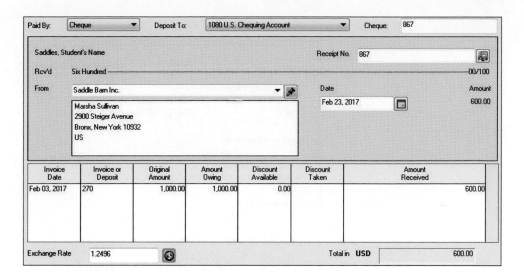

10 ➤ Display Receipts Journal Entry. It should resemble the following:

Receipts Journal Entry Feb 23, 2017 (J3)				
Account Number	Account Description	Foreign A...	Debits	Credits
1080	U.S. Chequing Account	US$600.00	749.76	-
5400	US Exchange Gains/Losses		3.30	-
1200	Accounts Receivable	US$600.00	-	753.06
1 United States Dollars equals 1.2496000 Canadian Dollar				
Additional Date:	Additional Field:			
			753.06	753.06

11 ➤ Exit the Receipts Journal Entry and **Post** when correct.

12 ➤ Exit to the Home window.

Similar procedures would be followed to record Vendor Purchases and Payments.

In Challenge Exercise 14-1 you will create a U.S. vendor and record a U.S. dollar purchase and a U.S. dollar payment.

Exercise 14-8—Reports

View the Customer Aged Detail report as follows.

1 ➤ Click **Reports, Receivables, Customer Aged, Detail** should be selected, click **Show Foreign Amounts**, select **Saddle Barn Inc.**, **OK**. The report displays the amounts in U.S. dollars.

Customer Aged Detail As at Feb 23, 2017					
Source	Date	Transaction Type	Cur Co	Total	Current
Saddle Barn Inc. (amounts in United States Dollars)					
270	Feb 03, 2017	Invoice	USD	1,000.00	1,000.00
867	Feb 23, 2017	Payment	USD	-600.00	-600.00
Total outstanding:				400.00	400.00
Total unpaid invoices:					
Canadian Dollar				-	-
United States Dollars				400.00	400.00

2 ➤ To view the report in Canadian Funds, click **Modify, Report Options**, unclick **Show Foreign Amounts**, click **OK**.

Customer Aged Detail As at Feb 23, 2017					
Source	Date	Transaction Type		Total	Current
Saddle Barn Inc.					
270	Feb 03, 2017	Invoice		1,255.10	1,255.10
867	Feb 23, 2017	Payment		-753.06	-753.06
Total outstanding:				502.04	502.04
Total unpaid invoices:				502.04	502.04
Total deposits/prepaid order:				-	-
Total outstanding:				502.04	502.04

3 ➤ **Exit** to the Home window.

4 ➤ Click **Reports, Receivables, Customer Aged**, select **Report Type** as **Summary**, click **Show Foreign Amounts**, **Select All**, **OK**. The report displays the amounts in Canadian and U.S. dollars.

Customer Aged Summary As at Feb 23, 2017			
Name △	Cur Co	Total	Current
Lonesome Ranch		1,695.00	1,695.00
Saddle Barn Inc. (amounts in Uni...	USD	400.00	400.00
Western Tack & Saddle Shop		1,017.00	1,017.00
Total outstanding in:			
Canadian Dollar		2,712.00	2,712.00
United States Dollars		400.00	400.00

5 ➤ **Exit** to the Home window.

Other Reports

1 ➤ Click **Reports, Financials, Realized Exchange Gain/Loss**, Start Date **Feb 01**, Finish Date **Feb 23**, **OK**.

This report will show the gain or loss difference between the Sale transaction exchange rate and the Receipt exchange rate.

Realized Exchange Gain/Loss Feb 01, 2017 to Feb 23, 2017								
Date	Name	Invoice/Source No.	Payment No.	Journal No.	Foreign Amt.	Original R...	Payment...	Gain/Loss
1200 Accounts Receivable								
Feb 23, 2017	Saddle Barn Inc.	270	867	J3	US$600.00	1.2551000	1.2496000	-3.30
Total Realized Exchange Gain/Loss								-3.30

2 ➤ **Exit** to the Home window.

3 ➤ Click **Reports, Financials, Unrealized Exchange Gain/Loss**.

The exchange rate would be changed when the financial statements are being prepared and all U.S. accounts need to be recalculated based on the exchange rate on that date.

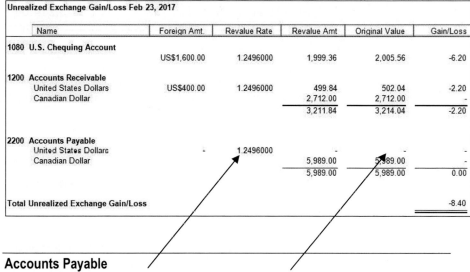

4 ➤   There are no changes required. Click **OK**.

Unrealized Exchange Gain/Loss Feb 23, 2017					
Name	Foreign Amt.	Revalue Rate	Revalue Amt	Original Value	Gain/Loss
1080 U.S. Chequing Account					
	US$1,600.00	1.2496000	1,999.36	2,005.56	-6.20
1200 Accounts Receivable					
United States Dollars	US$400.00	1.2496000	499.84	502.04	-2.20
Canadian Dollar			2,712.00	2,712.00	-
			3,211.84	3,214.04	-2.20
2200 Accounts Payable					
United States Dollars	-	1.2496000	-	-	-
Canadian Dollar			5,989.00	5,989.00	-
			5,989.00	5,989.00	0.00
Total Unrealized Exchange Gain/Loss					-8.40

Accounts Payable
Revalue Rate: The rate displays, but there is no dollar amount, because we have not recorded any U.S. purchases or payments.

5 ➤   **Exit** to the Home window.

To Print a Balance Sheet

6 ➤   Click **Reports, Financials, Balance Sheet**.

7 ➤   Click the **Yes** button to revalue the accounts. A drop-down exchange rate window appears.

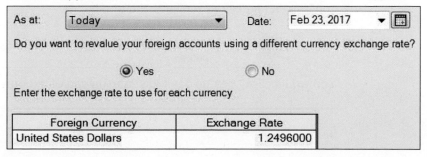

8 ➤ For this exercise, leave the choice as **Yes**, but do NOT change the exchange rate at 1.2496000 (today's rate). All outstanding U.S. dollar values will be revalued at this rate. Click **OK**. The Statement displays the Canadian equivalent for the U.S. accounts (Accounts Receivable and Payable).

Accounts Receivable	3,211.84

(**Yes** choice)

	Balance Sheet with Yes choice	Balance Sheet with No choice
Lonesome Ranch	1,695.00	1,695.00
Saddle Barn Inc.	502.04 CDN	502.04 CDN*
Western Tack & Saddle Shop	$1,017.00	1,017.00
Sub-Total	3,214.04	3,214.04
Add: Unrealized Gain/Loss on U.S.	(-2.20)**	
Accounts Receivable	3,211.84	3,214.04

* This is the Canadian equivalent of what the $400.00 U.S. was worth on the date the sale was made. Exchange rate was 1.2551.

** Applies to Saddle Barn Inc.

If you had selected No, the exchange rate would default to the original U.S. exchange rate for each transaction (which would include any unrealized gains or losses on the U.S. dollar values). The original exchange rate for the sale (Exercise 14-6) was 1.2551000. Click **OK**. The statement displays the Canadian equivalent for the U.S. accounts (Accounts Receivable and Payable).

Accounts Receivable	3,214.04

Accounts Payable	5,989.00

Specialty Saddles Ltd.	2,260.00
Western Clothing Manufacturing	3,729.00
Accounts Payable*	5,989.00

*No U.S. dollar accounts

Information only

If you were to use a different exchange rate during a session date (assuming you are recording all transactions on the same invoice/receipt date), you will receive a confirmation message similar to the one below.

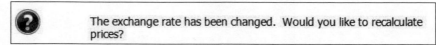

You would click "Yes" to save this rate instead of the previous rate used.

Before Moving On ...

There is no section for this chapter.

Relevant Appendix

WWW The following appendix is available in your course materials at www.nelson.com/student.

Appendix 2015 W **Transfer Funds—Transfer Money Between Bank Accounts**

Challenge Exercise 14 C14-1, Saddles
Foreign Currency Review

1 ➤ Be sure to back up before proceeding.

2 ➤ For the transactions below, continue to use your 14 Saddles solution data file to **create** a U.S. vendor and **post** a U.S. purchase and a U.S. payment.

Feb 23 Based on a customer's request, the manager has made arrangements to purchase model saddle #623 from the Hersay Stables, 258 RR#6, Millerton, New York, 12683, ignore phone number, Currency USD. Terms are payment on receipt of goods. Taxes for this vendor will be No taxes. The saddle will cost $1,300.00 U.S. (ignore Duty and HST taxes, etc., on this purchase to allow you to see the transaction without duty and taxes). The saddle will be delivered on Feb 25. Issued Purchase Order #15; exchange rate has not changed.

Feb 25 The saddle from Hersay Stables arrives in good condition. Invoice #1389 for $1,300.00 U.S., dated Feb 24, accompanies the shipment.

Feb 25 Issue U.S. cheque #101 to Hersay Stables for invoice #1389.

3 ➤ **Print** the following:

a) All Journal Entries, with Foreign Amounts for all entries.
b) Income Statement for Feb 1 to Feb 25.
c) Balance Sheet at Feb 25, without changing the currency exchange rate. Leave choice as No.

Sage 50 Premium Accounting 2015.0 Student Version Installation Instructions

Free to you as a software download from the Sage 50 server is the **Sage 50 Premium Accounting 2015 Release.0**—Student Version *(formerly Sage 50 or Sage Simply Accounting Premium—Student Version).*

These instructions assume that you have a previous version of Sage Simply Accounting or Sage 50 Premium Accounting—Student Version installed on your computer. You will need to uninstall the previous version of Sage 50 Accounting. If you do not have Sage 50 or Sage Simply Accounting installed, move to Exercise Appendix 2-3.

Make sure your computer meets the following minimum system requirements for optimal performance.

Sage 50 Pro Accounting 2015 and Sage 50 Premium Accounting 2015 System Requirements ✕

- Processor operating at 1.0 GHz or higher (2.0 GHz recommended)
- 512 MB of RAM (1 GB recommended)
- 2 GB hard disk space (additional 1 GB needed for installation)
- Internet Explorer 7.0 or later
- Microsoft® supported version of Windows Vista, Windows 7, or Windows 8 (with the latest updates from Microsoft)
- 256-colour or higher SVGA monitor, minimum resolution of 1024 x 768
- CD-ROM drive
- Forms that can be sent via email require MAPI-compliant email client, Internet connection, email service, and word processor
- Word and Excel integration requires 32-bit versions of Microsoft Word and Microsoft Excel 2007, 2010 or 2013
- Outlook synchronization requires 32-bit versions of Microsoft Outlook® 2007, 2010 or 2013 (Premium and higher)
- Multi-user (Premium and higher) optimized for Windows Vista and Windows 7. Dedicated server recommended: Windows Server 2008, Windows Server 2008 R2, Windows Small Business Server 2008, Windows Small Business Server, 2008 R2.
- Terminal Services: Windows Server 2008, Windows Server 2008 R2
- Connected Services: Online services such as Sage Drive require a high-speed internet connection

Conversion: Converts all data from previous versions of Sage 50 (formerly Sage Simply Accounting), excluding DOS and Macintosh® versions. However, it is not possible to convert to a lower-level version. Converts general ledger, customer, vendor, employee, and inventory data from QuickBooks® versions 2011-2012 and import IIF files from QuickBooks® versions 2001-2014; MYOB® versions 10 and 11; Quicken® versions XG 2003, XG 2004, and XG 2005; and Microsoft Excel.

Note to Microsoft XP Users: As of April 8, 2014 Microsoft no longer supports Windows XP, therefore going forward some features and functionality may not work with Windows XP. Any Sage 50 updates released after this date have not been tested for compatibility with Windows XP.

Note: If you do not have Word, Excel, or Outlook as noted, you can still use Sage 50 Accounting.

Restrictions and other information

The student edition of the Sage 50 Premium Accounting software has the following restrictions

1. Can be used for a maximum of 14 months after installation. The software will expire after 14 months.
2. CANNOT open data created in previous versions.
3. You will NOT be able to convert data from this version into future student versions.
4. Refer to the UPDATES/ERRATA section in your course materials at www.nelson.com/student for any updates/changes.

Due to different operating systems and various computer configurations, the following Exercise instructions may be different for your computer system.

Exercise Appendix 2-1: Remove Prior Sage Accounting Programs from Your Computer

IMPORTANT: If you have previously installed *any* version of Sage Accounting on your computer, you must uninstall that version first.

1 ➤ Click **Start, Settings, Control Panel**, double-click on **Add or Remove Programs**, scroll down to the Sage 50 Accounting 2014 or older software (e.g., Sage Simply Accounting different year), click on it, click **Remove**.

   After a brief time, you will then see a window similar to the following:

2 ➤ To continue click **Yes**.

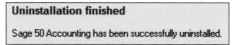

3 ➤ Click **Finish**.

4 ➤ Click **X** **X** to return to the Home page.

Exercise Appendix 2-2: Run the Student Version Utility from the Sage Website

1 ➤ Open **Internet Explorer**, or your browser.

2 ➤ In the address field, type the following:**http://na.sage.com/ca/about-us/education**

   You are taken to the Education Partner Program document for students

3 ➤ Scroll down to Sage 50 Accounting, click on **Step 4 Install link** and click on **Student Version Utility** (in blue).

4 ➤ In the next window, click on **Open** to open the StudentVerCleanup.zip file.

5 ➤ **Double-click** on StudentVerCleanUp.exe .

6 ➤ At Open File – Security Warning

. Click **Run**.

You should see the following message that the cleanup was successful.

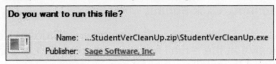

7 ➤ Click **OK** to close the window, and click X to return to the Sage 50 Student Download window.

Exercise Appendix 2-3: Student Registration and Install the Student Version software from the Sage Website

1 ➤ Open **Internet Explorer**, or your browser.

2 ➤ In the address field, type the following:

WWW   **http://na.sage.com/ca/about-us/education** Press **Enter**. You are taken to the Education Partner Program document for students.

If you do not have Internet access from your own computer, write the website link address on a piece of paper, or type it in a word processing document. You can use the school Internet access by typing the website into the Internet Address window and link to the Sage 50 Accounting website.

Note: Do **not** download any product updates for the Student versions unless you are advised to do so by an instructor.

As a student:

3 ➤ Scroll down to:

Sage 50 Accounting (formerly Sage Simply Accounting)

4 ➤ Step 1. Click on the Step 1 Read documentation link. Click on **System Requirements**. Click on **Sage 50 Pro and Premium Accounting** link. This will be the same information that is shown in Exercise Appendix 2-2 on the previous page.

5 ➤ Click X to close the System Requirements window.

6 ➤ To close the blue System Requirements window click X top right side.

7 ➤ If you see the following window, click on **Close current tab**. Otherwise you are returned to the Sage 50 **Step 1 Read** window.

8 ➤ Click on **Step 2**, **Register** link. Click on the blue **Register** button.

9 ➤ **Complete** the Student Version Registration. *Note*: Select **Version 2015 (Premium)**. Click **Submit** when done.

You are returned to the Sage 50 Accounting—Student Version Registration window. You will receive at the e-mail address you supplied, a serial number, and Key Code that is required to install your software.

10 ➤ **Open** your e-mail program and you should have received the activation codes. It may take from 5 to 15 minutes. **Print** the document, as you will need it in the next Exercise. It will be easier to enter the codes if you can read them. The document should be kept in a safe place in case you need to reinstall the software.

11 ➤ At the top of your window, click on [🗏 Education Partner Program ... ✕] to be returned to the Education Partner Program.

12 ➤ Continue with step 3 **Download**. Click on **2015.0**. At the bottom of window

Do you want to run or save **sa_20150cp1.exe** (337 MB) from **cdn.dlm.na.sage.com**?

13 ➤ Click on **Run** to install the software. You should see a User Account Control window to allow changes to this computer. Click **Yes**.

File location

The installation files will be saved in the folder shown below. Click Browse to choose another folder location.

Save files in this folder:

C:\Sage\Sage 50 Accounting Installer Files - CDN Release 2015.0

14 ➤ Choose **Next** to save at the default folder address.

15 ➤ Click **Install Sage 50**, select **English**, then **OK**.

Installation

▸ Install Sage 50

▸ View Installation and Getting Started Guides

16 ➤ Click **Install Sage 50**.

17 ➤ With a setting of English, click **OK**.

Question

An update has been detected on your computer, which may affect one or more files that Sage 50 uses. You should install this update and then restart your computer before installing Sage 50.

If you see this screen again after installing the update, you can safely install Sage 50.

Continue installing Sage 50?

Depending on the configuration of your computer, you may not see the previous window.

You should see a Windows Firewall window. With a setting of Yes, click **Next** to proceed.

Type of installation

Select either a Typical or Advanced installation:

⦿ **Typical:**   Install the most common components. (Recommended)

◯ **Advanced:**   Select which components are installed or use the server-only installation
                  option.

18 ➤ With a selection of Typical, click **Next**.

Product installation

Please enter the 14-character serial number provided by Sage 50 to continue your installation. If
you want to try Sage 50 for 30 days, select the trial option.

⦿ I have a serial number: [   ] - [   ]

◯ I will install the 30-day trial version for now.

19 ➤ Type the serial number from the Sage registration document received:
242P1U2 1000008 (5 zeros). Click Next.

License agreement   ⦿ English ◯ Français

Important changes have been made to the following license agreement. Please read it carefully.

> End User License Agreement for
> Sage 50 Accounting Products
>
> IMPORTANT - PLEASE READ CAREFULLY ALL OF THE FOLLOWING TERMS AND
> CONDITIONS:
> This End User License Agreement for Sage 50 Accounting products (this "Agreement") is
> a legal agreement between Sage Software Canada, Ltd. ("Sage") and you or the company
> or other persons you represent ("You" and "Your"). This Agreement governs the
> installation and use of the accompanying Sage 50 Accounting Canadian Edition computer
> software program and any add-on product or service, including but not limited to Sage 50
> EFT Direct, Sage 50 Intelligence Reporting, and the Sage Cloud Connector; all printed
> and electronic manuals, guides, bulletins and online help (the "Documentation"); and any
> modifications, updates, revisions or enhancements received by You from Sage or its

☐ I agree to accept the terms of the license agreement

20 ➤ Click the agreement box. With a setting that you agree to accept the terms of
the license agreement, click Install.

Installation successful

☑ Open Sage 50

☐ View product information in the README

☐ Learn how to configure Windows and folders so I can share company data with other
Sage 50 users

21 ➤ With a selection as shown, click **Finish** to open Sage 50 Accounting 2015.

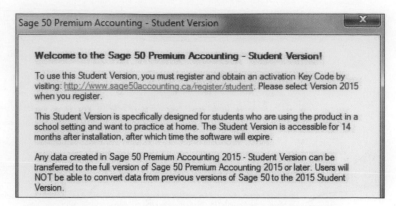

Appendix Fig. 2-1: Register and Activation window.

22 ➤ You have already registered and obtained an Activation key Code in step 10. Click **Activation Now**.

Exercise Appendix 2-4: Student Activation

---

1 ➤ **Open** your e-mail program. You should have received the activation codes, in step 10 in Exercise Appendix 2-3. It may take from 5 to 15 minutes. Put the document in a safe place in case you need to reinstall the software.

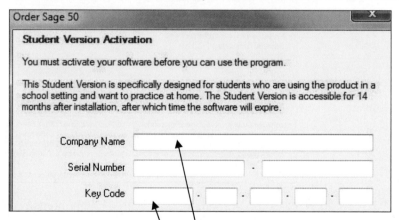

2 ➤ Company Name   Enter **your name** in the field exactly as it is spelled in the document received.

3 ➤ Key Code   Enter the **Key Code** in CAPITAL letters as indicated in the document. Click **OK** when complete.

     If you receive an error message, carefully double-check the information again.

4 ➤ Click **OK** when you are satisfied that the information is correct.

5 ➤ You will see the Sage 50 Premium Accounting window similar to Fig. 1-1a in Chapter 1. Click **Exit** to return to the Installation window.

 It is assumed that you have not completed Chapter 1, Exercise 1-1b: Unzipping the Master Data Files from your course materials at www.nelson.com/student. **WWW**

6 ➤ Click **Exit** to close the Installation window.

If you did not get a chance to enter the Activation code, you can Activate later (see Exercise 2-3, steps 8 to 10). When you open Sage 50 Premium Accounting to start the program, you will be prompted to enter the Activation code then.

You may see the following window.

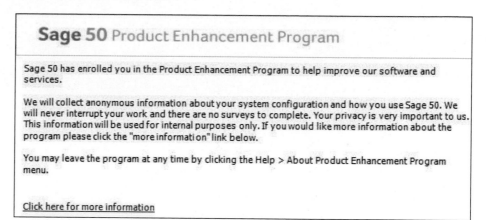

The Product Enhancement Program is meant for the retail market.

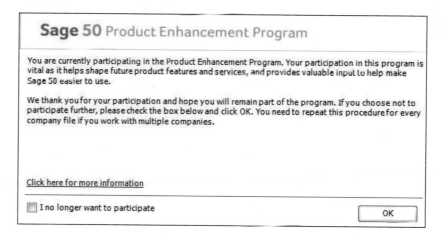

7 ➤ To leave the Product Enhancement Program, within each data file, you need to click **Help** on the Menu bar, and move down to **About Product Enhancement Program**. You would click the "**I no longer want to participate**" field, then **OK**.

Glossary

Account: A form in which transactions are recorded individually. Each account has a name (e.g., Cash, Accounts Receivable) and is identified with a number (e.g., 1010 to represent Cash, 1200 to represent Accounts Receivable). An account will have a left side (Debit) and a right side (Credit). Accounts are contained in a ledger.

Account Class: An identification for specific groups of accounts. The class identifies each group's main purpose or function; Cash, Bank, Payable, Debt, Expenses, etc. (refer to Exercise 4A-5, step 14 and Fig. 4A-33). This is different from Account Types or Account Numbers.

Account Numbers: A range of numbers established by Sage 50 Accounting for each particular type of account (Asset, Liability, Equity, Revenue, and Expense). This system is used in determining the normal balance of each account, and where the account is located in the Balance Sheet or Income Statement.

Account Type: An identification code, or category, for each account; e.g., Asset, Liability, Equity. Each code has a specific function and placement on financial statements.

Accrual: Recording the revenues and expenses for goods received and/or services completed but not paid for in a particular accounting period; e.g., salaries/wages owed to employees at the end of a period. The entries are normally reversed in the next period (see Exercise 10-4, To Reverse Prior Year Accrued Entries). The Accrual Method is the generally accepted accounting treatment in Canada, as it more accurately reflects revenues and expenses in a specific period. The alternative is to record revenue or expense when paid (Cash Method). The Cash Method, however, is not acceptable for income tax purposes in Canada.

Accrued Expenses: Expenses incurred in the period but no invoice or bill has been received (e.g., electricity or water bills attributable to the month ending). The amount is estimated and recorded for the month ending.

Accrued Revenue: Revenue earned in the period, but no sales invoice has been issued (e.g., a partial shipment made but an invoice was not issued). The amount is estimated and recorded for the month-end.

Accrued Salaries/Wages: If the pay period spans two months (i.e., the pay period starts in one month and the pay date falls in the following month), the pay amounts that relate to the previous month are referred to as "accrued salaries/wages." For example, if the work week goes from December 29 to January 4, the wages for December 29 to 31 must be accrued.

Adjustment: Journal entries recorded in order to bring the balance of an account up to date; e.g., to transfer the Prepaid Insurance amount used or consumed during a period from the Asset account to the Insurance Expense account.

Advance: An amount of money "borrowed" by an employee against future wages/salaries. This advance may be issued on a separate company cheque or it can be added to a regular paycheque. If the employee agrees to repay the advance with regular payments, the firm will reduce the regular net pay by the agreed-upon repayment. Advances are issued and repaid without any deductions for CPP, EI, or Income Tax.

Advance to a new year: This is a Sage 50 Accounting term that means advancing the Session Date to a new fiscal year. This results in the transfer of the balances of all Revenues and Expenses to Capital account (for a sole proprietorship) or Retained Earnings (for a Corporation). The closing entry is recorded automatically by the program when you perform year-end processing.

Advice: A detachable form on a cheque that provides the business receiving the cheque with details of the payment.

Aging: A process of sorting Accounts Receivable transactions in predefined categories: 30, 60, or 90 days based on the current session date; e.g., an invoice dated 26 days before the session date would appear in the "30 day" column in the Accounts Receivable Customer Aged report.

Allocate: To divide (split) revenues and/or expenses to various divisions (projects, jobs, etc.). By reviewing Division costs, the management can see the revenue, expense, and the profitability of each division.

Amortization: See *Depreciation*.

Approval Stamp: A stamp on the back of the vendor invoice on which an authorized person in the purchasing department indicates the G/L account number(s) to which the invoice must be charged. It is approved usually by showing the person's name or initials, and dated.

Back ordered: Goods or merchandise ordered by a customer but currently not in stock. The sales order will be filled at a later date when stock is available.

Backup: A copy of your data on another medium such as a USB storage device, CD-ROM, or DVD, using a computer operating system such as Windows or specialized software (e.g., CD-Creator). If the original storage device is lost or damaged, you can restore the data from the backup copy.

Balance Sheet: A financial report that shows a business's assets (what they own), liabilities (what they owe) and equity (owners' or shareholders' investment) at a certain date.

Bank: A basic definition used in the context of this text is: A financial institution that holds amounts of money for personal or commercial use.

Banking Codes:

    A (Adjustment) for transactions posted as adjustments to a bank account.

    C (Cleared) items (matched deposits with depositor cheques) that are recorded in your General Ledger bank account and that have been processed by the bank (on the bank statement).

    D (Deposit Error) is used for deposits that are recorded in your General Ledger bank account but which differ from the bank statement. The difference must be recorded with a journal entry and assigned the Deposit Error code. When both D codes are entered, they can be cleared with the C code. The original deposit coded as a D and the error correction coded as a D can be cleared together with a C (cleared) code.

    N (NSF) Means **N**ot **S**ufficient **F**unds. Cheques returned by the bank to the depositor when there is not enough money in the customer's bank account.

    P (Payment Error) is used for cheques that are recorded in your General Ledger bank account but which differ from the bank statement. The difference must be recorded with a journal entry and assigned the Payment Error code. When both P codes are entered, they can be cleared with the C code. The original cheque, coded as a P, and the error correction, coded as a P, can be cleared together with a C (Cleared) code.

    R (Reversed) When a cheque is received by the bank as a deposit, it is entered as a credit on the depositor's bank statement. When the cheque is cancelled (usually because of NSF), the entry in the depositor's bank statement is reversed, so the entry is assigned the **R** (Reversed) code. The reversing entry is normally recorded in the company's Sales Journal. A reversing entry is required and is then assigned the **A** (Adjustment) code.

    V (Void) is used to identify cheques that were cancelled because they were issued incorrectly. A reversing entry is required and is then assigned the **A** (Adjustment) code.

Bank Reconciliation: The process of determining and processing the differences in the company bank account(s) as shown in the company's records, and the balance as shown on the bank statement.

Benefit: Refers to items such as dental plans, life insurance, drug plans, for which the firm pays the cost of the items, either in full, or partly shares the cost with its employees.

Cash: In business terms this refers to actual cash, cheque, or credit card payment.

Cash Sale: Sale for which cash, cheque, credit card is received. In many businesses these sales are recorded in a cash register and are summarized daily.

Clear: To remove (delete) paid vendor invoices from the data records.

Close the books: See *Advance to a new year*.

Close the year: See *Advance to a new year*.

Codes: Abbreviations of words to indicate action taken. The code Rv indicates a reversal; the code Rt indicates a return item. (See Exercise 2A-16.)

Commission: Amount of money earned by an individual working in sales, based on a percentage of Net Sales made by the individual. The firm would keep records of sales by each staff member, and may pay the commission on a weekly, bi-weekly, semi-monthly, or any other agreed-upon time schedule.

Company Data: Transaction entries and general ledger files referring to one particular company, which are stored in one directory/folder separate from data belonging to other companies.

Conversion: The change from one accounting system to another, usually from manual accounting to a computerized system, or from one computerized accounting software to another.

Conversion Date: See *Earliest Transaction Date*.

Correction: An entry to correct errors in posting. These entries are made on a regular basis and are not necessarily part of the month-end/year-end procedures.

Cost Centre: Refers to a group of accounts where expenses and revenues are allocated and accumulated. This can also mean a division/department in a company.

Credit Memo (Seller): A memo similar to an invoice sent to customers to advise them that the amount owed to your company has been reduced as a result of a return of goods or price reductions.

Credit Memo (Vendor): A memorandum sent by a vendor to the purchaser to indicate that the purchaser's account has been **reduced**, usually because of a return of the purchased goods. It is a **credit** memo because the vendor is crediting **their** customer's ACCOUNTS RECEIVABLE account; therefore, the purchaser would **debit** ACCOUNTS PAYABLE in their books.

Customer Aged Report: A report of all amounts to be received from each customer in the CUSTOMERS subledger aged according to specified aging period; e.g., **Current, 30 days overdue, 60 days overdue**. The report may be listed in **Summary** (total owed by each customer) or **Detail** (individual outstanding invoices per customer not paid in full).

Debit Memo: A memo similar to an invoice sent to customers to advise them that the amount owed to your company has increased, usually as a result of errors in the original invoice, price changes that were overlooked in the original invoice, or extra charges for NSF cheques.

Deductions: Amounts of money deducted from an employee's earnings for items such as CPP, EI, Income Tax, charities, or employee benefits.

Default: A pre-set value; e.g., the default date format is month, day, year, unless the user changes it.

Deposit: 1) A sum of money paid in advance by customers for a guarantee that goods will be reserved for them. 2) Required of a new customer who has not yet established a good credit rating. 3) From a regular customer who has had trouble making payments on previous orders. May also be referred to as **Prepayment**.

Deposit: *See Prepayment*.

Depreciation: Represents the process of allocating the cost of the capital asset to expense over the useful life of the asset. The cost minus expected salvage value is divided by the estimated life of the asset. This amount would be the depreciation cost per year.

Distribute: See *Allocate*.

Drive Letter: **C:** in a standalone hard drive computer system, or D or any letter after C: for a USB or other storage device, CD-ROM, or DVD drive. The letter indicates that you are at the root directory of the current drive, or any letter after C in a network system, indicating that you are at the root directory of your current drive.

Earliest Transaction Date: This is the date when the manual books are converted to the computer system, or converted from one computerized system to another; e.g., May 31 month-end conversion. This is the conversion date as defined by Sage 50 Accounting.

Expense: Purchase of goods not for resale or services used in running a business.

Export: A feature that allows you to transfer reports produced in Sage 50 Accounting into a format that can be used by other software programs; e.g., PDF, Lotus 1-2-3, Excel, most word processing.

Finish Date: The end of the fiscal year.

Folders: A separate location, in Windows, where you can keep various reports or data files. May also be called directories or subdirectories.

GAAP: **G**enerally **A**ccepted **A**ccounting **P**rinciples are guidelines used by ethical practitioners in the Accounting field.

Garnishee: To deduct money from an employee's paycheque, due to a legal Court Order. See Appendix P, *Payroll Garnishment* in the course materials at www.nelson.com/student.

Gross Margin Income Statement: An Income Statement that breaks down the Expenses into two categories; **Cost of Goods Sold** and **Expenses**. The Gross Margin Income Statement can also be called the **Gross Profit Income Statement**.

Gross Pay: The amount of money earned by employees before deductions.

GST: **G**oods and **S**ervices **T**ax. See Appendix 1, *Taxes* (HST, GST, and PST), located at the end of Chapter 1.

GST Remittance: GST paid on purchases is deducted from GST collected from sales. If GST collected from sales is larger, the difference must be paid (remitted) to the government. If the reverse is true, a GST refund will be requested. The GST remittance may be made monthly, quarterly, or annually, depending on volume of business.

History: Account balances and other pertinent information in a module. Historical information needs to be entered before the module can be set to **Ready**.

HST: **H**armonized **G**oods and **S**ervices **T**ax. In the PAYABLES module, HST paid to vendors is posted to the account HST Paid On Purchases. It is based on 13% of the goods purchased amount. In the RECEIVABLES module, HST received from customers is posted to the account HST Charged on Sales. It is based on 13% of the goods sold amount.

HST Remittance: HST paid on purchases is deducted from HST collected from sales. If HST collected from sales is larger, the difference must be paid (remitted) to the government. If the reverse is true, an HST refund will be requested. The HST remittance may be made monthly, quarterly, or annually, depending on volume of business. See Appendix 1, *Taxes* (HST, GST, and PST), located at the end of Chapter 1.

Icon: A symbol, normally a graphic image that represents a menu item within Windows.

Import: To bring data into a file from another file or program; e.g., importing data from an Excel worksheet into Sage 50 Accounting.

Income Statement: A financial report that shows revenues (earnings) less expenses (costs) resulting in net profit/loss for a period.

Integrated Accounting Software: A type of accounting software in which the subledgers are linked to the General Ledger. When entries are posted in the subledgers, the General Ledger is updated.

Integration: See *Linking*.

Inventory Adjustment: The decrease or increase of inventory in the INVENTORY & SERVICES module, due to a difference between the actual physical count of inventory and the computer records (see Exercise 8-20).

Inventory Assembly Costs: The costs of the parts used when a business takes a number of parts and makes them into a product for sale (e.g., a number of different computer parts are made into a saleable computer system).

Invoice: A bill sent or given to a customer for goods or services sold.

Job: See *Project*.

Job Cost: See *Project*.

Journal Entry: The process of recording an accounting transaction, which may consist of one or more debit entries (DR) and one or more credit (CR) entries. Total Debits must equal total Credits.

Linking: A feature of Sage 50 Accounting that allows you to enter a transaction in one module and automatically update other modules.

Logbook: A dated record of activities, which will contain information on the material covered (the last page of text read or work completed), and the storage file name used for backup.

Manual Cheque: A cheque written by hand and not printed by Sage 50 Accounting. A numbering system different from computer-generated cheques may be used for manual cheques.

Markup Method: A method used for calculating gross profit by the following formula:
(Selling Price – Cost)/Cost. [($100 – $60)/$60 = 66.67%]

Matching Principle: This accounting principle requires that if revenues earned in an accounting period are recorded, then expenses incurred to earn those revenues must also be recorded in that period.

Merchandise: Goods that were purchased or manufactured by a company for the purpose of resale.

Minimum: A field in the INVENTORY ledger window that allows you to enter the lowest number of items that must be in stock. At any time, you can display a report of stock items that need to be reordered. The **Inventory Quantity** report shows the amount below minimum quantity in the **To Order** column.

Module: Refers to a part of a software program designed for a specific function. A module may be separate from the other parts of the program (as in a modularized accounting software), or it may be linked with other modules (as in integrated accounting packages such as Sage 50 Accounting).

Month-End Processing: Entering adjustments and accruals, to match Revenue with Expenses during the period.

Net Pay: The amount of money earned by employees after deductions are taken off. Also called **take-home pay**.

Network: Two or more computers connected directly or through a server, and able to share data files and peripheral equipment; e.g., printers or scanners.

NSF: **N**ot **S**ufficient **F**unds: A bank advice that a cheque received from a customer and deposited in your bank account was returned because the customer did not have enough money in their bank account to cover the cheque. You would ask the customer to issue a new cheque.

O/L (Outside Labour): The cost, to the company, of hiring individuals or companies outside the company (non-employees) to produce work/goods for sale, provide consulting services, or make deliveries, etc.

Obsolescence: When an inventory item has become outdated by new technology or upgrade, it is described as being obsolete. Normally, the realizable value (the amount the item could be sold for) drops (in many cases below original cost), and an adjustment should be made to reflect this loss in value. There are common accounting practices that should be followed in these cases.

Outstanding Cheque: Cheque issued by the company and recorded in the General Ledger, that has not been cashed by the bank by the statement date.

Outstanding Deposits: Deposits recorded in the company General Ledger that have not been deposited (credited) by the bank into the customer's account by the statement date. This could be due to a deposit being taken to the bank late in the day and the bank recording the deposit on the next day, or a deposit processed in the books but not yet taken to the bank.

Path: Also referred to as pathname; includes the computer drive and the folder/directory name directing the system to specific files. For example, if you have a set of company files on drive C in a folder called PHOTOS, the path or pathname would be **C:\01 PHOTOS\PHOTOS**. When indicating a path, one must be careful of the spelling, spacing between names, filename extensions, and backslashes.

Pay Period: A specified time interval for which employees are paid, usually every week, every two weeks (bi-weekly), middle and end of the month (bi-monthly), or every month.

Payroll: The record of wages/salaries earned by each employee, less deductions, which is completed on a regular basis.

Periodic Inventory Method: When goods are purchased for resale, they are recorded in the Purchases Account in the Cost of Goods Sold section of the Income Statement. The Cost Of Goods Sold section (Ending Inventory account) is adjusted at various times (periodically) during the year, usually at month-end and year-end.

Perpetual Inventory Method: When goods are purchased for resale, they are recorded in an Asset account (INVENTORY). When goods are sold, the INVENTORY account is reduced, and the Cost Of Goods Sold account is increased by the cost of the goods.

Physical Count: The actual counting of inventory in the store, warehouse, etc.

Physical Inventory: For a company that uses the periodic method of inventory control, the INVENTORY accounts are usually adjusted at the end of an accounting period (monthly, quarterly, semi-annually, yearly) by making a physical count of inventory on hand. The actual inventory on hand at this time is usually called the physical inventory. This amount is set up as INVENTORY ON HAND on the Balance Sheet, and COST OF GOODS SOLD Ending Inventory account is correspondingly reduced.

Post: To transfer the information recorded in a journal transaction to the appropriate subledger and/or general ledger, thus updating the company data.

Preferred Pricing: A reduction in the normal selling price of goods or services given to customers who buy a large amount (quantity) of merchandise and/or services.

Prepaid Expenses: These are expenses paid ahead of time; e.g., leases, insurance, subscriptions, etc. and are recorded as assets. The amounts in these accounts are reduced by an amount that corresponds to the portion used or consumed in the period. This amount is then entered as an expense. (Also see *Adjustment* above.)

Prepayment: An advance payment made to a vendor against a future invoice to show a commitment to purchase. In the RECEIVABLES module, Sage 50 Accounting refers to advance payments from a customer as a **deposit**. Also see *Deposit*.

Project: A job, division, activity, or enterprise, e.g., building a house (or houses); or a cost centre, e.g., a department or a branch of the company. It refers to a group of accounts where revenues and costs are allocated and accumulated.

PST: **P**rovincial **S**ales **T**ax. In provinces that do not have HST, companies selling to the public have to collect PST, except from companies involved in wholesale distribution that have an exemption licence.

Purchase: Includes transactions involving purchase of merchandise for resale, or the purchase of goods used to produce goods for resale.

Purchase Order (PO): A business form issued by a company, usually the Purchasing Department, to place an order for goods or services with a vendor or supplier. A purchase order, usually abbreviated "PO," is a formal request for goods or services to be shipped at a specified date, price, and quantity.

Purchase Quote: A business form issued by the vendor (supplier) to advise the customer that it can and will supply the products and/or services listed at the prices quoted by the date specified.

Purchase Return: A company may return goods to a vendor for a number of reasons: damaged goods, wrong items, late shipment, or over shipment. Purchase returns reduce Purchases and are recorded as a negative purchase invoice. This account refers only to goods purchased for resale. Returned items that are not for resale are recorded as a reduction to the original account charged when purchased. (e.g., Office Supplies).

QST: Quebec Sales Tax. See Appendix 1, *Taxes* (HST, GST, and PST), located at the end of Chapter 1.

Range of Dates: A time period, generally between two dates, in which data may be entered. The transaction date must be on or between the two dates.

Ready: The last step in the conversion process is to set the module to **Ready** for recording transactions. Before setting up a module from History to Ready mode, the total of individual subledger balances must agree with the corresponding General Ledger control accounts.

Reconciliation: See *Bank Reconciliation*.

Reimbursement: An amount of money repaid to an employee for money the employee paid on behalf of the business; e.g., travelling expenses, purchase of goods needed in a hurry, long-distance business calls from home phone, petty cash.

Release: Payment of vacation pay accumulated from prior periods. Vacation pay is set up as a payable each pay period. When vacation pay is released (just before the employee goes on vacation or when the employee leaves the company), the payable is reduced by the amount released to the employee. At this point, Sage 50 Accounting calculates deductions as though the released amount is gross pay. The employee receives a cheque for the vacation pay.

Relevé 1: Form provided to employers by the Quebec government for employers to indicate payroll information for each employee. See *T4 slip*.

Reversing Entries: Accrued revenues and expenses (usually adjustments) that pertain to a particular accounting period are reversed at the start of the next accounting period. This results in a zero balance (nil) in the original General Ledger account in the new period or fiscal year when the revenue or expense is finally recorded.

Salary: A fixed amount paid to an employee every pay period, expressed usually in total annual amount; e.g., $30,000 per annum (also see *Wages*).

Sales Order: A form issued to a customer to confirm that the goods or services listed on the Sales Quote are acceptable and will be shipped as indicated on the Sales Order form.

Sales Quote: A form requested by a customer advising them of selling price(s) for goods (merchandise) or services.

Sales Return: Goods returned from a previous sale for a number of reasons; e.g., wrong goods delivered, damaged goods received. In Sage 50 Accounting, it is entered in the RECEIVABLES module as a **negative** sale. The goods are added back into Inventory, and Cost of Goods Sold is adjusted accordingly.

Services: A sale not involving goods, but the seller provides assistance (auto or computer repair, etc.) or advice to the buyer.

Session Date: In Sage 50 Accounting, it is the actual working date when you are using the computer. In this text, the simulated date is advanced on a regular basis for classroom use.

Sole Proprietorship: A business owned by one individual.

Standalone: A computer system that is working on its own and not connected to a network.

Start Date: The beginning of the current calendar year, or fiscal year, or the date when the business started this year.

Supplier: *See Vendor.*

T4 slip: Form provided to employers by Canada Revenue Agency. The employer completes the form with a summary of each employee's earnings and deductions for the previous calendar year, and submits the four copies as follows: 1) for Canada Revenue Agency, 2) for the employee's use in completing their personal tax return, 3) for the employee, and 4) for the employer.

TD-1: Form supplied by Canada Revenue Agency to employers, to be completed by employees, which calculates the basic income exemption each employee is entitled to claim.

Take-home pay: See *Net Pay*.

Template: A data file supplied with the software that contains a set of linked and non-linked General Ledger accounts with section and group headings. Each of the templates has accounts that are similar in nature to specific businesses.

Terms (of Sale): The time allowed to pay an invoice; e.g., **net 30 days** to pay the full amount within 30 days. Terms of **2%/10, net 30** means that a 2% discount will be given if paid within 10 days; if not, the full amount is due within 30 days.

Unearned Revenue: Money received from customers (clients) before the work (service) or goods are delivered to the client, usually a deposit received in advance; e.g., prepaid subscriptions to a magazine company.

Unresolved Balance: The difference between the bank statement and the General Ledger bank account. The difference may be from bank errors or errors in processing transactions in Sage 50 Accounting.

Vendor: A business from which another firm buys goods or services. May also be called a Supplier.

Vendor Aged Report: A report of all amounts owing to each vendor in the VENDORS subledger aged according to specified aging period; e.g., **Current**, **30 days overdue**, **60 days overdue**. The report may be listed in **Summary** (total owed to each vendor) or **Detail** (individual outstanding invoices per vendor not paid in full).

Wages: Amount paid to an employee each pay period based on an hourly rate. This will also include overtime and any shift premiums (see *Salary*).

WCB: See *Workers Safety Insurance Board*.

Wizard: A smart step-by-step help feature in software that takes you through the necessary procedure in completing a process (e.g., setting up a new company).

Workers Safety Insurance Board (**WSIB**). As of January 1, 1998, in Ontario the name was changed from Workers Compensation Board (**WCB**). Sage 50 Accounting refers to this as WCB.

Write-off: Journal entry to reduce an outstanding balance from a customer's account, when the amount is no longer collectable for any reason; e.g., the customer is bankrupt or refuses to pay the amount. *Note:* A part or the full amount of the outstanding amount may be written off.

Index